BIOGRAPHICAL RECORD
of
Harford and Cecil Counties
Maryland

BIOGRAPHIES REPRINTED FROM THE ORIGINAL BOOK ENTITLED
Portrait and Biographical Record of Harford and Cecil Counties, Maryland

ORIGINALLY PUBLISHED IN 1897 BY
Chapman Publishing Company

WITH
NEW INDEX BY
HARFORD COUNTY GENEALOGICAL SOCIETY

HERITAGE BOOKS
2009

HERITAGE BOOKS
AN IMPRINT OF HERITAGE BOOKS, INC.

Books, CDs, and more—Worldwide

For our listing of thousands of titles see our website
at
www.HeritageBooks.com

A Facsimile Reprint
Published 2009 by
HERITAGE BOOKS, INC.
Publishing Division
100 Railroad Ave. #104
Westminster, Maryland 21157

Originally published in 1897 by
Chapman Publishing Company

Index Copyright © 1989
Harford County Genealogical Society

— Publisher's Notice —

The following illustration pages are missing:
149/150, 159/160, 475/476, 495/496

In reprints such as this, it is often not possible to remove blemishes from the original. We feel the contents of this book warrant its reissue despite these blemishes and hope you will agree and read it with pleasure.

International Standard Book Numbers
Paperbound: 978-1-58549-148-3
Clothbound: 978-0-7884-8085-0

INTRODUCTION

In the latter part of the 19th and the early part of the 20th Centuries, a number of publishing companies in this country produced hundreds of volumes of local biography, commonly referred to as "mug books." Representatives visited local communities and obtained data from persons of varying degrees of prominence, from which were prepared individual biographical sketches, sometimes flowery and patronizing. These were printed in large volumes, often in combination with state or local histories, and delivered to the subscribers, principally the biograpnees. Selected individuals, usually those who paid for the privilege, sometimes had a picture or "mug" of themselves included.

The accuracy of the information presented varies, depending on the subject's own sources and the care taken in its preparation, but it is generally considered credible as to contemporary generations and for personal histories. Material on earlier generations is often unreliable, but at least provides a basis for further research. Contrary to the usual tendency to embellish facts, the first remembered ancestor is frequently identified as the emigrant from Europe, while documented research often will extend the family in this country several more generations.

In 1897, Chapman Publishing Company, which produced several other Maryland area mug books, published <u>Portrait and Biographical Record of Harford and Cecil Counties Maryland</u>. To provide researchers better access to useful data, Family Line Publications has reprinted the local biographies from that volume, eliminating the sizeable presidential portrait and biography section.

To increase the utility of the reprint, an all-name index prepared by members of the Harford County Genealogical Society has been included. This index, keyed to the original page numbers, is of every personal name encountered, with married women listed by both married and maiden names. Except where a genealogical connection is indicated, references to non-local figures such as presidents, governors, generals, and the like, are not indexed. Subjects of biographies are indicated by an asterisk (*). Names were indexed as printed and the reader is advised that there are numerous instances of misspellings (e.g., Howard for Harward and Lacoflin for Loflin) and even one duplicated entry (Samuel A. S. Kyle). Page references to the local portraits are cited in the index in braces {}.

The index was initially prepared by Grace Currier, preliminarily checked by Reed and Gertrude DeForest, typed into the word processor by Helene Davis, and rechecked and revised by Margaret Bishop, Shirley Reightler, Doris Barben, and by the undersigned, who also incorporated the final corrections.

Aberdeen, Maryland, 1 September 1989   Jon Harlan Livezey

BIOGRAPHICAL

OF

HARFORD AND CECIL COUNTIES
MARYLAND

The original pages 1 through 116, giving the biographies of the U.S. Presidents, have been omitted.

HON. JOHN A. J. CRESWELL.

BIOGRAPHICAL

HON. JOHN A. J. CRESWELL. It may well be a matter of pride to the people of Maryland that the state has given to our country many men of large talents, recognized statesmanship and broad intelligence, men well qualified to lead in public affairs. Among its illustrious sons for many years stood the gentleman whose name introduces this biographical review, and who was the recipient of offices of honor from the commonwealth and the nation. Alike in the halls of congress and in the national cabinet, he ably represented his fellow-men and championed the cause of right and justice. In presenting to our readers a sketch of his long and eventful life, we are perpetuating the record of one of the most influential men, not alone of Cecil County, but of the state and nation as well.

The Creswell family is of English extraction and has been represented in America since a period very early in the settlement of this country. The name of Robert Creswell is enrolled as one of the subscribers to the company for Virginia previous to 1620, and from him sprang the branch of the family that settled on the banks of the Susquehanna River in Maryland. Col. John Creswell, grandfather of the subject of this sketch, had a brother Robert, who removed to Augusta, Ga., in 1795; his children were six in number: John, who remained in Augusta; Martha, who married John Phinezy, a planter near Augusta; Ann, Mrs. William Simms, of Montgomery, Ala.; Jane M., wife of Gassaway B. Lamar, formerly of Augusta, later of New York City, and she, with six of her children, was lost on the ill-fated steamer "Pulaski" off the coast of North Carolina, June 14, 1836; Samuel, who died without issue; and Mary, who married Gen. George W. Summers, of Augusta. The only child of Mrs. Lamar who escaped that deplorable disaster and shipwreck was Charles Augustus Lafayette, who was killed at Columbus, Ga., in 1865, while serving with conspicuous gallantry as an officer in the Confederate army.

The subject of this sketch was born November 18, 1828, in Port Deposit, Cecil County, Md., a thriving town on the eastern bank of the Susquehanna River, about five miles from its mouth. The place, prior to its incorporation in 1824, was known as Creswell's Ferry, and the larger part of the town is built on the estate formerly owned by Col. John Creswell. The only child of the latter was John Creswell, who represented his native county of Cecil in the house of delegates of Maryland, session of 1828-29, and died May 12, 1831, leaving the subject of this sketch, but little more than two years of age, and three infant daughters, to the sole care of their mother, Rebecca E. (Webb) Creswell, eldest daughter of Jonathan and Rachel (Ashe) Webb, of Pine Grove, Lancaster County, Pa. Mrs. Webb was the granddaughter of Dr. Daniel Heinrich Esch (Anglice Ashe or Ash), of Hackenburg, Germany, a physician, who emigrated to Philadelphia in 1741 and was lost at sea in 1747, when returning to his native land to secure an estate to which he had become entitled in his absence.

Through Jonathan Webb, his maternal grandfather, Mr. Creswell was descended in the fifth generation from Richard and Elizabeth Webb, who were prominent and influential members of the Society of Friends.

Jonathan Webb's father, James Webb (son of Richard), succeeded his brother, William Webb, as a member of the Provincial Assembly of Pennsylvania. William Webb was a member of that body from 1723 to 1736, and James Webb from 1747 to 1775. Among the many important committees on which James Webb served was the committee of correspondence, which assembled at Philadelphia, July 15, 1774.

After the return of Elizabeth Webb from a previous visit to America, in 1699, the Webbs emigrated from Gloucester, England, to the new world, and settled in Birmingham, Chester County, Pa., near Brandywine, where seventy-five years later was fought one of the most sanguinary battles of the Revolution. Elizabeth Webb was a most zealous and enthusiastic missionary in the cause of Christ, possessing the courage and fearlessness of character that fitted her for life in America at that time. In her diary, written in her strongly-marked chirography and still preserved, she recounts the details of a voyage she made to America with Mary Rogers as her companion, in 1697, "upon truth's service only." Leaving husband, children and all the comforts of home, she embarked at Bristol November 16, and braved the perils of a winter's voyage across the Atlantic. Courageous as the apostles of old, she stood as a pillar of strength amid the storms, and even when the ship was covered with waves and appeared to be sinking, she inspired by her exhortations and example a renewed fortitude in many who "were in great distress because death seemed to approach near unto them." February 5 they came to anchor within the capes of Virginia and a few days thereafter effected a landing. Regardless of the inclemency of the weather, she immediately started upon her missionary work. Crossing the bay, she traversed the eastern shore from Accomac to Cecil and proceeded through Delaware to Pennsylvania, making her first stop in Philadelphia, from there going through West and East Jersey, and traveling by water to New York, Long Island and Newport, where she arrived June 13, 1698. She then visited Boston, Salem, Salisbury, Hampton, Dover, Amesbury, Lynn and Scituate, and returning to Boston, held a "heavenly meeting there," which caused her to write, "It is the day of Boston's visitation after her great cruelty to the servants of the Lord." On the conclusion of her work in that city, she returned southward, crossing Massachusetts, going through Rhode Island, and via the sound to New York, thence to New Jersey, Pennsylvania, Delaware, Maryland, Virginia and fifty miles into Carolina "through the wilderness, the swamps and deep waters." After a journey, filled with hardships so great and perils so appalling that it seems almost impossible to have been taken by a woman, she reverted to the place of her debarkation, and took passage on the ship "Elizabeth and Mary," Frederick Johnson, master, for herself and companion, Elizabeth Lloyd, a daughter of Thomas Lloyd, who was deputy-governor of Pennsylvania, under William Penn. They set sail March 20, 1699, from the mouth of the Chesapeake, and on the 22d of May landed at Plymouth, "all in good health of body and peace of mind;" in thankfulness for which she piously wrote, "Our souls do bow before the Majesty of the Great God whose power and preserving hand we witnessed to be with us upon the mighty waters." Until her death she was unceasingly engaged in Christian work, without a thought of earthly compensation or reward. Anthony William Boehm, chaplain to Prince George of Denmark, the consort of Queen Anne, counted her among his friends.

The facts we have presented regarding the Creswell and Webb families show that the subject of this biography descended from ancestry in which conscience was as hereditary as intelligence and in which the results of generations of honest lives appear to have been transmitted. To the indirect influences of their lives was due much of the nobility that marked his character, and from them he inherited the liberal impulses that won the admiration of all. His education was thorough and broad, fitting him for the responsibilities of life. In June, 1848, he graduated from Dickinson College at Carlisle, Pa., sharing the first honors of the class with Prof. James W. Marshall, and delivering the valedictory oration on commencement day. Preparing himself for the legal profession, he was admitted to the bar of Maryland in 1850. In politics he was originally a Whig and cast his first presidential vote for General Scott in 1852. Upon the dissolution of the Whig party, he became a Democrat, and in 1856 was a delegate to the Cincinnati convention that nominated Mr. Buchanan for president. At the beginning of the Civil War he joined the Union movement and afterward was identified with the Republicans. In 1861 he was elected a member of the Maryland house of delegates, and in the summer of the following year was chosen acting adjutant-general of the state, which position gave him charge of the raising of the quota of Maryland troops.

The connection of Mr. Creswell with the affairs of the nation began in 1863, when he was elected to represent the first district of Maryland in the Thirty-eighth Congress. During his term he rendered efficient service on the committees on commerce and invalid pensions. In 1864 he was a delegate to the Republican national convention that nominated Mr. Lincoln. Further honors came to him the following year, when he was chosen by the Maryland legislature United States senator to fill the unexpired term of the recently deceased senator, Hon. Thomas H. Hicks. As in the other positions to which he had been called, he was distinguished in the senate as a man of keen intellect and wise judgment. In 1866 he was a delegate to the Philadelphia Loyalists convention and the next year took an active part in the border state convention held in Baltimore, also in 1868 was prominent in the councils of the Republican national convention. His position as an advanced Republican is clearly defined in his speech on the proposed thirteenth amendment to the constitution of the United States, delivered in the house of representatives January 5, 1865; in his speech in favor of manhood suffrage before the border state convention at Baltimore, September 12, 1867; and in his address on the life and character of his friend and colleague, Henry Winter Davis, delivered by request of the house of representatives, February 22, 1866. The friendship of Mr. Creswell for Mr. Davis was earnest and sincere, as is shown by the following eloquent and touching extract from his oration:—"At the portal of his tomb we may bid farewell to the faithful Christian, in the full assurance that a blessed life awaits him beyond the grave. Serenely and trustfully, he has passed from our sight, and gone down into the dark waters." * * * "For the Christian, scholar, statesman and orator, all good men are mourners; but what shall I say of that grief which none can share, the grief of sincere friendship? Oh, my friend! comforted by the belief that you, while living, deemed me worthy to be your companion, and loaded me with the proofs of your esteem, I shall fondly treasure during my remaining years the recollection of your smile and counsel. Lost to me is the strong arm whereon I have so often leaned; but in that path which in time past we trod most joyfully together, I shall continue, as God shall give me to see my duty, with unfaltering, though perhaps with unskillful steps, right onward to the end."

This eloquent oration was probably the crowning act of Mr. Creswell's eloquence. It furnishes proof conclusive that he was not only an orator and a statesman, but that he was a scholar of refined taste and literary culture, and a Christian gentleman, possessing all the tenderest emotions and graces of a human heart.

A warm personal friend of the illustrious General Grant, when the latter was honored by election to the presidency, Mr. Creswell was chosen a member of the cabinet, being tendered the position of postmaster-general in 1869, at the beginning of the first administration of President Grant. This important department of the government was under his charge for five years and four months. During that period almost every branch of the service was extended to meet the wants and convenience of the people. From June 30, 1869, to June 30, 1874, the number of postoffices was increased from twenty-six thousand four hundred and eighty-one to thirty-four thousand two hundred and ninety-four; the number of money-order offices from fourteen hundred and sixty-eight to thirty-four hundred and four; the number of postal clerks from two hundred and thirty-two to eight hundred and fifty; the number of free delivery cities from forty-eight to eighty-seven; the number of letter carriers from eleven hundred and ninety-eight to twenty hundred and forty-nine; the number of mail routes from eighty-two hundred and twenty-six to ninety-seven hundred and sixty-one; the aggregate length of all routes from two hundred and sixteen thousand nine hundred and twenty-eight miles to two hundred and sixty-nine thousand and ninety-seven; the aggregate annual transportation from eighty-four million two hundred and twenty-four thousand three hundred and twenty-five miles to one hundred and twenty-eight million six hundred and twenty-seven thousand four hundred and seventy-six miles; the length of the railroad routes from thirty-six thousand and eighteen to sixty-seven thousand seven hundred and thirty-four miles; the total annual transportation on rail routes from thirty-four million eight hundred and eighty-six thousand one hundred and seventy-eight to seventy-two million four hundred and sixty thousand five hundred and forty-five miles; the number of letters exchanged with foreign countries from thirteen million six hundred thousand to twenty-eight million five hundred and seventy-nine thousand and forty-five; the number of money orders issued from eight hundred and thirty-one thousand nine hundred and thirty-seven to four million four hundred and twenty thousand six hundred and thirty-three; the aggregate value of money orders issued from $16,197,858 to $74,424,854; the number of money orders paid from eight hundred and thirty-six thousand nine hundred and forty to four million four hundred and sixteen thousand one hundred and fourteen; the aggregate value of money orders paid from $15,976,501 to $74,210,156; the number of mail letters delivered by letter carriers from sixty-four million three hundred and forty-nine thousand four hundred and eighty-six to one hundred and seventy-seven million twenty-one thousand one hundred and seventy-nine; the number of local letters delivered by letter carriers from fourteen million eighty-one thousand nine hundred and six to fifty-four million one hundred and thirty-seven thousand four hundred and one; and the number of letters collected by letter carriers from sixty-three million one hundred and sixty-four thousand six hundred and twenty-five to one hundred and ninety-four million one hundred and ninety-six thousand seven hundred and forty-nine.

Notwithstanding the immense increase of business shown by these comparisons, and large concurrent reduction of postages and money-order charges, the cost of ocean transportation, including all subsidies, for the fiscal year ending June 30, 1874, was $22,492 less than for the year ending June 30, 1868, and the total deficiency for the former year was $1,178,058 less than for the latter. Mr. Creswell always kept within the aggregate of his appropriations. He returned to the treasury unexpended balances for the years 1870-71-72, amounting to $4,376,556, and when he retired from office he left on hand, after charging up all liabilities, a balance of $1,834,067. During his administration of the postoffice department many important reforms and improvements in the postal service were introduced and carried into successful operation, among which may be mentioned: First, a reduction of the cost of ocean mail transportation from eight to two cents per single letter rate; and a great acceleration of speed by abandoning the contract system as to ocean transportation and in lieu thereof awarding the mails at the reduced rate to the best and fastest steamers, appointed to sail on four days of every week, and then advertising the selections monthly in advance; second, the readjustment of the mail pay of railroads on an equitable basis; third, an extensive increase of railroad postoffice lines and postal clerks; fourth, a large increase of letter carriers in cities, and a free delivery for every city in the country having a population of twenty thousand inhabitants; fifth, a thorough revision of our postal arrangements with foreign countries; sixth, the general extension of the money-order system within the United States and to foreign countries; seventh, a complete codification of the laws relating to the postoffice department, with a systematic classification of offenses against the postal laws; eighth, a reform in letting mail contracts, which eventually led to the passage of such legislation against fraudulent bidding as secured fair competition among responsible bidders; ninth, the introduction of postal cards at a postage of one cent each, as a means of facilitating business correspondence, and a step toward a general reduction of domestic letter postage; tenth, the absolute repeal of the franking privilege.

The first efforts made by Mr. Creswell to secure a change of the law so as to exterminate fraudulent bidding were begun in the early part of 1870 and resulted in the act of May 5 of that year. Unfortunately, the vital provisions of the bill as proposed by him were stricken out by the senate and the objectionable feature of confining the postmaster-general in making mail contracts to the line of bidders inserted, against his protest. That act proving ineffectual, Mr. Creswell again called attention, in his report of 1871, to the pernicious practices to which bidders sometimes resorted, and recommended a series of remedies which he afterward embodied and presented in the form of bills. The passage of these measures he urged at the ensuing and subsequent sessions of congress, especially in 1872-74, but with only partial success. Finally, however, his views were adopted and the essential power of making contracts outside the line of bidders as a last resort was given to the postmaster general by the act of August 11, 1876. Thus, after a prolonged contest of six years, the department was relieved from the vicious contrivance known as straw bidding, and to Mr. Creswell more than to any other person is due the credit of devising and securing the adoption of an adequate remedy for that evil. He was also a zealous advocate for the adoption of postal savings depositories and the postal telegraph, and presented in his reports for the years 1871, 1872 and 1873, elaborate and exhaustive arguments in favor of both those measures. The sequel has shown, that if his views in relation to postal savings depositories had been adopted, many millions of dollars would have been saved to the mechanics and laborers of the country, and the financial condition of the government would have been greatly strengthened.

Although desirous of withdrawing from the cabinet at the expiration of General Grant's first term as president, Mr. Creswell accepted a reappointment upon urgent request, and continued in office until June 24, 1874, when he tendered his resignation. That this was greatly regretted by the president is shown by the following letter:

"EXECUTIVE MANSION,
WASHINGTON, D. C.,
June 24, 1874.

My Dear Sir:

As I expressed to you verbally this morning when you tendered your resignation of the office of postmaster-general, it is with the deepest regret to me that you should have felt such a course necessary. You are the last of the original members of the cabinet named by me as I was entering upon my present duties, and it makes me feel as if old associations were being broken up that I had hoped might be continued through my official life. In separating officially, I have but two hopes to express: first, that I may get a successor who will be as faithful and efficient in the performance of the duties of the office you resign; second, a personal friend that I can have the same attachment for. Your record has been satisfactory to me and I know it will so prove to the country.

Yours very truly,
(Signed) U. S. Grant."

That Mr. Creswell was one of the most influential members of President Grant's cabinet will be seen by the following account of his connection with the veto of the "Inflation Bill." Although the president did not submit the bill to the consideration of the cabinet as a body, he did talk with the different members about it. At the close of one of the meetings the President requested General Creswell to remain. When they were alone the bill was discussed, the President saying that although he had thought much upon the subject, he had been unable to come to a conclusion as to the true line of his duty. General Creswell urged him to veto the bill. The President replied that he was inclined to do so, but the pressure for approval of the measure, on the ground of party necessity, was greater than he had ever before experienced. He said that all but two members of his cabinet advised him to find reasons for signing the bill, and urged that a veto would imperil the prosperity of the country and perhaps wreck the party which had twice elected him. After considerable discussion the president said that his disposition of the measure would doubtless be the most important act of his administration; that in the midst of all the various contentions it was apparent that he must decide the matter for himself, that his judgment was opposed to the bill, and he thought he would veto it, although the weight of official recommendation was in its favor. He said he would have to see what he could do in the way of writing a message before the next cabinet meeting, and requested the postmaster-general to come to him an hour in advance of the next meeting to see what he should produce.

When General Creswell called prior to the next meeting, the president took from his desk and read a very carefully written memorandum setting forth the considerations which had led him reluctantly to determine to sign the bill, and asked the cabinet officer how he liked it, and if he did not think that, all things considered, he had reached the wisest conclusion. Upon being met with expressions of surprise and regret, he took from his desk another paper and read it. It was the since famous veto message. General Creswell said with enthusiasm: "Mr. President, if you will use that, it will put the substantial sense of the country under lasting obligations to you." "No matter what it does," was the reply, "it is the only thing I can write upon the subject and satisfy my judgment and conscience, and I shall adhere to it." He then explained that he had sometimes found that he could come to the safest conclusions by writing for himself the strongest possible paper on each side of controverted questions, and that he had worked until late into the previous night applying that test to the "Inflation Bill." He said that at first he had given himself up to the thought that he would sign the bill and file with it an explanatory memorandum. He had made this as strong and logical as he could. Then he turned to the other side and set to work to write the most convincing veto message of which he was capable. The result left no doubt in his mind as to which side had the weight of reason and argument. He felt sure of the right course, and, regardless of clamor and abuse, he would have pleasure in pursuing it.

Very shortly after resigning the position of postmaster-general, Mr. Creswell was appointed counsel for the United States before the court of commissioners of Alabama claims and continued to act in that capacity until the court expired by limitation of law, December 31, 1876. At the end of his labors as counsel for the United States before the court of commissioners of Alabama claims, the judges unanimously, and of their own motion, exhibited their appreciation of his services by an order in these words: "The court desire to place upon record an expression of their sense of the value of the services of the Hon. John A. J. Creswell in the discharge of his duties as counsel on behalf of the United States. He has exhibited unwearied industry in the investigation of the facts of the several cases, great research in examination of the difficult questions of law often arising, and great ability in presenting to the court his views, both of the facts and law. With an earnest zeal to protect the rights of the government, he has yet been entirely fair and just to claimants. His uniform courtesy and kindness of manner have made his official intercourse with the members of the court peculiarly agreeable to them. It is, therefore, alike proper and just that this expression of our opinion of his ability, fidelity and integrity should be placed upon the record."

Mr. Creswell was one of the commissioners for closing up the offices of the Freedman's Savings Bank & Trust Company and was president of the Citizens' National Bank of Washington. At the same time he acted as vice-president of the National Bank of Elkton.

A portion of every year he spent in the city of Washington with his family, where he devoted himself to the practice of his profession, and was often retained in important cases pending before the Supreme Court of the United States.

Though connected with the business and professional interests of Washington, he continued to make his home on the fine estate in the suburbs of Elkton, and here he died December 23, 1891.

The old homestead was the birthplace and is the present residence of his wife, who was Miss H. J. Richardson, and it is admired as one of the most beautiful and valuable estates in Maryland. Mrs. Creswell is of the seventh generation in direct descent from Robert Richardson, who was the progenitor of his branch of the Richardson family of Maryland, and whose patent to two thousand acres of land was confirmed by Charles Calvert in 1668. His son William was a member of the provincial assembly as early as 1678. On the maternal side of her father's family she is descended from Maj. Richard Ewen, who was speaker of the general assembly, also a member of the provincial court, and one of the commissioners who governed Maryland in 1654.

The life of Mr. Creswell furnishes an example well worthy of emulation by the young. While many others had opportunities fully equal to his, yet few of his co-laborers in youth attained the prominence and accomplished the good that he did. He left no descendants, but his example is not on that account by any means lost. In years to come the young men of Maryland will read the record of his life and by it will be inspired to greater love for and devotion to their state and country. He was a true patriot, and were he alive to-day, dictating the closing words of this life record, they would be words of encouragement, of advice to the young, urging them to guard carefully the honor of their nation and to assist in making America the fairest and best of the nations of earth.

The writer acknowledges indebtedness to the Biographical Cyclopedia of Maryland and the District of Columbia for information concerning the life of Mr. Creswell contained therein.

GEORGE W. BARNES. The years that have elapsed since the death of Mr. Barnes have not dimmed his memory in the hearts of his family or in the minds of those who were his co-laborers in life. His entire life was spent in northeastern Maryland. Some who were his playmates in boyhood sought homes in the remote west or went further south, but he was content to spend his entire life amid the associations familiar to his earliest recollections, for he believed this to be one of the garden spots of earth. He was born and reared in Havre de Grace, and from that place removed in 1854 to Carpenters Point, Cecil County, purchasing the property now owned and occupied by his family. The occupation in which he was principally engaged was that of fishing, and it proved the source of a fair income. In matters political his affiliations were with the Democratic party, while in religion he was a member of the Episcopal Church and in his fraternal relations belonged to the Independent Order of Odd Fellows; he never sought office in any of these organizations, for his tastes were domestic, and he was averse to public positions. Concerning his ancestry little is known, except that his father, Richard, who was born in Havre de Grace, was of English descent.

The first wife of George W. Barnes was Sarah Jane Morgan, member of one of the most highly respected families of the farming community of Cecil County. She died in 1857. Of her two children only one survives, Perry K., who was born in Havre de Grace, March 14, 1849. In 1859 Mr. Barnes was again married, choosing as his wife Rachel L. Kirby, daughter of Zebulon S. and Eliza Kirby, of this county, but formerly of Talbot County, Md., and being connected with some of the best families of that county. She died in 1893. To this union there were born five sons and four daughters, all of whom are living, with the exception of one son, who died in infancy. They are named as follows: Mary G., wife of J. Nelson Black, of Principio Furnace, who has two children, Edith C. and Mary B. Black; George W., Robert L., Richard K., Eliza B., Harry R., Emily E., Frederick M. (who died in infancy) and Edith R. Barnes. Richard K. is employed by the Pennsylvania Railroad Company, and all the other members of the family are at home. The estate is mutually conducted by the family and contains the most extensive shad, rock and herring fisheries on the bay. The eldest son of our subject, Perry K. Barnes, married Belle B. Black, of Charlestown, and they have two children, Harry H. and Emma M. Barnes.

WILLIAM STEEL EVANS, prosecuting attorney for Cecil County, was born at Rising Sun December 16, 1846, and spent the years of boyhood and youth upon the home farm. Being of an ambitious disposition, desirous of obtaining a good education in order that he might be fitted for the activities of life, he became a student in the West Nottingham Academy in Cecil County, later prosecuted his studies in Newark Academy, Newark, Del., and also took a special course of studies in Lafayette College, Easton, Pa., after which he turned his attention from literary to legal studies. He read under the supervision of the late Henry W. Archer, of Bel Air. In February, 1870, he was admitted to practice at the bar of Harford County, and shortly afterward removed to Cecil County, opening an office at Elkton, where he has since resided.

As a lawyer Mr. Evans is well versed in the intricacies of Blackstone. He is a man, less of brilliant, than of solid attainments, a safe counselor, familiar with the principles of wise statesmanship and public policy. Mentally vigorous, analytical and discriminative, he reaches his conclusions slowly, but certainly, and when once having resolved upon a course of action or theory for elucidation, is not easily swerved from his opinions. However, he is not prejudiced or unjust, but is calm in his judgment, and logical in his reasoning. He is a Democrat by political faith and a citizen on general principles. In the advocacy of his beliefs he is firm, pronounced in his political opinions, intelligently conversant with the political issues of the age, and at all times ready to openly discuss them. The high opinion in which he is held by others of his party is shown by his election to the responsible position of chairman of the Democratic state central committee. In 1887 he was chosen state's attorney, and served for four years. Again, in 1895 he was elected for a second term of four years. The duties of the office he discharges without fear or favor, and his policy is the terror of the evil doer. In addition to other duties, he has been council to the board of county commissioners. Fraternally he is connected with the Masonic lodge and Royal Arch Chapter, in Elkton, the Junior Order of American Mechanics, and the Ancient Order of United Workmen, and in religious belief he is identified with the Presbyterian Church, in which he holds the office of trustee.

April 24, 1872, Mr. Evans was united in marriage with Jennie, daughter of the late James Frazer, of Elkton, and sister of Dr. James H. Frazer, of Baltimore. They are the parents of eight children: James F., an alumnus of Princeton, and now engaged in practice in his father's office; Rebecca S.; John P., a student in the Baltimore Dental College; William S., Jr.; Emily, Harry C., Frank B. and Stanley.

Mr. Evans is a friend of the city in which he has spent the larger portion of his life, and any measure for the advancement of the place or the increased prosperity of the people is given his hearty support. The self-will that is one of his marked attributes is tempered by a calm, keen and discriminating judgment that always detects and advocates right and discovers and denounces wrong. These qualities qualify him to admirably discharge the duties of the office which he is now holding for a second term. He has always been actively and efficiently identified with the best interests of Elkton, and comes to the aid of worthy causes with a liberal and public-spirited response.

The subject of this sketch is the second son of John P. and Rebecca (Steel) Evans. James H. and Amos S., the two brothers of William S. Evans, are engaged in farming, Amos owning and residing on the home farm, and James owning and residing on what is known as the Robert Evans farm, near Rising Sun. The family is of Welsh origin. Johnston, in his History of Cecil County, says: "There is reason to believe that most of the name in this county are the descendants of three brothers, John, James and Robert Evans, who settled here about a century and a-half ago, and are believed to have been the sons of John Evans, who was probably born about the year 1680."

John Evans, who was born about the year 1680, was one of the early settlers of Pennsylvania in 1739. He had three sons, John, James and Robert. John, Thomas and Richard Penn conveyed unto James Evans, who was a son of the above-named John, four hundred acres of land at Drumore Township, Lancaster County, Pa., where he probably resided until 1752, when he sold it to his brother John Evans, the great-great-grandfather of William S. Evans.

Robert Evans settled on Big Elk Creek, Cecil County, in 1730. His son, Dr. Amos Alexander Evans, was a distinguished surgeon in the United States navy prior to and during the War of 1812. To this branch of the family belong Hon. Alexander Evans and Gen. Andrew Wallace Evans, a retired United States army officer. James Evans settled about the year 1750 in Cecil County, on a tract of land known as "Evans Choice," about four miles north of the town of Port Deposit, on the public road to the West Nottingham Presbyterian Church. From him comes the Rock Run branch of the family, of which Dr. John Evans, a successful surgeon and physician, was a member. James and Robert married sisters, daughters of John Kirkpatrick, who owned a large farm near Rising Sun. John Evans afterwards purchased the Kirkpatrick farm, but continued to reside at Drumore Township. His son, James Evans, became the owner of the Kirkpatrick farm, to which he removed, and where he resided until the time of his death, in 1817.

This memorandum relates more particularly to the descendants of John Evans, which is in the direct line to William S. Evans, the subject of this sketch.

John Evans, of Drumore, was born May 21, 1709, and died January 28, 1798. He married Sarah Denny, by whom he had the following children: James (the great-grandfather of William S. Evans), born February 16, 1749, and died January 22, 1817; Robert, born November 23, 1750, died July 15, 1779; Jane, born January 16, 1753, and died January 31, 1785, unmarried; Margery, born January 30, 1755, and died April 15, 1795, married to her cousin Robert Evans, who was a son of James, and her daughter was the wife of Cyrus Oldham; Margaret, born January 24, 1758, and died December 4, 1793, wife of William Ross, and her descendants, the Keyser family, are still living at Lower Chanceford, York County Pa.; Ann, born May 8, 1760, and died August 30, 1767; John, born November 2, 1762, and died July 4, 1797, the father of the Little Britian, now Lancaster City branch of the family; and David, born December 30, 1765, and the father of the Drumore Township branch of the family.

James Evans (the great-grandfather of William S. Evans), son of John, was born the 16th day of February, 1749. He was three times married, and died January 22, 1817. His first wife was Susan Allison. They were married on the 2d of December, 1776. To them were born the following children: John, born January 27, 1778, died January 17, 1861, and who was the father of the Erie branch of the family; Robert, born November 30, 1779, and died August 5, 1865, the father of Judge James M. Evans, of the orphans' court of Cecil County; Martha, born July 5, 1782, and died July 1, 1783; Susan, wife of James Evans, died July 1, 1783. For his second wife James Evans chose Catherine Porter, daughter of Capt. Andrew Porter, whom he married July 1, 1784. She was born July 14, 1755, and died July 22, 1801. Of their children we note the following: Andrew P., born September 28, 1785, was drowned in the Susquehanna River at Conowingo Bridge, September 11, 1817; he was unmarried. James (grandfather of William S. Evans) was born March 28, 1787, and died May 16, 1855; he was a volunteer in the War of 1812, and was at the battle of North Point. Sarah, who was the wife of William Patten, was born March 1, 1789, and died January 7, 1882, aged ninety-two years, ten months and six days. William Evans, born January 16, 1792, died September 29, 1795.

James Evans married his third wife, Martha Gillespie, October 28, 1802. There were no children by this marriage. James Evans, grandfather of William S. Evans, married Mary Patterson, daughter of John Patterson, who owned what is now known as the Marion Rawlings farm, near Port Deposit. They were married February 14, 1814. The following children were born of this marriage: John Patterson Evans, father of William S. Evans, born November 13, 1814, and died January 9, 1892; Catherine Porter Evans, born October 13, 1816, and died in July, 1897, the wife of W. W. Black, who resided near Charlestown, Cecil County, and was a man much respected for his sterling character; William James Evans, born September 21, 1821, and died January 6, 1892.

John Patterson Evans, the father of William S. Evans, married Rebecca Steel, on the 23d of November, 1843. She was the daughter of Hugh and Esther Steel, who resided on the "Steel Mount," near Port Deposit. She was born on the 27th of March, 1809, and died on the 5th of September, 1891. The following children were born of this marriage: James Hugh, born November 1, 1844; William Steel, born at date before stated, and Amos Standly, born August 5, 1847.

ISAAC W. COALE is one of the leading and representative farmers of District No. 3, Harford County. Not alone is there particular interest attaching to his career as one of the prominent citizens of the community, but in reviewing his genealogical record we find his lineage tracing back to the colonial history of the nation and to that period which marked the inception of the grandest republic the world has ever known. Through such sources have we attained the true American type, and along this line must our investigations proceed if we would learn of the steadfast and unyielding elements which constitute the basis on which has been reared the lofty and magnificent superstructure of an enlightened and favored commonwealth.

Mr. Coale was born in 1823, in the district where he still resides, and is a great-grandson of William Coale, who was probably among the first settlers of this region and made his home on Deer Creek. He was a native of England. His son Isaac was the grandfather of our subject. Dr. Skepwith H. Coale, the father, was for some years a practicing physician of Harford County and also carried on farming to some extent. He married Mrs. Eliza Dugan, whose father, Judge Samuel Chase, was one of America's most distinguished men. Born in Maryland in 1741, he was one of the immortal signers of the Declaration of Independence, a delegate to the continental congress that met in Philadelphia and a member of that body during the Revolution. After the close of the war he was appointed to the Supreme court of the United States by General Washington and so served until his death, in 1811. His father, Rev. Thomas Chase, who was an Episcopal clergyman and the third rector of St. Paul's Church of Baltimore, was a son of Samuel Chase, who came from England to America and resided in Somerset County, Md. Dr. and Mrs. Coale were the parents of six children, viz.: S. Chase, deceased; Eliza M., wife of Frederick D. Jackson; Dr. Skepwith H., Jr., deceased; Isaac W., of this sketch; William F., deceased; and Thomas C., who died in infancy. The father departed this life in 1832, at the age of forty-two years, and the mother in 1853, aged sixty-eight. The latter was given by Mrs. Washington a lock of George Washington's hair, after the death of the general, and this Mr. Coale now has in his possession.

Our subject was educated in a private school and the Baltimore College near the cathedral in that city, and subsequently became connected with the hardware firm of Richard Norris & Son, extensive importers of Baltimore, where he remained for several years. On returning to Harford County in 1843, he located on the old Coale homestead in District No. 3, where he was born and reared, and has since carried on general farming with good success. His fine farm of one hundred and fifty-two acres is under a high state of cultivation, and he has made a specialty of raising and feeding cattle, which has proved a profitable source of income.

In 1846 Mr. Coale married Miss Martha Davis,

of Harford County, a daughter of Joseph Davis, and to them were born the following children: Skepwith H., a resident of Glenville, Md.; William F., Harriet and Eliza, all deceased; Harry D., at home; Martha, deceased; and Charles, at home. The family are identified with Holy Trinity Episcopal Church, Mr. and Mrs. Coale being numbered among its oldest and most prominent members, and he has served as vestryman for a quarter of a century. Politically he is a supporter of Democratic principles, and has faithfully served his fellow-citizens in the capacity of chief judge of the orphans' court. In business affairs he is energetic, prompt and reliable, and in private life his career has ever been such as to commend him to the confidence and high regard of all with whom he has come in contact.

JOHN S. DALLAM. The history of a county, as well as that of a nation, is chiefly the chronicles of the lives and deeds of those who have conferred honor and dignity upon society. The world judges the character of a community by those of its representative citizens, and yields its tribute of admiration and respect for the genius or learning or virtues of those whose works and actions constitute the record of a county's prosperity and pride. As one of the leading and prominent citizens of Harford County we take pleasure in presenting to our readers the sketch of Mr. Dallam, now a resident of Bel Air, and who was for many years actively connected with its business interests.

Mr. Dallam was born near Darlington, Harford County, in 1816, and belongs to one of the old and honored families of the state, it having been founded here by Richard Dallam, a native of England. He was a nephew of the first Duchess of Marlborough, whose maiden name was Sara Jennings, and who was the most intimate personal friend of Queen Anne. Sara Jennings married John Churchill, who largely through her influence with the queen became the first Duke of Marlborough. Richard Dallam located at Joppa, where for many years he was a leading barrister. His wife, Elizabeth Martin, was better known as Betty Martin, famous in nursery rhyme as "Betty Martin, tiptoe, tiptoe fine, couldn't find a husband to suit her mind" (which, however, she finally did). One of their four sons was Richard Dallam, our subject's great-grandfather, who was born in Joppa, and during the Revolutionary War served as paymaster's treasurer, with the title of general of this district, including several states. In the war with England a number of the family bore an important part.

The great-grandfather located on Deer Creek, where he became the owner of a large tract of valuable land. In his family were four sons, John, Winston, William and Richard. William went to Europe and was never heard from afterwards. John had four sons, Samuel, Joseph, William and Richard (father of our subject), also several daughters. Richard, a farmer by occupation, spent much of his life at Darlington, but finally moved to Bel Air, where he died in 1870, when in his eighty-third year. Patriotic like his ancestors, he manifested his loyalty to the country by enlisting in the War of 1812, and gallantly serving in Smith's troop of cavalry. He married Sarah Wallis, and they had three children, who are still living: John S., Mary A. and Joseph W., of Baltimore. Another son, William H., was a major in the Union army during the Civil War. He held the position of secretary and treasurer of the Harford Mutual Fire Insurance Company for three terms, was state's attorney in his district, was also clerk of the circuit court for Harford County, and was filling the office of deputy collector of the port of Baltimore at the time of his death, in the spring of 1883. He was the father of Richard Dallam, the present secretary of state for Maryland.

John S. Dallam was reared in Harford County, where he acquired a common-school education. After starting out in life for himself he was for several years engaged in merchandising in Darlington. He was also interested in farming and the real-estate business. In 1853 he was elected sheriff of the county for a term of two years and also served acceptably as county commissioner for three terms, being president of the board for one term. In 1876 he was county assessor, and at one time was census enumerator, also held a responsible position as storekeeper in the internal revenue department in Baltimore. Whether in public or private life, he has always been found true to every trust reposed in him and is well entitled to the respect in which he is held.

In 1845 Mr. Dallam married Miss Amanda M. Prigg, and they have five children living: Sallie, wife of G. E. N. Ewing; Charles, a resident of Bel Air; Laura; Jefferson A., an attorney of Bel Air; and Frederick, a lawyer of Baltimore. The family is connected with the Presbyterian Church. For more than half a century Mr. Dallam has affiliated with the Masons, and now holds membership in Mt. Ararat Lodge in Bel Air.

DANIEL T. ARBUCKLE, the owner and occupant of a farm in Cecil County, is numbered among the progressive agriculturists of District No. 4. His estate comprises one hundred and fifty-three acres, bearing good improvements, and is devoted to the purposes of general farming. It lies on the Elkton road, five miles from the city of that name, and has been his home since 1894. He is a man of enterprise, and in his business and social relations his energetic character and judgment find ample field for exercise.

In the city of Philadelphia Daniel T. Arbuckle was born in 1852. He is a grandson of Daniel Arbuckle, one of four brothers who emigrated from Ireland and founded homes in the United States. Daniel, father of our subject, was born in Montgomery County, Pa., where in mature years he was engaged in the manufacture of woolen and cotton cloth, having a trade that extended to different parts of the country. Until 1869 his home continued to be in Philadelphia, but he then removed to Maryland and settled on the place now occupied by his son and namesake. He took no active part in politics aside from voting the Republican ticket at elections. In the years of his residence here his honorable and straightforward course won for him the confidence of the people, and it was felt that a good man had passed away when, in 1891, his eyes were closed in death. He was then seventy-eight years of age. By his marriage to Mary S. Magargle, of Philadelphia, he had five children, four of whom are living, namely: Samuel J.; Daniel T.; Paul T., of District No. 4, Cecil County; and Philip, who resides at Cherry Hill.

The education of our subject was obtained in the public schools of Philadelphia. At the age of sixteen he began to learn the plumber's trade, at which he served an apprenticeship of three years. On coming to Maryland, he worked on the home farm for two years, and then took charge of the chemical department of the plant owned by William M. Singerly, remaining in that position for seven years and then returning to the homestead in 1894.

Notwithstanding the fact that his personal interests have demanded much time and thought, he has always been a public-spirited citizen, giving his support to enterprises having for their object the welfare of the people around him. Politically he is a supporter of Republican principles, but has never sought office, preferring to devote his leisure hours to the quiet enjoyment of domestic happiness. He has been twice married, his first wife having been Miss Kate Culp, of Philadelphia, who died in 1891. The children born of this union are Samuel J., Ella May and Raymond. After the death of his first wife he was united with Miss Mary Spratt, an estimable lady residing in District No. 3. The family are identified with the Methodist Episcopal Church at Cherry Hill, to the maintenance of which Mr. Arbuckle is a contributor. Besides assisting materially in the development of the agricultural resources of the district, he has exerted an influence for good as a man of sound sense, unswerving integrity and the thoughtful disposition that makes him just and considerate in his dealings with others.

DAVID HARLAN, M. D.

DAVID HARLAN, medical director, U. S. N., was born November 30, 1809, at Strawberry Hill farm, near Stafford, Harford County, Md. He was a descendant in the fourth generation of Michael Harlan, who with his brother George came to America in 1687 and settled near Kennet (now Pennsbury), Pa. David's grandfather, who also bore the name of David, owned large tracts of land and several mills in Chester County, Pa., and at one time was very prosperous, but endorsed for a number of friends in Wilmington who were engaged in manufacturing and exporting flour; these merchants became bankrupt by the loss and seizure of their ships consequent upon the European wars, in which the property of neutrals (and they being members of the Society of Friends were neutral) suffered from the depredations on all sides, and David Harlan in his old age, through the endorsements for his friends, was brought to be in straitened circumstances.

Jeremiah, father of our subject, removed to Harford County from London Grove Township, about halfway between West Grove and Chatham, and six miles from Kennet, Chester County. The time of his arrival in Maryland was the last quarter of the eighteenth century. The knowledge he had acquired in his father's mills he turned to good account by building mills in Harford and Cecil Counties. In 1812 he bought the Strawberry Hill farm from Reuben Stump. In 1800 he married Esther Stump, daughter of Henry and Rachel (Perkins) Stump, and they had seven children, David being fifth in order of birth. The old homestead where the children were born and reared is most picturesquely situated high on the steep hillsides that form the precipitous banks of the Susquehanna River, about seven miles above where it mingles its waters with those of the Chesapeake Bay. From the house and the several hill tops of the farm one may see for miles up and down the beautiful Susquehanna, may catch a glimpse of the bay far off shining in the sun, while the old town of Port Deposit nestles close to the water's edge, beneath the rugged brows of a ledge of precipitous hills covered with a dark olive cloak of cedar trees, and on listening, the ear catches the subdued roar of the river as it rushes over its rocky bed, which led the Indians to call it the Susquehanna, "rippling over stones."

With wise forethought Jeremiah Harlan was anxious that his children should have the best possible education, and in the days when college graduates were not as commonly met with as now, he secured as tutor for his children Dr. Samuel Guile, a graduate of Harvard College. In his yard he built a stone schoolhouse, where Judge Price and his sister, Mrs. Rachel Parker, and John Stump, of Perry Point, and others of David's cousins came to attend school with him and his brothers and sisters. David also attended Rock Run Academy (or, as it is more popularly known, Stephenson's stone schoolhouse), which was originally erected by the Methodists for a meeting house. In 1829, when he was twenty years of age, he began the study of medicine under the tutelage of Dr. John Archer, of Rock Run. Afterward he attended the Maryland Hospital and Washington Medical School of Baltimore for two years, graduating in 1832 with the degree of M. D., and also receiving the diploma of the Medical and Chirurgical Faculty of Maryland. He immediately located near Chestertown, Kent County, Md., where he engaged in practice for three years. Upon the recommendation of Dr. John P. MacKenzie, he applied for admission to the United States navy, and was examined in 1835 and commissioned assistant surgeon. Forthwith he was ordered to report on board the United States ship "Peacock," then in the New York harbor preparing to start on a voyage around the world. This, his first voyage, was the longest and most eventful of his life. In the spring of 1835 he sailed out of the harbor of New York; four years later he returned to the same harbor, having sailed around the world, gone through many dangers, visited many lands and seen many strange sights.

The "Peacock" sailed first to Rio Janeiro, Brazil, thence around the Cape of Good Hope to Zanzibar, thence to Muscat, Bombay, Ceylon, Bangkok, Siam, China, across the Pacific to the Bonin Islands, thence to Monterey, Cal., via the Sandwich Islands, from there to Acapulco, Mexico, and Lima, Peru, then to Valparaiso, Chili; returning from there to Lima, where Dr. Harlan was transferred to the United States schooner "Enterprise," visiting a number of ports on the Pacific Coast of South and Central America, when he was transferred to the line of battle ship "North Carolina," of one hundred guns. In that ship he cruised on the Pacific Coast, rounded Cape Horn to Rio Janeiro, and thence to New York.

Voyages of circumnavigation were not so frequent in the '30s as they have since become, and this one contained more of interest than usual, both from the unusual route taken and from the fact that it included an embassy to Muscat and Siam for the purpose of exchanging ratifications of treaties of amity and commerce, which had been entered into the year previous, by the United States with the Sultan of Muscat and with "His Magnificent Majesty, the King of Siam." The limited space at command will permit only the most casual reference to the more striking events of this voyage. The diary of David Harlan records nothing more noteworthy than the usual courtesies received by the ship's officers in the hospitable port of Rio Janeiro, the glories of a phosphorescent sea in the tropics and the schools of flying fish, the nautilus and other wonders of the sea, interesting to a man on his first voyage, the capture of several sharks by the crew, one of which measured ten feet in length, etc., till, having passed the island of Zanzibar, while sailing along the coast of Africa, the ship grounded on a sunken reef not on any chart. The next day, upon the tide going out, the ship was left in a very precarious position, and to add to the dangers of her position, they were menaced by a number of daus filled with Bedouin Arab pirates, who while the ship was in a helpless condition and careened over on her side so that her guns were useless, showed plainly their hostile purpose and openly boasted that they would soon be joined by forty more boats. In this hazardous position, it was thought best to dispatch one of the ship's boats to Muscat to ask for assistance, while the rest of the ship's crew set to work to lighten the ship by throwing overboard half of the heavy guns and other things. Then by putting out anchors with hawsers attached, they succeeded after two or three days of unremitting toil, in warping the ship in water deep enough to float her. All the time they were threatened by the Arabs, who hovered around them and stole some of their stores, which they were obliged to put on an improvised raft. Fortunately the pirates were not sufficiently reinforced to venture an attack. It may be mentioned that the boat arrived safely in Muscat after a perilous voyage, in which they were chased by the Arabs, and that the Sultan of Muscat took the most energetic measures for the relief of the "Peacock," and sent the characteristic order to the Arab chiefs along the coast that he would hold them responsible "with their heads" for any injury to any of the "Peacock's" crew. On the ship's arrival at Muscat, she was supplied with everything necessary by the Sultan, who showed the greatest kindness to all her company. He also did her the very unusual honor of a personal visit and gave a banquet to her officers. Among the dishes at the banquet was one of boiled ant eggs, but Dr. Harlan is not on record as having tasted it.

The "Peacock" proceeded from Muscat to Bombay, where it was found necessary to put her in the dry dock for repairs. There was thus a delay of over a month in that typical city of the Orient, where can be seen every type of nationality of the east in most grotesque contact with the civilization and manners of the west. As one of Dr. Harlan's comrades writes: "It was a novel sight to see kummerbanded Hindoos, turbaned Banyans, and lofty capped Parsees in white, sitting in English built buggies, driving active horses, having a Hindoo in white costume running alongside with a hand on the shaft or just ahead, ever and anon crying out 'paish,' to warn foot passengers out of the way." The strange costumes of the females and their unbecoming employments; the absence of costume in the males; the variety of equipages; Brahmin priests in yellow robes; naked devotees smeared all over with clay or dust; the females of a better order attired in bright colored robes, but barefooted and loaded with tinkling ornaments about the ankles and rings on the toes. Did space permit, we would quote from Dr. Harlan's diary his description of some of the strange sights of this land of wonders, where one could have the services of four stalwart fellows to carry him about all day on their shoulders in a silk-cushioned palanquin, with a massol boy to run alongside to answers questions and wait on him, for the trifling sum of two and one-half rupees a day, about one dollar. Now he tells of a grave Hindoo reverently salaaming to the new moon and at another time going to bathe to cleanse himself from the supposed contamination of an eclipse of the sun; now, of the weird sight of eight funeral pyres all burning at the same time along the low sandy beach, the several bodies in all stages of consumption, some a mere heap of smoking ashes, while others, just arrived, are being placed on the pile prepared for them, and around each a few relatives or friends linger to keep the flames supplied with fresh faggots until their work is fully done; now he describes a marriage procession that he saw, with its brass bands, its six "floats" of artificial flowers, its thousands of torches and lanterns, with red, blue, green and yellow fire burning, its display of fireworks, including rockets and elaborate fixed pieces, its crowded procession of women gorgeously dressed and literally loaded down with jewelry and ornaments on wrists and ankles, fingers and toes, and in their ears and even noses, resembling more a Mardi Gras pageant than anything the western world has to compare with it,—and all to betroth a boy of ten years to a girl of six.

From Bombay an excursion was made to the island of Elephanta, with its wonderful cave-temple, which contains a colossal monolithic bust, supposed to represent the Hindoo trinity, viz.: Brahma, Vishnu and Siva. The plan of this temple is extremely grand and magnificent, and the whole is carved out of the solid rock of the hillside. It is believed to have been excavated more than a thousand years ago, and has been deserted by its priests and worshippers for several centuries. While at Bombay the "Peacock" received back the cannon which had been thrown overboard to lighten the ship when aground. The Sultan of Muscat had them fished up and sent on to her at Bombay, thus adding another to his many acts of courtesy to our government.

The voyage from Bombay to Ceylon was uneventful, the ship coasting along generally within sight of land and being constantly visited by natives with boat loads of fruit and poultry for sale. They arrived at Colombo in the middle of December, 1835, and stayed nine days, which were made most pleasant by the courtesies of the English governor of the island and the officers of the garrison stationed there. Dr. Harlan and his fellow-officers spent much time while there in driving about this most beautiful of tropical islands with its cinnamon plantations, its banyan trees with their descending branches forming true sylvan arcades, and its bread fruit trees. But this earthly paradise must have its serpent, and Ceylon has the venomous cobra de capello, whose bite is death, one of which they killed in a cinnamon garden, and the iguanas, an ugly lizard that grows to be two and one-half feet long.

From Colombo the "Peacock" sailed for the island of Java, passed through the Sunda Strait, and anchored off Batavia to secure ship's stores and provisions. Here they received their first letters from home, which had been written more than four months before. The water with which the ship's tanks were filled at Batavia proved to be very bad and caused much sickness. On the way to Bangkok two of the crew died of dysentery, and thirty were on the sick list at one time. For the fourth time on this voyage the "Peacock" crossed the equator and then coasted along within sight of the island of Borneo, the home of the Dyaks, the "head-hunting savages." Sailing up the Gulf of Siam, they passed several small floating islands, as they were called, and great numbers of water snakes of strange colors and shapes, specimens of which Dr. Harlan preserved in alcohol and brought home with him.

March 26 the ship anchored off Paknam, situated at the north of the Meinam River, and the port of Bangkok, the capital city of Siam. The object of this visit, as already stated, was to exchange ratifications of a treaty of amity and commerce negotiated the year previous by Edmond Roberts, as minister of the United States. Both copies of the treaty were written in English, Siamese, Chinese and Portugese. In accordance with Asiatic ideas, the copy of the treaty delivered to his "Magnificent Majesty, the King of Siam," was handsomely engrossed, bound in rich and costly binding and enclosed in an inlaid box. The seal of the United States attached to it was encased in a small round box of gold. The delivery of this treaty was also accompanied by the presentation to his Magnificent Majesty of costly presents, including two gold-mounted swords of exquisite workmanship and costing between thirteen and fourteen hundred dollars apiece, two very large and elegant mirrors, an American flag and other things.

It would be useless to attempt even the most casual reference to the incidents and events of interest that accompanied the "Peacock's" stay in Siam, where the whole life and manner of thought of the natives are so entirely different from ours that the most trivial features of every-day life are worthy of note. There could not fail to be found many things worthy of record in a land where the king's patent of nobility and commission to his governors are a tea-kettle, cups, spittoon and tobacco box, all of gold, on a gold tray, which is borne before the owner "whene'er he takes his walks abroad" and at the sight of which every native must prostrate himself to the ground. The Siamese name for Siam is Thai, literally "free country," yet the natives are virtually in a state of slavery to their rulers, and the sovereign of this free country is never mentioned except by such soft and flattering epithets as the "Sacred Lord of Heads," "The Sacred Lord of Life," "The Owner of All," "Lord of White Elephants," "Most Exalted Lord, Infallible and Infinitely Powerful." The habits of the Siamese often exhibit the most curious combination of luxury and magnificence with squalor and dirt. Lizards and snakes were seen hiding in the walls and rafters of the palace of his Magnificent Majesty himself, and at a dinner given to the "Peacock's" officers by the Rajah of Lagore, a tributary state of Siam, the viands were served on gold and silver dishes, there being by actual count not less than fifty-four gold vessels used in the entertainment, and yet the Rajah himself and his servants did not hesitate to mount upon the table and walk over it in their bare feet. At an audience given to the "Peacock's" officers by his Magnificent Majesty, they were permitted to wear their shoes in deference to American custom, but were required like the Siamese to salaam three times upon coming into his presence. The captain of a merchant ship was by his own request allowed to be present with the ship's officers at this audience, and shortly after they had entered and made their three salaams, his Majesty wished to inquire from him something about his ship and he was ordered to again salaam three times before answering. This so disgusted his American independence that while going through his salaams he said, sotto voce: "What a fool I was to come here. I have just got through this monkey business and now have got to do it again," which remark afforded much amusement to the Americans present.

While in Siam, the Asiatic cholera broke out aboard the "Peacock." One night a boat's crew of the sailors staid ashore. They built a large fire, cooked a lot of fowls and spent the night in a carouse. The next morning many of them were stricken with symptoms of the cholera, and within twenty-four hours out of the two hundred and one souls on the ship's register, twenty-three men were down with the cholera and one was dead. The fleet surgeon, Dr. Ruschenberger, was at Bangkok, two hundred miles in the interior, and the captain applied to Dr. Harlan to know what was to be done in the serious and alarming circumstances in which they were placed. He replied that it was necessary to get the ship out of the sultry miasmatic atmosphere of her present anchorage into the gulf, where by tacking across the gulf they could ventilate the ship, and by employing the men at light work keep their minds from dwelling on the sick and dead. This was serious advice to give, for it entailed on him the whole care and responsibility of their medical attendance through what promised to be a violent epidemic, but its wisdom was fully justified by the result which followed its adoption. The sick list was kept down to thirty-two and there was but one other death.

From Siam the "Peacock" proceeded to Cochin-China, which country Mr. Roberts was also commissioned to open negotiations with, looking to commercial treaty. For that purpose the vessel proceeded to Turon, but the visit was without results. The natives were very suspicious, and direct intercourse with their emperor was found to be very difficult and attended with so much loss of time that the attempt was given up. The great amount of sickness aboard both the "Peacock" and "Enterprise," Mr. Roberts himself being seriously ill, hastened this conclusion; in fact, it was absolutely necessary that the ship should proceed to some more hospitable port, where they could be properly supplied with provisions and stores. All on board were either enfeebled by disease or debilitated by the climate and the unwholesome water which they were often obliged to use. Their supply of bread had become worm-eaten and had to be cast overboard, and they were reduced to a diet of salt meat and rice. They therefore proceeded to Macao, the port of Canton. Here Dr. Ruschenberger, the fleet surgeon, rented a house and took all the sick ashore. Dr. Harlan stayed aboard the "Peacock" to care for the convalescent. Mr. Roberts, the diplomatic envoy, and Lieutenant-Commandant Campbell, the commanding officer of the "Enterprise," died here and were interred in the British burying ground. The other sick gradually improved in the hospital. After being again provided with stores, the "Peacock" and "Enterprise" started across the Pacific for the Sandwich Islands, but made a pleasant stop on the way to the Bonin Islands. While here the men caught about forty large sea turtles, any two of which furnished ample food for one hundred and eighty persons during a day. They weighed two or three hundred pounds each.

In the early part of September the ship arrived at the Sandwich Islands after a tedious and unpleasant passage of forty-nine days. During their stay of about a month on the islands, Dr. Harlan spent much of his time on horseback. He took daily baths in the cool mountain streams and gave himself up to a diet of fresh meats and vegetables, and took every means to recuperate from the state of debility that had taken hold upon him in common with all his shipmates, as a consequence of their long stay in the most unhealthy part of the tropics. His journal records a visit of ceremony to the king of the Sandwich Islands, a personage whom they often met in the billiard rooms and bowling alleys; a "louari" or native feast was given to the officers of the fleet, at which the king was present. One of the favorite dishes at the banquet was baked dog.

From Honolulu the "Peacock" made a quick voyage to Monterey, Upper California, then a part of Mexico. In this portion of the Pacific they constantly fell in with whalers, many of whom, in those days before the introduction of petroleum, made rapid fortunes for their owners in an industry that is now a thing of the past. The whales themselves were often seen, one day several of them appearing in the harbor of Monterey, and as Dr. Harlan and some others were coming out of the ship in a small boat, a huge whale came up to blow several times quite near their boat, so near as to make them desire to give him a wider berth. When he went down again, though it was difficult to tell where he would come up next, they pulled hard for the ship; as they did so, there was a ripple in the water behind them, the boat rocked with the impulse of a wave, and suddenly the whale reared his enormous head with open mouth, six or seven feet out of the water, and just behind the boat. The rowers were so startled that they stopped with oars in mid air; the next minute a lieutenant sang out "give way" and they did with a will. One second later, one stroke less, and the whale would have come up directly under the boat and capsized it.

From Monterey the "Peacock" went to Mazatlan, Mexico, thence proceeded southward and touched at San Blas, Acapulco and Payta, arriving at Callao, the port of Lima, to find it under a weak blockade by Chili, which was then at war with Peru. Commodore Kennedy was appealed to by the United States consul to remain and protect American interests, and though all on board were anxious to get home after their long voyage, he felt constrained to do so. The "Peacock" remained at Callao more than six weeks, which gave her officers a fine opportunity to become acquainted with the gay capital of Peru; for the Peruvians were gay, notwithstanding the fact that the country was at war and the Chilians were trying to blockade the port of their capital. Dull care sits lightly on the shoulders of the Spaniards and the ladies of Lima danced and sang, gambled and smoked as unconcernedly as if they knew nothing of war. They were fond of riding, were skillful horsewomen and rode fine spirited horses beautifully caparisoned, but they preferred to ride straddle, and fashion did not forbid it. They were fond of sea bathing and many of them spent much time at Chorillos, the fashionable seaside resort for Lima. The gayeties were increased by the occurrence of the carnival season. Then the torreo, the bull baiting, which is the national sport of the Spaniards, was entered into with zest by the inhabitants of Lima. Dr. Harlan found the torreo disgusting, the sickening slaughter (eight bulls and several horses were killed) and the cruelty of the show could not be compensated for, in his opinion, by the excitement to be derived from the hazard the metadors ran of being killed, or the skill and coolness they displayed in the encounter.

Lima is seven miles from Callao and the journey was generally made either in a stage or on horseback. Though a short distance, highwaymen infested the road and frequently asked for a traveler's purse and valuables at the point of the pistol. The authorities seem to have made no serious attempt to suppress these outrages. One Sunday the ship's sergeant of marines was halted by two highwaymen and forced to dismount and empty his pockets. Meanwhile several people rode by on donkeys and simply laughed at what was going on. While the ship was in the harbor of Callao, the blockade squadron had several skirmishes with some Peruvian gunboats protected by the fort, but no serious damage was done on either side.

From Callao they proceeded to Valparaiso, stopping one day at the island of Juan Fernandez, made famous by the romance of Robinson Crusoe, dear to every boy's heart. They found it a land of "milk and honey," beautiful in its verdure and abounding in fruits. From Valparaiso a visit was made to Santiago, and Dr. Harlan afterward spoke most gratefully of the hospitality and courtesy of its citizens. From Valparaiso the ship returned to Callao, where Dr. Harlan was transferred, July 3, 1837, to the "Enterprise," which was to stay in the Pacific squadron, while the "Peacock" was to return home. After he had left the "Peacock" he received a very grateful mark of the high esteem in which he was held by those who had been under his care. The crew, numbering over two hundred men, subscribed $1 each to purchase a handsome gold-mounted sword to be presented to Dr. Harlan as a mark of their appreciation for his attention to them throughout the cruise, but especially when they were attacked with cholera in Siam. Upon his return to the United States two years later he received a sword bearing this inscription: "Presented to Doctor David Harlan, by the crew of the U. S. ship Peacock, in grateful remembrance of his kind attentions to them in the hours of sickness during her late cruise, November 1, 1837."

The "Enterprise" sailed from Callao to Valparaiso, where she stayed about ten days and returned to Callao, whence she sailed for Mazatlan. She stopped at the Gallipagos Islands to catch terrapin, for which purpose and to gun, the officers and men were allowed to go ashore. At one o'clock the ship fired a gun to call all aboard, but when night came the purser and four men were missing. They were lost and could not find the ship. The captain became justly alarmed for their safety on this uninhabited island without fresh water. He sent a party ashore to build a watch fire on the highest point and to fire a musket every ten minutes during the night. Early the next morning the purser and one man came within sight of the ship, and the others were recovered before night. They had suffered all the agonies of men dying of thirst; they were pale, emaciated and racked with fever, though they had resorted to every expedient to allay the agonies of their thirst. They had killed turtles and birds and drunk their blood, had bathed their bodies in the sea and had tried to rest covered with wet sand, but with all their efforts they were almost delirious when they reached the ship. Though these five men suffered so much through their want of care, in losing their way, the rest of the crew, apart from the subsequent anxiety on account of the missing, spent a pleasant day at Hood's Island and captured many terrapin, twenty-five being taken the first day.

After a few days at Panama the ship started for Mazatlan. During the night of October 17, 1837, she was overtaken by such a furious tempest that nothing but the most strenuous efforts of every soul on board, from the captain to cabin boy, with the aid of divine Providence, kept her from sinking with all on board. All day there had been a fresh easterly wind and considerable sea, both of which increased toward sundown. In the middle watch the wind veered and came rushing upon the schooner with the violence of a tempest from a different direction. Great seas immediately broke over the struggling vessel and the water rushed down the hatches in such masses that the cry rose from the berth deck "The water is up to the hammocks." The rush of wind and water had extinguished all lights; there were occasional lurid flashes of lightning and the constant glimmer of the phosphorescent water rushing from side to side as the ship rolled, carrying with it everything that would float. We quote Dr. Harlan's own words as written in his journal just after the storm: "To look along the berth deck and behold the scene was awful. On deck was the roaring of the wind and the breaking of each wave over the ship; the shouting of officers and men, showing clearly the extreme distraction when sailors forget the silent obedience they are wont to give; in the midst of all this confusion and uproar, so violent a sea came upon the vessel that the starboard bulwarks were buried and so far did she sink, that those below and some on deck said she was on her beam ends. I was sitting at the larboard end of the ward room table, when the vessel was at the extreme point to which she sank; she remained stationary, how long I cannot say, but it seemed long; the situation of the vessel was so strange that the noise of voices on deck was hushed, there was a breathless involuntary pause; the sense of instant destruction was so apparent that the oldest seamen ceased momentarily their efforts, but when she rose a shout burst forth and the labors were resumed. After this the mass of waters below and on the spar deck seemed to hold her still in the water and she never careened so far again. A light was got and every hatch and scuttle was secured; the pumps were fully manned; the ward room skylight was raised for men to come down from on deck; a number came down to pass shot to throw overboard; I assisted. A line was formed and from hand to hand rapidly the round shot, twenty-four pounds, grape and canister, passed up the hatch and overboard. On deck they were working the pumps, trying to throw the guns overboard and keep the ports and skuppers open. Three times they were washed from the long forward gun, the water coming up to their waists, and the utmost exertion was necessary to hold on and prevent the reflux from carrying them out of the ports. Below there were about twelve of us in line passing shot; several hundred had passed each hand and not a word had escaped anyone; the perspiration flowed freely from the severe labor. At length some one said, 'What shall we do if we meet the Mexicans now?' and the quarter gunner of the gang replied, 'Beat them with our cutlasses.' Here ended the conversation, and it will appear strange to anyone acquainted with the talkative man-of-war sailor. The vessel seemed relieved, but so great was the quantity of water on the spar deck, that the forecastle, boats, trunk, binacle, armchests and guns were all that were to be seen within the bulwarks; the water seemed so permanent that it was the belief of Lieutenant Leigh that the vessel was settling, and he proposed to the captain to cut away the mainmast. The captain himself took off his overcoat to be free to swim if the ship sank. But the casting away of the guns and shot now evidently relieved and lightened the ship; the pumps gained fast on the water below; the hatches were so completely secured that they kept out the water. One long nine-pound gun and one twenty-four pounder were thrown overboard. The seamen began to talk, and it became evident that the ship was saved from the present gale."

After the storm, and without further mishap, the "Enterprise" arrived at Mazatlan, where she stayed twenty-two days. She then started to return to Callao, stopping at San Blas, the island of Tobogo in the bay of Panama, Payta, Lanbayéque, and Truxillo, and reaching Callao April 13, 1838. After a stay of five days, during which Dr. Harlan found time to visit Lima twice, the ship sailed for Valparaiso, where she arrived May 20, and after a stay of nine days set sail on her return to Callao, touching at Arica, Islay, the port of Arequipa, and Pisco. During his long stay at these various Spanish-American ports, Dr. Harlan became familiar with the language and habits of the Spaniards, and his journals are especially full in describing their manners and customs, their houses, their strange boats and the ease and freedom with which they receive strangers. He often mentioned the beauty of the phosphorescent sea, a phenomenon they often met with. Under the date of March 13, 1838, he writes: "This evening, as soon as it was dark, the whole sea was white from phosphorescence. The color was somewhat like the milky way, but more brilliant. At the verge of the visible horizon the luminous effect seemed increased, probably from the eye being nearer on the horizontal, and it shone a brilliant zone all around. Dark clouds were hanging about the horizon, contrasting strongly with the radiant arena of the ocean. The breeze was moderately fresh and wherever it ruffled the top of the waves or the wake of the ship or the log line or a bucket, or anything agitated the water, it showed the most brilliant phosphorescence I have ever seen. We took up some water and found it filled with animalculæ or ova. When a bottle of the water was agitated it shone with innumerable bright spots of strong light, which whirled around the bottle with the rapid motion of the water."

At Callao Dr. Harlan was transferred to the "North Carolina," a line of battle ship of one hundred guns, and as large and fine a ship as there was in the navy. While at Callao, a Chilian fleet of thirty-two sail, including men-of-war and transports, came into the harbor. They landed a force of five thousand and four hundred men, including one thousand horsemen, which while proceeding toward Lima were attacked by the Peruvians within sight of the "North Carolina." The engagement began about four o'clock and continued for two hours after dark. The scintilating flashes of the musketry and the dark bursts of flame offered a brilliant sight and occasioned the opinion on board the "North Carolina" that it was a hotly contested and sanguinary fight, but the killed on both sides did not exceed four hundred. The result was the Chilians entered Lima. The Peruvians had four men-of-war in the harbor of Callao. To prevent them from falling into the hands of the Chilians, they sold two of them and English flags were hoisted to cover them. The other two were dismantled and one of them sunk, the other was abandoned and the Chilians carried it off. These results were accomplished by a good deal of cannonading by sea and many skirmishes on land, most of which were in sight of the "North Carolina" and on one occasion she with other neutral ships found it necessary for her own safety to move out of range of the shot. The fortunes of Peru were now at a low ebb, and it looked as if the Chilians would conquer the whole country, but Santa Cruz and his army returned and the Chilians retired before him and embarked on board their fleet. Upon his return to Lima after driving out the Chilians, Santa Cruz was greeted by the people as their deliverer, with the most extravagant demonstrations of joy. He visited the "North Carolina" one day before she sailed.

February 9, 1839, the "North Carolina" sailed for New York. The home voyage was uneventful. She touched at Valparaiso, rounded Cape Horn, stopped about two weeks at Rio Janeiro and anchored within sight of Sandy Hook June 28, 1839, whence four years and two months before Dr. Harlan had started on his first voyage. After spending about three weeks in New York harbor on board the "North Carolina," he was granted the usual leave of absence for three months, which he spent at his home in Harford County. His leave of absence was extended and he went to Philadelphia, where he took a course of lectures at the University of Pennsylvania. He was next assigned to duty at the naval asylum, Philadelphia, and continued for two years to attend the medical lectures at the University and the clinics at the Pennsylvania and Blockly hospitals. July 8, 1841, he was examined and commissioned as past assistant surgeon, and in October was ordered to the schooner "Madison" for service on the coast of Florida, in pursuit of hostile Indians in the Everglades. In a few weeks he was attacked with yellow fever at Key West, and as soon as able to travel was sent home by a medical survey. After many months of convalescence he was assigned to shore duty at the Naval Rendezvous, Baltimore. In October, 1844, he joined the brig "Somers" of the West India squadron. Starting from Philadelphia, he went to several ports in the island of San Domingo, and thence to the Gulf of Mexico, visiting Key West, Pensacola and Vera Cruz. In October, 1845, he was transferred to the steamship "Princeton," of the gulf squadron, and December 6 was promoted to the rank of surgeon.

The following May war was declared with Mexico and the "Princeton" was employed in blockading Vera Cruz. The blockade continued many months and the ships engaged in it were frequently exposed to violent gales from the north and west, and in one of these northers the brig "Somers," from which he had so lately been transferred, was overturned and sunk with thirty-one of her men and two officers. March 9, 1847, the "Princeton" left Anton Lizardo, the place of rendezvous for General Scott's army of invasion, and proceeded to the point selected for landing the troops, opposite the island of Sacrificios. The "Princeton" had on board four hundred and eighty soldiers. They arrived at Sacrificios about two o'clock and before midnight the whole army of twelve thousand men had been landed without mishap or opposition from the enemy, though a succession of sand hills coming down close to the beach gave a good cover from which a small force could have seriously harassed them. Dr. Harlan's journal thus describes the landing of the first line as seen from the "Princeton's" deck: "The numerous vessels that had transported the second and third lines were still crowded with American braves, when the boats with the first division struck the beach. Instantly the men and officers jumped out, and as soon as they had planted their footsteps on Mexican soil they were greeted with three cheers. They immediately formed in line and charged to the top of the nearest hill, expecting to find Mexicans behind it. When the first ensign bearer reached the top and his standard was seen outlined against the western sky, the stars and stripes received such a united and spontaneous cheer from the thousands mounted in the tops and rigging of the ships that it thrilled every heart; no one with an American heart in his breast could remain quiet, and I cheered as loud as I could." We know now that this small army of twelve thousand men was destined to conquer an empire for their country and gain for themselves a reputation unsurpassed in the annals of the world for victories over superior numbers, strongly intrenched, a crown of glory for which one-fourth of them paid with their lives.

While Dr. Harlan did not actively participate in the four days' bombardment of Vera Cruz, he was always within sight of the flying shot and at times so near that they passed over his head. March 29 he was present at the surrender of the city, and with a small body of officers went into the city, where he found upon a wall the ensign of the fort, a small flag, trampled under foot. This he took as a memento of the surrender. The day of the surrender the "Princeton" left Vera Cruz to carry the news to the United States, stopping at Pensacola to deliver her dispatches, and then proceeding to Philadelphia, where Dr. Harlan was detached. He had been promoted, December 6, 1845, to the rank of surgeon, and the latter part of that winter received a short leave of absence while the "Princeton" was being repaired at Philadelphia. He went to his home in Harford County and was married March 3, 1846, to Miss Margaret R., only child of James B. and Mary A. (Baker) Herbert. After being detached from the "Princeton" he remained at home waiting orders until May 7, 1849, when he was ordered to the "Falmouth," at Boston, for a cruise in the Pacific. While en route to the Pacific, the ship had to pass around Cape Horn, which, in July, the mid-winter month in the southern hemisphere, is a thing very much dreaded by sailors. The ship met with severe cold weather, and for days sailed through seas of slush ice. The spray froze over the decks and rigging until her shrouds became a mass of ice as thick as a man's body. The sailors suffered much from the necessary exposure to the cold, and it was then that Dr. Harlan made an innovation in the practice of the navy. It had been customary upon such occasions to increase the rations of spirits "to splice the main brace," as the sailors say. In place of this Dr. Harlan had each man served with a pot of hot coffee as he went on and came off his night watches. Under this treatment the health of the men was excellent and the result of the experiment so satisfactory that he afterward received a letter from the surgeon-general of the navy, warmly commending his action. It may be worthy of note that in those days each seaman received a half pint of whiskey as his usual daily ration of spirits, just as he received his allowance of pork and beans. Since, as is well known, the allowance of spirits has been abolished in the navy. For about a year after passing the cape, the "Falmouth" cruised along the coast of South and North America, as far north as Astoria, at the mouth of the Columbia River in Oregon. All of the important points on the coast were visited, many of them several times. In 1850 the "Falmouth" sailed from San Francisco to the Sandwich Islands. From Hilo, in the island of Hawaii, Dr. Harlan made a four days' journey and ascent of the volcano of Kilauea, the largest in the world, its crater being nine miles in circumference. When he was there, its immense, deep, sunken area contained numerous small cones and chimneys, from which issued smoke and sulphurous fumes, and during the night which he spent on the crater's rim, he saw several glowing with flames and red hot lava. While exploring the crater he passed over lava so hot that his barefoot guide could not follow him. On his way to the mountains he passed what had once been a river of fiery lava, which had flowed through a cocoanut grove and had buried beneath it all the trees in its course. The lava was now hard and the trees beyond the reach of the stream were undisturbed in their growth.

At Honolulu, in the island of Cahu, Dr. Harlan frequently met his majesty, King Kauikeaouli, whom he had known on his first visit in 1836, and at a party took tea with the queen and many chiefs and their ladies. When the queen withdrew, she entered a low carriage drawn by natives, while the gentlemen of the court walked alongside. The "Falmouth" spent about eight months cruising among the islands of the Pacific, visiting the Marquesas, Samoan, Feejee and Society groups. Dr. Harlan saw much of the natives so lately converted from the most revolting cannibalism. He saw and talked with a Feejee man who had been the king's butcher and had killed and prepared for the table, so to speak, many of his fellow-beings. The most influential chief of Rakiraki embraced Christianity while Dr. Harlan was there. His father had been a most monstrous cannibal, notorious over all Feejee. He kept account of persons he ate by placing stones in rows. A man who saw and counted these stones said there were eight hundred and seventy-two of them, representing as many human beings devoured by this monster. That such a story, whether strictly true or not, could be current, shows the extent of this horrible practice.

In July, 1851, the "Falmouth" returned to San Francisco, and Dr. Harlan was detached. He then took the mail steamer to Panama, crossed the isthmus on mule-back to the Chagres River, which he descended in a small boat, and at Aspinwall took steamer for New York, going from there to his home. At the close of a three months' leave he was ordered to duty on the receiving ship at Boston, where he remained until October, 1854. The following year was spent at home, on leave waiting orders. On New Year's day of 1856 he was ordered to sea on the "Merrimack," a fine new steam frigate just put in commission. She had five hundred and eighty men and officers, including three medical officers, of whom Surgeon Harlan was chief. At Norfolk and Annapolis the ship was visited by many persons, including President Pierce, the secretary of the navy and members of congress, all of whom united in admiring the fine vessel. She then went to Havana, Cuba, and Key West, Fla., and having broken her propeller, returned to Boston for repairs, thence proceeded to New York, and September 9, 1856, sailed for England, spending fourteen days between Sandy Hook and Lizard Point. The month that the ship lay in harbor at Southampton, Dr. Harlan spent in London and in various places in Ireland, Scotland and England. He also had an opportunity to visit Paris, while the ship was at Brest, France. Two weeks and a-half were spent in Lisbon, Portugal, and over three weeks in Cadiz, Spain. The ocean was again crossed to the West Indies, visiting Barbadoes, St. Croix and St. Thomas, and at Boston, April 25, 1857, Dr. Harlan was detached and ordered to Norfolk to join the "Roanoke," a new ship of the same class as the "Merrimack." She proceeded to Aspinwall on the gulf side of the Isthmus of Panama, passing through the Mona Passage, then returned to New York, from there went to Boston, where the officers were given three months' leave of absence. December 1, 1860, Dr. Harlan was ordered to join the ship "Cyane" at Panama, and took the mail steamer from New York to Aspinwall, crossed the isthmus by railroad, and reached the ship in ten days. The "Cyane" proceeded to Acapulco, San Blas, Mazatlan, Cape St. Lucas, Guaymas, and returned to Panama, spending nearly nine months there; then sailed up the coast as far as Mazatlan, and returned to Acapulco, where, December 20, 1862, she was well situated to afford her officers a fine view of a bombardment of the old fort in the harbor by the French, and their assault upon and capture from the Mexicans of several small batteries of antiquated guns.

Dr. Harlan's medical journals show that he gave great attention to causes affecting the health of his ships' crews. On three occasions he received commendation from the surgeon-general for his studies in naval hygiene and his reports of his observations. While on the "Peacock" in the harbor of Acapulco, he noticed that the air from a marsh caused fever in a number of the crew who had not been ashore. Subsequent observation of the bad effect on the health of sailors of other vessels which anchored in that part of the harbor convinced him that it was very dangerous. During the four days the "Lancaster" anchored in that place, there were many cases of fever and eight deaths. He sent to the bureau of medicine and surgery a map of the harbor with a dotted line showing the anchorage that exposed the ship's company to the fevers, and the navy department has since marked the charts with "Dr. Harlan's danger line." He remained on the "Saranac" until June 8, 1863, when he was detached and returned home via the isthmus, reaching Harford County July 6, 1863, after an absence of more than two years and seven months. His son, Beatty, who had been born during his absence, was nearly two and one-half years old when his father first saw him.

Afterward being stationed at the naval asylum, Philadelphia, Dr. Harlan and his family remained there until May 18, 1865, when he was detached and ordered as fleet surgeon to Key West to join the United States frigate "Powhatan," the flagship of the blockading squadron in the Gulf of Mexico. The war was now coming to a close and directly afterward he joined the "Powhatan," she returned to Boston and he was detached. He was never a man to intrude his opinions on others, but throughout these troublous times of war, he was a stanch supporter of the Union and the government he served. During the spring and summer of 1866 he was a member of the board of visitors to the naval academy at Annapolis, Md., and of the board of surgeons to examine candidates for admission to the academy. September 3, 1866, he was stationed at the academy as surgeon and moved with his family to the surgeon's house next to the hospital in the academy grounds. He remained at this pleasant station until January 5, 1869, when he was detached on account of a tedious illness of more than four months and returned to his home at Churchville, Md. Afterward, for two months, he was stationed at the naval hospital on the government farm at Annapolis, Md. March 3, 1871, he was promoted to the rank of medical director, and was retired November 30, 1871, upon reaching the age of sixty-two years. Returning then to his home in Churchville, he continued to lead a most active life, devoting himself with his accustomed tireless energy to the improvements of his own and his wife's extensive farms. He died at his home in Churchville July 12, 1893.

While in Annapolis in 1866, Dr. Harlan began to carry into execution a plan which had long been forming in his mind. He purchased six acres of a pleasantly elevated piece of land about a quarter of a mile east of the village of Churchville and within easy view of his home. There he built a pretty little frame church of gothic design, which was called the Church of the Holy Trinity. The consent of the rectors and vestries of the adjacent parishes was obtained, and an act for the establishment of Churchville parish was secured from the convention of the Protestant Episcopal Church in the diocese of Maryland. Subsequently he secured the erection of a large rectory and a schoolhouse, and the rector, Rev. Edward A. Colburn, who had worked with him and ably seconded all his efforts, established a successful boarding and day school, where Dr. Harlan's sons received their early training. As the deed conveying the church property to the vestry recites, he was led to do this good work by "an earnest desire to aid in the extension of the Christian religion and as a slight manifestation of profound gratitude to Almighty God for many great mercies vouchsafed to him during many years." For many years he supplied or guaranteed the support of this missionary enterprise, and it was ever his delight to sustain and nourish it. Ten years after the frame church was built it was burned down, but was immediately replaced by a new and handsome stone structure. The debt incurred by its construction was paid by him.

The family of Dr. Harlan consisted of five children. His oldest child and only daughter, Oleita, died July 25, 1866, when just reaching womanhood. The oldest son, Dr. Herbert Harlan, was for many years demonstrator of anatomy in the medical department of the University of Maryland, but at this writing is one of the professors in the Baltimore City College. David E. graduated at Princeton in the class of '86 and is now a civil engineer at Lima, Ohio. Henry D., who is chief judge of the supreme bench at Baltimore, was born in 1858, graduated from St. John's College, Annapolis, in 1878, carrying off the second honors of his class, and for one year read law in the office of Hon. Henry D. Farnandis, the leader of the Harford County bar. He then entered the law department of the Maryland University, from which he graduated in 1881, with both honors, having secured the prize as first-grade student, and for the best thesis, his subject being "Contributory Negligence." Upon the committee that awarded the prize were Judge Brown and A. W. Machen. While a law student, he also read law in the office of John P. Poe. He was admitted to the bar in 1881, and two years later was chosen associate professor in the University of Maryland, to lecture on elementary common law and domestic relations. At the same time he was elected secretary and treasurer of the law faculty. These positions he held until he was made chief judge of the supreme bench in 1888. He is married and has two children. W. Beatty Harlan, of Bel Air, was given an excellent education, and after being prepared for college he passed through the sophomore class of St. John's College, Annapolis, and then went to the Johns Hopkins University of Baltimore, where he graduated with the degree of Bachelor of Arts in 1883. He then entered the law department of the Maryland University, from which he graduated in 1885. Opening an office at Bel Air, he has since been numbered among the attorneys of this village, although since the death of his father much of his time has been devoted to looking after the large family estate at Churchville. He makes his home with his mother, Mrs. Margaret Rebecca (Herbert) Harlan, on the estate at Churchville that has been in the possession of the family for generations. Mrs. Harlan was born June 25, 1826, and became the wife of Dr. Harlan March 3, 1846. Her father, James Beatty Herbert, was a son of Capt. John Herbert, of the War of 1812, and a brother of Dr. William Paul Herbert. Her maternal grandfather, Capt. Jeremiah Baker, of Cecil County, was an officer in the Revolution, and his tombstone at North East records his death as having taken place in May, 1814, when he was seventy-four. He married Rebecca Maulden, and their children were Jeremiah, Mary and Charlotte. Mary was the mother of Margaret Rebecca, the latter being her only child. Dr. William Paul Herbert left no heirs, and until the birth of Dr. Herbert Harlan there were no male members born in his mother's family for fifty-seven years (three generations), and only one female to represent each generation. Mrs. Harlan's grandmother, Margaret Beatty Herbert, died at the age of ninety-eight. The first representative of the family in America was Capt. John Herbert, who with his wife came from Ireland in 1794 and settled on the large estate at Churchville that is now in the possession of his great-grandchildren.

The facts contained in this biography of Dr. David Harlan were compiled by W. Beatty Harlan from his father's journals during his father's lifetime. They may therefore be relied upon as authentic by this and coming generations.

J. C. BUTLER, M. D., is engaged in the practice of medicine in Bel Air. The Butler family has for generations been identified with the history of Virginia, and its members have always been southern in sentiment, sympathies and opinions. The Doctor's grandfather, Reuben Butler, was a wholesale druggist in Norfolk, where he died of yellow fever in 1855; his wife had died of the same disease in 1852. He had three sons: Oceolo, who recently died in Savannah, Ga., where he had made a fortune in the wholesale drug business; Thomas F., who is in the real-estate business in Augusta, Ga., where he resides; and Reuben M., the Doctor's father. The latter was born in Norfolk, Va., and in youth embarked in the mercantile business, but soon gave up personal affairs in order to support the Confederacy. At the outbreak of the war he entered the army as captain in the Norfolk Light Artillery Blues and was a gallant soldier and excellent officer, but met his death in the battle of Petersburg, while bravely fighting at the head of his company. He was then a young man of twenty-eight. Very soon afterward his widow, with her child, sought safety in Bel Air. Here she continued to reside until her death, which occurred in February, 1886.

Born in Norfolk, July 5, 1860, the subject of this article was a child of three years when his father died. The changing tide of war caused his mother to come to Bel Air, and here he passed the days of youth in attendance at the academy. Later he took a special course at St. John's College, Annapolis. With a desire to enter the medical profession, he became a student in the medical department of the University of Maryland, where he graduated in 1881. At once opening an office in Bel Air, he has been in continuous practice here since, and has built up a large patronage. His father was a past master Mason, and he, too, is identified with this order, and is senior warden of Mt. Ararat Lodge. He is also connected with the Odd Fellows' Order and belongs to the grand lodge. Politically he is a believer in free trade, but not free silver. In 1888 he married Miss Louisa S. King, daughter of Henry S. King, a wholesale hardware merchant of the city of Baltimore. They have one child, Victor King Butler.

JAMES F. KENLY, a representative farmer and stock-raiser of District No. 2, Harford County, was born in District No. 1, August 20, 1845, his parents being George W. and Rebecca (Rouse) Kenly. His father was born and reared in District No. 2, and when a young man removed to District No. 1, where he followed the wheelwright's trade. He afterward added to this an undertaking business, his shop being located at Joppa Cross Roads, where he remained until 1862. He then purchased the farm on which our subject now resides and made it his home throughout the remainder of his life. He was one of the most extensive farmers of the neighborhood and also carried on stock dealing, buying cattle and feeding them for the market. The qualities essential to success were numbered among his characteristics, and his industry and enterprise made him one of the prosperous agriculturists of the neighborhood. He died at the age of seventy-six years, respected by all who knew him. His political support was given the Republican party, but he never sought or desired office. He was, however, one of the leading members and untiring workers in the Methodist Protestant Church. His father was Lemuel Kenly, also a native of Harford County. The mother of our subject was born in District No. 1, a daughter of John and Sarah (Cochran) Rouse. She, too, was a member of the Methodist Protestant Church, and was called to the home beyond at the advanced age of eighty-three years. They had two children, Mary E., the elder, being now the wife of Thomas W. Mather, of Carroll County, Md.

James F. Kenly early became familiar with the duties that fall to the lot of the agriculturist and assisted his father in the work of the farm until twenty-four years of age, when he was married and removed to the farm whereon he now resides, inheriting the same at his father's death. He married Miss Sarah Hanway, who was born in District No. 1, on the 21st of February, 1848, and is a sister of Hon. L. Littleton Hanway. They have nine children: Mary, Harriet, Leroy, Sarah, James F., Jessie, Julia, George W. and Marion. All are at home with the exception of Harriet, who has fitted herself for the duties of a librarian.

Mr. Kenly and his family reside on his farm of three hundred acres, where he is carrying on general farming and stock-raising. He thoroughly understands his business and has won the success which results from ability, industry and honorable dealing. He and his wife, also their children, hold membership in the Presbyterian Church. Their home is noted for its hospitality, and their friends throughout the community are many. Mr. Kenly gives his political support to the Republican party at national elections, but at local elections where no issue is involved votes independently of party ties. He has served as tax collector of his district, but has never been an aspirant for political honors. He belongs to Stephenson Lodge No. 135, F. & A. M., of Lapidum.

JOHN WESLEY GIFFORD. Of the citizens who have added to the prosperity of Cecil County, few have attained a reputation more enviable or a position more satisfactory than the gentleman named above. Through his long association with the agricultural interests of District No. 5 as the owner of a finely improved farm near Bay View, he has become well and favorably known. In every enterprise to which he gives his support he maintains a deep and unwavering interest, and his efforts have resulted in the promotion of the material welfare of the district.

The Gifford family is of English descent. The father of our subject, James Gifford, was born near Portsmouth, England, and from there emigrated to the United States about 1821, settling in Philadelphia County, Pa., near Germantown. He engaged in farming throughout the remaining years of his life, although he was a blacksmith by trade and had followed that occupation in the home land. After spending ten years in Philadelphia County he removed to Bucks County, and in 1855 came to Maryland, establishing his home in District No. 5, near Principio, about three miles from the present home of his son. He cast his ballot at one presidential election for General Jackson, the candidate of the Democratic party, but usually supported the men and measures brought forward by the Whig party. Fraternally he was identified with the Odd Fellows and in religious belief a member of the Methodist Episcopal Church.

Before coming to America James Gifford married Ruth Edmonds, and they became the parents of ten children, six of whom are living, viz.: Samuel, whose home is in District No. 9; Sarah, wife of Rev. James Cooke, of Iowa; Ellen, who is the widow of Thomas Gillespie, of Zion, Md.; John Wesley; George W., of Principio; and James, of District No. 9. The mother died October 6, 1861, and the father several years later. During the residence of his parents in Philadelphia County, Pa., our subject was born on the last day of the year 1828. He was quite small when the family removed to Bucks County and there his education was obtained in the common schools. At the age of sixteen his studies were discontinued, and he began to learn the trade of a carpenter. This, however, he did not long follow, as his time was given principally to assisting his father on the home place. In 1865 he purchased the farm where he has since resided, engaged in general farming. His right of franchise is used in favor of the Republican party. He is known for his constant championship of every measure calculated to benefit the community, and has always been progressive and enterprising. His religious belief is in sympathy with the doctrines of the Methodist Episcopal Church, the work of which he aids as far as possible.

January 20, 1858, Mr. Gifford was united in marriage with Catherine, daughter of Jesse Janney, of Cecil County. Unto their union were born six children, all but one of whom are living. They are named as follows: Jesse, who resides in Philadelphia; Grant, of Avondale, Pa.; Lotta, who is with her parents; Viola, wife of A. P. Rose, of North East; and Ida, who married H. Hamilton and resides in District No. 9.

A. HENRY STRASBAUGH, who is engaged in farming and merchandising at Creswell, District No. 1, Harford County, has been identified with business affairs since a lad of twelve years. Beginning at that time to earn his own livelihood, he had but little opportunity for obtaining an education, and the knowledge he acquired was principally the result of observation and the experiences of a busy life. At an early age he evinced the possession of industry, energy and fidelity to his employers' interests, and in consequence the greatest confidence was reposed in him. For years, when quite young, he was given entire charge of different stores for the same firm, and his long connection with them speaks volumes for his ability and trustworthy character.

The Strasbaugh family was represented among the early settlers of Pennsylvania and its members mostly followed milling pursuits. The father of our subject, Jacob Strasbaugh, was born and reared in Adams County, Pa., his birth occurring in 1805. For some time he followed the trade of a miller about ten miles from Hanover, in Adams County. In 1829 he married Dorothy, daughter of Frederick Bahn, a farmer in York County. Five children were born of their union, namely: Lucy, widow of John Kosher, formerly a merchant of Harrisburg, where she resides; Kate, who married Gregg Dellone, a cattle raiser and dealer in East Berlin and Abbottstown; Maria, deceased; Susie, who became the wife of Harry Fraley, a merchant of Harrisburg; and A. Henry, who was born in October, 1835.

When twelve years of age the subject of this sketch secured employment as a clerk in Baltimore County, and at fifteen he was transferred to a store at Sarah Furnace, the same county, of which he had charge for two years. Still continuing with the same firm, he was put in charge of a store at Ashland, and two years later was sent to Harford Furnace, Harford County. This was in 1855. Later he bought the store, which he continued to manage, at the same time keeping the books for the furnace company until 1870, when the firm sold out. He then opened a branch store in Abingdon, conducting that in addition to the store at Creswell, which he had started in 1865. In 1867 he went to the Chesapeake furnace in Baltimore for his brother-in-law, William F. Pannell, and remained in charge of the business until the death of the proprietor, when he was appointed administrator. This position was one that involved much labor and responsibility, and he spent four years, 1883 to 1887, in closing up the estate, which netted the heirs $55008.70. The implicit confidence reposed in him is shown by the fact that he was not limited as to time, but was allowed to close out the business in the manner that seemed to him wisest.

October 30, 1862, Mr. Strasbaugh married Isabella W., youngest daughter of the late James E. Pannell. They are the parents of one son, Harry P., who is engaged in the brokerage business in Baltimore. A lifelong Democrat, firm in his allegiance to party principles, Mr. Strasbaugh nevertheless declines the nominations which the members of his party would be glad to bestow upon him. The only exception to his decisions in this regard was in 1893, when he consented to serve as a member of the board of county commissioners, and of this body he has since been the president. In 1865 he became a member of the Presbyterian Church, and is now identified with the Churchville congregation, of which he has been a trustee for many years.

WILLIAM O. MICHAEL. The family which this gentleman represents is among the oldest of Harford County, where it was founded in ante-Revolutionary days by Balchior Michael, a native of Germany. The property that he purchased was situated near Aberdeen, in District No. 2, and is still owned by members of the family. One of his sons, Jacob, entered the American service during the war for independence, and rose to the rank of colonel in the army. Another son, Daniel, had a son, John C., who became the father of our subject, and spent his life as a farmer and business man of District No. 2. Besides agricultural pursuits, he engaged in the canning business, an industry that has become so profitable to Harford County residents. He did not take an active part in public affairs, but those who had any acquaintance with him knew him to be firm in his allegiance to the Democratic party. His death occurred at the old homestead in 1895, when he was sixty-nine years of age.

By his marriage to Martha, daughter of John Mitchell, of District No. 2, Mr. Michael had four children, namely: John, whose home is in Aberdeen; William O.; Lydia, wife of C. R. Kerwin; and Oleita G., wife of Rev. Archibald Jamison, now stationed at Brunswick, Md. The widowed mother still survives, her residence being on the old home place.

The subject of this sketch was born near Aberdeen in 1860, and received a practical education in the common schools and in Eaton's Business College, of Baltimore, completing his studies at the age of twenty-one. He continued to reside at the old homestead, interested in farming and the canning business, but in 1890 removed to his present home near Bel Air, where he has since engaged in general farming. The place where he now resides is one of the oldest in Harford County, and consists of two hundred and eighty-three acres of land. The property is under excellent cultivation. It needs only a glance at the farm with its appurtenances to determine the character of the man, and to indicate the industry and perseverance with which he has labored. Giving, as he does, his entire attention to agriculture, he has little leisure for public affairs, and aside from voting the Democratic ticket, takes no part in politics.

In 1890 Mr. Michael married Ida B. Gilbert, daughter of Bennett and Martha Gilbert, of District No. 2. She was reared in this county and educated in the public schools. In religious belief she is a Presbyterian, and is rearing her children, Martha Gilbert and Georgie Bell, in that faith.

GEORGE SMITH WEBSTER. The farm upon which Mr. Webster resides is situated in Churchville Precinct, District No. 3, Harford County. His residence, which is comfortable and comparatively new, stands on an eminence and is surrounded by forest and ornamental trees. One giant, a chestnut, is so large that a ten-foot pole laid along its side about a foot and a-half above the ground, does not extend beyond the breadth of the tree. When the main trunk reaches a height of about ten feet, it divides into four branches, three of which are larger than the average forest tree, while the fourth and smallest is at least eighteen inches in diameter.

A record of the life of Henry Webster, our subject's father, will be found in the sketch of William Webster, while the ancestral history appears under "The Webster Family," upon another page. Upon the old family homestead, now occupied by his brother William, our subject was born November 27, 1825. For some years, when a boy, he attended the academy at Churchville, which was built by his father and Mr. Finney. From there he went to the home of his uncle in Kent County, where he attended school a couple of winters, spending the intervening summer months at home. After completing his studies he assisted in the cultivation of the home farm until he was twenty-four, when he bought a farm of one hundred and ten acres near his father's place, and also one of one hundred and fifty acres that had belonged to the uncle for whom he was named.

After the death of his father, in October, 1872, Mr. Webster made his home in Bel Air for seventeen years, with his brother, Col. Edwin Webster, though he did not give up the care of his farm property, driving out each day to look after it. In 1865 he sold his one hundred and ten acre farm, but still retains the other, and since 1890 has occupied the neat residence he erected here in 1886. He is well-to-do, and not obliged to work unless he so desires, as he has a competency sufficient to provide every comfort for his declining years.

JACOB E. BULL, the leading contractor in Harford County, was born within two and one-half miles of Bel Air, his present home. The family of which he is a representative was founded in America by his grandfather, John Bull, a native of England, who came to Maryland in early manhood and settled in Harford County, where in after years he was a prosperous farmer and a large slave owner. The father of our subject, Edmund L. Bull, was a native of Harford County, born at what was then called Bulltown. During the progress of the War of 1812, when the city of Baltimore was threatened by the British forces, he enlisted in the American service and took part in the defense of the place. When a youth he learned the trade of a carpenter, and after following it for a time he took up contracting, in which line he was successful and prominent. He was well known throughout the state as one of its most efficient and extensive builders. Not only did he win confidence as a business man, but as a citizen and in private life as well, for his irreproachable character and exemplary life gained for him the esteem of all with whom he came in contact. As a citizen and in social circles, his standing was high.

The mother of our subject, Margaret Gay, was born in Harford County, being a member of one of the prominent old families of the county. Her children were four in number, and the three sons, Jacob E., Henry and Richard S. H., embarked in business life as carpenters; the daughter, Mary Susan, became the wife of John F. Forwood, a builder in the city of Baltimore, and a cousin of W. S. Forwood, of Bel Air.

Born in 1848, the subject of this notice had but a common-school education, supplemented by a brief attendance at the Bel Air Academy. When twenty years of age he commenced to learn the trade of a carpenter. In this business he has spent his entire life, and has gained the reputation of being one of the leading and most successful builders and contractors in the state. The most of the fine buildings of Harford County have been erected under his supervision, among these being the Masonic Temple of Bel Air, one of the most substantial and costly structures in northeastern Maryland. His reputation as a contractor extends through the state, and his business has not been limited to his native county, many of his contracts being made with parties elsewhere. In his profession his name is the synonym for ability, honesty and integrity. Fraternally he is identified with the Masons and Odd Fellows.

In 1861 Mr. Bull married Miss Mary Tustin

Sunderland, of Philadelphia. Eleven children were born of their union, and of this number eight are living. Lillie T. is the wife of William Wallace, a carpenter, residing in Baltimore; Charles A. is associated with his father in the building business, and possesses the talent in this direction that has been noticeable in the family for generations; Carrie P. and Emma V., accomplished young ladies, reside with their parents, brightening the home by their presence; Irene W. is the wife of Edward Wood, of Baltimore; William W., Alberta and Mary are at home.

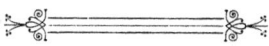

WILLIAM REED. Born and died,—such is the story of the individual man; but between the two words lies all that goes to make up the character of the person. The manner in which trials and sorrows are borne, the lessons of patience and determination to be learned, the friends made, the victories won upon life's great battlefield; these, and many more experiences, develop the character of the individual. The record of the life of Mr. Reed is not greatly different from those of others in Cecil County, but who can estimate the power for good his life has been and now is? Who can tabulate in cold figures the names of those whom he has helped, those whom he has encouraged, and those who have come to him, and not in vain, for the ready sympathy and practical advice?

A native of this county, the life-history of Mr. Reed has been interwoven with that of this locality, and naturally he is deeply interested in all movements tending toward the greater improvement and development of local resources. In his character he combines the sturdy honesty of his Welsh maternal ancestors with the genial kindliness of his Irish progenitors. His father, William, Sr., was born in District No. 5, this county, and always followed farm pursuits, dying on his homestead in 1865. Politically an old-line Whig, he took an active part in local affairs and was always a champion of progressive measures.

As supervisor he was instrumental in securing the opening and improvement of roads. In other ways he helped forward local enterprises. He was connected with the Methodist Protestant Church, and squared his life by the teachings of the Scriptures. His wife, who bore the maiden name of Amy McVey, was a member of an old family of District No. 5, and died here in 1833. Of their family the following survive: Joseph T., of Bay View; Benjamin M., whose sketch appears elsewhere in this volume; Martha, widow of John T. Slicer, of Calvert, Md.; and William, of this sketch.

Within a mile of his present place of residence our subject was born June 24, 1829, and in this neighborhood he obtained such education as he gleaned from text books. At the age of seventeen he began to take an active part in the management of the farm, assisting his father for two years. Wishing to try some other occupation, he left home in 1853 and secured employment on the Pennsylvania Railroad, where he was first fireman on an engine and afterward a baggage master on the train. Six years were spent with the company, but he finally concluded that railroading was less congenial and profitable than farm work, and accordingly resumed agricultural pursuits. In 1860 he purchased part of the farm known as the Jacobs purchase. On this tract of one hundred and thirty-seven acres he has since engaged in general farming. During the years he has spent upon the place he has succeeded in bringing the soil to a high state of cultivation and has erected farm buildings as needed.

In 1859 was solemnized the marriage of Mr. Reed and Miss Margaret Matilda Ferguson, daughter of James Ferguson, and of an old Cecil County family. Eight children comprised the family, and all but two of these are still living. They are named as follows: William J., of Bay View; Elizabeth E., who married George W. Fitzgerald and resides in Bay View; Thompson R.; Benjamin M.; Virginia and Mabel V., who are at home. The family attend the Methodist Protestant Church of Bay View, and have many friends in the congregation, whose work their co-operation and contributions have materially promoted. Politically Mr. Reed believes in the principles laid down in the Republican platform and therefore votes the straight ticket. He manifests an interest in measures for the benefit of the district, and may be counted upon to bear his part in all of these.

F. H. D. PUE. Many years have come and gone since the Civil War brought its blighting influence upon our nation. Old enemies have been forgotten and old prejudices wiped out. Over the graves of the past the soldier in blue and the one in gray clasp hands in friendship, and the North and South, once separated in thought, if not in reality, again find a common meeting place in the same hopes and aspirations. Looking back and impartially scanning the deeds of men, the student of history finds that both the Federal and the Confederate earnestly supported principles they believed to be right and just; both were chivalrous and brave, willing to die in defense of what they believed to be right.

On the Confederate side there was no soldier more brave, no officer more loyal than Captain Pue, the subject of this sketch. His long and active service in the army brought him into prominence among Southerners, and his comrades who still survive remember with pride how gallantly he led the men and how bravely he maintained his position, even when others were retreating and the day was lost. The leaders of the Confederacy placed the greatest confidence in his loyalty and courage. Among his friends was Jefferson Davis, who, some years after the war closed, visited him at his beautiful home in Harford County.

The Pue family is of Scotch extraction, but has been long identified with the history of Maryland. The records of the city of Baltimore show that Dr. Joshua Pue was the largest tax payer in the city in 1765. Our subject's father, Michael E., was the son of Caleb Pue, and was born in Elk Ridge, Howard County, Md., but at the age of eight years accompanied the family to Harford County, settling in District No. 1, near the line of No. 3. Here he engaged in farming until his death, which occurred in 1891. Politically he was a Whig in youth and a Democrat after the disintegration of the Whig party. In religious belief he was an Episcopalian. His wife, who also died in 1891, was Elizabeth Bull, daughter of Elisha Bull, of District No. 3, and a member of an old family of Harford County. They were the parents of six children, of whom five survive, namely: E. H. D.; Arthur, of Montana; Richard, also of Montana; Dr. Michael, residing in Delta, York County, Pa.; and Elizabeth, wife of Walter W. Preston, state's attorney of Harford County and a resident of Bel Air.

Where he now lives, the subject of this article was born April 28, 1840. In youth he attended the academy at Bel Air. He remained at home assisting his father in the management of the farm until the outbreak of the war, and his decided southern sympathies led him to enlist in the Confederate army. He enlisted in the Maryland Grays, of Baltimore, under the command of Capt. James Herbert. In every battle of the eastern army under General Lee, amounting to two hundred and fifty battles and skirmishes, Captain Pue took an active part. He was eleven times wounded, once at Petersburg, and twice at Gettysburg, the second battle of Manassas, Spottsylvania, battle of the Wilderness and five other places, two of the wounds being sabre cuts. In the seven days' fight before Richmond he was captured by the Federal troops, but succeeded in making his escape. His command started to join Johnston in 1865, but on learning that both that general and Lee had surrendered, they disbanded.

After the war, Captain Pue engaged in the mercantile business at Rectortown, Va., for seven years, and then returned to Harford County, where he has since occupied his beautiful country home, in District No. 2. Like his father he is a Democrat in politics and an Episcopalian in religious connections. He holds the office of vestryman in the Episcopal Church. November 12, 1879, he married Cornelia Dunn, who was born in New Orleans and is a lady of fine education,

They have had six children, and four are now living, Michael, Clara, Elizabeth and Barthena. The father of Mrs. Pue was Rev. Ballard S. Dunn, of the Episcopal Church, member of General Polk's staff during the Civil War, and chaplain of the Louisiana Rifles. Her maternal grandfather, Tobias Sternsbury, was a general in the army and assisted in defending Baltimore at the time it was attacked by the British, during the War of 1812. One of her uncles, Col. Smith Sternsbury, was chief engineer in the army and a colonel in Beauregard's staff. The family is of aristocratic southern lineage and its members have been cultured and well educated, as well as brave and loyal to southern institutions.

RANDALL W. ROSE. A man's lifework is the measure of his success, and he is the most successful man who, turning his powers into the channel of an honorable purpose, accomplishes the object of his endeavor. In the study of the life of every man we find some mainspring of action, something that he lives for. The chief ambition of Mr. Rose seems to have been to make the best use of his talents and secure for his family the comforts of life. A farmer by training and preference, he has led the quiet unpretentious and industrious life of an agriculturist, devoting himself to the cultivation of his farm in Cecil County. This place, which is the old family homestead, lies in the northern part of District No. 5, between Mechanics Valley and Bay View. It comprises one hundred and eighteen acres of land, planted to various cereals and improved with substantial buildings.

In Bucks County, Pa., Randall W. Rose was born October 3, 1845. His father, Timothy V., was a native of Humeville, that state, and was a son of John Rose, also a Pennsylvanian by birth. In 1857 the former removed to Maryland and settled in Cecil County, purchasing a farm in District No. 5, and making it his home until he died. While farming was his principal occupation in life, he was a stonemason by trade, and in his earlier days followed that calling. In the Methodist Protestant Church he was an active worker and a class leader. He was prominent in his locality, a Republican in politics, and exerted considerable influence among his fellow-men. June 21, 1840, he married Margaret A. Gillingham, daughter of J. P. Gillingham, of an old family of Bucks County. He died March 8, 1891, and his wife passed away September 26, 1886. Their family consisted of eleven children, and all but one member of this large family still survive. They are named as follows: Elizabeth D., wife of John White, of District No. 3, Cecil County; Harriet R., who married Thomas Miller, also of District No. 3; Randall W.; George G., of District No. 5; Mary F., Mrs. Joseph Miller, of this district; Alfred D., who resides at Wilmington, Del.; J. P., who makes his home in District No. 3; H. C. and Aquilla P., of District No. 5; and Edward W., residing in Baltimore.

The early childhood years of our subject were passed in Bucks County, and there he was a pupil in the Flushing school. In the spring of 1857 he accompanied his parents to Cecil County, where he has since resided. Until fifteen years of age he attended the local schools in winter and assisted in farm work during the summer months. In youth he learned the habits of industry and perseverance that have remained with him since and have been of the greatest assistance to him. In 1890, about one year before the death of his father, he purchased the old homestead, and this he has since operated, maintaining a high order of improvements upon the place. As a citizen he takes an intelligent interest in all public issues of the day, and is a Republican in politics. In addition to his business and agricultural enterprises, he is interested in religious movements and has devoted considerable attention to the work of the Methodist Protestant Church, of which he is a member.

December 28, 1869, occurred the marriage of Mr. Rose and Miss S. S. Alexander, whose ancestors were among the early settlers of this county. Her father, Benjamin Alexander, was a resident of District No. 5 until his death, which occurred when the daughter was very young. The seven children that comprise the family of Mr. and Mrs. Rose are named as follows: Caleb V., residing in Washington, D. C.; Marion E., at home; Rufus B., William C., Lucy Jane, Fred E. and Marvin B., who are still with their parents.

WILLIAM P. TAYLOR, M. D., of Abingdon, is regarded as one of the most efficient and skilled physicians of this section of the state. His professional brethren accord to him a foremost place in their ranks, and the public attest their confidence in his ability by a liberal patronage.

The Doctor is a native of the town which is still his home, his birth having here occurred August 2, 1851. His ancestral history is one of close connection with Maryland, although the family is probably of English lineage. His grandfather, James Taylor, and his father, William P. Taylor, both spent their entire lives here, following agricultural pursuits. The latter married Susan E. Norris, a daughter of Rheshea Norris, of Harford County, and they had seven children, of whom the following are living: Robert B., of Virginia; Amanda, wife of Frank C. Norris, of Baltimore; and the Doctor. William P. Taylor, Sr., was a member of the Methodist Protestant Church and a man of many excellencies of character. He died in 1879, and his wife survived until May, 1893, when she, too, passed away.

Dr. Taylor, of this review, began his education in the district schools near his home, pursuing his studies there until thirteen years of age, when he entered the Cumberland Valley Institute, of Pennsylvania. Later he matriculated in Calvert College, now known as New Windsor College, of Carroll County, Md. Determining to make the practice of medicine his life work, his professional studies were pursued in the medical department of the Washington University of Baltimore, which he entered in 1868. He there pursued a thorough and comprehensive course, and was graduated in 1872. He afterward spent a year in the hospitals of Baltimore, in order to still further perfect himself in his chosen calling, and during the following year practiced in that city. In 1874 Dr. Taylor came to Abingdon, opened an office and conducted a successful practice here until 1879, when he went to the West Indies to accept the position of surgeon for a phosphate company. Three years he remained in that place, and then returned to Abingdon, where he has since continued. His success in his profession was marked and immediate. He had gained an accurate and extensive knowledge of the science of medicine and its methods of application, and as the years have passed he has added to this by reading and study. His skill is attested by the splendid success that has crowned his efforts and accorded him a foremost place in professional circles.

WILLIAM W. HOLDEN. Farming has been the principal occupation of this gentleman, and the energetic manner in which he has taken advantage of every method tending toward the increased value of his property has had considerable to do with his present prosperity. When he started out for himself he had no capital with which to purchase lands and no influential friends to assist him; but he was determined, and with hope for his pilot and industry for the captain of his life boat, he surmounted the waves of adversity and finally steered safely into "snug harbor." While he is by no means a wealthy man, yet he has sufficient to enable him to provide desired comforts for his family and insure his declining years against the encroachments of poverty and want.

The farm owned and occupied by Mr. Holden is situated on Elk Neck, extending from Elk River a considerable distance to the westward. It is one of the best farms of the southeastern portion of District No. 5, which in turn is one of the best districts of Cecil County. At the time of coming here he rented the property, but in the following years he saved a sufficient amount to enable him to purchase the place. It includes two hundred and fourteen acres and is devoted to general farming purposes, the various cereals and vegetables being raised to which the soil of this section is adapted.

The father of our subject was Jacob, a son of William Holden, and a native of Cecil County, where he spent his entire life. Politically he was a Democrat, and in religious belief held membership in the Methodist Episcopal Church. His marriage united him with Margaret, daughter of Jesse Bolden, of this county. He died in 1859, but she survived for some years, passing away in 1881, when advanced in years. Of their children the following survive: Mary Ann, wife of William Potts, of Mechanics Valley, this district; Elizabeth, who married Lemuel Foster and resides in District No. 3; Helen, Mrs. John Cline, of District No. 5; Jacob, whose home is in Chester, Pa.; Mitchell, residing in Conshohocken, Montgomery County, Pa.; and William W., who was born in District No. 4, Cecil County, May 7, 1835.

In the schools of the home neighborhood our subject gained a knowledge of the three R's, but the principal portion of his present knowledge has been acquired through studious observation and through reading current literature. In 1865 he began as a renter and cultivated the farm he now owns, purchasing the same as soon as his means permitted. His long experience as a farmer renders his judgment sound and his opinion upon agricultural subjects valuable. He is not a man with any "hobbies" to ride; on the contrary, he is quiet, unobtrusive, unwilling to offend others, but desiring to live as an upright, law-abiding citizen, at peace with his fellow-men and his God. The Christian's faith has been his since boyhood, and he has long been connected with the Methodist Episcopal Church, in which he holds the office of trustee. Politically he is a Democrat.

January 29, 1859, occurred the marriage of Mr. Holden to Miss Talitha Mahoney, daughter of William R. Mahoney, of District No. 5. Eleven children were born of the union, and it may be noted as an unusual fact that death has not entered the home, the family circle still remaining unbroken by that dread visitor. However, not all of the children remain with their parents, as some have married and gone to homes of their own. By name the sons and daughters are as follows: Henry W., of Baltimore; William T., at home; John H., who is now in Wilmington, Del.; Theodore B., who cultivates a farm not far from that owned by his father; George, who is at the same place; Charles, at home; Harriet, who married Charles Racine and resides near the old homestead; Maggie, wife of Robert Graves, of Chester; Anna, Clementine and Sophia, who are with their parents.

FRANK E. GORRELL. Progress demands an exponent, and has ever had a medium for making known its discoveries and conquests. Rocks and tombs may be seen in ancient lands bearing hieroglyphics and cuneiform inscriptions. The stylus and parchment were for ages used as a means of preserving valuable records, but they were inefficient, and could be viewed by only a favored few. At length the art preservative was invented, and even the most casual, superficial student will observe that, with the introduction of the newspaper, all trades and arts received a fresh impetus, and commerce was enlarged. It is difficult to estimate the amount of our indebtedness to the printing art, or to conceive what would be our present condition were all our papers and magazines and books, our world of literature, to be suddenly taken away. As an eclipse of the sun to the physical world, so would this be to the intellectual world.

The modern journalist, he who endeavors to make his paper a medium, not alone for the propagation of local items, but a storehouse of broad general information, may be justly called a public benefactor. The good that he does is of a permanent nature and important in its bearing upon mankind. Of Mr. Gorrell it may be said that his ideal of journalism is high. It is ever his aim to produce a paper that will be attractive in appearance, perfect in typographical form, interesting locally and with a fund of general information that will be helpful to all. March 16, 1894, he bought an old, established paper, the *Aegis and Intelligencer*, at Bel Air, and has since been proprietor and editor, conducting it as a Democratic paper, and the organ of this party in the county.

Mr. Gorrell was born at Upper Cross Roads, Harford County, October 6, 1867, the son of Theodore and Margaret (Bullock) Gorrell. His paternal grandfather came from Scotland and located at Level, formerly Hopewell Cross Roads, in Harford County. Theodore Gorrell was in early life engaged in farming in Harford County, but in 1871 removed to Brooklyn, N. Y., where he carried on a mercantile business for some years. Returning to Maryland, he spent his closing years in Churchville. In politics he was a Republican, and during the war supported the Union. For sixteen years he served as a justice of the peace. His wife, who was born in Delaware County, Pa., bore him eight children, namely: Hiram D., of Brooklyn; Henry C., also of that city; M. Alice, wife of Charles L. Gorrell, of Baltimore; Joseph W., who lives in Brooklyn; Lida, wife of A. C. Barton; Charles E., of Baltimore; George P., who is in the United States government employ at Quebec; and Frank E. The father died at Churchville, June 2, 1882, at the age of sixty-five. His wife is still living and makes her home with her son in Bel Air.

In the public schools of Harford County and in Bel Air Academy, our subject obtained his education. For a few years he taught at Churchville and in Bel Air Academy. In 1885 he commenced to read law with Archer & Van Bibber, of Bel Air, and after three years was admitted to the bar of Harford County, October 6, 1888, after which he practiced law for six years in Bel Air. With a fondness for newspaper work, and a journalistic bent of mind, he determined to enter that field, and in 1894 bought the paper with which his name has since been identified. In 1893 he was elected town commissioner, and was re-elected in 1894, 1896 and 1897, serving as chairman of the board for three years. From 1890 to 1894 he was a notary public. He was interested in the organization of the National Guard of Bel Air, and one of the first projectors of the movement. Fraternally he is connected with Mt. Ararat Lodge of Masons, in which he is past master. He is also connected with Triumph Lodge, No. 16, I. O. O. F., in which he has been one of the trustees.

WILLIAM F. REASIN, who follows farming and stock-raising in District No. 2, Harford County, was born on the farm which he now owns, October 14, 1848, and comes of one of the prominent and honored families of this section of the state. His grandfather, Duty Reasin, was a native of Kent County, Md., and when a young man removed to Bush River Neck, Harford County, where he followed the carpenter's trade. He married a Miss Johnes, and they became parents of seven children, namely: James F.; Samuel W., who followed merchandising; William; Wesley; Mary, who became the wife of a Mr. Bradbury, who went to Africa and died there of yellow fever; Martha; and Amanda, who was the wife of Alexander Adams, a merchant of Havre de Grace. All of this family are now deceased.

James F. Reasin, father of our subject, was born at Bush River Neck, and reared on a farm. When a young man he went to Glenville, where he worked as a blacksmith and wheelwright until about 1861, when he sold his shop and devoted his time to the management of the farm, which he had purchased a few years previous, and which is now the property of our subject. He there spent his remaining days engaged in agricultural pursuits and in cattle feeding. His business was well and wisely conducted and was therefore quite profitable. He died in 1889, at the age of sixty-six years. In politics he was a stanch Democrat, recognized as one of the leaders of the party in this county, and twice served as county commissioner. He was an active member of the Presbyterian Church, served as trustee, was a member of the building committee and gave about $1,000 toward the erection of the Harmony Church. A true Christian man, he won the confidence and respect of all who knew him and the world is better for his having lived. His wife, who bore the maiden name of Matilda Courtney, was born in District No. 2, in 1808, and was a daughter of George Courtney. Her first husband was William Maxwell, who died, leaving three daughters. By her second marriage she had one daughter, Amanda V., widow of B. Hopkins, of Aberdeen, Md. Mrs. Reasin was a member of the Presbyterian Church.

William F. Reasin, the only son of James F. and Matilda Reasin, remained upon the home farm until his parents' death, and from an early age assisted in the cultivation and development of the land. His early education, acquired in the common schools, was supplemented by study in Columbia Academy, of Columbia, Pa., and in Newark Academy, of Newark, Del. On his father's death he inherited the old homestead, and in the management of his farm his time is now passed. The neat and thrifty appearance of his place indicates his progressiveness, and from the well-tilled fields he derives a good income.

Mr. Reasin married Miss Annie Hogsman, of District No. 2. He takes quite an active interest in local politics, giving his unwavering support to the Democratic party. Socially he is connected with Aberdeen Lodge No. 187, F. & A. M.

CHARLES W. SIMPERS. The most reliable information regarding the Simpers family indicates that its first representatives in America came hither from England and settled in Cecil County about two hundred years ago. From that day to this it has furnished the state with men and women of upright character and progressive spirit, whose influence has been felt in various lines of labor. Both the father of our subject, Jesse H., and the grandfather, William, were born in District No. 5, but in 1814 they removed to District No. 3, where the former engaged in farming and fishing, and also for a time followed the cooper's trade. A leader in public affairs, he was a Whig until the disintegration of the party, after which he allied himself with the Republicans. For years he was a trustee and active worker in the Methodist Episcopal Church. His marriage united him with Jane Miller, who died in February, 1845, when her children were small. She was a daughter of Rev. Thomas Miller, of an old family of District No. 3, Cecil County; one of her brothers, Thomas Miller, was sheriff of the county in 1827-28, and another brother, Benjamin, was magistrate for a long term of years. Of her nine children, six are living, namely: John W., of North East; Rachael J., whose first husband was John McCauley, and the second, John Cantwell; Joseph W., of North East; Jesse K., who makes his home in District No. 3; Charles W.; and Sam B., a resident of Chester County, Pa. The second marriage of Jesse H. Simpers united him with Elizabeth, daughter of Jacob Fulton, of this county; she died in 1886, and of her six children four are living, as follows: Wilmer F., of Bay View; Mary E., wife of Wilmer Bouchelle, of District No. 3; James A., of Elkton; and Henry E., who is the postmaster at Leslie.

On the old homestead in District No. 3, Cecil County, Charles W. Simpers was born June 30, 1840, and there the years of boyhood and youth were quietly passed. At the age of eighteen he began to learn the carpenter's trade, which he afterward followed for a time, meanwhile also having charge of a farm in District No. 3. In 1862 here moved to North East, where he has since made his home, at different times following various pursuits. For thirteen years he was proprietor of a livery establishment, after which he engaged in fishing and the mercantile business for ten years. A Democrat in politics, he has always been active in public affairs, and in 1870-71 was tax collector for District No. 5. In 1875 he was the Democratic nominee for the office of sheriff, and was defeated by only twenty-two votes, the county polling six thousand votes. At this writing he is one of the assessors of the county. Identified with the Methodist Episcopal Church, he has been a trustee of the congregation since 1882. Fraternally he was a charter member of the Knights of Pythias, and is still connected with the order.

January 1, 1868, Mr. Simpers married Sarah C. Roberson, a refined, cultured lady, well fitted to be the companion of his intellect as well as his heart. She is a member of one of the old families of the east, and a daughter of Dr. Elijah H. Roberson, of Newcastle County, Del., who was a relative of Gen. Robert E. Lee. The four children of Mr. and Mrs. Simpers are named as follows: Altha A., wife of Joseph J. Summerill, a lawyer of Woodbury, N. J.; Charles R., who is with his parents; Elizabeth Holliday and Gertrude Jane, deceased.

CHRISTIAN SMITH. It was once said by Gibbon that every man has two educations, one which is given him, and the other and more important, that which he gives himself. The same thought was emphasized by Sir Walter Scott, who said: "The best part of a man's education is that which he gives himself." The mind has been endowed with no ambition more powerful than that of self-advancement. The self-made man carries with him his own capital—a capital unaffected by monetary crises, and an investment whose interest is not regulated by success of speculation—a possession which none can dispute and of which no one can deprive him.

As a representative of the class who have attained success in life solely through their own exertions, we mention the name and present the biography of Christian Smith, a prominent farmer and canner of District No. 1, Harford County. He is a native of this county, born in District No. 3, near Churchville, May 29, 1859, being the son of Christian and Elizabeth (Burkley) Smith, natives of Germany. His father, who was a member of an excellent family in the old country, came to America about 1850, and settled on the farm where our subject was born. By trade he was a mason, but he followed farm pursuits through the most of his life. His death occurred in 1872. In religious belief he adhered to the faith of his forefathers, the Lutheran Church receiving his support. His wife is still living, and is now sixty-six years of age. Their six children were named as follows: Alexander, who resides near Churchville, in District No. 3; Christian; Frederick, a resident of Creswell; Anna, wife of George Walters, of Baltimore County; Emma, Mrs. William Gosweiler, who lives in District No. 3; and George, who died in boyhood.

Owing to the fact that his father's health was very poor, our subject was obliged to do far more work than falls to the lot of most boys. In planting, plowing, reaping and harvesting, his time in the summer was busily passed. Even during the winter months, work at home kept him so busy that he had little opportunity to attend school, and his knowledge has been mostly acquired by observation and experience. When he was twenty-one his uncle, Fred Burkley, took him into the canning business as a partner, and he continued in that connection for four years, but in 1883, withdrawing from the partnership, he and his brother, Alexander, embarked in the canning business on their own account. At the same time he purchased a farm at Carson's Run, District No. 2, where for seven years he engaged in farm pursuits, but especially in raising and canning fruit. With his brother, in 1886, he purchased ninety-seven acres near Harford Furnace, in District No. 1, to which place he at once moved. In 1890, Alexander wishing to withdraw from the business, Christian bought his interest and has since conducted alone the business of packing and the occupation of farming.

The Democratic party has in Mr. Smith a stanch adherent, and the Lutheran Church a faithful member. In addition to his personal farm and canning interests, he is a director in the First

National Bank of Aberdeen, a director in the Aberdeen Canning Company, and president of the Creswell Telephone Company. April 16, 1884, he was united in marriage with Miss Mollie Kammerer, daughter of Jacob Kammerer, of this district. They have a comfortable home and are numbered among the prosperous residents of the community.

THE STREETT FAMILY. Long residence in a community gives to a family a standing which can scarcely be otherwise acquired, especially if its members have made for themselves good records as citizens. If intelligent and actively interested in the welfare of the people around them, they become known as public-spirited and progressive, and their labors have a lasting influence for good in their locality. Within the limits of Harford County there are a number of families who have been represented here since colonial days and who, in each generation, have borne an honorable part in the upbuilding of the community. The first of the name in this country was Col. John Streett, a native of England, who came to America before the Revolutionary War and bore an active and valiant part in that historic struggle, holding the rank of colonel of his regiment. After the close of the conflict he returned to his home in Harford County, where the remainder of his life was devoted to farm work.

The Colonel's son, Maj. Thomas Streett, was born in District No. 4, Harford County, and here spent his life, with the exception of the time he was at the front in active service as an officer in the War of 1812. By occupation he was a tiller of the soil, in which calling he was very successful. The same vocation was followed by his son, Merryman, who was a native of this district, where he engaged in tilling the soil of the old homestead. Through his agricultural enterprises he became quite well-to-do, and at his death left his family in good circumstances. As an upright, conscientious man, his opinion had weight with others. He was active in the work of the Rock Spring Church, and aided those measures that would uplift humanity and elevate society. He believed in the principles of the Democratic party and used his influence in behalf of its candidates. At the old home, where his busy life was passed, his eyes were closed in death November 24, 1882, at the age of sixty-seven. He is survived by his widow, Priscilla D. (Bull) Streett, a native of Baltimore and a descendant of English ancestry, and by their two daughters, Mary V. and Mattie C. Four children have passed from earth.

THOMAS M. WILKINSON, now a resident of District No. 3, Harford County, was born in District No. 4 in 1825. He is of Irish descent, the first of his name in America being his grandfather, Thomas, who came from the Emerald Isle to Pennsylvania and settled at New London Cross Roads in Chester County. By occupation he was a tanner, he followed this trade and at the same time engaged in farming pursuits. Thomas, Jr., our subject's father, was born in Chester County, whence he removed to Harford County and engaged in farming and milling near Deer Creek. In politics he was a Whig, one who never swerved from the principles promulgated by that organization during its existence. He never held public office, preferring to give his attention to private affairs exclusively. His death occurred at his home in Harford County in 1862, when he was sixty-five years of age. By his marriage to Sarah Harkins, he had ten children, seven of whom are still living, namely: Rachel, whose home is in Lancaster County, Pa.; Hannah; Thomas M., of this sketch; Sarah, residing in Harford County; Charles, a minister in Indiana; Joseph, who lives near Hopewell; and Martha.

In his boyhood Mr. Wilkinson attended the district schools and assisted in farm work. Inheriting industrious and honest habits, he grew to be a manly, reliable youth, fitted to make his own way in the world. When but sixteen years of age, wishing to earn his livelihood, he embarked in the lumber business, in which he continued for many years, being a resident of Aberdeen from the time he was twenty-one until 1882. Meantime he purchased a farm near Aberdeen and from the village moved to his new purchase, where he remained for five years, but afterward went back to Aberdeen, continuing there, as above stated, until 1882. He then bought the farm where he has since resided. It consists of one hundred acres, devoted to the raising of cereals and tomatoes, the latter vegetable being utilized in the canning business.

Elizabeth Ordman became the wife of Mr. Wilkinson in 1850 and eight children were born of their union, namely: George; Robert; Ella, deceased; Edmund; Alice, wife of Edward Oldfield; Rosie, who married Frank Kimball; Irene, Mrs. Charles Carver; and Arthur, who has charge of the old homestead. The family attend Mt. Zion Methodist Episcopal Church, in which Mr. Wilkinson is trustee and steward, and formerly served as superintendent of the Sunday-school.

ANDREW W. HOLT. District No. 5 in Cecil County is divided by North East River into two sections of almost similar size. In the division further east lies that tract of land known as Elk Neck, bordering upon Elk River. Owing to its location, its inhabitants have for successive generations engaged principally in the fishing business. However, this is not the sole industry. Farming has been engaged in by many of the residents and with good success, where judgment and persevering industry are exercised. It is the latter occupation to which Mr. Holt gives his attention and in which he has gained a competency. The property of which he has been the owner since 1874 was prior to that known as the Lort farm and consists of one hundred and nineteen acres, a part of which lies upon the banks of Elk River.

Within two miles of his present place of residence the subject of this notice was born August 28, 1844. His father, Washington, was a son of Andrew Holt and of Welsh descent. He was born in this district and in early manhood ran a packet line of boats from Baltimore to Elkton. At this writing he is living retired from business cares, making his home in Elkton, and is strong for one of fourscore years. Since the organization of the Republican party he has always affiliated with it, though he never took an active part in politics. In religious belief he is identified with the Methodist Episcopal Church. In his chosen line of work he spent all the active years of his life, but, later desiring a more settled and less anxious existence, he left the water in 1877, and bought a farm on Elk Neck. From this place in 1892 he removed to Elkton, in which village he hopes to spend his remaining years. His wife, Ann, was a daughter of Jesse Foster, of one of the oldest families of Cecil County, and she is now seventy-five years of age. Of their six children four are living, all in this county, namely: Andrew W., Isaac Lumsden, Lizzie and May.

The active life of a business man was more attractive to our subject than the study of dry and dull text books, so it was not a matter of regret to him when he was allowed to leave school and begin to work. At the age of seventeen he secured employment on a steamboat line running between New York and Baltimore. His first position was a humble one and wages were exceedingly small, but gradually he worked his way upward until he was finally made first mate of the vessel. He remained on the water for eighteen years, and on his retirement from the business in 1874 he came to the farm where he has since resided. The uneventful life of a farmer presents a decided contrast to the stirring work of the sailor, but he finds the change quite congenial to his tastes, and intends to spend his remaining years upon the land. The fact that he was so long a time upon the water prevented him from participating in public affairs, though he aimed to keep posted concerning the issues of the age and questions before the nation for consideration. The Republican party embodies in its platform the principles that seem to him best adapted to the welfare of our government and he always votes the straight ticket. In religion he is a member of the Methodist Episcopal Church. In 1872 he married Annie Burns, daughter of Michael Burns and a resident of Baltimore. They are the parents of four children, Gertrude, May, Woodall and Charles.

GEORGE L. VAN BIBBER. The same diligence in study which characterized Mr. Van Bibber in youth, while preparing for his professional duties, has followed him through his whole career and fitted him for the first place in his profession. It has won for him a lucrative practice and placed him among the most influential and successful attorneys of Bel Air. When a young man he selected the law for his life work, and to master its intricacies gave months of arduous study. Nor did he cease to be a student when he entered upon active practice; on the contrary, he has maintained the custom of thoughtful investigation into laws, rulings, judicial decisions and jurisprudence in its entirety, the result being that he has become one of the best informed attorneys of Harford County.

The Van Bibber family is one of the oldest in America. When William Penn returned to Europe from his first visit to America, he set about forming a colony of Hollanders to make settlement upon his grant of land. One of those whom he secured as a settler was Jacob Isaac Van Bibber, and thus it was that the family took root upon American soil. This pioneer, in 1680, secured a grant to the property where now stands the suburban town of Germantown, Pa. About 1700, as nearly as can be ascertained from records extant, he removed to Cecil County, Md. Little is known concerning his personal characteristics, but the fact that he made the then perilous trip to America and endured all the hardships of pioneer life, would seem to indicate that he was a man of great courage, persistence and determination. There are indications that he was very influential and took a leading part in the affairs of his day.

Isaac Van Bibber, a native of Cecil County, was throughout much of his life a resident of Baltimore, where he amassed a fortune in business. His son, Washington, a native of Baltimore, was largely interested in farming lands, and died in Carroll County. Next in line of descent was George L., our subject's father, who was born either in Baltimore County or Carroll County, Md. (the exact place is unknown), and removed in early life to New Orleans, where for many years he was engaged in the mercantile business. He returned to Baltimore and there he died in 1855. His wife, Hannah C., was a daughter of Stevenson Archer, and a member of one of the most prominent of Harford's old families. One of her ancestors, Dr. John Archer, was the first graduate from a medical college in America, receiving a diploma and the degree of M. D. from the University of Pennsylvania. Stevenson Archer was a man of much prominence, and among other responsible positions held that of chief judge of the court of appeals. Our subject is an only son, and has one sister, Lucretia, wife of Frank M. Doan, who is superintendent of a gas plant at Jacksonville, Ill.

Noting the principal facts in the life of George L. Van Bibber, Jr., he was born near Churchville, Harford County, Md., December 14, 1845, and, being the only son, he was given the best educational advantages the country afforded, and in justice to him it should be said that he availed himself of these opportunities to the utmost. The knowledge acquired at the public school was supplemented by a course of study at Princeton, from which he graduated in 1865, with the degree of A. B. Under the preceptorship of his uncle, Stevenson Archer, he carried on his legal studies in Bel Air, where he was admitted to the bar.

His home, situated one and one-half miles from

Bel Air, is presided over by his wife, who prior to her marriage in 1871 was Miss Adele Franklin, of Sumner County, Tenn. Their family consists of three children, namely: Dr. A. F., a young physician; Harriet L. and Lena C., who have been educated in the leading schools of the country.

CLIFFORD C. BARNES. In this day and age of bustle and activity, very few people stop to consider what we eat and how to select it, but the skillful housewife is very careful in her purchases, for she realizes that on the purity and wholesomeness of her groceries depend in a great measure the health and happiness of her family. Among the many excellent grocery establishments of which Harford County can boast, which attract the eye and have secured an enduring hold upon public favor and confidence, that with which the subject of this sketch is connected ranks foremost. It is one of the best equipped stores of the kind in Bel Air, and its patrons can always rely upon getting a very superior article, satisfactory treatment and prompt attention. Mr. Barnes is a young man of pleasing manners, and combines push, enterprise and excellent business qualities, and without doubt a promising future lies before him.

He owes his nativity to Glenville, Harford County, Md., where he was born May 19, 1868, to Richard A. and Mary Frances (Noble) Barnes, both of whom belong to old and well-known families of Harford County. He and his wife are ranked among the first citizens of this section, support all worthy causes, and are in the enjoyment of a comfortable competency which their own industry has brought them. To their marriage three sons were given. Charles F. is a successful liveryman of Bel Air; W. L., who was born April 4, 1862, was associated with his brother, Clifford C. Barnes, in the grocery business at Bel Air, and now holds a responsible position with David Hanway of that place. All these gentlemen are wide awake, pushing and enterprising, upright and honorable in their methods of conducting their affairs, and they have already been rewarded with success. In recognition of the class of people he caters to, Clifford C. Barnes has made it his aim to keep only superior articles, and his patronage is already large and constantly on the increase.

In his boyhood days Clifford C. was engaged in such odd jobs of work as are necessary on a farm, but at the same time his education was not neglected, and such advantages as the public schools afforded were given him. Upon commencing life on his own account he continued to till the soil, and his time and attention were thus occupied until about ten years ago, when he removed to Bel Air and became bookkeeper for the extensive carriage works of this place. This position he ably filled until a short time ago, when, in connection with his brother, he opened his present establishment. His life has been one ceaseless round of activity, and he has by no means been inactive in political matters, for he is a stanch Republican, is in full harmony with the teachings and principles of that party, and he has ever given his unqualified support to the Republican candidates. Mr. Barnes received the appointment of magistrate from Governor Lowndes and he is also town tax collector. Socially he is a member of the Junior Order of American Mechanics. He is unmarried.

THOMAS H. ROBERTS, M. D. There are few, if any, of the citizens of Harford County who surpass the subject of this biography in ability and popularity; whether we view his life from the standpoint of profession, business or social relations. He is a very busy man, having, in addition to the management of a large practice, the responsibility of superintending the farm where he resides and the mill upon the place, as well as the raising of cattle and their sale in the markets.

The Roberts family is of Virginian descent.

Thomas H. Roberts, Sr., father of our subject, was born in the Old Dominion, whence he removed to Maryland about 1825, and settled in District No. 5, Harford County. Upon a farm here he spent the remaining years of his life, the land being cultivated by his slaves, of whom he owned a large number. Politically he supported Whig principles. When only thirty-six years of age, in 1841, he departed this life, leaving besides his wife, Margaret (Hudson) Roberts, four sons, who were named as follows: John B., now a resident of Baltimore; William G., whose home is in Harford County; Dr. George H., who died in District No. 5, in 1876; and Thomas H. The last-named was born on the old homestead at Mill Green, Harford County, in 1840, and grew to manhood surrounded by the refining and uplifting influences of old Maryland in the days before the war. His parents gave him the best educational advantages the state afforded. After completing the common-school studies he attended Bel Air Academy.

With the intention of becoming a physician, our subject began the study of medicine in Jefferson Medical College, one of the most celebrated institutions of its kind, not only in Philadelphia, but in the United States. Graduating in 1865, he at once commenced active practice. The day memorable throughout the world as that on which President Lincoln was assassinated is memorable in his life on account of the fact that he then came to Churchville and opened an office for professional practice. For twelve years he remained in the village, but in 1877, after his marriage to Susan, daughter of George C. Davis, he removed to the old Davis homestead in District No. 3, where he has since resided. Though living upon a farm, his practice has not been discontinued. On the contrary, it requires his almost constant attention, extending, as it does, through several districts of the county. When at leisure from professional cares, he may be found upon his country estate, which, with its three hundred acres of cultivated land, and its pastures for the cattle, presents a picture of rural comfort. It has been his custom, founded upon experience, to buy cattle in the west and south and fatten them for the market, selling in June and July of each year; and this business has brought him a considerable increase of revenue.

In religious connections Dr. and Mrs. Roberts are identified with Holy Trinity Episcopal Church. In him the Democratic party has one of its warm supporters. He is a patriotic citizen, an acknowledged friend and liberal supporter of every enterprise that looks toward the elevation of society and the progress of the county. Highly respected as a citizen, exemplary as a church member, sincere as a friend, with a pleasant word for all in the ordinary happenings of daily life, he has won a high place in the regard of the people of the county.

WILLIAM S. FORWOOD, Jr., clerk of Harford County, was born in District No. 5 of this county, May 12, 1864, and is a member of a family long and intimately connected with the history of this portion of Maryland. His father, William Smithson Forwood, Sr., also a native of Harford County, has been one of the prominent public men of the locality, and has filled various official positions, notably that of county sheriff, to which he was elected in 1871. The Smithson family, with which he is connected, is also an old and influential family, and one of its early representatives was the founder of the Smithsonian Institute in Washington. Dr. Parker Forwood, grandfather of our subject, was one of the leading physicians of his day, and his skill and ability in the diagnosis of disease brought him a large and profitable practice.

The boyhood years of the subject of this notice were uneventfully passed in Bel Air, and he was given an excellent academical education at this place. Trained to methodical business habits, later years bore the fruits of the ideas implanted in his nature in youth. His mind seemed to have a commercial rather than a literary bent, and, not desiring to take a thorough classical course in college, he prepared himself rather for the walks of business life. In his father's store, as clerk, he also gained practical experience that was of value to him. In 1884 he entered the clerk's office, being under the late Captain Jarrett, who had held the office for some forty years or more. After two years in that position, he accepted an appointment in the United States treasury under Secretary Manning. Eighteen months were spent in Washington, in the discharge of the duties as clerk in the treasury. On his return to Bel Air, he again resumed work in the clerk's office, this time as chief clerk. Courteous and obliging in manner and efficient in business transactions, he soon made many friends; in fact, everyone who had business in the office (and most of the people in the county did) had the highest regard for him and the greatest confidence in his ability.

When, in 1891, Mr. Forwood became a candidate for the office of county clerk, his popularity was at once proved. Not only those of his own party, but even some of different political belief, gave him an unwavering, cordial support. The result was that he gained the election by a large majority. He had the distinction of being the youngest man ever elected to the clerk's office in Harford County; but, in spite of his youth, he soon proved that he was fully able to cope with all the difficulties that arose. Since he became the head of the office he has made many reforms in the methods of work, for he is a champion of progress. His habit of close application to business does not prevent him from finding time to mingle in the enjoyment of social life; and in society, as well as in business, he is hailed as a genial comrade. He is not married, but continues to make his home with his father, who is living in Bel Air.

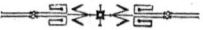

WILLIAM SAMUEL WEBSTER, who is engaged in farming and stock-raising in District No. 1, Harford County, was born June 18, 1838, upon the place where he now resides. His father, Capt. John Adams Webster, who was born here September 19, 1787, was a son of Samuel and Margaret (Adams) Webster, the latter a relative of John Quincy Adams, the former a son of Isaac Webster. Captain Webster was a seafaring man and spent the greater portion of his life upon the water. He entered the navy prior to the War of 1812, in which he served as a lieutenant on the privateer "Rosseau," being for a time in command of a battery between Forts McHenry and Covington. In the engagement of September 10, 1814, he was detailed with seventy-five men to take charge of the six-gun battery. They were busy until the 14th in making the battery as secure as possible. During the night of the 13th he detected the sound of the enemy's boats coming near, and at once opened fire on them. Skirmishing was kept up by both parties until one o'clock on the morning of the 14th, when the enemy retired, and as they passed Fort McHenry they were fired upon from there. In coming up they had passed the fort unnoticed, but later had, fortunately for the Americans, been detected by the young lieutenant, who drove them back. In recognition of this service the state of Maryland and citizens of Baltimore presented him with a handsome gold-mounted sword.

November 22, 1819, Captain Webster was commissioned captain of the revenue cutter, "Marine." May 19, 1846, he was detailed to control the operations of the revenue vessels employed in the Gulf of Mexico, and at the time of his death he was the senior captain in the service. In the battle of Bladensburg his horse was killed and the same ball knocked off his hat, another ball taking his thumb off. The sword which he carried in that battle is now in the possession of our subject. He was a man of fine physique, six feet tall and weighing over two hundred pounds, erect in carriage, well proportioned and of commanding appearance. In social characteristics he was genial and easily approached, possessing remarkably courteous manners and the hospitable traits that mark the true southerner. He was a patriot, ever loyal to the interests of the country, and an American in every fibre of his being. Had he been permitted to choose the day upon which his earth life should end, probably he would have selected the very day upon which his life went out, the anniversary of the independence of our country. He died at his home in 1877 and was buried beside his wife and deceased children in the family burial ground at Mt. Adams.

February 8, 1816, occurred the marriage of John Adams Webster and Rachel Biays, daughter of Col. Joseph Biays, a native of Frederick County, Md., and an officer in the Revolution. They became the parents of fourteen children. Margaret, who was born December 13, 1817, became the wife of William Bissell, who was killed at Gettysburg; she now resides at Bel Air. Elizabeth and John A. died in childhood. Josephine, who was born November 19, 1823, married Dr. William Dallam, of Harford County, and died July 25, 1869. John A. (2d) born June 26, 1825, passed away April 6, 1875. Mary Alice, who was born August 20, 1827, became the wife of Algernon S. Dorsey, July 3, 1851, and died in July, 1865. James Biays was born November 24, 1828, and died August 12, 1890. Susan Ann, who was born February 27, 1830, departed this life October 3, 1895. Benjamin M. was born October 23, 1831, and attained the age of forty-five, dying in October, 1876. Rachel Virginia died in girlhood. Laura Archer, whose birth occurred September 16, 1834, was married to John C. Patterson, of Wilmington, Del., June 19, 1861, and passed from earth March 21, 1892. Rachel Cassandra, who was born September 17, 1836, became the wife of Gen. Frank A. Bond, October 26, 1859, and died June 16, 1895. Isaac Pleasants, who was born April 19, 1840, died on the battlefield of Malvern Hill, Va., near Richmond, where he was fighting under General McClellan, July 1, 1862.

The next to the youngest of this large family was the subject of our sketch. He received his education principally at Bel Air and Elkton, and when about eighteen commenced to assist his father on the farm. In 1861 he enlisted as a member of a company formed at Leesburg, of Howard County men, and served in the army until May, 1865. Several times he almost miraculously escaped injury. Two horses were shot under him, a shot passed between his arm and side, and another through his hat. Returning home at the close of the war, he became an apprentice to the carpenter's trade, in Philadelphia. He now has in his possession a dining table, upon which he worked for a year during his apprenticeship; the legs of the table were made from the legs of an old piano that belonged to the family. He never actively engaged at his trade, but after the death of his father carried on the home farm until 1886, when he went to Colorado and there engaged in ranching for a few years. In October, 1892, he returned to Harford County and has since remained on the old homestead. June 4, 1889, he was united in marriage with Sarah Elizabeth Hutchison, who is of Scotch-Irish descent. They are members of the Presbyterian Church and actively interested in religious movements. In politics he votes the Democratic ticket, but has never taken part in public affairs, preferring to devote himself to his private business interests.

R OBERT P. MITCHELL, a farmer residing on District No. 2, Harford County, is a representative of one of the old and honored families of this locality, prominently identified with its farming interests for more than a century. His paternal grandfather, Parker Mitchell, was born in the same neighborhood, and as a means of livelihood followed both farming and fishing. He died at the early age of about thirty-eight years. John Mitchell, father of our subject, was a native of District No. 2, and throughout his entire life carried on agricultural pursuits, in connection with which he was also a fisherman for several years. He was twice married, his first union being with Miss Gilbert, who died leaving one son, John, whose death occurred at the age of seventy-one years. For his second wife he chose Miss Elizabeth Silver, a daughter of Gashen and Elizabeth (Bayless) Silver. She died at the age of sixty-nine years, but her husband reached the advanced age of ninety-two years. He voted with the Whig party in early life, and on its dissolution enlisted under the banner of the Democracy, but he never sought or desired political preferment, content to devote his time and attention

JAMES WEBSTER.

to his business and home interests. In his family were six children: Ann M., widow of J. Colvin Michael; Robert P.; Sarah, wife of John Archer Mitchell; Madison, who is engaged in the undertaking business at Baltimore; Mary E.; and Jerusha, wife of Charles B. Osborn, of District No. 2.

Robert P. Mitchell has always devoted his life to the pursuit to which he was reared, and industry and perseverance are marked characteristics of his business career. He was married to Miss Mary C. Hughes, a daughter of Amos H. Hughes, and they have a family of three children: Robert H., who is engaged in farming in District No. 2; Carrie G., who resides with her parents; and John O., who follows the undertaking business in Baltimore.

Mr. Mitchell is recognized as one of the leaders of the Democratic party in his county. He is well informed on the issues and questions of the day; in 1876 he served on the county assessment board, has been a member of the county board of control and review, and in 1881 and 1882 served as county commissioner. He has ever discharged his duties with promptness and fidelity, thus winning the commendation of all concerned, and in every relation of life he is found true and faithful to the trust reposed in him.

JAMES WEBSTER. There are few whose lives are prolonged to the age of more than four score and still fewer who are permitted, amid the vicissitudes of time and its constant mutations, to spend so long a period upon the same spot and within the same home. Such, however, has been the fortunate lot of Mr. Webster. The stone house where he now dwells was the place where his birth occurred February 14, 1814, and the farm, situated in Churchville precinct, District No. 3, Harford County, is the only home he has ever known. His own history is contemporaneous with that of our nation in its most interesting and important period of development. Born before the close of the War of 1812, as a child he witnessed the advancement of the interests and development of the resources of Maryland. He recalls the excitement of early presidential elections, the days when "Tippecanoe and Tyler too" was the popular campaign cry, the war with Mexico, the excitement caused by the discovery of gold in California, the introduction of steam railways, the settlement of the western lands, the exciting times prior to and during the Civil War and the period of reconstruction; all these, and many other incidents connected with our national history, he remembers as vividly as though but recently passed.

The Webster family, as stated upon another page, is one of the oldest and most influential of Harford County. The father of our subject, Richard, was born in Churchville precinct, District No. 3, in 1765, and was a son of Richard, Sr., born in 1741. Richard, Jr., engaged in farming and milling until his death. April 15, 1800, he married Rachel Mitchell, and to their union were born six children, namely: John, February 20, 1801; Phœbe, December 12, 1802; William, April 1, 1805; Noah, May 1, 1808; Mary, December 26, 1810; and James, of this sketch, the only one now living. Noah married Susanna Mitchell and died at sixty-five years of age.

Educated in the private schools of the county, the subject of this sketch assisted his father in the mill and upon the farm. Upon the decease of his father, September 10, 1855, he assumed control of the farm, which he still superintends, retaining its active management, notwithstanding his advanced years. May 23, 1839, he married Mary F., daughter of William W. and Mary Webster. Their married life was of brief duration, as she died December 4, 1840. His second marriage took place at Churchville January 10, 1848, his wife being Adaline, daughter of William Holland and Elizabeth (Osborn) Divers, both of old families of the county. Her father was for many years a school teacher here and was recognized as a very efficient educator. Should the lives of Mr. and Mrs. Webster be spared to January, 1898, they will celebrate their golden wedding anniversary. They are a well-preserved couple, in the enjoyment of excellent health, and it is the wish of their many friends that they may live to have many more happy years on earth. Mrs. Webster is identified with Calvary Methodist Episcopal Church, and while he is not a member of any denomination he is a believer in Christianity and aids church work by his contributions of money. In politics he is a Republican, and when in his prime would have been chosen to occupy public office had it not been distasteful to him; at no time has he been induced to hold public office, but he has always been willing to aid his friends in their candidacy. The farm where he resides consists of over two hundred acres of land and is devoted to farming and stock-raising purposes. The property is valuable, and under his efficient management the land has been very productive.

GEORGE B. JAMES, of Emmorton, is a leading representative of the agricultural and industrial interests of Harford County. He was born near Avondale, in this county, December 23, 1831, and belongs to one of the old and honored families which for more than a century have been identified with this region. He is also descended from good old Revolutionary stock, his great-grandfather having been one of the heroes who fought for the independence of the nation. His grandfather, Joseph James, was born in Pennsylvania, and came to Harford County about the year 1775. His son James, the father of our subject, was born about four miles from Emmorton, and was a chair turner and farmer. He married Sarah Gilbert, a daughter of Jarvis Gilbert, of this county. They held membership in the Methodist Episcopal Church, and were people of the highest respectability. The father died in 1874, and the mother passed away in 1895, at the age of ninety-one years. They had a family of ten children: William Joseph and Jarvis Gilbert, who are both residents of Indiana; Charles H., who makes his home in Churchville, Md.; George B.; John L., of Baltimore; Mary C., wife of James Sheridan, of Churchville; Elizabeth E., wife of Phil Hawkins, of Churchville; Sarah S., who is living in Churchville; Sophia Jane, wife of P. Lacoflin, of Aberdeen; and Jacob M., of Churchville.

George B. James, whose name forms the caption of this article, acquired his education in private schools, which he attended at intervals until twenty-one years of age. He then learned the trade of shoemaking, which he followed for a quarter of a century in Bel Air and Churchville. In May, 1884, he rented the Lettick farm, near Emmorton, and has since made his home thereon, extensively engaged in raising and canning tomatoes. He has here one hundred and fifty acres of land, of which thirty-five acres are planted in tomatoes, and from those vines he gathers enough of the vegetable to can five thousand cases. The excellent quality of his goods secures to him a ready market and his straightforward business dealing has won him the confidence and good-will of all with whom he has been brought in contact.

Mr. James married Miss Sarah E. Keithly, of Harford County. The wedding was celebrated on the 10th of January, 1861, and twenty years later Mrs. James died, in July, 1881. Their children were as follows: Mary C. and Annie, twins, the latter now deceased; Sarah, wife of Rev. George Cuddy, who is pastor of a large church in Tacoma, Wash.; Emma E., wife of George E. Wright, of Harford County; Stephen G and Paul S., at home; George B., who is living in the neighborhood; S. S., J. Gilbert and B. W. C., all yet with their father.

Mr. James formerly gave his political support to the Republican party, but believing the temperance question the most prominent issue before the people to-day, he allied his forces with the Prohibition party, and is now one of its stanch advocates. Socially he is connected with the Odd Fellows' Society, and in religious belief is a Methodist. He has served as trustee, steward and class leader of his church and for many years was an exhorter. He does all in his power to promote the cause of the church, and to advance all interests calculated to uplift and ennoble humanity. His own life is well worthy of emulation and all who know him retain for him the highest regard.

JOHN F. BULL, M. D., a retired physician of Harford County, was born in 1822 upon the farm in District No. 3 where he now resides. The family of which he is a member was established in America by five brothers who came to this country from England, but of these, his grandfather, John, was the only one who settled in Maryland. The Doctor's father, William Bull, combined the occupations of farming and tanning, and spent his entire life on the old homestead, dying here in 1853, at the age of eighty years. By his marriage to Elizabeth, daughter of Henry Ruff, there were born ten children, but only four survive, namely: Mary; Hannah; Eliza, wife of James Barrow, and John F., of this sketch.

In the days when Mr. Bull was young it was not as easy to obtain an education as it is now, however, he was enabled to acquire a broad knowledge of science, literature and philosophy, as well as an intimate acquaintance with the more practical and common branches of learning. After attending a private school for some time, he entered Bel Air Academy, where he was a student for three years. In 1849 he matriculated at the Washington University of Baltimore, but after a year left that institution and entered the University of Pennsylvania in Philadelphia, from the medical department of which he graduated in 1851. Returning to his home in Harford County he at once began practice and continued actively engaged there for some years. From 1867 to 1881 he resided upon a farm near the old homestead, giving his attention less to professional duties than to the supervision of the estate. In 1881 he went to Baltimore, where he made his home for three years, enjoying the advantages of city life. On his return to Harford County he established his home at Forest Hill, whence in 1890 he returned to the homestead where he was born. Living to some extent retired from professional cares and business affairs, with no weighty matters to engross his attention or perplex his mind, he is in a position to enjoy life to its utmost. His worth as a man is shown, among other things, by the fact that he is held in the highest regard by the people in whose midst much of his life has been passed. All unite in testifying to his nobility of character and integrity of life.

The marriage of Dr. Bull took place in 1855 and united him with Miss Cordelia Hollingsworth, of Baltimore. They are the parents of eight children, namely: Milton; Irving, a business man of Baltimore. Charles, who lives in Pennsylvania; Elma, Eugene, Harry, Clara and Bessie. One of the most important connections of Dr. Bull is his church relations. For sixty years he has been a Christian, striving in all things to exemplify his faith in the doctrines of the church. He is identified with the Methodist Episcopal Church, in which he has been steward and trustee for some time. In Sunday-school work he has been especially interested and has officiated as superintendent with efficiency and success. The people of this community hold him in the highest esteem and he is justly regarded as one of the public-spirited and progressive citizens of the locality.

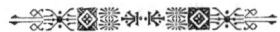

THE WEBSTER FAMILY, which is one of the oldest in Harford County, is interwoven by marriage with many of the best families of this locality. The date of the arrival of their first representatives in America is not definitely known, but it was about the time of Lord Baltimore, and some of the present generation have in their possession grants of land from him bearing dates as early as 1649 and 1652. The remote ancestors were of English and Scotch birth, and the traits of these nationalities are still noticeable in their American descendants. The first to cross the ocean were four brothers, named as follows: John, who settled in Virginia and was known as

John of Roanoke; Isaac, the progenitor of the Harford County branch; Samuel and Michael. Isaac took up land on the Bush River, extending back into the county for six miles.

The original representatives of the Websters in this country were of diversified religious belief, some being Quakers and others Episcopalians. Their descendants are now found among the Methodists and Presbyterians. The family coat-of-arms is a swan feeding its young. Miss M. Elizabeth, a sister of William and daughter of Henry Webster, has in her possession one of the old seals, showing this crest. John Webster was born in 1670 and left a family of three sons and two daughters, one son, John, having died prior to the father's death. His will, which was made in 1751, was recorded and is still extant. In it he provides for the following children: Sarah, Michael, Isaac, Samuel and Alisanna. The family has always been a long-lived one, and he is thought to have attained the age of eighty-five. His son, Samuel, was born in 1710, and married Elizabeth Dallam. He was a very prominent man and held the important and lucrative office of tobacco inspector at Joppa, which was then the principal port here, and raising and dealing in tobacco was the most important industry of the time.

Richard, son of Samuel, was born April 7, 1741, on a place adjoining the old homestead, now occupied by William Webster, and his death occurred in the old stone family residence. He was twice married, his first wife being a daughter of William Lester. By her he had three children, John, Samuel and Richard, the latter being the father of James Webster, a sketch of whose life will be found elsewhere in this work. After her death he married Phoebe, daughter of George Smith, of Chester County, Pa. To their union were born eight children, as follows: George, Elizabeth, William W., Sarah, Isaac, Wesley, Henry and Phoebe. Henry is the father of William Webster, who resides on the old homestead, and also of George S., whose sketches are presented in this volume.

It is perhaps unnecessary to dwell upon the characteristics of the Webster family, for they are well known to all our readers. They possess many of the noble traits that brought success to their ancestors, who were brave pioneers, developing the country that is now adorned with fine farms and busy towns. We who reap the harvest their hands have sown should honor them and hold their names in grateful remembrance. After their toils they rest in peace, leaving behind them a race that will read, with never-flagging interest, the records of their lives, which show so many examples of manly heroism and womanly graces. We, who are the heirs of the past, gladly acknowledge our indebtedness to all the pioneers, who, like the Websters, labored for the welfare of generations yet to come.

ROBERT L. MITCHELL is a member of a well-known family residing in the southeastern part of District No. 3, Harford County. Here he was born in 1847 and here he has continued to make his home, devoting his time to the business of a general wheelwright in addition to farming. He is the grandson of Elijah Mitchell and son of Robert Mitchell, a collier and farmer, who was born January 22, 1804. The latter spent his entire life in this district and resided on what was known as the Stony Ridge farm, making his home there until he passed away December 21, 1890, at the age of eighty-six. His wife, who was in maidenhood Arvilla Hawkins, died March 16, 1892, at the age of eighty-two. Their family consisted of seven children, namely: Mary Jane, the widow of John W. Hanby; George W., who lives in Indiana; Margaret, deceased; John T., who has continued to make his home in this district; Catherine, deceased; Robert L., of this sketch; and Samuel B., who occupies the old family homestead.

On the Stony Ridge farm, where he was born, the subject of this notice spent the years of boyhood and youth, early in life gaining a thorough knowledge of all the details of agricultural operations. It was not possible for him to spend much time in school, but the defects in his education have been remedied to a large extent by thoughtful reading and habits of close observation. For three years he served as an apprentice to the carpenter's trade, which he afterward followed for some years. In 1872 he turned his attention more particularly to work as a wheelwright, and in this he has since been interested. In addition, he carries on his farm of twenty-one acres situated in District No. 3.

The lady who in 1874 became the wife of Mr. Mitchell was Alice O. Gorrell, a resident of this district and a woman of estimable character. They are members of Calvary Methodist Episcopal Church, in which he has officiated as a trustee for twenty years. In Sunday-school work he is interested and as a teacher has been instrumental in promoting the cause among the children of the vicinity. He is a hard-working, upright man, and has the friendship of all who have been associated with him.

ADAM DE BAUGH, who is engaged in general merchandising in Earlton, is a wide-awake, energetic business man, and as a citizen is active in support of all measures which he believes calculated to benefit the community. During the Civil War he manifested his loyalty to the government by enlisting in his country's service and valiantly followed the old flag until the overthrow of the Confederacy. In all the relations of life he has ever been found true and faithful, and Harford County numbers him among its valued citizens.

A native of the neighboring state of Pennsylvania, Mr. De Baugh was born in York County, January 12, 1836, a son of Philip and Mary (Untonia) De Baugh, both of whom were born on the Rhine, in Germany. Their marriage was there celebrated and about 1830 they left the Fatherland for America, taking up their residence in York County. The father was a shoemaker by trade, but in Pennsylvania ran a huckster's wagon for several years. Later he purchased a farm in Baltimore County, Md., and in 1863 departed this life, at the age of sixty-three years. He came to this country a poor man, but his energy and perserverance enabled him to overcome the obstacles in his path and at his death he was the possessor of a comfortable property. Both he and his wife were members of the Catholic Church.

Under the parental roof Adam De Baugh was reared to manhood. He entered upon his business career as a farm hand, and worked in that capacity until about twenty-five years of age, when in 1861 he went to Ohio. He was there employed by the month until August 15, 1862, when, feeling that his country needed his services, he joined the boys in blue of Company A, One Hundred Twenty-third Ohio Infantry, for three years. At the battle of Winchester he was captured, spent four days in Libby prison, and was thence taken to Belle Isle, and from there to Annapolis. He was there paroled and although held as a prisoner only twenty-four days he was almost starved during that time. Going to Ohio, he there remained for two months, when he was exchanged and returned to his regiment. At the same time Mr. De Baugh was captured, his lieutenant and captain were taken prisoners, but they dug their way out of Libby and thus effected their escape. On the 6th of April, 1865, at the battle of High Bridge, Mr. De Baugh was shot through the right leg near the hip, which necessitated the amputation of that member. He was taken to City Point Hospital at Fortress Monroe, where he was confined for nine months, after which he returned to his home near Upper Sandusky, Ohio.

Not long after this he was appointed postmaster at Wortonsburg, in which capacity he served until 1867, when he removed to Towson, Md., and secured the appointment of postmaster at that place. After a term of five years in that office he was obliged to resign on account of his health and ran a stage line from Towson to Sherwood until 1881. In that year he came to Earlton, erected a store building and has since engaged in general merchandising. He carries a good stock, including everything usually found in a general store, and has secured from the public a liberal patronage which he richly merits, as his business methods are above question and he earnestly desires to please his customers.

Mr. De Baugh married Miss Elizabeth Passett, of Ohio. He is an unswerving Republican in his political affiliations and does all in his power to promote the growth and insure the success of his party. Socially he is connected with the Towson Lodge No. 79, I. O. O. F., and Dushane Post No. 3, G. A. R., of Baltimore. He is a member of the Christian Church, in which he has served as elder for the past two years, and is active in its work and upbuilding. In the discharge of his duties of citizenship he manifests the same loyalty that characterized his service when he followed the stars and stripes to victory on southern battlefields.

AMOS H. HUGHES, deceased, was born February 25, 1812, on what is known as the Eygh Trap farm in District No. 2, Harford County. His grandfather, John Hall Hughes, was probably a native of Scotland, but his father, John Hughes, was born on the homestead farm August 21, 1772. He there spent his entire life and was widely and favorably known throughout the community. He married Charlotte Mitchell, followed the mason's trade as a means of livelihood, and died upon the farm where his entire life was passed, at the age of fourscore years.

During a period of eighty years Amos H. Hughes witnessed the growth and development of his native county, saw the many changes that came with the passing of time, and ever bore his part in the work of public progress. He was married February 25, 1841, to Miss Hannah Catherine Adams, who was born in District No. 2, Harford County, December 3, 1821, a daughter of William and Catherine (Brown) Adams. Her father was born in England, and came with his parents to America during his childhood, spending his remaining days in Maryland. He was a self-made man, and the success that he achieved was due entirely to his own industrious efforts on the farm. In his political belief he was a Whig, while religiously he was connected with the Society of Friends. His death occurred at the age of fifty-seven years. His father, William Adams, was the first to engage in the manufacture of fine shoes in this portion of the state. He died in middle life. The mother of Mrs. Hughes, Catherine (Brown) Adams, was born in Cecil County, Md., was also a member of the Society of Friends, and died at the age of fifty-six years. Mrs. Hughes is now the only survivor of her family of nine children. She lives on the homestead left to her by her husband, and, although seventy-five years of age, is well preserved physically and mentally. She holds membership in the Methodist Church, and her many excellencies of character have won her the esteem of all and the love of family and friends.

To Mr. and Mrs. Hughes were born thirteen children, as follows: Charlotta Catharine, wife of George Silvers, a farmer of District No. 2; William Oliver, a prominent citizen of Bel Air, who formerly served as county sheriff; Mary, wife of Robert P. Mitchell, an agriculturist of District No. 2; Caroline, wife of Ambrose Cooley; Annie, wife of Thomas Vincen, of Baltimore; Henrietta, wife of Herman Spencer, a farmer and fisherman of District No. 2; Scott Hughes, a prosperous agriculturist of the same district; Lucy Virginia, widow of Martin Gilbert; Amos H., a farmer of the same neighborhood; Robert Henry, who is engaged in merchandising at Dorsey, Howard County, Md., and is a tobacco inspector in Baltimore; Hannah Emma, wife of William Smith, a merchant of Lapidum; Eugene Lee, who operates the old homestead and also runs a threshing machine during the harvest season; and one who died in infancy.

Amos H. Hughes spent his entire life upon the farm where he was born. He was reared to agricultural pursuits, and throughout his entire life followed that vocation. He placed his land under a high state of cultivation, made many substantial improvements, and in return for his care and labor the well-tilled fields yielded to him a golden tribute. In politics he was a stalwart advocate of the Democracy, who always kept well informed on the issues of the day and was active in support of his party. He held membership in the Methodist Episcopal Church. His death occurred October 4, 1892, and the community lost thereby a faithful citizen, his family a loving husband and father, and his neighbors a loyal friend.

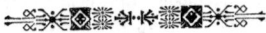

JOHN B. WYSONG. Few people deserve more credit for the property they have obtained and the prosperity they have enjoyed than do our honest, enterprising farmers, and of these Harford County has a large number. The farm owned and operated by Mr. Wysong is situated in District No. 3, and for fertility and productiveness is classed among the best in the neighborhood. It consists of three hundred and twenty acres, planted to the various cereals, and improved with substantial farm buildings. This has been the home of the present owner since 1872.

The Wysong family is of French extraction, and one of its early representatives was an officer in the French army. John Wysong, our subject's grandfather, was a merchant in Berkeley County, W. Va., and Rev. T. T. Wysong, the father, was also a native of that county, but has spent the principal portion of his life in Maryland, being engaged in the ministry of the Methodist Church for many years. His home has been near The Rocks, in Harford County, since 1867 and he is well known in this section. For some time he has not been active in ministerial work, but has lived retired. He married Fannie Preston, an estimable lady, who is now (1897) seventy years of age. Their children were named as follows: John B.; Annie; D. P., of Long Island, N. Y.; and Frank.

At the parental home in District No. 4, Harford County, the subject of this sketch was born in 1847, and here his childhood years were uneventfully passed. At an early age he was sent to the common school to obtain an education which would fit him for the duties and responsibilities of after days; although this education did not contain the studies now considered indispensable and did not include many text books now in vogue, it was nevertheless practical, and would have been very thorough had his health permitted him to remain in school for a satisfactory period. The fact that he was not strong rendered outdoor work a necessity to him, while the confinement in the school room proved detrimental. He therefore gave his attention mostly to farm duties, continuing at home for a number of years.

In January, 1895, Mr. Wysong was united in marriage with Ella J. Grymes, of King George County, Va., the great-granddaughter of George Mason. John Mason, the only child born of their union, died at the age of sixteen months. Mr. and Mrs. Wysong are members of the Rock Spring Episcopal Church, in which he has been registrar for fifteen years and vestryman for twenty-five years. Interested in matters pertaining to agriculture, he is an active member of the Deer Creek Farmers' Club and was its president in 1895. Politically he is a warm adherent of the Democratic party, and is interested in the current questions of government and civic import.

JOHN M. MACKLEM follows farming in District No. 2, Harford County. There are no thrilling events in his life, which has been devoted to quiet and honorable business pursuits, but such a career cannot fail to prove of interest, as he is a worthy representative of our best type of American citizenship in the faithful performance of his duty to his country, his neighbor and himself.

Mr. Macklem was born October 17, 1837, near Newark, Del., which was also the birthplace of his parents, William and Mary (Thompson) Macklem. The Macklem family is of Scotch origin, and was founded in America by John Macklem, the grandfather of our subject, who was born in the land of hills and heather, and came to America in early life. He served his adopted country in the War of 1812 and lived to an advanced age. The maternal grandparents were Andrew and Elizabeth Thompson, natives of Belfast County, Ireland, where they spent their childhood days and were married. Crossing the Atlantic to the New World, they took up their residence in Newcastle County, Del.

William Macklem, the father of our subject, was a stone mason by trade, and became an extensive contractor in that line, erecting many bridges for the Philadelphia, Wilmington & Baltimore Railroad, and many buildings in Newark, Del., and vicinity. His business methods were above question and his word was as good as his bond. Careful management and unfailing industry brought him success and he was the possessor of a good property at the time of his death, which occurred when he was fifty-six years of age. His wife was a member of the Presbyterian Church and died when about sixty-eight years of age. She had seven children, two sons and five daughters.

John M. Macklem, the youngest of the family, was reared under the parental roof and with his father learned the stone-mason's trade, perfecting himself in that business until he became an expert workman. Between the ages of twenty-five and thirty years he engaged in contracting on his own account. He then established a meat market in Wilmington, Del., where he successfully carried on business for about fifteen years, when he sold out and purchased his present farm, known as the Quaker Bottom farm, in District No. 2, Harford County. Here in connection with general farming, he conducts a large canning factory and raises sweet corn and tomatoes on an extensive scale for canning purposes.

Mr. Macklem married Miss Elizabeth Davies, of Wilmington, Del., and they have ten children, namely: Elizabeth T., wife of Amos Hughes, a farmer of District No. 2; Mary T., wife of John Gordon, of Wilmington; William J., a farmer of District No. 2; Levinia D., Annie M., Rebecca J., Lucy B., John W., Sarah L. and Bessie V., all at home.

Mr. Macklem is a most ardent worker in the Prohibition party. His earnest championship of the temperance cause led to his identification with the political party that embodied his views on this question, and he does all in his power to promote its growth and insure its success. He was its candidate for congress in 1893, has been its nominee for representative and county commissioner and his name was on its electoral ticket in 1896. When twenty-one years of age he united with the Methodist Episcopal Church, and on coming to Maryland joined the Methodist Protestant Church, with which he is now connected, serving as a member of its board of trustees. He now resides on his fine farm of two hundred and fifty acres, one of the best improved properties in this section of the state. In his business he has met with success, owing to his well-directed efforts. His perseverance has overcome all obstacles in his path and he has steadily worked his way upward to success.

J. P. WILSON is president of the Enterprise Carriage Works of Bel Air, and one of the leading representatives of business interests in Harford County. He was born four miles north of that city, February 19, 1865. His father, Humphrey Wilson, is a native of the same county, and a carpenter by trade, but has followed farming during the greater part of his life. He has served as magistrate and is a leading and influential factor in local affairs. His father was a native of Ireland, and in 1770 located on the farm where occurred the birth of our subject. Humphrey Wilson married Miss Sarah A. Durham, a native of Harford County, belonging to one of the old families of the state of English ancestry. Her father, Abel Durham, was one of the defenders of Baltimore in the War of 1812. Mr. and Mrs. Wilson have three sons and one daughter, of whom Abel and T. J. are engaged in farming at Forest Hill, where the parents reside. Mary F. is the widow of Charles Whitaker.

J. P. Wilson, of this review, was reared on the

GEORGE W. LOCKWOOD.

home farm, obtained his education in the common schools, and learned the blacksmith's trade at Forest Hill, When a young man he came to Bel Air, and has since been associated with its business interests. In 1891 he organized the Enterprise Carriage Company, of which he has since been president. This industry has prospered from the beginning and its patronage is constantly increasing, for they manufacture some of the finest carriages in the state, and have a reputation for good workmanship and honorable dealing that commends them to the confidence and support of all.

Mr. Wilson was married in 1895 to Miss Julia Billingslea, of Bel Air. He is an enterprising young business man, whose integrity stands an unquestioned fact in his history. Endowed by nature with a sound judgment and an accurate, discriminating mind he has not feared that laborious attention to business so necessary to achieve success, and this essential quality has ever been guided by a sense of moral right which would tolerate the employment of means that would bear the most rigid examination and require no disguise.

GEORGE W. LOCKWOOD. We are now permitted to touch briefly upon the life history of one who has retained a personal association with the affairs of Cecil County, and one whose ancestral line traces back to the colonial epoch. His life has been one of earnest and honest endeavor and due success has not been denied him.

Mr. Lockwood was born February 18, 1847, on the "Meadows" farm in Cecil County, Md., and is the oldest son of Edward Wilson and Sarah E. (Alrichs) Lockwood, both Delawareans by birth, belonging to families conspicuously associated with the earliest history of that state. On the maternal side he is a descendant of Peter Alrichs, who in 1660 was the third governor of Delaware, which was still in the hands of the Dutch. He was a nephew of Jacob Alrichs, the first vice-director (1651). The family had in its possession until recently the old Alrichs homestead, and the house is reputed to be the oldest north of St. Augustine, Fla. The grant for this land was obtained from the Dutch. On the paternal side Mr. Lockwood is descended from an old New England family, which was founded in America by two brothers, Edward and Robert Lockwood, who came from England and settled at Watertown, Mass., as early as 1630. From them the Lockwoods of Delaware sprang, and for many generations they have been prominently identified with the history of the Diamond State.

In the public schools of Middletown, Del., and Fredericktown, Cecil County, Md., George W. Lockwood, of this review, obtained his early education, which was supplemented by a course in the Georgetown University, of the District of Columbia, being a student there from 1862-66. He was there at the time of the grand review of the Union army at Washington directly after the late war. On leaving college, Mr. Lockwood went to New York, engaging in the fruit commission business with a large dealer of that city. He saw a good opportunity to become a member of the firm and had made all final arrangements for forming a partnership, when the head of the firm suddenly died. This turn of events made him determine to return to Maryland and take charge of one of his father's farms, devoting it to fruit culture. Engaging in this pursuit quite extensively, he met with excellent success, especially in raising peaches, and was one of the largest growers on the peninsula until a few years ago, when the peach blight made it necessary for him to remove and uproot all trees.

In 1871 Mr. Lockwood was united in marriage to Miss Adelaide Morton, of Strawberry Hill, Cecil County, the oldest daughter of Hamilton and Mary T. (Durkee) Morton. Her father was for many years a resident of Cecil County, but was born in Philadelphia and belonged to an old and honored family there. The Durkees were among the first settlers of Maryland, and many of the representatives of the family became quite distinguished and prominent during the colonization of the state, among whom was the third governor under the English (1647). Seven children were born to Mr. and Mrs. Lockwood, namely: Marie T., Blanche E., Harry M., Grace A., George I., Julia E. M. and James Booth. All are still living with the exception of Grace A.

Mr. Lockwood was baptized and reared as an Episcopalian, but while a student at Georgetown became converted to the Roman Catholic faith, to which he still adheres. In politics he is a Democrat, but takes no very active part in political affairs, the honors or emoluments of public office having no attraction for him. He has ever been a public-spirited, progressive citizen, cooperating in all that is calculated to promote the interests of his locality or state, and wherever he is found he is a sociable, affable, genial gentleman, whose friends are legion, and all honor and esteem him for his many virtues and genuine worth.

WILLIAM L. DERICKSON. The homestead of this well-to-do resident of Harford County is situated in District No. 3, and includes a large acreage of fertile land, with good improvements. A portion of the property is devoted to the cultivation of fruit, in which the owner is successfully engaged, he having found the canning business to be a profitable adjunct to agriculture. His real-estate possessions aggregate two hundred and eighty acres, divided into two farms, and containing the buildings necessary for the management of a country estate.

The birth of William L. Derickson occurred in 1862, in the neighboring county of Cecil, where his parents, John P. and Catherine I. (Miller) Derickson, owned and occupied a farm near Rock Springs, in District No. 8. The first representatives of the family in America settled in Delaware, and the old homestead in that state is now owned by a descendant of the original purchaser. About 1873 John P. Derickson removed from Cecil to Harford County and for three years made his home near Deer Creek, but in 1876 purchased and settled upon the Howard Grove place, where he engaged in general farming until his death, in 1896, at the age of seventy-two. Six of his ten children are now living, and they are named as follow: Joseph, Emma, Laura, William L., Florence I. and Lillian M.

Educated in the schools of Harford County, the subject of this notice learned perhaps as much from observation and experience as he did from text books. Reared to farm life, he selected agriculture as his occupation, and on the death of his father he succeeded to the ownership and management of the homestead. About 1886 he purchased an interest in a canning business, with which he has since been connected, and in addition to this and the cultivation of his farm he does considerable business in the sale of harvesting machinery and in the feeding of stock. As yet unmarried, he makes his home with his mother and two sisters. He is a member of the Bel Air Lodge of Odd Fellows and holds the office of steward in the Methodist Episcopal Church, in which he is an active worker. Interested in the Sunday-school, he has held the position of librarian, doing all within his power to advance this very important department of church work. He loses no opportunity to assist and encourage all measures looking toward the betterment of the condition of this district, religiously, educationally and morally.

HON. J. EDWIN WEBSTER. Although aristocracy is unknown in America, there are traits of character which descend from generation to generation and constitute a legacy of greater value than lands and titles. A good name is not only a priceless heritage, but it is an incentive to the highest aims and noblest purposes. Such it has proved to be in the career of J. Edwin Webster, attorney of Bel Air, who is a worthy representative of one of the oldest and most honored families of Harford County. The lineage is traced to Samuel Webster, who was employed as tobacco inspector in Joppa. Richard, son of Samuel, was a contemporary of John Wesley and had the distinction of being the second minister of the Methodist denomination born in America.

Henry, son of Richard, had a son, Col. Edwin Hanson Webster, father of our subject and one of the most influential citizens Harford County has ever had. He was born at the old homestead near Churchville March 31, 1829, and received an excellent education, attending the academy at Churchville, also the New London Academy in Chester County, Pa., and at the age of fifteen entering Dickinson College at Carlisle, Pa., from which he graduated in 1847. For a short time he taught a classical school near his father's home; but this occupation was but temporary, and preliminary to his life work. Desirous of becoming a lawyer, he studied law in the office of Otho Scott, at Bel Air. In 1851, prior to his admission to the bar, he was nominated by the Whig party for state's attorney, his opponent being Maj. William H. Dallam, a man of great personal popularity and family influence. The election was very close, Mr. Webster being defeated by only ten votes.

The public life of Mr. Webster may be said to date from 1855, four years after his admission to the bar. He then became the candidate for state senator on the American ticket and was elected by a majority of one thousand. During the second session he was president of the senate, which responsible position he filled with tact and impartiality. In 1856 he was presidential elector and gave his influence to the support of Mr. Fillmore. Three years later he was elected, after an exciting campaign, to represent the second congressional district in congress, his majority being two hundred. In that honorable body he served as a member of the committee on militia, special committee on the dedication of the Washington equestrian statue, and others of importance. During the period of excitement between the secession of South Carolina and the outbreak of the Civil War, he favored pacific measures, and took an active part in thwarting commissioners who were attempting to influence citizens of Maryland. When the war broke out, he declared in favor of the vigorous prosecution of war by the government and was re-elected to congress on that issue. During his second term as congressman he was a member of the committee on claims. The president of the United States, realizing the influence he wielded and the services he had rendered, wished to tender him an appointment as brigadier-general of volunteers, but he would not accept it. In 1862 he recruited the Seventh Regiment, Maryland Volunteer Infantry, and September 12th of that year the regiment marched from Baltimore under the command of Colonel Webster. Most of the time it formed a part of the army of the Potomac, and he was in active command more than twelve months, accepting no pay, and furnishing his own servants and horses. January 1, 1863, he took his seat in the house of representatives and served in the short session that followed.

In July, 1863, Colonel Webster, while in the field, was re-elected to congress, and resigning his military commission took up his duties as a public official. He voted for abolition of slavery by the United States. When Maryland was invaded by the Confederate forces in 1864, he tendered his services to the governor for the defense of the state, and received an appointment upon the committee that drafted a military code for the state militia. In November, 1864, he was for the fourth time elected to congress, but in August of the following year resigned to accept the appointment, made by President Lincoln, as collector of the port of Baltimore. This position he held for four years. When President Lincoln was shot he had in his pocket a list of appointments ready for announcement the following day, and among them was the appointment of Colonel Webster. Upon retirement from that office he was presented by his subordinates in the custom house with a handsome service of silver plate. On his retirement from office he returned to Bel Air and resumed the practice of law. Some years later, however, President Arthur appointed him collector of the port of Baltimore, and he served for four years, his withdrawal from the position signalizing his final retirement from politics. Afterward he was chosen president of the Harford National Bank on its organization and held that position until his death, which occurred after a lingering illness, April 24, 1893.

It may well be doubted if the generation now upon the scene of action can accurately measure or adequately appreciate the distinguished public services of Colonel Webster. To do this one must read backward, word by word, line by line, and page by page, the history of our country during the perilous days of war and the exciting period of reconstruction. Firm in his opinions, and possessing at all times the courage of his convictions, fearless in his expression of and adherence to what he believed to be right, it was but natural that he should meet with opposition from those of different opinions; yet to his credit be it said, that never was a word spoken against his character as a man or his integrity as a citizen. He evinced in every act a true and noble manhood, which invited the love of relatives and commanded the respect of all who knew him. His personal integrity and high sense of honor were never questioned.

"The elements so mixed in him, that Nature might stand up and say to all the world, 'This was a man.'"

Fraternally he was connected with Mt. Ararat Lodge of Masons, the Grand Army post at Havre de Grace, and in religious belief he was identified with the Presbyterian Church. In June, 1855, he married Mrs. Caroline H. Earl, daughter of James McCormick, Jr., of Washington, D. C., and Elizabeth (Henderson) McCormick, of Bel Air. Of their family three daughters and our subject survive. The former are Ida M., wife of J. Abell Hunter, who resides at Bel Air and is connected with the Baltimore & Ohio at Baltimore; Bessie, wife of William H. Harlan, who is in partnership with our subject; and Caroline H., who married E. P. H. Harrison, a civil engineer at Martinsburg, W. Va.

In the village of Bel Air, where he now resides, J. Edwin Webster was born September 24, 1857. His education was commenced in Bel Air Academy, and in 1872 he entered Brooklyn Collegiate and Polytechnic College. Three years later he matriculated at Princeton, graduating from that institution in 1879. His legal readings were conducted under his father's supervision and in the law school of the University of Maryland. Admitted to the bar in 1881, he began his professional practice in Bel Air, where he has since built up an extensive practice. In the fall of 1887 he was elected state's attorney and filled that position for four years. As a rule, however, he has not sought public office, but has been content with casting a straight Republican ticket at local and national elections. He has other interests, business and professional, the supervision of which engrosses his entire time. A Presbyterian in religious belief, he is a trustee and the treasurer of the church with which he is identified. June 6, 1896, he married Dora C., daughter of John G. Rouse, of Bel Air, and they reside on a well-improved farm near the village, their location enabling them to enjoy all the comforts of country life as well as the advantages of the town.

EDMUND S. WHITAKER. In the perusal of this volume the reader is doubtless impressed with the fact that it is not accident that helps a man in the world, but persistent energy, economy and industry. The life of Mr. Whitaker affords another illustration of the fact that he who is quick to see an opportunity, and equally quick to grasp it, will attain, if not wealth, at least a goodly amount of all that goes to make life happy—the esteem of acquaintances, the affection of relatives, and a position among the influential men of the locality. He is a hardworking, energetic man, and his life has been one of diligence and industry. Since early life he has been connected with the iron business, and is one of the well-known manufacturers of Principio Furnace, Cecil County.

The Whitaker family came to America from Wales about the time of the Revolution, and have since been loyal to our institutions and government. George P. Whitaker, the father of our subject, was born near Reading, Berks County, Pa., December 30, 1803, and was educated in the schools of his native place, where later he learned the business of an iron manufacturer. In 1832, with his brother Joseph, Robert Garrett, and others, he bought out the Elk Rolling Mills, near Elkton, Cecil County, and afterward, with the same partners, purchased the North East Rolling Mills; but these they sold in 1835, at the same time buying the mills at Principio Furnace. After they were remodeled, the company engaged in the manufacture of pig iron here. This property had been owned by the British government before and during the Revolution, and at one time Lawrence Washington, a relative of George Washington, owned an interest in the furnace. During the war the British destroyed the works to keep them from falling into the hands of the patriots. In 1861 George P. Whitaker and his brother, Joseph, dissolved partnership, and the former incorporated the business under the name of the George P. Whitaker Company, of which he was the head until his death, December 31, 1890, at the age of eighty-eight. Upon the disintegration of the Whig party, which he had supported, he became an adherent of Republican principles and a stanch advocate of the policy adopted by the new party. At the breaking out of the Civil War he was a delegate to the state legislature. Both in public life and in business affairs, he was undoubtedly the most prominent man of his locality, and no one wielded a more vital influence in its upbuilding than did he. For years he was a vestryman of St. Ann's Episcopal Church, and his wife was also identified with that congregation. Twice married, his first wife, who bore the maiden name of Eliza Ann Simmons, passed away in 1875. His second wife, Mrs. Mary Evans, is still living. The second union was childless, but by the first he had ten children, three now living: Mrs. Caroline Naudaine, who lives near the old homestead; Edmund S.; and Nelson E., of Wheeling, W. Va.

At the place where he still lives, the subject of this article was born April 10, 1838. He was given good educational advantages, first attending the schools here, later becoming a student in West Nottingham, Md., and afterward prosecuting his studies in an academy at New London, Pa., for two years. On leaving school in 1858, he became assistant manager of the Durham Iron Works, in Bucks County, Pa., but after two years in that position returned to Principio Furnace, where he has since been manager of the plant. A Republican in politics, he held the office of postmaster in 1862, but with that exception has never filled local positions. In religious belief he is identified with the Episcopal Church. March 4, 1862, occurred his marriage to Mary McFarland, of Philadelphia, and one child, Clifford C., was born of their union. The family is highly esteemed throughout this section of the county, where the members are well known.

BENJAMIN H. SILVER, who is engaged in farming and stock-raising in District No. 2; Harford County, was born here January 11, 1857. The family of which he is a member has been identified with the history of America for many generations and dates back to John Silver, who, with two brothers, emigrated from England to New York or New Jersey. The date of his emigration is unknown to the present generation. After some time his descendants removed to Harford County, establishing the family here. The father of our subject, Jeremiah, was a son of Benjamin and Effie Silver and one of their family of nine children. He was born at the family homestead in District No. 2, Harford County, where he still resides. Agriculture has been his life occupation and in it he has gained commendable success, having become known as one of the prosperous and efficient agriculturists of the locality. Notwithstanding his advanced years, seventy-four, he is quite active and physically is hale and robust. By his marriage to Mary E. Hoopman, he had six children, of whom four are now living.

Benjamin H., who was the third in order of birth, was reared on the home farm and received such educational advantages as the neighboring schools afforded, supplemented by a classical course in Lafayette College at Easton, Pa. With a natural fondness for agriculture, he chose it for his life occupation, and his thorough familiarity with every detail connected with the management of a farm has conduced to his prosperity. He continued on the homestead with his father until he was thirty-seven, when he married and settled upon an estate that he inherited from his aunt. The farm comprises one hundred acres, and is devoted to the raising of cereals and of cattle and sheep, the stock business forming an addition to Mr. Silver's income that is quite important. In politics he is a Democrat, but has never sought or desired office. In April, 1894, he married Miss Lillie M., daughter of Frank and Anna (Harper) Hopkins, and they have one son, Benjamin Stump Silver. In religious connections they are members of the Presbyterian Church.

HUGH F. SCARBOROUGH. Having been a resident of Cecil County throughout his entire life of almost seventy-two years, the name of Mr. Scarborough needs no special introduction to the readers of this volume. It is safe to say that few men in District No. 5 have been more closely identified with its development or have taken a more active part in its upbuilding than did he. Enterprises that tend to the public welfare always received his cordial support and he co-operated in measures for the advancement of local interests.

Between the dates of birth and death, August 9, 1825, and March 19, 1897, is encompassed a lifetime of toil and earnest endeavor on the part of Mr. Scarborough. The family of which he was a member originally came from England. Joseph, his father, was born in Bucks County, Pa., whence as a young man he came to Cecil County and embarked in general farming. He was called into active service at the time the British invaded Maryland and passed through Elkton on their march of devastation during the War of 1812. In private life he was energetic, industrious and honest, always exhibiting a helpful disposition to the unfortunate and needy. He continued to make his home in this county until his death, which occurred in May, 1848. By his marriage to Rebecca Boyd, of Port Deposit, he had four children, all now deceased. His second wife, Sarah Smith, also a native of this county, bore him seven children, of whom three are living: Ann E., wife of John O'Daniel, of Oxford, Pa.; Mary S., who married William Wright, also of Oxford; and Joseph S., a resident of District No. 4, Cecil County. Politically the father was a Democrat. In religious connections he was identified with the Methodist Protestant Church.

At Pleasant Hill, District No. 4, the subject of this memoir was born and reared. Schools in those days were of an inferior quality and his education therefore was limited. At the age of seventeen he began to learn the trade of cooper under the supervision of his father, and this occupation he followed for some time. In 1874 he purchased a farm and the grist mill at Mechanics Valley, and the latter he operated until 1888, when he sold the plant and retired from business. From that time until his death he lived in retirement. Upon the organization of the Republican party he became one of its enthusiastic supporters and continued to advocate its principles as long as he lived. He attended services at the Methodist Episcopal Church and was one of its active members, always maintaining an interest in its welfare. The faith which had cheered him in life sustained him in the hour when death came and he passed away in the Christian's hope of eternal life beyond the grave.

August 9, 1848, Mr. Scarborough was united in marriage with Francina Spence, a most estimable lady, to whose affectionate co-operation he owed much of his success in life. She was of English descent, a member of a family that has long been represented in District No. 4. Her father, Henry Spence, was one of the volunteers from this county who went to Baltimore in 1812 and 1813 to assist in defending that city against the attacks by the British forces. Seven children were born to the union of Mr. and Mrs. Scarborough and of these three are now living, namely: Amos H., of Wilmington, Del.; Annie, wife of Robert C. Larzelere, of District No. 4, Cecil County; and Nettie, wife of Walter A. Nowland, residing at the homestead with her mother.

The record of a useful life is of value not alone to the immediate relatives, but also to all who cherish the deeds of the good and the true. The life of Mr. Scarborough may well be an incentive to others and is worthy of emulation by those just starting out for themselves, with no capital but an unlimited amount of hope and a goodly stock of physical strength. His influence for good was felt throughout his district. All held him in the highest esteem. He left a record of good deeds as a legacy to his children and a well-spent life as an example to the world.

JOHN S. YOUNG, who has won distinctive honors at the bar of Harford County, and is numbered among the foremost attorneys of Bel Air, was born about six miles from his present home and near the village of Abingdon, June 10, 1855. His father, Col. William Young, also a native of the same county, engaged in commercial pursuits in early life, and served for one term as county sheriff. When about forty years of age he joined the legal fraternity and attained prominence at the bar of Harford County, being connected with much of the important litigation that was tried in its courts up to the time of his death. He won his title from service on the staff of governor.

He was a man of much prominence in public and professional circles and was numbered among the valued citizens of Harford County. The Young family is of English origin and was founded in America by the great-grandfather of our subject, a native of England, who came to the United States in command of a sailing-vessel. His son, William S. Young, was born in Baltimore, and was also a sea captain. He had four sons, one of whom lost his life in the Confederate army during the Civil War.

On the maternal side John S. Young is descended from an old Delaware family. His mother, Mary E. (Cochran) Young, was a sister of the founders of the Cochran & Ohle Ice Company, owners of the largest ice plant in Baltimore. Mrs. Young still makes her home in Bel Air, and has four sons: John S., of this review; and James, Charles and Harry L., who are engaged in merchandising.

In taking up the history of our subject we record the life of one who is well and favorably known in Harford County, having made his home here since the days of his infancy. He was educated in the Bel Air Academy and studied law under the direction of his father. Since his admission to the bar he has been actively engaged in practice and has met with a well-merited success that has gained him prestige among the attorneys of this section of the state. He has a broad and accurate knowledge of the science of jurisprudence, a keen analytical mind and in the arrangement of evidence so marshals his facts as to present the strongest possible front to the adversary. He has many times won the victor's laurels in forensic combat and enjoys a large and lucrative clientage.

Mr. Young was united in marriage to Miss Mary Fulton, a daughter of James Fulton, one of the prominent business men and highly respected citizens of Bel Air. Mr. Young has never aspired to political honors, but takes an active part in political matters on behalf of his friends. Of a social, genial nature, he easily wins the friendship of those with whom he comes in contact and their regard once gained is never lost.

AMBROSE COOLEY. The office of sheriff is one that was at one time filled by ex-President Cleveland and is a position that demands the exercise of great circumspection, personal courage and a general and apt intelligence. Harford County is fortunate in its choice of its present incumbent, Ambrose Cooley, who adds to strict integrity the other qualities essential to thorough discharge of the responsibilities connected with the station. All his life has been spent in Harford County, for on a farm in the vicinity of the Susquehanna River he first saw the light, December 24, 1842, and in the same locality his father, Daniel M. Cooley, and his grandfather, John Cooley, were also born, the former in 1790 and the latter in 1757. Daniel M. Cooley was engaged in farming throughout life, but when the War of 1812 opened he left his plow to take up arms in defense of his country, and while in the service held the rank of quartermaster. After a well-spent life he died in 1867. The patriotic spirit of John Cooley asserted itself during the Revolution and he saw some hard service in the colonial army. He died in 1809. Daniel M. Cooley was united in marriage with Miss Harriet Wiles, a native of Harford County, and a daughter of William Wiles, who was born on the ocean while his parents were en route to this country from Wales.

From this worthy ancestry comes the subject of his sketch, whose early life was spent like that of the average farmer's boy, in odd work about the farm and in attending the district schools in the vicinity of his home. As he grew to manhood he decided to follow the calling to which he had been reared and which was that of his father and grandfather before him, and through good management and industry he in time became the owner of a good farm, which he tills in an intelligent manner and with satisfactory results. Like others in the county he has given considerable attention to canning vegetables, and in this way utilizes all that he himself raises, also large quantities besides.

Although Mr. Cooley has always exercised his right of suffrage and has always shown the utmost interest in the welfare of his country, has never cared to hold official position, and the office of sheriff is the only one he has ever filled, with the exception of that of tax collector, which position he filled during 1876 and 1877. He is serving his first term and thus far has discharged his duties in a very satisfactory manner to all concerned. He is past master in the Masonic fraternity and is quite prominent in the work of the order. He was married in 1871 to Miss Clara A. Hughes, a sister of ex-Sheriff Hughes, and to them a family of twelve children was born, of whom eight are now living. Mr. Cooley is a very unostentatious man, but a valuable citizen, and one who possesses in a higher degree the esteem of the public, politics not considered, it would be hard to find. He has achieved his successes through labor and by strictly honorable methods and they are therefore the more estimable.

REV. E. D. FINNEY. "Man lives not unto himself alone" was said by one who was wise and good, and there is nothing in the world that presents a more inspiring spectacle than a man who devotes his life to the good of others, is ready to succor the needy and distressed, and upon whom the cries of the orphaned and the sorrows of the widowed are not lost. Such a man is Rev. E. D. Finney, who has devoted the greater part of his life to the saving of souls and who has made the world better for having lived in it. He was born at Churchville, Harford County, Md., September 12, 1825, the second son of Rev. William Finney, who was for half a century pastor of the Presbyterian Church at Churchville and one of the best known ministers of his day. He was universally beloved for his consistent Christian life, and the work that he performed in the interests of Christianity was Herculean.

Dr. John M. Finney, a brother of Rev. E. D. Finney, practiced the healing art at Churchville for half a century, having been a graduate of the University of Pennsylvania, and died June 25, 1896, after a long life spent in the interests of suffering humanity. Another brother, William Finney, was taken with the "gold fever" of 1849, went to California and died there. Charles McL., another brother, also went to the "Eldorado of the West" in that year, but finally returned to his eastern home and is now a resident of Churchville. George J. Finney is the present

WILLIAM A. SMITH.

clerk of the Board of County Commissioners of Harford County, and like the other members of the family is a useful, enterprising and public-spirited citizen.

The boyhood days of E. D. Finney were spent in his native village, and after the usual preparation in the common schools, entered La Fayette College, Pennsylvania, later Washington and Lee University of Lexington, Va., from which he was graduated. He was fitted for the ministry in Princeton Theological Seminary and soon after, in 1852, went South to Mississippi, where he taught school and preached until after the close of the great Civil War, when he returned to his native county and for twenty-five years thereafter was pastor of the Presbyterian Church of Bel Air, during which time he did noble work in the interests of the Christian cause, and during his pastorate the new church building was erected. At the end of the above mentioned time he resigned and since that time has lived a quiet and retired life.

Rev. Finney has been twice married, first to Miss Anna L. Parker, of Long Island, who died leaving two sons: Rev. William Parker Finney, a Presbyterian minister of New Jersey, and John M. T., assistant surgeon in Johns Hopkins Hospital of Baltimore. The second marriage was to Miss Elizabeth McCormick, of Bel Air, by whom he became the father of two children, both of whom died. The life of this worthy man has been full of good and charitable deeds and he is now enjoying a serene and peaceful old age.

WILLIAM A. SMITH. The lands of Harford County afford such excellent pasturage that it is not surprising that the stock business should be a special feature of agricultural operations here. Among those who have engaged in it with success is Mr. Smith, the well-known farmer and stockman of District No. 2. He is the owner of about three hundred acres of valuable land, upon which he engages in raising stock and also the various cereals to which the soil is adapted.

In the district where he now resides, Mr. Smith was born September 2, 1861, the son of James and Harriet E. (Jewens) Smith, also natives of Harford County. The former, who has been very successful in life, accumulated his fortune chiefly through his operations as a farmer and stockman. Though now eighty years of age, he is quite hearty and in full possession of his faculties. He has not been active in politics, and, aside from voting the Democratic ticket, never identified himself with campaigns or election affairs. Now to some extent retired from active business duties, he has turned over to his son, William A., the management of his large and important interests, while he himself enjoys the leisure he has justly earned as the fruits of former labor. Little is known concerning his ancestral history, except that his father, James, was born in Massachusetts and in young manhood removed from there to Harford County. The mother of our subject is still living and is hale and hearty for one of her age, sixty-five. There are only two children in her family, her son and a daughter, Annie F., the latter being the wife of John M. Michael, who is engaged in farming and the canning business in this district.

The early life of Mr. Smith, the subject of this sketch, did not differ materially from that of the average Maryland boy of the present generation. Born at the opening of the Civil War, his earliest recollections are of the exciting scenes and times that marked the '60s. As soon as old enough he was sent to school, it being the desire of his parents that he should have a good education. Afterward he attended school with reasonable regularity a portion of each year for some years. While the family were well-to-do, they were too wise to rear him in idleness, but he was expected to contribute to his own support as soon as he became physically able to perform any kind of manual labor, and probably the most important part of his education was his manual training. He is not one of those who have gained success in spite of poverty and reverses, for his life has been singularly free from adversity and its blighting influences. He did not have the humble origin, the hard experiences or the early privations that fall to the lot of some; but on the other hand, few enjoying his advantages have turned them to such excellent account. He had a fair start in life, and the wisdom, energy and perseverance with which he has pushed his way along furnish an example for others. He continues to make his home with his parents, and their declining years are brightened by his filial devotion.

J TAYLOR JANNEY. Undoubtedly no family now residing within the limits of Cecil County has contributed to the prosperity and development of District No. 5 to a greater extent than has that of which Mr. Janney is an honored and able representative. Coming hither from England many generations ago, they labored, not alone for personal advancement, but also for the welfare of the community, and their services entitle them to honorable mention in this volume.

The subject of this sketch is worthy of the name he bears. He has spent his entire life in this district and is numbered among its best known residents. His paternal ancestors have long been prominent in agricultural circles, the most of them following farm pursuits. Jesse, son of Thomas, and father of our subject, was born about one mile from the present family residence. He was reared upon a farm, and having a taste for the occupation, became an agriculturist, to which calling his life was devoted. During the existence of the Whig party he advocated its principles, and upon its disintegration became a supporter of the principles of the newly organized Republican party. At one time he held the office of county commissioner from this district. In religious associations he was a member of the Methodist Episcopal Church. A man of intense patriotic spirit, he was glad to render service as a soldier during the War of 1812. When the Civil War broke out he was too aged and infirm to go to the front and take part in the contest, but he was deeply interested in the results. About the time of the close of the war, in April, 1865, he passed from earth.

The mother of our subject was born in England and bore the maiden name of Maria Taylor. She died in 1863, at the family homestead. Eleven children were born of her marriage, and of these the following survive: Mary, widow of Silas Carter, of Zion, this county; Catherine, who married John W. Gifford, and resides in this district; Charlotte, wife of T. W. S. Kidd, of Illinois; and J. Taylor, of this sketch. The last-named was born February 24, 1833, on the farm where he now lives. Spending the days of boyhood in this locality, he attended the district schools, and, reared upon his father's farm, was thoroughly trained to a practical knowledge of agriculture. Day after day, through the spring, summer and autumn, he was busy sowing, plowing, reaping and harvesting, and when he could be spared, he improved the moments in the public schools of the neighborhood. From his early years he was a boy of ambition and enterprise, and carefully supplemented the limited education he received at school with the knowledge gained by observation and reading. He was an intelligent and quick-witted youth, and at maturity was self-reliant, ready to win his way to assured success. From the age of seventeen, when he left school, he assisted in the management of the homestead, and on the death of his father he bought the place, which he has since cultivated. Both as a general farmer and stock-raiser he has been prospered. The success attained by him and the prosperity he now enjoys may be attributed to his sterling qualities and his perseverance. With the exception of the amount received from his father's estate, all of his possessions have been secured by his unaided toil, and represent many years of unremitting labor.

Politically a Republican and intelligently posted upon all vital questions of the day, Mr. Janney is ever ready to do his full duty as a man and a citizen. However, he is not an office seeker, preferring to give his time to personal matters. In religious connections he is a member of the Methodist Episcopal Church. His first wife was Sarah T. England, of this county, and their two children are Annie M., wife of Russell Reed, of Bay View; and J. Kirk, who lives at Buena Vista, Va. In 1894 Mr. Janney married Charlotte M. Reed, daughter of Joseph T. Reed, of Bay View.

GEORGE V. DEVER. The life of this venerable citizen of Harford County covers almost the entire period of the nineteenth century. Born during the progress of the second war with England, reared under the elevating influences of a free, liberty-loving country, the witness of constant and remarkable improvements, spared to see the present growth of the country now recovered from the depressing influences of the Civil War; during all these years and amid all the changes that have gone on about him, he has led the quiet and comparatively uneventful life of a farmer. In 1837 he purchased a part of the Christopher Camp farm in the southern part of District No. 3, and here he has since resided, a period of sixty years. The property comprises two hundred and seven acres of land, upon which the various cereals are raised, and some attention is also given to stock-raising.

The Dever family came to Maryland from Pennsylvania, our subject's grandfather being the first of the name to locate in Harford County. Samuel Dever, father of our subject, was a blacksmith by trade, and in addition to work at that occupation he also carried on general farming. He died on what is now the Webster place, at the age of sixty years. His wife, who bore the maiden name of Nancy Vandergrift and was a member of an old Philadelphia family, died when sixty-two years of age. They were the parents of ten children, but George V., of this once large family, alone survives. When he was a boy his educational advantages were exceedingly limited, and the knowledge that he acquired was gained principally by observation and experience. At the age of sixteen he began to cultivate a rented farm, and afterward continued as a renter until 1837, when he purchased his present property. Advancing years, with attendant infirmities, prevent him from engaging in manual labor, as in former days, but he still takes an interest in farm work and his happiest hours are spent in noting the improvements and cultivation of the old home place.

The first marriage of Mr. Dever took place in 1848, when Margaret Forsyth became his wife. She died, and all of their family, comprising eight children, have also passed away. His second wife, Mary Arnold, was a descendant of an old family of Harford County and was a daughter of Henry Arnold, who lived near Aberdeen. The nine children that came to their home were named as follows: Ella and Edwin, now deceased; Carrie; Benjamin, who carries on the old homestead, and is an energetic, successful farmer; Mamie; David, who is also at home; Charles and Hattie, who are twins; and Addie. The family attend the Calvary Methodist Episcopal Church.

SAMUEL M. LEE was formerly well known as a practical and successful agriculturist of Harford County in District No. 3, but has now ceased active labor. He was born here in 1814, the son of William D. and Anna (Wilson) Lee. His grandfather, Parker H., who held the rank of lieutenant in the colonial army during the Revolution, was a son of Samuel, and a grandson of James Lee, who came to this country from England, about 1600, being sent here as the representative of an English company. Capt. William D. Lee, who served as an officer during the entire period of the War of 1812, engaged in farming on the old Lee homestead and there he died in 1828, at the age of forty-five years. He and his wife were the parents of ten children, but the only survivors are Samuel M., John, Lycurgus and Priscilla. After the death of her husband, the widowed mother reared her children, training them for useful positions in the business and social world; in return for her care and affection, they tenderly ministered to her in her declining years and made happy her last days by their attention. She passed away at the age of ninety-three, and was buried by the side of her husband in the family cemetery.

When our subject was a boy of fourteen, his father died, and afterwards he assisted in the management of the home place, with its eight hundred acres of land. Though so young he proved industrious, efficient and reliable, and soon had in charge the entire management of the property. As a farmer he was active and energetic, always anxious to do all within his power for the advancement of his own interests and those of others. Of late years he has not done so much as in his younger days, for the infirmities of age render manual labor impossible; however, he continues to be interested in the cultivation of the place and in all new improvements. Though not desirous of taking part in public affairs, he has always been a man of firm convictions in politics, uniformly supporting the Republican party. In 1844 he married Miss Cassandra Gover, who died June 8, 1867. Their family consisted of six children, Priscilla, Lydia, Cassandra, Laura, William and Fannie.

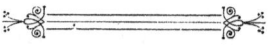

NICHOLAS N. NOCK, whose devotion to his duties of citizenship and active interest in the welfare of the community with which he is connected have made him one of the valued residents of Harford County, is *engaged in journalistic pursuits in Bel Air. He was born in Accomac County, Va., on the 3d of April, 1846. His grandfather, Littleton Nock, was a native of Scotland, and on crossing the Atlantic to America took up his residence in Virginia. The father, also named Littleton, was a native of the Old Dominion, and a man of much prominence in the locality where he made his home. He was a ship owner, and also had extensive property interests, but he died during the early childhood of our subject. His wife, who bore the maiden name of Susan Dix, was a member of the prominent Virginia family of that name. They had three sons: Nicholas N.; Littleton H., who was engaged at the time of his death in the insurance business in southern Maryland; and John W., a farmer and carriage manufacturer at Crisfield, Md.

Mr. Nock, whose name introduces this review, came to Maryland in early life, and obtained his education in private schools at Snow Hill, and at Buckingham Academy. Before attaining his majority he responded to the call of his country and enlisted in the Union army in Coles' Maryland Cavalry, in which he served until the close of the war, when he was mustered out as first sergeant of Company E. On many a southern battlefield he displayed his loyalty to the old flag and the cause it represented. He was with General Sheridan in the Shenandoah Valley, and had many narrow escapes, at one time having his horse shot from under him.

When the war was over, and the country no longer needed his services, he returned to Maryland and engaged in journalistic work, being employed on several papers in Baltimore. In 1881 he came to Bel Air and established the *Times*, the only Republican paper in the county. He has made it one of the leading weekly journals in the state and receives a liberal patronage. He is a forceful writer, handling fairly and squarely all the public issues, and his editorials are both instructive and interesting. Through the columns of his paper he also supports all measures calculated to prove of public benefit and upholds every interest tending to uplift humanity. He is a pronounced advocate of the temperance cause, active in its work, and is now president of the County Temperance Alliance, and vice-president of State Temperance Alliance. He is treasurer of the Harford Historical and also of the State Editorial Association, and is a recognized leader in Republican circles. A man of broad general culture, he exerts a wide influence in behalf of education and all that will advance the general knowledge. He has left the impress of his individuality upon his adopted county and is well numbered among its prominent citizens.

Mr. Nock was united in marriage to Miss Gamma Long, a member of a prominent old Virginian family, and they have three children, John Dix, Alan Page and Ivan Finney.

JOHN B. GARRISON stands among the foremost of the progressive, enlightened and enterprising farmers who have assisted in rebuilding the fortunes of Harford County since the war. Doubtless few men within the past few decades have done more for the development of the agricultural resources of District No. 4 than has he. His farm, which is situated near Taylor postoffice, is one of the best managed for miles around and is devoted both to raising cereals and to the dairy business. Upon it may be noticed an excellent class of buildings and all the improvements of a first-class estate.

Upon the farm where he now resides the subject of this article was born October 7, 1849, he and his sister, Mary A., being the only children of James B. and Mary E. (Carman) Garrison. The family is an old one in this county. His great-grandfather, Cornelius Garrison, was born in New Jersey, and from there removed to Maryland, establishing his home in Harford County. The date of his arrival on the family homestead was November 15, 1776, and from that day to this the property has been in the possession of some member of the family. Four generations in turn have tilled the soil of its one hundred and eighty acres and have left the imprint of their energy in various valuable improvements. Our subject's grandfather, John Garrison, was born on this place and here spent his entire life, except that period when he was serving in the War of 1812. He married Mary Birmingham, a native of Harford County, and daughter of an Englishman, who crossed the Atlantic about the beginning of the Revolution and settled in District No. 4, this county. Thereafter he engaged in farm work, becoming well-to-do and prominent.

At the age of twenty-six the subject of this sketch married Anna P. Curry, of District No. 4, daughter of John B. Curry, Jr., a merchant at Upper Cross Roads, and granddaughter of John B. Curry, a farmer of this county. The children of Mr. and Mrs. Garrison are named as follows: Philip M. (deceased), William M., Sannie S., Alfred S., Frank B., Elsie (deceased), Ernest B. and Mary A. While Mr. Garrison is not active in politics, he is well informed upon public questions and is an advocate of Republican principles. He attends the Methodist Church, of which Mrs. Garrison is a member.

P. A. DIETRICH. The family represented by this well-known citizen of District No. 1, Harford County, was founded in America by his father, C. Dietrich, a native of France, who crossed the ocean and established his home in America about 1830. Unlike many who seek a home and fortune on the shores of the new world, he was not penniless, but brought with him a modest competency inherited from his parents, who were well-to-do. Added to this small capital, he possessed what was even more important, boundless energy, shrewd judgment and force of will. With a thorough knowledge of a money-making business at his finger-ends, and an energetic temperament as a portion of his stock in trade, he settled in Cincinnati, Ohio, where he engaged in the manufacture of soap and candles, and was a member of the firm of Gross & Dietrich. He rapidly rose in fortune and prominence, and in time becoming identified with railroad interests, was chosen president of the Dayton & Michigan Railroad.

In this position, as in all others that he occupied, he was characterized by a strong mind, a determined will and a firm perseverance that knew no defeat. In some respects he was a man of decided and inflexible traits of mind, but no man questioned his honesty. In political faith he was a Democrat in national issues, but maintained an independent attitude in local affairs, voting for the best men, without regard to their political connections. His participation in politics was confined to voting. He was an excellent representative of the progressive men in this country who are of French birth or parentage, and who retain the thrifty, industrious habits of that nationality. When a young man he was active in the work of the Catholic Church, but as the pressure of his business affairs became greater, he had little time to participate personally in religious enterprises and was obliged to limit his activities, though he always continued a generous contributor. In 1862 he retired from business, after a most successful career, and soon went to Europe, where he spent several years. Returning to this country in 1868, he purchased the Harford Furnace property, consisting of seven thousand acres, which made him the largest land owner of Harford County. His death occurred in 1884. He and his wife, Catherine, who died in 1892, were the parents of ten children, and of that number seven are living, the others besides our subject being as follows: C. W., whose home is near Baltimore; Dr. Louise, wife of Charles O'Leary, of Providence, R. I.; Josephine, who married L. A. Dochez, of Indianapolis, Ind.; Mary, wife of James Walsh, residing at Harford Furnace, Md.; Caroline, Mrs. A. J. Garesche, of St. Louis, Mo:; and Catherine, wife of M. O. Shriver, of Baltimore.

In Cincinnati, Ohio, where he was born, the subject of this sketch attended the public schools for a time. He had the advantage of foreign travel and study, being for three years in Paris and for a similar period in Strassburg. Returning to the United States in 1878, he spent one year at Annapolis, Md., after which he came to Harford County and engaged in business with his father for five years. He then transferred his attention to farming and the packing business, in which we find him engaged to-day. In politics he is independent. He is interested in educational matters and has acceptably served as school commissioner and trustee. In religious belief he is identified with the Catholic Church. June 3, 1891, he was united in marriage with Caroline Farish, daughter of Edward Farish, member of a prominent old family of St. Louis, Mo. They are the parents of three children, Alexander, Mimika and Catherine.

J NELSON BLACK. A large number of farmers of Cecil County lead such quiet and unobtrusive lives that they are seldom heard of outside of their own county. In their own community they are doing excellent work, but do not care to mingle in the more public activities of politics, but devote their entire time to the cultivation of their farms and the development of the resources of their locality. Such men deserve more mention than is always given them, for upon their efforts depends the prosperity of the county. If they are indifferent and idle, the county is injured; but by their activity and industry the progress of every industry and the happiness of every resident is promoted. We are glad to here present one of these capable farmers in the person of J. Nelson Black, of District No. 5. He is prominent in social, agricultural and church circles, and has long been identified with all movements of importance in this part of the county. The farm which he occupies and cultivates is situated in the western part of the district, near Principio Furnace, and is one of the best-improved estates in the neighborhood.

In the village of Charlestown, Cecil County, our subject was born April 15, 1851, being a son of W. W. and Catherine P. (Evans) Black. His father, who was born in the same house as he, was engaged as proprietor of a store in Charlestown for some time, but deciding to become a farmer he purchased a place some miles northwest of the village, moving there two years later. This continued to be his home until his death, which took place January 4, 1888. The property then fell into the possession of our subject and his brother, William W. A Democrat in politics, he always voted that ticket, but took no further interest in public matters. He was deeply interested in church affairs and was a Presbyterian in belief. Of his four children two are living, J. Nelson and William W., the latter being a resident of Middletown, Del. The wife and mother died July 4, 1897.

The education of our subject was begun in the common schools. In 1872 he entered the State Normal School at Millersville, Pa., and later took a business course in Crittenden's Commercial College, Philadelphia. Returning to the home farm in 1873, he has since engaged in cultivating its acres, and is also a dealer in a fertilizer. Politically he advocates Democratic principles, and in 1884-85 served as tax collector of District No. 5. By training and preference he is a Presbyterian, and always takes an interest in the work of that denomination. In 1894 he became a member of Union Lodge No. 41, F. & A. M., at Elkton. His marriage took place June 17, 1891, and united him with Mary G. Barnes, daughter of George W. Barnes, a well-known resident of Carpenter's Point, this district. They are the parents of two daughters, Edith C. and Mary.

ORLANDO W. BENJAMIN. Now in the prime of life, Mr. Benjamin has attained considerable influence in the community where he resides, a fact that is easily accounted for by his strong principles, his active interest in the welfare of all around him, and his good judgment as a business man. His ancestors were numbered among the pioneers of Cecil County, to whom great honor is due for the manner in which they bore hardships, and the toils which they underwent in preparing for later generations a beautiful country with all the blessings of civilization. It would be strange, indeed, if the descendant of such ancestors should not possess the qualities which would bring him a high place in the regard of his fellow-men.

Now engaged in the mercantile business at Leslie, Mr. Benjamin was born on the old homestead near this village, February 18, 1852. The family has been connected with American history since colonial days. He is a great-grandson of Joseph Benjamin, who was born and reared in England, but ran away from home in order to come to America, and here took a valiant part with the patriots in the Revolutionary War. In Charlestown, Cecil County, where he established a permanent home, his son, George, was born and reared, and there he spent his life as a farmer. Joseph, son of the latter and father of our subject, was born in Charlestown, but when very young removed to the place now occupied by our subject, and here he carried on general farming. In addition, he took a part in local enterprises for the advancement of the community. During the war he was employed as a wagon master. For fifteen years he held the office of magistrate. The industry which he exhibited met with its reward and he became one of the prosperous farmers of the district. Not only so, but he also secured the esteem of his neighbors, who found that his Christianity was real and sincere, for in his daily actions he endeavored to live faithful to the doctrines of his church, the Methodist Episcopal. He died October 13, 1895.

The mother of our subject was Mary A. Johnson, daughter of Jethro Johnson, a well-known resident of District No. 5, Cecil County. She is a most estimable lady, beloved by all who know her. Of her marriage fourteen children were born, and of these the following survive: Charles A., who makes his home at Leslie; Emeline A., wife of George W. Phillips, of California; Indiana, Mrs. A.J. Kelly, of Newark, Del.; James E. W., who resides at Harper's Ferry; Orlando W.; Anna S., who married W. B. Minor and lives in Baltimore; Zella A., who is the wife of John Whitehead and resides in Leslie; Sarah, Mrs. John McNamara, of Zion, Cecil County;

Minnie, who is the wife of Walter B. Logan, of Leslie; and Joseph, residing in Baltimore. In their various communities the sons and daughters are highly respected, and the majority of them have been prospered financially.

The years of our subject's boyhood were passed on the home farm and in attendance at the local schools. At the age of twenty he secured employment in a woolen factory, where he learned the trade. Later he resumed farming and engaged in agricultural pursuits until 1886. He then built a store building in Leslie, purchased a stock of goods and embarked in general merchandising. This enterprise he has since conducted with fair success, in addition to which he owns a farm and superintends its management. He has officiated as a trustee in the Methodist Protestant Church, and politically is a stanch Republican, taking an intelligent interest in the political issues of the age.

HENRY WOOLSEY. One of the many pleasing characteristics of the people of Maryland is their loving remembrance of the dead. Those who once were in their midst, assisting in the development of business, professional or agricultural interests, but who have passed away from the scenes of former usefulness, are not forgotten, but cherished with an affection that years do not weaken or age dim. It has been a long time since Mr. Woolsey departed this life, for his death occurred in 1867. To the present generation he is known only by name, but those of his former associates who survive dwell often in thought and conversation upon the many kindly deeds that gave character to his career.

The life of Mr. Woolsey covered a period very important in the history of the United States. When he was born, in 1787, the country had not recovered from the effects of the protracted war with England; when he died, the people were still suffering from the effects of the Civil War. He was born on a farm near Bel Air, to which place his father, Joseph, had removed from New Jersey, establishing his permanent home there. The latter was a soldier in the Revolution and a man who cherished the deepest love for his country.

During the opening years of the nineteenth century, advantages were few, especially in an educational way. Mr. Woolsey had very limited opportunities for obtaining an education, but he was an observing, thoughtful man and gained a broad fund of knowledge most helpful to him in life's activities. He continued to reside on the old homestead in District No. 3, cultivating its one hundred and fifty acres and acquiring a competency through industry and honesty. On this place he died at the age of eighty years. By his marriage to Rebecca Cochron, who died in 1877, he had ten children, namely: Catherine, Sophia, Jason M., William, Elizabeth, Henry, James, Harriet, Sarah and Rebecca. The sons William and Jason purchased the old Hall's Rich Neck farm about 1845, and on that place remained until their death, cultivating the three hundred acres that constituted the estate. Here the youngest daughter, Rebecca, makes her home. Of the once large family she alone survives. In memory of her parents, and with a spirit of filial devotion to them, she gives these facts for publication in a volume containing a record of the lives and deeds of many prominent men of Harford and Cecil Counties.

JARRETT B. MOORE, the owner of a well-improved farm in District No. 3, Harford County, was born near Bel Air in 1837. The family is of Scotch descent, and was founded in Maryland by his grandfather, Alexander, a native of Scotland, who came to America and settled near Fallston, Harford County, where he devoted the remaining years of his life to the cultivation of a farm. The father of our subject, James Moore, was born October 30, 1801, and in youth learned the trade of a carpenter, which he followed throughout much of his life, in conjunction with

WILLIAM E. WHITEFORD.

the cultivation of a farm. By his marriage to Johanna Boddin, he had four sons, named as follows: Elijah, now a resident of Bel Air; Jarrett B.; Van Buren and James, deceased.

In the schools of Bel Air and Johnson's private school, the subject of this sketch was given fair educational advantages. When he was eighteen he began to learn the trade of a carpenter, at which he worked under his father's supervision. He soon acquired a thorough knowledge of the occupation and familiarity with all its details. His work being done with painstaking care, he became known as an honest, reliable and efficient workman. However, when he was twenty-nine he abandoned the occupation and bought a part of the Stony Ridge farm, where he has since resided. This place is not a large one, consisting of only about fifty-nine acres, but the land has been placed under such excellent cultivation that the results are very gratifying, and the amount of grain raised compares favorably with farms much larger. One of the special features of the place is the raising of tomatoes for canning.

In 1865 Mr. Moore married Sarah Cole, who was born near Aberdeen, and is a daughter of James Cole. They have three children, all sons, namely: Archer, who resides at Aberdeen; Harry and Charles G., both at home. The two latter are identified with the Junior Order of American Mechanics. The family attend Smith's Chapel and are active workers in the interests of the Methodist Episcopal Church.

MRS. MARGARET L. WHITEFORD.

From the biography of every one may be gleaned some lessons of genuine worth, and this is particularly true with regard to Mrs. Margaret L. Whiteford, who is an intelligent lady and a native of the district and county in which she is now living. She is the widow of the late William E. Whiteford and the daughter of James and Elizabeth (Slade) Streett, all of whom were born and reared in Harford County. To Mrs. Whiteford's parents were born three children, Geraldine, deceased; Margaret L., Mrs. Whiteford; and James P. Mr. Streett was first married, however, to Miss Margaret Miles, a native of the city of Baltimore, and to them were born four children: Ann R.; Martha J. and John J., deceased; and Cordelia. The paternal grandfather of Mrs. Whiteford was Col. John Streett, a native and farmer of Harford County, from which section he enlisted as a soldier in the colonial army during the Revolution. Harford County was the birthplace of James Streett also, and there he, like his immediate progenitor, was engaged in tilling the soil, in which occupation he was quite successful. He showed his love for his native land by enlisting as a soldier in the War of 1812 and throughout life upheld her laws and institutions by every means in his power.

The early life of Mrs. Whiteford was spent at the rural home of the family in this county, and until she was fourteen years of age she was an attendant of the district schools near by. She was then placed in McDermott school, a private institution of Baltimore, where she completed her education three years later. After remaining at home with her parents for two years, she was united in marriage with William E. Whiteford and they immediately afterward established a home of their own. In course of time three children were born to them: James S., deceased; Mary E. and William M. The daughter, Mary E., is the wife of Harry W. Baldwin, a native of Baltimore County, and they have two interesting children, H. Streett and Margaret.

William E. Whiteford was the eldest of a family of seven children born to his parents and his early life was spent in the various duties of farm life, for his father was a successful tiller of the soil. After acquiring such knowledge as the common schools afforded, he was for two years an attendant of the school at Uniontown, Md., where he made rapid advancement in his studies and acquired an excellent education. Upon commencing the battle of life it was as a tiller of the soil and this occupation he pursued with marked success all his life. He was possessed of business ability of a high order and all his efforts were crowned with success and a competency secured for himself and family, which was the result of his own unaided efforts. His attention was not wholly confined to business, however, for he found time to devote considerable attention to the political affairs of his county, and in the fall of 1881 he was elected to the office of county sheriff by the Democratic party, of which he had always been an ardent supporter. He discharged his duties for two years with marked ability, and for two years also held the position of tax collector of District No. 4.

Mr. Whiteford was always of a genial, social disposition and was an active member of the Independent Order of Odd Fellows and the Knights of Pythias fraternities. On the 15th of October, 1894, at the age of sixty years, he was called from this life, having for many years been an earnest and consistent member of the Presbyterian Church and one of its trustees. Mrs. Whiteford and her children are also members of that church. Her son, William M., who is an intelligent and well-educated gentleman, makes his home with her and oversees the home farm. He is unmarried.

JOSHUA R. GREEN, deceased, was for many years a successful farmer and dairyman of Harford County, where he owned a well-improved estate in District No. 4. A native of Baltimore County, born in 1829, he was reared upon a farm and on reaching mature years naturally adopted for his occupation the calling with which he was most familiar. That he did not make a mistake in his choice of a vocation the subsequent years proved. As time passed by, he added to his possessions until he became the owner of more than three hundred acres, all lying in Harford County, with the exception of a small portion in Baltimore County. This land he brought under cultivation, raising upon it the various cereals to which the soil was adapted. He also gave some attention to the raising of cattle and always kept on his place forty or more head of Jersey cows. Through his ability as a financier he was enabled to secure success in farming and the dairy business, and at the time of his death he was one of the richest farmers in the district. His contributions to charitable and religious enterprises were always generous, for his was a liberal and large-hearted nature. In the Chestnut Grove Presbyterian Church of Baltimore County he officiated as an elder for more than thirty years. When a young man he enlisted under the standard of the Democratic party and from that time forward he never wavered in his allegiance to that organization. On the farm where so many useful years had been passed, he died May 1, 1892, at the age of sixty-three years.

Mrs. Sarah R. Green, widow of the late Joshua R. Green, was born and reared on a farm in Baltimore County, whither her parents, Moses and Sarah (Gemmill) Rankin, had removed from their native county of York, Pa. She was next to the youngest of five children, of whom the others were named as follows: Samuel, now a large land owner and retired business man of Baltimore; Dr. Robert G., a noted physician of Baltimore; Margaret A. and Hannah J., both deceased. The Rankin and Gemmill families were prominent in York County and were farmers as far back as the genealogy has been traced. Sarah Rankin remained in the home of her parents until she went to the one prepared for her by her husband. She was about twenty years of age when she became the wife of Mr. Green. Seven children were born to them, viz.: Moses I., who is unmarried and resides with his mother; Dr. John S., a successful physician practicing at Long Green, Baltimore County; Mollie E., who married Rev. A. L. Hyde, of Slate Ridge, Pa., and died September 2, 1896, aged thirty-eight years, leaving two children, Rosa and Hazen; Sallie R., who married Rev. R. L. Clark, of Center, Pa., and they have one child, Robert; Robert C., who runs the home place; L. May and Joshua R., the latter a member of the class of 1899, medical department of the University of Maryland. The large farm that Mrs. Green inherited on the death of her husband she has since managed, but the work of cultivation is carried on by her sons. She is a lady of Christian character, an earnest member of the Presbyterian Church, and kind and true in every relation of life.

JAMES W. McNABB. It being generally believed that heredity has much to do with the formation of character, and that our lives are stimulated by the immediate or indirect influence of our ancestors, a short résumé of the ancestral history of the McNabb family may serve as an index to the impulses that mark the daily lives of the present representatives. The first of the name in America was Thomas McNabb, a sturdy Scotchman, whose enthusiastic devotion to his beloved native land cost him dear. Owing to his participation in the rebellion in 1716, he was banished from the country, and came, a prisoner, to America, on the then famous ship, "Speedwell." He settled in Harford County, Md., and in 1740 acquired the title to a tract of land lying near Prospect, in District No. 5. During the Revolution his son, James, took an active part as a soldier in the colonial army, patiently bearing the hardships and privations of war, in the hope that the country might gain freedom from England.

Practically the same characteristics are noticeable in the various generations of the family. They have been honest and honorable, interested in public affairs and leading citizens of their day, yet never seeking political honors. In physique, they have been uniformly stalwart, rugged and of commanding appearance. For generations the male representatives have been six feet or more in height, the sole exception, so far as known, being the subject of this sketch, who is less than six feet tall. His father's four brothers, John, William, James and Isaac, all stood over six feet in height; all are deceased but the father of our subject. The latter, David G., who was born on the old homestead in 1820, has been a wheelwright and farmer, but is now living somewhat retired from business cares. His home is still on the place where he was born and which is called Macton, in honor of the family. His wife, Nancy Martin, who was born in Harford County and died here in 1876, was a daughter of Luther Martin, a German, who came to America in 1805.

The oldest son of David G. and Nancy McNabb is Hon. Joseph Martin McNabb, who was born on the homestead at Macton, October 18, 1847, and received his education in the Harford Central Academy. He began active life as a school teacher, after which he held the office of county surveyor for a number of years, meantime reading law. In 1874 he was admitted to the bar and began in professional practice at Bel Air and Macton, in both of which places he still has offices. He is an able advocate and counselor, and justly ranks high in the legal fraternity. As a Democrat, he takes an active part in the politics of the county, and upon his party ticket he was elected to represent the county in the legislature in 1884 and 1886. In religious connections he is identified with the Methodist Episcopal Church. By his marriage to Miss Sarah E. Savin, he has one son, now a student at St. John's College, Annapolis.

The other brother of our subject is Luther H., a merchant at Macton and also a justice of the peace; and the sister is Anna M., wife of William Stamp, of Susquehanna, Pa. The subject of this sketch was born at the family home in District No. 5, February 25, 1850. He spent his early years on the farm and in attendance at public schools and Harford Central Academy. On the completion of his literary education, he taught school for a time, meanwhile devoting his leisure hours to the study of law, which he carried on under the preceptorship of the late Col. E. H. Webster. In 1876 he was admitted to the bar and the same year became surveyor of the county. For four years he was counsel to the board of county commissioners. In addition to his professional duties, he takes an active part in agricultural affairs, and has been secretary and treasurer of the Harford County Agricultural Society since

1890. He makes his home at Prospect, not far from his birthplace, and has an office there, as well as in Bel Air.

The first wife of our subject was Laura, a daughter of Daniel P. Thomas. Some time after her death he was united with Hannah J. Scarboro, daughter of a leading farmer and member of an old Harford family. They have one child, David Paul. In religious belief they are connected with the Methodist Episcopal Church, in which he has been prominent as an official and as superintendent of the Sunday-school. A man of recognized professional ability, liberal ideas and keen intellect, always looking forward into the future for a broader evolution and wider knowledge, he is justly regarded as one of the most influential citizens of Harford County.

HERMAN W. HANSON has spent almost his entire life in District No. 1, Harford County. He was born where he now resides, January 30, 1859, and is well known as one of the principal canners and packers of this locality. The place which he owns and occupies, situated near Magnolia station, consists of about one hundred and sixty acres, and is planted principally to tomatoes. The annual yield of this vegetable amounts to about thirty-two thousand bushels and he purchases about as much more from his neighbors, so that he is enabled to sell each year about seventeen thousand cases. He has made a science of his chosen occupation, and his success has encouraged others to embark in the business, thus tending towards the enlargement of the industries of the county and the development of its material resources.

For several successive generations our subject's forefathers were seafaring men. His father, Thomas Hanson, was born in Holland and was a sailor by occupation. Coming to America in early manhood, he settled in Baltimore, and from there sailed upon the high seas. Later, however, he retired from that occupation, and purchasing a farm in District No. 1, Harford County, stocked it with cattle and carried on a dairy business in Baltimore. He continued in that occupation until about six years prior to his death, which occurred November 20, 1887, at Seneca Ridge farm. His wife, who passed away February 22, 1895, was Sophia Gunther, daughter of Frederick Gunther, who was born in Germany. They were the parents of six children, but only three are now living, our subject and his two sisters, Dena, Mrs. William Maloney; and Lucy, Mrs. Fred Lantz, both of whom reside in District No. 1.

In the Lutheran parochial schools of Baltimore the subject of this sketch obtained his literary education. He was prepared for a business life by a course of study in Bryant & Stratton's Business College. At the age of sixteen he began to carry on the dairy business in Baltimore that was owned by his father, but after a short time in that employment he took a clerkship in the city. In 1881 he came to Harford County and has since engaged in farming and the canning business. His attention is given closely to his business affairs, and he has little time or inclination to enter public life. Aside from voting the Democratic ticket he takes no part in elections. He is a member of the Lutheran Church, taking an active interest in all its work and having served as its president. Fraternally he is connected with the Junior Order of American Mechanics. November 4, 1881, he was united in marriage with Emelie, daughter of Frederick Emmord, of this district. Eight children were born of their union, and of these five are living, Amelia, Ada, Irene, Ruth and Emmord.

ALLEN HOFFMAN, who was one of the heroes of the late war that valiantly aided in the preservation of the Union when rebellion would have overthrown it, was born in Waterloo, in the province of Ontario, Canada, in 1846. His ancestors, natives of Switzerland, left that country during the time of war and sought a home in Pennsylvania. John Hoffman, father of our subject, was a native of Pennsylvania, and removed to Waterloo, Canada, where he became a man of much local prominence, serving as mayor of the city and as magistrate. He died in 1878.

Allen Hoffman was pursuing his education in Buffalo, N. Y., at the time of the Civil War, and though a boy of only sixteen years he left school and joined the Seventy-sixth New York Infantry, participating in the campaign in the Shenandoah Valley, where for meritorious conduct he was raised to the rank of second lieutenant. At the explosion of the mine in front of Petersburg, July 30, 1864, he was seriously wounded, and was sent to the hospital at Annapolis, where, on account of his injuries, he was honorably discharged. He started for his home in Canada, but was unable to travel, and for some time remained at Aberdeen, Harford County, Md. Becoming deeply interested in the place and its people, he afterwards located here, where for a time he was engaged with George Walker in dealing in general merchandise. Subsequently he went to Edgewood, on the Pennsylvania Railroad, where he conducted a hotel and was also engaged in the canning business. In his business undertakings there he met with excellent success, and accumulated a handsome capital.

In 1884 Mr. Hoffman removed to Bel Air, where he engaged in loaning money and did an extensive business as a broker in canned goods, besides carrying on a fire and life insurance business. He was also a director of the Harford National Bank from the time of its organization, and was the promoter of many other enterprises which materially advanced the prosperity and welfare of the city. He erected one of the finest residences in Bel Air and was accounted a wealthy citizen, but in his last years lost heavily by signing bonds for others. He was a man of excellent business and executive ability, reliable in all transactions, and his methods were above question.

In Harford County, in 1877, Mr. Hoffman was united in marriage with Miss Sallie R. Sheridan, daughter of the late Richard C. Sheridan, and a representative of a prominent family of this section of the state. Mr. Hoffman never fully recovered from the wounds sustained in the war, and this, combined with the worry and trouble caused by the loss of his money, terminated his life. He passed away January 26, 1897. He was a prominent Mason, holding membership in Mt. Ararat Lodge of Bel Air, and his upright and honorable life exemplified the teachings of that noble and beneficent fraternity.

J. M. STREETT, the well-known editor of the *Harford Democrat*, is one of the distinguished and popular citizens of Bel Air. He was born February 8, 1838, and belongs to one of the old and honored families of Maryland, his ancestors having come from England and located here prior to the Revolutionary War. The founder of the family in the new world is described in the court records of 1774 as a planter residing near Deer Creek in Upper Harford. Our subject's parents were A. J. and Elizabeth Streett, lifelong residents of Harford County, while his grandfather was Col. John Streett, who commanded a regiment of Harford Cavalry in the defense of Baltimore in 1814, and for the thirteen succeeding years represented Harford County in the state legislature.

J. M. Streett, of this review, acquired his early education in the Sweet Air Academy in Baltimore County and then completed the three years' course at Princeton University, of New Jersey, from which he graduated in 1858, receiving the degree of A. M. some years following. After leaving school he took up the study of law under the direction of the late Otho Scott, and in 1860 was admitted to the Harford bar.

In 1866 was celebrated the marriage of Mr. Streett and Miss Juliet E. Gover, the eldest daughter of the late George P. Gover, of Baltimore. As a representative and prominent citizen of Harford County, Mr. Streett was elected to the general assembly of Maryland in 1869, and in 1871 was re-elected, serving with distinction for two terms. About this time he bought the *Har-*

ford Democrat, and by the application of good business methods soon succeeded in placing it on a firm foundation. By continued good management, it has steadily grown in usefulness and popularity and to-day probably has a larger circulation than any newspaper in the state outside of the city of Baltimore. Five years ago the Democratic editors of Maryland formed a state editors' association, of which he was elected president, a distinction he continues to enjoy by virtue of as many annual re-elections. Of a large brain and kindly heart, he is interesting and instructive in conversation, courteous and genial in deportment, and affable and agreeable at all times. He is a fluent and forcible speaker, an attractive and correct writer and a gentleman of ripe scholarship and large information.

JOHN H. WHITE. There are many citizens of Cecil County whose unaided exertions have resulted in prosperity, and an excellent representative of this class may be found in Mr. White. The business of which he is in charge has been built up by his industrious application, and is one of the leading industries of North East. In addition to the ownership of that concern he has a neat and comfortable home and forty acres of land, carrying on farming to some extent. His energy and determination have enabled him to overcome such obstacles as he has met. Early years of labor and the hardships of army life during the late war combined to develop in his character sturdy traits of self-reliance, which lie dormant far too often.

Mr. White represents the first generation of the family that has resided in Maryland, those before him having lived in Massachusetts, to which colony the first settlers came from England and Scotland. His grandfather, John White, was born in Berry, Mass., and the father, Silas, was also a native of the same locality, the latter being a resident of Boston throughout his entire active life. For years he engaged in the meat business,

but his leisure hours were given largely to music, of which he was very fond. It is said that he was a fine violin player. In politics he was a Republican, and held some town offices, to which he was elected upon that ticket. Though not identified with any denomination, he usually attended the Congregational Church. He married Maria Hearndon, a native of Massachusetts, whose brother, Lieut.-Col. Henry Hearndon, commanded the troops that captured Jefferson Davis. Our subject has seen the $3,000 that was paid Colonel Hearndon for the capture.

Silas and Maria White had seven children, named as follows: Lorenzo, of Boston; John H., who was born in Boston, March 4, 1843; Inez, widow of William Hunt; Henry, whose home is in Lynn, Mass.; Sidney, of Ohio; Helen, Mrs. Charles Nichols; and Mrs. Mary Bissell, of Massachusetts.

The education of our subject was obtained in the public schools of Woburn, Mass. It was abruptly terminated at the age of sixteen, when, his patriotic spirit having been fired by the outbreak of the war, he ran away from home and sought for and secured admission into the army. A company was raised, of which he was made first sergeant, but when the men were mustered into the service he was rejected because he lacked a few inches of the regulation height. However, this did not daunt him, and shortly afterward he started to the front as a drummer in the Second Massachusetts Regiment of infantry, the first regiment that was mustered in for three years' service. With the others of the company he was present at Cedar Mountain, Antietam and Gettysburg, and was within one hundred yards of "Stonewall" Jackson when that illustrious general was shot. He was also at Lookout Mountain and at Resaca, Ga., together with many other smaller engagements. Three times he was wounded, but not seriously. At the expiration of his term of service he was honorably discharged.

Going to Philadelphia, the youthful war veteran sought to earn a livelihood in business affairs. He entered a shop where razor strops and morocco goods were manufactured and learned the business thoroughly, after which he was made foreman. In 1876 he purchased the business and moved it to North East, where he has since conducted the enterprise. He has never cared to enter politics and has not allied himself with any party, voting for the man whom he deems best qualified for the office in question. In religious belief he is an Episcopalian. In 1872 he married Catherine E. Birmingham, member of a family that long engaged in the manufacture of morocco goods in Philadelphia. Five children were born of the marriage, of whom one is deceased, and the others are at home: Herbert, Irene, Anne and Rhoda.

WILLIAM ENFIELD is one of those men who are able to successfully conduct different enterprises at the same time. His interests are varied and some of them quite important, involving large responsibility and entailing upon him considerable work. While he learned the blacksmith's trade in youth, he followed the occupation a short time only, having turned his attention to other lines of labor. To farming he has given some attention, and in addition he has engaged in the milling business at Cooper, and for some time has also been the proprietor of a general store building in that village.

Harford County, the present home of Mr. Enfield, is also his birthplace. He was born July 22, 1836, the son of Jacob and Nancy (Howlett) Enfield, natives respectively of York County, Pa., and Harford County, Md. The family of which he is a member consisted of eight children, namely. William, of this sketch; Eliza, deceased; Mary; Julia A. and Nancy, both of whom are dead; James; John S., who died in infancy; and John. The paternal grandfather was a native of Germany and in an early day came to America, settling in York County, Pa. Jacob Enfield was born on a farm in Harford County in 1811 and early became familiar with agricultural pursuits, but for some years when a young man he followed the milling trade. About 1845 he retired from that business and purchased a farm in Harford County, to the cultivation of which he afterward gave his attention.

When a mere boy our subject became familiar with the various employments of farm life and assisted in the cultivation of the place. His education was obtained in the common schools, and by a steady course of reading he has kept himself well informed. At the age of twenty-two he began to learn the blacksmith's trade, but spent only six months in that occupation, it being uncongenial. His marriage, at twenty-six years, united him to Tacy A. Weeks, a native of this district. Seven children were born of their union, namely: Alice, Elida, Willametta, Bertha, Estella, Dora (deceased) and Harry. Alice is the wife of William McNutt, proprietor of a general store at Berkley, this county. Elida is married to William Cox, a farmer of this county. Willametta is the wife of Nelson Scarborough, a farmer of this district. Bertha is a teacher and has successfully followed that profession about three years.

Harry, the only son, is in charge of the home farm, his efficient assistance being very valuable in the management of the property. Mr. Enfield is in sympathy with the principles of the Christian religion and contributes to religious enterprises, being interested particularly in the Presbyterian Church, of which his wife is a member. A Democrat by early training and inclinations, he has continued a firm adherent of the old party and takes an interest in local politics.

ELISHA ENGLAND KIRK. The homestead owned and occupied by Mr. Kirk is one of the most desirable within the limits of Cecil County and has been brought to a high state of cultivation by the owner. It is located in District No. 9, and comprises one hundred and twenty acres, embellished with a substantial residence, flanked by a barn, and having the other outbuildings required for the successful prosecution of agriculture. In all its appointments the place indicates in a marked manner the hand of thrift and industry. While general farming is the main occupation, dairying has also been carried on to some extent, and with fair success.

While Mr. Kirk is a native of Chester County, Pa., born there February 28, 1819, he is a member of an old Cecil County family. His grandfather, Levi, and father, William M., were born in District No. 9, and were farmers by occupation, the latter, in addition, having a saw and grist mill on Big Creek. In political belief he was a Whig. He married a daughter of Elisha England, and had six children, but Elisha E. is the sole survivor. With the exception of a short time spent in Chester County, he continued to reside here until his death, which occurred in 1832. He was buried in the old cemetery at this place.

The educational advantages received by our subject were exceedingly meager, for at an early age he was obliged to become self-supporting. After the death of his father he made his home with his grandmother Kirk, who carefully trained him for a position of usefulness in the world. When nineteen he secured work as an agent on the Pennsylvania Railroad and continued in that capacity for seven years, being at different times freight and passenger agent. On his return to Cecil County he took charge of the farm owned by his grandmother, and after her death he bought the place from the other heirs. In politics he is a Republican and takes an interest in national questions, also in local affairs. Frequently he has been called to serve on the jury. Shortly after the opening of the Civil War in 1861, he enlisted as a member of Company E, Parnell Legion, and served at the front for almost two years, when he was honorably discharged. Among the most important engagements in which he took part were the battles of Rappahannock and Antietam and the second battle of Bull Run. During the first-named engagement his nephew, L. K. Brown, of Washington, who was with him, was wounded by the enemy and lost a limb.

Mr. Kirk married Rebecca Hannah, daughter of James Hannah, of Lancaster County, Pa. Eleven children were born of the union, and of these six are now living, as follows: Hattie, wife of John Simpers; James, who is engaged in mining in Mexico; Harry, Eugene and Walter, mining engineers, also in Mexico; and Martha, wife of Isborn Brown. After the death of his first wife he married Isabelle Taylor, daughter of James Taylor, of District No. 9, Cecil County. The family are identified with the Quaker Church and exemplify in their lives the beautiful teachings of that society. The high principles which have characterized Mr. Kirk throughout his life have given him a good reputation as a man and a citizen, while his intelligence and enterprising spirit and his kindly nature give him a still higher place in the esteem of his fellow-men.

JOHN B. GRAHAM. From a perusal of the life records of our prominent citizens may be gleaned much that is interesting to readers of mature years, as well as many lessons that may serve as examples to the young. Mr. Graham is one of those who have made their way to the front in his special line of trade. While during his long business life he has met with his share of reverses, he has not grown discouraged, but has worked steadily and energetically toward the fruition of his hopes. It is worthy of especial mention that, on the site where he now engages in business, members of his family have followed the same occupation for one hundred and twenty years, a record perhaps unequaled by any other family in Cecil County.

In Charlestown, where he now resides, John B. Graham was born September 5, 1822, and his entire life has been passed at his present home. It is thought that the family is of Scotch descent. His grandfather, William Graham, was born in Chester County, Pa., but removed from there to Cecil County, Md., where his remaining years were spent. The father of our subject, Zachariah

HON. JOHN S. WIRT.

Butcher Graham, was born in Charlestown, a short distance from the place where his son began his earthly career. Like his father, he too engaged in business as a cabinet-maker and undertaker, and being very handy with tools, he was kept busy at work in his shop. In the possession of our subject are some of the tools used by his father and grandfather, but they are so different from those now in vogue that cabinet-makers of to-day cannot tell for what they should be used. In politics Z. B. Graham was a Democrat. He was a leading man of the village and held the office of magistrate for thirty years. By all who knew him he was highly regarded. Considering the limited advantages he had, he was a well-informed man. In religious belief he was a Presbyterian, and in that faith he passed from earth in 1854. His wife, who bore the maiden name of Rebecca Lewis, was a native of Charlestown, Cecil County, and died in 1848; her maternal ancestors, the Cunninghams, were among the most prominent early settlers of the county, and two of her uncles were soldiers in the Revolutionary War. The parental family consisted of twelve children, and of these three are living, namely: John B., the subject of this narrative; Charles, whose home is in Baltimore; and Lafayette, a resident of Wilmington, Del.

When our subject was young the schools were inferior to those of the present day, both as to quantity and quality of instruction; but then, as now, one who was studious and anxious to learn could gain considerable knowledge, no matter how discouraging the environments. He attended the neighboring schools and from the text books then used stored in his mind a valuable fund of information for future use. After leaving school he assisted his father in the work of a cabinet-maker and also built bridges and sailing scows. In 1854 he succeeded his father in the management of the business, which he has since conducted, besides dealing in sand and clay, selling fish, and building boats. During the war, in 1864–65, he held the office of county collector. He keeps well posted regarding public issues, and favors protection of home industries. Though not a member of any denomination, he inclines to the Methodist Episcopal Church, with which his wife is identified. In addition to the business of which he is sole owner, he owns considerable property in town and also seventy acres of farming land. Twice married, his first wife, Elizabeth Cooper, bore him one child, John C., who is with his father. His second wife was Caroline Richardson, daughter of Henry Richardson, and member of an old family of the county. Two children blessed their union, namely: Helen, wife of George Matting, of Wilmington, Del.; and William H., also of Wilmington.

HON. JOHN S. WIRT. To write the history of Cecil County and omit the name of John S. Wirt would be to do injustice to a man of rare intelligence, extended information and broad culture, with clear and concise opinions upon all important questions, one whose public life of usefulness has covered all his years since early manhood, and one whose voice has been heard, directly or indirectly, upon almost every public issue. As the representative of his district in the state senate, he secured the complete confidence of his constituents and the respect of his co-laborers who, like himself, were striving to promote the interests of the people of Maryland. During the more than twenty years in which he has followed the profession of an attorney-at-law, he has proved his ability to cope with the most intricate questions and grasp the often overlooked technical points of the law.

In considering the life of a man who has attained prominence, it is always appropriate to dwell upon his ancestry, for the character is moulded by the influence of preceding generations. The family of which Mr. Wirt is a member is among the oldest and most highly respected of Maryland. His great-grandfather, Thomas Wirt, was a member of the United States navy during the Revolutionary War and took an active part in the stirring events of that day. Next in line of descent was Samuel, born on Bohemia

Manor, which his forefathers had assisted in founding, and married to Francina Bayard, a relative of Thomas Bayard, United States senator from Delaware and one of the most prominent public men of the age. Dr. John W. Wirt, father of our subject, was born in 1808 on Bohemia Manor, and was quite young when his father died; his educational advantages were excellent, and he was a graduate both of Delaware College and the medical department of the University of Maryland. However, he never entered upon active professional work, but settled upon the old homestead, in the quiet life of a farmer. His death occurred in 1855. A portion of the original tract of Bohemia Manor is now in the possession of the subject of this sketch.

The mother of our subject bore the maiden name of Margaret Savin Biddle, and was a daughter of Peregrine Biddle and an aunt of Hon. George Biddle, in whose sketch will be found further mention of the Biddle family. She was born April 7, 1818, and died February 15, 1896. Her family consisted of three sons: William Bayard, John S., and Henry Biddle, of whom mention is made in this volume. The eldest son, William Bayard, was born July 27, 1849, graduated from Washington College and in early life went to Chicago, where he became clerk in the United States circuit court. He continued to advance until he was chosen chief clerk at a very large salary. He was one of the brightest lights connected with the courts in Chicago and had the confidence of the entire legal fraternity of that city. Chief Justice Fuller and many other illustrious men were numbered among his warm personal friends. At the time of his death, March 4, 1896, no man had brighter prospects than he, and his untimely death was a public loss.

A member of this family, so many of whose representatives have been gifted public men, John S. Wirt was born November 16, 1851, at the old homestead in Cecil County. He was but a child when his parents left the old estate and moved to Elkton, where he was orphaned by his father's death when he was only four years of age. He received his primary education in the Elkton Academy, and in 1868 entered St. John's College, Annapolis, where he graduated four years later with the degree of A. B., carrying off the highest honors of the class. In 1882 St. John's conferred upon him the degree of M. A. In 1874 he graduated from the law department of the University of Maryland, standing second in his class, and with a general average of ninety-nine and one-half. For three years after graduation he engaged in practice in Baltimore, in partnership with Gen. L. A. Wilmer, but in 1878 he accepted a position in Chicago, where he would doubtless have remained had it not been for the death of his brother, Henry Biddle, in 1881. This necessitated his return to Elkton to look after the business interests that his brother had previously managed. Here he at once commenced professional practice. His advent into the political world was unsolicited by him. In 1884 he was a delegate to the Democratic national convention at Chicago and was a strong supporter of Grover Cleveland throughout the entire convention, being one of six of the Maryland delegates that supported him on every ballot. In 1892 he was a delegate-at-large to the national convention at Chicago and again was one of six who constantly voted for Cleveland. A stanch Democrat, he has always been an admirer of Cleveland and a firm supporter of his principles. In 1889 he was his party's candidate for state senator and was elected by the largest majority given any candidate in his district since 1867. As a member of the senate he took an active part in public measures and commanded the attention of many of the older members of that body. It was largely due to his efforts that the Australian ballot system became a law. He took a firm stand against the gas bill, which was defeated principally through his efforts. He wrote a review of the proceedings of the Maryland legislature that was published in the *Baltimore Sun* and attracted attention from people throughout the entire country, being quoted in all the leading papers of the United States. In 1892 he was a candidate for United States senator, and was third in the race when the balloting began, but withdrew in favor of Gibson, who was elected.

In his chosen field, the law, Mr. Wirt is a recognized authority. While in Chicago he published the general laws of the state of Illinois, relative to warehouses and railroads. Learned in the law and well equipped for his profession, he is ready to cross swords with the best and is fearless of any controversy. As a public speaker he has been heard with pleasure upon many important occasions. Perhaps the best known of his addresses was that delivered before the alumni of St. John's College, in 1890, on the subject, "The Relation of Men of Liberal Education to the Civil Service Reform Movement," which was largely circulated both in the daily press and in pamphlet form. For many years he has been vice-president of the Civil Service Reform Association of Maryland, and is also vice-president of the Maryland State Bar Association, and since 1884 a trustee of St. John's College. Since his retirement from the senate he has given his attention principally to his legal and property interests, yet he has often been a delegate to state, congressional and county conventions. Since 1882 he has been counselor for the Baltimore & Ohio Railroad, Whitaker Iron Company, Scott Fertilizer Company, Fidelity and Deposit Company of Maryland, the board of school commissioners, Rowland Manufacturing Company, Port Deposit Water Company, and other corporations. In religious belief he is an Episcopalian and since 1881 has been a member of the vestry of Trinity parish and since 1885 treasurer of the parish. He has frequently been a lay delegate to the conventions and in 1895 was a lay delegate of the diocese of Easton to the national convention at Minneapolis. In addition to his other business enterprises, he is president of the Cecil Democrat Publishing Company and director in various local companies. Fraternally he is connected with the Masons, the Knights of Pythias, Independent Order of Odd Fellows and Ancient Order of United Workmen. His attractive home on East Main Street is presided over by his wife, whom he married April 28, 1886, and who was Miss Anne Rebecca, youngest daughter of Benjamin C. and Ann J. Pearce.

From this résumé of the life of Mr. Wirt it will be seen that he is one of the busiest as well as one of the most influential men of Elkton. The people among whom his boyhood days were passed have watched with interest and pride his upward course and have counted his successes their own. Now in the prime of manhood, it may be safely predicted that he has before him years of usefulness in the public service, and certainly, to whatever position he may be called, he will be as painstaking, as efficient and as honorably loyal to the interests of his fellow-citizens as he has ever been in the past.

JOHN W. WEBSTER was born in September, 1819, on the old Webster homestead, situated near Calvary, in Harford County, and he died on the Ball Hill farm in June, 1872. Much of his active life was spent in Baltimore, where he was numbered among the efficient business men of the city. In 1850, however, he purchased land in District No. 3, Harford County, and here he established a pleasant home, engaging in the cultivation of the land and in other work incident to the development of an estate. Patient application and perseverance bring their reward in due time, and by industry and thrift Mr. Webster was able to accumulate a sufficient amount of this world's goods to ease his mind with regard to the necessities of old age. However, his life was not prolonged to old age, but he passed away at the age of fifty-two, while he was surrounded by a loving family and the friends who had learned to honor him for his sterling manhood and conscientious character. He is survived by his intelligent and capable wife, who had bravely stood by his side in storm as well as sunshine, and who in every respect did her share in the accumulating of a competency and in maintaining the reputation of the family.

The history of the Webster family appears upon another page of this volume. John W., who was a son of Henry Webster, spent his childhood days on the old homestead in District No.

3, and upon reaching man's estate embarked in merchandising in Baltimore; but in 1850 he purchased a farm near Allibone, and there he engaged in farm work until his death. A stanch Republican politically, President Lincoln tendered him the appointment of assessor for Baltimore County, which he held for four years. He and his family always affiliated with the Methodists in religious belief. December 3, 1844, he married Priscilla Smithson, daughter of William Smithson, an old resident of District No. 3. His widow and their six children survive him, the latter being named as follows: Henry, of New York City; John W., who lives in District No. 4; Edwin H., a well-known citizen of Bel Air; Franklin and William, of District No. 3; and Anna, wife of William H. Hines.

JAMES A. FULTON, after a long and useful life in the business world, is now living retired in Bel Air, enjoying a rest which he richly deserves. Through his entire business career he has been looked upon as a model of integrity and honor, never making an engagement that he has not fulfilled, and standing today an example of what determination and force, combined with the highest degree of business integrity, can accomplish for a man of natural ability and strength of character. He has justly won the proud American title of a self-made man, and in business and social life he has gained the confidence and regard of all with whom he has been brought in contact.

Mr. Fulton was born in Harford County, September 2, 1811. His paternal grandfather was a native of Scotland, and in 1748 sought a home in America. With the rank of lieutenant he served in the Revolution, which made this country "the land of the free," and for many years his sword was in possession of William Fulton, brother of our subject. His children were Thomas, who lived in Lancaster County, Pa.; William, of Cecil County, Md.; David, who removed to Ohio in 1830; Philip; James, father of our subject; and John, who went to Ohio about 1812.

James Fulton, the father of our subject, was born about 1763, in Cecil County, and in 1808 removed to Harford County. He was by trade a fuller and carder. He served as an elder in the Presbyterian Church at Churchville, and all of his family were connected with the Seceder Church. He married Susan Trago, a native of Harford County, and they became the parents of four children: Joseph M., who followed carpentering; John C., a carder and fuller, who also followed farming on the old homestead; William H., a carpenter; and James A. There were also three daughters in the family: Mary, wife of Stephen B. Hanna, the grandfather of John B. Hanna, a leading young Republican politician and merchant of Bel Air; Avarella, wife of John Barnes, an elder in the Presbyterian Church, who was the maternal grandfather of John B. Hanna; and Mrs. Margaret McCall.

James A. Fulton, of this review, received but meager educational advantages and at the early age of sixteen years started out in life for himself by learning the trade of harness-making. After a time he removed to Wilmington, Del., where he served a four years' apprenticeship. On the expiration of that period he returned to Harford County, establishing a little shop in Churchville, where he carried on business from 1833 until 1839. He then came to Bel Air, and for fifty-two years was prominently connected with the mercantile interests of the latter city. He was an expert in his line and his work always gave the utmost satisfaction, so that he won a large patronage, which his honorable dealing enabled him to retain. From the time he embarked in business in 1833 until his retirement to private life in 1891 he purchased his goods of Edward Jenkins and his successors, always maintaining the most friendly relations with that house.

Mr. Fulton was married in 1838 to Miss Bridget McGonigal, who was for forty-three years a faithful companion and helpmeet to him. She died in 1881, leaving three children: Mary, wife of John S. Young, a lawyer of Bel Air;

Susan, wife of Joseph P. Weisel, of Cumberland; and John, who is engaged in the stationery business in Cumberland.

The name of Mr. Fulton is inseparably connected with the varied interests which go to form the history of his county. During President Tyler's administration he was postmaster of Bel Air, during which time he had to keep a list of every letter that was received at or sent from his office, and the postage was from five to twenty-five cents, according to distance. He was a great admirer of Henry Clay and in early life was a stanch Whig, but since the dissolution of that party has been a Democrat. He was county commissioner two years, clerk of the county twelve years and justice of the peace twenty-five years, discharging his duties with a promptness and fidelity that won him high commendation. Since the organization of the Presbyterian Church in 1850 he has been one of its elders, and has been very active in promoting its work and upbuilding.

WILLIAM WEBSTER. We record as noteworthy, because unusual, the fact that the farm owned and occupied by Mr. Webster has been in the possession of the family for seven generations. One of his most valued souvenirs is the original grant for two hundred and sixty-five acres given by Lord Baltimore to Isaac Webster, November 14, 1747; this is printed and written on sheepskin. There is also extant, in the hands of other members of the family, grants bearing dates of 1649 and 1652. The old homestead is situated in Churchville precinct, District No. 3, Harford County. A portion of the residence has been built in modern times, but the old part, which is of stone, is practically a castle, built for protection from the Indians. The walls are fully two feet thick, and in one place, where repairs were being made, it was found to be seven feet thick.

At this place William Webster was born January 4, 1831, and here much of his life has been spent. His father, Henry, who was a son of Richard (1st) by his second wife, was born here March 16, 1791, and in October, 1818, married Martha Hanson, of Kent County, Md. They became the parents of twelve children, named as follows: John Wesley; Benjamin Franklin and Phœbe, who died in childhood; Richard Henry; George Smith, whose sketch appears upon another page; Benjamin Franklin (2d), Edwin Hanson, William, M. Elizabeth, Martha Ann, Phœbe Smith and Sarah Frances. The only members of this once large family that now survive are George Smith, William, M. Elizabeth, and Phœbe Smith, the latter being the widow of Joshua Rutledge, and residing on Deer Creek. Henry Webster made farming his life work, and avoided politics and public office. Interested in religious affairs, upon the separation of the Methodist Protestant from the Methodist Episcopal Church, although with the majority, he resigned all claim to Calvary Church, as he wished to avoid contention. With Mr. Finney he built the Churchville Academy.

In spite of the fact that his family was large, Henry Webster succeeded in giving all of his children fair educational advantages. His son, William, our subject, was educated in the Churchville Academy and a private school at Christopher Camp, afterwards completing the course in Bel Air Academy. During the time of the gold excitement in California, he determined to seek his fortune in that far distant land. Accordingly, in 1851 he went to the Pacific coast, where he engaged in mining and merchandising until 1856. Having been moderately successful in his undertakings, he returned home and soon afterward assumed the control of the farm of two hundred and sixty acres. Here he engaged in general farming and stock-raising, and was prospered as the years passed by. About 1883 he retired from the active management of the estate and has since given his time and attention to the Mutual Fire Insurance Company in Harford County, of which he is the agent and a director. Politically he is a Democrat, but not active in public affairs. He and his family are connected with the Churchville Presbyterian Church, in which he has been a trustee for twenty-five years or more.

October 5, 1865, Mr. Webster married Anna J., daughter of John and Mary Aleicia (Mitchell) Stump, of Perryville, Cecil County. The six children born of their union were named as follows: Martha Hanson, who died in childhood; Mary Aleicia, who married Rev. C. D. Wilson, then of Washington County, Pa., now residing in Franklin, Ohio; Richard Henry, cashier of the bank at Aberdeen; Annie Stump, wife of Willard G. Rouse, a prominent attorney of Bel Air; John Stump, who has charge of the old homestead; and Caroline Henderson, who died at the age of seven years.

JOSHUA HUSBAND. Harford County has been the home and scene of labor of many men who have not only led lives that should serve as an example to those who come after them, but have also been of important service to their community through various avenues of usefulness. Among them must be named Mr. Husband, who passed away in 1896, after a life of industry and rich in those rare possessions which only a high character can give. For many years he labored with all the strength of his great nature and all the earnestness of a true heart for the bettering of the world about him; and when he was called to the rest and the reward of the higher world his best monument was found in the love and respect of the community in which he lived for so many years.

Mr. Husband was born near Deer Creek, in District No. 5, Harford County, in 1807, and was a son of Joshua Husband, Sr., whose birth occurred in 1764, in Cecil County, Md. The grandfather, also a native of Cecil County, was born near Rising Sun, on the Actoraro Creek, while the great-grandfather, William Husband, was born on the eastern shore prior to 1737, where he engaged in the manufacture of iron and in milling. His son, Herman, became one of the leaders in the rebellion of North Carolina previous to the outbreak of the Revolutionary War, and the British government offered a reward of one thousand pounds for his capture, either dead or alive.

His home at one time was in North Carolina. Members of the family have principally been engaged in the manufacture of iron and flint grinding and have become prosperous and useful citizens in the communities where they have lived.

Joshua Husband, Sr., the father of our subject, married Miss Margaret Jewett, and to them were born eight children, of whom Joshua, Jr., was the fourth son; the only one now living, Thomas J., is engaged in the manufacture of Husband's magnesia, in Philadelphia. The father died in 1837, at the age of seventy-three years.

Throughout his entire life Joshua Husband, Jr., remained a resident of Harford County, and early became familiar with the business in which the other members of the family had been engaged. Succeeding to his father's manufactory, he successfully carried on the business until his life's labors were ended, and was numbered among the most substantial and reliable citizens of the community.

In early manhood Mr. Husband was united in marriage to Miss Ruth W. Pennock, of Chester County, Pa., and three children blessed their union: Hannah P., William P., and Joshua, deceased; the latter for some time successfully carried on the business left by his father. For three generations the family has been identified with the Society of Friends, and our subject was one of its most faithful and earnest members, doing all in his power to promote the cause of Christianity and advance the welfare of his fellow-men. His political support was given to the men and measures of the Republican party.

It is but just and merited praise to say of Mr. Husband, that as a business man he ranked with the ablest, as a citizen he was honorable, prompt and true to every engagement, as a man he held the honor and esteem of all classes of people, as a husband and father was a model worthy of all imitation, unassuming in his manner, sincere in his friendships, steadfast and unswerving in his loyalty to the right.

GEORGE W. McCOMAS, who resides in District No. 1, Harford County, is a successful business man, who in the prosecution of the enterprises that have claimed his attention has ever manifested a strong desire to carry forward to the highest perfection attainable anything he undertakes. This has formed one of the important elements in the success that has crowned his efforts.

Mr. McComas was born near his present home April 13, 1841, and comes of a family long prominently connected with the history of Maryland. His grandfather, William McComas, a native of Baltimore, was one of three brothers who at the battle of North Point, near that city, performed distinguished service in defending their country against the attack of the British and killed the British commander in that engagement. A monument now stands in Baltimore in commemoration of their brave and noble service.

Henry G. McComas, father of our subject, was born in Baltimore, and for many years followed the sea, being captain of a vessel. In 1840 he purchased the farm upon which our subject now resides and made it his summer home until 1857, when he retired from the sea and located permanently on this place. During the excitement over the discovery of gold in California, he went around Cape Horn in the "George Washington," a one-hundred-ton vessel, loaded with boots and shoes. This is the smallest vessel that ever rounded the Horn and the feat was considered a very daring one. Captain McComas married Miss Keziah Cunningham, a daughter of George K. Cunningham, a native of Ireland. He was not long permitted to enjoy his home in Harford County, for he passed away in 1858. His wife, however, still survives him at the age of eighty-five. Their children are George W.; Henry Clay, of Baltimore; and Isabelle, wife of Joseph Turner, of New York.

George W. McComas attended the public schools of Baltimore until fourteen years of age and then came with the family to the farm whereon he has since made his home. His earlier years were devoted to general farming, but for the past sixteen years he has been extensively engaged in canning corn and tomatoes, which business has proved a profitable undertaking. In business affairs he is energetic, prompt and notably reliable, and tireless energy and honesty of purpose have brought to him a well-merited success.

On the 3d of December, 1874, was celebrated the marriage of Mr. McComas and Miss Virginia G. Norris, a daughter of Cardiff Norris, of Bel Air. They have four children: H. G., C. N., George W. and Nona Mary. The family attend the Methodist Church, and occupy an enviable position in social circles. In his political affiliations Mr. McComas is a Democrat.

GEORGE W. CRAIG. This name will be recognized by many of our readers as that of a gentleman who has borne an important part in the advancement of the business interests of Cecil County, and who has been a potent factor in municipal affairs in the village of North East. For a number of years he has held the office of president of the Green Hill Fire Brick Company, which was organized by his father, William Craig, in 1876, and in which for a long time he has been a stockholder and director, succeeding his father to the presidency on the death of the latter.

The exact date of the establishment of the Craig family in Cecil County is not known, though it was probably in colonial days. The first of the name in this country came here from England. William Craig was born in District No. 5, this county, and here spent his entire life, engaged principally in agricultural pursuits.

For years prior to his death, which occurred in 1893, he was president of the Green Hill Fire Brick Company, organized by himself and others. In early life he was a Whig and became a Republican upon the organization of that party. For several years he was supervisor of roads; where he rendered effective service in the opening and improving of roads in the district. In religious belief he was connected with the Episcopal Church. He was a man of progressive ideas and endeavored to give his children the best possible educational advantages, that they might be fitted for the duties of life. His wife, Elizabeth J., was a daughter of Henry Baker, whose ancestors were prominent in Revolutionary times and were among the founders of the Episcopal Church at this place. She is still living, at the age of seventy-seven, and is active and energetic for one of her years. In her family there were five sons and three daughters, of whom the following survive: George W.; Anna L., wife of James N. Cameron, of this county; Ella M. and Henrietta C., who are with their mother; Philip; Christopher, of Philadelphia; and Merryman D., whose home is in Perryville, this state.

At the parental home in District No. 5, Cecil County, George W. Craig was born February 22, 1846. When a boy he attended school during the winter months and worked on the home farm in the summer. When his father started in the fire-brick business, in 1876, he became an assistant in the work and learned to make stove linings and fire brick. He held considerable stock in the enterprise and was a director of the company for some years, succeeding his father as president in 1893. In addition to his interest in this business, he owns a farm and has some stock in the Stevenson Wrench Factory. In his political affiliations he is a Republican, zealous in everything pertaining to the welfare of the party, but not an office seeker. He is not a member of any secret society or church, but contributes to the Methodist Church, which his family attends. Of recent years he has been connected with the Mutual Guarantee Building and Loan Association of Richmond, Va. March 4, 1880, he was united in marriage with Miss Elizabeth A. Sentman, of this county, and they are the parents of six children now living: Martha Washington, Laura E., William Evan, George Ferris, Aldridge B. and Bessie Pauline.

WASHINGTON FOSTER. In giving honor to whom honor is due in the development of Cecil County, mention should certainly be made of Mr. Foster, who has labored long as a farmer and has shown himself to be a man of energy and industrious habits. He has been a lifelong resident of this county and is now engaged in cultivating a farm in District No. 5. He forms one of the class of men who have rendered excellent service in bringing a portion of the district to a state of cultivation, and is highly regarded as a practical man and useful citizen. At all times he has striven to advance the interests of the community in which he makes his home.

Near his present place of residence, the subject of this sketch was born January 22, 1842, to the union of Jesse and Elizabeth (Rutter) Foster. His paternal grandfather was a native of Ireland and an early settler of Cecil County. Jesse Foster was born two miles from the place where our subject now lives, and throughout his life he was interested in agricultural pursuits. In every relation of life he sustained a high character. Though not active in politics, he always voted the Democratic ticket and was interested in the success of his party. In religious belief he was connected with the Methodist Protestant Church. While still a young man, he passed away, in 1845, leaving his wife with a family of small children to care for and rear. She was a daughter of John Rutter, of this district, and was a lady of genuine worth of character, devoting herself, with the utmost self-sacrifice, to the welfare of her sons and daughters. When she was called from earth in 1872, she was deeply mourned by relatives and friends. Of her nine children five are now living, namely: Ann, wife of Washington Holt, of Elk-

RICHARD E. WEBSTER.

ton; James, whose home is in Baltimore; John, a resident of Chesapeake City; William, who cultivates the home farm; and Washington.

As a student in the schools of the neighborhood, Washington Foster gained a knowledge of the three R's. His education was thorough enough to enable him to look after his business interests with sound judgment. In 1857 he began to work upon the home farm for his father, continuing successfully as a tiller of the soil, and gaining a complete knowledge of every department of the work. The Robinson farm, as the place he owns is usually called, has been his property and home since 1875, and consists of three hundred and forty acres, upon which have been erected substantial buildings. While farming has been his principal occupation, it has not been his sole means of gaining a livelihood. In 1861 he commenced to run a line of freight steamers between Baltimore and New York, and in that connection was engaged until 1891, when he retired from the business. Like his father, he is a Democrat in politics and in religion a member of the Methodist Protestant Church. He has never married, but finds a pleasant home with his brother, William T. The latter was united in marriage, December 28, 1867, with Elizabeth Talley, daughter of William Talley, of this district; they are the parents of eight children, all of whom are at home, namely: William, Dora, Carrie, Raymond, Ernest, Ethel, Ellis and Edna.

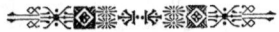

RICHARD E. WEBSTER. In the house where he now lives Mr. Webster was born September 18, 1833. He has known no other home than this, and is therefore more deeply interested in its development and more affectionately devoted to the old associations, than any stranger could possibly be. The place where he resides, and which descended to him from his father, is situated in District No. 3, Harford County, and comprises two hundred acres of land. The larger portion of the property is under cultivation, though some is devoted to the pasturage of the cattle, large numbers of which are here raised and fattened for market. Some of the land is planted to fruit, for the owner is one of the many who have found the canning industry a profitable and pleasant business in which to engage.

Richard Webster, grandfather of our subject, was a farmer and miller on James Run, and spent his entire life in this locality, dying when eighty-six years of age. The father of our subject, Noah Webster, was born in District No. 3, and engaged in farming on the place now owned by Richard E. A man of great energy and industry, his life was busily and usefully, but uneventfully, passed in the supervision of his interests. He died at the age of sixty-seven, and his wife when seventy-four. The latter was Susan, daughter of Richard Mitchell, who lived near Perryman, in District No. 2. The three children that comprise the family are Richard E.; Joseph, who is engaged in the livery business in Baltimore; and Priscilla, widow of Charles Saddler.

The rudiments of his education our subject obtained in the common schools and afterward he was a student in Hillsboro Academy, at Leesburg, Va. On his return from school he assisted his father in conducting the home farm, to the management of which he succeeded at the age of thirty years. Since then he has engaged in its cultivation, devoting his energies to the development of its acres. He is a man who keeps himself well posted upon matters of general interest, and politically is a firm Republican. His father, a man of public spirit, was for two terms county commissioner, and he himself has also assisted local enterprises in every possible way. While he has never sought office, the office of road supervisor sought him, and he consented to fill the position, his service in that capacity resulting beneficially to the country in the improved system of roads. Such men as he are a source of great strength to an agricultural community, and the farming interests of Harford County have been materially advanced by his instrumentality.

In 1866 Mr. Webster was united in marriage with Sophia Norris, daughter of William B.

Norris, of Baltimore. Their union was blessed and their home is still brightened by two children, Richard and Sophia C. The family attend the Calvary Methodist Episcopal Church, in which Mr. Webster has been steward for some years and also holds office as one of the trustees.

WILLIAM C. KARSNER, M. D. The medical profession offers an inviting field for men of energy, decision of purpose, discriminating powers and persevering industry. To such a one the study of the science is attractive, and through its practice a wide realm of helpfulness is assured. In no country of the world, with the exception, perhaps, of Germany, are there to be found physicians of such energy, broad information and skill, as the United States may boast. Nor are the physicians of Maryland deficient to others in skill and intellectual acumen; in fact, in many respects they lead the profession in the east, and by their knowledge of the medical science have enlarged the usefulness of the work.

These words aptly apply to the subject of this notice, a physician of Chesapeake City. While he does not belong to the small class of men who have gained national renown for scientific discoveries or newly attempted operations, he is a member of that larger, but equally useful, class of physicians who, in their own locality, have built up a good practice. He is skillful in the diagnosis of cases and wise in the selection of remedial agencies. His experience has been a varied one, including practice in almost every department of the profession, and in that manner he has gained a knowledge that is most helpful to him in his work.

A native of Cecil County, Dr. Karsner was born at what is known as the brick meeting house, District No. 6, October 27, 1831. His father, Daniel Karsner, was born in Elkton, this county, where he was educated and where later he engaged in the mercantile business. Afterward he was proprietor of the old Cross Keys Hotel at the brick meeting house, and still later resumed mercantile enterprises, but was obliged to retire from the business on account of failing health. In 1840 he came to Chesapeake City, and accepted the appointment of collector for the Chesapeake and Delaware Canal Company, at this place, a position that he held more than eighteen years. His death occurred in this village at the age of eighty-eight. Though not an active partisan, he never failed to support the Democratic party, believing its principles best adapted to promote the welfare of the people. At one time he was collector of taxes for his district. In religious connections he was identified with the Methodist Episcopal Church, in which he officiated as steward and trustee for many years. At the time of the building of the first house of worship erected by that denomination in Chesapeake City, he was one of the leading workers, and it was largely through his instrumentality that the building was erected. In the War of 1812 he served as an officer in what was called a troop of horse (cavalry), being orderly sergeant. His wife, who bore the maiden name of Eleanor F. Millechop, was born on a farm near Elkton and died at Chesapeake City in 1871, when eighty-one years of age. She was a woman of estimable character, a devoted Christian and an active worker in the Methodist Episcopal Church, a faithful friend and especially kind to those who were sick or in need. Of her nine children, the sole survivors are William C. and Cornelia H., wife of Thomas J. Cleaver, of whom a sketch is presented elsewhere in this volume.

In the schools of Elkton and Chesapeake City, and in Hopewell Academy, near Oxford, Pa., the subject of this sketch received fair educational advantages. When about nineteen he began to read medicine under Drs. Tyndall and Trites, in Chesapeake City, and later took a course of lectures in Jefferson Medical College, one of the most famous institutions of the kind in the United States. From this he graduated March 9, 1853, and at once went to Kent County, Md., where he practiced his profession for two years, but was then obliged to leave on account of poor health.

His next location was at Warwick, Md., whence, in 1857, he came to Chesapeake City, and here he has since been in continuous practice, with the exception of about three years during the war. He was then assistant surgeon in the United States army, and had charge of three wards in the general hospital at Newark, N. J.

The marriage of Dr. Karsner united him with Sarah C. Bouchelle, of Cecil County, and they are the parents of one daughter, Elsie Eleanor, who is an accomplished musician and a popular young lady. The family are connected with the Methodist Episcopal Church, in which for a number of years the doctor has been steward and trustee. In politics he is an active Democrat. In 1891 he was chosen, under Gov. Frank Brown, to serve in the position of Weigher General of Grain, of Baltimore City, and during his incumbency of the office he went to Baltimore once or twice a month, the detail work being in charge of five assistants there. For two years he was collector of taxes for this district. Fraternally he is associated with Cecil Lodge No. 125, F. & A. M., of Chesapeake City.

H. E. CLEMSON, M. D. The calling of a physician is not only one of the most arduous, but one of the most responsible professions in which man can engage, and he who attains a high reputation in it must necessarily be endowed with physical endurance, keen intelligence and excellent judgment. While the subject of this sketch has not been engaged in practice many years, he has already secured a high standing in professional circles, and to this he is entitled by his mental endowments, his careful culture, and his painstaking efforts to continually add to his theoretical knowledge and practical skill. As a private citizen he is highly esteemed for his public spirit, personal example, and interest in all that is beneficial to the people of the village and county where he resides. Since his gradua-

tion he has carried on practice in Elkton, of which place he is a native, born November 17, 1872.

The Clemson family is one of the oldest in the neighboring county of Lancaster, Pa. There Oliver P. Clemson, the doctor's father, was born and reared, and thence, about 1865, he removed to a farm in Cecil County, where he died in 1893. He was a man of retiring disposition, but greatly respected by those to whom he was intimately known. He took an interest in all that pertained to the welfare of Cecil County, his public spirit and liberality helping forward all schemes for its improvement. He married Mrs. Sarah Louisa (Rea) Wilson, a native of Lancaster County, who, by her first marriage, had a daughter, Rachel J., now the wife of Hon. Frank R. Scott, of Elkton. Of her second union only one child was born, Harry E.

The best advantages which the schools of the state afforded were given to our subject in his boyhood and youth, and being a diligent and ambitious student he availed himself of these opportunities to the utmost. For a time he prosecuted his studies in the Elkton Academy and West Nottingham Academy, after which he was a student in Delaware College for two years, and by taking advantage of every opportunity offered by these time-honored institutions he secured a broad literary culture. With the intention of becoming a physician, he matriculated in the University of Maryland and in 1894 graduated from its medical department. During his studies there he assisted in the University Hospital, and the practical experience there gained was perhaps as helpful as the theoretical knowledge acquired under the able professors of the institution. After his graduation he returned to his native village, where he opened an office and has since engaged in professional practice. In addition to his private practice he held the position of coroner's physician under the Democratic administration. He is regarded as one of the rising young physicians of the county and one whose future prospects are exceedingly bright. His home is in this village, with his widowed mother. Fraternally he is connected with the

Independent Order of Odd Fellows and is noble grand of the local lodge. He is also a member of the Improved Order of Red Men. As a young man of clear, well-balanced mind, with a good insight into professional matters, he is considered one of the men whose presence adds value to the citizenship of Elkton.

WILLIAM B. HEATZIG. Many of the patriotic citizens of our country have emigrated hither from foreign lands, and among them are some of the stalwart sons of Germany. With keen intuition they have foreseen future prosperity in America, such as could never be obtained in their native land, and coming across the ocean they have, almost invariably, been successful in their undertakings. A representative example of this class is the gentleman named, who is engaged in the general mercantile business in Elkton, and is one of the well-known citizens of the village. A native of Dresden, Saxony, born in 1822, his education was received in his home locality prior to his fourteenth year, when he began an apprenticeship to the cabinet-maker's trade. This he followed until 1854, when he was led, for political reasons, to decide to come to America. Crossing the Atlantic, he at first settled in Long Island and engaged in business at Flat Bush; but the surroundings were not entirely to his liking, and he resolved to remove further south. Therefore, after a short time, he came to Elkton, and here he has since resided. Opening a furniture store, he gradually built up a remunerative trade and accumulated a large property, but in 1891 his store and four of his houses were destroyed by fire, entailing a heavy loss. Without allowing himself to become discouraged by this catastrophe, he at once rebuilt, erecting the substantial store building in which he and his son, as partners, are now engaged in the mercantile business.

Prior to leaving Saxony, Mr. Heatzig was united in marriage with Eleanor Stein, who died in Elkton in 1891, about the time he met with his losses by fire. They were the parents of eight children, three of whom are living: Charles A., who is in partnership with his father; Laura, who is married and lives in Elkton; and Emma, who remains at home and brightens her father's declining years by her devotion to his welfare. Mr. Heatzig was reared in the Lutheran faith, but is now a member of the Presbyterian Church and a contributor to its good works. Upon coming to this country he made a study of our government and its institutions, and was led, as a result, to identify himself with the Democratic party. In the campaign of 1896, when the Democrats were divided upon the financial question, he strongly advocated the free coinage of silver and voted for William J. Bryan for president. While the ticket was not successful, he is hopeful that in coming years there will be a change of sentiment and the cause of silver will yet win. He never loses an opportunity to advance the welfare of his adopted home, favoring at all times such enterprises as will promote the progress of Elkton.

When thirteen years of age our subject was orphaned by the death of his father, John Heatzig, who was a cabinet-maker by trade. One of the sons of the latter, Adolph, remained in his native country and amassed a fortune of millions as a speculator in lumber, large quantities of which he furnished the government in 1866, during the Austro-Prussian War. At that time the secretary of war for Prussia came to him to purchase lumber for fortifications, stating that if he refused to supply it he (the secretary of war) would fell all the trees in Grosse Garten, the finest park in all Saxony and the pride of every resident in Dresden. Mr. Heatzig sold him the lumber, thus saving the beautiful park and at the same time clearing the snug sum of half a million in the transaction. He was the owner of several fine villas in the vicinity of Dresden and his private mansion adjoined the castle of the King of Saxony, with whom he was on the most intimate terms. On one occasion the king came to him in person and offered to knight him for his services to the country, but he refused to accept the honor, as he did not care to sacrifice his fortune in order that he might write "Van" before his name. He was one of the leading and wealthy citizens of Dresden, where he died in 1878. He had a sister, Dr. Neumann, a widow, who is a noted specialist of Dresden. Our subject has made two trips to his native land. In 1873, accompanied by his family, he returned to the old home and was the guest of his brother, remaining there for one and a-half years, during which time his son, Charles, attended school in Dresden.

ARCHER HAYS JARRETT. The natural advantages of this section attracted at an early day a superior class of settlers, thrifty, industrious, progressive and law-abiding, whose influence gave permanent direction to the development of the locality. Among the worthy pioneers of Harford County the Jarrett family hold a prominent place, and in their honor the village of Jarrettsville was named.

At that place the subject of this sketch first opened his eyes to the light of day in the home of his parents, William Bosley and Mary Virginia (Cairnes) Jarrett, who were born, reared and married in Harford County, and were numbered among its most valued and honored citizens. (A more extended mention of this worthy couple can be found in the sketch of Dr. Jarrett, of Jarrettsville, on another page of this volume.) Five children constituted their family, namely: Archer Hays, of this review; James Henry, a successful merchant of Jarrettsville; Ida Virginia, wife of Jesse Clinton Taylor, a manufacturer of and dealer in granite and marble at the same place; Sallie Leona, at home; and William Hope, who is also engaged in the marble business in Jarrettsville.

In his native village A. H. Jarrett passed the days of his boyhood and youth, acquiring a good practical education in the public schools, which has well fitted him for the responsible duties of business life. He has now for some time been a resident of Baltimore, his home being at No. 516 North Charles Street, and he is serving as head clerk in the New York Clothing House, Nos. 102 and 104 East Baltimore Street. Mr. Jarrett was united in marriage to Miss Margaret McMaster, of Cecil County, a daughter of Robert and Caroline E. (Gwinn) McMaster. Her mother was born in Port Deposit, Md., and belonged to one of the oldest and most prominent families of that section of the state. Mr. McMaster, who has now been dead about twenty-eight years, devoted his entire life to agricultural pursuits, and always made his home in Cecil County.

William Hope Jarrett led to the marriage altar Miss Mary Virginia Streett, who is a daughter of Samuel and Mary Ellen (Miller) Streett, the former of English and the latter of English and German descent. Her father is engaged in the hotel business. These brothers are men of much force of character, strong individuality, and their pleasant social manners have won them a host of friends who recognize their true worth. They have figured quite prominently in local affairs and their popularity is well deserved.

JAMES CORNER ROBINSON. From an early period in its history, Harford County has been fortunate in its representative men, those who, thrown upon their own resources early in life, have displayed the metal that was in them; and to such sterling characters the county is indebted for its development and prosperity. Among this class was James C. Robinson, of District No. 3, a man of sterling worth, and one who during the whole course of his career commanded the esteem of his fellow-men. Strictly a farmer, he was one of the most industrious of his class, and through his industry and perseverance he accumulated a competency, and at his demise left his family comfortably provided for.

The son of Edwin and Mary (Corner) Robinson, of Baltimore, the subject of this sketch was born in that city in 1836, and was the eldest of four children, the others being Mary; Hannah, widow of Samuel Richardson; and Edwin, deceased. The father died in Baltimore, at the age of forty, and the mother died at the same place. The first of the family to locate in Harford County was James C., who removed here in 1862 and settled on the farm in District No. 3, now occupied by his family. Here he carried on general agricultural pursuits the remainder of his life. Having received a good education in the common schools, he had the inclination and ability to turn his knowledge to good account, and with energy worked his way to a position of influence among the farmers of the district. He cared little for public life and nothing for official positions, but, had he chosen, he could have held local offices creditably to himself and satisfactorily to those who honored him with a public trust.

In 1865 Mr. Robinson married Susan Beaman, of Churchville, and three children came to bless their union, namely: Mary, wife of Robert Preston; Emily B. and Nannie H., accomplished young ladies, who, with their mother, hold a prominent position in society, and are active in the work of the Presbyterian Church at Fallston. Mr. Robinson passed away in March, 1897, aged sixty-one years. His life had been well and worthily passed and in death he was mourned.

J HENRY BREUNINGER. There is no element which has entered into our composite national fabric which has been of more practical strength, value and utility than that furnished by the sturdy, persevering and honorable sons of Germany, and in the progress of our Union this element has played an important part. Intensely practical and ever having a clear comprehension of the ethics of life, the German contingent has wielded a powerful influence, and this service cannot be held in light estimation by those who appreciate true civilization and true advancement.

Prominent among the German-American citizens of Harford County is Mr. Breuninger, of Castleton, whose birth occurred in the Fatherland in 1818. His grandfather, Henry Breuninger, a jeweler by trade, spent his entire life in Germany; and his father, Jacob F. Breuninger, only came to America on a visit. The latter was also a jeweler and was a highly respected citizen of his locality. He died in Germany in 1856, aged seventy-four years; and his wife, who bore the maiden name of Dora Kraut, died in 1860. Their children were Frederick, now deceased; J. Henry, of this sketch; and William, a jeweler of Washington, D. C.

In the schools of his native land, J. Henry Breuninger secured a good practical education, and remained in the old world until 1847, when he crossed the broad Atlantic for the purpose of trying his fortune in America, where he believed that better opportunities were furnished enterprising and industrious young men. Having learned the tanner's trade, he followed it for three years in Baltimore County, Md., after his arrival here, but in 1850 took up his residence in Harford County, where he worked for George P. Cook in his tannery at Cooksville on Deer Creek for the same length of time. The following four years were spent in the employ of James D. Wiley & Son, at Peach Bottom, Pa., and for seven years he was with John Moore at Bel Air, Md.

Having accumulated some capital, Mr. Breuninger, in 1864, purchased a place in the wilderness on a small stream, and there established a tannery, which he has since successfully conducted. He has not confined his attention strictly to the tanning business, but has engaged in the manufacture of all kinds of leather, including some very fine qualities, and has devoted some attention to farming. His tannery is located in what is now called Lafayette Valley and he has taken a prominent and active part in the upbuilding and improvement of the locality where he has made his home for over a third of a century.

In 1846 was celebrated the marriage of Mr. Breuninger and Miss Lizzie Sommer, also a native of Germany, and to them were born three sons, namely: Henry, who died in Washington while in the government employ; George, a merchant of Castleton, Md.; and Louis E., who is conducting a government restaurant in the treasury department in Washington. The wife and mother was called to her final rest in 1878, and the following year Mr. Breuninger married Miss Josie Eckolt, of Lancaster County, Pa.

In his social affiliations, Mr. Breuninger is a member of Mt. Hebron Lodge No. 516, I. O. O. F., of Delta, Md., and in his church relations is connected with the Methodist Episcopal denomination. His family attend the same church, and are widely and favorably known throughout the community. Upright and honorable in business life, Mr. Breuninger has gained the confidence of all with whom he has had any dealings and has the respect and esteem of all with whom he has come in contact.

ANDREW ANDERSON, who is engaged in business at North East, has been successful in the affairs of life and is in good circumstances. His means have not been accumulated without hard work and the exercise of prudence, and those who know him feel that he has won no more than he deserves. About 1888 he embarked in the livery business, which he has since carried on, and in addition he has a large trade in hardware, harness and agricultural implements, his place being stocked with a full assortment of goods to be found in his line, in the disposal of which he is thoroughly honest and reliable.

The birth of Mr. Anderson occurred in Lancaster County, Pa., October 4, 1848, his parents being John and Sarah (Winters) Anderson, of the same county. His father, who was a farmer by occupation, a Whig in politics and a Methodist in religious convictions, died in 1866, when in the prime of life. There were nine children in his family and six of these are living, namely: William, a resident of Chester County, Pa.; Andrew; George, who lives in New London, Pa.; Mrs. Rebecca McVey, of Harford County, Md.; Henry, living in Chester County, Pa.; and John,

of Lancaster County, that state. At the age of nine years our subject left home with a friend and for a few years afterwards he attended the schools of Lancaster County, but when seventeen began to work for others in farming. Two years later he came to Cecil County, where he learned the coachmaker's trade and then went west to follow this occupation, but not being satisfied with the country he soon returned to North East. For some years he worked in the employ of others here, in the manufacture of carriages, but finally embarked in business for himself.

In public life Mr. Anderson is a man of much prominence. Numerous business enterprises engage his attention outside of his personal affairs. At this writing he is president of the Wakefield Fire Brick Company and president of the Stevenson Wrench Company. An enthusiastic Democrat in politics, in 1891 he was elected on that ticket to the office of county commissioner and for four years served as president of the board, his services in that position being most helpful and satisfactory. For four years he held the office of president of the board of town commissioners and for a similar period he was president of the county board of health. At this writing he holds the office of school trustee. A member of the local lodge of Knights of Pythias, he has been through all the chairs. In 1877 he married Mary E. Gardy, of Philadelphia, Pa., and they are the parents of a daughter, Nellie V., an accomplished and popular young lady. The family attend the Methodist Church and have many friends among the residents of the village.

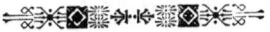

HENRY B. WIRT. Of all the young alumni of St. John's few were cherished as was the subject of this brief sketch. His gifts of intellect commanded the respect of his associates, and his noble traits of character made him dear to his intimates and a favorite in the social circle, where his presence was ever welcomed. Cut off in the first stage of manhood, he had but laid the foundations of the success he must have attained, had he been permitted to crown his career. As a member of the great army of toilers for fame, he fell early in the fight, but as a man he was as great as he could have hoped to be, had he lived to the limit that is wont to fall to the lot of mortals. Honest, sincere, generous and pure, unswerving in his friendship, devoted to his loved ones, reverent to his elders, kindly with his inferiors and humbly striving to serve God and keep His law, he has measured up as few do to the standard by which all that is great and admirable in manhood must be judged.

Henry Biddle Wirt was born in Elkton, Cecil County, Md., April 30, 1854. In early infancy he lost his father, Dr. John W. Wirt, who, like him, passed away in early manhood. Yet, valuable as would have been a father's care, he was blessed with a mother, who combined the graces and powers of womanhood, and who reared him with a tenderness and control that won for her his fondest affection and guided him in the path of duty. The writer first met him in the winter of 1866-67 at the Elkton Academy and the friendship there formed strengthened with the years until it became as abiding as brotherhood. At the academy young Wirt ever commanded the regard of his instructors and the esteem of his companions. He won successive medals for scholarship and deportment and always stood at the head of the roll. In the spring of 1868 he repaired to the time-honored academy at West Nottingham, where he gave renewed evidence of his abilities. In October, 1868, in company with the writer and others of his schoolmates at the Elkton Academy, he matriculated at St. John's, whither his brother had preceded him the previous term.

Mr. Wirt entered the first preparatory class and immediately took a high rank, which steadily rose until he stood first in a class than which few stronger have ever quitted St. John's. No undergraduate ever stood higher in the esteem of the faculty and the regard of his fellow-students. As a further evidence of his great abilities it may be noted that, while maintaining his class precedence, he stood among the first of the talented members that then composed the Philokalian Society and was ever prepared to discuss the questions that arose at its sessions. He filled every office in the gift of the society and enjoyed in his senior year the crowning distinction of being chosen to represent the Philokalians in the annual public debate, which was decided in his favor. Yet, despite his close attention to his studies as a student and a Philokalian, he always found time to enjoy the delights for which the Society of the Ancient City has ever been renowned. At the commencement in 1873 he graduated at the head of his class, delivering the valedictory oration, which, in the judgment of his hearers, was a marvel of pathos, voicing as it did the impulses of the generous boy, whose friendships were so tender and so true.

Immediately after graduating, Mr. Wirt was appointed tutor at St. John's College by the board of visitors and governors, among whom he numbered many warm friends. This position he filled for two years to the satisfaction of his associates in the faculty and the delight of the students. None more sincerely mourned his untimely death than those whom he helped to usher upon their collegiate careers. While tutor he laid the foundations of his legal education, and on quitting St. John's, in the fall of 1875, he entered the law school of the University of Maryland at Baltimore, where in an able class he stood first, completing the curriculum in a single year. Here, too, his manly traits and generous impulses won the regard of those around him, and he was elected president of his class. Receiving his diploma he returned to Elkton, where, on the invitation of George W. Cruikshank, he entered into a law partnership which was satisfactory and successful. At the bar he commanded the utmost courtesy from the bench and his associates, and had he been spared, must have risen to high distinction.

In April, 1879, Mr. Wirt was married to Miss Nellie Knight, a daughter of William Knight, Esq., an honored citizen of Cecil. Two years of blissful happiness followed this union, when the dread summons came, and he quitted this mortal

MISS MARTHA FINLEY.

sphere for the realms of the blessed. In February, 1881, he accompanied his wife on a visit to Winchester, Va. Returning through Baltimore during the intensely cold weather then prevailing he contracted a severe cold, which speedily developed into pneumonia and he steadily sank. Despite the fond care of his loving wife and devoted mother, he died on the 8th of February, at the early age of twenty-six years, after a brief week of suffering, but with hope unshaken in the blessed promises of God.

The years glide by, and soon his mortal form will have found its kindred dust, but his grand spirit calls to us from out the great unknown in tones of fondness as of yore, in the words of the grand old bard, whose end, crowned with earth's homage and distinctions, was calm and confident as his:

"There is no death! What seems so is transition.
This life of mortal breath
Is but a suburb of the life elysian,
Whose portal we call death."

MISS MARTHA FINLEY. That women, girls and children throughout the length and breadth of the land should be interested in Miss Martha Finley is not to be wondered at when it is known that she is the famous authoress of the "Elsie books," for while there are books and books, there are few that have, as do hers, the interesting situations, the pleasing romance, the wise religious suggestion, the pure lovemaking, and better than all, the pure womanly tone. But few of the people of eastern Maryland, while they know of her and have read her books, know that most of them were written in the quiet village of Elkton, Md., where her home has been for many years. Miss Finley comes of illustrious Irish ancestry. Her grandfather, Gen. Samuel Finley, was born in Westmoreland County, Pa., in 1752. He graduated from Princeton College, under his uncle, Dr. Samuel Finley, and upon the opening of the Revolutionary War, espoused the cause of the colonists, and rose to the rank of major. He was captured at Ft. Washington and held a prisoner by the British for three years. During the War of 1812 he again entered the army, in which he distinguished himself and attained the rank of general. He was a warm personal friend of General Washington, and served under him as receiver of public money at Chillicothe, Ohio. His uncle, James Finley, was the first Presbyterian minister at Elkton, Md.

Miss Finley's father was Dr. James Brown Finley, who was born in Pennsylvania June 7, 1794. At the age of eighteen years he enlisted in the War of 1812, with his father, and served until the surrender of Detroit, when he was paroled and returned home. Later he was graduated from Dickinson College, of Carlisle, Pa., after which he studied medicine. He was married to his first cousin, Maria Theresa Brown, who was visiting at that time at Chillicothe, Ohio, where Miss Finley was born April 26, 1828. In 1836 her parents moved to South Bend, Ind., where the father practiced medicine until his death in 1852. The girlhood of Miss Finley was spent in South Bend and there she received an excellent education in private schools. She then taught for a time in a private school for small children, and here she frequently entertained her little pupils with stories which were doubtless the nucleus of tales published in later years. Her first effort in a literary way was as a writer of short stories for religious papers, which were under the direction of the Presbyterian Publishing Company. The manuscript of her first story was taken to the Baptist Board, was accepted and published, and upon its appearance was well received.

After the death of her father Miss Finley had come east and her early articles were written in New York and Philadelphia. In 1876 she made a visit to Elkton, Md., and finally decided to make this place her home. She has a beautiful residence in the most aristocratic part of the village, surrounded by extensive grounds and a neat hedge fence. In this place much of her best work has been done. She has written more than one hundred books, all for children (with the exception of the Finley series). To anyone who has read her books her love for young girls and her strong religious feeling are most evident. No writer of the nineteenth century is better beloved. Her great aim has been to interest the little ones and in this she has succeeded far beyond her expectations. While all her works have attracted wide attention her Elsie books are without doubt the most popular, the principal ones being as follows: Elsie Dinsmore; Elsie's Holidays at Roselands; Elsie's Girlhood; Elsie's Womanhood; Elsie's Motherhood; Elsie's Children; Elsie's Widowhood; Grandmother Elsie; Elsie's New Relations; Elsie at Nantucket; The Two Elsies; Elsie's Kith and Kin; Elsie's Friends at Woodburn, and others of the Elsie series. Some of her other works are: Signing the Contract; Wanted, a Pedigree; The Mildred Series; The Finley Series; and the Tragedy of Wild River Valley.

It can be truly said that Miss Finley's Elsie books made her famous, although all have been well received. At one time some of the newspapers of the country made an effort to stop the publication of any more Elsie books, saying that "they had had enough of Elsie," and one editor of a large daily remarked in the columns of his paper: "For God's sake, give us something besides Elsie." Notwithstanding this Miss Finley "pursued the even tenor of her way" and continued to write "Elsie books." She was not writing to please the editors or publishers, but her little friends, and as long as they were pleased and satisfied she was content to give them Elsie in every phase. When she first began writing her publishers refused to let her get her books copyrighted and paid her only what they saw fit for her manuscript, but when fame came to her, she determined that she, instead of the publishing houses, would copyright her books and that royalty must be paid her for them. Her publishers are Dodd, Meade & Co., of New York.

Miss Finley is easily accessible, and although her health is poor her work goes on. She freely discusses her early struggles for fame and fortune and is an easy, fluent and agreeable talker. She has a matronly, graceful figure, a gentle face, lighted up with bright, intelligent eyes, and her finely shaped head is crowned with a wealth of gray hair. Her personality is very pleasing and she has a sweetly modulated voice, expressive and animated. Her surroundings are pretty and exquisitely neat, comfortable and convenient, and her study is well supplied with standard works and books of reference; but few of her own publications, however, are found on the shelves. She is a member of the Authors' Club of New York City.

JOHN STREETT. The life whose main events are herewith chronicled has been closed upon earth; the book is finished, its record completed, but those who have been helped by contact with Mr. Streett and who remember his many noble attributes of character will welcome this memoir with especial interest. He was a progressive farmer of Harford County and rose to a position in the agricultural circles of District No. 3 which many might envy. He was respected by all who knew him, and such was his integrity that his word was as good as his bond.

Of English descent, the subject of this sketch was born in District No. 5, in 1815, being the son of Maj. Thomas Streett, and grandson of Col. John Streett. Reared upon a farm, he early turned his attention to agriculture, in which he manifested such a lively interest and so much industry and integrity of purpose that he easily met with success. Until thirty years of age he remained on the old homestead near Highland, but he then removed to Chestnut Spring and made his home upon a farm near Clement Mills for fourteen years. In 1858 he purchased a portion of the Francis Delight farm, and here he afterward continued to reside until his death, which occurred December 25, 1895, at the age of eighty-one years.

January 16, 1844, Mr. Streett was united in marriage to Priscilla A. Ruff, and their union was blessed with two children, Sophia Priscilla and James Ruff. Mrs. Streett, now seventy-eight years of age, continues to reside at the old homestead and, notwithstanding her advanced age, is quite active and bright. The farm is now carried on by her son, J. Ruff, who was born in 1854 and in 1891 married Hannah Baldwin, of this county. The family hold membership in the Episcopal Church and are respected wherever known.

WILLIAM CHARLES COOPER is well known in Cecil County, and the fact that he is favorably spoken of by high and low, rich and poor, is sufficient indication of his character. One of the prosperous farmers of this section, he occupies a pleasant home in District No. 5. Like many of the best residents of the county, he has spent his entire life here and is a member of one of its old families. The old homestead where he resides was purchased by his grandfather, John Cooper, in 1754, and has been in the possession of the family ever since. John Cooper was the owner of a ship yard at Seneca Point and later carried on the same business in Baltimore until his death, which occurred in 1794.

The father of our subject, John Cooper, Jr., was born on the Cecil County farm, to the cultivation of which his active years were given. While he never acquired wealth, he accumulated a competency and was able to surround his family with the comforts of life. He never cared to identify himself with politics, and aside from casting a straight Democratic ticket at elections took no part in public affairs. He was a member of the Episcopal Church and in his life and character endeavored to carry out the lofty teachings of that faith. His marriage united him with Jane Little, whose parents were farmers and respected residents of this county. She passed away in 1861, having long survived her husband, whose death occurred in 1844. They were the parents of four children, but the only survivors are William Charles and Mary Jane, the latter the wife of Benoni Cooling, of Charlestown.

Where he now resides, William Charles Cooper was born August 12, 1833. In boyhood he alternated attendance at school with work on the home farm, and a little later learned the trade of a bricklayer. Leaving school when seventeen, he turned his entire attention to farming and work at his trade. Since 1860 he has been in charge of the old homestead of one hundred and thirty acres, which is one of the fine estates of the district, containing an excellent class of buildings fitted for their varied purposes. One of the attractions of the place is a pond with carp and cat fish. The land produces large harvests and is very fertile, responding readily to cultivation.

Mr. Cooper has never been interested in politics in the sense of office-seeking, but is well informed regarding the issues of the age, and at elections always casts a ballot in favor of Republican candidates. He takes an active part in everything pertaining to the welfare of the community, and, with his family, attends the Methodist Episcopal Church. In January, 1860, he married Rachael Bryson, of Elk Neck. The eleven children born of their union are named as follows: Rebecca Jane, of Baltimore; Mary Lizzie, wife of Curtis Taylor, of Blythedale, Cecil County; William H. Seward, who resides near his father and is a farmer by occupation; Charles P., of Charlestown; Cecil C., who lives near the old homestead; John, who resides near Baltimore; Ella and Edith (twins), George F., Bert and Herbert, all at home.

CHARLES REMBOLD. Many men on coming to this country from a foreign land find circumstances here so different from what they have been accustomed to that frequent mistakes are made in choosing their occupations, and this they very often find to be the case when it is too late. Fortunate is he who has the discernment to choose a congenial calling—one for which he is suited, and can adapt himself to the changed condition of affairs. In such a case he will be as congenially and suitably employed as is Charles Rembold, who is the capable overseer of ten thousand acres of land, divided up into sixteen farms, and owned by John Cadwalader, of Philadelphia. Mr. Rembold owes his nativity to Wurtemberg, Germany, where he was born March 26, 1820, a son of Henry Rembold, whose life occupation was that of a weaver. He had several brothers, and all became farmers. He was an industrious, worthy man and died when in the prime of life, in 1825. He was married to Miss Victoria Neff, also a native of Wurtemberg, who died in 1839.

The early life of Charles Rembold was like that of the average German youth, for upon attaining a suitable age he was placed in a school where he acquired a practical and, as far as he went, a thorough education. He had sufficient discernment to perceive the advantages that were offered to young foreigners who put themselves under the protection of "Uncle Sam," and on May 24, 1847, arrived in the United States and at once made his way to Harford County, Md. He tilled various farms in this county for a number of years, and his thrift, industry and good judgment soon won him the notice of Mr. Cudwalader, who about 1870 tendered him his present position. This he has filled with marked ability up to the present time, and fortunately the calling has been one for which he has a natural aptitude and a decided liking. These farms he rents to different men, who work them on shares.

Mr. Rembold was married in 1848 to Miss Fredericka Pershing, a native of Baden, Germany, and to them ten children were given, eight of whom survive: Katie, wife of Charles Fisher, of Baltimore; Lizzie, wife of Harry Carroll, of District No. 1; August and John, also of this district; Rebecca, who is still with her father; Charles, at home; Mary, wife of Joseph Jeffrey, of Virginia; and Frank. The mother of these children has been dead about one year. Mr. Rembold has supported the principles of the Democratic party since coming to this country, but is by no means an office seeker or a partisan. He is a Catholic. As a business man he is esteemed for his honest methods, and as a citizen for the interest he has taken in the welfare of his adopted country. Like the great majority of Germans he has been industrious and economical and his efforts have won him a competency and universal respect.

WILLIAM H. HAINES. In the neighboring county of Harford the subject of this sketch was born June 19, 1834. Throughout his entire life, covering a period of more than threescore years, he has been identified with the history of the northeastern part of Maryland. His home is now in Cecil County, whither he was brought by his parents when a child of one year. A resident of Charlestown, he has many friends in this village and the surrounding district, and all who know him recognize in his character the qualities of perseverance, industry and honesty that mark the best citizenship.

The Haines family originated in Scotland. The representatives in this country have inherited, from a long line of honorable, industrious forefathers, the heritage of a good name and the qualities of thrift and uprightness so characteristic of the Scotch people. Thomas, the grandfather of our subject, was born in Cecil County, his parents having emigrated here from Scotland. He was reared upon a farm near Port Deposit and followed agricultural pursuits as long as his strength permitted him to engage in manual labor. During the War of 1812 he was a soldier in the American army. He attained an advanced age, dying at eighty-eight years.

The father of our subject, Samuel Haines, was born near Port Deposit, Cecil County, and made farming his chief occupation in life. He did not have the advantages in youth which fall to the lot of the children of this age, but while he lacked in learning and scholarly attainments, he was not lacking in industry and perseverance, without which success cannot be secured. Politically an old-line Whig, he desired the public welfare, and, being a good citizen with a liberal spirit, he aided in all matters tending to the promotion of local interests and industries. He was identified with the Methodist Protestant Church. His death occurred in 1880, five years before the demise of his wife, Mary Ann (Rockwell) Haines, who was a native of Harford County. They were the parents of eleven children, of whom four sons and one daughter are living. They are named as follows: William H.; George, residing at Principio Furnace; Ann Eliza, wife of William Culbertson; James, who lives at Wilmington, Del.; and Frank, a traveling salesman. The boyhood years of our subject were passed at Port Deposit, where he attended the public schools. At the age of seventeen he began to learn the trade of a blacksmith, but this he followed only six months, as the work was not congenial and he preferred to enter other lines of employment. His life has been passed principally in general farm pursuits, although he has also given considerable attention to fishing and has been quite successful in that occupation.

September 26, 1861, occurred the marriage of Mr. Haines and Miss Hannah Jane Harris, whose parents, Wilder and Alice (McMullen) Harris, were descendants of early settlers of this district and county. The six children born to the union of Mr. and Mrs. Haines have, with one exception, been spared to years of maturity. They are Joe Edward, living in Philadelphia; Alice, wife of Joseph Lynch and a resident of Charlestown, Cecil County; Will, Harry and George, who are at home.

JAMES A. BOULDEN. The varied wants of mankind give rise to varied occupations. In one part of the country may be found those who, within the recesses of the earth, mine the coal; in another place there are stone quarries, or gold fields, or wide-stretching fields of grain. But there is no place where the merchant is not needed and where the sale of household goods, groceries and articles of clothing, is not carried on. In every community the merchant is indispensable. If he is energetic, he may advance the commercial importance of his locality; on the other hand, if he is shiftless, idle or aimless, he may immeasurably retard local progress. Of Mr. Boulden it may be said that he is one of the leading business men of Chesapeake City, and his activity has been very helpful in promoting the interests of the place. Since the time when he first established himself in business here, in 1865, he has been identified with local industries, and has been especially interested in the grain and phosphate business, though he also carries in stock a full line of hardware and modern farm machinery.

The birth of Mr. Boulden occurred in this village December 29, 1837, his parents being Levi and Elizabeth (Bennett) Boulden. His father, who was born near the village of Chesapeake City, spent his entire life in Cecil County, with the exception of two years, when he resided in Wilmington, Del. Reared upon a farm, he did not, however, make agriculture his life work, but in 1832 secured employment as collector for the Chesapeake & Delaware Canal at this place, retaining the position for six years. His life was a sad one, for ill health cast a gloom over his later days and rendered him unable to engage in any line of labor for a long time prior to his death. He suffered intensely with rheumatism, so severely, indeed, that he was confined to his bed for sixteen years before he passed away, and his death, at the age of forty-seven, brought him welcomed release from pain. His wife, also a native of Chesapeake City, is now over eighty years of age, but is in good health.

Reared upon a farm, our subject devoted the years of youth and early manhood to agricultural pursuits, but in 1865 embarked in business and has since given his entire time to the enterprise with which his name is connected. He takes an interest in all matters relating to local affairs and also keeps himself well posted regarding questions before the nation to-day. Politically his sympathies are with the Democratic party and he has always been firm in his allegiance to that organization. For four terms he held the office of commissioner and he has also rendered efficient service as mayor. He has been twice married. His first wife, Mary E. Clark, of this place, died in 1864, having been the mother of two children: Alice M., who is with her father; and Harry, who died in boyhood. The present wife of Mr. Boulden was Emma Doble, of Wisconsin, a cousin of Budd Doble, the well-known horseman. They are the parents of six children, namely: Laura, wife of I. G. Griffith, Jr., of Chesapeake City; Fannie, who married William A. Stubbs; D. Palmer, who is employed as a clerk for his father; Nellie E.; Elizabeth and Carlisle, who died in infancy.

JOSEPH VEAZEY WALLACE, M. D., of Chesapeake City. It has been well said that "If the virtues of strangers be so attractive to us, how infinitely more should be those of our own kindred; and with what additional energy should the precepts of our parents influence us when we trace the transmission of those precepts from father to son, through successive generations, each bearing the testimony of a useful and honorable life through their truth and excellence." This is forcibly pertinent to the ancestry of Dr. Wallace. He comes of that old Maryland stock noted for its zeal in the cause of freedom during the Revolution, for its course in danger and its principles of honor carried into even the smallest details of life. Nor were his remote ancestors less upright; they were of the Scotch race, known the world over for thrift, probity, industry and high-minded, spotless characters.

The Wallace family was founded in America by Andrew Wallace, who was born in Scotland in 1672 and settled in Cecil County, Md., prior to the year 1700. In Johnson's History of Cecil County he is mentioned as one of the first elders in the old Presbyterian Church, at the head of Christiana Creek, which was erected in 1708. His gravestone in the cemetery adjoining the church shows that he died "on ye 3d of March, 1751, aged 79 years." His wife, Ellinor Wallace, who was also his cousin, departed this life "ye 8th of Dec., 1753, aged 78 years." They had three children, Jeannette, Margaret and Joseph. The last-named was born in Cecil County, Md., in 1713, and married Mary Black, of Delaware, by whom he had four children, Andrew, Joseph, George and Ann. April 15, 1755, he was commissioned by "Horatio Sharpe, governor and commander-in-chief in and over the province of Maryland" to be first lieutenant of the foot company commanded by Capt. Zebulon Hollingsworth, of Cecil County; the commission is now in the possession of the subject of this sketch. Joseph Wallace died in Cecil County May 28, 1776, at the age of sixty-three. His wife, Mary, died January 7, 1794, aged seventy-four years.

Dr. George Wallace, son of Joseph Wallace, was born in Cecil County, Md., in 1752. He studied medicine under Dr. Phineas Bond, in Philadelphia, and graduated from the University of Pennsylvania August 3, 1773, his diploma being signed by Dr. Thomas and Dr. Phineas Bond, two of the incorporators of the university. After his graduation he removed to Delaware to practice his profession. When war was declared against Great Britain he was commissioned first lieutenant in Capt. Joseph Caldwell's company of the southern district of Kent County. His commission, which is in possession of his grandson, our subject, was signed by J. W. McKinley, president of the council of safety, and bears date January 23, 1776. In answer to an inquiry from a subscriber as to the origin of the name "Blue Hens' Chickens," the *Philadelphia Record* made the following reply: "One of Delaware's most gallant fighters in the war of the Revolution was Capt. Joseph Caldwell, who was notorious for his love for cock fighting. He drilled his men admirably, they being known throughout the army as Caldwell's Game Cocks. This same Caldwell also held the peculiar theory that no cock was really game unless its mother was a blue hen. As months wore away Caldwell's men became known as Blue Hens' Chickens, a title which only increased their respect for the old game cock captain. The nickname became famous, and, after the war, was applied indiscriminately to all natives of the Diamond State." After the close of the war Dr. George Wallace returned to Cecil County, and locating at Elkton, resumed the practice of medicine. January 27, 1787, he married Elizabeth Black, of Newcastle County, Del. The following-named children were born to them: James; Mary, who married Thomas W. Veazey, governor of Maryland 1835-37; and Joseph. He died in Elkton June 17, 1796, aged forty-four years. His widow, Elizabeth, became the wife of Dr. John Groome, August 31, 1799, and by that marriage had three children: Hon. John C. Groome, father of ex-Governor James Black Groome; Dr. Samuel W. Groome, and Eliza Jeannette, who married Capt. Mathew C. Pearce.

Dr. Joseph Wallace, son of Dr. George and father of Dr. Joseph V. Wallace, was born in Elkton, Md., February 5, 1791, and was the youngest of three children of his mother's first marriage, his brother and sister being James, born June 10, 1788; and Mary, September 17, 1789. He attended the school in Elkton and finished his education at Nottingham Academy. His medical studies were begun in the office of Philip Syng Dorsey, of Philadelphia, and in 1812 he graduated from the University of Pennsylvania. The faculty at that time contained Benjamin Rush, signer of the Declaration of Independence; Philip Syng Phipsic, John Redman Cox, Benjamin Smith Barton, C. Wistar and Philip Syng Dorsey. July 9, 1813, he was appointed hospital surgeon's mate by Dr. James Tilton, surgeon-general, U. S. A., and was ordered to Ft. Mifflin for duty. Having passed an examination before the army board of surgeons he was appointed by the secretary of war, John Armstrong, acting assistant surgeon, which appointment was confirmed September 28, 1813, and he was ordered to join General Wilkinson's army on the Canada frontier. He remained with the army until the declaration of peace. By John C. Calhoun, secretary of war, he was appointed, April 21, 1818, surgeon of the Fifth United States Infantry, which appointment being declined and a preference expressed for that of post surgeon, he was appointed by President Monroe to the post at Annapolis, Md., where he reported to Captain Read, commandant, July 23, 1818. While stationed at Ft. McHenry, June 17, 1825, he married Elizabeth Ward, daughter of Joshua and Sarah (Veazey) Ward, and niece of Gov. Thomas W. Veazey, of Maryland. The children born to them were named as follows: George F., James, Joseph Veazey, John Charles Groome, Mary C. Ward and Laura V. After resigning from the army in 1827, Dr. Joseph Wallace returned to Elkton, where he continued to reside until his death, September 12, 1872, at the age of eighty-two. His wife was born January 22, 1797, and died February 3, 1876, aged seventy-nine years.

The subject of this sketch was born in Cincinnati, Ohio, April 12, 1830, and was five years of age when his father returned to Elkton. He was educated in private schools here, and in October, 1850, began the study of medicine in the office of his uncle, Dr. James R. Ward, in Clearspring, Washington County, Md. In the fall of 1851 he entered the University of Maryland, in the city of Baltimore, where he attended two full courses of lectures, graduating March 8, 1853. Returning to Washington County, he engaged in practice with his former preceptor until March, 1854, when he came back to Cecil County and opened an office at Chesapeake City March 13. Here he has since engaged in general practice and in the management of the property interests he has gradually established. In politics he is a Democrat, but has never held office. At this writing he is a member of the board of examining surgeons for pensions at Elkton and a member of the Society of the Sons of the American Revolution. April 25, 1867, he married Cornelia C. Price, daughter of John R. and Mary A. (Lum) Price. Mary E. Wallace, their daughter, was born May 15, 1868, and November 5, 1891, was married to Rev. Frank Edwin Williams, pastor of Boundary Avenue Presbyterian Church, Baltimore; they have three children, Wallace, Frank Edwin and Fletcher Price. Veazey Ward Wallace, only son of the doctor, was born February 10, 1870, and died May 25, 1878, aged eight years, three months and fifteen days.

JOHN W. ANDREW, who has been identified with the interests of the people of Darlington since 1849, was born in 1820 in the eastern part of District No. 3, near Hall's Cross Roads, being the son of William H. and Nancy (McVay) Andrew, also natives of Harford County. On the maternal side he is of direct Irish descent, his grandfather, John McVay, having been a native of the Emerald Isle. For generations his paternal ancestors have been identified with the history of Maryland, and particularly with the agricultural interests of Baltimore and Harford Counties. His grandfather, Abram, spent his life near Aberdeen, and his great-grandfather, Abram Andrew, lived near Baltimore. In early years William H. Andrew followed the cooper's trade, but later he returned to the place where he was born and there he engaged in farming until he passed from earth, in 1877, at the age of eighty-nine. His wife died at the age of sixty-eight. They were the parents of eight children, but only two are living, John W. and Benjamin F., the latter a resident of Barton, Allegany County, Md.

At the family home near Aberdeen the subject of this sketch was reared and his education was obtained in the neighboring common schools. At the age of sixteen he went to Perryman and learned the blacksmith's trade under Joseph E. Taylor, following this occupation for thirty-five years afterward, the most of the time in Darlington. After coming here in 1849, he was for seven years in partnership with Samuel Harper, but at the expiration of that time they divided the business and each carried on his own shop under the same roof. In 1865, after years of hard work at the trade, Mr. Andrew engaged in farming near the village, being connected with Samuel H.

Mathews for eight years, and later, in 1875, he retired from active work, since which time he has lived quietly in the village, enjoying the comforts made possible by years of continuous application.

In politics a Democrat, Mr. Andrew for some years officiated as magistrate for the district and also held the position of road supervisor, filling both in a manner satisfactory to all. Fraternally he is connected with Mt. Pisgah Lodge of Odd Fellows, and in religious belief he is a member of the Methodist Episcopal Church, in which he has held office as steward and class leader. His marriage, which occurred in 1843, united him with Miss Mary E. Keene, member of an old family of Harford County, and daughter of Quila Keene. They became the parents of eight children, namely: Georgia K., wife of Rev. W. E. Miller; Hannah E., who married P. F. Forwood; William H., deceased at the age of thirty-five; Quila; Mary, deceased; Rev. J. Robert, of Middletown, Va.; Joseph F., who resides near Darlington; and Charles A., who lives at Burkleyville.

HENRY E. SELFE. Known to be a man of undoubted integrity, Mr. Selfe is regarded by his friends and neighbors in the village of Darlington as one of their most substantial and industrious citizens. While perhaps others are better fixed financially or have become more prominent in politics and public affairs, yet when we take into consideration the fact that he started without capital, that he had obstacles to overcome and that he is still but a young man, the success he has so far achieved is certainly very commendable.

Unlike many of the residents of Maryland, whose ancestors were identified with the early history of this state, Mr. Selfe is a member of a family established in this country in comparatively recent years. His parents, James and Catherine (Moon) Selfe, were born in Chilcompton, England, and came to America in 1855, settling in Havre de Grace. The father, who was a ma-

JAMES GIFFORD.

chinist by trade, was for ten years employed as engineer on the Philadelphia, Wilmington & Baltimore Railroad, but died at the early age of thirty-two, January 6, 1866. His wife passed away January 6, 1897, exactly thirty-one years after his demise. Two of their children are now living, our subject's brother being William B., the subject of a sketch presented on another page.

Born in Havre de Grace in 1861, Henry E. Selfe remained in that place, attending the public schools, until 1879, when he came to Darlington, his present place of residence. Here he learned the blacksmith's trade, after which he worked for some time in the employ of others; but in 1892 he opened a blacksmith and repair shop and this he has since conducted, in addition to which, since 1896, he has been proprietor of a general mercantile store. Taking considerable interest in local politics, he is a firm Democrat, but does not desire public office. He has held the various offices in Deer Creek Lodge of Odd Fellows. In religious belief he is connected with the Episcopal Church, and is a vestryman at this writing. His marriage, in 1887, united him with Sadie Burton, by whom he is the father of three children, Edith, Walter and James.

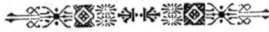

JAMES GIFFORD. The present high standing of District No. 9 among the agricultural regions of Cecil County may be attributed to the patient, well-directed efforts of the men who have for years conducted general farming pursuits here. As a representative of this class mention should be made of James Gifford, a successful farmer residing on the Stony Lane Road. Since establishing his home on his present place in 1865, he has witnessed the advancement of the district and contributed to its material prosperity, and while advancing his personal interests he has also promoted the welfare of his neighbors. His property, formerly known as the England farm, is not large, consisting of seventy-two and one-half acres, but it is well improved and produces perhaps as much as many farms that are larger.

The Gifford family is of English origin. The father of our subject, James, was a son of Joseph Gifford, both natives of England. In youth he learned the trade of a blacksmith, but did not follow the occupation long. Coming to the United States when young, he first settled in Philadelphia County, but afterward removed to Bucks County, Pa., where he became the owner of a large farm. He made a specialty of raising fine stock, and had the best grades of horses, hogs and sheep upon his place. His energy may be judged from the fact that he started out in life empty-handed, but became the possessor of a valuable property. He was a supporter of the principles of the Republican party. The farm in Bucks County continued to be his home until about 1856, when he sold it and removed to Cecil County, Md., where he became the possessor of three farms. He died near Principio, this county, in 1882, in his eighty-fourth year.

Before leaving England he married Ruth Edmonds, a native of that country. Ten children were born of their union and six of these are now living, namely: Samuel, whose home is in District No. 9, Cecil County; Sarah, wife of Joseph Cook, of Iowa; Wesley, of District No. 5, Cecil County; James, Jr.; George, residing in District No. 7, Cecil County; and Ellen E., the widow of Thomas Gillispie, now residing in Zion, this county.

In Bucks County, Pa., James Gifford, Jr., was born November 3, 1832. In boyhood he attended the neighboring district schools, his education being completed at the age of nineteen years. He remained on the home farm until twenty-five years of age, and at that time was united in marriage with Rhoda A. Scarborough, daughter of Sutton Scarborough, of District No. 9, Cecil County. After his marriage he was a resident of District No. 7 for six years, engaged there in farming and stock dealing. In 1865 he bought the Joseph England farm, one of the oldest places in District No. 9, and here he has since carried on agricultural pursuits. He and his family attend the Zion Presbyterian Church and are interested in all its works. Of his five children three are now living, namely: Joseph, who is a business man of Philadelphia, but living in Cecil County; Harry M., who is interested in a printing concern in Philadelphia; and Gertrude, who is with her parents. As every public-spirited citizen should, Mr. Gifford takes an intelligent interest in local and national issues, and in matters political gives the weight of his influence, and his ballot, to the principles of the Republican party. He is a man of energy, not afraid to work, and his perseverance and good management have achieved for him a success that has numbered him among the substantial farmers of the district.

HON. WILLIAM S. BOWMAN is one of the honored pioneer farmers and surveyors of Harford County and one of the most prominent and influential citizens. His entire life has been passed in the county which is still his home, and from an early age he has been an important factor in its public affairs and business interests. The development and substantial improvement of the county have been largely advanced through his efforts and he is both widely and favorably known, having the warm regard of his extensive circle of friends.

Mr. Bowman was born at Hopewell Cross Roads, near his present home in District No. 2, December 17, 1822, and traces his ancestry back to Germany. His great-grandfather, Henry Bowman, was a native of that land, and when a young man came to America, taking up his residence at what is now Hopewell Cross Roads, among the pioneers in this section of the state. He aided in the primitive development of the county and assisted in the advancement of civilization. He became a member of the Methodist Protestant Church in 1769. This was then called the Bush Forest Church, afterward known as the Log Meeting House, and is now called Bush Chapel. He died at the advanced age of ninety-six years, at which time he was the oldest member of the church, having been identified with its congregation for sixty years. He was twice married and had a large family. By occupation he was a chair maker and followed that pursuit as a means of support.

The grandfather of our subject, Henry Bowman, was born near Hopewell Cross Roads, February 14, 1762, and spent his entire life in this district. He was a farmer and carpenter and in his business dealings met with a fair degree of success. His life was ever upright and honorable, in harmony with his professions as an attendant of the Methodist Episcopal Church. He passed away at the age of seventy-four years, and all who knew him mourned his loss. The parents of our subject were Henry and Priscilla (Keen) Bowman, both natives of District No. 2, Harford County. The father carried on agricultural pursuits and also conducted a cooper shop at Hopewell Cross Roads for many years. In 1836 he removed to Ohio, but after two years returned to his native county and never again left the old neighborhood. He purchased the farm on which our subject now resides, and by the careful conduct of his business secured a comfortable competence. By his ballot he supported the men and measures of the Democracy, but was not active in political affairs. Throughout his life he held membership in the Methodist Episcopal Church, and did all in his power to advance its interests. He was ever faithful to his duties of citizenship, and during the War of 1812 earnestly desired to enter the service, but on account of his youth his parents refused to allow him to join the army. He died in his seventy-fifth year. His wife, who was born January 9, 1803, died in 1896. She ably supplemented her husband in his church work, and her many excellencies of character won her the love of all.

In the family of this worthy couple were twelve children: William S.; Rachel, deceased wife of James B. Gallion; Henry C., a farmer of Harford County; Mary Ann, who died in infancy; Eliza, deceased wife of George Gray; Priscilla, deceased wife of William Bailey; George W., who died at the age of thirty years; Rebecca J., widow of

John Bowman; James H., who lives in Virginia; John B. and David Thomas, both deceased; and Sophia Ann, wife of John Gorrell.

Mr. Bowman, whose name introduces this review, remained at home with his parents until about twenty-three years of age, when he was married and removed to the farm which he now owns. It was given him by his father, and in connection with the cultivation of his land he also conducted a cooper and cabinet shop until 1853. He then accepted the position of assistant civil engineer for the Baltimore & Ohio Railroad Company, laying out that road for two hundred miles and locating the divisions. For three years he remained in that service, and in 1856 resumed the operation of his farm. In 1860 he was elected county surveyor, and served in that capacity for ten years, discharging his duties with marked fidelity and ability. He then refused longer to hold the office, but since that time he has been prevailed upon to accept the office on three different occasions. No higher testimonial of his faithful service can be given than the fact that he has so often been called to the office. He still follows surveying to a limited extent, and is now the oldest surveyor in the county.

On the 27th of June, 1846, Mr. Bowman was united in marriage to Miss Mary Bailey, a native of District No. 2, Harford County, who traveled life's journey with him for forty-eight years and was to him ever a faithful companion and helpmeet. She died March 1, 1894, and many friends beside her immediate family mourned her loss. Mr. and Mrs. Bowman had seven children: John H., a carpenter of District No. 2; George W., who also follows the same pursuit here; James L., who died in middle life, leaving a family of seven children; William S., a farmer of Harford County; Rebecca, who died in infancy; Mary Emma, wife of George L. Mitchell; and Charles C., a farmer of District No. 2.

Mr. Bowman now resides upon his farm of fifty acres. His life has been well spent, benefiting not only himself, but also the community with which he has been connected. In 1888 he was elected to the state legislature, where he served on the committee on the Chesapeake Bay and its tributaries and on the road committee. His political support has ever been given to the Democratic party, and he is recognized as one of the leaders of the Democracy in this section of the state. He holds membership in the American Mechanics Lodge, and in Mt. Ararat Lodge, F. &. A. M., of Bel Air.

JOSEPH T. REED. The record of the life of Mr. Reed may be read with profit, for it illustrates the power of self-help and untiring perseverance. While in many respects his career has been uneventful, unmarked by stirring events, yet it has been very useful to others and successful as regards himself. Though he has met with his share of reverses in business, he has nevertheless attained a position of prominence in his locality. In addition to the management of the mercantile business in which he succeeded his father, he has for thirty years or more held the office of postmaster at Bay View, and in that way has made the acquaintance of almost every resident of the village and surrounding country. His long tenure of the office proves him to be a man of ability, with the accommodating disposition that wins and retains friends.

A native of Cecil County, Mr. Reed was born at Mechanics Valley, District No. 3, February 19, 1821. His father, William, who was born in the same district, of Irish descent, followed the occupation of a farmer all through his active life, and also took a lively interest in public affairs, being a supporter of old-line Whig principles, and for some years was the incumbent of the office of road supervisor. In religious belief he was identified with the Methodist Protestant Church. He continued to reside in this county until his death, which occurred in 1865. His wife bore the maiden name of Amy McVey, and was a member of a Welsh family long resident in this portion of Maryland. She died in 1833, when still a young woman. The four surviving children born of this union are named as follows:

Joseph T.; Benjamin M., whose home is in District No. 5; Martha, widow of John T. Slicer, of Calvert, Md.; and William, a resident of District No. 5.

About two months of each year when he was a boy, our subject had an opportunity to attend school, but the remainder of his time he was employed on the farm. He continued as a tiller of the soil until 1856. At that time his father, who had conducted a store at Bay View with a partner, purchased his partner's interest and took his son into the business, with which the latter has since been connected. Besides the store, he owns considerable property in the county and is in fair circumstances financially. In early life he affiliated with the Whigs, and when that party gave way to the rising organization of Republicans, he joined the ranks of the new party and has since voted for its men and measures, though never seeking its emoluments for himself. He is a member of the Methodist Protestant Church, in which he has been treasurer and trustee for years. In former years he was identified with the Independent Order of Odd Fellows, but does not now retain his membership in the local lodge. In 1849 he was united in marriage to Miss I. A. Russell, daughter of James Russell, whose grandfather was from Ireland, and her grandmother a native of England. Six children were born of the union, of whom three daughters and one son are living, namely: Charlotte, wife of Jesse Taylor Jennings, who lives near his father-in-law; Russell James, who is manager of the store; Pocahontas, who is with her parents; and Ruth R., now in New York City.

HENRY HESS, for many years a resident of Cecil County, and a successful farmer of District No. 4, has been identified with the progress of his community during the entire period of his residence here. The farm which he owns and upon which he engages in general agricultural pursuits, consists of one hundred and twenty-one acres, and under his energetic efforts has been brought to a high state of cultivation. This place has been his home since 1861. In addition to farming he has been interested in the hotel business, and as an accommodating landlord has become well known to people who travel through this section of the county.

The Hess family came to this country from Germany. Our subject's father, Christian, was a son of Christian, Sr., and was born in Lancaster County, Pa., where he spent his entire life, being the owner of a farm and a grist, saw and plaster mill, also engaging in the manufacture of woolen goods. He was the largest mill owner in his part of the county, and did much to develop the industry. A prominent man in public life, he was chosen by his fellow-citizens to serve in the office of county commissioner, and also held other positions of trust. Politically he was a stanch Whig. He married Elizabeth Roop, and they became the parents of nine children, but only three are now living. They are: Christian, whose home is in Ohio; Henry, of this sketch; and Moses, a resident of Perry County, Pa. His death occurred in 1857, when he was seventy years of age.

At the home of his parents, in Lancaster County, Pa., the subject of this sketch was born in 1819, and in the neighboring schools his education was obtained. At the age of seventeen he left school, and thenceforward gave his attention to obtaining a livelihood. For four years he was connected with his father as an assistant in the carding of wool. He then became interested in the cattle business and was employed as a drover for some years, driving cattle from the west to New York. After four years he settled at Intercourse, Lancaster County, where for a similar period he was proprietor of the Cross Keys Hotel. Selling out there in 1855, he went to Baltimore County, Md., and had charge of a hotel for a year. In 1857 he came to District No. 4, where he at once began farming, and also for four years was proprietor of the Fox Chase Hotel. Moving to Fair Hill in 1861, he kept the hotel and engaged in the cultivation of his farm. Politically a Democrat, he was for two years supervisor from this district upon the county board, and for a similar period held the position of county commissioner. At this writing he is a director of the Farmers' Mutual Fire Insurance Company of this county.

The marriage of Mr. Hess, which was solemnized in 1849, united him with Elizabeth N. Clemson, of Lancaster County, Pa. Five children were born to their union, named as follows: Hiester, an attorney of Elkton; Henry C., of this place; George E. L., at home; Maria Elizabeth, who married A. T. McCrery, and is now deceased; and Louisa Frances, wife of Benjamin D. Bowen. The family attend the Episcopal Church, of which Mrs. Hess is a member. Not only has Mr. Hess carried on his private affairs with energy, but he has manifested an almost equal amount of zeal for the public welfare. He may be counted upon to bear a part in every worthy enterprise which is promulgated in the neighborhood. A man of energy, not afraid of work, his good management and perseverance have brought him a success that has numbered him among the substantial business men and farmers of the community.

RUFUS LOW is one of the extensive land owners of Harford County, his possessions aggregating more than six hundred acres. To a student of human nature there is nothing of greater interest than to examine into the life of a self-made man and analyze the principles by which he has been governed, the methods he has pursued, to know what means he has employed for advancement and to study the plans which have given him prominence. In the history of Mr. Low there is much food for thought, and if one so desires he may profit by the obvious lessons therein contained, for his career demonstrates the possibilities that are open to the ambitious young men of America.

Mr. Low resides in District No. 4, of which he is a native son. He was born December 3, 1826, one of the ten children of Jeremiah and Rebecca (Fifer) Low, who were natives of Pennsylvania. The ancestry of the family can be traced back to Hulo Low, the great-grandfather, who was a native of England, and with his five brothers came to America, taking up his residence in the colony of Pennsylvania, in what is now York County. He became very wealthy and was at one time owner of more than one thousand acres of good land. The grandfather, John Low, was also a native of Pennsylvania, and was a farmer by occupation. Jeremiah Low, the father, gave his attention to agricultural pursuits and during the War of 1812 served his country as a commissioned officer. His children were Rezin, deceased; Harriett; Grace; Martin; Ennis; Rufus; Obediah; Amon and Festus, both deceased; and Laban.

On the family homestead Rufus Low spent his boyhood days. He obtained a good common-school education and in early life learned the carpenter's trade, which he followed for fifteen years. He did a good business along that line and as his financial resources increased he invested in land, to which he has added from time to time until he is now the owner of more than six hundred acres, the greater part of which is under a high state of cultivation. Good buildings and well-kept fences also add to the value and attractive appearance of the place, which is accounted one of the fine farms of Harford County.

When thirty-three years of age Mr. Low was united in marriage to Miss Rachel A. Marstillar, a native of Pennsylvania. Her grandfather was one of the heroes of the Revolution and was of German lineage, the family having been founded on American soil in the days of colonial history. Mr. and Mrs. Low are the parents of the following children: Benjamin F., Rebecca M., Henry M., John F., David and Jeremiah L. (twins), Simon G. and Lizzie M.

Mr. Low has been active in public affairs and is one of the leaders of the Republican party, in the principles of which he strongly believes. He served as tax collector of District No. 4 for two years, and in 1891 was the candidate of his party for the legislature, but was defeated by a small majority. His duties of citizenship are ever faithfully and promptly performed and he is true to every trust reposed in him. His wife is a member of the Methodist Episcopal Church, but the Low family were connected with the Society of Friends. Honesty of purpose permeates his every act and straightforward dealing characterizes his business career. His worth as a man and a citizen is widely recognized and he well deserves representation in this volume.

ARCHIBALD WILSON represents the third generation of the Wilson family that has resided in District No. 5, Harford County. His grandfather, whose name was the same as his own, came to America from his native land of Scotland and settled here, buying a farm upon which he engaged successfully in agricultural pursuits. The family characteristic of longevity was apparent in his own life. The father of our subject, James Wilson, was born on the home farm, where his subsequent years were busily passed and where his death occurred in 1870. During the War of 1812 he enlisted in the American army and assisted in defending the property and lives of the citizens of Maryland. By his marriage to Letitia J. Wilson, of this county, he had six children, namely: William H., Archibald, Margaret J., Cassandra, James (deceased) and Samuel.

Trained to a knowledge of farm work, our subject has always continued in this occupation and of it he has made a success. In the division of the estate he inherited a portion of the property, which was of much benefit to him financially; but even without this help there is no doubt but that he would have succeeded, for he has many of the qualities that are necessary for success, and these, coupled with the industry and economy of his faithful wife, made prosperity a sure result. At the age of twenty-seven he married Hannah J. Gladden, who was born in this county, being a sister of James W. Gladden, mentioned on another page. To the union seven children were born, but one died in infancy, and another, Harry S., in boyhood. The survivors are James J., William F., Edward A., Cyrus H. and Anna L., all of whom are married but Cyrus and all are well-to-do.

Born June 2, 1830, Mr. Wilson is not yet an old man, and his family being a long-lived one, he may reasonably hope to enjoy many more years of happiness on earth. Among the people of the district where his entire life has been passed he is well known and highly esteemed. On account of his intelligence, and his firm allegiance to Democratic principles, he has been a man of some prominence in the politics of the township. In 1872 he was elected county commissioner, which office he filled for two years. For eight years he was register of voters and for more than twenty years a member of the county executive committee. In 1857 he was made a Mason and he has since been identified with the order, his membership being in Mt. Ararat Lodge No. 44, at Bel Air. His wife is connected with the Presbyterian Church, with the work of which he is in sympathy, though not a member of the denomination.

HON. JOSEPH H. STEELE. To secure success in business, a man must be energetic, persevering, capable and judicious; with these characteristics, he need have no fear of failure. It is largely due to these qualities, which he possesses in a large degree, that Mr. Steele owes the prosperity that has attended his efforts in business. He is recognized as one of the stirring and progressive men of Chesapeake City, where he owns and conducts a grain, coal, lime and phosphate business. His success is especially worthy of commendation when we consider the fact that he had few educational advantages, his parents were poor, and the opportunities which fell to the lot of most boys did not come to him.

A record of the life of one so closely identified with the growth of Chesapeake City will be of interest to the people of this locality. A lifelong resident of this village, Mr. Steele was born here December 13, 1836, the son of George A. and Rebecca R. (Sharp) Steele, natives respectively of Districts No. 9 and 5, Cecil County. His father spent the years of youth upon a farm, but in early manhood settled in Chesapeake City, where he worked at the carpenter's trade for a number of years. In his political views he was a pronounced Democrat. He remained in this village until his death, which occurred at seventy-six years of age. He was a son of Joseph Steele, a native of Cecil County, a soldier in the American army during the War of 1812, and throughout active life engaged in farming pursuits, remaining a resident of Cecil County until his death, at the age of about ninety years. Our subject's mother attained the age of ninety-three; she had but two children, Joseph H. and Caroline, Mrs. William Young, deceased.

Amid the surroundings familiar to him from earliest childhood, the subject of this article passed the years of youth. At the age of fourteen he entered the office of the late George W. Bennett as a clerk, and so efficient was he in the discharge of duties that he finally became associated with Mr. Bennett as a partner in the lumber and grain business. Upon the death of the senior member of the firm in 1869, Mr. Steele succeeded to the entire management of the grain, coal, lime and phosphate business, which he has since successfully conducted. While his time and attention have been closely given to the oversight of his business interests, his is not a narrow mind, but he is capable of superintending various interests at the same time. With a true insight into the importance of the insurance business, he early became identified with it, and for a number of years has represented the Mutual Fire Insurance Company of Cecil County in his native place.

Nothing that has tended to the benefit of the village and county has been refused Mr. Steele's support, both in time and money, and to his efforts much of the advancement of local industries is due. In his political belief he is firm in his allegiance to the principles of the Democratic party, which he upholds by his influence and his vote. Honoring the party, he has in turn been honored by it. Under the administration of President Johnson he was appointed postmaster of Chesapeake City, in which position he sustained his reputation as a careful and reliable business man. During the years 1871 and 1872 he served as collector of state and county taxes for the second division of this county. In 1879 a high honor was tendered him in his election, upon the Democratic ticket, to the Maryland house of delegates, with the late Hon. Hiram McCullough and James M. Touchstone. While in the legislature he established an excellent record as a capable worker in the committee room and rendered service on the committee of ways and means, as well as on other committees equally important. His public life has been an active and honorable one, such as to reflect credit upon his citizenship and establish his reputation as a man of ability. In religious belief he is an Episcopalian and holds the position of vestryman in the church, to the building and support of which he has been a liberal contributor.

January 25, 1871, Mr. Steele was united in marriage with Caradora, daughter of John W. and Hannah L. (Bayard) Bouchelle, and like her husband an active member of the Episcopal Church. They are the parents of five children, namely: Bennett, who is associated with his father in business; Stanley, a practicing dentist in Elkton, Md.; J. Groome, Harold and Dora B. Mr. Bouchelle, the father of Mrs. Steele, was born at Bohemia Manor in 1807 and is still living, quite active and strong for one so advanced in years. Farming has been his life-work and in it he has been successful, accumulating a competency. For sixty-five years or more he has resided on the same farm, situated in District No. 2. Politically he has been a Democrat ever since he was old enough to have opinions for himself, and upon the Democratic ticket he was, in 1842, elected to the state legislature. He was a son of Peter and Alice (Cannon) Bouchelle, and Peter Bouchelle in turn was the son of Thomas, who was a son of Peter, whose father, Lege de Bouchelle, established the family in America, settling on Bohemia Manor, Cecil County, in 1640. As the name indicates, the family is of French origin, and it is said that the ancestors were very prominent in that country. The present generation is the seventh that has been identified with the history of Cecil County. The mother of Mrs. Steele was born on Bohemia Manor and died there at the age of seventy-seven years. She had fifteen children, and of that large family nine attained years of maturity.

HON. THOMAS WARD VEAZEY, governor of Maryland 1835-38. Cecil County numbered among her favorite sons one who was honored in halls of legislature and councils of state, one whose public service extended through a period most eventful in our country's history, and one upon whom was bestowed the highest office within the gift of the people in Maryland. The records of the official life of Governor Veazey are to be found in the archives of the state and in its historical literature, but the influence of his gifted mind, in giving direction to events and in shaping the destiny of the commonwealth, is not to be measured by official records or the writings of the historian; it is as measureless as the soul and as enduring as time.

While the history of the remote representatives of the Veazey family is shrouded in obscurity, it is thought that the first of the name in America came from England about 1687. In 1749 Col. John Veazey, an officer in the militia of Maryland, secured a patent from Frederick Lord Baltimore for a large tract of land in District No. 1, Cecil County. Upon this place he settled and here he spent his remaining years. The property has since been occupied by succeeding generations and is now owned by the two daughters of Governor Veazey. Col. John Veazey, Jr., and his son Edward, who was the father of our subject, were born in District No. 1, and followed farm pursuits throughout their entire lives. With few exceptions, the members of the family have been identified with the Protestant Episcopal Church.

Upon the old Cecil County homestead Thomas Ward Veazey was born January 31, 1774. When he was an infant, war between the colonists and England was declared and the succeeding years were filled with hardships and bloodshed, all of which doubtless had its effect upon him in the impressionable years of youth. Surrounded by influences that would tend to make him intensely patriotic, he grew to manhood. His parents being well-to-do were able to give him every educational advantage the country afforded and of every opportunity he availed himself to the utmost, acquiring an excellent education in Washington College, at Chestertown, Kent County, from which he graduated. At an early age he became closely identified with public affairs and associated with men of prominence throughout the state. He was chosen a presidential elector in 1809 and 1813, and voted for James Madison. There had been implanted in his nature in boyhood a love of country and devotion to its welfare, hence the War of 1812 found him enthusiastically supporting the American cause, and during that conflict he served as a colonel of state militia. When peace was declared he returned to civic pursuits. He was soon called to serve his fellow-citizens in an official capacity, being chosen to represent the district as a member of the legislature, and later he became a member of the state senate. The fidelity to the interests of the people which he displayed in every position led to his selection as the incumbent of the highest office within the gift of the state. In 1835 he took his seat as governor of the state, and during the three years that followed represented the interests of the people with the utmost faithfulness and with the high order of ability ever characteristic of his actions and decisions. When he retired from office in 1838 he carried with him to private life the best wishes of all, for he had won the respect of even his political opponents by his wise administration. Like others of his name, he was an Episcopalian in religious belief, his membership being in St. Stephen's Church.

From whatever point of view we may study the life of Governor Veazey he was a man to be admired. Whether we view him as a private cit-

JOHN H. HESSEY.

izen, true in even the smallest detail, kind to all, generous to the needy; as a soldier, gallantly defending the old village of Fredericktown when it was assaulted by the British, May 4, 1812; or as the chief executive of the state, maintaining a watchful oversight of all public affairs,—we recognize in him the qualities that bring a man influence, power and success. After sixty-eight useful and honorable years, he passed away, July 1, 1842.

JOHN H. HESSEY. Though not a native of Maryland, Mr. Hessey has spent his entire life here, with the exception of the first year. He resides in District No. 1, Cecil County, where he owns a valuable farm of two hundred and ninety-seven acres. By practical experience he has found that the soil of this locality is well adapted to the raising of fruits, and, believing the business to be profitable, he turned his attention to it a number of years ago. As a result of his efforts he now has on his place over thirty-five hundred bearing pear trees and smaller numbers of other fruit trees, and has met with flattering success in this department of agriculture. Success has not been won easily, but through constant effort and exercise of sound common sense in the management of affairs. He can bear testimony to the fact that it is not luck, but hard work, that brings prosperity.

In Ohio, June 25, 1819, John H. Hessey was born to the union of Henry and Ann (Sutton) Hessey, natives of Delaware. The family of which he is a member originated in France, but has been represented in this country many years. His father was a soldier in the War of 1812, and a farmer by occupation, but died when in his prime. Of his five children, William S., George W., John H., Mary A. and Ellen H., only our subject and Ellen H. survive. The former was a year old when brought to Maryland by his parents in 1820, and here he was educated in the public schools. When he was ten years of age his father died, and afterward he and his brother George remained with their mother until her death. At the age of twenty-seven he married Laura E. Morgan, who was born in District No. 1, Cecil County. They became the parents of seven children, but four died in infancy. The others are Frank H., Ellen M. and Dr. John H., the latter of whom is a practicing physician of Kent County, Md.

Like all public-spirited citizens Mr. Hessey keeps himself posted concerning public affairs. He is a decided Democrat in his opinions and always votes that ticket. At one time he was tax collector and also constable. He is not connected with any denomination, but is ready to assist religious enterprises, and inclines toward the Methodist Episcopal Church, of which his wife is an active member.

JOHN LIGHT. The true patriot is one who, from love of country, does, or tries to do, all that appears necessary to promote her honor, prosperity and peace, and no one has proven himself more deserving of public gratitude than has the farmer who has redeemed this country from the wilderness and made it to blossom and bear fruit so abundantly. Not only is John Light a thorough practical and progressive farmer, but he is also descended from one of those grand old patriots who fought for the freedom of American colonies during the Revolution. This patriot was Adam Light, great-grandfather of the subject of this sketch, a German by descent. John Light was named in honor of his sire, whose native place was Little York, Pa., in the vicinity of which he was first engaged in farming. However, the last thirty-five years of his life were spent in Baltimore County, Md., where he kept a hostelry. During his early manhood he was engaged in teaching for some time, in fact, his entire life was one of activity, and every opportunity which presented itself was improved to the utmost. The men and measures of the Democratic party always received his earnest support, and in his church relations he was a Presbyterian.

Mary Hartman, daughter of John Hartman, of York, Pa., became his wife, and as years passed nine children were born to them, only four of whom survive at the present writing: John, William, Samuel and Thomas, the last three being residents of Baltimore County. The father's death occurred in 1862, preceded many years by that of his wife. Upon reaching the required age, John Light was placed in the public schools of York, Pa., but about 1857 was taken by his father to Baltimore, where, after a time, his school days closed. When he had reached the age of fifteen years he began learning the miller's trade, and for the following six years his time was devoted to this occupation. The three subsequent years were spent in railroading, and he then, in 1850, settled down on his present farm of one hundred and sixty-three acres near Monkton, Baltimore County, and for five years devoted his attention to its cultivation. The following six years were spent in Edgewood, then for six more years he resided on the Price farm near Clayton. At the end of that time he rented a farm on Long Bar, where his home continued to be for sixteen years, at the end of which time he decided to come to Harford County.

The date of his arrival in this section was 1885, in which year he purchased the farm on which he is now living, consisting of four hundred acres. In connection with his farm, which is admirably managed, he conducts a canning establishment and puts up about five thousand cases each summer. In every detail of his work he has shown good judgment and a knowledge of his business which is most thorough, and his comfortable home is but the just reward of his industry. A member of the Presbyterian Church and a Democrat politically, his work for both has been steadfast and earnest, and in his work in the former he has been warmly seconded by his worthy wife. She was formerly Miss Sophia Kroh, a daughter of Philip Kroh, of Harford County, and her marriage with Mr. Light occurred December 21, 1847. To them an old-fashioned family of eleven children was born, the following of whom survive: John, of Abingdon; James, also of that place; George; Joseph; Nicholas; Robert; Eliza, wife of Frank Kroh, of Joppa; and Mary, wife of C. C. Smith, of Joppa.

Mr. Light has always labored for the best interests of the sections in which he has made his home and is a worthy type of the true American citizen, for he is loyal, public-spirited and charitable, and his influence is always on the side of justice and right.

WILLIAM H. REASIN, Jr. The life of Mr. Reasin has been a busy one, and from an early age he has been familiar with telegraphy. His experience has been such as to prove that he possesses energy, wise judgment and perseverance, and these qualities have brought him the confidence of the company in whose employ he has been for many years. His character and business equipment have made him an acquisition to the citizenship of Aberdeen, and he stands well among the people here. During the years in which he has held the position of agent for the Baltimore & Ohio Railroad at this point, he has become known, not only to railroad men, but to the traveling public and the residents of this portion of the state.

In the city of Baltimore the subject of this sketch was born March 27, 1853, to the union of William H. and Hannah E. (Cole) Reasin, both of whom were born near Aberdeen, in Harford County. His father was reared on a farm here, but when a youth went to Baltimore, where he studied architecture, and as he possessed a natural taste for the occupation, and was a thorough student, he became in time one of the leading architects of Baltimore, where he made his home many years. After removing his residence to Havre de Grace, he still retained his office in Baltimore. He was one of the most prominent architects of his time in the state. In politics, also, he was active and influential, and was a decided Democrat in his views. Among his principal characteristics was that of frankness. He was a plain, outspoken man, firm in his convictions and never hesitating to express them, no matter what the sentiments of others might be. He died at the age of fifty-six years. His father, Dooley Reasin, was a planter in Maryland. The mother of our subject, who now makes her home with him, had four children, one of whom died in infancy. The others are William H., Gertrude and Jennie. William H. was a child of about eight years when his parents removed to a farm in Harford County, and there he remained until twenty-one years of age, meantime attending the common schools and Eaton and Burnett's Commercial College. When a young man he learned telegraphy, and his first employment in that capacity was in the office of the Baltimore city water works as an operator. He remained in Baltimore until 1886, and since that time has been employed as agent for the Baltimore & Ohio Railroad at Aberdeen. Interested in politics as a stanch Democrat, he has, however, never taken an active part in such matters, but his unobtrusive and quiet disposition has led him to confine his attention to private business affairs. Fraternally he is connected with Harford Lodge No. 42, Order of the Golden Chain, in Aberdeen. In 1887 he married Miss Fannie Cole, of Harford County, who died January 17, 1897, leaving two children, Claude Nelson and Florence Aline.

HENRY H. BRADY. The fact that Chesapeake City is the terminus of the Chesapeake & Delaware Canal has been the means of securing to the place, as permanent residents, a number of men of ability, energy and excellent judgment. Such a one is the subject of this article, who came here in 1857, and during the forty years that have since elapsed has established a high reputation in business circles. At first, in partnership with his brothers, George F., William and Samuel, he had charge of the towing on the canal and has for several years been interested in the tug boats at this end of the canal, employing as many as seventy-five men and one hundred mules to do the towing. A change was made in the firm about 1887, when he and John T. Cheairs bought out the interests of his three brothers, and they have since conducted the business, Mr. Brady having charge of the work at this terminus of the canal, while his partner has charge at the other terminus, Delaware City, Del.

The parents of our subject, James and Margaret (McCrone) Brady, were born in Dublin, Ireland, where the former was engaged in the manufacture of linen and was fairly successful as a business man. Wishing to seek a home in the new world, in 1829 he crossed the Atlantic and settled near Wilmington, Del., purchasing a farm, to the cultivation of which his remaining years were devoted. He died about 1850, and his wife in 1866. Henry H. Brady was born in Newcastle County, Del., January 24, 1831, and received his education principally in New London, Chester County, Pa. After completing his studies he taught a district school for three years, then turned his attention to merchandising and opened a store at St. Georges, Newcastle County, Del., where he remained until 1857. From that place he removed to Chesapeake City, and with his brothers, George F., William and Samuel, at once began in the towing business. In addition to his private business affairs he has taken part in local public enterprises and has always been ready to contribute his share to public-spirited projects. For a time he held the position of commissioner for the county. At this writing he is a director and vice-president in the National Bank of Elkton. He and his family are active members of the Presbyterian Church, and he officiates as an elder.

March 27, 1861, occurred the marriage of Mr. Brady to Miss Rebecca, daughter of Joseph and Rebecca (Small) Cooper. She is a direct descendant of William and Margaret Cooper, who, in 1679, crossed the Atlantic and settled in what is now Camden, N. J. Her father, who was born in Bucks County, Pa., engaged in farming during the earlier part of his life, but afterward became a lumberman in Bristol, that county, and was following that business when he died, at fifty-four years of age. He married Rebecca Small, who was born in Burlington County, N. J., and died in Cecil County at the age of seventy-six. Mrs. Brady was born July 21, 1837, and under the careful training of her parents was prepared for a useful and honorable life. She is a notable housewife, busy and energetic, and is tireless in her devotion to husband and children. Her eldest daughter, Lucy Cooper Brady, is the wife of Charles H. Cook, proprietor of the Cook Pottery Company, of Trenton, N. J. Carrie, the younger daughter, married Henry M. McCullough, an attorney of Elkton, Cecil County. Henry H., Jr., graduated from Princeton with the class of 1895, and is now connected with the Roebling Manufacturing Company.

JOHN G. DOLLMAN. Though a native of another country, all but the first seven years in the life of Mr. Dollman have been spent in the United States. When he came to Darlington, his present place of business, he made his home in an old log house, but as business increased and prosperity crowned his efforts, he was enabled to surround himself with advantages more suited to his position in life. In 1894 he erected a block in the village, and the first floor of the building he utilizes for a store, while the upper floor is occupied as a lodge room for the Deer Creek Lodge, I. O. O. F. He has also built a new residence on the same foundation as the old one, but larger in dimensions and more modern in finish.

Born in Germany in 1847, the subject of this sketch is a son of John and Christina (Heim) Dollman, who emigrated to America about 1854 and settled in Pottsville, Pa., continuing to reside there for many years. In 1874 the father brought his family to Darlington and opened a tin shop, which he carried on for some time. Owing to ill-health he returned to his native land, where he revisited the scenes familiar to him in early childhood, and his sojourn there of two years proved pleasant and physically beneficial to him. Returning to Darlington, he remained here until his death in 1882. He and his wife were the parents of five children, namely: Christina, widow of Daniel F. Loudman; Mary, who is the wife of Frederick Clyne; John G., of this sketch; Charles, who went to the west and is now in Utah; and Hettie, deceased.

At the age of seven years, our subject was brought to America by his parents. He was educated in the common schools of Pennsylvania and spent the principal part of his youthful days on a farm. Shortly after his father came to Darlington, he joined him here, and under his supervision learned the trade of a tinsmith, in which occupation he has engaged since 1875. He is a hard-working, painstaking man, and deserves the commendation of all for his honest and upright life. Since 1872 he has been identified with the Deer Creek Lodge of Odd Fellows, in which he has passed through all the chairs, and of which he is an active member. In religion he follows the teachings of his parents and inclines toward the Lutheran faith. Through his unaided efforts he has acquired a modest competency, sufficient to provide his declining years with every comfort; he has the satisfaction of knowing that he is not indebted to anyone for the property he has acquired or for the success with which his efforts have been attended. In his views he is practical, looking at matters from a business point of view. Politically he adheres to the Democratic party.

DANIEL CALLAHAN has worked his way upward from an humble position to one of affluence, and the obstacles which he has met in his path have been overcome by determined purpose and unflagging perseverance. He is now successfully engaged in farming and in the canning business near Creswell. He was born near Gunpowder Neck, in District No. 1. Harford County, November 7, 1862, and is a son of Patrick and Ann (Ready) Callahan. His father was a native of the Emerald Isle, whence he crossed the Atlantic to America, believing he might better his financial condition in the new world, where superior advantages were afforded to those who sought to rise by their own efforts. He first located in Pennsylvania, but after a time took up his residence at the Ashland Furnace, in Baltimore County, Md., and subsequently purchased a tract of land near Creswell, in District No. 1, Harford County. Here he has since engaged in farming, and is actively superintending his farm, at the age of sixty-five. His mother is also living and has reached the advanced age of eighty-four. In politics he is a Democrat, and in religious belief is a Catholic. His wife is a native of Baltimore, and by her marriage she became the mother of seven children, as follows: Daniel, of this review; John, deceased; Joseph and David, who are assisting their father in the cultivation of the home farm; Timothy, who is studying medicine; and Mary and Ann, who complete the family.

Daniel Callahan was reared in the county of his birth, and acquired his elementary education in the school of Harford Furnace. Later he pursued his studies in Aberdeen, and at the age of seventeen years he began working for his father, assisting in the cultivation of the home farm until 1887, when he embarked in business on his own account. He purchased one hundred and sixty-five acres of land, known as the Roberts' place, and carries on general farming. However, he is making a specialty of the raising of vegetables for canning purposes, and each year prepares large quantities for the market in this way. This is one of the leading industries of Harford County, and Mr. Callahan's business is ably and successfully conducted.

On the 30th of January, 1889, was celebrated the marriage of our subject and Miss Daisy Kahoe, a daughter of Michael Kahoe, of Churchville. Five children grace their union: John, Frank, Helen, Ann and Mary. Mr. Callahan and his family hold membership in the Catholic Church. He is quite a prominent leader in local politics, and advocates the principles of Democracy. In his business undertakings he has prospered and throughout the community he is regarded as one of its most highly respected citizens.

DAVID EDWARDS THOMAS, for many years a distinguished and honored citizen of Harford County, was born in Baltimore, Md., on the 7th of February, 1825, a son of David Edwards Thomas, Sr., who settled there in early life and became a very successful lumber merchant. The grandparents, Seth and Prudence (Edwards) Thomas, were residents of Media, Pa.

Our subject was provided with excellent educational privileges, having been a student at Dickinson College, and on completing the course returned to Baltimore, where he entered the lumber business with his brother-in-law, Richard Price, forming the well-known firm of Thomas & Price. Tireless energy, keen perception, honesty of purpose, genius for devising and executing the right thing at the right time, joined to everyday common sense, guided by resistless will power, were his chief characteristics and brought to him remarkable success.

In 1865 Mr. Thomas was united in marriage to a daughter of Rev. John Davis, and a descendant of the old Webster family of Harford County. After his marriage he spent his summers at his large country place, Wayside, near Darlington, in Harford County, and in 1877, his health becoming impaired, he retired from business and made his permanent residence here. As far back as 1720 Wayside was the property of Michael Webster, a planter of Baltimore County, which at that time embraced all of what is now Harford County.

In politics Mr. Thomas was a stanch Democrat, and always identified himself prominently with the interests of the county. Being greatly opposed to the liquor traffic, he served as president of the County Temperance Alliance for some time, and was chiefly instrumental in securing the passage of the local option laws, which banished the licensed saloon from Harford County. He was a man of strict integrity and honor, was always willing to lend a helping hand to the poor and needy, gave liberally to the church and to all objects tending to promote the moral, intellectual or material welfare of the community, and was as fearless in defense of his convictions as he was large-hearted. After an active and useful career of sixty-five years, he passed away at his residence, Wayside, October 12, 1889, his death resulting from a paralytic stroke. His loss was deeply felt throughout the entire county, and particularly by the members of the church at Darlington, with which he was connected, as he had been the chief promoter of many of its improvements.

Webster Thomas, one of his sons, died a few months prior to the father's death. The members of the family still living are David Edwards, who resides with his mother at Wayside; Mrs. Edward M. Allen, Jr.; and his step daughter, Mrs. John H. Price. The family is one of prominence, holding a high position in social circles.

JOHN F. SIMPERS, of North East, justice of the peace, was born in this village February 7, 1860. The family of which he is a representative is among the oldest in Cecil County, some of its members having settled here from England about the time of Lord Baltimore's arrival. As a rule they have followed agricultural pursuits, though some have engaged in the mercantile business. The father of our subject, Johnson, was a son of John Simpers, both natives of District No. 5. He was born in 1793, and for years was one of the prominent and leading citizens of North East. At the time of the second war with England he was a member of a local militia, but being employed in the post-office as postmaster was unable to engage in active service. Politically he was first a Whig and later a Republican. In 1837-38 he represented his district in the legislature, for years held the position of postmaster, and was also a justice of the peace and county commissioner. A sincere Christian, he held membership in the Methodist Episcopal Church and was for years a trustee of the congregation. He attained the advanced age of ninety-four, passing away in 1887. Twice married, his first wife was Milicent Ford, by whom he had three children, but only one survives, Dr. C. T. Simpers, living near Aikin, Cecil County. His second wife was Rachael E. Whitaker, who was born in Cecil County, of Welsh descent, and a niece of George P. Whitaker, who for many years was prominent in the iron business here, and grand-niece of Oliver Evans, the great inventor. The two children born of this union are John F. and Edward E., both residents of District No. 5.

The rudiments of his education our subject obtained in local schools, after which, at the age of sixteen, he took a course of study in the Keystone boarding school in Philadelphia, Pa., remaining there for two terms. On his return to Cecil County he assisted in the management of the home farm. In 1885 he entered the postal mail service as a postal clerk, having received his appointment from the postmaster general, John A. J. Creswell. After about one year he returned to the farm. In 1890 he became baggage agent for the Pennsylvania Railroad at Dover, Del., but in a short time met with an accident, through the falling of a stone upon him, that compelled him to resign his place and seek other employment. Politically he is a firm champion of Republican principles, and has the greatest faith in the advancement of our country through the adoption of Republican principles. May 1, 1896, he was appointed by the governor to the position of justice of the peace, which he has since held. Fraternally he is connected with the Knights of Pythias and has been prelate in the order. His connections, religiously, are with the Methodist Episcopal Church. In 1885 he was united in marriage with Anne M. Ferguson, of North East, and they have four children, Johnson, J. Scott, Annie M. and Gertrude. As a citizen he is public-spirited. He deserves credit for his disinterested efforts in sustaining many enterprises of importance in his community and justly has the confidence of the people of North East.

WAKEMAN H. BEVARD bears a name that is deeply engraved on the history of the county, for his family is one of long and honorable identification with Harford. He now resides in District No. 1, but was born in District No. 5, in Dublin, on the 28th of July, 1826. His great-grandfather, Charles Bevard, came to America in colonial days, and when the oppression of Great Britain became too great to be longer meekly borne he took up arms in defense of the colonies, which Richard Lee said "are and of right ought to be free and independent states." He lived to be ninety-five years of age and his wife also reached the same age.

His son, James Bevard, the grandfather of our subject, engaged in merchandising at Bush, but afterward removed to District No. 5, where he purchased a farm and carried on agricultural pursuits. His son, George Bevard, was born in an old house in Bush which was long used as a tavern, and accompanied his father on his removal to District No. 5, locating on a farm which is still in possession of the family. He learned the cooper's trade and did an extensive business in that line. During the War of 1812 he aided in defense of the city of Baltimore. His political support was given the Democracy, and he was a man of considerable influence in his party, but would never consent to hold office. In religious belief he was a Presbyterian. He wedded Mary Wallace, a daughter of Randall Wallace, of District No. 5, who belonged to one of the prominent old families of Harford County. They had a family of ten children, but only three are now living: James, who resides in District No. 4; Wakeman H., of this review; and George, who lives on the old homestead. The parents have also passed away.

Mr. Bevard, whose name begins this sketch, acquired his education in the schools near his home, and lived on the farm until twenty-eight years of age, when he was married and removed to the Bel Air District. Seventeen years were there passed, during which he industriously devoted his energies to the cultivation of his land. In May, 1873, he purchased the Willow Valley farm of one hundred and forty-five acres, and has since made it his home. He carries on general farming and his well-tilled fields are an evidence of his thrift and enterprise. He has never found time nor inclination to seek political preferment, but by his ballot upholds the principles of Democracy. His church relationship is with the Methodist denomination.

In 1864 was celebrated the marriage of Mr. Bevard and Miss E. M. Strett, a daughter of Samuel Strett, of District No. 4, Harford County. Seven children have been born of this union. Samuel is associated in business with his father; Harry is living in Carroll County, Md.; Mary is the wife of Ed C. Kirkwood, of District No. 4; Howard W. is also living in District No. 4; Louisa is the wife of Rev. Charles H. Day, a minister of the Methodist Protestant Church in New York; Alethia is the wife of Rev. G. A. Getty, a Lutheran minister of Baltimore; and Marion completes the family.

THE BARROLL FAMILY. Cecil County owes much to its early settlers, those who established their homes within its borders at an early period and thenceforward contributed to its development and progress. Some came hither from the north, bringing with them the Puritan firmness and conviction of principle; a few came from Germany and other countries of continental Europe, but, perhaps, the largest number came from England, bringing with them the determination, force of will and energy for which that nation is noted. In the list of these prominent pioneers we should not omit the name of Rev. William Barroll, who was born in England, the son of Sir Knight Barroll, and settled in America in the early colonial days. As a minister of the Gospel he accomplished a great amount of good. He became rector of St. Stephen's Protestant Episcopal Church at Sassafras Neck, in charge of which he remained for many years. During his long period of service he endeared himself to all the people of the parish, and his earnest efforts in Christian work were followed with excellent results. It is said of him that he was a man of superior intellect and culture, a scholarly expounder of Bible truths and a fluent and eloquent speaker.

The only son of this pioneer preacher was William Barroll, who settled in Chestertown, Md., and became a prominent attorney. Twice married, he had two sons, James E. and William, but of the latter we have no reliable information. James E. was born in Easton, Talbot County, afterwards removing to Chestertown, and was a graduate of Yale College and a lawyer of more than local note, practicing his profession for many years in Chestertown, but in 1854 removing to Baltimore, where he was an influential member of the bar until 1860. Then having acquired an ample fortune, he retired to his country home, Holly Hall, in the suburbs of Elkton, where the remainder of his life was quietly passed. Not only was he well informed in the theory and practice of law, and familiar with legal technicalities, but he also possessed extensive information of a historical nature, and was a man of cultured literary tastes. He died in 1875, at the age of eighty-seven, having been born in 1788. His wife, Henrietta J. Bedford Hackett, was a daughter of Major Hackett, of Queen Anne County, Md., and his wife was a lineal descendant of Gunning Bedford, of Delaware, one of the framers of the Constitution of the United States, but whose name, owing to his illness at the time, does not appear on the Declaration of Independence. She died in March, 1877, fifteen months after her husband had passed away.

Nine children were born to the union of James E. and Henrietta Barroll, but only three are now living. Henrietta J. married Charles Medcalf, a commission merchant in Baltimore, but she is now deceased. Laura is living in Elkton and is unmarried. John Leeds Barroll, who graduated from St. Mary's, of Baltimore, was a prominent attorney at Chestertown, where he died in 1866, leaving three sons. John Leeds, Jr., now of Philadelphia; Hopewell H., a graduate of St. John's College of Annapolis, now the leading attorney at Chestertown and said to be making money faster than any attorney on the eastern shore; and Morris K., a graduate of West Point, now a lieutenant, stationed at San Francisco, Cal. Sallie, the fourth child of James and Henrietta Barroll, died when a child of four years. S. Rose died unmarried. Ellen resides in Elkton. James E. died when quite young. Victoria, deceased, was the wife of R. E. Jamar, register of wills for Cecil County; she died in February, 1878, leaving three children, Henrietta Barroll, Laura C. and Victoria Barroll.

TOWARD N. LORAINE, chief engineer at the power house of the Chesapeake & Delaware Canal, was born September 7, 1862, in Chesapeake City, Cecil County, where he has since resided. The family of which he is a member consisted of five children: Ruth E.; Elizabeth W., Henry W., Toward N. and Kate I.; whose parents were Toward and Catherine (Lodge) Loraine, natives of England. When about thirty years of age his father came to America and at first was employed in Philadelphia, where he followed the trade of a machinist. In 1854 he removed to Chesapeake City for the purpose of putting in place an engine he had built to run the canal water power. His ability soon became manifest and he was considered one of the most efficient employes of the canal company, with which he was connected for thirty-eight years, or until his death. Their recognition of his ability led to his promotion to the position of chief engineer, and that responsible place he filled most satisfactorily to all concerned. It was

MRS. ANNA A. REYNOLDS.

STEPHEN J. REYNOLDS.

felt to be a loss to the company and a loss to the village in which he had so long made his home when at the age of sixty-five, November 18, 1892, death removed him from the scene of his usefulness. His time, thought and talents were given entirely to his business duties. He had no interest in politics other than that which every patriotic citizen should feel, in the election of good men to make our laws and good men to see that these laws are executed. Even had he desired to hold public office (which he did not) his business cares would have prevented him from so doing. He is remembered as one of the most capable engineers the county has ever had.

Under the careful supervision of his father, the subject of this sketch gained a thorough knowledge of engineering, and finally was made assistant engineer. January 1, 1897, he was promoted to chief engineer of the company's power house. The water is pumped from the pond to the canal by means of the largest water wheel in the United States. The position is a responsible one, but he is fully equal to every emergency. Politically he votes the Democratic ticket, and fraternally is identified with Bohemia Lodge No. 68, I. O. O. F., at Chesapeake City. In 1894 he married Miss Willie R. Cavender, who was born in Maryland. They are the parents of two sons, Toward N., Jr., and John C.

STEPHEN J. REYNOLDS. The subject of this sketch stands second to none among the energetic and progressive agriculturists of District No. 6, Cecil County, whose record it has been deemed wise to preserve in this manner for the perusal of coming generations. As a judicious tiller of the soil he has met with success, and as a man and a citizen he holds a good position among his neighbors. He is the owner of eighty-seven acres of rich and arable land, a part of the old homestead, on which his birth occurred September 17, 1832.

The father, Jacob Reynolds, was born May 8, 1791, in the house now owned and occupied by our subject, it having been erected by the grandfather. Throughout life Jacob Reynolds followed agricultural pursuits, and both he and his wife were consistent members of the Society of Friends. On attaining man's estate he married Miss Annie Moore, who was born August 31, 1793, and they became the parents of eleven children, as follows: William M., born August 27, 1814, died September 6, 1869; Mercy A., born May 29, 1816, died February 5, 1885; Esther, born May 9, 1819, died October 28, 1824; Jacob H., born August 16, 1821, died July 23, 1893; Adrianna, born August 14, 1823, is the wife of Alexander Kirk; Benjamin C., born September 17, 1825, is a resident of Oxford, Pa.; Joseph T., born June 29, 1827, also makes his home in Oxford, Pa.; Granville T., born August 8, 1829, lives near Zion, in Cecil County, Md.; Stephen J., of this review, is next in order of birth; Anna, born July 23, 1835, is the wife of Charles S. Lincoln, and lives in Philadelphia; and Susan J., born July 18, 1837, died September 16, 1838. The death of the father occurred May 13, 1869, and the mother was called to her final rest September 19, 1874.

Reared on the old homestead, Stephen J. Reynolds received his early education in the common schools of the neighborhood, but was later a student in the Rising Sun Seminary, a private school. He remained under the parental roof until eighteen years of age, when he began learning the machinist's trade in the shops at Stone Run, Cecil County, where he served a three years' apprenticeship, receiving $3 per month for the first year, $4 for the second, and $5 for the third. He then continued with the same firm for twelve years longer, but at the end of that time purchased the Drew Moore farm of sixty-eight acres in Lancaster County, Pa., where he engaged in farming for four years. Having greatly improved the place, he sold it at an advance of $2,000. He then purchased a part of the old homestead farm in District No. 6, Cecil County, where he still continues to reside.

In 1861 was celebrated the marriage of Mr. Reynolds and Miss Anna A. Phillips, who was born in May, 1841, and died September 21,

1893. She was a most estimable lady, beloved by all who knew her, and a faithful member of the Society of Friends, taking an active and prominent part in the work of that church, and for a number of years was a prominent minister in the society to which she belonged. By her marriage she became the mother of three children, namely: Anna, now the wife of David T. Benson, of Benson, Harford County, Md.; Narcissa, who died at the age of eight years; and William, who is attending the normal school of Rising Sun.

In connection with general farming, Mr. Reynolds is successfully engaged in the dairy business. He is a prominent member of the Grange, and, like his wife, he holds membership in the Friends' Church, in which he has served as clerk and overseer. He possesses a large share of benevolence, which induces him to take an active interest in what is going on around him, and which most nearly affects the welfare of his community.

RICHARD D. HALL. Though dead, Mr. Hall yet lives in the memory of all who knew him and who held him in high regard for the good deeds that marked his pilgrimage on earth. His memory is cherished by those most closely connected with him by ties of love and is to them an inspiration to higher purposes and nobler deeds. A lifelong resident of Cecil County, he engaged in agricultural pursuits from boyhood to the close of his life. He mastered nature's obstacles and made a successful record as a farmer. In many respects his character was an ideal one. His family, its comfort, its best interests, were, as they should have been, his first care, but with an unselfish spirit he also aimed to help those about him and to advance the interests of the community where he lived. His unselfish spirit is a splendid heritage to those who in life were nearer and dearer to him than life itself.

In the house now occupied by William E. Porter, in District No. 8, Cecil County, the subject of this sketch was born June 7, 1824, being a son of Washington and Ann (Guinn) Hall. The family has always been characterized by patriotism, a spirit of self-sacrificing loyalty to the government and its institutions. His grandfather was Colonel Hall, of Revolutionary fame, and the latter had a brother, Elisha, also a participant in the struggle with Great Britain. Washington Hall was a prominent and wealthy farmer of Cecil County and his landed possessions aggregated many acres in this locality. By his marriage to Ann Guinn thirteen children were born, but all are deceased; Richard D., who was the youngest of the sons, passed away April 16, 1893; and Mrs. Robert Rogers, of Baltimore, who was the youngest daughter, died in 1896.

The education acquired by our subject was an excellent one, considering the times in which he lived. It began in a private school at Baltimore, was continued in Bel Air Academy, and finally concluded in Nottingham Academy. After his return home he took charge of his father's farm and soon gained a thorough knowledge of every department of agriculture. He resided on Mt. Welcome farm until 1885, when he removed to Hy Field's farm, and there his death occurred in 1893. In the work of the Nottingham Presbyterian Church he took a keen interest and was ever ready to assist in its activities. By those who knew him best he is said to have been a man of exemplary character, and true in every relation of life. The lady who co-operated with him in all his efforts and who is now his widow, bore the maiden name of Margaret Mitchell, and was a daughter of Abram D. Mitchell, member of an old family residing near Elkton. Their marriage was a union of purpose and aspirations as well as of hand and heart, and they gathered together many of the comforts of life for their own use and to leave as a heritage to those who came after. Their family consisted of three children, and these are now living, namely: Anna, wife of Harry Porter; Washington H., who resides with his mother and has charge of the old homestead; and Richard D., a civil engineer living in South Bethlehem, Pa.

A man of more than ordinary intelligence, Mr.

Hall was active in those measures tending to the advancement of local industries. The people among whom he lived so long and before whom he acquitted himself so creditably, learned to respect him for his excellent traits of character, which combined integrity with excellent business capacities. It was, however, the wife upon whom the loss fell heaviest, for their union had been a happy one and its termination left her desolate; comforted by the thought of a re-union in the eternal home where partings shall never come.

"There is no death! What seems so is transition.
This life of mortal breath
Is but the suburb of the life elysian,
Whose portal we call death."

NICHOLAS R. BELL. The homestead owned and occupied by the subject of this sketch is one of the finely improved estates of District No. 5, Harford County. It was in 1866 that he moved to this district and bought the mill and farm he has since owned. After a long and busy career, he retired some years ago from his business interests, and has since enjoyed the leisure well merited by his former efforts. The fact that he has retired, however, does not mean that he has ceased to take an interest in the management of his property; on the other hand, he still superintends his varied holdings and directs his affairs personally.

The city of Baltimore was the place of our subject's birth, and July 7, 1812, the date of the same. He is the sole survivor of the six children born to the union of Isaiah and Catherine (Wygart) Bell, natives of Baltimore. His paternal ancestors were farmers and owned large tracts of land granted under Lord Baltimore. His grandmother, the wife of John Bell, attained the great age of one hundred and five years. During the Revolution Isaiah Bell was a soldier in the colonial army.

Reared upon a farm, at the age of fifteen, tiring of the quiet life and longing for adventure, our subject went to sea with a friend, remaining for sixteen months. On his return to Maryland, he learned the millwright and miller's trade, which he followed for a time in Baltimore, and later in Harford County. At the age of twenty-three he married Henrietta Spurrier, who was born in Baltimore. They had three children that died in infancy, and a daughter, Georgietta, who married George Robinson, a native of Baltimore, and became the mother of two sons, Ernest and Clayton. Mrs. Bell was a lady of kind heart and possessed those traits of character that make a woman's influence so widely felt throughout a community. Her co-laborers in the Methodist Episcopal Church testified to her worth of character and sweet Christian spirit. She died in 1895, at the age of seventy-six, mourned by all by whom she was known.

The advantages which Mr. Bell received in boyhood were greatly inferior to those of the present time, but he improved them to the utmost and they were supplemented by extensive reading during later years. The scenes amid which his early life was passed, while sailing, were of a nature to make him content to settle down to the quiet life of a landsman. By his industry and energy he was able to provide his wife and daughter with the comforts of life. He has always stood ready to assist financially in enterprises, the benefit of which he perceives will be lasting. He gives his suffrage to the candidates of the Democratic party.

CHARLES E. CRESWELL. The self-made man is entitled to respect and he gets it in America, for he represents all that is vigorous and substantial in our institutions. When he has made his way to prominence by hard and persistent endeavor in tilling the soil, he is all the more worthy of esteem, for fortunes are not made in a day by the "sons of the soil," but through weeks, months and years of earnest effort. That he is a true son of America cannot be denied when it is known that his paternal grandfather fought on many a bloody battlefield to free this country from the yoke of England, as did his own father, William Creswell, during the War of 1812. It is then but natural that Charles E. Creswell should be patriotic, a lover of liberty and interested in all that pertains to the welfare of his country.

William Creswell was born and reared near Clayton, Md., and his father, James Creswell, was also a native of this county. The former was a farmer and cooper by trade, a worthy and law-abiding citizen, and a man of more than average intelligence. He was married to Margaret Cramer, a daughter of Ludwig Cramer, a native German, and eventually a family of eight children was born to them, two of whom are deceased. Those living are: Margaret, wife of Ernest Sweckendeik, of Baltimore: Charles E.; Mary C., wife of Davis P. Smith, of Peoria County, Ill.; Hannah, the widow of Joseph Walter; Emma, wife of Wesley Travers, of Aberdeen; and Ellen, wife of H. A. Vokes. Mr. Creswell was a Democrat politically, and he and his wife were members of the Christian Church. He was called from this life in 1869.

Charles E. Creswell was born on the farm on which he is now living, May 14, 1849, and while growing to manhood pursued his studies in the common schools in the vicinity of his home, acquiring a practical education. When he was about twenty years of age his father died and he at once took upon himself the management of the old homestead of sixty acres and it has ever since remained in his charge. In his views of matters and things he is thoroughly practical and sensible, and having resided in this section all his life, he has ever had its interests at heart. In his business relations with his fellows he has been upright and honorable, and his correct mode of living has gathered about him a large circle of friends and well-wishers. A Democrat in his political views he served in the capacity of justice of the peace, from 1892 to 1895, but has never cared for political preferment. He has shown his appreciation of secret organizations by becoming a member of the Independent Order of Odd Fellows and the Junior Order of American Mechanics, being doorkeeper in the last-mentioned order.

He and his wife are members of the Christian Church, in which he is a deacon. The maiden name of Mrs. Creswell was Laura V. Granger, daughter of William Granger, of Baltimore, and their marriage was celebrated February 23, 1872. They have three children : Alice, wife of John A. Norris, Charles C. and Harry.

A. J. MICHENER. The student of biography finds a subject of interest to him in the life of one who starts out on a business career with no advantageous surroundings, but by conscientious endeavor, honorable purpose and well-directed effort works his way steadily upward until he reaches the plains of prosperity. Such is the history of Mr. Michener, one of the representative and highly respected citizens of Cecil County.

He was born in Bucks County, Pa., July 16, 1830, a son of John D. and Harriet B. (Jones) Michener, who had a family of six children, namely : Huldah, widow of James D. Headley ; Joseph, deceased ; A. J.; Sarah, deceased ; Mary J., widow of David M. Reynolds; and Amos J., who is now living a retired life in Philadelphia. In 1849 John D. Michener removed with his family to Cecil County, and purchased what is known as the Rev. James McGrow homestead, where he lived for four years. He then bought the farm upon which A. J. Michener now resides, and made it his home until his death in 1867, at the age of sixty-five years. His wife passed away in 1868, in her sixty-fourth year. They were both members of the Friends' Church and were people of the highest respectability.

Mr. Michener, whose name introduced this review, remained with his father until twenty-one years of age, and then engaged in merchandising near the old home in Pennsylvania. For two years he was thus employed, after which he returned to Maryland and purchased a tract of land near his present home. In connection with general farming he carried on an implement business, adding not a little to his income in this way. In

1868 he removed to his present farm and has since made it his home. In 1874, in partnership with his brother, Amos J., he leased the Glen Mountain House, of Watkins, N. Y., and for four years conducted that popular hotel, but during that time he continued his residence in Cecil County. He is a progressive agriculturist, and the neat and thrifty appearance of his place, with its many improvements, well indicates the careful superintendence of the owner. He is also one of the directors of the Farmers and Mechanics' Fire Insurance Company, and for fifteen years was a director of the Chester County Agricultural Society.

Mr. Michener was married in 1852 to Miss Esther Reynolds, who died in 1855. In 1856 he wedded Martha J. Reynolds, and they had three children: Amanda M., wife of A. O. Reynolds; Harriet J., wife of E. H. Worthington; and John D., who died May 12, 1882, at the age of nineteen years. Mr. and Mrs. Michener hold membership in the Friends' Church, and he also belongs to Harmony Lodge No. 53, F. & A. M. He is a genial, courteous gentleman and has many stanch and admiring friends among all classes of men. As an energetic and honorable agriculturist he stands high in the estimation of the entire community.

ISAAC R. TAYLOR, Esq., an honored and highly respected citizen of Rising Sun, has throughout life been prominently identified with the interests of Cecil County. He was born in District No. 6, January 19, 1821, was reared upon a farm, and was educated in the district and subscription schools, completing his literary training in the old stone school house one mile east of Rising Sun.

At the age of eighteen Mr. Taylor started out to make his own way in the world, and going to Chester County, Pa., there served a three years' apprenticeship to the cabinet-maker's trade, at which he worked in Philadelphia for the following year, but at the end of that time, he returned to Rising Sun, where he has since conducted a shop. He is also engaged in the undertaking business.

In 1846 Mr. Taylor was united in marriage with Miss M. Harlan, and of the twelve children born to this worthy couple, nine are still living: George H., Laura R., Albert G., Clarissa J., Eugene, Benjamin F., William L., Annie M., and Helen M.

Mr. Taylor was first appointed justice of the peace in 1856 during Governor T. Watkins Ligon's administration, and has held that position continuously since, with the exception of the term of Governor Bradford and two years during the term of Governor Frank Brown, serving in all for about thirty-five years. He was also twice elected to the board of public school commissioners for Cecil County when that system was first put in operation, and was deputy postmaster at Rising Sun for two years. Politically he is a strong Jeffersonian Democrat, casting his first ballot for James K. Polk for president in 1844. Religiously he is connected with the Society of Friends, and fraternally is one of the charter members of Excelsior Lodge No. 67, I. O. O. F., of Rising Sun, which was instituted in 1849, having thus been a member of the order for fifty-two years. In the discharge of every duty, whether public or private, he is true to every trust reposed in him, and by all who know him he is held in that reverence and respect tacitly accorded those whose lives have been distinguished by integrity and usefulness.

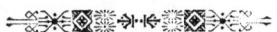

HENRY R. CARTER. It is fitting that those who spend the morning of life's brief day in ceaseless activity, who labor for the welfare of their children and their fellow-men, and who strive to discharge every domestic and public duty,—it is fitting that when the day sinks into twilight and approaches its close, one should enjoy a rest from former toils. Mr. Carter's life has been a busy, active and useful one, and he deserves its closing days of ease and rest. On the old homestead in District No. 4, Cecil County, he is living in comparative retirement from cares and labors, and in the enjoyment of an income that renders further exertion unnecessary.

The home where Mr. Carter now lives was the place of his birth, which occurred in 1821. The family of which he is a member settled in Chester County, Pa., about 1630 and was thenceforward connected with the growth of that locality. The father of our subject, Robert Carter, was born there, but removed in early life to Delaware County, and in 1815 came to Cecil County, where he established a paper mill, the first in the entire state, and known as the Cecil Paper Mill. All kinds of paper were manufactured and the industry proved so successful that similar plants were afterward established. In political opinion he was a Whig, but at no time took an active part in public affairs, preferring to devote himself to the paper business, which he continued to carry on as long as he lived. By his marriage to Lydia Levis he became the father of seven children, namely: Harriet, Joseph, Lottie, John, William, Edward and Lydia. Some time after the death of his first wife he was united with Mary Reynolds, and their union resulted in the birth of four children, as follows: Henry R., of this sketch; Robert C., Israel and Mary, all deceased. The father passed away at the home place in 1852, when seventy-three years of age.

Leaving school at the age of eighteen years, the subject of this sketch turned his attention to farming and assumed the management of the home place in behalf of his father. On the death of the latter he succeeded to the ownership of the property, and his entire active life was spent in its development and cultivation. Some years ago he retired and has since lived a life of leisure, with the exception of the oversight of his varied interests. In politics he is a Republican and evinces an intelligent interest in all the public questions of the age. As a citizen he is interested in local matters, liberal in contributing toward worthy movements, and among the residents of the district he holds a prominent position, to which his intelligence, generous social spirit, and good character entitle him. He has never married, but has been content to lead the life of a bachelor. A sincere Christian, he holds membership in the Methodist Episcopal Church of Cherry Hill, and for several years has been trustee and steward. When young he took an active interest and assisted in Sunday-school work.

JOHN MORRIS. Success is comparatively easy to attain when circumstances are favorable and surroundings auspicious, but the path to prosperity is a rough and rugged one when obstacles are many. It was the fate of Mr. Morris to be orphaned when eleven years of age and afterward he worked with William Kersey until sixteen years of age. Few educational advantages were given him, but through reading and observation he has acquired a fund of information equal to that possessed by many a college-bred man. He has won a large degree of success in spite of discouragements and hardships, and now holds a position among the prosperous business men of Cecilton, where he is the proprietor of a furniture and undertaking establishment.

The only child of James and Mary (Tate) Morris, natives of Delaware, our subject was born in that state, April 25, 1828. At the age of sixteen years he came to District No. 1, Cecil County, where he has since made his home. Learning the carpenter's trade he made this his occupation until about 1883, when he retired from it permanently and opened a furniture and undertaking establishment in Cecilton, and this he has since conducted.

At the age of twenty-two years Mr. Morris married Lydia Price, who was born in Middletown, Del., but was brought by her parents to Maryland in 1834, when she was an infant. Six children were born of the union, but one died in infancy. Those living are Mary E., William H., Panola, Arabella and Ruth. The children were reared in the faith of the Methodist Episcopal Church, in which their father holds the offices of secretary and treasurer. He keeps well posted in the politics of the country and is in sympathy with Republican principles. For fifteen years he has acted as town commissioner. Any measure for the benefit of the people receives his active support. He has the greatest faith in the future of Cecilton and believes in years to come it will have large influence as a business center; for the accomplishment of this purpose he has labored and to it he has largely contributed. Fraternally he was at one time connected with the Odd Fellows, but does not retain his membership in the order.

JAMES WHITELOCK, one of the valued and highly respected citizens of Darlington, was born in Perryville, Cecil County, Md., in 1822, and is a worthy representative of one of the pioneer families of the state, its founder having come from England and located in Cecil County as early as 1630. Its members have since been prominently identified with the growth and development of this region. Abram Gorrell, a maternal uncle of our subject, and a native of Harford County, joined the continental army during the Revolutionary War and gallantly fought for the establishment of our glorious republic.

John Whitelock, our subject's father, was a son of Charles Whitelock, and a farmer by occupation. In 1824 he left his old home in Cecil County, locating near Hopewell, in Harford County, and there resided until called to his final rest in 1858, at the age of seventy-three years. He married Ann Gorrell, by whom he had eleven children, but only three are now living: James, who was seventh in order of birth; Eveline, widow of William Brown; and A. J.

In Harford County James Whitelock, of this sketch, was reared and educated in much the usual manner of boys of his day, and at the age of seventeen began learning the miller's trade at Rock Run Mills, serving a three years' apprenticeship. After mastering the business, he returned to his birthplace in Cecil County, and remained there thirteen years, conducting a grist mill at Port Deposit. In 1860, however, he returned to Harford County, where he has since made his home. For five years he operated a mill near Lapidum, but with that exception he has principally devoted his energies to agricultural pursuits, in which he has met with a well-merited success.

In 1846 was performed a wedding ceremony which united the destinies of Mr. Whitelock and Miss Caroline Bowman, and they have three children yet living: George D., who is represented elsewhere in this volume; Euphemie, wife of Charles H. Stamford, of Darlington; and Emma, widow of R. E. Spencer, of Wyoming, Del. The family attend the Baptist Church and are the center of a cultured society circle, while Mr. Whitelock has long been an active and prominent member of the Odd Fellows' Society, serving as noble grand and secretary of the local lodge. His ambition has been to acquit himself of life's duties honorably before all men, to improve his capabilities and opportunities, and to become of use in the world; and it is this spirit that has made him one of Harford County's eminent citizens.

ZEPHANIAH HEAPS, who cultivates a farm in District No. 5, is a member of an old family of Harford County, one that has contributed men of intelligence, energy and ability to the agricultural circles and the public affairs of the locality. The family was founded here by his great-grandfather, Robert Heaps, who emigrated from England to America and settled in the county where his descendants now reside. The grandfather, Robert, who was born in Harford County, took part in the Revolution, defending the interests of the colonies against British tyranny and fighting for freedom from the mother land.

Robert L. Heaps, father of our subject, was

born in this county and like his father, he was intensely patriotic. During the War of 1812 he went to the front with the American army. His life work was farming and in it he met with fair success. By his marriage to Sarah Stokes, he had six children, namely: David H., Robert, Mary C., Zephaniah, Sarah C. and Nathan W., the two last-named being deceased. The schools of this locality furnished our subject a fair education and the knowledge there obtained was subsequently supplemented by information gained in the school of experience and through contact with men of affairs.

At the age of thirty-one years Mr. Heaps married Laura L. Tate, a native of Harford County, and the daughter of James and Sarah A. (McFadden) Tate, the former a miller in this county. Mrs. Laura Heaps was a sincere Christian, a member of the Methodist Episcopal Church, and a lady whose kind disposition won for her the friendship of every acquaintance. She died in 1872, at the age of thirty-two. The children born of this union were twins, named Osborne H. and Ida B. The son married Martha J. Harry, of this county, and they reside on the home farm, which he cultivates on shares. The present wife of our subject was Belle M. Cameron, a native of York County, Pa. Two children (twins) were born of the union, but both died in infancy. Mrs. Heaps is a daughter of James and Lydia Cameron, of Pennsylvania, and is an active member of the Presbyterian Church.

In all matters pertaining to the welfare of the county Mr. Heaps takes an interest, assisting therein by his co-operation. Politically he votes the straight Democratic ticket. For more than fifteen years he was judge of elections in the district. He is a director of the Miles National Bank of Delta, Pa., and one of its large stockholders. For some years he has acted as agent for the Susquehanna fertilizer and farm implements. The farm which he owns and operates comprises one hundred and eighty-five acres. Its neat residence, convenient outbuildings, and other appurtenances indicate the supervision of a proprietor more than ordinarily intelligent and enterprising.

FRANKLIN T. MACKIE. A visitor in Cecil County would not long remain in ignorance of the name and character of Mr. Mackie, who is classed among the best agriculturists of District No. 4. His farm consists of one hundred acres of well-improved land, a portion of the old family homestead, upon which stands a complete line of buildings. The property inherited from his father gave him a fair start in life, and as he has been diligent and persevering, he has increased the value of his possessions during the years of his active life. While general farming has been his principal occupation, other departments of agriculture have received attention. He has been interested in stock-raising and has also carried on a dairy business.

The parents of our subject, John and Catherine (Andrews) Mackie, were natives, respectively, of District No. 4, Cecil County, and Natchez, Miss., and their family consisted of four sons and one daughter. The third in order of birth was Franklin T., who was born at the Mackie homestead in 1844. His father was a tanner by trade and followed that occupation for several years, but the greater part of his life was devoted to farming. Throughout his community he was highly esteemed as a man of worth and upright character. He died at the age of fifty-four. His eldest son, J. Alfred, is represented upon another page of this volume.

After completing the studies of the common schools, the subject of this sketch became a student in a college in Cincinnati, Ohio, where he remained until eighteen years of age. On his return home he began to assist in the tilling of the soil, and in conjunction with his brothers had the management of the farm, which, on the death of his father, was divided among the children. About 1864 he was given a position in the government employ, which required his presence near Cincinnati about two years, but since that time he has resided continuously in Cecil County. The one hundred acres which comprise his farm bear excellent improvements and are situated on the Telegraph road in District No. 4, the land being devoted to the raising of cereals. He has also taken an interest in the stock business and in

JOHN HOLLINGSWORTH.

dairying, and finds these lines remunerative. In his political relations he is independent. Fraternally he is identified with New London Lodge No. 218, K. of P., at Lewisville, Pa., and is an attendant of the Rock Presbyterian Church. His marriage took place in March, 1873, and united him with Elizabeth Mackey, daughter of David and Catherine Mackey, of this county. Their children are named as follows: Eugene, Dora, Amos, Osborne, Lillie and Nellie. The pleasant home of Mr. and Mrs. Mackie is the abode of hospitality, and in social circles they hold an enviable position.

AMOS HOLLINGSWORTH. In all the expanse of Maryland there is no county that affords a better maintenance to agriculturists than Harford, for its productive soil and advanced development make it pre-eminently the farmer's home. One of its comfortable rural abodes lies in District No. 3, and is owned and occupied by Mr. Hollingsworth, who was born here in 1844, and has made Montland farm his lifelong home. This property, as well as the adjoining tracts owned by Silas and Thomas Hollingsworth, belongs to the old homestead, originally purchased by his grandfather, Nathaniel, a native of Delaware County, Pa., but an early settler of Harford County, where he accumulated landed possessions aggregating thousands of acres.

The father of our subject, John Hollingsworth, was born in Pennsylvania, and when about two years old accompanied his parents and here spent his whole life, becoming known as one of the leading agriculturists of his day. Energetic and public-spirited, he was a leading factor in local improvements and in the development of his district. By his marriage to Rachel Benson, he became the father of six children, of whom John was killed by a horse; and William and Margaret are also deceased. The surviving sisters, Lydia and Eliza, reside on the old home place with their brother, Amos. The father was deeply interested in the welfare of his children, and was a man whose greatest happiness consisted in promoting the prosperity of his family. With an appreciation of what he had lost by not having a good education, he was especially anxious that his children should have the best educational advantages the community afforded, and he was therefore always ready to bear a part in movements to promote the public schools and enhance their usefulness. In 1874, when sixty-nine years of age, his earth life was brought to a close. His wife passed away in 1886, at the age of seventy-four.

Spending the years of boyhood and youth on the home farm, the subject of this sketch succeeded to its management on the death of his father, and has since superintended the cultivation of its one hundred and thirty acres. Some of the land is used for pasturage, some for market gardening, and some for the raising of cereals, in which various departments of agricultural work Mr. Hollingsworth engages. Following the example of his ancestors, he has retained membership in the Friends' Church, and in his congregation serves as a trustee. Politically he adhered to the protection principles of the Republican party, and always voted the ticket in early life, but he came to believe that the protection of American manufactories, important as it seems, is of less vital importance to our national life and prosperity than the protection of the American homes from the curse of drink, and he has therefore identified himself with the Prohibition party, upholding its total abstinence platform both in theory and practice.

JOSHUA W. WRIGHT. Everywhere in our land are found men who have worked their own way upward to leadership in business, who by their individual effort have achieved success. It is one of the glories of our nation that this is so, and it should be a strong incentive and encouragement to those just starting out in business life. After a successful career as a farmer, Mr. Wright is now practically living retired, enjoying a well-earned rest, the fruits of his former toil, and the confidence of all with whom he has been brought in contact.

His home is in District No. 4, Harford County, which is also the place of his birth. His natal day was February 13, 1826, and his parents were William and Amelia (Smithon) Wright, the former a native of Baltimore County, and the latter of Harford County. They had eleven children, but only four are now living, namely: Daniel, Emily, John W. and Joshua W. The paternal grandfather was a native of Pennsylvania, and throughout his life followed farming.

Although born on the farm where he now makes his home, Joshua W. Wright was reared in the city of Baltimore until twelve years of age. He received good educational privileges, and reading, practical experience and observation have made him one of the well-informed men of the county. His life work has been farming, and has been successfully conducted. He is a man of great industry, of resolute purpose and firm determination, and has carried forward to successful completion whatever he undertakes. In connection with his son William, he owns more than four hundred acres of rich and arable land, which is divided into fields of convenient size, that return good harvests as a tribute to his care and cultivation. The place is improved with substantial buildings, and is accounted one of the fine farms of this section of the state. Mr. Wright is now practically living retired, but still oversees the operation of his land.

When twenty-five years of age, Mr. Wright was united in marriage to Miss Margaret Anderson, a native of Pennsylvania, and to them were born three children: William A., Margaret W. and one who died in infancy. The mother of this family was a faithful member of the Methodist Episcopal Church, and died at the age of twenty-seven years. Three years later, Mr. Wright was again married, his second union being with Hannah Amos, who was born in District No. 4, Harford County. They became the parents of two children: Sallie R., now deceased, and one who died in infancy.

In his political affiliations, Mr. Wright is a Democrat, and believes in the free coinage of silver, at the ratio of sixteen to one. Active in church work, he is now serving as trustee of St. Paul's Methodist Protestant Church, which is located on a part of his farm. His life has been a busy and useful one, characterized by an honorable purpose, and fidelity to duty in all relations. Thus he has won a name that is above reproach, and gained the confidence and good-will of his fellow-townsmen.

JOSEPH ANDREW, one of the most progressive and energetic business men of District No. 5, Harford County, was born in the village of Darlington, in 1857, and is a son of John Andrew, whose sketch appears elsewhere in this work. He completed his literary education in the Darlington Academy, and on laying aside his text books operated the farm of Samuel Mathews for about eight years.

In 1882 Mr. Andrew purchased the Thomas Dallam farm near Darlington, where he has since made his home, and the same year established a canning factory, which he has conducted in connection with the cultivation of his land, turning out about six thousand cases per year. His farm, which comprises one hundred and seventy-five acres of rich and arable land, he has placed under a high state of cultivation, and the well-tilled fields yield bountiful returns for the care and labor bestowed upon them. Mr. Andrew has not confined his attention to these lines of endeavor alone, but was for some years engaged in teaching, and for a number of years has acted as agent in Harford County for the firm of Sanders & Staman, piano and organ dealers of Baltimore.

In 1887 was solemnized the marriage of Mr. Andrew and Mrs. Maggie (Cook) Willis, and they now have a little daughter, Annie T. He is a member of the Methodist Episcopal Church at Darlington, in which he is serving as class leader and trustee, and also as superintendent of the Sunday-school. Mrs. Andrew is a member of the Friends' Church. Being a strong temperance man, Mr. Andrew affiliates with the Prohibition party, and is one of its most ardent advocates. Social, educational and moral interests have been promoted by him, and anything that tends to uplift and benefit humanity secures his hearty cooperation. By energy, perseverance and fine business ability he has been enabled to secure a comfortable competence, and to-day enjoys the reward of his painstaking and conscientious work.

SAMUEL J. KEYS. In the business circles of Elkton Mr. Keys is, by universal consent, accorded a high place. Successful in a financial sense, he has throughout his entire career exhibited clearness of perception and soundness of judgment, and also enjoys a high reputation for integrity of purpose and moral worth. Public-spirited when matters affecting local enterprises are in question, he uses his influence to enhance the best interests of village and county, and all worthy measures for their development meet with his hearty support. It is the testimony of the people that his course in life has been such as to reflect credit upon the citizenship of Elkton. Since 1872 his home has been in this village, where he has engaged extensively in the lumber business, and he is now president of the Keys & Miller Lumber Company, one of the flourishing industries of the place.

In Dorchester County, on the eastern shore of Maryland, the subject of this article was born in August, 1847. The family of which he is a member has been identified with the history of the eastern shore for about a century, and there several successive generations have been born. Our subject's grandfather, Charles Keys, the son of a Scotchman, was born on the eastern shore and during the War of 1812 was one of the brave soldiers who defended our country against threatened encroachments by the British. The father of our subject, Samuel Keys, was born in Dorchester County, in September, 1804, and in youth had very limited educational advantages, as schools were then few in number and inferior in quality. A hard worker throughout his entire life, his principal business was the manufacture and sale of shoes, and in this he continued up to the time of his death, in 1892. In religious belief he was identified with the Methodist Episcopal Church, and was one of the active workers of the congregation. Fraternally he was connected with the Independent Order of Odd Fellows and the Sons of Temperance. He married Ann M. Spedden, who was born in Dorchester County, Md., member of an old family that resided at what is known as Spedden's Neck, below Cambridge.

Of the children born to the union of Samuel and Ann M. Keys, the subject of this sketch was the only son that attained years of maturity. He received his education in Vienna Academy, and was for some years engaged in the produce business in that place. In 1872 he came to Elkton, of which place he has since been a resident. Soon after removing here he became connected with the Davis & Miller Lumber Company, in which he purchased the interest of Mr. Miller, the firm name then being changed to Davis & Keys. In 1883 another change was made and the firm became Davis, Keys & Co., in which manner the business was conducted until 1893, when it was incorporated as the Keys & Miller Lumber Company. He is the head of the concern, and has associated with him some of the leading business men of Elkton, doing an extensive business in the sale of lumber and coal both here and throughout the surrounding country. He has led a purely business life and his expert judgment and ability to control and direct important undertakings very largely give to the firm the reputation it enjoys. He has always devoted himself untiringly to the work in hand and cares little for public life, though a stanch Democrat in politics. In religious connections he is a member of the Methodist Episcopal Church, and fraternally is connected with the Masonic Order, the Independent Order of Odd Fellows, the Royal Arch Chapter of

Masonry, the Junior Order of American Mechanics, Ancient Order of United Workmen, and Improved Order of Red Men. In 1873, the year after coming to Elkton, he was united in marriage with Miss Mary H. Hopkins, daughter of Ezekiel Hopkins, of this place, and cousin of Johns Hopkins, who founded the famous Johns Hopkins University, of Baltimore. They are the parents of a daughter, Mabel, now attending school.

J ALFRED MACKIE. It is not necessary for a visitor to the country to understand agriculture in order that he may know which are the good farmers of the locality. The sight of the tumbled-down fences, weedy fence-corners, machinery exposed to the weather, and grain inadequately sheltered, is sufficient to stamp the proprietor of a farm as one lacking in enterprise and judgment. On the other hand, well-built farm houses, neat fences and well-tilled fields, are equally conclusive proof of the energy of the owner of the place. The farm which Mr. Mackie owns belongs to the latter class. It comprises one hundred and forty-four acres. The house which he occupies is a substantial, old-fashioned structure, and, though used as the family residence for more than one hundred years, is still in good repair, and from appearance may brave the storms of winter for as many years to come.

Here occurred the birth of Mr. Mackie in 1838. His father, John, was a son of John and a grandson of David, who in turn was a son of Robert Mackie. John, Jr., was born at the old homestead in District No. 4, Cecil County, and in youth learned the tanner's trade, which he followed about thirty-five years. However, in later life he gave his attention principally to general farming and stock-raising, and continued to reside at the old home until he died, when fifty-four years of age. In politics he supported Democratic principles and was twice the candidate of his party for the position of representative. By his marriage to Catherine Andrews, of Natchez, Miss.,
he had five children, all of whom live near the old home. They are J. Alfred, Arthur A., Franklin T., David A. and Ella, wife of Frank Houston.

The public schools of District No. 4, Cecil County, and Chester County, Pa., afforded Mr. Mackie his educational privileges. On the completion of his studies at Hopewell Academy, in Chester County, Pa., he began to work for his father on the home farm of four hundred acres, having it in charge until the death of his father. In addition to general farming, he has been interested to some extent in the raising of horses and cattle, and in this line has been fairly successful. He has always been interested in educational matters and has served efficiently as trustee of schools, doing all in his power to advance the welfare of the common schools. Politically he votes the Democratic ticket. For some years he was secretary of the Lewisville Grange, to which he belongs. In religious belief a Presbyterian, he and his family attend services at that church. His marriage united him with Miss Mary McVey, of Lancaster County, Pa. The five sons born of their union are named as follows: Frank H.; John C., who lives in Chester County, Pa.; Harry M., who assists in the management of the home farm; Clement L., who also assists in the cultivation of the homestead; and James A. C., a student in the local schools.

WILSON L. COUDON, proprietor of the Cecil Fire Brick Company at North East and editor of the Perryville *Record*, was born near Perryville, Cecil County, August 14, 1858, the son of Henry Stump and Martha B. (Levering) Coudon, natives, respectively, of Cecil County and the city of Baltimore. On both the paternal and maternal sides he is descended from ancestors who were prominently identified with the early history of Maryland and bore an influential part in many of its activities. His grandfather, Joseph Coudon, farmer and merchant of Cecil County and member of the state legislature, married Ann Stump, and died May 23, 1860, at the age of seventy-three years. The great-grandfather, Rev. Joseph Coudon, had the distinction of being the first Episcopalian rector ordained in this county and his remains lie interred under the chancel of St. Mary Anne's Church, North East, the slab bearing this inscription: "Here lies the Rev. Joseph Coudon, rector of Saint Mary Anne's parish; a zealous and indefatigable preacher of the Gospel; who departed this life on the 13th of April, A. D. 1792, and in the fifty-first year of his age."

Still a resident of Cecil County, where his entire life has been passed, Henry Stump Coudon has devoted himself principally to the occupation of a planter, but, being a man of broad information and large talents, his activities have not been restricted to that calling. Prominent in public affairs, he could have held almost any local office he desired, but his inclinations have not been in that direction. In his political belief he is a Democrat, stanch and loyal to the principles of the party. In earlier years he wrote many articles on political subjects during the local campaigns, and these writings, marked by a keen sense of humor and a thorough knowledge of men and times, show that he might have achieved success in literature, had he entered that profession. Many of his leisure hours have been spent in hunting and he has quite a reputation as a sportsman and a crack shot. For years he was a vestryman of St. Mary Anne's Church, and is always interested in religious enterprises. His home is near Perryville, where he has long resided. By his marriage he had eight children, of whom four are living, Anna, Wilson Levering, Joseph and Martha.

The maternal grandfather of our subject, Thomas W. Levering, was a prominent coffee merchant of Baltimore, and a member of an influential family of that city. Rosier Levering, the first of the name of whom there is any record, is supposed to have been a native of France, born about 1600; on account of religious persecution he fled, either to Holland or Germany. The earliest representatives of the family in this country were Wigard and Gerhard Levering, brothers (the former born in 1648), who emigrated to America in 1685 and settled at Germantown, Philadelphia County, Pa. Their coming to America was the result of inducements held out by William Penn on his visit to Germany a short time previous. The first of the family to locate in Baltimore was Enoch Levering in 1773, senior member of Levering & Barge, grocers. From him the members of the family now resident in Maryland are descended.

Educated in the local schools and at St. Clement's Hall, Ellicott City, Howard County, Md., the subject of this sketch went to Baltimore at nineteen years of age and embarked in the grain commission business, assisting his grandfather, Thomas W. Levering. After four years there, in 1881 he came to North East and took charge of the Cecil Fire Brick Company, in which his father owned a large interest. With this concern he has since been connected, and from the manufacture of fire brick and stove linings is in receipt of a good income. As a diversion, he began the publication of the Perryville *Record* in 1892, and has since continued its management, writing for it articles upon political and social matters that have attracted considerable attention. Politically he is a Democrat, but inclined to be independent in his opinions and beliefs. Following the example set by his paternal ancestors, he adheres to the Episcopal faith and for a number of years has been a member of the vestry. He and his wife, who was formerly Alice E. Wroth, have a pleasant home at Perryville.

Doubtless Mr. Coudon is as well known through his record as an athlete as through his business connections. In 1882 he entered and won the championship of America in throwing the sixteen-pound hammer, and this he held for four years. In this, and in the throwing of the fifty-six-pound weight three times, he broke all existing records. He made a record of ten feet and three inches in height for pole vaulting, this being done without any special preparation. At his first attempt he broke the world's record for pole vaulting for distance. A man of perfect physique, six feet tall and over two hundred pounds in weight, he is not only large, but strong as well, possessing a powerful frame and muscles capable of long endurance and great pressure. He has the reputation of being the strongest man in Maryland, having a record for lifting six hundred and eighty-two pounds with either hand, and over one thousand pounds with both hands; this has been done without special effort on his part or without any particular attention having been given to the development of his strength. In one afternoon he broke thirteen world's records, and he has broken more records with hammers than any man living. He also excels as a boxer and skater, and is foremost in all athletic sports.

J. WARREN BROWN. The prosperity of any locality depends almost solely upon the character of the people who inhabit it, and if the citizens are pushing, energetic and intelligent the country will prosper accordingly. In Harford County there is not a more pleasant or agreeable member of society, or a more thorough and sagacious business man than J. Warren Brown, in which respect he is but illustrating that he is "a chip off the old block," for his father, George W. Brown, before him was and is a man of sound and practical views on all matters of general interest and one who has made his own way in life unaided by others. This substantial and useful citizen was born in the city of Baltimore, January 4, 1835, and at the age of two years was left fatherless. His sire, Jesse Brown, was a native of Scotland and from early boyhood followed the sea. He attained the rank of captain, was in the coffee trade, and on one of his voyages died and was buried at sea. His wife was Eleanor, daughter of John Sweeting, of Baltimore, and his death left her with a family of five small children to care for, of whom George W. is the only survivor. Her death occurred about eighteen years ago.

During his boyhood George W. Brown attended the public schools of Baltimore and later the old school built by Capt. Joe Downey at Gunpowder Neck, but owing to force of circumstances his school life closed when he was nine years old, and at that extremely youthful age he started out to fight the battles of life as best he could. He soon secured employment with an uncle on a farm in this district, but five years later he gave this up to learn the trade of book-binding. He continued to follow this occupation until he was twenty-two years of age, at which time he was taken with the "western fever" and eventually made his way to California, where he experienced the usual ups and downs of fortune. Three years later he returned to Baltimore and until 1866 his trade occupied his time and attention. He subsequently erected a store building at Magnolia and embarked in the general mercantile business. This work seemed suited to him and through good management and energy his business prospered and he continued to devote to it his attention until about twelve years ago, when he turned the care of its management over to his son, J. Warren, under whom it has prospered, and began giving his whole attention to farming and his canning establishment, which is a flourishing enterprise.

Formerly an influential and prominent Democrat, he came out during the last presidential campaign as a stanch free silver man, in which views he is supported by his son, J. Warren. He was married to Miss Mary A. Lee, a daughter of Nathaniel Lee, of Baltimore, and of eight children born to them the following are living: J. Warren; Godell, who is at present in Baltimore; John William, at home; Mary Eleanor, wife of W. S. Hering, of Baltimore; and Carrie Elizabeth, at home. Mr. Brown and his wife are members of the Methodist Episcopal Church and take a keen interest in religious and charitable work; in fact they are in sympathy with all worthy interests. Mr. Brown is well known in Harford County, for his present honorable position in life has been gained through his own efforts, and he deserves much credit therefor.

The birth of J. Warren Brown occurred in Baltimore, August 10, 1860, and in Knapp's Institute of that city he was educated. Upon leaving school he entered his father's store at Magnolia as a clerk, but June 2, 1884, was given complete control of the establishment and has managed it with marked ability ever since. In 1891 he opened a canning establishment, the output of which is about twelve thousand cases of tomatoes annually. He is a member of Mt. Ararat Lodge No. 44, F. & A. M. at Bel Air, and also belongs to Lodge No. 7 of the Elks of Baltimore. His wife was formerly Miss Laura, daughter of John Wesley Knight, of an old Virginia family. They were married March 20, 1882, and have three children: George C., Edith L. and Beulah M.

BASIL GRAFTON, who carries on general farming in District No. 1, Harford County, was born near Forest Hill on the 16th of September, 1832. His father, Martin Grafton, was born in the same district, and was a son of Nathan Grafton, who came from England to America and took up his residence in Maryland. Martin Grafton served his country in the War of 1812, and as a means of livelihood followed the occupation of farming. He was a member of the old-school Baptist Church, in which he served as deacon, and politically he affiliated with the Whig party. He married Miss Hannah Lee, a native of Harford County, and they became the parents of eleven children, of whom the following are now living: Liza, wife of John Watkins, of Harford County; Crobin M., who is living in District No. 1; Rev. William, a Baptist minister of the same district; Nathan, who resides at Forest Hill; the subject of this sketch; Alexander, of Baltimore County; and R. L., who makes his home in the city of Baltimore. Both parents are now deceased.

Mr. Grafton, whose name introduces this article, is indebted to the public schools near his boyhood home for the educational advantages which he enjoyed. At the age of seventeen he learned the trade of a wheelwright, serving a three years' apprenticeship, after which he embarked in business on his own account in that line, and pursued the trade for ten years. On the expiration of that decade, however, he returned to the pursuit to which he was reared, and in 1867 purchased the farm on which he has since lived—a tract of eighty acres of rich and arable land. He has since given his attention to its cultivation, and the well-tilled fields and good improvements on the place indicate his careful management and the progressive methods which he pursues in the care of his farm. His political associations are with the Democratic party.

As a companion and helpmeet on life's journey Mr. Grafton chose Miss Ann Elizabeth Hines, a daughter of John T. Hines, of Abingdon. Their marriage was celebrated on the 16th of December, 1857, and to them were born five children: Martha H., at home; Mary Jane, wife of William Cochran, of Baltimore; Ann L., wife of Ed Hooker, who is living in District No. 1, Harford County; Maggie L. and Sarah Maud, both of whom are successfully engaged in school teaching.

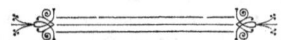

THOMAS ADY, whose long and well-spent life has been identified with the farming interests of Harford County, is one of its native sons, his birth having occurred in the Marshall District. His grandfather, William Ady, was of English descent, the family having been founded in America at an early day. The father of our subject, Samuel Ady, was born near Rock Creek Church in Harford County, and he and a brother served in the American army during the War of 1812. He learned the cooper's trade, and followed that pursuit in connection with farming. He also conducted a store for some time at Cooktown. An earnest advocate of the Whig principles, he was twice nominated by his party for the office of county sheriff. He and his family were prominent in church work, and the Adys have ever been foremost in support of all measures calculated to prove of public benefit. He married Miss Mary Ayres, a daughter of Thomas Ayres, of Harford County, and they became the parents of seven children, two of whom are living, Thomas and Mary.

Thomas Ady acquired his education in the school which was conducted in Rocky Spring Church, and at the age of sixteen he began work on the farm. He also learned the cooper's trade, which he followed to some extent during his early manhood. In 1859 he purchased the farm whereon he now resides, and has since carried on agricultural pursuits. Here he makes his home, faithfully devoting his time and energies to the cultivation of his land. His sister Mary keeps house for him. His life has been well spent, and all who know him esteem him for his sterling worth. He belongs to the Episcopal Church and is a Democrat in his political views.

CHARLES L. HECK. Numerous instances might be cited of men in Harford County who, by dint of persevering application and determined energy, have risen from a position of poverty to one of usefulness and influence. They furnish proofs of cheerful, honest labor, and a zealous determination to make the most of every advantage offered. Among this class of prosperous men, mention belongs to the gentleman with whose name we introduce this sketch, and who is known as a farmer of District No. 3.

In tracing the lineage of our subject, we find that he is a son of Philip Martin and Elizabeth (Hoffman) Heck, the former of whom was a government officer in Germany for fifty years, and died in his native land at eighty-one years of age. The parental family consisted of six children, namely: Philipine, who died in Harford County; Laura; Louisa, wife of Josiah Morgan, of this county; Mary; Charles Henry, who died at the age of eighty-one years; and Charles L. The last-named was born in Germany in 1818, and received his education in the excellent schools of that land. Emigrating to the United States in 1840, he made a sojourn of two years in Baltimore, where he was employed in the brewery business. In 1842 he located near Sandy Hook, in the northern part of District No. 3, and here he has since owned and operated an eighty-acre tract.

The marriage of Mr. Heck, in 1842, united him with Miss Cassandra E. Morgan, by whom he had four children: Elizabeth E., Philip, Martha P., and Cassandra (deceased). In his native land he was confirmed in the Lutheran Church, the doctrines of which he has since upheld. His wife is connected with the Presbyterian Church of Bel Air. In fraternal relations he is a member of Mt. Ararat Lodge No. 44, A. F. & A. M., of Bel Air, in which he has held several of the minor offices. He is one of that class of German settlers of whom our country has reason to be proud, and he is a loyal citizen of his adopted country, upholding its laws, and cherishing a patriotic regard for its institutions. Upon his farm he has many improvements and the best machinery, a fact that indicates his thrift and energy of character.

CHARLES A. ANDREW. Honored and respected by all, there is no man in Harford County who occupies a more enviable position than our subject in business circles, not alone on account of the success he has achieved, but also on account of the honorable, straightforward business policy he has ever followed. He possesses untiring energy, is quick of perception, forms his plans readily and is determined in their execution; and his close application to business and his excellent management have brought to him the high degree of prosperity which is to-day his.

Mr. Andrew is a native of the county, his birth occurring in Darlington, in 1857, and is a son of John W. Andrew. There he was reared and educated, completing his literary studies in the

CHRISTIAN H. WALKER.

Darlington Academy. About 1881 he embarked in the canning business at that place, and successfully followed the same for six years, but at the end of that time sold out to his brother Joseph, and came to Berkley, where he has since made his home. Here he also established a canning factory in 1887, and in connection with its operation also engages in general farming, and in 1893 purchased the warehouse of Emlow Brothers at Berkley. He also owns another warehouse at Conowingo, Md., and is now extensively interested in the hay, grain and feed business.

In 1883 Mr. Andrew was joined in wedlock with Miss Julia A. Jackson, of Baltimore County, Md., and they now have two children, Estelle K. and Mary, both at home. With the Methodist Church the family holds membership and occupies a high place in social circles. In the ranks of the local Democratic organization, Mr. Andrew is a recognized leader, was the candidate of his party for high sheriff in 1891, and in 1897 his name was again placed on the ticket as the nominee for county clerk. He is a prominent and honored member of Stephen Lodge, F. & A. M., of Lapidum, in which he has passed the chairs, and has also held the office of treasurer in the Odd Fellows Lodge at Darlington. For four years he has been president of the Berkley Building and Loan Association, and has been actively identified with almost every enterprise calculated to prove of public benefit or that will in any way advance the welfare of the community.

CHRISTIAN H. WALKER. The chief industry of the people of Harford County is agriculture, in which the principal part of the population is engaged. Directly upon the shoulders of the tillers of the soil rests the prosperity of every other class of men; they hold in their hands the destinies of all. Their prosperity means universal prosperity, their failure universal distress. The highest honor is due to those agriculturists who have, through their entire lives whether long or short, endeavored to promote the welfare of this county and increase the prosperity of its residents. To this class belongs Mr. Walker, the owner and occupant of a farm in District No. 2. He was born in this district November 18, 1827, the son of Robert and Catherine (Hoopman) Walker.

A native of Ireland, Robert Walker crossed the Atlantic and settled in America when a young man. For a time he sojourned in Portland, Me. After the close of the War of 1812 he came to Harford County, where he worked on a farm and was also employed as a fisherman. Here he met and married a daughter of Christian Hoopman, of District No. 2, and afterward he engaged in cultivating a small farm that belonged to her. To the property he added from time to time, and upon the place he spent the remaining years of his life. When he passed away, at the age of about seventy, his landed possessions were extensive and valuable. He was a member of the Methodist Protestant Church and in politics a pronounced Republican. He and his wife were the parents of twelve children.

When our subject arrived at the age of maturity he purchased a small farm in District No. 2, but after a short time sold the property and removed to Virginia, where he engaged in farming for four years. On his return to Harford County he bought the farm where he has since made his home. His marriage, June 23, 1857, united him with Cornelia A., daughter of Joseph R. and Sarah A. (Watson) Cole, natives of Cecil County. Her father, who was reared upon a farm, in early manhood purchased a tract of land in District No. 3, and here remained until his death, which took place at the age of about fifty-six years. In politics he was a Democrat. While he never attained wealth, he was fairly successful and was able to secure the comforts of life for his family. In religion he was a member of the Presbyterian Church. He is survived by his wife, a most estimable lady, who is now seventy-eight years of age. Mrs. Walker was born in this county July 31, 1837, and has a family of six children, namely: Winfield Scott, who is a farmer residing in this district; Annie L., wife of William J.

Keene, of this county; Mary V., who married Theodore J. Hetrick, of this county; Sadie, Mrs. William J. Macklin, also of this county; Cornelia, who died at four years of age; Ella H., who is with her parents.

Avowedly Republican in his political doctrine, Mr. Walker has been honored by his party with the nomination for various local offices. At three different times he was candidate for county commissioner, but the Democrats having a majority in the county he has always met with defeat. He and his wife are identified with the Methodist Protestant Church, in which he is now a trustee. He is deeply interested in Sunday-school work, and in the office of superintendent has been instrumental in advancing the interests of the school.

E. H. REYNOLDS, who has been prominently identified with the business interests of Cecil County for many years, was born in District No. 6, a mile and a-half northwest of Rising Sun, and is a representative of one of the oldest families of this locality. He traces his ancestry back to Henry Reynolds, who was born in England about 1655, and established the family in America. His son, Jacob Reynolds, was born in 1727, and was the father of Jonathan Reynolds, the grandfather of our subject, who was born on the old family homestead in this county, April 9, 1755. The original farm purchased by the family comprised four hundred and ninety-one acres of land near Rising Sun, a part of which property is now in possession of our subject. The grandfather was a drover and dealer in stock, and was numbered among the prominent citizens of the community.

Haines Reynolds, the father, was born on the old homestead, and married Phoebe Moore, daughter of David and Sarah Moore. He made milling his life work, and also established the machine shop and foundry on Stone Run, and owned and operated a saw and grist mill on his farm. His business interests were extensive and were profitably managed. He died in 1865, and his wife passed away in 1861, their remains being interred in West Nottingham Friends' burying ground. They were members of the Friends' Church, and had a family of ten children, namely: Sarah, widow of John Nice; Elizabeth, David and Jacob, all deceased; Theodore; E. H.; Mary J., deceased wife of Coulton Kimball; Anna E., wife of J. P. Kirk, who is living near Liberty Grove; Phoebe, deceased wife of William Thomas; and Reuben, who has also passed away.

The boyhood and youth of E. H. Reynolds were quietly passed upon the home farm. His elementary education, acquired in the common schools, was supplemented by a course in Kennett's Academy, and at the age of seventeen he began teaching, which profession he followed through five winter terms. He also assisted in the work of the foundry and saw and grist mills, remaining on the old homestead until twenty-two years of age. He then rented the farm and machine shops and continued the foundry business in connection with agricultural pursuits for two years. In 1867, when his father's estate was sold, he purchased the original Reynolds homestead, and is now the owner of ninety-eight acres of valuable land. He also engaged in superintending the operation of the stone quarries in West Nottingham Township, Chester County, Pa., following that business for six years. He afterward carried on general farming until 1893, when he removed to Rising Sun, where he has since been engaged in the business of plumbing and steam heating. He is a progressive business man, whose energy and perseverance enable him to overcome all obstacles in his path and work his way upward to success.

On the 23d of February, 1859, Mr. Reynolds married Miss Lydia Lincoln, daughter of John Lincoln. Their children are: Ella, wife of Edwin M. Hunt, of Rising Sun; Maggie S. Rosine, wife of Benjamin Stubbs; Lizzie, wife of U. Grant Brown, of West Nottingham Township, Chester County, Pa.; and Jannette, at home. Mr. Reynolds and his wife are members of the Society of Friends, and are highly esteemed citizens of the community in which they reside. In all the relations of life, Mr. Reynolds is true to duty and to the trust reposed in him, and fully merits the warm regard of his many friends.

NATHANIEL T. HOLLINGSWORTH. More than sixty years of residence upon a farm must create an affection for the place, a fact that is doubtless understood by Mr. Hollingsworth, for his entire life has been passed upon the homestead which he now occupies. Not only is this place dear to him, but the entire locality has a warm place in his heart and he cherishes an affection for all the old landmarks with which time has made him so familiar. His landed possessions consist of one hundred and twenty-five acres of land, lying in the southwestern part of District No. 3, Harford County; but he has not devoted himself exclusively to the cultivation of this tract, for, in addition, he has had extensive and profitable milling interests.

Upon the place where he still makes his home, Nathaniel T. Hollingsworth was born in 1834. He is the grandson and namesake of Nathaniel Hollingsworth, a native of Goshen, Lancaster County, Pa., who migrated to Harford County in 1806 and settled upon the farm now occupied by Silas W. Hollingsworth. Further reference to the family, as well as the life of our subject's father, will be found in the sketch of Joel C. Hollingsworth, presented upon another page of this volume. When a boy our subject did not have the excellent advantages enjoyed by the boys of the present generation, but such opportunities as came to him he improved to the utmost, and in that way he gained considerable information that proved of value in subsequent years. At the age of nineteen he began to work at the turning business, and later, with his brother Joel C., he became interested in the manufacture of spokes and rims, the two remaining together about thirteen years, when the partnership was dissolved. Afterward, for fourteen years or more, Nathaniel gave his time entirely to the rim and saw-mill business, but in 1890 he erected a gristmill and four years later added a flour mill, in which various lines he is now engaged, as well as in the cultivation of his farm.

In 1869 Mr. Hollingsworth established a home of his own, being in that year united in marriage with Hannah S. Carter, a native of Ohio. Three children came to bless their union, but only one is now living, a son, Samuel H., who resides with his parents and assists his father in the various mill and farm interests with which the latter is connected. The family is of Quaker faith and holds membership in the Friends' Church. Mr. Hollingsworth is a man of genial and kindly disposition, one whose friendship is sought, and with whom an acquaintance always develops into a feeling of friendship and a warm personal regard. He is one of the substantial business men of his vicinity, and a loyal, patriotic citizen, interested in all measures for the advancement of county and state.

GEORGE M. CHRISTIE is a prominent representative of the industrial interests of Cecil County, and belongs to that class of enterprising, progressive citizens to whom a community always owes its prosperity and advancement. He was born in District No. 7, Cecil County, in 1844, a son of John and Sophia (Logan) Christie. His maternal grandfather, Robert Logan, came from Ireland to America in the last decade of the eighteenth century. The paternal grandfather, James Christie, also a native of the Emerald Isle, located in New York at the time of his emigration to the new world, but afterward came to Cecil County. He served as a lieutenant in the regular army during the War of 1812, and was on the Canadian border with General Pike when that commander was killed.

John S. Christie was prominently identified with the business interests of Cecil County. For a time he engaged in milling in Harford County, and in 1856 built the mill which is now owned and operated by our subject. The greater part of his life was devoted to that vocation. In politics he was first a Whig and then a Republican. He served as county commissioner for some time and was a very prominent and influential citizen. In 1862 he entered the Union army and became captain of Campany G, Sixth Maryland Infantry. but was compelled to resign on account of ill health. He married Sophia Logan, of Cecil County, a niece of Hiram McCullough, and they became the parents of eight children. George M., Mary J., deceased; Robert L., of Colora; Anna, deceased; Frank S., of District No. 7; Fannie, wife of Dr. R. R. Crothers, of Colora; India S., deceased wife of William H. Moore; and Cornelia. The father of this family died in 1869, at the age of fifty-four years.

George M. Christie obtained his elementary education in the common schools, and later attended the West Nottingham Academy, where he pursued his studies until seventeen years of age. He then joined his father's company and was in the military service of his country for three years. When honorably discharged at the close of the war he held the office of quartermaster-sergeant of his regiment

In 1865 Mr. Christie returned to Cecil County, and joined his father in the milling business. He was afterward employed for some time by the firm of Hill & Alexander at Elkton, and at the age of twenty-five he took charge of his father's business, having since carried on operations along that line. The milling property was formerly owned by Davis & Christie, but in 1895 our subject became sole proprietor of the plant, which is equipped with the latest improved machinery and supplied with all accessories for turning out first-class work. He thoroughly understands the business in every particular and his straightforward dealing and courteous treatment of his patrons have secured to him a liberal patronage. Throughout the community he is recognized as one of its leading business men.

Mr. Christie was united in marriage to Priscilla G. Stevenson, of Port Deposit, daughter of Robert and Agnes Stevenson. He and his wife attend the Methodist Church, and occupy a high position in social circles. By his ballot he supports the men and measures of the Republican party. Integrity, activity and energy have been the crowning points in his career and his connection with various business enterprises and industries has been a decided advantage to this section of Maryland, promoting its material welfare in no uncertain manner, while at the same time bringing to him a handsome competence.

WILLIAM ARMSTRONG. This name will be recognized as that of a resident of Cecil County who is extensively engaged in farming. He is the possessor of one hundred and seventy-five acres of as fine land as can be found in District No. 4. Every acre is well improved, and its excellent condition is due entirely to his own good taste and management. The estate is supplied with improvements in the way of machinery, and the horses to be found here are second to none in the county. Considerable attention is also paid to the dairy business. One of the principal features of the place is the family residence, where home comforts and general hospitality abound.

It is a noteworthy fact that the Armstrong homestead has been held in the name of William Armstrong for a period of one hundred and thirty years. It is a part of a tract of one thousand acres granted by William Penn to one Haley, some time early in the seventeenth century, and is undoubtedly the oldest farm in Cecil County. The first of the Armstrongs to own it was our subject's grandfather, William, and the latter's son, William, was born here and made the place his lifelong home, engaging in agricultural pursuits. During the War of 1812 he served in the American army. He voted the Democratic ticket but never fancied public affairs or cared to enter official life. His death occurred in 1837, when he was forty-eight years of age. By his marriage to Ann Booth, of New London Township, Chester County, he had nine children, and five of these are now living: Catherine, wife of William Holland; Mary, Mrs. Jacob D. McConnell, of Chester County, Pa.; Susan, who married William Houston, of Chester County; James, also a resident of Chester County; and William.

On the place where he has since lived, Mr. Armstrong, of this sketch, was born August 26, 1822. His education in the common schools was completed at the age of seventeen, and afterward he assisted in the cultivation of the farm. On the death of his father he succeeded to the ownership of the estate, where he has since engaged in farming, stock-raising and dairying. He has led a busy and useful life, with so many personal duties that he has never desired to enter public life, and confines his connection with politics to the casting of a Democratic vote. He is a strong advocate of the public schools, believing that education is the best foundation for good government.

An important event in the life of Mr. Armstrong was his marriage, which took place in 1849, uniting him with Mary Smith, of Delaware. Three daughters were born of the union, one of whom, Addie G., died at the age of eighteen years. The others are Amelia E., wife of T. H. Armstrong; and Mary D., Mrs. John R. Armstrong, all of Newcastle County, Del. Mr. and Mrs. Armstrong are identified with Rock Presbyterian Church, the oldest in the state. Of this congregation he was a trustee for some years, and he has also held the office of Sunday-school superintendent. His busy life, characterized by diligence and judicious management, has won for him a comfortable competence.

ALEXANDER B. KAY. There are no rules for building character; there are no rules for achieving success. The man who can rise from the ranks to a position of eminence is he who can see and utilize the opportunities that surround his path. The essential conditions of human life are ever the same; the surroundings of individuals differ but slightly; and, when one passes another on the highway to reach the goal of prosperity before others who perhaps started out before him, it is because he has the power to use advantages which probably encompass the whole human race. For many years, Mr. Kay ranked among the most prominent business men of Cecil County, and the success that he achieved was due entirely to his own efforts, but he is now practically living retired upon his farm in District No. 6.

A native of Scotland, he was born near the city of Edinburgh, in 1823, and was there reared. The opportunities afforded him for securing an education were very limited, and at the age of thirteen he began serving a seven years' apprenticeship in a paper mill, where he continued to work until coming to America in 1844.

On reaching the shores of the new world, Mr. Kay located at Morristown, N. J., where he served as manager in a paper mill for a time, and then accepted a similar position in a large mill at Greenville, S. C. At the end of two years, however, he returned to Morristown and purchased a mill, which he conducted for two years. He next went to Trenton, N. J., where he became part owner in a large paper mill, but at the end of five years sold his interest and removed to Manchester, N. H., making his home there two years, during which time he superintended the erection of a large paper mill at that place. He then established a mill at St. Johns, New Brunswick, which he operated for three years, and on selling out there returned to Morristown, N. J., where he conducted a mill on shares for one year. The following two years were spent at St. Johns, New Brunswick, where he erected another mill, but at the end of that time he embarked in merchandising at Morristown, N. J. Subsequently he became manager of a mill near Elwood, N. J., and continued the manufacture of paper in that state until 1873, when he accepted the position of manager of the Cecil Paper Mills, with which he was connected until 1894. He then bought his present farm, which comprises seventy acres, and in addition to this tract owns another place of seventy-five acres at Harrisonville, Md.

Mr. Kay was married in 1869, the lady of his choice being Miss Elizabeth Talmadge, and they had ten children, eight of whom are living, namely: John, a machinist, now on board the battleship "Maine;" Lewis D., clerk in the Iron National Bank of Morristown, N. J.; Robert H., who completed a collegiate education, and is now a successful mining engineer; Howard B., Stewart W., Bradford Ramsey, Charlotte and Ellen.

In politics, Mr. Kay has always been identified with the Democratic party. Socially he is a Royal Arch Mason, belonging to the blue lodge of Port Deposit, Md., and Mt. Holly Chapter, of Manchester, N. H. His life has been in keeping with the teachings of that ancient and honored fraternity, and his career has ever been such as to warrant the trust and confidence which he receives from all with whom he comes in contact, either in business or social circles.

WILLIAM H. H. WHITEFORD. There is scarcely a child in our land who has not heard of Mason and Dixon's Line, and to older persons the expression is a very familiar one. Some, however, are unacquainted with its origin and history. It lies in latitude thirty-nine degrees, forty-three minutes, and twenty-six seconds, and was run between 1763 and 1767 by Charles Mason and Jeremiah Dixon, two English surveyors, whose names it bears. In location it was the imaginary line that separated the free state of Pennsylvania from the slave states of Maryland and Virginia. In 1820, when congress was in the midst of its exciting debate on the question of excluding slavery from Missouri, the illustrious John Randolph of Roanoke made frequent use of this phrase, which was at once caught up and echoed by the newspapers all over the land, thus bringing it the prominence it has ever since retained.

To the subject of this sketch Mason and Dixon's Line is of especial interest because of the fact that it was there he was born in 1840. The family was first represented in America by his great-grandfather, Michael Whiteford, who with a brother, William, emigrated to this country from Ireland and about 1720 located on the spot through which, years later, the famous line was run. He became a large land owner and a successful man. His son, Dr. Hugh Whiteford, was a surgeon in the War of 1812 and for many years was one of the foremost citizens of Harford County, Md., and York County, Pa. Next in line of descent was our subject's father, Doddridge Whiteford, who was born and reared in Harford County, and throughout active life engaged in farming and mechanical construction, manufacturing a large number of the old-fashioned spinning wheels. By his marriage to Elizabeth A. Silver, he had ten children, eight now living, as follows: William H. H.; Horace F., whose home is in Missouri; Cassie F., widow of Fred Anderson; Silas S., residing in Kansas; Philip D., of Baltimore; Mattie; Frederick T., of Kansas; and Joseph S. The father died at his home in Harford County, February 27, 1883, when nearly seventy-two years of age.

In District No. 5, where he now resides, William H. H. Whiteford was reared, receiving his education in the common schools here and in West Bangor, Pa. In early manhood he was interested in farming, having his home on his father's place. Afterwards he was engaged in business with his uncle at Dublin, this county, but in 1869 he purchased the general store owned by Philip Silver. That enterprise he carried on until 1877, when he sold it and began in the undertaking business, which he has since efficiently conducted. His home and business interests are in the village of Darlington. In politics a stanch Democrat, he held the office of school commissioner for ten years, being elected to the position on the regular party ticket. In 1869 he was united in marriage with Annie E., daughter of Philip W. Silver, of this county. He and his wife are identified with the Presbyterian Church, and in fraternal connections he is a member of the lodge of Odd Fellows at Delta, Pa. A man of excellent executive ability, he has made his way in business unaided, and is now a prominent factor in the enterprises of Darlington.

JAMES CUMMINGS. No life has been lived in vain that has exerted a helpful influence upon other lives. The names of those who have assisted in the advancement of Cecil County will be remembered by a grateful posterity long after their clay tenements have crumbled into dust. While a number of years have elapsed since Mr. Cummings passed away, the services he rendered in promoting the best interests of the people were of such a permanent and uplifting nature that his name will not soon be forgotten. For a period of thirty-five years he officiated as magistrate of District No. 8, and it is a noteworthy fact that this office has been in the family for forty-five or more years, he being succeeded by his son, James F., and the latter by a brother, Thomas, in 1891.

The life here sketched began in 1814, and ended in 1887. It was marked by no thrilling events, but was characterized by the quiet discharge of every duty, by deeds of kindness and charity. The family was in moderate circumstances, and the boy did not have the advantages now enjoyed by children. His father had come from Ireland a poor man, and settled in Philadelphia, where James was born and educated. After the usual custom of those days he learned a trade, selecting the occupation of a tailor, and this he followed for many years. When a young man he went to Pleasant Grove, Pa., where, in addition to working at his trade, he acted as magistrate for five years. On coming to Oakwood, District No. 8, Cecil County, he opened a general country store and built up a good trade. In 1859, purchasing a farm near Pilot Town, he settled there, making it his home the balance of his life. About 1860 he was appointed magistrate, and continued to fill the position as long as he lived. For several years he was tax collector for the district. Politically he voted the Republican ticket.

By the marriage of James Cummings and Jane McColgan, of Lancaster County, Pa., nine children were born, namely: Margaret, Lewis, John, James F., a colonel in the army during the war, for five years a magistrate, and deceased in 1891, at the age of forty-eight; Henry Clay, a resident of Rising Sun; William Penn, of Port Deposit; Samuel R., a resident of Philadelphia; Thomas H., who was commissioned magistrate by Governor Brown in 1891, and still holds the office; and one who died in infancy. The family adheres to the Presbyterian faith, following the example set by its forefathers.

When a long life is ended, it affords satisfaction to friends and relatives to know that the world has been benefited by the presence in it of a good, upright and energetic man. Far more to be desired than mere success in accumulating a fortune, is the building up of an upright, honest character, the cherishing of honorable principles, and the encouragement of lofty and public-spirited opinions and sentiments. Such was the success Mr. Cummings achieved, and such the reputation he enjoyed. He was a man of excellent judgment, a keen thinker, with a kind and loving heart, and no worthy object failed to elicit from him a tangible assistance. In all public improvements and in the advancement of the community he was prominent, while in the family circle it was his desire to enhance, by any means in his power, the pleasure and happiness of those dear to him.

REUBEN HAINES. In Elkton there is no man who in a higher degree enjoys the confidence of the people than the subject of this sketch, who is identified with many of the important professional and financial interests of the village. By his energy and resolute character, coupled with force of will, he has partially overcome the serious obstacle which ill health presented to his success. His public spirit has given an impetus to the growth of the locality and he is actively forwarding various enterprises for its advancement in important directions.

Before presenting in detail the principal events in the life of Mr. Haines, a few words regarding his ancestors will not be amiss. The family has been represented in America since an early period of its history. His grandfather, Reuben Haines, was born in Cecil County and was a leading member of the Society of Friends. During the early days of the settlement of this locality, the Indians always found a true friend in him, and they often came to his farm to camp and hold their "pow wows." He died in 1828, when advanced in years. He was the son of Eli and grandson of Joseph Haines, both of whom took active parts in the stirring events connected with the early history of Maryland, and both were prominent members of the Quaker Church.

The father of our subject, Joseph Haines, was born in Cecil County in 1798, and, like his forefathers, held membership in the Society of Friends. His principal business was that of storekeeper, but he also held numerous public positions, including that of deputy clerk of the county courts and for six years judge of the orphans' court. Highly esteemed by all who knew him, he led an exemplary life and died a Christian's peaceful death, January 23, 1866. His wife, whose maiden name was Harriet Kirk, was born near Rising Sun, Cecil County, the descendant of Scotch and Quaker ancestors. Her father, William Kirk, was born in this county, where he was occupied as a farmer and storekeeper. The Kirk family, on coming to America, settled in Pennsylvania, but afterward removed to Maryland. Mrs. Harriet Haines died in November, 1858, having been the mother of six children, five of whom survived her. Charles H., who was clerk of the circuit court of Cecil County and for many years cashier of the Cecil National Bank of Port Deposit, died January 23, 1866, a day rendered doubly sad to the family because on it their father was also taken from earth; Cornelia H. is the widow of Dr. James Turner and resides in Washington, D. C.; her husband was formerly a practicing physician in Cecil County, but after his death the widow removed to Washington; Mary E. is the wife of John M. Ireland, a real-estate dealer in the city of Washington; Robert died when young, and William L., who was a farmer, died in 1891.

At the old homestead in Cecil County, situated near what was then known as the brick meeting house, the subject of this article was born June 29, 1840. He was a delicate child, slight in figure, and with none of the sturdy robustness usually displayed by boys. Though physically weak, he was mentally strong and vigorous, and with an ambitious spirit prosecuted his studies in the New London Academy in Chester County, Pa., West Nottingham Academy and Lafayette College, Easton, Pa., graduating from the last-named institution in July, 1862, with the degree of A. B. After the completion of his education he taught school for a term. April 14, 1863, he came to Elkton and entered as a student in the law office of John A. J. Creswell, who was later a United States senator and postmaster-general in President Grant's cabinet. He was admitted to practice at the bar October 14, 1864, and two years later was elected state's attorney, serving until 1868. In his youth he was regarded as one of the most promising young men of the county, and he would undoubtedly have attained conspicuous positions of honor and trust had he been equal, physically, to their responsibilities, but poor health has interfered to a great extent with his practice and political advancement. Stanch in his advocacy of Republican principles, he is regarded as one of the active members of that party in Elkton. Among his interests are those of stockholder and director in the National Bank of Rising Sun and stockholder and for twenty-five years a director of the National Bank of Elkton.

Amid the muliplicity of other duties, Mr. Haines has never allowed his religious duties to be neglected. In the Presbyterian Church he has been an official for years, holding the important position of elder. He carries his religious belief into the practical affairs of life, thereby gaining a reputation for probity, honor and uprightness, which is far too seldom seen among

PHILIP F. COALE.

professional and business men. Fraternally he is connected with the Masonic order. His marriage was solemnized February 8, 1866, and united him with Amanda M. Brown, daughter of Edward and Martha Brown, of Elkton. They and their two daughters, Mary C. and Estella, have a pleasant home in Elkton.

Such, in brief, is a sketch of one of the best-known men in this village, one who has, in spite of obstacles, gained a fair measure of success, and who at the same time has promoted the prosperity of the place by his progressive spirit and enterprise.

PHILIP F. COALE. Among the residents of Harford County who are successfully engaging in general farming and the canning business, mention belongs to Mr. Coale, of District No. 3. On the farm where he now resides, he was born June 3, 1852, the son of Joseph R. and Sarah A. (Watson) Coale. The family is of English origin, and the first of the name in Maryland was his paternal great-grandfather, who on crossing the ocean from England settled in District No. 6, Cecil County. Joseph R. Coale, son of William, was a farmer in that district for some years, but at the time of the building of the Philadelphia, Wilmington & Baltimore Railroad, he sold his land to that company and soon afterward removed to Harford County, where he purchased a portion of the Stony Ridge farm. Upon this place he conducted general farm pursuits. He was a well-informed man, and in politics supported Democratic principles. At the age of fifty-six years, in 1867, he fell a victim to small-pox, which terminated fatally. His wife, Sarah A., who is still living, is a daughter of Abraham Watson, and a member of an old Cecil County family. They were the parents of fourteen children, of whom eight are living, as follows: Maria, wife of C. H. James; Cornelia, Mrs. C. H. Walker; Clara, who married J. L. James, of Baltimore County; William and Joseph, of Bel Air; Philip F.; Alice, wife of W. Arthur Trago; and Ella, Mrs. Robert Lilley. The mother of this family makes her home with our subject and is in the enjoyment of excellent health, though now seventy-eight years of age.

When his father died, our subject was fifteen years of age. He at once began the management of the home farm, and has since resided here, cultivating the one hundred and thirty-three acres that comprise the estate. The canning of fruit is a special feature of his work, and he also does a very large business in the canning of tomatoes. His private affairs require his entire attention and he has never found leisure to identify himself with public affairs, but keeps posted regarding politics and is a pronounced Republican. In 1877 he married Miss Ella Loflin, daughter of William Loflin, of this district. They have seven children now living, namely: Ida, Walter, Ira, Sadie, Howard, Roy and Amy. The family are members of the Methodist Episcopal Church and for several years Mr. Coale has been a steward in Smith's Chapel, as well as trustee, secretary and treasurer, and superintendent of the Sunday-school.

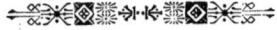

SILAS J. LOWE. By the exercise of industry and perseverance, Mr. Lowe has amassed a comfortable fortune and established a reputation as a citizen of more than ordinary worth and usefulness. His entire life has been spent amid rural scenes and employments, and he bears the reputation of being one of the most prosperous farmers of Cecil County. Upon the old family homestead, originally purchased by his grandfather, and located in District No. 8, he is engaged in general farm work, planting the land to such cereals and vegetables as are best adapted to the soil. The one hundred and thirty acres constituting the farm bear an excellent grade of improvements, including substantial buildings. In addition to his work as an agriculturist, he has been postmaster of Rock Springs for twenty-two years, during all of which time the post-office has been in his house. This, and his interest in public affairs, have brought him into prominence among the people of the neighborhood. While he did not have in early life the advantages that are common to the youth of to-day, yet he has kept his eyes open to what is going on in the world, and has perhaps received from his observation of men and things a more practical schooling than he could have obtained from a collegiate course.

At the home of his parents, Joshua and Sarah (Ales) Lowe, in District No. 5, Harford County, the birth of Silas J. Lowe occurred February 27, 1842. His grandfather, Joshua R. Lowe, came probably from England and on arriving in Cecil County settled upon three hundred acres, a portion of which comprises our subject's present home. The father of our subject was born in Cecil County and there spent some part of his life, engaged in farming and mining, but for thirty years he was a resident of Harford County and the owner of a farm in District No. 5. Politically he always voted the Democratic ticket, though not taking an active part in public affairs. He died at his home in Harford County when seventy years of age, in 1870. Of the seven children that constituted his family, only three are living, namely: Jane, wife of Isaac Scarborough; John, whose home is in Ohio; and Silas J.

The common schools of Harford County afforded our subject all the education that he obtained from text books. Remaining at home and assisting in the cultivation of the farm, upon the death of his father he removed to Rock Springs, Cecil County, and settled upon the farm where he has since resided. He leads a busy life, having in charge the management of his land, the supervision of the post-office and the carrying on of a general store. Fortunate in possessing a good constitution, he has been able to do an immense amount of work, without seriously impairing his health. He meddles little in politics, but is a Democrat first, last and all the time. Realizing the advantage to be derived from a good education, he has always maintained an interest in the cause of good schools and in the capacity of school trustee has been enabled to assist in advancing the grade of local schools and efficiency of their work. For some time he was agent, and is now collector for the Farmers and Mechanics' Mutual Fire Insurance Company, handling large sums of money for the concern.

The family of Mr. Lowe consists of his wife and daughter, Sarah D. The former was Miss Sarah E. T. Durham, of Harford County, daughter of D. D. Durham. They attend the Baptist Church and take a part in all the movements inaugurated by that denomination. In fraternal relations Mr. Lowe is connected with Excelsior Lodge No. 67, I. O. O. F., of Rising Sun. During the long period of his residence in Cecil County, he has proved himself to be one of the most valued members of his community. He is foremost in local enterprises, and the substantial encourager of every plan calculated to benefit the district and advance the interests of the people.

REV. EDWARD A. COLBURN. How much our country owes to the ministers of the Gospel can never be known. Their loyal sacrifices, their heroic achievements, their ceaseless labor for the moral and spiritual elevation of mankind, all entitle them to lasting remembrance. The life of Mr. Colburn has perhaps had less of adversity and hardship than falls to the lot of many ministers, for he has not been obliged to change pastorates frequently nor has he suffered, as many do, the ingratitude and unkindness of others. However, he has found the profession one of the greatest responsibility, and his time has been fully occupied in endeavoring to faithfully discharge every duty that falls to him. In August, 1861, he came to Harford County and assumed charge of the Trap Church, and since 1867 he has been rector of Holy Trinity Church at Churchville, and during that long period has become deeply attached to his field of work and his parishioners. Rejoicing in their successes and sympathizing with them in sorrow, the members of his congregation feel sure of his unchanging interest in their welfare, and the ties of long association that bind pastor and people are of golden threads.

In the city of Baltimore Mr Colburn was born July 20, 1830, the son of Dr. Harvey and Elizabeth (Knight) Colburn. His father, who was a son of Fletcher Colburn, of Massachusetts, came to Maryland about 1828 and embarked in business in Baltimore, but later studied medicine and engaged in practice for a short time. Afterward he carried on a dental practice. In 1861 he was appointed clerk in the quartermaster's department in Washington, D. C., where he remained for twenty-seven years. He died at the home of our subject in 1890, when eighty-five years of age; his wife passed away in 1887, at the age of seventy-nine. Of their eight children two are now living, namely: Edward A. and Rollinson, the latter a government employe since 1861.

In 1851 the subject of this article graduated from St. James' College, Hagerstown, Md., and three years later completed the studies of the theological department. On being ordained to the ministry of the Episcopal Church, he accepted a position as assistant pastor of St. Luke's Church, Baltimore, where he remained for three years. Three years were then spent in Prince George County, Md., from which place he came to Trap Church in August, 1861, and in 1867 entered upon the pastorate of Holy Trinity Church, where he has since remained. He has labored long and faithfully in the church, and in both his public and private life has exhibited the generous mind, noble heart and charity toward the faults of others, which have gained him the confidence of those among whom he has lived, thus establishing his influence and making him the instrument of much good. In addition to his ministerial duties, he has held other important positions, having been trustee of the public schools, secretary of the Baltimore convocation, and president of the Harford Historical Society. He is the Rural Dean of Harford County.

In 1859 Mr. Colburn was united in marriage with Miss Hannah Rogers, member of an old Baltimore family. This lady died in 1863, leaving an only child, James R., now a resident of Elmira, N. Y. The second marriage of Mr. Colburn took place in 1865 and united him with Miss Mary Brooke, of Havre de Grace. They are the parents of seven children, named as follows: Alice B.; Edward H., who resides in Elmira, N. Y.; William H., who is connected with the Pennsylvania Railroad in Jersey City; Florence P., a trained nurse at the Johns Hopkins Hospital, of Baltimore; Alfred A., of Churchville; Mary R. and George S., who are at home.

WILLIAM E. PORTER. This name is familiar to most of the citizens of Cecil County and is borne by a man of high moral character, excellent business ability; one who, in all respects, is a valued member of his community. After an active life in the railroad business, he has returned to the scenes of childhood and now resides in District No. 8, within one and one-half miles of the place where he was born. Though now practically retired, his life is not an idle or aimless one, for the supervision of his extensive interests requires considerable thought and attention. He is the owner of six hundred acres of well-cultivated land here and also several buildings in Piedmont, W. Va.

Born October 30, 1829, the subject of this sketch is the son of John H. and Mary (Toy) Porter, a grandson of James, and great-grandson of James Porter, the latter a native of Ireland, who settled at Peach Bottom, Lancaster County, Pa., during the early portion of the eighteenth century; after some time devoted to mercantile pursuits in that place, in 1753 he removed to Cecil County and purchased the Hopewell farm in District No. 8. From that time to this the property has remained in the possession of the family and is now owned by William E. Porter, who derives a good income from the rental of its two hundred and fifty acres. Capt. Andrew Porter, uncle of John H. Porter, took a conspicuous and valiant part in the War of 1812, and one of the lieutenants in his company was his brother, John H. The latter was born in District No. 8 and here spent his entire life, engaged in general farm pursuits. In his political opinions he was a Democrat. He died at his home in 1859, aged seventy-four years, and his body was interred in the old cemetery in this district.

Ten children comprised the family of John H. and Mary Porter, and five of these are now living: Robert; Mary E., widow of E. W. Gillespie; William E., George, and Anna E., widow of William Morrison, of Baltimore. Our subject attended the common schools in boyhood and at the age of seventeen went to Baltimore, where he served four years as an apprentice to the carpenter and builder's trade. In 1851 he secured employment with the Baltimore & Ohio Railroad Company as superintendent of construction and building. Eight years later he was made general assistant to the road master, and while acting in that capacity he had charge of the building of the Parkersburg bridge over the Ohio River, the completion of the Benwood bridge over the same river, and the arching of tunnels. He remained with the company until 1878, when he resigned in order to accept the more lucrative position of superintendent of the Chesapeake & Ohio Canal, and in that capacity the two following years were spent. In 1880 he was made general superintendent of construction for the West Virginia Central Railroad at the time of its building and remained with it until the work was completed in 1893.

Meantime Mr. Porter had rented to tenants the old family homestead, of which he had become the owner. About 1878 he purchased the Mt. Welcome farm of three hundred and fifty acres and here he established his home about eight years later. In 1851 he married Sarah Paxson, of Chester County, and they became the parents of seven children, named as follows: William, a lawyer in Baltimore; George H., who is interested in a banking business in that city; Henry T., who has held the position of general road master for the Toledo & St. Louis Railroad since 1887; Augustus H., superintendent of the Macon & Northern Railroad; A. Lee, a practicing physician of Cumberland, Md.; Elizabeth, wife of P. S. Shaffer, of Baltimore; and Anna M., Mrs. Louis Traddell, whose home is in Philadelphia. Henry T. married Anna, daughter of Richard Hall and granddaughter of Washington Hall, who was a member of a prominent old family of Revolutionary fame.

Public spirited and liberal, Mr. Porter is always ready to encourage worthy projects and has proved an important factor in progressive movements. He votes the Democratic ticket, but has never been active in politics, owing probably to the fact that his business duties required a frequent change of location. Personally he is genial and social, having inherited in a marked degree many of the traits peculiar to his ancient and honorable ancestry.

JOHN T. MOORE. Among the leading and influential agriculturists of District No. 3, Cecil County, who thoroughly understand their business, and pursue the avocation of their chosen calling in a methodical and workmanlike manner, is the subject of this biography. He is the owner of twenty-seven and a-half acres of timber land, besides his homestead, which comprises one hundred and forty-four acres of valuable and productive land, on which he is successfully engaged in general farming and dairying.

Mr. Moore was born near Newport, in Newcastle County, Del., January 15, 1849, a son of William V. and Jane (Stewart) Moore, who were the parents of ten children, seven sons and three daughters. In the year of his birth, the family removed to Cecil County, Md., locating in District No. 3, where the father purchased a farm on which they made their home for four years, but at the end of that time they removed to our subject's present homestead. The father was born in 1818, and died on the 9th of April, 1896, respected by all who knew him.

In the common schools of Cecil County, John T. Moore acquired a fair education, sufficient to fit him for the responsible duties of business life, and he was reared to manhood upon his present farm, remaining with his father until twenty-six years of age, when he rented a farm, which he operated for one year. At the end of that time, however, he returned home, and has since had the management of the place, which is made to yield bountiful returns for the care and labor bestowed upon it.

On the 2d of March, 1881, was celebrated the marriage of Mr. Moore and Miss Henrietta Shaw, of Newcastle County, Del., and to them were born six children, Ethel J., William T., Bertha H., John C., who died in infancy, Lulu May, and James H. Mr. Moore uses his right of franchise in support of the men and measures of the Democratic party, and has served his fellow-citizens as a member of the county board of supervisors. Fraternally he is a member of the American Mechanics. They are attendants at the Methodist Episcopal Church of Cherry Hill.

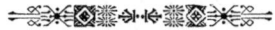

HON. WILLIAM J. SMITH. Doubtless few men have done more for the upbuilding of Cecil County and its general improvement than the subject of this sketch, who has proved a valuable acquisition to its citizenship. His tact in the management of affairs, his recognized ability and his devotion to the interests of his locality have brought him before the public as a desirable official. He has frequently been chosen by his fellow-citizens to represent them in offices of trust and honor, and at this writing is a member of the Maryland legislature. To that responsible position he brings the same energy of character and devotion to principle that marked his career in positions of lesser importance. He is a man of intelligent and pronounced views upon all subjects, and particularly in the matter of politics, where he always acts with the Republican party.

To rightly judge character, it is necessary to note the ancestral record. The family of which our subject is a member is an honorable one. His grandfather, Rev. James Smith, was well known in his home neighborhood as a local Methodist preacher, and accomplished much in the cause of religion through his self-sacrificing efforts. He had a son, Stephen, who was in the railroad service throughout his entire life; another son, Samuel, our subject's father, born in Cecil County in 1804, who was for many years engaged in the construction of railroads, principally on the Pennsylvania system and the branches since secured by that road. Late in life he settled upon his farm, where he died in 1862. His wife, who bore the maiden name of Sarah J. Batton, was born in Newcastle, Del., and died in Cecil County in March, 1891. Her father, William Batton, was a prominent farmer in Delaware, a soldier in the War of 1812, and a member of the Methodist Episcopal Church. Her family consisted of four sons and two daughters, namely: Thaddeus S., who was a soldier in the Sixth Maryland regiment of Federal infantry, and after the war went to Illinois, where he died in 1877; Samuel C., who was a farmer and died in Cecil County; George P., a Methodist minister, having a pastorate in Dorchester County, Md.; Mary A., wife of T. B. Brown, of Baltimore County; Anna J., who is employed in the post-office department in Washington, D. C.; and William J., who was born in District No. 2, of this county, June 26, 1850.

Upon the home farm the early years of our subject were uneventfully passed, his education being obtained in the neighboring public schools. At the age of twenty-one he began for himself in the painting and paper-hanging business, and his careful work and industry soon brought him a favorable reputation. From early manhood he has taken an active part in local politics as a stanch supporter of the principles of the Republican party, and he is one of the leaders of this political organization in the county. In 1883 he was elected to fill the responsible position of county sheriff, where the value of his services were soon apparent. In 1891 he was a candidate, on the Republican ticket, for the office of clerk of the circuit court, but was defeated. In

1895 he was elected to the state legislature and at this writing is a member of the house. In 1896 he was a delegate to the St. Louis convention that nominated Major McKinley for the presidency, and he took an active part in the heated campaign that followed. As a member of the house he has served on a number of important committees and has taken an active part in all the important proceedings. Among his fellow-citizens in Elkton he has many warm personal friends, who appreciate his genial qualities of character. He is now a candidate for register of wills of Cecil County.

The marriage of Mr. Smith took place in 1876, and united him with Miss Mary A. Ash, by whom he has four children, Gertrude, Estelle, Julian C. and Mary B.

J. WESLEY FALLS, attorney-at-law, of North East, was born May 31, 1835, in District No. 5, three miles from this place. He is a son of Elijah Falls, a native of the same district, and by trade a cooper, but throughout much of his life a farmer, cultivating a tract which he purchased in 1844, and which is still in the possession of the family. In early years he supported Whig principles, and upon the disintegration of that party, became a Republican. Though well informed regarding public matters, he never allowed the use of his name as a candidate for office, but preferred to give his attention to private affairs. His death occurred at his home October 4, 1876. He was a son of Hugh Falls, who emigrated from Ireland, and died in Cecil County in 1816. The mother of our subject, Emily Riddle, was born in the house where the eyes of her son, J. W., opened to the light. She was a daughter of William and Mary Riddle, and died in 1886, at an advanced age. Her grandfather, Humphrey Riddle, was born in Ireland in 1732, and about 1750 established his home in the United States; he married Bridget Shannon, who was born in 1737.

In youth the subject of this sketch learned the cooper's trade, but never worked at it afterward. He was sick much of the time from twenty-one to twenty-six years of age, but, though sick, he was never idle. He was ambitious to learn, and devoted himself closely to helpful reading and the study of such branches as he believed would be of assistance to him. For two years, while still in poor health, he studied law with Hiram McCullough. In 1858 he became teacher of the Marion school, one mile from his home, and was thus engaged until the spring of 1861. From that time until 1866 he cultivated the old homestead, but in the latter year removed to Philadelphia, and for two years carried on a produce commission business. In 1868 he returned to North East, and for some time afterward gave his attention to teaching school, being three years at Charlestown, two years in Elkton and eleven years at North East as principal of schools. He taught under a first-grade certificate, and was recognized as one of the best instructors of the county.

In spite of these years of work in the teacher's profession, Mr. Falls had never abandoned his hope of becoming a lawyer, and at last his desire was fulfilled, and he was enabled to study law with William S. Evans, the present state's attorney. In 1886 he was admitted to practice at the bar of Maryland, and at once opened a law office in North East, where he has since built up an extensive practice. While studying law, he did a large surveying and real-estate business. He is now well-to-do, his possessions comprising the old homestead where his boyhood days were passed. Fraternally he is connected with the Knights of Pythias, has passed all the chairs in the lodge, and is a member of the grand lodge. He is also connected with the Odd Fellows. In 1873 he allowed his name to be used as candidate on the Republican ticket, for the house of delegates, but the large Democratic majority in the district made election impossible. In addition to his practice, he has various business interests. He is vice-president of the Wakefield Fire Brick Company, and a stockholder and director in it, and the Stevenson Wrench Company. February 9, 1860, he married Miss Rachel Thompson, of Cecil County, an estimable lady, and a member of the Methodist Episcopal Church. They are the parents of three children now living: Emily Elizabeth, wife of William H. Lynch, of Cecil County; Rachael T., who married Worden Rambo, of North East; and Wilmer J., who is engaged in the insurance business in this place.

FRANK R. SCOTT, postmaster of Elkton, has an exceptional record as a local leader in the Democratic party, and as one of the best business men of the village. It is conceded by all that Elkton has never had a more public-spirited and judicious official than Mr. Scott, for he has carried in his official relations the same good judgment and superior ability which he has always manifested in the marts of trade. A man of strong convictions, when once he makes up his mind what is best to do, he is not easily swerved from his decision.

The connection of the Scott family with the history of Cecil County was begun at a very early period, when our subject's great-grandfather crossed the ocean from Scotland and made settlement here, he being then a young man. Succeeding generations have been closely identified with the development of this community. To its progress they have contributed liberally of their toil and their means, and it stands to-day conspicuous as a monument to their thrift, assisted by other pioneers; a spot to which the entire state can point as a fitting result of the labor and intelligence of early settlers, whose brain and brawn have planted villages and built up large plantations.

One of the most influential and prominent members the family has ever had was David Scott, father of our subject. He was born in District No. 4, Cecil County, six miles north of Elkton, in January, 1824, and received a liberal academic education, becoming a man of cultured literary tastes. When a young man he taught school and also acted as clerk to the board of county commissioners. In 1867 he was elected clerk of the circuit court, which position he filled efficiently for six years. In 1875 Gov. John Lee Carroll tendered him the position of State Weigher of live stock with office in Baltimore, and he was filling his second term in this capacity at the time of his death, which occurred May 13, 1879. Interested in religious and educational enterprises, he was a trustee in the Presbyterian Church and the Elkton Academy. In the organization of the National Bank at Elkton he was actively interested and in it he served as a director from its inception until his decease. In his love of literature he resembled his cousin, whose name was the same as his own and who was an author of note. In the course of his active public life he made many friends and even those who differed with him in opinion had the highest regard for his integrity of purpose and action. His first wife, who bore the maiden name of Mary J. Wilson, died in 1858, leaving three children, one of whom, Ella M., is the wife of Edwin M. Miller, of Newton, Kan. By his second marriage, which united him with Anna Elizabeth Craig, he had one son and three daughters, namely: Henry D., who resides with his widowed mother; Eva C., wife of J. F. Frazer, of Elkton; Bessie F. and Helen, who are with their mother.

The subject of this article was born in Elkton August 11, 1856, and was only two years of age when deprived by death of his mother. He was educated in the Elkton Academy and also took a business course in Eastman's commercial college, of Poughkeepsie, N. Y. In 1875 he entered his father's office as an assistant, and four years later succeeded to the fertilizer business that had been established by his father and uncle. In partnership with the latter and William H. Mackall our subject carried on the enterprise, under the old firm name, until 1887, when the Scott Fertilizer Company was organized, with him as the president, and he has since continued as its head, conducting an extensive business. He succeeded his father as a director of The National Bank of

Elkton and continued as such until January 1, 1897, when he sold his stock in the bank. Always actively interested in politics and well informed regarding the public issues of the day, he has been prominent as a member of the Democratic party. The first important office to which he was elected was that of representative to the state legislature, in 1883, and during his incumbency of this office he held membership on a number of important committees. For two years he was treasurer of the town. Another honor tendered him was that of World's Fair Commissioner for Maryland, which appointment was made by Gov. Frank Brown. Under the second administration of President Cleveland, in April, 1894, he was appointed postmaster of Elkton, and in this position he has displayed the same energy of purpose and accuracy of system characteristic of him in every relation of life.

The marriage of Mr. Scott took place in 1882 and united him with Miss Rachael J. Wilson, who was born in Chester County, Pa., but came to Elkton at an early age. Their family consists of five children: Edith W., David, DeLancey, Elizabeth and John Wirt.

ISRAEL R. DEAN. In the suburbs of the village of North East lies the place usually known as the Scotten farm, consisting of a large acreage of well-improved land and containing all the buildings to be found upon a model farm. This is the home of Mr. Dean and his family, and here they are surrounded by all the comforts that can enhance the happiness of existence. He is a busy man, for it requires all of his time to cultivate the two hundred and sixty acres in his charge, but this he does in a manner that proves his ability and good common sense. He and his wife, who have ever been economical and thrifty, are classed among the representative residents of District No. 5, and are highly esteemed by all.

The Dean family is one of the oldest in Cecil County. John Dean, our subject's grandfather, was born near Elk Forge, in this county, and was an iron worker by trade; his father owned the land where now stands the Howard House, of Elkton. Moses Dean, father of our subject, was born in Cecil County, and throughout life followed the trade of an iron worker, never taking an active part in politics or in public affairs. In religious belief he was a Methodist. He was killed at the works here in 1865. His wife, who died in 1869, was in maidenhood Julia Ann Alexander, and was a member of an old family of Cecil County, the Alexanders having come here from Scotland about 1700. Six sons and six daughters comprised the parental family, of whom the following survive: Israel R.; Mary J., who married Benjamin R. Rocky, a railroad man residing in Philadelphia; Ann Rebecca, wife of Isaac Nyman, a farmer of Chester County, Pa.; Jacob, who makes his home at Elk Neck; Susan, widow of George Williams, and a resident of New Jersey; and William G., an iron worker employed at McKeesport, Pa.

In Lancaster County, Pa., our subject was born May 8, 1838, and there he resided until the spring of 1861, when he came to North East and secured employment at the trade of an iron worker with the McCullough Iron Company, holding a position with the same concern for twenty-one years. In June, 1882, he went to McKeesport, Pa., where he worked at his trade for ten months. On his return to North East he took charge of the Scotten farm, formerly the property of his father-in-law, who had been manager of the iron works for forty years. He carries on general farming and keeps the place under excellent cultivation. Fraternally he is connected with the Knights of Pythias and in religious connections is a member of the Methodist Episcopal Church, in which he has been steward. In politics he is now and always has been a Republican, voting with and working for the success of the party ticket. However others may have faltered in devotion to the principles of this organization, he has always remained firm, and through evil and good report has labored for the success of the party. Honoring the party,

JOSEPH B. HANWAY.

he has in turn been honored by it, and is at present a member of the state central committee. In 1891 he was nominated for county commissioner by the Republican party.

February 13, 1862, he married Minerva A. Scotten, a native of Cecil County, and nine children were born of their union. The seven now living are named as follows: Martha Ann, wife of Schuyler Boyd, of this county; Sarah E., Mrs. Samuel S. Biles, of Chester County, Pa.; John H., an iron worker by trade; Joel H., who assists in the cultivation of the farm; George Herbert, William S. and Minerva, who are at home.

JOSEPH B. HANWAY. "Self-made" is the word that affords the clue to this enterprising business man's rise to his present influential and honorable position. Back of that lies a sterling character derived from worthy Scotch ancestors, and it is of the utmost interest to the student of human nature to trace his career from his first start up to the present, for it is only in this way that one can realize the difficulties and discouragements that he has surmounted — difficulties and discouragements that would have caused any one of less determined will to abandon the struggle and sink back into insignificance. Such was not the stuff of which Mr. Hanway was made, however, for every buffet of fortune's wheel but made him the more determined to bend the force of circumstances to his will, and the result may be seen in the fine fortune he has accumulated.

Mr. Hanway was born at Hall's Cross Roads (now called Aberdeen), Harford County, Md., April 12, 1842, a son of Thomas and Sarah (Keen) Hanway, both natives of Harford County, the latter a daughter of Timothy Keen, of District No. 2. In his early manhood Thomas Hanway was engaged in the manufacture of woolen goods, but later devoted his attention to merchandising and farming, carrying on the former occupation at Creswell. He was a pronounced Democrat in his political views and for years prior to his death, which occurred in 1862, he was a member of the Friends' Church. To Mr. and Mrs. Hanway the following children were born: B. F., a resident of Creswell; Mrs. J. G. Rouse, of Bel Air; George William, who served in the Confederacy during the war, and died in Philadelphia; J. B., the subject of this sketch; Timothy L., a resident of Aberdeen; Sarah B., wife of James Kenly, of Hopewell; Thomas, who was a hardware merchant of Bel Air, where he died; David, of Bel Air; E. C., who also lives in Bel Air; and Ella, wife of Adolph Ahrens, of Philadelphia The mother of these children has attained to the advanced age of eighty-two years.

The first schooling received by J. B. Hanway was at Calvary, and for three years he attended the Grove Academy at Aberdeen, and in 1862 began the occupation of teaching, his pedagogic career being confined to the country districts. He finally opened a mercantile establishment at Creswell, but later removed to Churchville, where he had control of a similar establishment, but he eventually gave up this occupation to engage in the retail grocery business in Baltimore. In 1873, upon the death of his father-in-law, C. C. Rouse, he purchased the Rouse property at the crossroads, where he now lives, and at the same time had charge of thirteen miles of the Baltimore & Philadelphia Turnpike for Colonel Gittings. At the time the Baltimore & Ohio Railroad was built, Joppa station was established, and he at once began clearing his tract of land in the vicinity, and may be said to be the owner of the town, which was built up through his push and enterprise.

His attention has not alone been confined to these enterprises, for during the past fifteen years he has been a director of the Harford Mutual Fire Insurance Company of Bel Air and a director of the Second National Bank of the same place. For the past twenty years he has been the proprietor of a large canning concern, where all sorts of vegetables are put up. This fine establishment is complete in every detail, fitted up with the finest and latest improved machinery, which is run by steam. He manufactures his own cans, and as an illustration of the capacity of his plant it may be stated that twenty-four thousand cans of tomatoes are put up daily, and other vegetables in like proportion. This establishment has been a blessing to the community in which he lives, for it furnishes a ready market for farm produce and has greatly stimulated that industry in his vicinity. The purchase and sale of coal and fertilizers have also occupied his attention, and without doubt he is the largest dealer in the latter commodity in his section.

The tenets of the Democratic party have always met his approval, and in his religious proclivities he is a Presbyterian. Public spirit is one of his distinguishing characteristics and generosity is a scarcely less conspicuous one. Taken all in all, he is the sort of man who is pointed to as a shining example of good citizenship, the kind of man whom one knows to one's pleasure and edification. He is a member of Mt. Ararat Lodge No. 44, F. & A. M., of Bel Air, but owing to his remoteness from the lodge has never taken the higher degrees. On November 24, 1865, he was united in marriage with S. E. Rouse.

HON. DAVID P. DAVIS, chief judge of the orphans' court of Cecil County, is a representative of a family known and honored in the annals of Maryland. The origin of the family is not definitely known, though it is thought that the ancestors were Welshmen. Their connection with the history of America dates from a very early period in the settlement of this country, when some of the name established their home in Prince George County, Md. From that time forward succeeding generations assisted in the development of the resources of this state and the progress of its institutions. Not a few of the name have gained more than local fame. Rev. Henry L. Davis, second cousin of our subject, was elected president of Dickinson College when but eighteen years of age. Hon. David Davis, a third cousin, of Bloomington, Ill., was one of the most famous men of the west in his day, and for years held the office of supreme judge of the United States. In 1876 he was appointed a member of the electoral college in the celebrated Tilden-Hayes presidential contest, but declined to serve. Cecil County claims the proud distinction of having been the birthplace of this illustrious man; he was born in 1815. In 1847 he was a member of the constitutional convention; 1848, judge of the eighth judicial circuit, and in 1862 became associate justice of the supreme court of Illinois. On the bench he was a perfect model of a judge, full of dignity and decision, and as an associate judge his decisions were learned and able. In the senate, to which he was elected, he introduced legislation based upon equity and justice, with a view to resulting to the greatest good to the greatest number.

Born in Cecil County, Md., December 7, 1833, the subject of this sketch is a son of Dr. David and Emmaline L. (Wickes) Davis, both natives of this state. He was fifth among eight children, the others being Ann A., James L., Mary V., Susanna R., Louisa M., John O. and George N. His mother was a daughter of Lambert Wickes and a great-niece of Capt. Lambert Wickes, the first officer who commanded a naval vessel in foreign waters. He was deputed by congress to convey Benjamin Franklin to the court of France in 1776, and on his return trip the vessel was wrecked off the coast of Newfoundland, all on board perishing except the cook.

Reared on a farm until fourteen years of age, our subject then entered the general store of Alfred C. Nowland, of Cecilton, Md., where he remained for three years. On leaving the store he went to make his home with his grandmother, Mrs. Alethea Wickes, on a farm in District No. 1, Cecil County, and there he remained until 1881. In the fall of 1879 he was elected associate judge of the orphans' court of Cecil County, in which position he served four terms, and since the fall of 1895 he has been chief judge of the same court. Though he has not engaged in farming since 1881, he still oversees his large estate. In politics he is a Democrat. In 1862 he married Henrietta W. Cruikshank, daughter of Thomas C. and Sarah E. (Morgan) Cruikshank, natives of this state. The three children born of their union were named Sarah E., Lambert W. and Mary P., but the son alone survives. In girlhood Mrs. Davis spent three years in the Wesleyan Female College at Wilmington, Del. She is identified with St. Stephen's Episcopal Church, as is also Judge Davis, the latter being secretary, treasurer, warden and vestryman of the church.

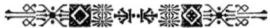

JOHN M. RAWLINGS. While traveling through Harford and Cecil Counties, the writer found that a large proportion of their residents are natives of the localities where they still reside. The majority of them are descendants, in the third or fourth generation, of people from other lands who came hither, and by their industry prepared the way for those to follow. The work for which they laid the foundation was carried forward by those who came after them, and by degrees the educational, commercial and agricultural interests of the locality were placed upon a substantial basis.

The Rawlings family is of Irish origin, but has been represented in Cecil County for several generations. Robert, father of our subject, and a son of John Rawlings, was born on the family homestead, to the ownership and management of which he succeeded, and upon which he remained until his earth life was ended, at the age of sixty-two years. The property is now owned and occupied by Z. T. Rawlings. The mother of our subject was Mary McVey, member of an old family of District No. 9, Cecil County. In her family there were five children, named as follows: Elizabeth, wife of John Brown; John M., of this sketch; Z. Taylor, who resides at the old homestead; Hannah M., Mrs. William Peoples; and Roberta E., wife of David B. Boyle.

In District No. 8, Cecil County, where he still resides, John M. Rawlings was born in 1844. His education was begun in the common schools, and afterward continued in Nottingham (Md.) Academy. He remained on the home farm, assisting in its cultivation, until he was twenty-four years of age, when he married Eliza M. Hindman, and then settled upon the place he has since occupied. The property consists of sixty acres, and bears first-class improvements. In addition to its management, he has been surveyor for the Mutual Fire Insurance Company for six years, and was also tax collector for two years. Politically he supports Democratic principles, and fraternally was formerly connected with the Knights of Pythias lodge at Colora, the Odd Fellows lodge at Rising Sun, and has been the incumbent of all the offices in the former organization. He and his wife are parents of four children: R. Lee, who is employed on the Pennsylvania Railroad; Emory C., Llewellyn H. and Mary P. The family attend the Presbyterian Church.

JOHN J. WILLIAMS. The family of which this gentleman is a member has been represented in America for many successive generations. It was founded in Pennsylvania by his great-great-grandfather, who purchased from William Penn a large tract of land that for a long time constituted the family homestead, remaining in the possession of one of the members in each generation until 1892, when Thomas Williams, brother of our subject, sold it to a railroad syndicate. Through all these years the family was closely identified with the growth and development of the state and the increase of its material resources. Upon the old homestead the boyhood years of the subject of this sketch were uneventfully passed, and from there he marched forth to take a part in the Civil War; but at the close of the conflict he established his home in Maryland, and since the fall of 1865 has resided upon a farm in District No. 2, Cecil County, where he owns three hundred and forty-six acres of well-improved and valuable land, comprising one of the best farms in this locality.

Born in Montgomery County, Pa., February 17, 1838, the subject of this article is a son of John J. and Lydia (Knight) Williams, also natives of Pennsylvania. He was the youngest of five children, the others being Mary K., Thomas W., Jonathan K. and Harriet, deceased. John J. was reared to farm work, early gaining a thorough knowledge of agricultural pursuits that was of great assistance to him in starting out for himself. August 17, 1862, his name was enrolled as a member of Company G, One Hundred and Nineteenth Pennsylvania Infantry, in which he served until the close of the war, when he was honorably discharged, May 26, 1865, at Annapolis, Md. For a time he held the rank of first sergeant and afterward was commissioned second lieutenant. Among the important engagements in which he took part were Fredericksburg, Chancellorsville, Gettysburg, Hatcher's Run, Wilderness and Petersburg, together with all the battles from the siege of Petersburg to the surrender of Lee. In the battle of the Wilderness he was wounded in the limb by a grape shot and was obliged to remain in a hospital in Philadelphia four months. He was also wounded at Hatcher's Run. At Sailor's Creek he was again wounded, but not seriously. His record as a soldier was that of a brave man, whom no danger daunts nor perils affright.

The marriage of Mr. Williams, in 1869, united him with Laura L. Peach, who was born in Maryland, grew to womanhood upon a farm and was given an excellent education. In religious belief she is identified with the Methodist Episcopal Church. In her family there are five children, namely: Howard P., Frederick P., Adelaide P., Roger K. and John J. The family of which she is a member was founded in America by her grandfather, John Peach, a native of England, who settled in Delaware in an early day and there engaged in farming. While the principal portion of his time Mr. Williams devotes to farm work, he yet keeps abreast with current events and national problems, and in matters political is a firm Republican. Among the public offices which he has held are those of town commissioner and school trustee, and he also held the position of postmaster of St. Augustine for nine years, from 1872 to 1881.

ALBERT McCRERY. The subject of this notice is certainly entitled to be considered not only one of the enterprising farmers of District No. 3, Cecil County, but one of its most respected and honored citizens, and a man of more than ordinary ability. Upon the farm where he still resides his birth occurred December 8, 1845, and there his father, John McCrery, was born in 1804. The place has now been in the possession of the family for over a century, the first to locate thereon being the grandfather of our subject, John McCrery, Sr., who purchased two hundred acres of land. He had five children, namely: William, Samuel, Sarah, Mary and John.

The last-named married Sophia Perry, who departed this life in 1853, at the age of forty years. They became the parents of six children. John T., born August 5, 1834, died in 1872; James, born August 6, 1836, is now living retired at Zion, Md.; Sarah, born October 29, 1838, died February 24, 1864; William, born October 26, 1840, died October 6, 1893; Harriet was born December 31, 1842; and Albert is the youngest of the family. The father spent his entire life upon the old homestead and was numbered among the prominent and highly esteemed citizens of the community. In religious belief he was a Presbyterian.

Upon the home farm, Albert McCrery early became familiar with the duties that fall to the lot of the agriculturist, and received a good education in the common schools of the neighborhood. Going to Philadelphia, Pa., in 1863, he clerked in a store until his enlistment, February 27, 1864, in Company I, Second Pennsylvania Heavy Artillery, as a private. The command was first sent to Washington, D. C., after which it participated in the battle of Cold Harbor and took part in the entire siege of Petersburg. At the end of that time Mr. McCrery was taken ill with typhoid fever, and was confined in the hospital at Washington for three months. He was finally discharged at Philadelphia in January, 1866, and returned to the home farm, to the cultivation of which he has since devoted his time and attention with most satisfactory results. The place comprises one hundred and thirty-five acres of rich and arable land.

Mr. McCrery was married in February, 1881, the lady of his choice being Miss Maria E. Hess, who died in August, 1890, at the age of forty years. Two children graced their union: Louise, born in May, 1882; and Florence, born in July, 1884. Politically, Mr. McCrery is a Republican and heartily indorses the measures of that party, while socially he is a prominent member of Grant Post No. 10, G. A. R., of Cherry Hill. He is an active and consistent member of the Presbyterian Church, and is now serving as a member of the board of trustees.

BARCLAY REYNOLDS, the subject of this review, is one whose history touches the pioneer epoch in the annals of Cecil County. In reviewing his genealogical record we find his lineage tracing back to the colonial history of the nation and to that period which marked the inception of the grandest republic the world has ever known. Through such sources have we attained the true American type, and along this line must our investigation proceed if we would learn of the steadfast and unyielding elements which constitute the basis upon which has been reared the lofty and magnificent superstructure of an enlightened and favored commonwealth. Mr. Reynolds traces his ancestry back to Benjamin Reynolds, the first of the family to locate in Cecil County, where he secured a tract of land, obtaining the title from William Penn. His son Jacob was the father of Jacob Reynolds, Jr., the grandfather of our subject, who was born in District No. 6, Cecil County.

Taylor Reynolds, the father of Barclay, was also born in the same district, and on attaining to man's estate he married Miss Eliza Taylor. They became the parents of eight children, who in order of birth are as follows: Ann T., widow of Jacob Kirk, and a resident of Rising Sun; Barclay, of this review; Charles, Henrietta and Jacob, who are all deceased; John T., who makes his home in Virginia; Hetty, deceased; and Samuel T., who is clerking for Mr. Buffington in Rising Sun.

Barclay Reynolds was born October 22, 1819, on the farm in District No. 6, Cecil County, where he still resides, and was there reared to manhood. Although his early school privileges were meager, he has become a well-informed man by reading and observation in later years. At the age of nineteen he began teaching, and successfully followed the profession for four years, after which he engaged in merchandising at Harrisville for twelve years. At the end of that time, however, he returned to the old homestead, where he still resides.

In 1854 Mr. Reynolds was united in marriage with Miss Amanda C. Carter, a native of Chester County, Pa., and to them were born six children, namely: Howard H., who resides on the farm with his father; Charles T., a hardware merchant of Wilmington, Del.; Sophia C., wife of Elmer Reynolds; H. Mitchell, deceased; Eugene A., a teacher residing at home; and Barclay, Jr., a professor in the high school of Philadelphia.

In the fall of 1857 Mr. Reynolds was elected sheriff of Cecil County, which position he efficiently filled for two years, during which time he lived in Elkton, but with that exception his entire life has been passed on the old homestead. Casting his first presidential vote for William Henry Harrison, in 1840, he continued to support the men and measures of the Whig party until its dissolution, since which time he has been an ardent Republican. He has served as school director in his district, and for the long period of forty years was one of the directors of the Cecil

County Fire Insurance Company. The home farm, which comprises one hundred and forty acres, he has placed under a high state of cultivation, but is now practically living a retired life, leaving its management to his son. Socially he affiliates with the Odd Fellows' Society of Rising Sun, and religiously both himself and wife are consistent and faithful members of the Society of Friends. He is now serving as trustee of the church. They are widely and favorably known throughout the community where they have so long resided, and endeavor by lives of kindness and charity to set an example worthy of imitation.

ADAM HETRICK, a wide-awake and energetic farmer, of District No. 5, Harford County, first opened his eyes to the light in Perry County, Pa., in 1821. His grandfather, Nicholas Hetrick, a native of Germany, emigrated to America about 1790, and located in Perry County, where he first worked in the mines, but later followed farming. Before leaving the Fatherland he had married Miss Elizabeth Rator, and they became the parents of five sons.

John Hetrick, our subject's father, was the third of the family, and was born in Perry County, Pa., where he devoted his entire life to general farming. By his marriage with Susan Bird, he had two children: Adam, of this sketch; and John C., a resident of Newport, Pa. The father died at that place in 1827, at the early age of thirty years, and his wife passed away in 1823, when our subject was only two years old. Her father, Andrew Bird, enlisted as a musician in the Colonial army during the Revolutionary war, and for seven long years was fifer of his regiment. He was also a resident of Perry County, Pa., making his home near Millerstown.

In the county of his nativity, Adam Hetrick passed the days of his boyhood and youth, acquiring his education in the common schools near his home, and at the age of seventeen began learning the carpenter's trade, serving a three and a-half years' apprenticeship. When he had completely mastered the business, he followed it until 1877, but now devoted his attention almost exclusively to his farming interests. He continued to make his home in Perry County, Pa., until his removal to Harford County, Md., in 1850, at which time he purchased the Henry Wilson place of eighty acres, near Darlington, where he has since carried on agricultural pursuits with most gratifying results.

In 1846 Mr. Hetrick was joined in wedlock with Miss Catherine Wendt, of Perry County, Pa., a daughter of Major Wendt, who belonged to an old and honored family of the Keystone State, and won his title by gallant service in the War of 1812. Five children graced this union, namely: Clara and Jane, at home; Theodore J., who married Mollie V. Walker, and resides near Darlington; Annie, wife of Samuel G. Hopkins; and Cassie, wife of George W. Bailey. While in Pennsylvania, Mr. Hetrick held membership in the Lutheran Church, but now attends the Methodist Episcopal Church of Darlington, of which his son Theodore is serving as steward. Our subject is one of the representative and prominent farmers of his district, and is widely and favorably known throughout the county, where he is recognized as one of the valuable and highly respected citizens.

THOMAS A. REES. During the long period that Mr. Rees has made his home in Cecil County he has not only accumulated a competency, but he has achieved that which is more important and valuable, a position among the honorable, capable and public-spirited men of the locality. Farming has been his vocation in life and in it he has been very successful. Since the spring of 1864 he has made his home upon a farm in District No. 2, where he owns a valuable and well-improved place, containing all the improvements of a model estate. During his long and continuous residence here, he has given his attention to the raising of the cereals to which the soil is adapted, and has also taken an active part in matters pertaining to the welfare of the people.

As far back as the record can be traced, the Rees family resided in Delaware and assisted in the agricultural development of that state. There our subject was born September 25, 1839, and there, too, occurred the birth of both his parents, John R. and Anna E. (Sevil) Rees. He was the eldest of three children, the others being John R., deceased, and William. Reared upon a farm and early initiated into the details of planting, plowing and reaping, he gained a thorough knowledge of agriculture, and upon arriving at manhood chose farm work for his life occupation. In the meantime he fitted himself for his work by acquiring a practical education, and attended school at New London, Pa., and for three terms in York, Del. In 1864 he came to Maryland, and for three years lived alone on the farm, but in 1867 married and brought his wife to his home. She was Georgia A. Griffin, a native of Delaware, and an estimable lady of energetic disposition and untiring industry. Two children were born of the union, but Annie E. died in childhood, and the son, Ralph H., alone survives. He was carefully trained by his parents and was given excellent educational advantages at Dickinson College, and also took a business course in Wilmington Commercial College. Since the completion of his studies he has assisted his father in the cultivation of the home place, his activity and energy proving an invaluable aid in the work. In 1895 he married Lizzie V. Woolford, a native of Dorchester County, Md., and they reside on the farm with his parents.

Believing in the principles of Christianity, Mr. and Mrs. Rees are identified with the Methodist Episcopal Church, and endeavor, in their daily lives, to exemplify the truth and reality of their religious convictions. "To do unto others as they would be done by" has been their aim at all times, and as a result they have made many friends during their long residence here. The poor and needy never appeal to them in vain for help and no hand stretched out to them for aid is turned empty away. Their ample means enable them to give generously to worthy enterprises and to the upbuilding of the church with which they are connected, and they have never refused to assist, by their time, money and influence, charitable projects and benevolent enterprises.

JAMES S. WHITAKER, M. D. In comparison of the relative value to mankind of the various professions and pursuits, it is widely recognized that none is so important as the medical profession. From the cradle to the grave human destiny is largely in the hands of the physician. An able and prominent representative of this calling is Dr. Whitaker, who has for several years successfully engaged in practice at Cherry Hill, Md.

The birth of the doctor occurred February 27, 1848, in Center County, Pa., but since 1851 he has made his home in Cecil County, Md., passing the days of his boyhood and youth in the village of North East. The common schools afforded him his early educational privileges, but at the age of seventeen he entered the State Normal School of Maryland, where he pursued his studies for three years. For the following two years he clerked in a drug store in North East, and then turned his attention to farming for seven years. Entering the Jefferson Medical College of Philadelphia, Pa., he graduated from that noted institution with the class of 1879, and the following year located at Fair Haven, Md., where he engaged in practice until coming to Cherry Hill, in 1889. In connection with general practice he also conducts a drug store, and is recognized as one of the most skillful physicians and surgeons of Cecil County.

In 1885 Dr. Whitaker led to the marriage altar Miss Clara Engall, and they now have five children, namely: Maggie, Hattie, Emily, Maria and Hilda. Being an ardent Democrat in politics, the doctor has three times been appointed postmaster of Cherry Hill, the duties of which office he discharged in a most acceptable manner, and he has also served as physician of the county alms house for two years. He holds membership in a number of important medical societies and also belongs to the Order of American Mechanics. As a citizen as well as a physician, he stands high in the esteem of all who know him, and has a host of warm personal friends.

ROSS REYNOLDS SMITH. A long residence in a community gives an individual a standing which can scarcely be otherwise acquired, especially if he has made for himself a good record as a citizen and a business man. "The rolling stone gathers no moss," but the man who through a long term of years has shown the possession of energy and honesty and has labored continuously among the same associations gains a warm place in the hearts of others and almost invariably attains financial success. While Mr. Smith is not a native of Cecil County, he has spent the principal part of his life here, and is favorably known to the people. The fact that he is uniformly well spoken of is sufficient indication of his true character. A stranger upon meeting him recognizes him at once as a man of intelligence, one possessing the companionable disposition that is a free passport to the regard of others.

Now a farmer in District No. 9, Cecil County, Mr. Smith was born in Kittanning, Armstrong County, Pa., in 1850. The family of which he is a member has always been noted for patriotic spirit. His grandfather, Gen. Samuel A. Smith, was a captain in the Revolution and a general in the War of 1812, enlisting in the latter war when he was old in years, but with an enthusiastic valor that had characterized him in the conflict thirty-five years before. His son, George W., father of our subject, was born in Bucks County, Pa., and was an officer in the War of 1812, after which he carried on an extensive legal practice in Kittanning, Pa. He was well posted regarding politics and was a pronounced Republican. He married Isabel Reynolds, daughter of David Reynolds, one of the first settlers of Kittanning. They had eight children, six of whom are living: Mary, wife of Matthias Hurst; Ann W.; David R., of Cecil County; Virginia, who married R. H. Cameron, of Baltimore; Ross R. and Panama W. The father died in Cecil County at the age of eighty-four.

Brought to Cecil County in 1855, the subject of this sketch was educated in West Nottingham, after which he was employed as clerk for a firm in Oxford for two years. In 1882 he bought the farm which he has since cultivated and on which he has engaged in general farming and stock-raising. The place consists of one hundred and thirteen acres, all under cultivation, and improved with good buildings. In politics he is a Republican, believing the principles of this party best adapted to the advancement of the nation. He has had no political aspirations, and aside from serving as judge of election of this district has occupied no public office. He is a member of Zion Presbyterian Church and in fraternal relations he is identified with the Cecil Grange. In 1882 he married Anna Whitaker, of Cecil County, and they have an only son, P. Jenks Smith, now a student in school. Mr. Smith is now (1897) a candidate for the assembly on the Republican ticket.

JOHN SPRIGG POOLE, M. D., who practices medicine and surgery at Dublin, District No. 5, Harford County, was born in 1862, in Montgomery County, Md, of which his father, Dr. Thomas Poole, and grandfather, John Poole, were also natives. The family, which is of English extraction, was established here as early as 1637, and has since been actively and prominently identified with the growth and prosperity of the state. Dr. Thomas Poole spent his entire life in the county of his birth, and after completing his medical studies in the Maryland

HON. MURRAY VANDIVER.

University at Baltimore, successfully engaged in general practice there, his office being in Poolesville. He was united in marriage with Miss Eveline Hyde, of the same county, and they became the parents of five children, but John Sprigg, of this review, and two sisters, residing in Poolesville, are the only ones now living. The father's death occurred in 1870, when in his sixty-sixth year.

Dr. Poole, whose name introduces this sketch, also attended medical lectures at the University of Maryland, from which he graduated with the degree of M. D. in the class of 1887. Coming to Harford County the following year, he located in Dublin, where he has resided ever since. The doctor was married in 1891 to Miss Georgia, daughter of Dr. Silas Scarboro, and to them have been born two children, Mary and Thomas. Both the doctor and his wife are members of the Episcopal Church.

HON. MURRAY VANDIVER. Before reviewing the life of a successful man it is always well to consider briefly his parentage and ancestry, in order that we may better understand the principles that have guided his actions and the personal characteristics that have made him a power among his fellow-men. As indicated by the name, the Vandiver family originated in Holland. However, it has had representatives in this country for more than three centuries, and its members have always been men and women of upright characters, unwavering integrity and more than ordinary ability. At different times the name has been variously spelled, Van der Weer, Vanderweer, Vanderveer, Vandeveer, Vandever and Vandiver.

The family was founded in America by Jacob Van der Weer, who came to this country about 1655, and in that year assisted in the capture of Ft. Christiana from the Swedes. This fort, which was built by the Swedes in 1638, was situated on the south side of Christiana Creek, near The Rocks, in Wilmington, Del., and around it some fifteen or twenty houses were clustered. The Dutch, after capturing the place, changed its name to Ft. Altena, and the little town laid out west of the fort was called Christianham (now Wilmington). Jacob Van der Weer was a sergeant in the garrison at Ft. Altena, but in 1660 he made application for his discharge, upon the ground that he wished to leave with the first vessel after the river was open. It was his plan to command a ship to be used in trading along the coast, but for some reason his plans were changed, and he remained in Delaware. April 8, 1661, he secured a deed for a tract of land in Christianham, near the fort. Three years later the English captured the fort, which they allowed to fall in ruins, and the town was abandoned. March 24, 1668, he received a patent and settled on a tract of land north of the Brandywine, where his descendants resided for many generations.

At Brandywine Hundred, opposite the old Dutch fort, was a piece of land called Cooper's Island, on account of the fact that it was occupied by two Dutch coopers. March 2, 1682, Jacob Van der Weer obtained a warrant for this land, which comprised one hundred and forty-seven acres, and the island was afterward known as Van der Weer's Island. It appears to have been the neck of land where the railroad bridge now crosses, and the early records show that the family residence was situated near Brandywine Creek. By order of court, May 13, 1675, a ferry was established at this place, and this was in charge of Jacob Van der Weer and his descendants until a bridge was built near the present Eleventh Street bridge in Wilmington. In 1764 the state legislature authorized the building of a bridge higher up the Brandywine, on the site of the present Market Street bridge, and when this was completed the old bridge was ordered destroyed, but it continued to be used until 1767.

When William Penn assumed the government of the country in October, 1682, he immediately inaugurated proceedings looking toward the transfer of the Swedes and Dutch into English citizenship. A court was held at Newcastle February 21, 22, 1683, at which Penn presented a form of naturalization; and upon its adoption, among those who took the oath of allegiance was Jacob Van der Weer (whose name was there spelled Vandever). May 18, 1664, he was given a warrant for another tract of land, which, together with his previous purchases, was re-surveyed in April, 1688, and found to contain five hundred and thirty-two acres. It included what is now the village of Brandywine, and elevations known as Timber Island and Thatcher's Hook. For over one hundred and fifty years the property was in the possession of this family, but it afterward passed into the hands of many owners.

Within the limited space at our command it would be impossible to trace the history of the members of the family; suffice it to say that many of them attained prominence in Delaware and Maryland, and exerted a powerful influence in the promotion of progressive measures. At the outbreak of the War of 1812, Peter Vandiver was elected to the Delaware legislature, and during the years that followed, while acting as legislator, he gave his support to the government in the maintenance of the war against England. Among the family characteristics may be mentioned industry, energy and a progressive spirit. Some of the members were agriculturists, giving especial attention to the propagation of fruit trees, and the Vandervere apple is well known as one of the best that is grown in the Middle States.

The father of our subject, Hon. Robert R. Vandiver, was born July 22, 1805, at the old Delaware homestead, whence he removed to Harford County and became engaged as a contractor. He built the Protestant Episcopal Church at Easton, Talbot County, the Methodist Episcopal Church at Havre de Grace, the outlet lock of the Susquehanna and Tidewater Canal at Lapidum, Harford County. He superintended the digging of the cut through which the Philadelphia, Wilmington & Baltimore Railway Company ran their cars to be transferred over the Susquehanna River from Havre de Grace to Perryville on their large steamer. A decided Democrat and a leader in political affairs, in 1868 he was elected to the house of delegates, where he rendered efficient service in the interests of the people. He possessed an energetic nature and strong will, in disposition was cheerful and hopeful, and to the circle of his intimate friends he displayed social qualities of a rare order. In business he was very successful, and his contracts were always carried out in spirit as well as letter. Comprehensive reading gave him accurate information upon all subjects. He attained the age of eighty-one and passed away in 1885.

The mother of our subject was Mary Russell, who was born in 1810, and died in January, 1886, aged seventy-six. She was of English descent and a daughter of Thomas Russell, who took part in the War of 1812. His wife was a member of the Murray family, which was among the first English settlers of Cecil County. Mrs. Vandiver was the mother of four sons and three daughters. George T., who was a soldier in the Confederate army, was a prisoner of war at Point Lookout in 1864, but was afterwards exchanged; he died a few years later. Another son, Robert R., Jr., was an attorney in Cecil and Harford Counties, and died in December, 1884. The others were Jacob, Martha, Alice and Ellen.

Born September 14, 1845, Murray Vandiver was educated in the public schools and academy at Havre de Grace and in Eastman's Business College, Poughkeepsie, from which he graduated in December, 1864. With a predilection for the mercantile business, he decided to embark in the lumber business, and this he did at Havre de Grace in 1865. Some years were spent in that occupation, but in 1878 he joined his father in the business of shipping brick moulding sand to Baltimore, Philadelphia and other cities, the two continuing together until the death of the father in 1885. The son then continued the business on his own account until 1890.

Any sketch of Mr. Vandiver would be incomplete were there no mention made of his public life, for that forms one of the most important chapters in his history. He was but a young man when he entered politics as a champion of Democratic principles, and from that time to this he has been known as a firm advocate of Jeffersonian doctrines. Honoring the party, he was in turn honored by it. The first position of prominence to which he was called was that of membership upon the Harford County Democratic executive committee in 1873. In 1875 he was elected to the house of delegates, where he was a member of various important committees, discharging every duty with such ability and faithfulness that he was re-elected to the assembly of 1877. During his terms in the house he introduced a number of measures of benefit to his constituents, among them a bill incorporating Havre de Grace as a city, which became a law, greatly to the subsequent benefit of this place. He also secured an appropriation from the state to erect hay and cattle scales here, and authority to permit the commissioners of Harford County to fund the school debt of the county. During the session he was frequently chosen temporary speaker and made an honorable record as presiding officer. In 1880 he was again elected to the house of delegates, where, as before, he often served as temporary speaker and on important committees, besides being chairman of the committee on claims. His party chose him again as their nominee in 1881, but disruptions and divisions caused his defeat, together with that of Hon. Herman Stump, Democratic candidate from Harford County for the state senate.

Realizing that his services were too valuable to be dispensed with, the Democratic party afterward brought Mr. Vandiver into frequent prominence. In 1885 his fellow-citizens, on that ticket, chose him to serve as mayor of Havre de Grace, and the following year he was re-elected. During his administrations many reforms were instituted and improvements were introduced, including a new sewerage system and the pavement of the streets. The qualities that had made him successful in other positions brought him the commendation of all in the discharge of his duties as mayor, and he retired from office with an enviable record. In 1891 he was again elected to the legislature, and unanimously chosen speaker of the house, where his service was as able as before. From 1887 to 1892, he was secretary and treasurer of the Democratic state executive committee, and secretary and treasurer of the Democratic state central committee. A high and merited honor was bestowed upon him under the second administration of Grover Cleveland, in June, 1893, when he was appointed collector of internal revenue for Maryland, his district including not only this state, but Delaware, the District of Columbia, and the counties of Accomac and Northampton, Va. He took the oath of office July 1, 1893, and has since discharged the responsible duties of the position with the diligence and fidelity that have marked his every act, business or official. In 1892 he was delegate to the Chicago convention, and voted for A. P. Gorman for president. Four years later he was delegate-at-large to the Chicago convention that nominated Bryan.

At Philadelphia, June 23, 1886, occurred the marriage of Mr. Vandiver and Miss Annie Clayton, who was born in Tamaqua, Pa. Two children comprise their family, Robert M. and Dorothy. Mrs. Vandiver is a daughter of Henry Clayton, a civil engineer and lessee and operator of the Little Schuylkill (now the Philadelphia & Reading) Railroad, but who died at thirty-two years. Fraternally Mr. Vandiver is a member of Susquehanna Lodge No. 130, A. F. & A. M. In addition to other interests he is a director in the First National Bank of Havre de Grace, the Commonwealth Bank of Baltimore, and director and one of the organizers of the Commonwealth Savings Bank and the American Banking & Trust Company of Baltimore, a director in the Harford Agricultural Society for six years, director in the Havre de Grace Improvement Company and Havre de Grace Water Company, trustee of the Maryland Agricultural College, colonel on Gov. Robert McLane's staff, and custodian of the United States post-office and court house buildings in Baltimore. August 12, 1897, he sent his resignation as collector of internal revenue, to President McKinley, to accept the chairmanship of the Democratic state central committee, which he assumed August 12, 1897, and called the committee together to meet at Carrollton Hotel, noon, Wednesday, August 18,

1897, to map out the campaign of 1897 for the state of Maryland. He was one of the subcommittee of the state of Maryland for the centennial of 1876, also one of the World's Fair managers of the state of Maryland at the World's Fair in 1893.

The public life of Mr. Vandiver has been of such a character as to place him among the eminent men of Maryland. While acting as legislator, his acts were marked by prudence and economy, as well as energy and a progressive spirit, and a due regard for the will of his constituents. As mayor of Havre de Grace he was in sympathy with the local plans for improvement. As collector of internal revenue he was reliable and efficient, true to the administration he represented. In all offices of public trust he has been characterized by energy, integrity, business-like methods, and judicious actions, and the sequel of his success shows how, with these qualities, it is possible for a young man to attain a position of prominence and influence in this free land of ours.

MARSHALL HAINES, who is an attorney-at-law, of Elkton, was born near Rising Sun, Cecil County, Md., December 10, 1846. His father, Eli Haines, who was born in the same neighborhood in 1811, was one of the first manufacturers of stone and earthenware in the country, and owned a pottery located a mile east of the village of Rising Sun. He did an extensive business in that line, his ware being sold in all parts of the United States. At the time of his death, in 1855, he was the owner of a pottery at North East, Cecil County. For the management of large business interests he was admirably fitted, both by nature and training. He cared little for political matters and held no public office except that of county commissioner. He had a brother, Samuel, who was a farmer and served both as county and school commissioner.

Eli Haines, Sr., grandfather of our subject, was a native of Cecil County and a member of the Society of Friends; he was a man of ability, and had he lived to middle life or old age would doubtless have become prominent, but he died when young. His father, Job Haines, was an influential resident of this locality both before and after the Revolution and was acquainted with all the prominent men of his day. In 1781, at his home near Rising Sun (the property now owned by Edwin M. Hunt), he entertained the illustrious Lafayette, who was one of his warm friends. He was a member of the Maryland legislature at the time of General Washington's death, and as a representative of the state attended the funeral of that eminent man.

The Haines family is one of the oldest in Cecil County, its residence here dating back many years. In 1682, while Richard and Margaret Haines were en route from Northampton County, England, to America on the ship "Amity," their son, Joseph, was born. Shortly afterward, and before the ship cast anchor in this country, Richard died. The widowed mother settled in Burlington County, N. J., where Joseph grew to manhood. In 1714 he removed from there to the western part of Nottingham Township, Cecil County, which, however, at that time was within the bounds of Chester County, Pa. He soon became prominent and was called to fill public positions, among others serving as justice of the peace for Chester County. His oldest brother had preceded the family to America about 1679 and obtained for his father a grant of land in West Jersey; or it is possible that the father himself had been in America, and, securing possession of large tracts of land, returned to his native country and then sent his eldest son, John, to America to look after the property until he himself could arrange to bring his family over. The papers for this original grant of land are still in the possession of the family. Joseph Haines had a large family, Job being his sixth child, and Job had nineteen children, of whom Eli, our subject's grandfather, was the sixth, and the latter in turn had six children, of whom Eli, Jr., was the youngest.

The mother of our subject bore the maiden name of Hannah Marshall and was born in Chester County, Pa., near Brandywine. Her father, Humphrey Marshall, was a native of Chester County and a member of one of its oldest families. He was a member of the Society of Friends and lived up to the lofty teachings upheld by that organization. L. Marshall Haines was one of seven children, of whom only three attained years of maturity. Rachel A. married Isaiah Buddy, of Philadelphia, where she died. Samuel E. is a dentist in Philadelphia. When he was but a child our subject was left an orphan and was taken into the home of an uncle, Absalom Roman, father of Dr. Samuel T. Roman, but after three years he went to live with another uncle, Samuel Haines, near Rising Sun. His primary education was obtained in the district schools near Rising Sun, after which he entered the Pennsylvania State Normal School, near Lancaster. During his course of study there, in 1864, while still in his teens, he entered the Union army, enlisting in Company C, Eighth Pennsylvania Calvary, and joining the army of the Potomac. He served with his regiment in Virginia until August, 1865, when, peace having been declared, he was mustered out and returned to the normal school.

After graduating, Mr. Haines taught school for a time, but in 1868 turned his attention to the study of law, which he had resolved to make his life work. His readings were carried on under the preceptorship of Hon. William J. Jones, of Elkton, and he was admitted to the bar in June, 1870. January 1, 1872, he formed a partnership with his former preceptor and this continued until the death of Mr. Jones in 1894, when Mr. Haines succeeded to the lucrative practice of the firm. He has twice been a candidate for state's attorney and has been the candidate of the Republican party for the house of delegates and the state senate, but the Republicans being in the minority he has failed of election. In 1893, when a candidate for the state senate, he came within twenty-six votes of being elected, and it was claimed by some that he had fairly won, but he refused to make a contest for the seat. In July, 1897, he was nominated as candidate for circuit judge, to be chosen in the following fall, and should he be elected he would undoubtedly render as able service on the bench as he has at the bar. In addition to his lucrative law practice he has various other interests. He is a director in the Mutual Building & Loan Association and in the Mutual Fire Insurance Company of Cecil County. Well known in Grand Army circles, he is past commander of the Elkton Post, and is also past master of the Masonic lodge of Elkton. While he has a birthright in the Society of Friends, he does not adhere to the faith as closely as did his ancestors.

In 1873 Mr. Haines married Elizabeth Jackson, of Chester County, Pa. They have two sons: Frederick Taylor Haines, a graduate of Lehigh University as a civil engineer and now a law student in his father's office; and Warren Jackson Haines, a graduate of Princeton, and now with his uncle, J. T. Jackson, in the real-estate business in Philadelphia.

The success which Mr. Haines has attained illustrates the reward of merit. He has worked long and arduously to gain the position to which his talents entitle him and in which he can exert a larger influence for the welfare of his fellowmen. He has demonstrated that there is no genius like the genius of hard work, and that no success is as lasting as that obtained through laborious efforts through the years of one's prime.

WILLIAM BENJAMIN was born January 12, 1826, about one and one-fourth miles from Bay View, upon the farm where he now resides. Here his entire life has been spent, and amid the scenes familiar to him from earliest childhood he is passing the twilight of his useful career. A man of influence in the community, he is highly respected and is regarded as a man of sound judgment in public affairs, as well as in matters relating to the management of his farm.

From his father he inherited a portion of his present possessions, which include his valuable homestead of one hundred and fifteen acres. The cultivation of this place he superintends, and also directs the investment of his capital, thus finding plenty to occupy his time and attention.

Mr. Benjamin represents the third generation of his family in the United States. His grandfather, Joseph Benjamin, was the son of a rich man in England, but through a love of adventure or restlessness under parental authority (the records do not tell us which) he ran away from home, and crossing the Atlantic, settled in Maryland, where he afterward remained. The father of our subject, George Benjamin, was born in Cecil County in April, 1780, and in early life was a farmer near Charlestown, but about 1825 removed to the place where his son now lives. Politically he was a lifelong Democrat, and for years served as a magistrate, but was not a politician in the ordinary usage of that word. He held membership in the Methodist Protestant Church and was influential in the congregation, as among his neighbors generally. He attained advanced years, dying on the last day of 1864, when eighty-four years of age. His marriage, which took place March 14, 1805, united him with Sarah Taylor, member of an old family of this locality. Their family consisted of twelve children, of whom the following are living: John, of Annapolis; Thomas, who lives near Bay View; Eliza Jane, wife of Washington Alexander, of Havre de Grace; Albert, of Baltimore; and William, of this sketch.

In boyhood the subject of this article alternated attendance at the district schools during winter with work on the home farm in the summer. At first he worked for his father, but afterwards became the owner of the home farm, where he has since engaged in raising the various cereals to which the soil is adapted. In political affiliations a Democrat, he was elected to the position of assessor in 1897 upon that ticket, and has held other minor offices, the duties of all of which he has discharged with credit to himself. For years he was a trustee in the Methodist Protestant Church, and he has also been one of its class leaders. January 12, 1847, he was united in marriage with Sarah J. Mahoney, of District No. 5, member of a family that has resided in Cecil County for several generations. There were born to the union ten children, and of these seven are living, namely: Lavinia A., wife of William R. Campbell, of Bay View; Henry T., whose home is in Chester, Pa.; Deborah M., widow of William B. Tyson, of Trainor, Pa.; William W., a resident of Cecil County, living near the old homestead; Martha E., wife of William F. Thompson, of Chester, Pa.; Winfield Scott, a farmer living in District No. 5; and Jeremiah John, who makes his home in Wilmington, Del.

GEORGE O. GAREY. A successful newspaper is generally representative of the people of the place in which it is located, and its value to a community is beyond estimate. Prominent among the papers of Cecil County is *The Star*, published by Mr. Garey at North East. In every respect it is a progressive paper, and exerts a potent influence in all matters pertaining to the welfare of the people of the county. Its zealous advocacy of local interests has made it popular with the citizens of North East, whose advancement it has materially aided. Its success is due to the energy of its founder, who is its present editor and publisher, and who is fitted to make a success of the venture, both by natural inclinations and by years of experience.

The Garey family is well known in Talbot County, this state. The subject of this sketch was born in Easton, Talbot County, September 8, 1855, the eldest of a family of nine children, of whom seven are living, namely: George O.; Milton, who is in the newspaper business in Jersey City, N. J.; Alfred and Frank, merchants of Easton; Walter, who has a bakery in Easton; Mrs. R. C. Lambert and Miss Carrie Garey, both of that place. The father, George W. Garey, was born in Talbot County, and throughout much of his life carried on a boot and shoe business. He held numerous public positions, including that of assistant postmaster of Easton for four years, and justice of the peace. During the war he was one of the few men in Easton who supported the Union cause. In politics, though not specially active, he advocated the principles of the Republican party until the "reconstruction" period, at which time he identified himself with the Democratic party. He was a man of genial disposition, modest and retiring, and his amiable disposition won many friends for him. He died in Easton in 1890.

The mother of our subject was Emmaline Benjamin, a native of Cecil County and a member of one of its old families. Her father, Isaac Benjamin, ran the ferry at Perryville until the bridge was completed, and afterward he had a line of stages from Perryville to Easton, still later conducting a hotel in Easton. His grandfather, Joseph Benjamin, came to this country from London in 1766 and settled in Virginia. During the Revolution he served in the army under Light Horse Harry Lee. On the close of the conflict he came to Cecil County and took up large tracts of land, much of which still remains in possession of the family. When a boy the subject of this sketch attended the district and high schools of Easton, and at the age of nineteen he entered the Western Maryland College at Westminster, Carroll County, in which he was a student for three years. Prior to this he had served an apprenticeship to the printer's trade in the composing room of the *Easton Star*, and on leaving college he returned to that place, where he remained a year or more, later going to Philadelphia, where he worked at his trade. In 1882 he came to North East and found for sale the plant and good-will of the *North East Record*, which had recently failed. He purchased the plant and began to issue The Star. For some years he continued, meeting with success and building up a large circulation. He had long cherished a desire to gain experience on the metropolitan papers, and it happened that in 1891 he had an opportunity to gratify this ambition and at the same time to sell his paper.

Going to New York, he accepted a position on the city staff of the *Tribune*, and remained there several months. However, he soon found life was not so pleasant when under the dictation of others, and concluding he preferred the independent life of the country editor, in April, 1892, he purchased his old paper, which he has since published.

Politically Mr. Garey is an independent Democrat, and is well informed regarding politics. He has never held office nor allowed his name to be used as a candidate. A member of the Knights of Pythias, and its representative twice to the grand lodge, he has been through the chairs of his lodge, and has many warm friends among the members of the order. In November, 1894, he started the *Maryland Pythian*, representative of the order in the state, and backed by both the grand lodge of Maryland and Delaware, in both of which states it has met a cordial reception. He is a member of the Methodist Episcopal Church. In 1884 he married Addie Alexander, of Oxford, Pa., and they have had six children, one deceased.

JOSEPH R. ELY, justice of the peace at Darlington, Harford County, is a descendant of an old English family that settled in Pennsylvania in 1734. The first who settled in Maryland was his grandfather, Joseph, a native of Bucks County, but through much of his life a resident of Harford County, where he carried on agricultural pursuits. Isaac J. Ely, father of our subject, learned the wheelwright's trade in youth, and this he followed, in connection with the business of an undertaker, in Darlington, for many years, also at the same time superintending the cultivation of the old home farm. He married Sarah Rogers, who survived him thirty years, dying in 1879, at the age of eighty-six. His death occurred in 1849, when he was fifty-six. His family consisted of three children: Sarah,

Mrs. S. T. Prigg, formerly of Darlington, but now deceased; Joseph R., of this sketch, and Mary R., who is dead.

After attending the common schools and Darlington Academy for some years, our subject, at the age of sixteen, began to assist his father in the store, continuing to make his home in his native village of Darlington. In 1849, when his father died, he was a youth of seventeen years. Notwithstanding his lack of experience, he carried on the business successfully for four years afterward, closing it out in 1853. For ten years he held a clerkship in a general store, and during a portion of this time, from 1852 to 1860, he held the office of postmaster at Darlington. The lime business engaged his attention for five years. In 1867 he was elected register of wills for the county, in which capacity he remained for six years. Later he accepted an appointment as deputy clerk of the circuit court for Harford County at Bel Air, which position he filled efficiently for eighteen years, winning deserved commendation for the accurate manner in which he discharged every duty. Governor Brown appointed him justice of the peace in 1892; in 1896 he was reappointed, holding the position at the present time. He has never married; however his home is not a lonely one, for he has residing with him two of his sister's children, Mary R. Whitelock and Robert E. Prigg, and his niece, Mrs. Sallie E. Whiteford, is also a resident of Darlington.

JAMES N. CAMERON stands well in the business circles of North East, and has an excellent financial record, his present position being the result of his ability and sound judgment. His life of industry and usefulness, and his record for uprightness, have given him an influence in the community which all might well desire to share. The position which the village of North East holds to-day as a business center is due to the energy of such men as he. For years he was connected with and manager of the Green Hill Fire Brick Company, but in 1890 secured the incorporation of the Wakefield Fire Brick Company, of which he has since been the head, and which has a large business in the manufacture of fire brick and stove linings.

The Cameron family was founded in Cecil County by Robert Cameron, grandfather of the subject of this sketch, who came hither from Scotland, and established his home in District No. 5. Here was born his son, Amor, our subject's father, and for many years a large and influential farmer. In early life he advocated Whig principles, and after the disintegration of that party he became a Republican. Like many of the Scotch people he inclined to the faith of the Presbyterian Church. He married Emeline Brown, daughter of Hugh Brown, who came to Cecil County from Ireland in early manhood. She died in 1850, and her husband in 1885. Of their five children three are living, namely: Robert, who lives near the old homestead; James N., of this sketch; and Alice M., Mrs. Jacob Minker, of Wilmington, Del. Those deceased are Hugh B. and Margaret Elizabeth.

Within one-half mile of where he now lives the subject of this sketch was born July 10, 1841. His educational privileges were limited to an attendance, during the winter months, in the neighboring schools, where he laid the foundation of the knowledge he now possesses. From an early age he has been interested in farming, and, while he has other interests now, he still owns and superintends the cultivation of twenty-three acres of the old homestead, in District No. 5. At the opening of the Civil War he enlisted in the Union service, and in August, 1862, his name was enrolled as a private in Company A, Eighth Maryland Infantry. At the close of the war he was honorably discharged as a first sergeant, the date of his discharge being May 28, 1865. During his active service he participated in twenty engagements, but was fortunate in escaping injury, though several times he was struck by spent balls. When the war was ended he returned to his home in Cecil County. In 1876 he assisted in incorporating the Green Hill Fire Brick Com-

REV. J. ALPHONSE FREDERICK.

pany, of which he was manager until 1890, and since the latter year he has been in charge of the Wakefield Fire Brick Company.

For twenty-five years Mr. Cameron has been a steward in the Methodist Episcopal Church. He is now master-at-arms in Fellowship Lodge, K. P., and captain of the Uniform Rank. In Wingate Post No. 9, G. A. R., he has had several offices, including that of past commander. In 1867 he married Margaret, daughter of William H. Baker, of Elk Neck, and member of an old family to which belonged Captain Baker, of Revolutionary fame. She died in 1868, leaving a son, William A., who is associated with his father in business. In 1870 Mr. Cameron married Annie L. Craig, whose father, William Craig, is represented elsewhere in this volume. Eight children were born of this union, four of whom are living, namely: George N., who is telegraph operator at Havre de Grace; Abel C. and Murray H., who are connected with their father in the fire brick business; and Ruth H., who is at home.

REV. J. ALPHONSE FREDERICK. Of the various professions in which men engage there is none more unselfish in its aims and more important in its results than that of the ministry, nor is there any that calls for higher powers, for greater devotion or for a deeper consecration of purpose. He who would enter upon the calling must be of superior intelligence, broad knowledge and self-sacrificing disposition. It is to the possession of these qualities that the subject of this article owes the large measure of success he has achieved in the priesthood of the Catholic Church, while in addition he has many attractive personal qualities that bring him the respect and admiration of people of every phase of religious belief.

The parish of St. Ignatius, of which Father Frederick is rector, was originally known as St. Joseph's Mission, Deer Creek. It is older than any Catholic parish in the city of Baltimore, for it dates its beginning back to within a century after the landing of the Maryland pilgrims under Leonard Calvert, in 1634. At one time extending from the Susquehanna River to Baltimore and beyond, it is now confined to far narrower limits, although it still embraces an area of more than a hundred square miles and includes Bel Air, the county seat. The present congregation numbers more than seven hundred souls, and, with the exception of those resident at Bel Air, is composed chiefly of such as follow the pursuit of agriculture.

Joseph Alphonse Aloisius Frederick was born in Baltimore, Md., August 1, 1848, and is the third child and youngest son of a family of eight children. His father, John M. Frederick, bookseller, is proprietor of a Catholic book concern, which, with a single exception, is the oldest of its kind in Baltimore City. The mother, now deceased, was Margaret Ann, youngest daughter of Georgius Hild, burgomaster of Soden, in Germany. Under the care of the Christian Brothers, in Baltimore, our subject received his primary schooling. When sixteen years of age his father sent him to St. Charles College near Ellicott City, Md., to take a six years' course in the classics. There he graduated, in June, 1870. In September of the same year he entered St. Mary's Seminary, Baltimore, and, in order to qualify himself for the reception of orders, he applied himself for four and one-half years to the study of philosophy, theology and kindred branches. He was ordained deacon in 1873, and just one year later, December 19, 1874, at the cathedral in Baltimore, he was raised by the Most Rev. James Roosevelt Bayley, D. D., to the dignity of the priesthood. Immediately afterward an appointment was given him as assistant priest to the Rt.-Rev. John S. Foley, D. D., then pastor of St. Martin's Church, Baltimore, but since elevated to the Episcopal see of Detroit, Mich.

In October, 1876, Father Frederick was promoted to the pastorate of St. Mary's Church, Deer Creek, Harford County, Md. Having labored strenuously in these parts for more than three years, he was, in February of 1880, assigned a larger and more important field in an appointment to St. Mary's Church, Hagerstown, to which were attached the missions of Williamsport, Boonsboro and South Mountain, and later, when he had received an assistant, the missions also of Moorsville and Clear Springs. On account of failing health he petitioned for a return to his country mission at St. Mary's, Deer Creek, of which he again took charge in February, 1883. His second term of ministration here lasted a little over six years. At this time his eminence, Cardinal Gibbons, offered him a rectorship in Baltimore City, which kind offer, however, he thought best to decline, as considerations of health and a passionate fondness for the country dissuaded him too strongly.

Out of deference to the wishes of his superiors, in March, 1890, Father Frederick accepted an appointment as pastor of St. Joseph's Church on the Bel Air road near Baltimore City. To this charge he attended for nearly three years, preaching every Sunday both in English and in German. He resigned in September, 1892, in order to pursue some higher studies at the Catholic University, in Washington, D. C. After having for a short time supplied the place of pastor to St. Augustine's Church, Elkridge Landing, Md., he was honored by the Cardinal, in January, 1894, with an appointment to his present charge of St. Ignatius Church, Hickory (Bynum P. O.), Harford County. His immediate predecessor here was his old college chum and bosom friend, Rev. Francis M. Fowler, who for sixteen years had, against many odds, labored faithfully and with abundant success in this part of the Lord's vineyard.

The founding of Sunday-schools, the establishment of circulating libraries and the unremitting care of the spiritual needs, especially of the young of the flock, have been some of the marked features of his ministry wherever Father Frederick has labored. He has also taken particular pains to improve the material surroundings of the church, and for this purpose he makes it a practice to call upon the members to lend whatever manual or mechanical help they are able. He holds that men must pay or toil for what they are to prize. If a man's religion costs him no trouble or sacrifice, it lacks something vital and essential. Here, as in other matters, a thing is worth to you the bother and the pay expended upon it. It must be dear to you in more than one sense to be rightly appreciated. To increase, if possible, the revenues of the church, or, at least, to guard against any marked decrease in the finances, has been the endeavor of Father Frederick at all times and everywhere, and this not for any selfish end, as is readily understood; for no matter how large may be the income of a place, the amount fixed as salary by diocesan statute, and which is the same for all churches or missions, can alone be appropriated. To stimulate by example the generosity of his parishioners, he has often taxed his own liberality severely, as grants, donations and cancelling of dues, etc., here and elsewhere, amply testify.

In stature Father Frederick is not large, but above medium height, of rather slight build. His cast of countenance inclines rather to the serious, with lineaments that suggest refinement of thought and feeling, earnestness, benevolence, sincerity and appreciativeness. In deportment and dress he exhibits the priest and the scholar. He is broad-minded and conciliatory in his views, and hence enjoys the friendship or good-will of many who differ with him in points of religion. Retiring in disposition, he visits but little outside of official calls. Most of his time is devoted to serious study. His library is large and valuable, containing more than fifteen hundred volumes that have been selected with great care. His tastes turn strongly toward the scientific, and next to the studies peculiar to his calling, he delights most in what are known as nature-studies. For years he has been the possessor of telescope and microscope. Concerning the flora and avi-fauna of this region he has gained considerable information, and he also interests himself in the study of entomology, although not a collector in any of these departments. He possesses, however, a cabinet of Indian relics with some rare and beautiful specimens, and the greater portion of these he has himself gathered from various localities in many a delightful tramp and hunt. It is by reason of such tastes and habits that he is very happy and contented in his country parish, with no desire to exchange his rural surroundings for the excitement of city life, even though accompanied with high honors and prominence in the ministry.

ST. IGNATIUS CHURCH.
HARFORD COUNTY, MD.

The writer of the following hasty sketch acknowledges his great indebtedness to the labors of G. W. Archer, M. D.; John Gilmary Shea, LL. D.; Rev. Wm. P. Treacy, and others. He desires also to state that, owing to the shortness of time allowed him for gathering and verifying facts and dates, he can only consider his work in many respects incomplete and merely tentative.

The privilege of reprinting in part or in whole is reserved.

THE pious ancestors of the devout generation that now gathers for religious service in the venerable church of St. Ignatius, in colonial times worshiped in ruder and less appropriate structures, chiefly on the uplands of Deer Creek. Of these edifices several are still in a fair state of preservation, notably the old Wheeler residence near Kalmia P. O., and St. Joseph's Chapel House at Priest's Ford. A tradition of some weight informs us, that prior even to St. Joseph's there was a priest's house, or chapel, "on the north side of Deer Creek, on the high hills back from Nottingham Forge, which stood about a half-mile above the mouth of Thomas' Run."

Who were the first missionaries to labor in the northern part of our state is not known with any certainty. The Recollects, or Franciscan Fathers, came to Maryland as early as the year 1673, and are believed to have exercised the ministry chiefly northward, but in what locality is still questioned. What is certain, however, is that the Jesuits, who were with the colony from the very beginning, in the year 1704, established themselves near Bohemia Manor in Cecil County, Md., and it is very probable that from this point the Fathers attended the missions in the region of Deer Creek.

The first priest of whom we have certain knowledge in connection with this district is Rev. Benedict (Bennet) Neale, who was a relative of Archbishop Neale, and like him a descendant of Capt. James Neale, a favorite of the Crown and Privy Councellor of Maryland. Father Neale was certainly in charge of St. Joseph's Mission, Deer Creek, then Baltimore County, in the year 1747. In 1750 he purchased land near a spot still called Priest's Ford, on the south side of Deer Creek, and he, possibly, even erected a mill for the purpose of procuring a living. "At this time," writes Bishop Carroll, "Catholics contributed nothing to the support of religion or its ministers; the whole charge of their maintenance, of furnishing the altars, of all traveling expenses, fell on the priests themselves, and no compensation was ever offered for any services performed by them, nor did they require any so long as the produce of their lands was sufficient to answer their demands. But it must have been forseen that if religion should make considerable progress, this could not always be the case."

In an "Examination of Wm. Johnson," in the year 1756, we find mention made of "Priest Neale's Mass House." Both Dr. G. W. Archer and Mr. John Gilmary Shea are of opinion that we have here an allusion to the building which is still standing, and is now the property of George Archer, architect, of Baltimore. But whether Father Neale erected the old chapel building or simply adapted it to serve its religious purpose is now beyond telling. What is known, however, is that on the 8th of October, 1764, Thomas Shea conveyed to Rev. Benedict Neale, in consideration of "lodging, board, and all things necessary during his life," one hundred and fifteen acres of land, "without any manner of exception, only that one-half of an acre of ground, where the burying place now is, be reserved, which the said Thomas Shea reserves for a burying place for himself and family."

In respect to mass-houses or private chapel-rooms the following quotations from the author of the "Catholic Church in Colonial Days" will serve as an elucidation. "By a law passed in 1702, which received the royal sanction, the English acts of toleration were extended to Protestant dissenters in Maryland, who were permitted to have service in their meeting-houses when registered." But Catholics fared not so well. Rev. Dr. Hawks, himself a minister of the Church of England, notes with evident disapproval that "Maryland presented the picture of a province founded for the sake of religious opinion by the toil and treasure of Roman Catholics, in which, of all who called themselves Christians, none save Roman Catholics were denied toleration." ("Contributions" II, p. 117.)

"An exemption, however, granted temporarily and confirmed perpetually by Queen Anne's direction (1705), allowed the office of the Catholic Church to be performed only in a private family. Henceforward to the end of British rule no separate Catholic church or chapel was allowed. The step taken by the early missionaries in securing lands was now to show its providential character. The houses of the missionaries were adapted or new ones erected in such a form, that while to all intents and purposes each was a dwelling house, a large room within was a chapel for the Catholics of the district. The house of some Catholic planter at a convenient distance would, by the zeal and piety of the owner, have under the general roof a chapel-room, where his family and neighbors could gather to join" in the solemn rites of the church.

Father Neale resided at Deer Creek, with some probable intervals of absence, from 1747 to about the year 1770. He died at Newtown, St. Mary's County, Md., March 20, 1787, aged seventy-eight years. The next resident priest, as far as has been ascertained, was Rev. Ignatius Matthews, who came apparently about 1770, and stayed probably until the year 1779. For a time, in 1774 and 1775, he had residing with him Rev. Bernard Diderick. This is the priest who is first mentioned as attending Baltimore and Elkridge, landing, namely, from 1775 to 1784. Rev. Charles Sewall had charge of St. Joseph's Mission probably from 1779 to 1784, in which latter year he took up his residence in Baltimore. He was related to Charles Calvert, third Lord Baltimore, who married a daughter of Hon. Henry Sewall.

He died November 10, 1806. Rev. Sylvester Boarman exercised the ministry for many years in Harford County. He probably succeeded Father Sewall in 1784, and stayed certainly as late as 1797.

It was during Father Boarman's administration that the building of St. Ignatius' Church near the Hickory was probably begun. If we are to credit tradition it was five years in the course of erection. In the year 1793 Col. Ignatius Wheeler is said to have contracted with "Jack Reardon, stonemason" for the building of the walls at his expense. It is also claimed that Josiah Wheeler, in his will of 1791, bequeathed seventy-five pounds, and that Benjamin and Thomas Wheeler, brothers, furnished conjointly a negro slave to wait upon the builder. No doubt, many other members of the parish contributed very considerably toward the erection of the new church, but neither their names nor their contributions have been handed down. The year and day of its dedication, or opening, have been lost, but it was most probably some time in 1797 or 1798. It is said to have received the name St. Ignatius in honor of Col. Ignatius Wheeler's patron saint. Father Boarman was closely related to the Boarmans and Wheelers of Harford County. He died at Newport, Charles County, on the 11th of January, 1811.

The foregoing pastors were all Jesuits, and, with the single exception of Fr. Diderick, to the manor born in Maryland. Henceforth we meet with the names of those not Jesuits.

Rev. Charles Leander Lusson, a Recollect, or Franciscan friar, was manager of the Deer Creek estate for about two years, that is, between 1795 and 1797. He was under the directions of Father Boarman, and may have been the first priest to attend the new St. Ignatius. Next on the list appears the name of Rev. Dr. Cornelius Mahoney, whom Bishop Carroll transferred later to Albany, N. Y. He was probably in Harford during the years 1798 and 1799. Rev. W. Pasquet came probably before 1800. He remained until 1806, when he was appointed to St. Francis', Bohemia, in Cecil County, Md. Rev. Joseph Eden, or more fully, Edenschinck, was the first resident priest in Alexandria, Va. He came thence to the Deer Creek mission in the year 1806. He resided at Priest's Ford, where, probably, he also died December 22, 1813. His remains now rest under the sanctuary of St. Ignatius', but they may have been originally interred under the entrance of old St. Joseph's. For eighteen months after Father Eden's death there was no priest residing in the mission, and the Priest's Ford property was meanwhile sold; but after the middle of the year 1815 the Rev. Roger Smith was appointed, who is said to have made his home with his brother, Samuel Smith, then living one mile west of St. Ignatius', where James M. Cain now resides. The stone rectory adjoining St. Ignatius' was not built till seven years later.

In this connection it may be stated that Mrs. Angus Greme's house on Tobacco Run, now the residence of John Kerr, was for a time a quasi-home for the clergy. Like another Martha, she received the Master in his representatives. Father Pasquet, writing to Archbishop Carroll in 1814, speaks in glowing terms of her kindness to Fathers "Boarman, Mahoney, Eden and myself," and he says her house "has been and will always be the priest's house."

Father Roger Smith opened a new baptismal and matrimonial register on the 22d of June, 1817, which contains the earliest parish records now on hand, all the preceding ones having disappeared.

St. Ignatius' Church was incorporated by a special act of legislature in 1818. The first meeting of the trustees took place on the 31st of May, 1819. The following are some of the names which appear on the earliest records: Capt. Henry Macatee, John Kean, Robert Boarman, Edw. F. Bussey, Clement Green, Augustus I. Greme, John Butler, Samuel Smith, Samuel Brown, Matthew Cain, Bennet Wheeler, George Rider, Stephen I. Raphel, Benjamin W. Boarman, Francis Delmas, James Kean, and others.

Father Smith was transferred to Baltimore in 1820 and became a member of the archbishop's household. He was succeeded by Rev. Timothy O'Brien, who in the year 1822 built the pastoral residence, a modest stone structure adjoining the church. Father O'Brien's term ended in April 1832, and his place was taken by Rev. Francis T. Todrig. The latter was succeeded by Rev. Dr. Henry B. Coskery in December, 1834. Dr. Coskery was afterwards for many years rector of the cathedral in Baltimore, and Vicar-General of the archdiocese. He severed his connection with St. Ignatius' in December, 1839. The pastorate of Rev. James Reid extended from the latter date to about the middle of the year 1845.

Following closely upon Fr. Reid came Rev. Thomas O'Neil, who was in charge till some time in 1851. He tore away in 1848 the semi-circular sacristy in the rear of the church and built an extension. He also built St. Patrick's, Havre de Grace, Md. Rev. John Joseph McNally was the next pastor. His ministry began toward the end of the year 1851, and closed in October, 1854. He was for many years in charge of St. Stephen's in Washington, D. C. Father Jacob A. Walter resided at St. Ignatius' from October, 1854, to July, 1858, when he concluded to make his residence at St. John's Church, Long Green, Baltimore County, after having built the present church to replace the old chapel which had been destroyed by fire. In his time, also (1855), St. Mary's Church, Deer Creek, was erected chiefly through the exertion of the Macatee family. Father Walter was for many years pastor of St. Patrick's Church, which he built in Washington, D. C. It was he that assisted the poor, guiltless Mrs. Surratt at the gallows. In July, 1858, Rev. John Gloyd succeeded Fr. Walter at St. Ignatius', just as he has more recently supplied his place at St. Patrick's, Washington. Rev. James McDevitt took charge of St. Ignatius' in July, 1859; he was transferred about the middle of the year 1863, and had for his successor Rev. Henry Hoffman, who served the mission till the beginning of 1865. Rev. D. De Wulf was at the Hickory for only a few weeks.

The name of Rev. Patrick Francis O'Connor will be always associated with St. Ignatius' Church. Father O'Connor was appointed the 26th of March, 1865. A man of wonderful energy, he set to work at once, building an imposing belfry to the church. He next began the erection of the fine new parsonage, and almost at the same time, a similar one at St. Mary's, Deer Creek (Clermont Mills). He also built St. Francis' Church, Abingdon. He severed his connection with St. Ignatius' October 19, 1873, and retired to Baltimore, whence he was some time after transferred to Mt. Savage, Md., where, worn out with good works, he went to his reward in the spring of 1894.

Rev. Joseph A. Gallen attended St. Ignatius' from St. Mary's, Deer Creek, after the departure of Father O'Connor in 1873; later, however, in October, 1876, he became pastor, which position he held until April, 1878. On the 21st day of that same month and year Rev. Francis M. Fowler relieved Fr. Gallen of his charge. Of all the pastors in charge of this mission, with the exception, perhaps, of Rev. Benedict Neale, Father Fowler held the responsible office longest. Through his efforts much good was accomplished and a new spirit infused into the flock. He made several additions to the church, notably the commodius and well-furnished sacristy. He enlarged the dimensions of the choir, purchased a superb organ and procured the services of Prof. John Mahoney. He resigned his office in favor of the present pastor. Rev. J. Alphonse Frederick took up the work of his predecessor on the 1st of February, 1894.

The plot on which St. Ignatius' was erected contained originally not more than three acres of land. Whether it was donated or purchased is now uncertain. To this plot were added, by purchase, in 1852, about two more acres; in 1873, partly by purchase, five additional acres; and finally, by gift from the pastor, in 1895, an adjoining lot with ice-pond and embracing about one and a-quarter of an acre.

In the cemetery, the hallowed God's acre, but for too many years much neglected, lie the remains of whole generations of the faithful awaiting the call of the final trump. Some of the bodies were removed from former resting places and interred here under the shadow of the cross. A few graves are hid from view by later additions to the church edifice, and among these are the tombs of Col. Ignatius Wheeler and his wife, née, Henrietta Maria Neale, and of some of their children. Stately shaft and lowly head-stone record for our remembrance and emulation such old, cherished names as Wheeler, Macatee, Boarman, Brown, Greme, Delmas, Quinlan, Scott, Kean, Lochary, Cain, Ady, Richardson, Rider, and a host of others not less honorable. May their rest be peaceful in the Lord, and may their awakening be glorious.

I D. CARTER, deceased. It is an important public duty to honor and perpetuate, as far as is possible the memory of an eminent citizen, one who, by his blameless and honorable life and distinguished career, reflected credit not only on his city and state, but also upon the whole country. Through such memorials as this at hand the individual and the character of his services are kept in remembrance, and the importance of those services acknowledged. His example, in whatever field his work may have been done, thus speaks as an object lesson to those who come after him, and though dead he still speaks. Long after all recollection of his personality shall have faded from the minds of men, the less perishable record may tell the story of his life and commend his example for imitation.

Mr. Carter was born March 15, 1826, in District No. 3, Cecil County, where his entire life was passed. Upon that farm, his father, Robert Carter, had located at a very early day, being one of the pioneers of Cecil County, where he erected the Cecil Paper Mills, which he owned and operated for many years. He was twice married, his first union being with Lydia Lewis, and for his second wife he chose Mary Reynolds.

Upon the home farm our subject was reared to habits of industry, and in the schools of Newark and Strousburg, he acquired a good practical education. On laying aside his text books, he entered a paper mill, where he soon mastered the business in its various departments, and on returning home he took charge of the Cecil Paper Mills, which he successfully operated throughout the remainder of his life. An enterprising, industrious and capable business man, he accumulated considerable property, and was numbered among the most substantial and prosperous men of the community.

In 1854 was celebrated the marriage of Mr. Carter and Miss Eliza Levis, who was born in Elkton District, Cecil County. Her father, Norris Levis, the first of the family to locate in the county, and her grandfather, Joshua Levis, owned and operated the first paper mill established in the United States. This was conducted in Delaware County, Pa., where he and his son were both born.

Eight children blessed the union of Mr. and Mrs. Carter, namely: Harry L., a paper manufacturer of Overbrook, Pa.; Mary, wife of H. M. Brown, of Chestertown, Md.; Annie; Robert D., a paper manufacturer of Wanaque, N. J.; Emily, wife of Henry L. Patterson, of Philadelphia, Pa.; Daisy, wife of Eugene Kitterlinus; Charles, at home; and Helen, who is attending Dresden Musical College.

Mr. Carter, who was a consistent member of the Methodist Church, was called to his final rest in September, 1893, his death being caused from heart disease. His political support was given the men and measures of the Republican party, and he took an active and prominent part in promoting those enterprises calculated to benefit the community or advance the general welfare. Whether in public or private life he was always a courteous genial gentleman, well deserving the high regard in which he was held.

MERRITT S. McNAMEE. The home of Mr. McNamee is situated in District No. 8, Cecil County, near the village of Rock Springs, and consists of seventy acres. The place invariably attracts the attention of the traveler through this section of the country, and with its surroundings, its stretch of meadowland and cultivated fields, presents a pleasant picture to the eye. Judging from his wise management and prudent investments, the owner well deserves the position he is accorded among the leading agriculturists of the district.

The McNamee family is of Irish origin. Francis, grandfather of our subject, was born in Ireland and received an excellent education, being a student for the orders of priesthood. However, his plans were entirely changed, and instead of entering upon professional work, he was married and came to America. Here he followed the trade of a shoemaker. The father of our subject, Frederick McNamee, was a weaver by trade, and this occupation he followed in his younger days in the employ of David Caldwell, at Farmington. In 1843 he removed to what is now District No. 8, and here he engaged in general farming the remainder of his life. Politically he advocated Democratic principles. By his marriage to Sarah A. Hollowell, of Chester County, Pa., he had a family of five children that are now living. They are named as follows: Merritt S., of this sketch; William A., a resident of District No. 5; Stephen D.; Elizabeth, wife of John Kirkwood, of North East; and Cornelia J., who resides in District No. 8. The father died in 1879, at the age of sixty-eight years, and the mother about 1894.

During the residence of his parents at Farmington, District No. 6, the subject of this sketch was born September 8, 1836. He was educated in the common schools and Millersville Normal School, from which he graduated at the age of twenty-four years. Qualified both by training and natural talents for the arduous work of a school teacher, he began in the profession, in which he met with considerable success, winning the friendship of both pupils and parents. He was in charge of schools in Lancaster County until 1865, when he returned to Cecil County and settled near Rock Springs. However, he continued to teach until 1880, when he retired from the profession and turned his attention entirely to agricultural work. He is now engaged in cultivating his farm of seventy acres, which contains a good set of frame buildings, substantial fences, live stock, modern machinery and all the appliances of a country estate. Politically a Democrat, he was tax collector for the district two years, judge of the orphans' court eight months and county commissioner one term (1890-92).

When a young man Mr. McNamee established domestic ties and has since had the assistance and co-operation of his wife in every undertaking. She was Martha J. Keetley, of Lancaster County, Pa. Three children were born of their union, one of whom is deceased, and the others, Cecil and Berenice, are at home. Fraternally a Mason, Mr. McNamee is connected with Harmony Lodge at Port Deposit. In former years he was identified with the Odd Fellows and Knights of Pythias lodges at Rising Sun, and passed all the chairs in both organizations. Cecil Grange numbers him among its active members. Believing in the doctrines of the Presbyterian Church, he and his family assist in the work of that denomination.

CHARLES SCOTT ELLISON was born in Delaware, December 27, 1842, and is descended from Scotch ancestors, who came to America in a very early day. His parents, Jonathan L. and Susan D. (Scott) Ellison, were natives, respectively, of New Jersey and Delaware, and had a family of ten children, all natives of Delaware, namely: Harry C., L. Frank, Charles S., Susan B., Sallie, James T., Emma L., Clayton L., Lizzie B. and Nellie. The paternal grandfather, Lewis Ellison, was born in New Jersey and throughout active life engaged in farming.

Reared on a farm in Delaware, Charles Scott Ellison was a student in the academy at Newark for three terms, and thus gained the foundation of the knowledge to which he afterward added by reading and observation. In 1868 he came to Maryland, and one year later married Adelaide Young Clayton, who was born in Delaware, grew to womanhood upon a farm there and for one term was a student in the academy at Wilmington. The five children born of their union are named as follows: Mary C., Edgar L., L. Frank, Addie Y. and Charles S., Jr. They have been given every advantage and under careful parental training are being fitted for useful and honorable positions in the business and social world. In religious connections Mr. and Mrs. Ellison are identified with the Methodist Episcopal Church and contribute to religious enterprises as their means permit. Politically he is a Republican, ever loyal to the principles of the party.

The farm upon which Mr. and Mrs. Ellison reside is situated in District No. 2 and has been in continuous possession of the Clayton family ever since it was given to an ancestor by patent from the Duke of York. This is one of the oldest families of the Middle States and was founded in America by Joshua Clayton, who came to America with William Penn in 1682 and whose body was interred in a cemetery in Kent County, Del. John, son of Joshua, was high sheriff 1752-57, justice 1754, captain of Kent County militia 1756, member of assembly 1759, and was buried in Delaware. James, son of John, had a son, Dr. Joshua Clayton, who was one of the most prominent men of his day. He was the first mayor of Bohemia, Baltimore, Md., 1776, state treasurer 1786, judge of court of appeals 1788, member of colonial congress 1778-83, first governor of Delaware under the constitution of 1789-96, president of council 1789-93, United States senator 1798, and in all the public issues of the eventful period in which he lived was most conspicuous. He died while doctoring yellow fever patients in Philadelphia August 11, 1798, being then in his fifty-fourth year; his body was buried in Bethel churchyard in Cecil County, Md.

Thomas, son of Dr. Joshua Clayton, was scarcely less prominent than his distinguished father. He became an attorney and was regarded as one of the finest lawyers of Delaware. In 1810 he was chosen attorney-general of the state, and two years later was elected to represent his district in congress. In 1824 he became a United States senator and four years later was appointed chief justice of Delaware. He was buried in Dover, Del. Col. Joshua Clayton of Thomas, son of Thomas Clayton, was born Au-

JOHN SAPPINGTON, M. D.

gust 2, 1802, and died February 12, 1888. In early life he was a lawyer at Dover, but later settled upon his farm, "Choptank on the Hill" near Middletown, Del., and had the reputation of being the largest land owner in the state. His title was gained through his service as colonel of the Eighth Delaware Regiment. Among the public positions which he held were those of secretary of legation, Brazil, and Argentine Republic, 1823, and charge d'affaires, 1825. Twice married, his first wife was his cousin, Lydia A. Clayton, who died in 1849, leaving him three sons: Thomas and Henry, who died in 1896, and Richard, a resident of Middletown, Del. His second wife, Martha E. Lockwood, died in 1887, their union having resulted in the birth of the following-named children: Adelaide Young, Mrs. Ellison; Macomb, of Philadelphia; Edgar, who died young; Dr. Joshua, a physician of Philadelphia; Mary W., widow of J. Fletcher Price, superintendent of the Chesapeake & Delaware Canal; Elizabeth, who resides in New York; Eugene Y., who died in 1887; and Fannie, wife of Nathaniel J. Williams, whose home is in Middletown, Del.

HON. JOHN SAPPINGTON, M. D., ex-state senator, is an influential citizen of Darlington, where he was born in October, 1847. The family of which he is a member has been represented in Harford County for many years. They were the founders of the station at Sappington, named in their honor. It is a noteworthy fact that he represents the fourth generation, in direct line, that has been connected with the medical profession and won distinction in that honorable vocation. The first of these was Mark Sappington, M. D., a native of England, but from early manhood a resident of Maryland, where he wielded a large influence among the people of his day. He was one of the men who went on board the ship "Peggy Stewart," at Annapolis, Md., and told Captain Stewart what he might expect in case he revealed the parties who caused him to burn the tea brought over by that ship.

Next in line of descent was Richard Sappington, M. D., a surgeon in the Revolutionary War, and also a physician of local prominence. His son, John, our subject's father, was born near Havre de Grace in 1801. Following in the footsteps of his ancestors he chose medicine for his profession. After his graduation from the medical department of the University of Pennsylvania in 1824, he removed to Darlington and at once began the practice that he carried on uninterruptedly for forty-five years. He was a member of the constitutional convention that met at Annapolis in 1851. In all public affairs he bore an honorable and active part. As a citizen he was public spirited and loyal to the interests of town and county. He died at Darlington in 1869, aged sixty-eight years.

Twice married, by his first wife, Sarah Bagley, Dr. John Sappington, Sr., had only one child, Richard and he became a prominent physician of Baltimore. Though now seventy years of age, he still carries on practice in Waverly, which is within the city limits. The doctor's second wife was Mary O'Neal, and they had three children: Florence, deceased; John, M. D.; and Walter, deceased. The mother of these children died in 1885, at the age of sixty-five.

Reared in Darlington, the subject of this sketch, as a boy attended the academy here and one in Norwalk, Conn., graduating from the latter in 1865. The following year he attended the University of Virginia, where he began the study of medicine. He then entered the Jefferson Medical College, graduating in 1868. At once he returned to the old homestead, where the happy days of boyhood had been spent, and here in useful professional labor the active years of manhood are being passed. While his profession has engrossed his close attention, yet it has not done so to the exclusion of public enterprises and local measures. He believes it to be the duty of a citizen to maintain an interest in the questions of the age, and accordingly he has always been a thoughtful reader and close student of the times. His political affiliations are with the Democratic party, which expresses his personal opinions regarding public questions. Upon that ticket he was elected to the state senate in 1885, and served for a term with credit to himself.

In 1874 Dr. Sappington married Mary Hays, and they have three sons: Walter H., a medical student; William F., who is preparing for Johns Hopkins University; and Earl Neilson, a student in the Maryland Agricultural College. Fraternally the doctor is connected with the Stephenson Lodge of Masons, in which he has held the various chairs and is now past master. He is also a member of Deer Creek Lodge of Odd Fellows. In religious belief an Episcopalian, for some time he has officiated as vestryman and treasurer of Grace Memorial Church.

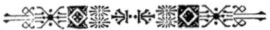

HOLLIS COURTNEY, Jr. The growth and prosperity of any city or village depend almost entirely upon the efforts of a comparatively small number of her residents, to whose faith in the future of the place and wise judgment as to methods by which to secure a steady progress, other citizens owe the benefits that accrue to them. An important part in local enterprises for the advancement of Havre de Grace has been taken by Mr. Courtney, who is a native of this place and for many years has been agent for the Philadelphia, Wilmington & Baltimore Railroad here. In the civic positions which he has held it has always been his aim to promote local enterprises and enlarge the prosperity of the people. As a director of the cemetery association he has borne a part in fitting up a last resting place for our dead. As a director in the building and loan association he has helped forward the building enterprises of the locality; and as a director in the water company he has aided materially in securing an adequate supply of pure water for local use. Other schemes and projects have from time to time had the advantage of his assistance and influence.

In this city the birth of our subject occurred October 14, 1842, his parents being George W. and Ellen (Baker) Courtney. He was a namesake of his uncle, Hollis Courtney, Sr., a wheelwright by trade, a prominent worker in the local lodge of Odd Fellows, and a resident of Havre de Grace until his death, at the age of about ninety years. George W. Courtney was born and reared in Hartford County and having learned the blacksmith's trade, came in early manhood to Havre de Grace, where he opened a shop. In this occupation he continued here until his death, when seventy years of age. Though not active in public affairs, he was interested in the success of the Democratic party and kept himself well posted regarding current events. His wife was born in Cecil County, and died in Harford County when about sixty-seven. Of their family of eight children, five are now living.

Educated in private schools, our subject cared less for study than for active work, and at an early age began to assist his father in the shop. About 1862 he became a member of an engineering corps that built the bridge for the Philadelphia, Wilmington & Baltimore Railroad across the Susquehanna River at Havre de Grace. In 1864 he was made freight agent at this point and October 1, 1874, was given the more responsible position of station agent, which he has since filled. October 30, 1860, he was united in marriage with Miss Lydia A. Foster, of this place, and they had an only child, George H., who died at the age of twenty-three years.

A history of the life of Mr. Courtney would be incomplete were no mention made of his connection with public affairs. A stanch Democrat in his political opinions, he has been very active in local politics and in all matters relating to the welfare of the city and county. In 1874-75 he was a member of the old board of commissioners of this place, and in 1879, at the time of the reorganization of the place and its incorporation as a city, he was president of the council. In 1880 he was elected mayor of the new city, which position he filled for one year. Twice he was appointed by Governor Brown one of three supervisors of elections of Harford County, and for ten years he was one of the district trustees of the public schools. Since 1886 he has held membership in the executive committee of the Democratic party, where his advice is most helpful in important decisions. Fraternally he is connected with Susquehanna Lodge No. 130, F. & A. M., of Havre de Grace, Morning Star Lodge No. 20, I. O. O. F., and Eden Conclave No. 6, of Baltimore.

WILLIAM H. TUCKER has owned and occupied Castle Blaney farm, in District No. 3, Harford County, for a number of years. He was born in this district in 1854, the son of William H. and Sarah A. (Jones) Tucker, and grandson of David Tucker. The latter was the first of the family to settle in Maryland, he having come from Bucks County, Pa., to Harford County, where he spent the remaining years of his life. He was a man of consistent Christian character, an earnest worker in the church, and was held in the highest esteem by all with whom he came in contact. William H. Tucker, Sr., was reared in this county, where for some years he engaged in business as a carpenter and contractor, and also carried on agricultural pursuits. However, in 1857, he removed to the west, believing that it offered better advantages than the east to the farmer. A stay of four years in Marshall County, Ill., was sufficient to convince him that his opinion was an erroneous one, and he made up his mind to return to old Maryland. Returning about 1860, he resumed work at his trade, and continued in that occupation until his death, in September, 1889, at the age of sixty-four. His wife passed away in November, 1893, at the age of sixty-two years. They were the parents of six children, named as follows: Rebecca, wife of George W. Preston; Elizabeth, who married John W. Preston; William H.; David R.; Mary B., deceased; and Florence E., Mrs. Walter O. Myres.

At the age of sixteen our subject left school and began an apprenticeship to the trade of coachsmithing. After he became familiar with the work he went to Illinois and followed the trade in Quincy for six months. He made his home there for eight years, but, like his father, in 1883 returned to make his permanent home in the east. In February of the same year he was united in marriage with Miss Georgia A. Grafton, daughter of Corbin M. Grafton. For four years subsequently he resided on the Bond place, and then spent five years in cultivating the farm owned by the late Joseph Harlan. In 1892 he went to Jersey City, where for eight months he was proprietor of a grocery and provision store, but then sold out the business and returned to Harford County. In the spring of 1893 he purchased Castle Blaney farm, near Hickory postoffice, and here he has since engaged in general farming, devoting his time to the cultivation of the one hundred and forty-six acres that comprise the place. In addition to raising grain, he has large pastures, in which his cattle graze; he prepares the cattle for the market, and finds this branch of agriculture profitable. He and his wife are members of the Methodist Church, and actively interested in everything that pertains to the success of the cause of Christianity. Their family consists of two sons, Willard Leroy and Lester Winfield. In his fraternal relations he is connected with Columbus Lodge of Odd Fellows, and has held a number of the offices in the lodge.

THOMAS HOLLINGSWORTH. A number of the best citizens of Harford County are descendants of Quaker ancestors, who were identified with the history of Pennsylvania from the earliest period of its settlement. One of this class is the subject of our sketch, a well-known farmer residing in District No. 3. For many successive generations his forefathers continued to reside in the state where the family first settled, but in 1806 his grandfather, Nathaniel Hollingsworth, removed from western Pennsylvania to Maryland, settling upon the property now owned by our subject. Here the remainder of his life was spent in the cultivation of the soil and general farm pursuits. After his death the estate fell to the ownership of his son, Nathaniel, who carried on general farming here as long as he lived, and made a number of valuable improvements to the place, having it as his home until he died in 1851, at the age of about fifty. By his marriage to Mary Warner he had seven children, Silas W., Thomas, Sarah, Rebecca G., Nathaniel (deceased), Mary and Edward.

Upon that portion of the estate now owned by his older brother, the subject of this notice was born in 1837. When a boy he was a pupil in a private school conducted by the Friends, and also attended the Springdale Academy, in Virginia, for one term. Upon completing his studies he returned home and assisted in the work of the home farm, where he remained until 1863, and then removed to Baltimore, becoming a conductor on the Baltimore & Towson Railway. Four years later he returned to Harford County, when the farm was divided between himself and his brother, he retaining the older part. The fifty acres have been placed under excellent cultivation, new buildings have been erected, and the various improvements introduced which mark the farm as the home of a thrifty agriculturist.

Though never caring to hold office, Mr Hollingsworth takes an interest in politics and public affairs, and at elections votes the Republican ticket. In his party he is active as a local worker. He is a member of the Friends' Church, and in his daily intercourse with others endeavors to live up to the lofty teachings of that society.

PATRICK ANDERSON. The growth of the village of Cecilton has been largely due to the energy and efforts of Mr. Anderson, who has made this place his home for many years, and is one of its most successful business men. In his youth he served an apprenticeship to the trades of wheelwright and carriage-maker, and to that line of work he gave his attention for some time, in the employ of others. However, his was not a nature to be contented with salaried positions; he wished to engage in business independently for himself, and this he did, as soon as he had saved a sufficient sum of money to warrant the undertaking. At this writing he is proprietor of a general store in Cecilton, where, in addition to the stock usually found in such stores, he carries a line of hardware and machinery, and also does general repairing.

The birth of our subject took place on New Year's day of 1838, his parents being William and Ellen (McKelvey) Anderson, who, like himself, were natives of Ireland. He was one of eleven children, of whom eight attained years of maturity: Rebecca, now deceased; Ann J.; John, deceased; William, Elizabeth, Patrick, Robert and Mary. During the Civil War John enlisted in Company E, Tenth Ohio Infantry, and was killed while in an engagement. When fourteen years of age our subject came to America, in 1852, and for twelve months was employed in a cotton factory in Philadelphia, after which he went to Chatham, Chester County, Pa., and for three years was an apprentice under James A. Kendall. The year 1859 witnessed his arrival in Cecilton, where he has since made his home. For ten years he worked at his trade here under the same man, but in 1869 began in business for himself, and has since built up an excellent trade. His success is certainly commendable, especially when we consider the fact that he commenced without capital or influence, and was obliged to overcome many obstacles before establishing his finances on a firm basis. Much of his money is invested in real-estate in Cecilton, and he has ever been foremost in promoting enterprises for the benefit of this place.

In 1862, at the age of twenty-four, Mr. Anderson married Henrietta Register, who was born in District No. 1, Cecil County, and has always resided here. Eight children were born of their union, but death has claimed four of the number: Susan E., Clara, Robert H. and William. The others are Mary E., Henrietta, John and Anna B. The children have been reared in the faith of the Methodist Episcopal Church, to which both Mr. and Mrs. Anderson belong. A few years ago, when the new edifice was erected, he was treasurer of the building committee having its construction in charge. He has also held the office of steward, and is now superintendent of the Sunday-school. Politically he has not allied himself with either of the prominent political parties, but maintains an independence of opinion that finds expression in the support of the best man for office, irrespective of party ties.

JOSEPH T. ENGLAND. A representative of the class of farmers to whom the world is indebted for its prosperity, Mr. England is pursuing his chosen calling with energy and perseverance. In every movement that is likely to advance the material and moral welfare of the people of Cecil County, he is always ready to bear his part, and for many years he has been connected with the agricultural development of District No. 9. Having followed farming throughout his entire life, he has acquired a thorough practical knowledge of all its departments and has become known as one of the successful farmers of the vicinity. He is the owner of the old family homestead, which consists of three hundred and fifteen acres, and contains all the improvements so necessary to the proper management of a first-class estate.

On the property that now belongs to him, Mr. England was born in 1821, being a son of Isaac, and grandson of John, and great-grandson of Samuel England, who in turn was the son of an Englishman, the founder of the family in America. Isaac England was born on the homestead, to the cultivation of which he gave all the years of his active life. Though having few opportunities, he yet was a well-informed man, and his sound common sense was visible in all his actions. Politically he advocated Democratic principles. His life was prolonged to an age attained by few and was brought to a close when he was ninety-two years and seven months. His wife, Maria, was a daughter of Reuben Haines, of District No. 9, and they were the parents of five children, namely: Hannah P., Joseph T., Reuben H., Mary E. (deceased) and Deborah.

From the age of eighteen, when he completed his education, Joseph T. England gave his attention to farm work. He has known no other home than his present place, and its excellent condition bears testimony to his energy and good judgment. He keeps abreast with every advance made in agriculture and has placed first-class improvements upon his estate. His political views bring him into sympathy with the Democratic party and he generally votes for the men and measures brought forward on that ticket. However, he has not been active in political matters, preferring to devote himself to his private duties. In 1850 he was united in marriage with Mary A. Alexander, who is an attendant at the Presbyterian Church. Mr. England's people were of the Quaker faith and were members of the Friends' Church. Their three children are named as follows: Isaac, Leroy and Helen, wife of Clifford Cook, of Lancaster County, Pa.

CORBIN GRAFTON has for nearly sixty years made his home upon a farm in District No. 3, Harford County, and this tract, which comprises about ninety acres, he still continues to cultivate. Born near his present home, July 31, 1820, he has been a lifelong resident of this locality, and has seen the wonderful changes that cultivation has made in the country. He has seen many people come and go, but whatever the changes, he has continued his pleasant relations with all, for he is by nature a man who easily makes and retains friends.

Mr. Grafton represents the fourth generation in descent from the founder of the family in this country, an Englishman, who settled about two miles from Chestnut Hill. James, father of Corbin, and son of William Grafton, was a carpenter by trade, and followed his occupation in this district throughout his whole life. By his marriage to Phoebe Grafton, three children were born, namely: Jesse; Bennett, who died on the old homestead in 1891, at the age of eighty-five; and Corbin. The last-named had few advantages when he was a boy, as at an early age he was obliged to begin work for himself. For some time he worked in the employ of various farmers of the neighborhood. Meanwhile he saved his earnings until he was enabled, in 1840, to purchase a farm of his own, and then he bought the place near Chestnut Hill, where he has since resided.

The marriage of Mr. Grafton took place in 1839, his wife being Miss Eliza Ward, a native of Harford County, and a lady of amiable character. Three children came to bless their union. The eldest, Mary, is the wife of Lee Bowman; the only son, James O., resides on the home place, the cultivation of which is now largely in his charge; and the youngest of the family is Margaret C., the widow of Samuel Tucker. The family are identified with the Methodist Protestant Church, to the maintenance of which Mr. Grafton contributes. Honest and upright, he gives to all what is due in just measure, and accords to every man what he claims for himself, the right to his own opinions.

HON. T. LITTLETON HANWAY. The name borne by this well-known citizen of Aberdeen is one that is honored throughout the entire extent of Harford County. The family has been an influential one in this part of the state, where three successive generations have resided, each contributing to the growth and development of local interests, and giving to their community men of energy, industry and wise judgment. Under all circumstances they have borne their part as law-abiding citizens, whose aim it has been to promote the welfare of county and state. Nor has the subject of our sketch been less active in this respect than other members of the family. His influence and prominence may be judged, not alone from the fact that he has for years been a successful merchant of Aberdeen, but even more from the fact that he has been chosen by the people of his district to represent them in the legislature of the state.

In 1846, when the present village of Aberdeen was known by the name of Hall's Cross Roads, the subject of this sketch was born here, to the union of Thomas and Sarah Ann (Keen) Hanway. His father was born and reared in District No. 4, Harford County, and when a young man came to Aberdeen, where he opened a general mercantile store, though at the same time continuing as a farmer. In 1847 he removed to Creswell, District No. 1, where he was engaged in merchandising and farming until his death, at sixty-five years of age. While he never cared to hold public office, he was well posted regarding current events and was a stanch Democrat. From his father, who was an Englishman, he inherited the determination of will characteristic of that race, and doubtless it was due to this quality that he became well-to-do. His wife, who was born in what is now Aberdeen, is still living in this village, and at the age of eighty-three, is in possession of her mental and physical faculties.

Educated in the public schools and the academy at Bel Air, the subject of this sketch, at the age of twenty, went to Wilmington, Del., where he became a clerk in the leather department of the manufactory of H. S. McCombs. After a year there the firm transferred him to Philadelphia, where he remained eighteen months. Returning to Harford County, for two years he was employed as clerk in a store at Michaelsville, and from that village came to Aberdeen in 1870, purchasing Jacob J. Gallion's store, which he still owns and has since conducted. A decided Democrat in politics, he held the office of postmaster at Aberdeen under the first administration of President Cleveland. In 1895 he was elected a member of the legislature, and during his service in that body was a member of the committees on elections and inspection. His other interests have been important and he has been foremost in plans looking to the benefit of Aberdeen. He has been president, vice-president and a director of the First National Bank, secretary and treasurer of the Aberdeen Land Company and a director in the Aberdeen Canning Company. In the Presbyterian Church to which he belongs, he holds the office of trustee. In January, 1875, he was united in marriage with Miss Libbie A. Morgan, of Aberdeen. They are the parents of four children: Stanley, who is employed as bookkeeper in the bank at this place; Carroll, Walter and Lillian.

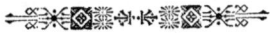

JOSEPH W. REYNOLDS, M. D. The subject of this sketch, who is one of the oldest practicing physicians of Cecil County, has been for many years devoted to his profession, and has achieved much more than the average meed of success. While engaging in general practice, he has, however, made a specialty of the treatment of cancer. This dread disease, so insidious in its approach and so deadly in its consequences, for ages defied all forms of treatment, and only within modern times has it been successfully mastered. Believing the use of the knife to be fatal to the patient, Dr. Reynolds has adopted a plan and method of treatment whereby the cancer is drawn out, rendering an operation unnecessary. Out of over one thousand cases that he has treated, he has lost less than seventy-five, and doubtless these could have been successfully removed had treatment been sought in time. Certainly humanity owes a debt of gratitude to the persevering, skillful physicians, who have through so many years and with such untiring patience sought to conquer the disease.

While making the practice of medicine his calling and an answer to the summons of his patients a duty, Dr. Reynolds has found time and opportunity to superintend the management of the farm on which he resides, and which is situated at Mt. Pleasant, in District No. 8. As a matter of recreation from the cares of his profession, he gives some attention to the cultivation of his estate, and in this, as in his profession, he has been prospered. For four years he had an office in Baltimore, but still retained his residence on the farm, preferring rural life on account of its healthfulness and conveniences.

Born in Lancaster County, Pa., in 1834, Dr. Reynolds is a son of Josiah and Mary (Swagert) Reynolds, also natives of that county. His grandfather, Samuel, who came to Lancaster County from the northern part of the state, was a descendant of John Reynolds, one of three brothers who came to America from England, settling in Pennsylvania. Josiah Reynolds remained a continuous resident of Lancaster County until death, and there followed the trade of a potter, and the occupation of a farmer. Politically he was a Republican, and in local affairs wielded considerable influence. He died in 1887, at the age of eighty-four, and his remains are interred in East Land cemetery. His eight children were named as follows: Kirk S., who resides in Christiana, Pa.; Joseph W., of this sketch; Melissa; Anna E., wife of Morris Reynolds; Andrew, living in Harford County; Tyson, who remains on the old homestead; Hannah, wife of Philip Carter, of Ohio; and Alice, Mrs. Thomas Brown, of Liberty Grove, Cecil County.

After the conclusion of his literary studies our subject spent five years at home, assisting in the cultivation of the farm. At the same time he studied medicine under Dr. Wood. In 1856 he married Margaret A. Tucker, of Baltimore, and about the same time came to Cecil County. He and his wife are the parents of eleven children now living, namely: Kirk E.; Elmer, who is station agent at Burmont, Del.; Anna; Eli, a druggist at Rising Sun; Mary, Arthur, Walter, Alva, Margaret; Alfred, who is in the drug business with his brother in Rising Sun; and Stella, who is the youngest of the family. The family are identified with the Friends' Church and exemplify in their lives the beautiful teachings of this society. Whatever part Dr. Reynolds takes in politics is to the advantage of the Republican party, of which he is a supporter. He has never indulged in politics with a view to becoming a seeker after the spoils of office, and whatever activity he has displayed has been through purely patriotic motives. He is a liberal-minded citizen and warmly endorses all projects that will promote the welfare of the district.

PATRICK BOYLE. A large proportion of the farmers of Cecil County have labored on the maxim that "a rolling stone gathers no moss," and have wisely clung to the associations of youth and the old family homesteads. Among this number is Mr. Boyle, who, though not an occupant of the farm where he was born, lives only about a mile from that place, and carries on general agricultural pursuits in the midst of the surroundings familiar to him from childhood and among the people known to him from earliest years. It was in 1870 that he bought the old Love farm, comprising one hundred acres and pleasantly situated in District No. 8. Here the ensuing years were busily passed in the raising of crops and other work incident to life upon a farm; and here he is still living, surrounded by the comforts his industry has rendered possible.

Born in 1830, the subject of this sketch is a son of Patrick and Hannah (Harland) Boyle. The first of the family in Cecil County was his grandfather, Patrick, a native of Ireland, who emigrated to America about 1730 and made settlement upon the property now owned by John E. Boyle. His principal occupation in life was that of a tailor and much of his time was spent along that line of business. The father of our subject engaged in farming upon the homestead, where he died at the age of eighty-four years. By his marriage to Hannah Harland, who died at seventy-two years, he had a family of eight children, four of whom are living, namely: John, Granville, Cromwell and Patrick. The last-named was educated in the common schools, which, however, were of a character greatly inferior to those of the present day. When still quite young he was obliged to discontinue his studies and assist in the cultivation of the farm. Remaining with his father until twenty-four years of age, he then hired out to work for a farmer and was employed by others for five years. After his marriage to Sarah J. Hill, of District No. 8, he and his wife set up housekeeping, renting the Andrew Lowe place. For eight years he worked in the iron quarries, and afterward, receiving the appointment of road commissioner, he devoted much of his time for four years to the duties of this office, though he carried on a small farm besides. In 1870 he bought the farm where he has since resided and where he engages in general farming.

In addition to the office of road commissioner, which, as already stated, Mr. Boyle held for four years, he has been judge of elections. In politics he is a decided Democrat, always stanch in his allegiance to party principles. His family consists of two children; Steward L., of Philadelphia, and Hannah M., at home. As a representative citizen of Cecil County, whose industry and good judgment have surmounted the obstacles that stand in the way to success, and a progressive citizen, he is worthy of the respect so universally accorded him.

H. D. M. HOWARD is a native of the county, his birth occurring in Elkton, April 28, 1838, and there he grew to manhood. His early education, which was acquired in the public schools of that city, was supplemented by a course in the schools of New London, Pa., and he completed his literary training in St. Timothy's and St. John's College.

On starting out in life for himself, Mr. Howard engaged in the lumber business at Elkton from 1855 until 1868, and he served as grain inspector at Baltimore in 1876 and 1877. Subsequently he was connected with the Maryland Live Stock

ABRAM P. McCOMBS.

Scales Company until 1881, when he removed to Philadelphia, engaging in the real-estate business until 1888. He was similarly employed at Atlantic City, N. J. until his removal to the farm of his stepson, C. Monteith Gilpin, in 1893, since which time he has lived retired. As a business man he possessed more than ordinary ability, was energetic, enterprising and progressive, and met with a well-deserved success in his undertakings. He is always courteous, kindly and affable, and those who know him personally have for him warm regard. In his political affiliations he is a Democrat.

In 1866 Mr. Howard was joined in wedlock with Miss Lavina Ford, of Elkton, Md., and to them was born a daughter, Eveline. Our subject was again married in 1875, his second union being with Mrs. Sally Gilpin, widow of Thomas Gilpin, and four children blessed their union: Veleska, who is now attending college in Philadelphia; Guy, who is taking a commercial course in Wilmington, Del.; Henry M., who died in 1882; and Ethel, who is also attending college. The family is one of prominence in the community, holding a high place in social circles.

ABRAM P. McCOMBS. Whoever labors to secure the advancement of his community, striving to develop its resources and promote its commercial interests; who is devoted to the welfare of the people; who seeks to promote the cause of justice and morality, and to advance our civilization through educational, professional, business and agricultural channels, becomes a public benefactor, and is worthy of especial mention in the pages of history.

Such is the character and such the record of Mr. McCombs, long one of the most influential citizens of Havre de Grace and the promoter of many important local enterprises. A man of versatile ability, he has successfully carried to a consummation enterprises of a widely divergent nature. However, it is perhaps as a newspaper man that he is best known and has wielded the greatest influence. In the field of journalism he has championed with his pen the cause of truth and honorable, independent manhood; has ably represented the best citizenship of the county and state, and has accomplished not a little toward the progress of the city where he resides.

His business ability, enterprise and integrity of character, are evidenced by the number of positions of honor and trust he now occupies. He is president of the First National Bank of Havre de Grace; president of the City Building and Loan Association; president of the Havre de Grace Improvement Company; president of the Water Company; president of the Real Estate and Power Company; vice-president of the Havre de Grace Shoe Manufacturing Company, and interested in other industrial enterprises.

The life now sketched began in Coventry, Chester County, Pa., June 16, 1824. The McCombs family is of Scotch origin, but later representatives resided in Ireland. William McCombs was born in the city of Armagh, Ireland, in 1765, and his wife, Elizabeth, was born in the same place in 1769. In 1787, at that time unmarried, they came to the United States, landing at Newcastle, Del., where they were married. The following year they bought a small farm near Newark, Del., where the eldest son, George T., father of our subject, was born July 19, 1797. The latter married Ellen Prizer, of Chester County, Pa., July 19, 1823, and was assassinated near Allentown, Pa., in October, 1836. At the age of seventeen he marched with other volunteers from Delaware to the defense of Baltimore in 1814. He was a licensed preacher in the Methodist Church, as were his brothers, James and William, the latter a member of the Philadelphia conference for fifty years.

The subject of this sketch began his education in the common schools and later attended an academy in Hatboro, Montgomery County, for two terms. His opportunities for gaining knowledge were limited, but with a love for reading and a taste for the best in literature, he early stored his mind with a fund of useful information, upon which he was accustomed to draw at will in his later years. When he was still quite young, he made his first literary efforts, and various of his compositions, both prose and poetical, appeared in standard papers, among them the *Philadelphia Weekly Ledger* and the *Saturday Evening Post*. Three years of work upon the farm were followed by three years as a clerk in a store and by a similar period spent as a teacher of public schools, near Reading. In the latter place he met Miss Maria C. Schott, daughter of Louis Schott, of Lebanon, Pa., and they were united in marriage March 29, 1849.

After some years spent as clerk and assistant manager of the iron works of Robeson, Brooks & Co., twelve miles above Reading, in the spring of 1855, Mr. McCombs became general manager of the Sarah Furnace Company's iron works, and removed to Harford County, Md. Ten years later he accepted a similar position in the Ashland iron works, of Baltimore County, owned by the same parties. Associated with others, in the spring of 1866 he organized a stock company known as the Havre Iron Company and purchased the iron furnaces at Havre de Grace from George P. Whitaker. Accepting the general management of the works, he moved to the place that has since been his home. For the purpose of saving a claim in the *Havre Independent*, a small temperance paper that had died after a precarious existence of some months, in 1868 he bought the printing office, and at once commenced to publish the *Havre de Grace Republican*, which he still, in association with his son, edits and publishes.

In 1862 Mr. McCombs organized a company of home guards, and by Governor Bradford was commissioned captain October 16 of the same year. In May, 1869, he was appointed deputy collector of the port of Havre de Grace, which position he held for eight years. He was an original Republican, identified with the organization of the party, and supported its platform until the principles of liberty, justice, and equality of all men before the law, upon which it was founded, had been engrafted in the constitution and laws. For the past twenty years he has maintained an independent position toward party politics. As stated, he came of Methodist ancestry; his grandfather was among the pioneer Methodists in the state of Delaware, and his house was one of the stopping places of Bishops Asbury, Coke and others of the early fathers of the church in this country. Mr. McCombs is not a member of any church; his religion consists in charity toward all mankind and in doing unto others as he would have others do to him.

His family consists of a son and two daughters. The son, William, has been mayor of Havre de Grace, and was elected to the city council several terms. The daughters are both married; one resides in Salisbury, Md., and the other in Brooklyn, N. Y.

JOHN KEILHOLTZ. Cecil County has many well-to-do and successful farmers, who have accumulated what they have of this world's goods through individual effort. Among this class the name of the subject of this notice is entitled to a place. He is now the owner of a valuable and well-improved farm of one hundred and seventeen acres in District No. 6, where he is industriously engaged in the prosecution of his noble calling, and is meeting with far more than ordinary success.

Born in the city of Baltimore, September 15, 1821, Mr. Keilholtz was there reared and educated until coming to Cecil County, in 1834. In District No. 6 he began learning the cooper's trade, at which he served a three years' apprenticeship, during which time he received only his board and clothes. He continued to work at his trade in connection with farming until 1855. In 1847 he purchased forty acres of land, which he improved and cultivated, and added to the amount until he had one hundred and eighty-six acres. On selling that place he purchased a farm of two hundred and twelve acres of a Mr. Kimball, and continued to make his home there until 1884, when he disposed of the property and bought his present fine farm, whose neat and thrifty appearance indicates the supervision of a careful and painstaking owner.

Mr. Keilholtz has been twice married, the first time in 1843, Miss Sarah Mossey becoming his wife. To them were born the following children: Henry C., Mary, Mary A., Amos E., William K., Charles M., Clara C., Ada B. and Ella N. For his second wife he chose Miss Martha E. Kirk, and they have become the parents of four children: Ellis H., Emma Beatrice, Clara C. and Lillie R.

Mr. Keilholtz cast his first ballot for Henry Clay, the Whig candidate, and since the organization of the Republican party he has been a stanch supporter of its principles. Public-spirited and progressive, he has always taken an active interest in local affairs and given his aid to all matters pertaining to the progress and development of his country.

HON. GEORGE BIDDLE. Doubtless few of the residents of Cecil County have promoted its educational interests in such an important degree as has Mr. Biddle, whose long service as a member of the board of school commissioners, and as school examiner for the county, renders him thoroughly familiar with the work and qualifies him for the intelligent management of affairs. His long retention in the position and the advancement which the schools have made under his administration, prove his fitness for the work better than mere words could do.

His is a historic family, related to many of the leading people of the eastern shore of Maryland. The progenitors of the family in this country were John Biddle and Mary, his wife, who emigrated from England some time before 1692; the exact date is not definitely known. Settling in what is now District No. 1, Cecil County, he at once took a prominent position among the people of that early day. In religious activities he was earnest and successful, and for many years officiated as warden and vestryman of St. Stephen's Episcopal Church. His son, John, who was born October 1, 1695, married Mary Mouned, whose birth occurred February 2, 1715. Their son Stephen, born March 1, 1733, married Mary Savin. Next in line of descent was Peregrine Biddle, our subject's grandfather, who was born July 14, 1775, and married Martha Bateman, daughter of William Bateman. He was an extensive landowner and for twenty-eight years vestryman of St. Stephen's Church, during all of which time he never missed a meeting of the church. In addition to being a large property holder, he was engaged in settling estates and had other important business of that nature. He died April 18, 1828.

George, son of Peregrine Biddle, and father of our subject, was born December 27, 1804, and was a man of prominence in his day. Like his ancestors he was for many years a vestryman in St. Stephen's Church. His sister, Susan, married Col. George W. Oldham, who was a direct descendant of Augustine Herman, the founder of the Bohemia Manor; one of their children, Mary Amanda, married Dr. Charles H. B. Massey, of Massey, Kent County, Md., whose ancestors were among the earliest settlers of Kent County and had an extensive grant of land there. Mrs. Massey is now living in Chestertown, Kent County. Another sister of our subject's father, Margaret Savin Biddle, married Dr. John W. Wirt, father of Hon. John S. Wirt, of Elkton. The mother of our subject was Frances A. Perkins, daughter of Dr. John D. Perkins, of Queen Anne County, Md., and a relative of Hon. James B. Ricaud, who was a member of congress and leading politician of Kent County; also closely related to Hon. Thomas J. Keating, of Queen Anne County, who was for many years comptroller of the state of Maryland, and is at this writing state tax commissioner. Mrs. Frances A. Biddle died October 18, 1887.

Born August 20, 1836, the only child of George and Frances A. Biddle, the subject of this sketch was given the best advantages the schools of the east afforded. The rudiments of his education were obtained in the common and select schools of this neighborhood and Wilmington, Del., after which he went to Charlottesville, N. Y., and in 1855 graduated from Delaware College. During the four years of his collegiate course he was never absent a day from his classes, but put his whole life and energy into his work. Although he graduated before he was nineteen years of age, he carried off the honors of his class. Since then his entire time has been devoted to education and the improvement of the school system. He was one of the very first to advocate the establishment of free public schools, and commenced the agitation as early as 1860. He was one of the first to advocate the appointment of school commissioners by the judges of the circuit court, believing that this was the proper way for them to be appointed, as it would entirely remove politics from schools. In 1870 he was elected to the legislature on this issue and was the author of the bill that became a law to have the school commissioners of the state appointed by the circuit judges. This law was in force for twenty years, when it was taken away from the judges and the appointing power given to the governor of the state.

After spending one term in the house and accomplishing the object he had in view in taking the position, Mr. Biddle did not aspire to a reelection, but in 1872 was appointed a school commissioner and served in that capacity for twenty years, resigning in 1892 to accept the more important position of school examiner for Cecil County. At the same time he is secretary and treasurer of the board of school commissioners. His whole active life has been devoted to the improvement of the school system and no man is better versed in the wants of the schools of Cecil County than is he. The building of good schoolhouses is one of his "hobbies," and the fine new high school building at Elkton stands as a monument of his untiring zeal and energy. He has the confidence, not only of the school commissioners but of the entire community, and to it he is justly entitled, for he is a conscientious worker, a thorough student and an excellent judge of human nature. For years he has been active in the work of St. Stephen's Protestant Episcopal Church and is keeping up the reputation of his ancestors by his long service as an official of the parish, having served for thirty-four years as a member of the vestry; at the expiration of that time he tendered his resignation but the congregation refused to accept it. January 4, 1866, he married Miss Katherine Kettell, daughter of Rev. George F. Kettell, D. D., a Methodist minister of Brooklyn, N. Y.

THOMAS JEFFERSON McCAUSLAND was born March 5, 1834, in District No. 5, Harford County, where he now resides. He is the son of Robert and Ann (Higginbotham) McCausland, natives, respectively, of this county and Ireland, and the parents of eight children, namely: George W., John C. and Andrew J., all of whom are deceased; Robert, who is unmarried and owns a farm in Darlington, this district; Thomas Jefferson; Mary J.; Sarah A.; and Maria, who married Joseph R. Hopkins, a farmer and butcher residing in this county. The father of this family was a farmer. During the War of 1812 he was captain of a battalion, but was never called into active service.

The grandfather of our subject, George McCausland, was born in Ireland, and from there came to America, establishing his permanent home in Maryland, and carrying on a general store in Dublin. He was also a surveyor. His property possessions were large, aggregating more than two thousand acres, all situated in Harford County. During the War of 1812 he was a major in the American army. Our subject was reared on the home place and received a fair education in the common schools. In 1867 he married Melissa R. Hopkins, a native of Harford County, and there were born to bless their union three children, namely: Marcus H., who is married and resides near his father; Inez, who is at home; and Paul C., deceased.

In the northeastern part of his district, Mr. McCausland is especially well known, for he has always resided in that locality and naturally has many friends among his neighbors. By a course of industry and good management, he has become well-to-do, and his valuable property shows in a marked degree to what good purpose the proprietor has labored. In politics he was reared a Democrat, of the most pronounced kind, and the party with which he votes nominated and elected him to the position of supervisor, which he filled for two years. Formerly he was connected with the Independent Order of Odd Fellows, but at this writing is no longer an active worker in this lodge. He and his family are connected with the Presbyterian Church.

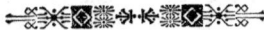

JACOB B. WEBSTER. Of the various occupations in which men engage not one is so free from the cares and anxieties of the world as the occupation of farming. To watch the seeds spring into life, developing into the plant that is finally enriched by the wealth of ripened fruit and grain; to watch the soil respond to the care and cultivation bestowed upon it; and to enjoy the harvests which kind nature almost invariably bestows upon man; this is a privilege granted only to the farmer. In this calling Mr. Webster has spent his entire life and from it he has become the possessor of a competency, the deserved reward of diligent labor. The one hundred and sixty acres which constitute his farm are situated in District No. 3, Harford County, and are devoted to the raising of cereals and of stock.

Upon this place Mr. Webster was born in 1840. He is a son of John L., and grandson of John Webster, and a lineal descendant of the same ancestors as those to whom James Webster traces his lineage. In early life John L. Webster was interested in a saw mill, but the most of his life was devoted to agriculture, and he resided in District No. 3 until his death, in 1869, at the age of seventy. During the existence of the Whig party he was a supporter of its principles, but upon its disintegration he identified himself with the Democrats. His wife, who bore the maiden name of Susan Brown, died in 1884, at the age of seventy-three. They were the parents of six children, named as follows: Jacob B., J. Thomas, William E., Mary E., M. Sophia (Mrs. Joseph Mitchell) and Sarah.

The boyhood years of our subject were spent in school and upon the home farm. Early gaining a thorough knowledge of agriculture in every department, and having a partiality for country life, he naturally selected farming as his life occupation, and he has had no reason to regret his choice. On the death of his father he succeeded to the ownership of the old homestead, which he has since occupied and cultivated. In matters of politics he gives his influence and vote in behalf of the Democratic party, because to him it embodies those principles best adapted to the government of a free country. He is prompt to meet every obligation and therefore stands well in business circles. In the management of his affairs he is systematic, and in his dealings with others, careful and considerate. In 1881 he married Miss Sarah J. Fletcher, daughter of carpenter Fletcher, and a member of the Presbyterian Church. He has the moral and material welfare of the community at heart, and earnestly uses his influence to promote it.

LOUIS H. OSBORNE. On the banks of the Sassafras River lies the village of Fredericktown, where the subject of this sketch was reared and where he is now engaged in the mercantile business. While much of his life has been passed in this place, he has been in many other portions of the United States and has become familiar with customs of people in other sections of the country. However, he believes there is no state like old Maryland and no county that can compare with Cecil. The place where for generations his forefathers dwelt is the one most dear to him, and here he expects to spend his remaining years.

A native of Kent County, Md., Mr. Osborne

was born in 1852 upon the anniversary of the day remembered by American people as that upon which George Washington was born. His parents, Edward L. and Christiana J. (Hall) Osborne, were natives, respectively, of Maryland and New Jersey and had a family of five children, namely: Charles T., deceased; Mary F.; Edward L., deceased; Louis H. and Emma. The paternal grandfather, Groom Osborne, was born in Maryland and here spent his entire active life engaged in mercantile pursuits. In the schools of Fredericktown our subject received a fair education that fitted him to make his own way in the world. In early manhood he took up fishing and was thus employed on the Chesapeake Bay about six years. Afterward for five years he followed railroading and was engaged in construction work in Indiana, Michigan and Illinois. For four years prior to going west he was interested in the lime business in Fredericktown. After his return to this place, he opened a general store in 1889 and has since conducted a profitable business among the people of the surrounding country. He is not active in politics, but always votes the Democratic ticket and is interested in the success of his party.

Mr. Osborne married Grace Hopkins, who was born in Maryland, a member of a family identified with the history of this state for many generations. The only child born of this union was Mary, who died at the age of eleven months.

NELSON K. WARNER. The family of which this gentleman is a representative came to this country from Scotland, and has since been identified with the history of Maryland and southern Pennsylvania, where its members have become known for energy of disposition and probity of character. One of their most distinguishing traits has been prtriotic devotion to country. Not only in times of peace were they loyal citizens, but they proved their patriotism on many a closely contested battlefield, where they stood firm for the principles they believed to be just and right. This trait, so noticeable in preceding generations, is equally conspicuous in the lives of those now living, and causes them to be numbered among the best citizens wherever they may reside.

Reviewing the genealogical record, we find that the grandfather of the subject of this sketch, Richard Warner, was a native of Harford County, Md., and died near Woodlawn, Cecil County. He had several sons who bore a valiant part in the Union cause during the Civil War, among them Jacob, now living at Woodlawn, a member of Snow's Battery; Edward, also a Union soldier, and now residing at North East; William, who was taken prisoner while in active service, but was afterward released, and now lives in Linwood, Chester County, Pa., and Frank, of Ilion, Herkimer County, N. Y., who was a member of the United States navy during the war. Our subject's father, Henry Warner, was born in Lancaster County, Pa., August 4, 1828, and followed the trade of an iron worker. For twenty-eight years he was manager of the McCullough iron works, near Elkton, but then resigned the position, and is now living on his farm near Zion, in Cecil County. His wife, who is still living, was Ellen M., daughter of Thomas Caldwell, owner of a sawmill in this county, and the descendant of Irish ancestors. She had several brothers, one of whom, Harvey, now a resident of Liberty Grove, Md., is a veteran of the late war. In her family there are but two children, our subject and Sophia, wife of D. M. Lee, who is a farmer near Zion, and one of the board of county commissioners.

In the little village of Rowlandsville, five miles from Port Deposit, Cecil County, the subject of this article was born, January 14, 1855. He was twelve years of age when his father was made manager of the McCullough iron works, near Elkton, and he then removed with his family to this place, receiving his subsequent education in the Elkton Academy, later embarking for himself in the mercantile business. His good judgment brought him a fair measure of success; both as a dry-goods merchant and as the proprietor of an agricultural implement business. In May, 1896, he was commissioned magistrate by Governor Lowndes, and has since efficiently filled the office at Elkton. In his political belief he has always been stanch in his adherence to Republican principles. Fraternally he is connected with the Heptasophs. In 1891 he was united in marriage with Miss M. Allie Dougherty, of Lewisville, Pa., and they have one child, a son, named Henry E.

HENRY VAN BIBBER CRAWFORD. Identified throughout his entire life with the history of this locality, and well known as one of its most influential citizens, the subject of this memoir was laid to rest, at his death, amid the scenes familiar to him through so many years. He was born at Middletown, Newcastle County, Del., September 16, 1833, and died suddenly of heart disease January 14, 1897, at his home near Warwick, Md. The family of which he was a member was among the oldest in Maryland and was connected with the Youngs and Culbreths, of Caroline, the Mackeys, of Talbot, the Turpins, of Queen Anne, and the McKims, of Baltimore. Upon his mother's side he was connected with the Petersons and Van Bibbers, of Cecil County, and the Gilmores, of Baltimore. He was the youngest son of William Hazlett and Catherine A. (Reading) Crawford, the former a native of Delaware, an influential farmer, a private in the ranks at the battle of North Point and at Ft. McHenry, and a nephew of Col. William Hazlett, a Revolutionary hero, whose body lies buried in Dover, Del.

The advantages given Mr. Crawford in boyhood were those common to the aristocratic families of the central south, prior to the war. It is said of him that when a youth he was one of the most popular young men in his neighborhood, and this quality of winning and retaining friends remained one of his principal characteristics through life. At the outbreak of the late war he was living quietly at the old homestead in Middletown, engaged in general farming. His sympathies were with the south, and soon he enlisted for active service, becoming a member of Company B, First Maryland Cavalry, under Capt. George M. Emack and Col. Ridgley Brown. In all the engagements of the First he bore a valiant part and was one of those who "rode with Stuart." It was the testimony of his comrades that under fire he was calm and collected, never evincing any excitement, even when peril was greatest. His regiment was ordered to General Ewell's Corps to lead the advance into Pennsylvania in 1863, and was in the three days' battle at Gettysburg. During the retreat, on the night of the 4th of July, while guarding a part of Ewell's wagon train, they held in check for more than two hours a brigade of Federal cavalry, for which they received meritorious mention from General Lee in his report of the campaign. They participated in the disastrous valley skirmishes of 1864, and during that time he was one of a force of men, under Sergeant Tunis, who succeeded in burning a bridge, despite the efforts of a company of Federal cavalry to dislodge them. Returning home at the close of the war, Mr. Crawford resumed farm work. When about forty years of age, April 30, 1873, he married Miss Margaret Price, with whom he lived happily until his death came to separate them. His home was on a farm in District No. 1, Cecil County, and it was while superintending some of the farm work that he succumbed to heart disease. Returning from the barn to the house, he sank into a chair near the fire, shivered as from cold, and in an instant was dead. He was buried from St. Francis Xavier Church, which he joined after his marriage. Besides his widow, he left a son, Charles, a capable and well-educated young man, who succeeds to the management of the estate.

Mrs. Crawford was born March 10, 1839, upon the farm where she now lives. Her parents, John V. and Ann (Nowland) Price, were natives of Cecil County and had a family of four children, namely: Thomas, Susanna, Margaret C., and John N., deceased. She received a good education, which fitted her for the responsibilities of life, and at an early age became a member of the Roman Catholic Church, with which she has since been connected. Her father was a soldier in the War of 1812, and she is justly proud of the fact that both he and her husband were brave soldiers, with the courage to fight for what they believed was right. Among the people of District No. 1, she has many warm friends, to whom she is endeared by her many noble traits of character.

DAVID A. MACKIE. The farming community of Cecil County recognizes in Mr. Mackie one of its leading men, a citizen prosperous and public spirited, and favorably known by the people of the locality. He owns and operates eighty acres lying in District No. 4, near the place where, in 1848, his eyes first opened to the light. Of his parents, John and Catherine (Andrews) Mackie, mention is made in the sketch of J. Alfred Mackie, which appears elsewhere in this volume. He and his brothers were well educated and are following the example set by their honored father, as good and useful members of the community, having contributed in no small degree to the encouragement of various enterprises calculated to benefit the people, socially, morally and financially.

On the farm where his brother Arthur resides, the subject of this sketch was born, and there his earlier years were uneventfully passed, his education being obtained in the neighboring district schools. After leaving school he turned his attention to the cultivation of the home farm, in which work he assisted his brothers, J. Alfred, Franklin T. and Arthur A. The place consisted of about four hundred and fifty acres, and upon the death of the father it was divided among the children. About 1870 our subject purchased the Dr. Brookens farm that adjoins a portion of the old homestead, and here he has since engaged in general farming pursuits. Although a steadfast Democrat, he has taken no part in politics other than to cast his vote at local and national elections. His family attend the Rock Presbyterian Church, in the welfare of which, though not a member,

he is deeply interested, believing that the progress of a community depends upon the honest, upright Christian character of its people. Fraternally he is connected with New London Lodge No. 218, K. of P., Lewisville, Pa., and is also a member of Little Elk Tribe of Red Men of Cherry Hill.

In 1869 Mr. Mackie was united in marriage with Miss Cornelia J. Read, daughter of Walden and Martha L. Read, and a native of District No. 5, where the years of girlhood were passed. She has been a most efficient helpmate to her husband in all his undertakings and has contributed to securing the financial success that has marked his career. They are the parents of an only son, Arthur A., who is now traveling for a tobacco firm. Mr. Mackie takes quite an active interest in everything that will tend to the improvement of the district, and by his upright life has gained the esteem of those around him. Intelligent and of good principles, he is regarded with respect by his neighbors and fellow-citizens, and his wife shares in their good-will.

GEORGE W. POIST. For many years this gentleman has been connected with the agricultural interests of Cecil County, and as the result of his untiring labors, his ambition, his energy and well-directed effort, he is to-day the possessor of a handsome competence and a good farm, where, in the midst of his family, he is surrounded with all the comforts that go to make life worth the living. A native of the Keystone State, he was born in Lancaster County, at Columbia, on the 10th of May, 1834, and for nine years remained at that place. In 1843 he accompanied his parents on their removal to Baltimore County, Md., where Mr. Poist lived until eighteen years of age. Through the three succeeding years he was a resident of the city of Baltimore, and served an apprenticeship to the butcher's trade, in which he became very proficient. On the expiration of that period he removed to Colora and established a meat market, which he has since

ALEXANDER HAMILTON GEORGE.

successfully conducted. He now enjoys a good trade, which has come to him as the reward of his honorable dealing and straightforward business methods and his courteous treatment of his patrons. In addition to this industry he has other property interests, including two farms in District No. 6, Cecil County. One tract comprises fifty-four acres of land, and his home farm embraces sixty-three acres, which is under a high state of cultivation and yields to him a good return for the care and labor bestowed upon it.

In 1856 was celebrated the marriage of Mr. Poist and Miss Elizabeth A. White, who was born on the farm where he now resides. They have a family of six children: Mary, George H., Charles D., Annie C., Fannie and Harry, and the family circle yet remains unbroken by the hand of death. Mr. Poist and his wife are members of the Presbyterian Church of West Nottingham, and by his ballot he supports the men and measures of the Democracy. His life is an honorable and useful one, actuated by unselfish motives, and he has thereby won the confidence and esteem of many friends.

ALEXANDER HAMILTON GEORGE, of Elk Neck, is postmaster and proprietor of the general store in this village. No resident of the place has been of greater value as a citizen than he. His life and character are worthy of emulation by those who, like himself, must be the architects of their own fortunes. He is very unostentatious, a plain, practical man of affairs, with the sound common sense necessary to success in any department of activity, and with the energy that almost invariably brings its possessor prosperity. The name which he bears was given him in honor of his ancestor, Alexander Hamilton, illustrious in the annals of history, and among his most prized possessions is the gold watch worn by that statesman at the time he was killed in the duel with Aaron Burr.

The grandfather of our subject, Anthony George, was born in Cuba and in early manhood came to the United States, settling in Philadelphia. However, much of his time was spent upon the ocean, as he was a sea captain by occupation. He was an intimate friend of the philanthropist, Stephen Girard. In religious belief he was a Catholic and his children were reared in that faith. His son, Anthony, Jr., was born in Philadelphia, and there engaged in the manufacture of block tin metal cups and saucers, dying in Cecil County at the age of seventy-six, in 1892. A Whig in politics, he took no interest in official matters, but contented himself with depositing his ballot at elections. He married Lucinda, daughter of Alexander Hamilton, and member of one of the oldest families of America; she attained a very advanced age, dying in 1889. Of her four children, two are living, the subject of this sketch and Louisa, who resides in Cecil County.

In the city of Philadelphia Alexander Hamilton George was born April 20, 1833. When he was a child he accompanied his parents on their removal to a farm near Elk Neck, on the Elk River. His education was obtained principally in the schools of Philadelphia and Mt. Holly, N. J. At the age of sixteen he began to learn the trade of a machinist and was thus employed for six years. At Philadelphia, July 17, 1861, he enlisted in Company B, Twenty-third Pennsylvania Infantry, and took part in eighteen of the engagements of the war, being discharged September 8, 1864, at the expiration of his period of service. At once after his return home he opened a store at Elk Neck, and this he has since carried on, besides having charge of the post-office. He was appointed postmaster in July, 1864, under the administration of Abraham Lincoln, and has perhaps held his commission longer than any one now in the service. In addition to his home in Elk Neck he owns property in North East and has an interest in the old homestead, which is now occupied by his sister. In politics he is independent, in religion a member of the Methodist Episcopal Church, and fraternally is identified with the Junior Order of American Mechanics. April 20, 1882, he was united in marriage with

Mary A., daughter of James Clark, of Elk Neck. They are the parents of three children, Louis O., Harriet Lucinda and A. Hamilton.

Starting out in life a poor boy, without means or influential friends to aid him, Mr. George has made his own way in the world, and by honest methods has gradually advanced until he is now well-to-do. His honorable way of doing business commends him to the people, among whom he has built up an excellent trade.

JOSEPH K. LEVIS. The life of this gentleman has been marked by energy and perseverance, and his well-directed efforts have been rewarded by the accumulation of a valuable property. For forty years he owned and operated a grist and saw mill in Cecil County, and still has in his possession the plant, which, however, is now conducted by his son, while he is living practically retired from business. His home is situated in District No. 4, where he is well and favorably known. He was born in this county, near Rock Springs, August 28, 1833, and is a son of Norris Levis, who came to this country and settled in District No. 3 when a young man, removing hither from Delaware County, Pa. For fifty years or more he engaged in the manufacture of paper and was proprietor of a paper mill that brought him in a profitable income. He was a supporter of the Democratic party and its principles. While he never sought public office, he was chosen by his fellow-citizens to serve as county commissioner and acted in other local positions of trust. He took an intelligent interest in everything pertaining to the welfare of the district and county, and certainly deserves mention among the representative men of the locality. Through energy he achieved a success that ranked him among the substantial men of this community. His death occurred here in 1875, when he was seventy-nine years of age. By his marriage to Eliza Kirk, of Cecil County, he became the father of nine children, and six of these are now living, namely: Joseph K., of this sketch; Eliza, widow of I. D. Carter; Amelia K., who married Slater B. Russell, of West Chester; Robert C., residing in Elkton; Harriet, wife of V. R. Alexander and a resident of Lancaster, Pa.; and Mary, wife of A. W. Mitchell, of Elkton.

When our subject was a boy the schools were not as good as those of the present day, and his education was therefore limited, at least in regard to school attendance, but through reading and observation he has become well informed. For a time he was connected with his father in the manufacture of paper, but his principal business has been the operation of the grist and saw mill he still owns. He has also been interested in the flour business. A Democrat, he is true at all times to the interests of his party. His marriage in 1863 united him with Anna M. Armstrong, daughter of Walter Armstrong, and they have four children. Norris, who is now in charge of the mill, married Miss May W. Kessler, of Pensacola, Fla., and they have one son, Norris K.; Eliza, wife of D. E. Weston, of Philadelphia, has two children, Levis Belknap and Elizabeth; Emma A. is the wife of Dr. David Mackey, of Lewisville, Pa., and has two children, David Levis and Barton Hurst; William is in Philadelphia. In the Rock Presbyterian Church, of which Mr. Levis and his wife are members, he has been trustee and treasurer, and contributed, while the incumbent of these offices, to the financial oversight and business management of the church.

CHRISTOPHER WILSON, now living retired, is a prominent citizen of Darlington, and is a representative of one of the old and distinguished families of Harford County. About 1760 John Wilson, our subject's great-grandfather, left his early home in England to come to America, and first located in York County, Pa., but subsequently removed to Stafford, Harford County, where he was associated in business with the Stump Brothers, under the firm name of

Wilson & Stump. His father, Christopher Wilson, a celebrated Quaker preacher, whose home was in Yorkshire, England, near the Scottish border, had previously come to Maryland on a visit and was well pleased with the country. His son John being engaged to a Yorkshire girl who was not a member of the Society of Friends, he was opposed to the union and proposed that the son come to the new world. This he agreed to do, and accordingly gave up the young lady and by his father was provided with the means to start in life for himself here. In a sailing-vessel he crossed the Atlantic, landing at the little town of Joppa, on the Gunpowder River. Among the people of the settlement who saw the newcomers arrive was a young lady, Miss Webster, who, when the others were selecting their future husbands, decided upon Mr. Wilson, with whom she later became acquainted. Subsequently he made a visit to his native land, and on his return to this country they were married, July 11, 1764. They located at Stafford, where they spent their remaining days, and reared their family of ten children. One of these, Christopher Wilson, the grandfather of our subject, was born December 12, 1766, and spent most of his life on the farm now owned by the heirs of Judge Price.

The father of our subject, who also bore the name of Christopher Wilson, was born February 25, 1792, near Darlington, in Harford County, and made his home in the same neighborhood throughout life, devoting his energies to agricultural pursuits. On attaining to man's estate he married Miss Hettie Smith, who was born January 4, 1794. Her paternal grandfather ran the ferry at Lapidum, which at that time was known as Smith's Ferry. Of the nine children born of this union, one died in infancy, and only four are now living: Mary S., wife of David E. Wilson; Christopher, of this sketch; Edward, a resident of Virginia; and Margaret, widow of Reuben Stump, of Baltimore County. The father departed this life March 23, 1876, at the advanced age of eighty-four years. His wife died July 19, 1844.

Mr. Wilson, whose name introduces this review, began his earthly career September 1, 1827, in Harford County, near Darlington, where he was reared and educated, attending the common schools, and completing his literary course in the Darlington Academy. For some years he was engaged in farming, and later was employed as clerk and bookkeeper in mercantile establishments here. In 1857 he went to Illinois, where he spent the twenty-one succeeding years in clerical work and grain dealing. Since returning to Darlington in 1878, he has practically lived retired, enjoying a well-earned rest, free from the cares and reponsibilities of business life.

December 14, 1880, Mr. Wilson was united in marriage with Miss Susanna Lyon, of Cecil County. They are members of the Presbyterian Church, and occupy a high social position. During his residence in Illinois Mr. Wilson was a prominent member of the Masonic order, belonging to the blue lodge, chapter and commandery, and passed all the chairs in the local organization. His pleasant, genial manner makes him popular with all classes of people, and he well deserves the high regard in which he is universally held.

GEORGE S. RITTENHOUSE, M. D., a well-known physician and surgeon, practicing his profession in North East, is a graduate of the Jefferson Medical College, and in his subsequent practice, by his devotion to his work and the careful study and diagnosis of the various diseases that have come under his observation, he has been unusually successful, and has gained quite a reputation as a skilled practitioner.

The doctor was born on the 23d of December, 1856, in Kingwood, Hunterdon County, N. J., near Frenchtown, but when only four years old was taken by his parents to Philadelphia, where his father, who was also a physician, located to engage in the practice of his profession. There our subject grew to manhood and received his literary education in the public schools. At the age of fifteen he began the study of medicine under his father's able direction, and later attended lectures at the Jefferson Medical College, entering that institution in 1877 and graduating in 1880. Opening an office in Philadelphia, he there engaged in practice until 1887, when he came to North East, Md., where his skill and ability were soon widely recognized. He now ranks among the most proficient physicians and surgeons of Cecil County, and enjoys a large and lucrative practice.

In October, 1884, Dr. Rittenhouse led to the marriage altar Miss Lida P. Eppelsheimer, and since coming to North East they have made many warm friends. The doctor belongs to the Cecil County Medical Society, the Masonic lodge of Philadelphia, and the Knights of Pythias of North East. He is medical examiner for a number of important insurance societies, including the Equitable of New York; the Washington Life; the Baltimore Mutual Aid; the Prudential of Newark, N. J.; the Home Mutual of Baltimore; and the Merchants and Mechanics' of Baltimore. He has won his way in the regard of the people with whom he comes in contact in his daily rounds by his ready tact and kindly sympathy.

JOHN McCLEARY. The present standing of Cecil County among the agricultural regions of the eastern shore may be attributed to the careful, painstaking labors of the men who for years have conducted general farming pursuits here. As a representative of this class mention may appropriately be made of Mr. McCleary, of District No. 4, who, now in the twilight of his busy, useful life, is in the enjoyment of the fruits of former days of labor, surrounded by the friends of his earlier years and respected by the younger generation that has succeeded to the active management of affairs. It is with feelings of deepest respect that we look up to those men, advanced in years, whose lives have been filled with good deeds and acts of kindness, and who now stand, like lighthouses on the rocky coast, to warn the young of the dangers that threaten to engulf them. In their long lives they have seen many changes in the surrounding country. The years that have slipped from them as noiselessly as the autumn leaves drop in the forest have not been uneventful ones, but have been characterized by marked improvements and advances in every realm of activity, and their part in this development is no small one.

In the neighboring state of Delaware the birth of John McCleary took place in 1814. His family is of Irish origin, the first of the name to come to America being his father, John McCleary, a shoemaker by trade, and thus engaged in his native land and in Delaware and Fair Hill, Md. He spent two years in Pennsylvania and in 1817 came to Cecil County and settled in the central part of District No. 4, where his remaining years were passed. In the days when political excitement ran high and party strife often became objectionable, he kept himself posted concerning local matters and national issues, but never took any part in political contests, preferring to give his time wholly to his trade. He voted the Democratic ticket and supported its principles. By his marriage to Ann Robinson he had nine children, of whom four are now living, namely: John, of this sketch; Mary, wife of Joseph McMaster; William, who lives in Pennsylvania; and Joseph, of Philadelphia. The father died in Cecil County at the age of sixty years.

The family not being well-to-do and schools being inferior, our subject's education was limited. He did not have the opportunities that fall to the lot of most boys of this generation, but from early days was obliged to earn his own livelihood. Under his father's instruction he learned the trade of a shoemaker, which he followed in this district and other places. However, about 1847 he bought his present farm of about sixty acres and afterward gave less attention to shoemaking, as he preferred agricultural pursuits. Imbibing from his father Democratic opinions, he early became an advocate of that party, but on the organization of the Republican party he identified himself with it, and has since voted for its men and measures. For two years or more he was supervisor and has also served in the office of judge of elections, but of late years has been less active in public affairs than formerly. His family are connected with the Rock Presbyterian Church and take an active part in religious enterprises.

October 1, 1839, occurred the marriage of John McCleary to Miss Elizabeth Gallagher. Nine children were born of this union, and all but two are still living. They are named as follows: Mary H., who is the wife of William Hughes and lives in Elkton; Annie, Mrs. David McMaster; Melissa, wife of William Kerr, of Pennsylvania; Elmira, who married William Younker; Emma, Mrs. Edward Taylor; Theodore F., who has relieved his father of the active management of the home farm and now superintends its cultivation; and Robert J., a farmer of District No. 4.

W. T. MILLER, a representative and prominent farmer, residing in District No. 3, Cecil County, was born in the same district, November 9, 1821, and is a worthy descendant of one of the honored pioneer families of the county. His great-grandfather, Thomas Miller, a native of Ireland, located near the present home of our subject on crossing the Atlantic to the new world, and in Cecil County, the grandfather, Thomas Miller, first opened his eyes to the light. The latter was for forty years a prominent minister of the Methodist Episcopal Church, and in 1813 he purchased a tract of land in District No. 3, where he spent his remaining days, his death occurring at the ripe old age of seventy-nine years.

In that district the father of our subject, Thomas Miller, was born and reared. He married Miss Ann Simpers, a daughter of William Simpers, who was of English descent and also one of the early settlers of Cecil County. Eight children were born of this union, as follows: W. T., of this review; Sarah, who married Franklin Mearns, but is now deceased; Rachel, now the wife of Andrew Cameron, a resident of Zion, Cecil County; John W., who is now living retired at Cherry Hill, the same county; Rebecca, wife of Joseph W. Nowland; Samuel, a resident of Avondale, Chester County, Pa.; Catherine, wife of William A. Miller, a farmer living near Bay View, in Cecil County; and Joseph, who died in infancy.

Upon a farm in District No. 3, W. T. Miller was reared in much the usual manner of farmer lads of his period, assisting in the labors of the fields and attending the public schools of the neighborhood when his services were not needed at home. He continued under the parental roof until he had attained his majority, and in the meantime learned the carpenter's trade, which he successfully followed for thirty years after leaving home, becoming one of the best contractors and builders in his locality. In 1847 he removed to his present farm, which comprises one hundred and twenty-five acres of valuable and fertile land, which he has placed under a high state of cultivation and improved with good and substantial buildings. In connection with the cultivation of his land, he continued carpentering until 1883, when he retired from that business.

In 1847 Mr. Miller was united in marriage with Miss Sarah J. McCullough, by whom he had nine children, as follows: Andrew T., Jane, deceased; John E., Frank, James, Hester, Sarah, Mary and Rachel. After the death of his first wife he wedded Miss Annie Whitson, and to them were born seven children, namely: William W., Annie M., George H., Charles, Philip, Elva, and Harry.

Mr. Miller has ever taken an active and prominent part in public affairs, and has been called upon to fill a number of important positions of honor and trust. In 1866 he was elected county treasurer, in which capacity he faithfully and satisfactorily served for six years, and at three different times he was appointed clerk of the board of county commissioners. He was also notary public for one year, and refused to become a candidate for state senator after having received the nomination, from the reason that in 1858 he was licensed a local preacher, and, owing to the constitution of Maryland, he was not eligible to the office. Originally he was a Whig in politics, but since the dissolution of that party he has been a pronounced Democrat. As an earnest, conscientious Christian gentleman, he is an active worker in the Methodist Episcopal Church, of which he has been a member for many years, and in which he has filled all the offices. In all places and under all circumstances he is loyal to truth, honor and right, justly valuing his own self-respect as infinitely more preferable than wealth, fame and position.

SYLVESTER E. PENNING. A close observer in studying the history of the advancement of Harford County will find golden threads running through the web and woof of events connected with both the past and the present. These are indicative of the lives of the men whose public spirit and energy have increased the county's growth and promoted her welfare. A true representative of such men is found in the subject of this article, who for years has been one of the well-known residents of Havre de Grace, and is engaged in practice at the bar in this place. His life has been full of varied experiences and incidents. Orphaned when very young, he was compelled to become self-supporting at an age when boys are carrying on their studies in school. When, after years of arduous effort, success seemed to have rewarded his efforts in business, through fire he lost what represented the self-sacrifices of a lifetime of labor. It was not until some time after that, receiving the appointment of justice of the peace, that he began to turn his attention to the law. Since then he has built up an excellent practice in the courts of the county.

One of the native-born sons of Maryland, the city of Baltimore was the birthplace of Mr. Penning, and April 24, 1841, the date of his birth. His father, John Penning, was born in Boston, Mass., where he was reared and educated. When a young man he removed to Philadelphia, where he secured a clerkship. After a time, however, he changed his place of residence to Baltimore, where he engaged in the boot and shoe business a number of years. He was only thirty-one years of age when death terminated his career. Though he never took an active part in politics, he was interested in public affairs and always voted the Democratic ticket. His wife, who bore the maiden name of Sarah Cooke, was born in Frederick County, Md., and died at thirty years, leaving two children, Sylvester E., then a child of four years, and Thomas Jefferson, who became a prominent politician of Baltimore, and died in that city when fifty-three years of age.

The subject of this sketch has only a vague memory of his parents, for his mother died when he was four, and his father eighteen months later. He was then taken into the home of his maternal grandmother, Mrs. Sarah Cooke, who cared for him until he was able to become self-supporting. When twelve years of age, he began to learn the carriage-maker's trade, and this occupation he followed for seventeen years. In 1859-60, he read law in Baltimore, but did not complete his studies, instead, resuming work at his trade, opening a carriage manufactory in Baltimore and conducting it successfully about seven years. February 19, 1867, his place was burned, entailing a heavy loss, and forcing him to retire from the business. Shortly afterward he secured employment as traveling salesman for the Wheeler & Wilson Sewing Machine Company, in whose employ he remained from 1867 to 1878, his route covering mainly the counties of Baltimore, Harford and Cecil. In 1878 he took a position with the Singer Sewing Machine Company, and represented this firm from that year until 1890, traveling over the same territory he had when with the other company. During this time he made his home in Havre de Grace. In 1885, upon receiving the appointment of justice of the peace, he took up the study of law, of which he had gained a rudimentary knowledge years before. In 1893 he entered the law department of the Baltimore University School of Law, from which he graduated in 1895, although previous to his graduation he had done considerable practicing. Fraternally he is connected with the Knights of Pythias, Improved Order of Red Men and Independent Order of Odd Fellows; in religious belief he is connected with the Episcopal Church, and in politics he is a Democrat, loyal to party principle. In 1863 he married Miss Alice E. Markland, of Baltimore. They became the parents of six children, of whom four are living, namely: Elsie M., a teacher in the high school of Havre de Grace; Dr. Oliver P., a graduate of the University of Maryland, and now a practicing physician with office in Baltimore; William E., also a graduate of the Baltimore University School of Law, where he studied law at the same time with his father; and Sarah E., who is a student in the State Normal School.

JAMES B. BAKER. As a man of sound understanding, of prompt business methods and great energy, Mr. Baker has been influential in the commercial and public life of Aberdeen and Harford County. In his life may be found an illustration of the value of good principles and habits of industry. Inheriting from his father a considerable sum, this proved the nucleus to which he afterward added by intelligent supervision of business affairs. Like other members of the family, his success has been secured in the canning industry, and he was among the first to show the possibilities of this line of business to the people here.

Through the years of the century now drawing to a close, the Baker family has been identified with the history of Harford County, its members having borne an honorable part in many of its important enterprises. Further reference to the ancestry will be found in the sketch of George A. Baker, presented upon another page of this volume. James B. Baker was born upon the home farm near Aberdeen, December 24, 1845, and in his boyhood and youth was a student in the local schools, there laying the foundation to the education he afterward obtained through habits of close observation and reading. When about twenty-three years of age he went to Shelbyville, Ky., and with his brother, Charles W., began butchering, a business that he followed for three years in the same place. On his return to Aberdeen, he turned his attention to farming and the canning business, having a factory near Odessa, Del., but making his home in Aberdeen. He is the owner of two valuable farms near this place.

During his residence in Shelbyville, Ky., Mr. Baker was united in marriage with Miss Fannie Richardson, of that place; they have three children, Bertha, Harold and Maude. In political belief he adheres strongly to Republican principles, but has never cared to be a local leader of his party. For four years he held the office of commissioner of Aberdeen and under the administration of President Grant he was given charge of the post-office at Aberdeen. In his religious connections he is identified with the Methodist Episcopal Church. While he is unpretentious and rather retiring in his disposition, the people among whom he has dwelt throughout the principal part of his life hold him in high regard, knowing him to be a man of principle and integrity. Any measure that tends to the benefit of the people or the advancement of the place receives his unqualified support, and he is generous, both of time and means, in aiding it.

ALBERT S. HOLLOWAY, of Darlington, is a prominent representative of the agricultural interests of Harford County, where he has spent his entire life, his birth occurring near Stafford, in 1845. His grandfather, Richard Holloway, was a native of England, and on coming to the United States located near Darlington, in Harford County, where Hugh S. Holloway, the father of our subject, was born and reared. Throughout life he followed general farming and in 1850 purchased the old Hopkins farm in the same county, where he continued to make his home until his death, in 1868, when in his sixty-third year. He had married Hester N. Stump, and to them were born five children: Albert S., William R., Samuel S., Eliza D., and Mary R., wife of Levi B. Kirk.

Mr. Holloway, whose name introduces this review, obtained a good education in the Darlington Academy, and upon the home farm was trained to habits of thrift and industry, so that he has become a thorough and capable business man. At the age of eighteen he took charge of the old homestead—a valuable tract of two hundred acres—which under his able management has been converted into one of the most productive farms of Harford County, yielding bountiful returns for the care and labor bestowed upon it.

In 1882 Mr. Holloway led to the marriage altar Miss Abbie Cook, and they now have three children: Rowland C., Margerie and Edwin. With the Society of Friends he and his family hold membership, while politically he is connected with the Republican party. He is a pleasant, genial gentleman of high social qualities and is very popular, having a most extensive circle of friends and acquaintances who esteem him highly for his genuine worth. He has ever been a loyal citizen, co-operating in all that is calculated to promote the interests of county, state or country.

CAPT. HENRY E. O'NEILL. To be descended from ancestors whose names are honorably associated with the annals of our country is an honor in which one may take just pride, but it is equally gratifying to the biographical writer to record the deeds of those who, through active and useful careers, have preserved untarnished the good name they bear, and have even added lustre to the ancestral history.

It is therefore a pleasure to present the life sketch of Captain O'Neill for the benefit of this and coming generations. His position in Havre de Grace is one of influence, and a narration of the events of his life and his ancestry will be of common interest to all. First, however, it will be appropriate to dwell upon the connection of his ancestors with the early settlement and later history of Maryland. His grandfather, John O'Neill, the first of the name in this country, crossed the Atlantic when about eighteen years of age. He was born in Ireland November 22, 1768, and it was in 1805 that he established his permanent home in Havre de Grace, where he started a nail factory, nails being then made by hand. He met with uniform success until the destruction of the town by the British, which temporarily ruined his business, but afterward he again started the factory and was again prospered as before.

In 1813 the village of Havre de Grace consisted of only a few dozen dwellings, the population not being more than four hundred. These houses stood on the shore of the Susquehanna River, and about a quarter of a mile below them a small earthwork had been thrown up, on which were mounted two or three small cannon. To man this battery there were about fifty raw militia, who were supposed to be somewhere in the neighborhood. This was the condition of things when, at break of day, May 3, 1813, a British fleet fired on the town, arousing the peaceful inhabitants from their hitherto undisturbed slumbers. At once the greatest consternation prevailed. People hurried hither and thither, uncertain what course of action to pursue. Among them was John O'Neill, at that time forty-five years of age. He was second lieutenant of the company of militia of Harford County, belonging to the Forty-second Regiment. He seems to have been the only officer present on that occasion, at least, there is no record of any other. He was one of the few citizens who were not frightened at the unceremonious attack of the British. Going with the greatest speed possible to the little battery, he found there one of the militiamen, and they were soon joined by two or three more. The little group fired a few shots at the barges, but the bursting bombs and grape shot that rattled around them was too much for their composure, and they all fled except the lieutenant. He was left alone to man the battery as best he could. With a courage that few would exhibit under such dangerous circumstances, he worked one of the pieces until the enemy had almost reached him, when the last discharge of the cannon recoiled upon him, knocking him down and severely injuring him, thus disabling him from further service. He hobbled off amid a shower of grape shot just as the enemy entered the battery, but being unable to make any speed with his injured limb, he was soon captured and taken prisoner to one of the barges.

The news of the capture of Lieutenant O'Neill reached the capitol at Washington, and the story of his bravery was told to many prominent people, among them the president of the United States. The latter at once became interested, and going to the secretary of war directed that a message should be immediately sent to General Miller, commanding at Baltimore, ordering him to take measures without delay for the prisoner's release. A part of this communication reads as follows: "But, sir, in the event of O'Neill's execution, painful as may be the duty, it becomes unavoidable, and I am authorized and commanded to state to your excellency that two British subjects shall be immediately executed." O'Neill was at once paroled. In 1829, when the present lighthouse was built, only a few steps from the little battery he had defended, he was appointed its keeper and held the position until the time of his death, which occurred January 26, 1838. This position, by common consent, has descended from father to son as a sort of heirloom, and his grandson, our subject, holds it to-day.

The father of our subject, John O'Neill, was born and reared in Havre de Grace, and spent much of his life working at the brickmason's trade. In 1861 he was appointed keeper of the lighthouse, and continued in that capacity until his death two years later, at the age of sixty-five. His wife, Esther Mullen, was born in Fulton, N. Y., and after her husband's death, in 1863, she was appointed the keeper of the lighthouse, holding the position for eighteen years, when impaired eyesight caused her to resign in favor of her son. She was very active until a short time before her death, which occurred at the age of eighty-six. In religious belief she was a member of St. John's Episcopal Church. In her family there were seven children, but one died in infancy. Of the others we note the following: Mary is the widow of William L. Moore, of Havre de Grace; Virginia died at the age of sixty years; Charles Z. enlisted in 1861 and was commissioned captain of Company H, Fourth Maryland Infantry, continuing to serve until he was killed at Spottsylvania, May 9, 1863, by a minieball; Indiana is the wife of John Martin, of Philadelphia; our subject is next in order of birth; Martha died at the age of eleven years.

Born in Havre de Grace June 6, 1841, the subject of this record accompanied his parents to Baltimore at nine years of age and remained there until 1861, when the family returned to his native place. While in Baltimore he learned the bricklayer's trade, and at this he was employed until September 12, 1861, the date of his enlistment as a private in Company D, Fifth Maryland Infantry. He soon received promotion, and in the spring of 1863 was commissioned lieutenant. September 17, 1863, he was struck five times by a minie-ball in the battle of Antietam, one ball passing through the left wrist, another through the little finger of the right hand, two through his clothing, and one, a spent ball, lodging in his ankle. After being wounded he walked about twenty miles, to Frederick, filling his position of orderly sergeant. At Frederick he went to a hospital and had his wounds dressed, after which he was removed to the Baltimore Hospital, where he remained three months. On his recovery he rejoined his regiment at Harper's Ferry, as orderly sergeant. June 16, 17 and 18, 1863, he participated in the battle of Winchester, Va., where two-thirds of the regiment was captured. He was imprisoned in a tobacco warehouse in Richmond, later was transferred to Belle Island, from there to Libby Prison and after two months was paroled, reporting to his command at Brandywine Springs, Del. The company was there reorganized and sent to Ft. Delaware to guard prisoners, remaining in that place from May to June, 1864. While there he was promoted to the rank of lieutenant. Among the other engagements in which he took part were the siege of Petersburg, battle of Chapin's Farm, Fair Oaks, and the fall of Richmond. In June, 1865, he was discharged at Fredericksburg, and returned to Baltimore, working at his trade there until 1878, when he came to Havre de Grace and took charge of the lighthouse.

While in Baltimore Captain O'Neill was for three years employed as a letter-carrier. In his political views he is a pronounced Republican and is actively interested in public affairs. Fraternally he is connected with Admiral Rogers Post No. 28, G. A. R., at Havre de Grace. November 12, 1863, he married Miss Fannie Kirby, of Baltimore, who died July 24, 1896, leaving three children. They are Mary B., wife of Millard F. Tydings, of Baltimore; Warren E., who is employed as a printer in Havre de Grace; and Harry F., a fisherman and hunter by occupation.

J WILLIAM O'NEILL. There is no occupation or calling for which there is more universal need than that of general merchant, and those who follow it, whether in a large city or small village, if they possess industry, perseverance and good judgment, cannot fail to succeed. In the list of prosperous merchants of Havre de Grace we mention John W. O'Neill, who for years has carried on a large and profitable trade at this place. In his life are visible the effects of invincible determination, coupled with sound common sense, and he justly occupies a position among the energetic business men of his native town.

The O'Neill family has been represented among the residents of this part of Maryland for a number of generations. Full reference to the genealogical history is made in the sketch of Capt. Henry E. O'Neill, upon another page of this volume. The father of our subject, William, youngest son of John O'Neill, was born in Havre de Grace and here spent his entire life, succeeding, on the death of his father, to the nail manufacturing business established by the latter. He was thus engaged at the time of his death, when thirty-six years of age. He was numbered among the influential citizens of the place, and was active in the ranks of the Democratic party. For a time he held the position of commissioner. His property included four slaves, who worked in his nail factory.

After the death of William O'Neill his widow, Eliza J. (Latour) O'Neill, who was a native of Lewistown, Pa., built the store now owned by our subject and here she embarked in the millinery business, later adding a stock of notions. After her son was old enough, he assisted her in the management of the business. She had but two children and one of these died in infancy. Her life was prolonged for fifty years after the death of her husband, and she continued active and vigorous until shortly before her death, which occurred when she was eighty-two. J. William was born in Havre de Grace November 15, 1845, and was an infant when his father died. His youthful years were spent in Havre de Grace, with the exception of the period when he was a student in the Maryland Agricultural College near Hyattsville, two years being spent in study in that institution. February 4, 1879, he married Miss Augusta Burke, of this place, but their wedded life was of brief duration, for she passed away in October of 1883.

In political belief Mr. O'Neill is firm in his allegiance to the principles for which the Democratic party stands. He has never wavered in his fidelity to his party, and has ever rejoiced in its successes and deplored its defeats. His interest, however, has not been that of an office seeker, but of a public-spirited, patriotic citizen. For eight years or more he has been a director of the First National Bank of Havre de Grace. In the Episcopal Church he is a member of the vestry, of which he has been the treasurer for fourteen years. Local enterprises receive his support, and all measures for the benefit of the place his hearty sympathy. He is one of the original members and a stockholder in the Havre de Grace Improvement Company, also a stockholder in the shoe factory here, and in addition owns a substantial store building, stocked with a full line of goods suited to the needs of the people.

CHARLES W. BAKER. The business men of Aberdeen are well known throughout Harford County and are highly regarded on account of their thorough-going integrity, their enterprise and their promptness in responding to the necessities of a business life. They have advanced the financial interests of the village and brought it to a flourishing condition in trade, through their efforts not only promoting their own success, but also materially advancing the welfare of others in the locality. Of no others can this be said in a greater degree than of the Baker brothers, who have been instrumental in securing the advancement of Aberdeen along business lines. While they were assisted by their father, who was a man of means, yet their success was not due alone to his assistance, for had they lacked energy and good judgment they could have achieved little for themselves or others. They have been pioneers in the introduction and development of the canning industry, now one of the principal lines of business in the county.

The record of the Baker family appears elsewhere, in the sketch of George A. Baker. The subject of this sketch was born January 14, 1848, in District No. 2, Harford County, about two miles west of Aberdeen. The early years of his life were spent upon the home farm, and his education was obtained in the public schools. When about eighteen years of age he became interested in the meat business, and this he carried on in Aberdeen about three years. Then, for a similar period, he was interested with his brother, James B., in the same business in Shelbyville, Ky. On his return to Aberdeen, he engaged in farming and the canning business. He now owns a large factory here, another at Kenton, Del., and one at Wyoming, that state, the corn for which is raised upon his eight large and valuable farms. About 1880 he embarked in the canning brokerage business as a member of the firm of Baker & Morgan, well known throughout the entire country at this time. He also has mercantile interests here. Fraternally he is connected with Aberdeen Lodge No. 187, F. & A. M., of Aberdeen, in religious belief holds membership in the Methodist Episcopal Church here, and politically he is a pronounced Republican, but not active in public affairs. His marriage was solemnized in 1874, and united him with Miss Emma F. Michael, daughter of William B. Michael. They are the parents of four children, namely: P. Tevis, Frank Emerson, Beulah and Austin L., who are being reared for honorable positions in the business and social world.

As a man of genuine public spirit, Mr. Baker interests himself in everything that will in any way promote the welfare of Aberdeen, and contributes liberally toward all plans for improvement. A careful and conscientious business man, he has endeavored to adhere strictly to the dictates of his own conscience in matters both of a public and private nature, and has won the respect of his fellow-citizens.

ELLIS J. TUCKER. Among the energetic and progressive farmers of Harford County none is more deserving of mention than the subject of this sketch, whose fine farm of one hundred and thirty-seven acres is pleasantly situated on the Susquehanna River at the mouth of Deer Creek, and six miles above Havre de Grace. He is a native of the county, born at Forest Hill, in 1831, and is a son of David Tucker. His paternal grandfather, who also bore the name of David, came from Bucks County, Pa., and located at Forest Hill about 1810, here spending his remaining days. Of his three sons David was the second in order of birth, and was a lad of about ten years when he accompanied his parents to their new home in Harford County. In 1840 he succeeded to the old homestead where Mrs. Margaret Tucker now resides. By occupation he was a general farmer and devoted his energies principally to the cultivation and improvement of that farm, where almost his entire life was passed. After his marriage, however, he removed to Peach Bottom, York County, Pa., but after spending three years there decided that the old home place in Harford County was good enough for him and accordingly returned. He also made two different trips on horse back to Indiana, where he secured a quarter-section of land and built a cabin, but finally sold out and returned to his birthplace to spend his remaining days.

As a companion and helpmeet on life's journey David Tucker chose Miss Sarah Carter, of Lancaster County, Pa., and by their marriage they became the parents of eleven children, eight still living, namely: Elizabeth, widow of Amos Benson; Sarah, wife of M. Smith, of Illinois; Ellis J.; John C.; Isabel, wife of John Stonebraker; Mary Ann, wife of John Stridehoff; Margaret C., wife of D. Deaver; and David, who married Sarah Stewart and lives at Forest Hill. The father of this family was called to his final rest in 1883, at the age of eighty-three years, and the mother some years afterwards.

In the quiet, uneventful manner of most farmer boys Ellis J. Tucker spent the days of his boyhood and youth on the old homestead at Forest Hill and obtained his education in the schools of that place. In 1854, at the age of twenty-three, he moved to the Ridgby Hope farm, where he has since continued to reside, and in connection with general farming makes a specialty of raising fruits for canning.

In 1857 was celebrated the marriage of Mr. Tucker and Miss Melissa E. Reynolds, of Lancaster County, Pa., a daughter of Josiah and Mary Reynolds. Three children have been born to them: Alva J., born in 1861; Elizabeth, now the wife of Price Hoopes, of Vale, Md.; and Ellis R. The family is one of the highest respectability and is connected with the Society of Friends. Mr. Tucker is a man of the times, broad minded, public spirited and progressive. His influence is great and always for good, and his goodness, his benevolence, his kindly greeting, will long be remembered after he has passed to the unseen world.

JEREMIAH C. PRICE, Jr. The old homestead in District No. 1, Cecil County, where Mr. Price has spent his entire life, has been in the possession of the family for five or six generations and consists of four hundred acres of land, the most of which is under cultivation. The substantial house that is the family residence is one of the oldest places in the district; there our subject was born, and within its walls, too, the eyes of his grandfather, Fredus Price, first opened to the light. Could the lifeless timber speak, many a tale might it tell of the early days when settlers were few and when the improvements that are now conspicuous in the county were undreamed of, by even the most sanguine.

Born May 7, 1852, the subject of this sketch is a son of Jeremiah C. and Ellen (Price) Price, also natives of this district. He was one of ten children, of whom, besides himself, only three survive, Eugene, Anna W. and Fredus A. Reared to a knowledge of farm pursuits, he chose for his life-work the occupation in which his ancestors, almost without exception, had engaged. His education, which was quite thorough, was gained in a Catholic college in Washington, D. C., and in St. Mary's College, at Wilmington, Del., in each of which he was a student for a year and a-half. On leaving college he returned to the homestead and has since resided here, giving his attention to the cultivation of the place. Local enterprises receive his assistance, to the extent of his ability. In politics a strong Democrat, he was elected on that ticket commissioner of Cecil County and held the office for four years, from 1892 to 1896. He has also acted efficiently as school trustee of the district.

At the age of twenty-eight Mr. Price married

Belle Veach, who was born in Delaware, received a good education and is a lady of amiable disposition and an active member of the Protestant Episcopal Church. Her great-grandfather, John Veach, founded the family in America, coming to Maryland from Ireland in an early day and settling upon a farm. The six children of Mr. and Mrs. Price are Ellen A., Emily, Lindsey, Belle, Anna and Jeremiah C., the latter deceased.

GEORGE WALKER, of the village of Aberdeen, stands high in business circles and has an excellent record. His present position is the result of his ability and wise judgment. Through a life of industry and usefulness, he has been given a position of influence in the community which all might well desire to share. As a merchant, it is his aim to be honorable in every transaction; as a citizen, he strives to aid such measures as will advance the welfare of the town; and as a man, he gives his influence to the cause of justice and morality.

The Walker family has been represented in Harford County for several successive generations. The first of the name to establish a home here was our subject's great-grandfather, George, a native of Scotland, and from early manhood a resident of America, where he probably settled in what is now Harford County. The grandfather, George, was born here and engaged in farming pursuits until old age rendered manual labor impossible. He died at the age of eighty-six. The father, who likewise bore the name of George, was born in Churchville, this county, and spent the greater part of his life near Perryman, where he owned and operated a farm. He died here at the age of about sixty. His wife, who bore the maiden name of Susan Cole, was born in this county and died here at fifty-eight years of age. Of her three children, Elizabeth was the eldest; and Cornelius died at the age of twenty-seven.

On the home farm the boyhood years of our subject were uneventfully passed. By careful training he was fitted for active contact with the business world, and the habits of industry and perseverance formed in youth, were of the utmost value to him in after years. He was born August 8, 1847, and was about sixteen years of age when he began to clerk in a general store near his home in Perryman. During the seven years spent there he gained a thorough familiarity with his work that fitted him for the management of an establishment of his own. He then came to Aberdeen where he has since built up an excellent trade among the people of the locality. In June, 1870, he married Miss Anna Russell, of Baltimore, and they have three children: William R., who assists his father in the store, Percival and Marienne L.

Politically Mr. Walker is a Democrat, active and aggressive, and always interested in local and national affairs. His interest, however, has rather been for the good of the country, than through any selfish motive, for he has never been prevailed upon to accept office. Fraternally he is a member of Aberdeen Lodge No. 187, F. & A. M., Concordia Chapter, R. A. M., and Monumental Commandery No. 3, K. T., of Baltimore. In religion he is a Presbyterian.

GEORGE A. BAKER. In reviewing the history of any community, there are always a few names that stand out pre-eminently among others, because those who bear them are men of ability, energy and force of character. Such names and such men add to the prosperity of a place, elevating its moral tone and increasing its commercial importance. Their wealth, put into circulation in the home neighborhood, becomes a factor in the prosperity of every citizen. Their intelligence is a power that cannot be lightly estimated.

To this class belongs George A. Baker, one of the most successful business men of Havre de

Grace, where he has resided since 1891. He was born, of remote Scotch descent, in District No. 2, near Aberdeen, Harford County, the son of George W. and Elizabeth (Greenland) Baker. His father, who was born in District No. 2, spent his entire life on the homestead where he was born, and had the distinction of being the pioneer canning packer of this county, which is now the banner canning county in the world. About 1866 he began on a very small scale, somewhat similar to the canning operations of thousands of housewives all over the land. The fruit was pared, then put into a wash boiler on the stove and cooked until ready for the cans. From that small beginning he worked his way to the ownership of several large canning factories, which he built, and in which were prepared for the market the products of about three thousand acres planted to fruit and corn. He was remarkably successful, when we take into consideration the obstacles he was obliged to overcome and the difficulties that impeded his progress in those early days of the canning industry. In early years he had been a cabinet maker, and later engaged in the ship timber business, but the enterprise in which he met with the most marked success was the canning of fruit. Politically he was a Republican, but never took an active part in local conventions or elections. In religion he was a member of the Methodist Episcopal Church. He led a very active, busy life until 1887, when a stroke of paralysis warned him that his earthly career was nearing an end. He died in 1889, at seventy-three years of age.

The grandfather of our subject, Nicholas Baker, was born in District No. 2, and was a farmer and country merchant, and quite a prominent man in his day. Our subject's mother was a native of this county, and passed away here in 1897, at the age of seventy-three. Like her husband she was a consistent member of the Methodist Episcopal Church. Their family consisted of fifteen children, but six of these died in infancy. Of the others we note the following: Sarah R. is the wife of John Carty; William B., whose sketch will be found elsewhere in this volume, is a resident of Aberdeen, Harford County, and is at this writing a member of congress from the second congressional district of Maryland; Lydia C. married Wesley Howard; James B., of Aberdeen, is represented upon another page, as is also Charles W.; John H. was the sixth of the family; Susie E. is the wife of C. R. Courtney; Alice C. married C. Tollinger; and George A. is the youngest.

Reared upon the old homestead, our subject's life has been a busy one from his early youth. When he became of age he assumed the management of a farm, and in connection with his father, had charge of a canning factory. In this way he gained the experience that has since been so helpful to him. During the latter years of the life of his father, he managed the canning business, and when sickness obliged the founder of the enterprise to withdraw from all active cares, the son was ready to assist in carrying forward the enterprise to the best of his ability. The property was divided among the children, George A. receiving his share. In 1891 he came to Havre de Grace, and has since been the owner and proprietor of two canning factories at Perryman, which are the largest in the county. These are situated on his valuable farm near Aberdeen, which, though he still owns, he has not personally operated since 1894. Like his brothers, he uses the brand established by his father, and ships goods throughout the entire country. His property holdings include the ownership of a fine residence in Havre de Grace and large mining interests in Colorado. In 1889 he married Miss Mary W. Sumption, of this place, who presides with graceful hospitality over his elegant home. Fraternally he is identified with Aberdeen Lodge No. 180, F. & A. M., of Aberdeen. Politically a Republican, he is one of the prominent members of the party here, and in 1892 was its candidate for congress from the second congressional district, but, the party being in the minority, he was defeated. Though always active in politics, he has never cared to accept office, and the defeat which he experienced he regretted more on account of his party than himself. He is not indebted to luck for the measure of success he has obtained, for, aside from his portion of the family estate, no legacies have descended to him and no accidents have befriended him. His watchword, work, has been the secret of his success, and it stands for a long road and one hard to travel, but he has traversed it perseveringly in youth and has secured good results.

JACOB T. BIDDLE. Having retired from active participation in the agricultural pursuits that formerly engaged his attention, Mr. Biddle is spending the closing years of his life in the enjoyment of the competency accumulated by toil in his younger years. The property which he has owned from early manhood and from the rental of which he derives a good income, is situated in District No. 4, Cecil County, and comprises one hundred and twelve acres of well-cultivated land. In addition to the raising of cereals he gave some attention to the dairy business, which he found to be profitable and congenial.

In this county, in District No. 2, Mr. Biddle was born in 1832, being a son of Rensselaer and Mary (Egner) Biddle, natives, respectively, of Districts Nos. 2 and 3. His father, who in youth learned the miller's trade, devoted some time to that occupation, but afterward transferred his attention to farming and in that calling his remaining years were spent. He was a lifelong resident of Cecil County and had many warm friends among the people here. On the organization of the Republican party, being in sympathy with its policy, he became one of its adherents and ever afterward voted that ticket. He was spared to attain an advanced age, his death occurring in 1877, when he was seventy-four. By his marriage to Miss Egner, three children were born, those besides our subject being George, deceased; and Mary, wife of David Devlin, District No. 4.

At the age of fifteen, Mr. Biddle discontinued his studies which he had previously carried on in the common schools. From that time he assisted his father until the death of the latter, since which he has had the old homestead in charge, from its acres reaping bountiful harvests in return for the labor he has bestowed upon them. He has been an industrious, hard-working man and deserves the success he has attained. He has never married, but while he does not have the domestic ties that form so important a part of most lives, he has a large number of near friends, in whose companionship many happy hours have been spent. The tenets and platform of the Republican party he has advocated ever since the inception of that organization. He attends services at the Methodist Church and contributes to its maintenance. In him the district has one of its useful citizens, a man of shrewd business qualifications, of upright life and generous heart. He is attached by long association to this locality and would exchange it for no other home in the world. The long stretches of grain-laden fields; the towns with their busy merchants, their canning factories and their little homes; the waters of the bay in the distance, into which flows the old Susquehanna; and the quiet, happy faces that bespeak a contented, industrious population,—these represent all that is dearest and best on earth to him, and amid the scenes so familiar to him he hopes to quietly pass what may remain to him of life.

GOLDSMITH BOTTS, who is engaged in farming in District No. 2, Harford County, is a native of the locality which is still his home, his birth having occurred on the 25th of February, 1837. His parents, John B. and Anna (Miller) Botts, were also natives of the same neighborhood, and spent their entire lives as respected farming people of the community. When the country became engaged in the second war with England, the father patriotically responded to the call for troops and aided in the defense of the republic. He made farming his life work and successfully carried on his business until he became owner of an extensive and valuable tract of land. His political support was given the Democracy, but he never sought or desired political preferment. His death occurred at the age of seventy-seven years, and his wife passed away at the age of seventy-two. They had a family of six children, three of whom are now deceased, those living being Asel M., Avarilla and Goldsmith.

Mr. Botts, of this review, through his boyhood and youth assisted in the cultivation of the home farm and remained with his father until his death, when he inherited the homestead upon which he has spent his entire life. He here owns sixty acres of rich land, which he has placed under a high state of cultivation. He has good improvements upon the place in the way of substantial buildings and has added to it all the accessories and conveniences of a model farm of the nineteenth century. In all his business dealings he is straightforward and honorable, never taking undue advantage of any one, and has gained thereby not only a comfortable competence, but has also secured the high regard of those with whom he has been brought in contact.

Mr. Botts married Miss Melissa Gardner, of New York, and they have a family of four children, three sons and a daughter, namely: Archie M., a farmer of District No. 2, Harford County; Winfield, who also follows farming in the same district; Lester and Libbie, at home. Mr. Botts is a stalwart advocate of Democratic principles and is a public-spirited, progressive citizen.

THOMAS J. CLEAVER. The long period of Mr. Cleaver's residence in Chesapeake City and his equally long connection with the Chesapeake & Delaware Canal Company, have brought him into prominence among the business men of the village. Among the towns of Cecil County that of Chesapeake City is known chiefly through the fact that it is the western terminus of the canal, which connects it with Delaware City. Therefore those who have been connected with the canal company have also been very influential in the advancement of the village, and of these men Mr. Cleaver is one. Beginning in their employ in a humble position, where the wages were very small, he gradually worked his way to increased responsibilities and larger salary, and now for many years has been collector at this point. In June, 1896, he was appointed superintendent and now holds both positions.

The son of Peter and Anna (Jeffreys) Cleaver, natives of Pennsylvania, the subject of this sketch was born December 15, 1836, in Newcastle County, Del. His father, who was a member of the Society of Friends, was consistent in adhering to the rules of that sect, until their removal to Delaware, when they united with the Methodist Episcopal Church. He devoted the principal portion of his life to agricultural pursuits, and died at seventy years of age. The wife and mother died when fifty years old. Their son, our subject, was reared upon the home farm and received a common-school education, supplemented by one year of study in the Newcastle Academy. In 1849 he accompanied his parents to District No. 2, Cecil County, settling upon a farm, where he continued to reside until twenty-one years of age. Returning to Newcastle, he attended school for one year and then secured a clerkship in a country store, where he remained for two years and three months. His wages for the first year were $10 per month; for the second $15 per month, and it was arranged that he was to receive $20 the third year, but on account of failing health he was obliged to resign the position. The president of the Chesapeake & Delaware Canal Company, being one of his personal friends, gave him a position as clerk in the collector's office at Chesapeake City, and he came here in August, 1858. After being at this place for two months his salary was raised, and his greatly improved health enabled him to better discharge his duties. At the expiration of the first year of his connection with the company, his salary was made $50 per month, and after four years it was raised to $60, and in 1874 another advance was made to $70. He remained in the collector's office until October, 1879, when he was appointed collector at this terminus of the canal. In June, 1896, he became

WILLIAM T. WARBURTON.

superintendent of the entire canal, a position of great responsibility, but one which he is capable of filling satisfactorily. He is also part owner and in charge of two tugs and three barges at this port.

January 12, 1862, Mr. Cleaver was united in marriage with Cornelia H. Karsner, daughter of Daniel and Eleanor Karsner, and sister of Dr. Karsner, mentioned upon another page of this volume. Three children were born to bless the union, but two died in infancy. The only one now living is Harry Archer Cleaver, M. D., to whom every educational advantage was given, and who graduated from Wesleyan University and Chester Military Academy. He then spent one year in the medical department of Columbia College of New York City, and later was for three years in the medical department of the University of Pennsylvania. After receiving his degree, for about two years he at different times filled vacancies in various hospitals, and is now employed as resident physician in the Episcopal Hospital of Philadelphia. Both Mr. and Mrs. Cleaver are identified with the Presbyterian Church, and are attendants at its services.

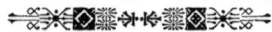

WILLIAM T. WARBURTON. The practice of banking and the establishment of banks belongs entirely to the modern world. The first bank which the civilized world boasted was the bank of Venice, which was founded in 1157. According to some authorities, it was founded in consequence of a loan which the state had felt the necessity of raising in order to carry on a war. At the settlement of this country the colonists brought over with them the financial theories and practices which prevailed at the time in the mother country. The first bank established was at Boston in 1784. From that year to this there has been a steady growth in the volume and importance of the banking business, and now these financial institutions may be found in every town of any size. One of the reliable banks of Cecil County is the Second National, of Elkton, of which Mr. Warburton has been president since the time of its organization. He is a capable financier and has placed the finances of the concern upon a firm basis, thereby gaining the confidence of the business men of this locality.

Not only is Mr. Warburton known as president of the Second National Bank, but also as an able attorney and successful practitioner at the bar. His business interests, too, are important. He is president of the Elkton Electric Light & Power Company, that is doing so much for the improvement of the place. He is a director in the Singerly Pulp and Paper Mills of Elkton and a director in the Lancaster, Cecil & Southern Railroad Company, both of which are aiding in promoting the growth of Elkton; also president of the Maryland Water Company and president of the Citizens' Mutual Fire Insurance Company of Cecil County. For all the corporations with which he is connected, he holds the position of attorney. Educational matters receive a due proportion of his time and he is now a trustee in the Elkton Academy.

The life of a man so intimately connected with the history and business interests of Elkton will be of general interest. Mr. Warburton was born on a farm near Bay View, District No. 9, Cecil County, July 16, 1852, the son of William T. and Elizabeth (McCauley) Warburton. His father, who was born on the home farm in 1809 and died there in 1885, spent the intervening years in the occupation of a farmer, in which he met with success. Fraternally he was a Mason, in religious belief a member of the Methodist Episcopal Church, and in public affairs prominent and active. His father, Thomas Warburton, who was an Englishman by birth and a direct descendant of Bishop Warburton of Gloucestershire, England, came to America in young manhood and settled upon a farm in Cecil County, where he engaged in farming and also ministerial work as a local Methodist preacher. He died in 1857, at the age of eighty-four years. He had only one son, William T.

The mother of our subject was born in Cecil County and was a daughter of John and Elizabeth

McCauley, and a member of an old Scotch family that settled here in an early day. She is still living, now eighty-one years of age. Her intellect is as bright as in the past, and her memory, both of events far remote and those recently occurring, is excellent. One of her marked characteristics is her happy disposition, which makes her a cheerful companion and genial friend. Her brother, the late Judge James McCauley, was a man of remarkable parts, possessing literary ability and broad knowledge of public affairs. For a long time he was register of wills for Cecil County, and for thirty years held the position of chief judge of the orphans' court, his long service on this bench bringing him in contact with nearly every family in the county. He was retired from the bench on account of failing health and soon after died. Another brother, Daniel McCauley, was a leading citizen of Baltimore County until his decease and served on the board of county commissioners.

The subject of this article was third among five children, the others being Hannah, who resides in Cecil County; Elizabeth, wife of John P. Ruley, who is connected with a clothing house in Philadelphia; Thomas H. and Mary, who reside on the old homestead. The boyhood days of our subject were spent on his father's farm. At the age of fifteen he entered West Nottingham Academy, and in 1871 graduated from Delaware College. The following year, before he had attained his majority, he commenced the study of law in the office of Reuben Haines, then a prominent member of the Cecil County bar. In 1874 he was admitted to practice, and at once became identified with politics and public affairs. However, he had no political aspirations for himself, but contented himself in working for the advancement of the Republican party. In 1888 he was a delegate to the Republican national convention. Honoring the party, he would in turn be honored by it if he cared to give up his business interests for public life, but such is not his desire.

January 2, 1877, Mr. Warburton married Matilda McFarland, daughter of Richard McFarland, who, at the time of his death, was cashier of the National Bank of Elkton. Two sons and one daughter came to bless the union. The sons, Charles E. and Henry A., are school students. The daughter, Emma, who was a singularly gifted girl and the pride of the family, was a student in the Elkton Academy, where for four successive years she secured a gold medal offered by the trustees of that institution for the highest general average in all studies. Later she entered the Woman's College, of Baltimore, where she was recognized as a young lady of rare attainments. Personally she was very attractive and no one looked into her bright, cultured face without being deeply impressed with the superiority of her intellect. Her death, which occurred December 9, 1896, when she was nineteen, was a deep bereavement to her parents, the only sorrow that has come to their otherwise happy life. Mr. and Mrs. Warburton reside in a pleasant home on North Main Street, in the finest part of Elkton.

JESSE W. HAMBLETON. Within the bounds of Cecil County no better representative of the farming community can be found than the above-named gentleman, who throughout the most of his life has been identified with the work of the county, and especially of District No. 9, in which his home is located. His farm comprises one hundred and sixty-two acres and is devoted to general agriculture. It is a place which any man might be contented with owning. Even a casual observer would recognize it as the abode of people of intelligence as well as of assured financial standing, for everything about it indicates the qualities that make a dwelling-place a home indeed.

The Hambleton family came to Maryland from the neighboring state of Pennsylvania. The father of our subject, Joseph, and his grandfather, Samuel, were born in Chester County, and there engaged in general farming, but in 1838 the former came to Cecil County and settled at College Green. His last years were spent in District No.

9, where he died. Politically he was a Republican. Interested in educational matters, he rendered effective service as trustee of schools. He was also the road supervisor of his district for some time. By his marriage to Mary Conard, of Lancaster County, Pa., he had eight children, but only three of these are now living: William C., of Calvert, Md.; Jesse W.; and Samuel, whose home is at Rising Sun, Md. At the time of his death, in October, 1893, he was eighty-four years of age.

In 1838, shortly before the family removed to Maryland, Jesse W. Hambleton was born on the old homestead in Chester County. He was educated in the district schools and early gained a knowledge of farm pursuits, which occupation he selected for his life calling. In 1861 he enlisted as a member of Company E, Purnell Legion of Maryland Volunteer Infantry, and served for a period of thirty-eight months. Among the most important engagements in which he took part were those at Antietam, Cold Harbor, second battle of Bull Run and Weldon Railroad. He was honorably discharged from the service in 1864 and returned to his Cecil County home, where the next few years were spent in the cultivation of the farm. Thinking that the west might offer better opportunities, in 1870 he went to Iowa and from there to Kansas, engaging in general farm work for two years. The surroundings, however, were undesirable and the prospects less hopeful than he had anticipated, so in 1872 he came back to the old homestead, which he has since managed and cultivated. He has never taken an active part in politics, aside from casting a straight Republican ticket at elections.

In 1861 Mr. Hambleton married Rachel Lewis, of District No. 3, member of an old family there. The four children born of their union are as follows: Frank, who resides in District No. 6; Harry, who assists his father in the cultivation of the home farm; Mary E. and Carrie. Fraternally Mr. Hambleton is connected with Excelsior Lodge of Odd Fellows, in which he has passed all the chairs. He is also identified with the Junior Order of American Mechanics and Cecil Grange. For some years he has been steward of the Methodist Episcopal Church and at this writing is also a trustee of the congregation. He and his wife are interested in all matters of local importance, both of a social and public nature, and wield an influence for good throughout their community.

NICHOLAS MILBURN. In days of old a philosopher exclaimed, "Account no man happy until he is dead." Ages have swept away since he uttered these words, but they still contain a lesson for all mankind. The mutations of life, the shadows of adversity, the loss of loved ones, the waiting chalice of disgrace and defeat—all these the future may bring even to the most joyous and gay. But, when temptations have been resisted, when the life has been kept spotless, when prosperity has not elated nor adversity rendered bitter, when every duty has been faithfully discharged to mankind and to God, at the going out of such a life one may truly say, "How blest are the dead that die in the Lord."

The life which this biography chronicles began in Elkton June 14, 1817, and closed near Bay View April 28, 1893. After nearly seventy-six years of earth-life, the body was laid to rest in the midst of the old familiar scenes, just as nature was budding forth in all the rich beauty of spring after the chill barrenness of winter,—fitting type of the entrance of the spirit into the splendors of heaven. His death was not unexpected, either by himself or his friends. Realizing that the end approached, he made such preparations as were needed regarding his business affairs. He even selected the hymns to be sung at his funeral and the text for the discourse: "I am the resurrection and the life; he that believeth in Me, though he were dead, yet shall he live."

In view of the prominence of Mr. Milburn in the agricultural circles and public affairs of District No. 5, Cecil County, a record of his life will be welcomed by all readers. He was a member of a family long resident in the United States and was a first cousin of the famous blind chaplain of the United States congress. His parents, Benjamin and Catherine (Boyce) Milburn, were natives, respectively, of Elkton and Baltimore, and had four children, but all are now dead. The father was the son of a Revolutionary soldier, and was himself a man of loyal, patriotic spirit. By trade he was a stone mason.

The entire life of our subject was spent in his native county, principally engaged in agricultural pursuits. Prospered financially, he was able to provide his family with every comfort, and everything around his pleasant home indicated good taste and convenience, as well as an orderly spirit. There was always a sufficiency of the material things requisite for happiness, these having been provided by his industry through long years of toil. In 1858 he was converted in the old Shelemiah Church under the preaching of Rev. Mr. Helmbold, then the minister in charge of the Cecil circuit. He became connected with the church that stood within what is now Bay View cemetery, but long since the building was torn down and replaced by a stately building a few rods distant. The faith which had brightened and blessed his life filled his dying moments with hope, and he passed away in the glorious assurance that all was well with his soul. For many years he was a trustee in the Methodist Protestant Church of Bay View, and his active co-operation was always given to measures for the benefit of the congregation. As every citizen should, he bore his part in matters relative to the public welfare. A Democrat in politics, he was, however, not narrow in his opinions, but conceded to others that liberty of thought he demanded for himself and that is the most precious birthright of the citizens of the United States.

January 7, 1847, Mr. Milburn married Amy A. Ramsey, whose father, William Ramsey, was of Irish descent. Her grandfather came from Ireland to the United States and settled in Chester County, Pa., where he resided until his death. Her mother, who bore the maiden name of Martha Mevay, was of Scotch descent, and was a member of a wealthy family of Cecil County. She was reared in this district, and owns a valuable farm of ninety-seven acres here. Four children were born of her marriage, but two are deceased. Mattie J. is the wife of I. T. Rogers, and lives near the old homestead; A. Virginia married Levi Plank, of Chester County, Pa. One of the principal characteristics of Mr. Milburn was his generosity to others. In his personal expenses he was careful and economical, but he loved to surround his family with comforts, and he was very kind to the needy and distressed. He was a man of moral worth and pure character, and in all positions, under all circumstances, a gentleman.

HON. WILLIAM B. BAKER, M. C. No resident of Aberdeen has pursued a more honorable course in life or been of greater value as a citizen than the subject of this article, who is the present representative of the second district of Maryland in congress. As one of the influential men of Harford County, he has been largely instrumental in advancing the material, educational and commercial interests of this part of the state, and few have done more than he in building up the village of Aberdeen. In public life he has been prominent and popular; in financial circles, as president of the First National Bank of Aberdeen, discriminating, judicious and wise; and as a business man, shrewd and far sighted.

A record of the life of one so influential will possess general interest. A member of an old family of Harford County, reference to whom will be found in the sketch of George A. Baker, the subject of this sketch was born July 22, 1840, on the old homestead, three miles from Aberdeen, in District No. 2. His education was obtained in the public and private schools of the neighborhood and he remained at home with his parents until thirty-two years of age. In 1872, with his brother, Charles W., he built a large canning factory in this district, and continued to operate it until the fall of 1876, when the factory was destroyed by fire. He sold the property and then purchased a large farm, comprising two hundred and eighty acres, one and one-half miles from the village of Aberdeen, and here he built a canning factory, the management of which he superintended for some years.

The connection of Mr. Baker with politics began when he was quite young. In 1875 he was the Republican candidate for the house of delegates and at the election ran ahead of his ticket, but was defeated with the remainder of the ticket, the county being then strongly Democratic. In 1881 he was again a candidate for the position and was elected, serving one term. At the following election, in 1883, he was defeated by a small majority. The Republicans, in 1889, placed him in nomination for the state senate, but he was defeated, though by only five hundred and fifty votes. In 1893 he was again the candidate on the Republican ticket and was elected, but after one year of service he resigned in consequence of his election as congressman from the second district of Maryland. To this responsible position he was elected by a majority of one hundred and ninety-one, with the distinction of being the first Republican ever chosen to that office from the district. As a member of the Fifty-fourth Congress, he ably represented his constituents, whose welfare he ever had in mind, and was a member of the committee on agriculture. That the people were pleased with his service is proved by his re-election in 1896, when he carried the district by a majority of about five thousand three hundred and sixty-seven, having a majority in every county and ward in the district. This fact, without any comment, shows the high order of his service and the regard in which he is held by the people.

With important public duties on hand, it might be supposed that Mr. Baker would lose interest in the village where, since 1894, he has made his home; but not so. No one takes a greater interest in the welfare of Aberdeen than he, and if the place should ever gain a position among the commercial centers of the state, it would be largely due to the efforts of himself and his relatives. He aided in the organization of the First National Bank of Aberdeen, of which he has been president since the first, and his ability in banking is no less than in other lines of activity. Since the organization of the First National Bank of Havre de Grace, in which he aided, he has been one of its directors, and he is a heavy stockholder, both in it and in the bank here. Another local enterprise which he has assisted is the Harford County Telephone Company, of which he is president. Among his possessions are four large farms in this district. Fraternally he is connected with Blenheim Lodge No. 102, I. O. O. F., at Aberdeen, and has been its secretary for twenty-four years; he is also a member of Aberdeen Lodge No. 187, F. & A. M. In 1868 he married Miss Alevia Wells, of Aberdeen, who died sixteen months later. His second marriage, which took place in 1872, was to Miss Mary C. Hollis, and they are the parents of two daughters and a son, namely: Jessie M.; Hollis R., a student in Westminster College; and Nettie F. The family are members of the Methodist Church, with the exception of Mr. Baker, who, however, is an attendant at the same.

CHARLES W. WILSON. There is ever interest attaching to the life of one whose success in life is worthily achieved by honorable endeavor and unfaltering perseverance. Such a life demonstrates the possibilities that are open to a young man in a land unhampered by caste or class. Almost the same opportunities surround every individual, and it is the use which one makes of these which determines his success and his standing in life. Mr. Wilson has won a position of prominence in Cecil County, for his career has gained him the respect and confidence of all with whom he has been brought in contact.

Born in Oxford, Chester County, Pa., January 7, 1837, he was reared on a farm until sixteen years of age, when he attended school at Jordan Bank Academy, Chester County, Pa., under the distinguished Dr. Evan Pugh. He also attended Hopewell Academy, under John M. Kennedy. He then began working at the carpenter's trade, a pursuit which he followed until attaining his majority. He then became a student in the State

Normal School of Pennsylvania, and afterwards engaged in teaching for four years, until he put aside all personal considerations in order to aid his country.

Mr. Wilson enlisted in August, 1862, in the One Hundred and Twenty-fourth Pennsylvania Infantry, for nine months' service, and was mustered in at Harrisburg. The first engagement in which he participated was at Antietam, and later he took part in the battles of South Mountain, Chancellorsville and Fredericksburg. He was honorably discharged in May, 1863. When President Lincoln made a call for state troops, he aided in organizing a company and was elected first lieutenant of Company A, Forty-third Pennsylvania Infantry, with which he went down the Potomac, doing patrol and guard duty along the canal. After returning home he soon made his way to Rising Sun, Md., where he taught in the public schools for two terms. He then went to Washington and accepted a position in the quartermaster's department, where he remained until the close of the war. He was in Ford's Theatre the night President Lincoln was assassinated.

When hostilities had ceased Mr. Wilson removed to Rising Sun, where he has since engaged in contracting and building with excellent success. He built the bank building, the Methodist Episcopal Church, the town hall and the fine residences of Edwin Haines and George H. Fox, together with many of the other buildings of the town. He is one of the leading contractors of the county, and his high standing as a business man is unquestioned.

In 1864 Mr. Wilson was united in marriage to Elizabeth Fisher, formerly of Philadelphia. They have six children living and have lost four. Those who still survive are Rhoda V., who has attended the Conservatory of Music in Boston, and is now a teacher of vocal and instrumental music; Fred C., a carpenter; Emma E., who is engaged in the millinery business in Union, S. C.; Howard M., who is attending the Normal Institute of Rising Sun; and Armenia H. and Edna, who are also in school.

Mr. Wilson is a Republican in politics and has twice been the candidate of his party for the state legislature. For one term he served as town commissioner. He is a member of Garfield Post No. 18, G. A. R., and is frequently called upon to deliver addresses on memorial day. He is past commander of the Independent Order of Odd Fellows; has filled all of the offices, and is now financial secretary. He is a leading member of the Methodist Episcopal Church, and has served as superintendent of the Sunday-school.

JAMES STEPHENSON. So many years have elapsed since the subject of this memoir laid down the burdens of life and entered into rest, that comparatively few now living ever saw him; yet, as one of the once influential men of Harford County, as one who contributed to the upbuilding of local industries and was instrumental in promoting local progress, his name deserves to be perpetuated in a volume dedicated to the public-spirited men of Harford and Cecil. His life began in Cecil County when the colonies were still under English domination, and he was a boy when the patriots rose in arms to fight for the freedom there then seemed so little hope of ever gaining. When the second struggle with Great Britain began, he at once enlisted and rendered good service as captain of a militia. He witnessed the rapid development of the country in the years that followed and was permitted to assist therein. Attaining an advanced age, he died before the dark clouds arose in our national sky that presaged the horrors of a civil strife.

In what is now Perryville, Cecil County, the subject of this article was born August 10, 1767, being a son of William and Rachel (Barnes) Stephenson, natives, respectively, of Scotland and Maryland. His father came to America in young manhood, and settled in Harford or Cecil County, Md. During the Revolution he was proprietor of a hotel at Perryville, and soon after the conflict closed he purchased a large tract of land in District No. 2, Harford County, a portion of which is still in possession of the family. He was a man of honest Christian character, energetic in business, and a hard worker. His death occurred when he was about seventy-four. His wife, who was a woman of religious nature, was one of the first Methodists of this neighborhood, and possessed the zeal and fervor for which this denomination is remarkable. Her six children were named as follows: George, born March 18, 1763, who was a prominent farmer of District No. 2; William, born February 12, 1765, who was a farmer and a local preacher in the Methodist Church; James; Mary, who was born March 9, 1769; Rachael, March 21, 1773; and Ann, in 1776.

The early boyhood years of our subject were spent in Perryville, and from there he accompanied his parents to the farm in District No. 2. Inheriting a portion of that place, he added to his possessions by purchase, and owned a large tract of land at the time of his death. In addition to his land he also owned many slaves, to some of whom he gave their freedom before he died. During the War of 1812 he served in the American army, loyally supporting the government. While not a member of any church, he was a believer in Christianity, and endeavored to lead an honest, upright Christian life, and was always generous in his contributions to religious enterprises. His death occurred in 1838, when he was about seventy-one years of age.

By the marriage of James Stephenson to Priscilla Hopkins twelve children were born. Rachel, the eldest, was born December 23, 1799, and died in December, 1818. Mary was born March 18, 1801, and died September 18, 1837. William, whose birth occurred June 16, 1802, was a colonel in the militia and a prominent man; he died February 13, 1884; James was born in 1804, and died in 1879; Robert, who was born July 1, 1806, was murdered by Union soldiers at Port Deposit, September 21, 1861; he, like the other members of the family, was strongly southern in his sympathies. Eliza was born July 25, 1807, and died in October, 1861. Ann was born March 11, 1810; Susan, June 23, 1812; George, who was born March 14, 1814, was a man of prominence in public affairs, a member of the legislature for two terms, and died October 24, 1878. Margaret, the only one of the family now living, was born February 23, 1816, in the house where she still resides. Hannah was born February 22, 1818, and died in April, 1848. Miss Margaret Stephenson has spent her whole life in this place, and is highly respected as a sincere Christian and kind-hearted woman. Though now in her eighty-second year, she is active and strong, retaining to a large degree the possession of her faculties.

WILLIAM H. LYNCH. If to one class of people more than another the United States owes a debt of gratitude, it is to the diligent, persevering farmers, on whom our prosperity as a nation so largely depends. Among those who for years have followed agricultural pursuits in Cecil County may be mentioned Mr. Lynch, a well-known resident of District No. 5. His farm is not a large one, being only forty acres in extent, but every portion of it has been brought under excellent cultivation and consequently it is more productive than some farms of larger acreage. It lies in the northern part of the district, and prior to its purchase by the present owner was known as the Elijah Falls estate.

Within one-half mile of his present residence, William H. Lynch was born September 30, 1836. He is of Irish descent, his grandfather, John, having been a native of the Emerald Isle. The father, William, was born at Principio Furnace, in this district, and for some years worked in the employ of Mr. Whitaker at the furnace, but in addition thereto conducted a farm. A Whig in early life, he became a Republican upon the organization of the party and was always deeply interested in the welfare and success of that ticket. His children were reared in the faith of the Methodist Episcopal Church, in the work of which he aided. He married Lydia Baker, daughter of Nathan Baker, of Cecil County. Ten children were born of their union and of these the following are living: John T., a resident of District No. 5; Eliza J., who married Benjamin Flounders and lives at Cherry Hill; William H.; Rachel A., the wife of Benjamin F. McVey, residing at Wilmington, Del.; George W., living in Chester, Pa.; Stephen, who resides at Principio; Edmund, of North East; and Clinton, of Washington.

The boyhood years of our subject were uneventfully passed. For some years he was a pupil in the old Washington school, where he gained a practical education. At the age of nineteen he began for himself as a peddler, going first to Wilmington, Del., where he spent a year. From that occupation he drifted into the business of buying rags, traveling through all parts of the country. After twelve years spent in this manner, in 1874 he began in the business of a cattle drover, buying cattle in the lower counties and selling them in this county. Four years of this occupation convinced him that it was less desirable than a calling that would enable him to remain at home, and in 1878 he purchased a farm, intending to turn his attention permanently to agricultural operations. In this work he has been prospered and it has proved very congenial to him.

In everything pertaining to the welfare and best interests of the district and county, Mr. Lynch takes an intelligent and active part, and while by no means a politician, he nevertheless adheres with firmness and fidelity to the Republican party. In religious convictions he is identified with Ebenezer Methodist Episcopal Church and so far as possible, gives his active support to all worthy benevolent and church enterprises. For thirty years he has held the office of trustee of the congregation and has also been a class leader for fourteen years. Possessing information upon every subject connected with farm work, he is considered one of the thorough agriculturists of his neighborhood.

In January, 1878, shortly before he settled at his present place of residence, Mr. Lynch was united in marriage with Miss Emily E. Falls, daughter of J. W. Falls, the well-known and popular attorney of North East. Their family consists of six children, named as follows: Nettie C., who resides in North East; Percival F., Anna E., Herbert W., Helen B. and Wilmer J., who are being given the best educational and social advantages that the district affords.

GEORGE GILBERT has passed his life in agricultural pursuits upon the farm in District No. 2, Harford County, where his birth occurred July 29, 1814. The family of which he is a member has been identified with the history of this part of Maryland for perhaps one hundred and fifty years, and has contributed to the development of its farming interests. Longevity is one of their noticeable characteristics. The grandfather of our subject, Mickey Gilbert, was a native of this county and here engaged in farming until the infirmities of age rendered manual labor an impossibility. He lived to be ninety-four years of age. He was a man of religious nature and always maintained an interest in the church.

The father of our subject, Amos Gilbert, was born in District No. 2, and in youth learned the shoemaker's trade, but gave his attention mainly to agriculture. He remained a resident of this district until his death, which occurred when he was about sixty-six, and his wife, Sarah Bailey, also died the same year, 1836. In politics he was a Jacksonian Democrat, ever adhering closely to the principles of the party as laid down by one of its most famous leaders. Like his father, he was a sincere Christian and an exemplary member of the Presbyterian Church. He and his wife were the parents of nine children, of whom our subject was the fifth in order of birth. The first-born, Mary, died when young. Bennett, who was a farmer of District No. 2, a stanch Democrat in politics, for several years an elder in the Churchville Presbyterian Church, for a long time justice of the peace and also one of the assessors of the county, was killed by the cars at Aberdeen, Md., when sixty-five years of age. Quillar was a carpenter and attained the age of eighty-six years. Elizabeth married James Gilbert and is still living, being now eighty-six years of age. Amos, formerly a school teacher, later a farmer, and for many years justice of the peace, died at seventy-five years. Sarah married Hosea Barnes, of District No. 2, and is now seventy-six years old. Arabella, Mrs. Amos Barnes, lives in Ohio and is now sixty-seven years of age.

On the death of his father our subject inherited the old homestead and here his whole life has been quietly, but busily, passed. A stanch Democrat, he has served as judge of elections, but has paid little attention to politics or public life further than supporting good men for office and favoring the principles proclaimed by his party. Twice married, his first wife was Ellen McComas, and his second, Henrietta Laughlin, who was born in Avondale. He is a man of warm heart and generous impulses, always ready and willing to assist the needy to the extent of his ability. His long life has been one of busy industry, and he has witnessed the growth of Harford County through the principal part of the nineteenth century. He is one of the few men who, after a long life in a community, is spoken well of by everybody; one who has sustained the character of a gentleman and who now, after eighty-six years of active life, has the satisfaction of knowing that he has wronged no man, but has endeavored in every respect to fulfill his duty to his Creator and his fellow-men.

JAMES HOPPER is one of the men—of whom the number is not few—who have worked their way from poverty to independence, from a humble position to a prosperous one. Now a resident of Havre de Grace, he is known as one of the honest, industrious business men of the city, and as a public-spirited citizen, interested in progressive measures. The enterprise of which he is the head and in which he has been engaged for many years, is one of the important ones of the place. He has on sale all kinds of coal and wood and also carries a full line of builders' materials, in which he has gradually established a large and profitable trade.

The family of which our subject is a member was founded in America by his ancestor, John Hopper, who with two brothers came from England early in the eighteenth century and made settlement in New Jersey. Our subject's father, Thomas Hopper, was born in Woodbury, N. J., where he was reared and educated. . In youth learning the trade of a wheelwright, he worked at this occupation in New Jersey for a time, but about 1838 removed to Delaware City, Del., and there his death occurred in 1844, when he was fifty-two years of age. His wife, who bore the maiden name of Keziah Hufsee, was born in New Jersey and died in Chesapeake City at the advanced age of ninety-eight. Notwithstanding her great age, she was active and mentally vigorous until the time of her demise. In her family there were three sons, of whom Thomas, the eldest, is deceased; and Seth, the youngest, is a resident of Baltimore. In religious belief she was identified with the Presbyterian Church and in her life bore witness of the sincerity of her faith. She was of direct Dutch descent, her father having been born in Holland, whence in youth he came to America, being sold to pay his passage to this country.

In the village of Woodbury, N. J., the subject of this notice was born December 3, 1832. When he was less than twelve years of age his father died and shortly after he came to Havre de Grace, where he made his home with an uncle in a hotel and attended school about four years. Upon the purchase of a store by his uncle, he was put to work as a clerk, and in that occupation showed considerable ability. After two years he became the owner of a one-fourth interest in the business, and five years later purchased the store, which he continued to manage successfully until July, 1875. He then embarked in the business which he has since conducted. As a business man he is conservative and judicious, never hasty in decision or reckless in financial ventures. Politically he has adopted for his own the principles set forth in the platform of the Republican party. Elected to the city council, he served as a member for several terms, and under the old town charter held the office of commissioner for several years. In religious connections he and his family are identified with the Presbyterian Church.

January 31, 1861, occurred the marriage of Mr. Hopper to Miss Sallie E. Barnes, who was born in Havre de Grace May 8, 1842, the daughter of Henry Barnes, of this place. She died April 1, 1897. Seven children were born of their union, five of whom are deceased. Those living are Henry Barnes Hopper, who is connected with his father in the coal business, while the younger, Mabel Leslie, is at home. Henry married Miss Kate Mathews, of Havre de Grace, and they have a daughter, Helen.

ROBERT J. WALKER. Among the farmers of Harford County Mr. Walker occupies a position of influence. While there are other estates larger than his, there are certainly few that bear such indications of thorough cultivation and efficient management. All the modern improvements have been introduced, including a neat residence, substantial barn, and the outbuildings necessary for the shelter of stock and storage of grain. The property includes one hundred and seventy-three acres, lying in District No. 2, in the midst of an excellent farming community.

Reference to the Walker genealogy will be found in the sketch of our subject's brother, Christopher H., presented upon another page. Robert J. was born in District No. 2, September 18, 1831, and was reared upon the home farm, attending the public and subscription schools of the locality. At the age of twenty-two he was given by his father a farm of thirty-seven acres, which he cultivated for years, and then sold in 1874, purchasing the place that he now owns.

January 22, 1857, he married Sarah R. Spencer daughter of John W. Spencer, of this district. They have three daughters, namely: Mary L., wife of George W. Wilkinson, who is engaged in farming and the canning business in this district; C. Rebecca, who married E. L. Wilkinson, a merchant, also residing in this district; and Nellie S., Mrs. Howard Carter, who lives near Oak Hill, Lancaster County, Pa.

In early life a Whig, upon the disintegration of that party Mr. Walker allied himself with the Republicans, and at the time of the Civil War was in favor of freeing the slaves. Since the close of the war he has been a Democrat, and takes an active part in party councils. In November, 1883, he was elected county commissioner and served in that capacity until 1887, being president of the board in 1886-87. For about thirty years he has been an officer in the Methodist Protestant Church, rendering excellent service as class leader and superintendent of the Sunday-school. He has been leader of the choir for forty-five years, and his regularity and punctuality in attendance at all church services have proved very helpful to the work.

The father of Mrs. Walker, John W. Spencer, was born on the farm now owned by our subject, and here he spent his whole life engaged as a farmer, fisher and cooper. At his death, which occurred when he was sixty-one years of age, he left about six hundred acres of land, being one of the largest property owners of the district. This represented the earnings of a lifetime, for he started out without capital and all he made was the result of his economy and industry. Though not a member of any denomination, he attended the Methodist Episcopal Church. In politics he was a Whig. His wife, Rebecca Keene, was born on the ocean, when her parents were coming to this country from England; she died in this district at seventy-seven years of age. She was an earnest Christian and a faithful member of the Methodist Episcopal Church. In her family there were twelve children, but two of these died in childhood. The others were, Sophy, widow of George W. Hopkins, of this district; Jarrett, a resident of this district; John R., a farmer; Elizabeth, who married George Bailey and died at fifty-two years; Eli, who died at the age of twenty-seven years; Silas L., who is interested in farming and the canning business; William T.; Sarah R.; Priscilla, widow of Thomas Robinson; and Noah, whose death occurred when he was twenty-one.

HENRY B. McCAY. To trace the history of a successful life, be it in the electrical world of business where competition is rife, or in the calm and peaceful pursuits which have to do with the source of all supplies (the calling forth from the earth her benefices and goodly returns), must ever prove profitable and interesting, showing, as it does, the methods that have been followed to attain success and thus pointing out to others the way that they may follow. A work of this nature exercises its most important function when it enters the memoir of the life and accomplishments of a successful man, one who has been in the fullest sense the architect of his own fortunes and whose virile strength has marked his entire career.

Mr. McCay eminently deserves classification among those who have thus attained prosperity. He was born in District No. 7, Cecil County, April 6, 1822. His great-grandfather, John McCay, was a native of Scotland, and located in Maryland in colonial days. As a valiant soldier of the American army he aided the colonists in their struggle for independence. He was a large slave owner and the possessor of a handsome estate of twelve hundred acres.

The grandfather, John McCay, Jr., was a native of District No. 7, and made farming his life work. The father, James McCay, was born in Baltimore, and served in the War of 1812 as captain in the valiant Twenty-seventh Regiment of Maryland. He was joined in wedlock with Mary Broughton, and they had eleven children: Henry B., James G., John and William B., deceased; Joshua P.; Washington N. and George B., deceased; Marcus, who is living in Richmond, Va.; Mary A., deceased; Beulah, wife of John H. Baynes; and Elma, deceased. The father of this family died when in his eighty-seventh year and was laid to rest in West Nottingham Cemetery. His wife died at the age of seventy-eight.

Henry B. McCay was born and reared in District No. 7, and acquired his education in West Nottingham Academy. He bore his part in the cultivation and improvement of the home farm until 1852, when he removed to Baltimore, and there engaged in the wholesale liquor business for twelve years, meeting with success in his undertakings. He then returned to Cecil County, purchased eighty acres of land, and has since carried on general farming. He has been three times married. He first wedded Caroline Bettley, and they had four children, as follows: John J., Mary, Cora B. and Elma. His second wife bore the maiden name of Annie Emmons, and died leaving one daughter, Ella V. For his third wife he chose Maggie Pennington, and six children have been born of their union, namely: Henry B., George P., Emily G., Laura S., Isabella C. and Eva C.

R. J. ROWLAND is one of the enterprising and progressive business men of Cecil County. In past ages the history of a country was the record of its wars and conquests; to-day it is the record of its commercial activity, and those whose names are foremost in its annals are the leaders in business circles. It is as a wide-awake merchant of Liberty Grove that Mr. Rowland occupies a foremost place among his fellow-townsmen. He was born in District No. 7, Cecil County, and is a son of William L. Rowland, who in his youth served an apprenticeship to the miller's trade, and afterward followed that occupation for a brief period.

R. J. Rowland spent the days of his boyhood and youth on his father's farm, assisting in the labors of field and meadow in the summer months, while in the winter season he attended the public schools, acquiring there a good English education. To his father he gave the benefit of his services until twenty-one years of age, when he began farming on his own account. He successfully followed that pursuit until 1877, when he came to Liberty Grove and embarked in general merchandising. He carries a full and complete line of goods and has studied the various tastes of his customers, so that he knows how to select his stock to please them. Straightforward dealing characterizes all his transactions, and his uniform courtesy has won him the good will of his many patrons.

In 1871 Mr. Rowland was united in marriage with Miss Emma Brown, now deceased, and their only child, Annie, died in infancy. In 1873 he married Emma H. Stricklen, and they have one child, Ernest, a graduate of the Baltimore Medical College, who though only twenty-three years of age, is now recognized as a leading physician of Liberty Grove. Fraternally he is a Royal Arch Mason of the Port Deposit lodge.

Mr. Rowland has served as postmaster of Liberty Grove at different intervals, his term of service covering altogether fourteen years. In politics he is an ardent advocate of the Democracy, and affiliates with the Masons, belonging to the lodge of Bel Air. He also holds membership in the Presbyterian Church, and is a man whom to know is to honor.

HON. RICHARD DALLAM, secretary of state for Maryland. In this free country of America, precocious mentality and youth have not proved a bar to advancement; on the contrary they have frequently been rewarded by promotions to places of honor and trust, and almost invariably the recipient has shown himself worthy of the confidence reposed in him. Although the subject of this sketch is young in years, he has demonstrated over and over again that upon his shoulders rests wisdom far beyond his age,

and that sound judgment and tried experience guide his actions. The name of Dallam is frequently mentioned in Scott's works, and the family is supposed to be of Scotch lineage. Sara Jennings married the first Duke of Marlborough, and became the intimate personal friend of Queen Anne of England, over whom she exercised great influence and greatly enhanced the interests of her husband, the Duke. One of her nephews came to this country many years ago, settled in the colony of Maryland and practiced law. He met and married Elizabeth Martin, who was made famous in the old nursery rhyme of—

"Pretty Betty Martin, tip-toe, tip-toe,
Pretty Betty Martin, tip-toe fine.
Couldn't get a husband to please her, please her,
Couldn't get a husband to please her mind."

From this couple are descended the well-known Dallam family of Maryland, members of which have been prominent in the affairs of the state for generations. The Dallams have in their possession a dress and a ring that once belonged to Betty Martin, and these articles were on exhibition at the World's Fair at Chicago in 1893. Members of the family took part in the Revolutionary War, and were also members of the constitutional convention of Maryland. The paternal grandfather was a wealthy farmer, a man of excellent parts, and bore the name of Richard. His son, William H., was born at Darlington, Harford County, Md., in 1825, and as a successful legal practitioner made a name for himself, and was honored with the position of state's attorney, and at one time was also clerk of the courts. At the opening of the great civil strife in this country, he was made major of the Seventh Maryland Regiment, U. S. A.; made a brave and daring officer and supported the cause of the Union until the surrender at Appomattox. In recognition of his ability and the service he had rendered his country in her time of need, he was made deputy collector of the port of Baltimore and was discharging his duties at the time of his death in 1883.

John S. Dallam, brother of William H., is residing in Bel Air, and has reached an advanced age. He has been foremost in the public affairs of the county, and has served as a director of the Harford County Mutual Fire Insurance Company for half a century. His intellect is of a high order, and his influence has ever been on the side of justice and right. Another brother, Joseph, has been with the Baltimore & Ohio Railroad for more than forty years. The wife of William H. Dallam was Mary C. Maulsby, a native of Harford County, born in the house in which the subject of this sketch now lives, and which she inherited from her father, Hon. J. D. Maulsby, who was a member of the Harford bar. He represented his county in the state legislature for twenty-nine years, and was a member of the governor's council. His son, William P. Maulsby, was colonel of the Fourth Maryland Infantry during the Civil War, and in later years became one of the judges of the court of appeals.

The subject of this sketch was one of four children born to his parents, the other three members of the family being sisters, only two of whom are living at the present time: Mrs. A. H. O'Brien, of Philadelphia, and Mrs. William B. Nelson, whose husband is a business man of Baltimore but makes his home in Bel Air. In the home in which he is now living, Hon. Richard Dallam was born May 11, 1865. His education was received in Bel Air Academy, and in the law department of the University of Maryland, from which he graduated in 1888. He at once began practicing his profession in his native village, where his ability soon won him recognition, and he received the appointment of deputy in the Baltimore custom house under Colonel Webster, with whom he served until 1889. He then resigned his position to continue his law practice in Bel Air, and at once leaped into popularity, for he conducted his cases with skill and shrewdness, and his success up to the present time has remained unbroken.

Young as he is, Mr. Dallam wields a wide influence in political matters and in the interests of the Republican party. He was appointed by Governor Lowndes in 1896 to the position of secretary of state. That this selection was a most wise one is universally acknowledged by political friend and opponent alike, for he has discharged his duties with distinguished ability and with a conscientious regard to the interests of the state. In his vocabulary there is no such word as "fail," and success has tended but to stimulate his brain to greater energy. He is president of the Harford County Mutual Fire Insurance Company, treasurer of the Bel Air Water Works Company, and is connected with various other local interests. He was married in 1892 to Miss Josephine Evans, daughter of Dr. John Evans, of Cecil County, and they have a daughter, Rebecca. Mr. and Mrs. Dallam are church members, and he is a member of the Masonic and Odd Fellows' fraternities. He is a man of remarkable executive talent, and with his unbroken success and his wide popularity, it is well known that he is but fairly started upon his career, and that much better and greater things await him.

JOHN R. ALLEN. The credit for a share of the enterprises that help to make No. 9 one of the best districts in Cecil County belongs to Mr. Allen, who, although he has not resided here so long as many of the other citizens, has nevertheless contributed greatly to the advancement of local interests. His farm is conceded to be one of the best in the locality and comprises one hundred and fifty-two acres of land. Here he may usually be found engaged actively in tilling the soil or gathering in the large harvests. While general farming principally engages his attention, he also finds time to devote to stock-raising and to the creamery business, in which he has been successful.

In looking up the genealogy of the Allen family, we find that our subject is a grandson of Patrick Allen, who was born in Ireland, came from there to America at the age of eighteen years and settled first in Delaware, where he engaged in the manufacture of woolen cloth, but afterward he removed to Pennsylvania. The father of our subject, Thomas C. Allen, was born in Delaware County, Pa., and followed the blacksmith's and machinist's trades in Burmont, that county, where he spent all the years of active life. In politics he adhered to Democratic principles. His death occurred in a hospital in Philadelphia in 1876, when he was fifty-nine years of age. He married Elizabeth Rudolph, of Delaware County, daughter of William Rudolph and member of a well-known family of that locality. They became the parents of five children, but only two survive, John R., and Mary A., wife of J. E. Dougherty, of Delaware County.

Delaware County, Pa., was our subject's native place, and October 2, 1843, the date of his birth. He was educated in the schools of the home neighborhood and in Crittenden's Commercial College, Philadelphia, where he completed the course at the age of twenty-four. In 1861 he enlisted as a member of Company F, Ninety-first Pennsylvania Infantry, and remained in the army for four years, meanwhile holding a commission as first lieutenant of his company and as adjutant of the regiment. He was present at the siege of Fredericksburg and took an active part at Chancellorsville and Gettysburg, as well as in the other engagements of the army of the Potomac. He was wounded at Fredericksburg July 10, 1865, and again at Jerusalem Plank Road, where a shell struck him in the face. On his return to Delaware County at the close of the war, his father gave him a position as bookkeeper and he soon obtained a financial interest in the concern, remaining there about seven years. He then accepted an appointment as assistant assessor of internal revenue for the Seventh District, Twenty-fifth Division of Pennsylvania, in which capacity he was employed for one year. His next venture was in the mercantile business at Clifton Heights, Delaware County, but after three years there he sold out and went to Armstrong County, Pa., where he was chosen secretary to the president of the Grant Pipe Company. Several years were thus passed, when he became secretary and treasurer of the Parker City Oil Exchange of Armstrong County, Pa., and while holding that position he was also treasurer of the town of Parker and treasurer of the board of directors of the poor. Later he was manager and bookkeeper for W. H. Spain, in the general hardware and oil supplies business, where he continued for three years. Failing health caused him to retire from the business and seek more congenial pursuits. In 1881 he came to Cecil County and settled upon the William Kirk place, which is one of the oldest farms in District No. 9. In the different places where he has resided he has taken a part in local affairs and has ranked among the leading Democrats.

In 1870 Mr. Allen married Sarah D. Hall, of Delaware County, Pa., daughter of James C. Hall. Their children are named as follows: Frederick H., who carries on the home farm; Bessie I., Mattie D., James C., Rudolph S. and Thomas C. The family are identified with Zion Presbyterian Church. In fraternal connections he is a member of Chester Lodge of Masons at Chester, Pa.; Media Chapter, R. A. M., in which he has held several offices; and Pittsburg Commandery No. 1, K. T.

GEORGE SIMCOE. Especial interest attaches to the histories of the families that have been identified with the advancement of Maryland from a very early period of its settlement. Their first representatives in the state laid the foundation upon which later generations builded. They bore the hardships and endured all the privations of pioneer life. The traveler to-day, as he passes through the state, comfortably ensconced in a palace car, looks out upon either side on cities and towns, churches and schoolhouses, and finely cultivated plantations. But the pioneer who sought a home here a century or more ago, braved the dangers from attacks by hostile Indians and tories and had experiences that are but little understood or appreciated at this late day.

The records show that the first member of the Simcoe family who came to America was George, a felt-maker by trade, and first a resident of Queen Anne County, Md., but after 1720 a farmer of Cecil County, where he purchased two hundred acres of land. From Johnson's history of Cecil County we quote as follows:

"The first settlement in Cecil County was made in 1658, upon the farm which for more than a century and a-half has been in the possession of the Simcoe family of this county. This farm may be found on the map of the county and is located a short distance northwest of Carpenter's Point fishery. It appears from papers in the possession of George Simcoe, of Bay View, the present owner of the farm, that it was part of a tract of four hundred acres taken up and patented on the 20th of July, 1658, by one William Carpenter."

This George Simcoe who founded the family in Cecil County was a Scotchman by birth and possessed the perseverance and uprightness characteristic of the Scotch people the world around. His son, William, father of our subject, was born at Carpenter's Point, the old homestead in District No. 5, and upon attaining manhood engaged for himself in farming pursuits. A popular citizen and a prominent man of affairs, he supported Whig principles and by his party was elected to the state legislature in 1840, serving in that capacity with satisfaction to all. In the days when the popular cry was "Tippecanoe and Tyler too," he gave his influence toward the election of General Harrison and was active in the campaign. For years he was a trustee and steward in the Methodist Episcopal Church, to which he belonged. He married Rebecca Cazier, who was born in Cecil County, of Irish descent; she was a daughter of Capt. Thomas Cazier, an officer in the state militia and a soldier in the War of 1812. The marriage resulted in the birth of thirteen children, of whom three are living, our subject being the eldest. J. S. is a resident of North East; and Louisa J., Mrs. Manley, makes her home in Elkton.

At the old homestead in District No. 5, the subject of this sketch was born July 13, 1822, and he has been a lifelong resident of the locality. His education was obtained in the country schools and West Nottingham Academy. While still quite young he established domestic ties, choosing as his wife Miss Elizabeth Poinsett, member of an old New Jersey family. The young couple at once settled on a farm located in what is now the center of North East, and this place Mr. Simcoe carried on for some years. Meantime he also became interested in merchandising and the lumber business, in which, as in agriculture, he met with fair success. After twenty-eight years in the one place, he sold out to his son, William H., and moving to Bay View, settled upon the farm of two hundred and forty-seven acres where he has since made his home. The supervision of this property he oversees, and by his judicious management it has proved remunerative. The attractive family residence is presided over by his wife, and two of their children still remain with them, brightening their declining days by their devotion. Of the seven originally in the family five are living, namely: William H., of North East; Benjamin P. and C. Annie, who are with their parents; Thomas C., a resident of Allentown, Pa.; and Lulu R., wife of E. A. Gillespie, of Nottingham, Pa. Politically Mr. Simcoe is a Democrat and in religion a member of the Methodist Episcopal Church. In addition to his farm he has considerable property in North East.

WILLIAM C. HENDERSON. The results of industry and persevering, intelligent effort are exhibited in the life of Mr. Henderson, who for some years has been proprietor of a country store at Appleton and also the owner and manager of a farm in District No. 4, Cecil County. While this place is not so large as some others in the county, being ninety-six acres in extent, it nevertheless is more productive than many, for especial attention has been given to securing the very best results from every acre.

Born in this district in 1846, Mr. Henderson is a son of Capt. John Henderson, who was born and reared in Ireland, emigrated thence to America and took part in the War of 1812, where he gained the title by which he was afterward known. His first home was in Baltimore, but afterward he removed to Elkton, and from there in 1840 came to District No. 4, where his death occurred in 1856, at the age of seventy-four. Upon the ticket of his party, the Democratic, he was elected to the legislature of Maryland, and remained a member of that body for two years. By his marriage to his first wife he had four children, one of whom died in infancy. The others are John S., Rebecca and Ann. After the death of his first wife he married Rebecca A. Groves, and they became the parents of the following-named children: Gustavus, now deceased; Alice J., wife of J. Henderson, of Baltimore; Nora and Susan, deceased; Emily, wife of J. P. Smith, who resides in Delaware; Benjamina, Mrs. George Coyle, of Wilmington, Del.; Martha, who married John Armstrong; and William C.

The youngest of this large family, our subject remembers his father only as a man advanced in years, and the latter died when the son was ten years of age. His education, begun in the district schools, was continued in Newark Academy and Ft. Edward Institute in New York. At the age of nineteen he left school, and for three years afterward he worked at the machinist's trade in Baltimore, after which he went to sea as an engineer. In a short time, however, he abandoned that occupation, and came to Appleton, District No. 4, Cecil County, where he has resided since 1874. In 1892 he opened a general country store at Appleton and this he has since conducted, in addition to the management of his farm. Since attaining manhood his unqualified support has been given to the Democratic party. In 1881-82 he was tax collector for the district. He has placed himself on record as one of the progressive citizens whose endeavor it is to advance the interests of Maryland, and especially of Cecil County.

The first marriage of Mr. Henderson, in December, 1874, united him with Anna B. Smith, of Cherry Hill, and they became the parents of four children that are now living: John T., Mary, Helen and William. She died in May, 1889. His second wife, to whom he was married in 1891, bore the maiden name of Alma Best and was born in Oxford, Md., this union being blessed by two children, James and Armstrong. The family attend the Methodist Church at Cherry Hill and are active workers in its movements. Fraternally Mr. Henderson is connected with Lodge No. 925, Junior Order of American Mechanics, and is also a member of Hiram Lodge No. 25, F. & A. M., in Newark, Del. As a citizen he possesses public spirit and enterprise. Nature endowed him with common sense and the force of character that has led him to follow his judgment as to the right, refusing to countenance measures that may be questioned. With a good education and more than ordinary ability, he endeavors to keep himself acquainted with the progress of the world in current events, and so complete his character and acquirements, instead of becoming one of those "men with one idea" who are occasionally to be found. The sturdy characteristics which are his, coupled with intelligence and courtesy, make him an object of respect in the community, and give promise of his future years being even more useful and prosperous than those which are past.

SOLOMON RUSSELL EWING. Considering the subject of success from a material standpoint, the opportunities which Maryland offers are as great to-day as ever before. Perhaps fortunes are not made so rapidly here as in some of the newer states, but on the other hand the risks are not so great. He who labors persistently and judiciously almost invariably wins a competency sufficient to supply the comforts of life. Some of the young men of the state, allured by El Dorado stories of the west, have sought homes in other and far distant states, among strangers; but not a few of our best and most aggressive young men have preferred to remain at home, amid the associations familiar to them from their earliest recollections. Of the latter class Mr. Ewing is one. While he resides in

WALTER B. KIRK, M. D.

Harford County and has spent most of his life here, he is a westerner by birth, a native of Pike County, Ill., born April 16, 1865. However, he is as devoted to the advancement and welfare of old Harford as any of its native-born sons, and as a citizen is public spirited and progressive.

The occupation by which Mr. Ewing is best known and in which he is gaining financial success, is that of merchandising. He is the proprietor of a general store situated in the village of Level, in the northern part of District No. 2, and having carried on this business for a number of years and in a most efficient manner, he has gained the confidence of the people of the community, who recognize in his character those honest and reliable traits that make a man a desirable citizen. His first connection with the business dates from 1888, when he and his brother took charge of his present store. They continued together until January, 1894, when his brother's interest was bought by T. K. Price.

The record of the Ewing family will be found upon another page, in the sketch of Lawson Ewing, father of S. Russell. The latter has had the advantage of a fair education, that qualified him for an active business life. The influence he exerts upon the community is an important one. In social circles he is considered a decided acquisition. Fraternally he is connected with Blenheim Lodge No. 102, I. O. O. F., of Aberdeen; Columbus Lodge No. 27, K. of P., at Baltimore; and Venus Council No. 44, American Mechanics, at Havre de Grace.

WALTER B. KIRK, M. D., of Darlington, Harford County, is a member of one of the pioneer Quaker families of the adjoining county of Cecil, his great-grandfather, Josiah Kirk, having been numbered among the original settlers of Blue Ball, District No. 4. Josiah P. Kirk, son of Ellis P. Kirk, and father of the doctor, was born and reared at the homestead of Blue Ball, in the western part of the district, and in that locality his entire life has been passed. Since 1870 he has been proprietor of a grist mill at Liberty Grove. His early education was limited, being confined to a brief schooling, but his intelligence and forethought have enabled him to make the most of his opportunities, and there are few men in his neighborhood better read than he. He takes no part in politics and has never been an office-seeker. However, he has his views upon political matters and is an earnest supporter of the Democratic party.

The marriage of Josiah P. Kirk united him with Annie E., daughter of Haines Reynolds and sister of Edward H. Reynolds, of whom mention is elsewhere made. Their family comprised four children: Walter B.; Sherwood H., who resides in Lancaster, Pa.; Ada and Lewis, living at the parental home in Liberty Grove. The subject of this sketch is a young man, born in 1868, and is a native of the village of Rising Sun. When he was two years of age his parents removed to Liberty Grove, and he was educated in the school there and in West Nottingham Academy, graduating from the latter institution in 1886. On completing his literary studies, he taught school at Blythedale and Chapel. With the intention of becoming a physician, in 1890 he entered the medical department of the University of Maryland at Baltimore, where he took the regular course of medical studies, graduating in 1893. In June of the same year he came to Darlington, where he opened an office and began in professional practice. He has since gained the confidence of the people by his reliability, accurate methods of diagnosis and skillful treatment of intricate diseases, and his practice now extends through several districts.

While giving his attention mainly to the demands of his profession, Dr. Kirk has not been unmindful of the benefits to be derived from fraternal organizations. He has been quite active in the Independent Order of Odd Fellows and has passed all the chairs in Deer Lodge at Darlington, besides being a member of the grand lodge. In former years he was connected with the Junior Order of American Mechanics and held all the chairs in the local lodge. Now, in the prime of his career, his life promises to be one of usefulness to his fellow-men. His earnest advocacy of all plans for the public good and his well-known breadth of culture, have gained for him a warm place in the regard of all who know him.

CLINTON J. WHITE. The citizens whose sound judgment has promoted the industrial growth of their community and whose energy has brought an enlarged prosperity to every line of human activity, deservedly occupy positions of prominence in local history. A volume wherein reference is made to leading residents of Cecil County should not omit mention of Mr. White, who has officiated as county sheriff, and in every relation of life, both public and private, has proved his stability of character and energy of disposition. He has exerted a marked influence on the civil and political life of the county, has taken a deep interest in its welfare, and has borne a prominent part in promoting its rise and progress to its present high standing among its sister counties. In youth he became a Republican and has since been a zealous supporter of that party's principles. Upon its ticket he was elected to the office of county sheriff, a fact that proves his personal popularity, for the Democrats usually carry the county by a considerable majority,

The birth of Clinton J. White occurred in West Philadelphia, Pa:, in 1841. His father, Clinton Johnson White, Sr., was born in the city of Washington, August 16, 1810, and in youth learned the trade of a carpenter. In early manhood he removed to Port Deposit, Cecil County, where he married Barbara H. Dennison, daughter of William Dennison. After remaining there for a time, working at his trade, he went to Philadelphia and engaged in the contracting business. Soon after the birth of our subject, the family returned to Port Deposit, where the father continued to reside until his death, in 1883. In religious belief he was identified with the Methodist Episcopal Church. An active temperance worker through his entire life, it is said that he signed one of the first temperance pledges in the state. He had several brothers and sisters, of whom, however, but little is known. Jefferson W., who was a quarryman at Port Deposit, died of cholera October 9, 1834, and his wife died of the same disease three days later, leaving no children. Another brother, Milton J. R. White, was born in Washington October 23, 1807. Napoleon P., a carpenter by trade, resided at Port Deposit until his death.

The grandfather of our subject, Levi White, was born May 4, 1768, but the place of his birth is unknown, nor is there any definite information to be obtained in regard to the ancestral history. He was a son of John and Sarah (Smith) White, and made his home at Port Deposit, where he had a small nail factory in the days when nails were made by hand. Of the brothers and sisters of our subject, we note the following: Adaliza M., who was born in 1836, married John A. Mitchell, a carpenter at Havre de Grace, where they reside; Elizabeth, born in 1838, is the widow of Charles Woolley, who was a carpenter, and she now resides in Annapolis; William L. died in infancy; John D., who was born in Port Deposit in 1843, learned the carpenter's trade, and at the outbreak of the Civil War enlisted in the First Eastern Shore Regiment, re-enlisting at the expiration of his term and serving until the close of the war; Mary F. died in infancy; Rufus is employed in the railroad service and resides at Port Deposit; Alfred, also a resident of Port Deposit, is a mechanic by trade; Maria died when young; Lucius G. is employed in the National Bank of Port Deposit; Emmett T. was drowned when a boy; Harry is in the employ of the Pennsylvania Railroad Company and makes his home at Perryville.

Our subject was less than one year old when his parents left Philadelphia to make their permanent home in Port Deposit, and there his boyhood days were passed and his education obtained in the Port Deposit Academy, under Professor Hawkins. He learned the trade of a carpenter with his father, and assisted the latter in his duties as inspector of lumber at that port. When the Civil War broke out he joined the construction corps and was engaged in the building of bridges for the government, remaining in the service until the close of the war. He then returned to his home in Port Deposit and resumed work as a carpenter. About 1880 he was made deputy clerk of courts under James A. Davis, the Republican incumbent of the office, under whom he served two terms. In 1893 he was made the candidate of the Republican party for sheriff of Cecil County, and was elected by a small margin, being the only Republican on the ticket who was elected. Since the expiration of his term he has been conducting a grocery business in Elkton. He is a member of the Methodist Episcopal Church, and fraternally has been connected with the Independent Order of Odd Fellows, the Knights of Pythias and the Ancient Order of United Workmen. His marriage in 1866 united him with Miss Martha Williams, daughter of George P. Williams, of Port Deposit. They are the parents of three sons and three daughters, namely: Mary, wife of Charles J. Rudolph, a telegraph operator living in Elkton; Emmett, a telegraph operator; Bertie, who is at home; Charles W., a telegraph operator in Rhode Island; George and Maggie, who are at home.

EPHRAIM B. McCLUNG, a retired farmer residing in District No. 4, Harford County, is a representative of a family that has long been identified with the history of the country. His ancestors took part in the events which shaped the destiny of the nation and their names are found on the military records of the Republic. The great-grandfather of our subject, coming from Ireland in early colonial days and locating in Baltimore County, Md., devoted his energies to agricultural pursuits. When the colonies attempted to throw off the yoke of British oppression and secure their independence, Joseph McClung, the grandfather of our subject, became one of the heroes of that long and sanguinary struggle. He was a native of Baltimore County, and in his business career was very successful, becoming one of the extensive planters of that section of the state. He owned more than one thousand acres of land and was a large slave owner, operating his plantation by negro help.

Robert McClung, father of our subject, was born on the family homestead, and when his country again became engaged in war with England he fought for the supremacy of the American arms. His life was devoted to agricultural pursuits with good success. He married Miss Mary Payne, a native of Harford County, wherein they established a home. Seven children were born of their union, of whom three are now living: John P., Mary C. and Ephraim B.

The last-named was born June 25, 1831, in District No. 4, Harford County. His educational privileges were limited to three months' attendance at the common schools during each year. His training at farm labor, however, was such as to early prepare him for agricultural duties, and throughout his life he has followed the occupation to which he was reared. As a companion and helpmate on life's journey he chose Miss Hannah E. Wiley, a native of District No. 4, Harford County, their marriage taking place when he was twenty-six years of age.

Twelve children were born to the union of Mr. and Mrs. McClung, of whom four died in infancy: Wiley P., Robert R., Benton N., and one unnamed. Those still living are Webster C., who married Cynthia J. Strawbridge and taught school about eleven years, but is now engaged in the lumber business in Stewartstown, Pa.; John T., who married Mary Jane Leib and follows farming; Lizzie M., wife of J. Nelson Wiley, a farmer, by whom she has two children, Webster L. and Goldy; Laura B., wife of E. Milton Anderson, a farmer, by whom she has two children, John C. and Raymond; Amanda Z., wife of M. Tidings McGinnis, an agriculturist; Margaret C., at home; Lovisa R., wife of C. Harry Yost, who follows farming; and Morgan E., who is working by the month on his father's farm.

Mr. McClung owns a valuable farm property, comprising one hundred and thirty-two acres of rich and productive land, the care of which he has now given in charge of his youngest son, while he is practically living retired, enjoying the rest which is the just reward of a long and useful business career. He has served as juryman and as road supervisor of Harford County. His political support is given the Democracy, and he firmly believes its tenets are best calculated to secure the greatest good to the nation. He and most of his family are members of the Methodist Protestant Church, of Norrisville, and he has been very active in its work, serving as treasurer, steward and trustee. His well-spent life commends him to the confidence of all, and he has the warm regard of a large circle of friends and acquaintances.

HON. WALTER W. PRESTON. Ever since the days when Harford County was a trackless forest, in which lurked Indians not yet accustomed to the sight of white faces or the presence of strange visitors, the Preston family has had representatives in this part of Maryland. Two hundred and fifty years have passed since the first of the name in America sought a home here, and in common with other pioneers endured the vicissitudes of life in a strange country. There have been many changes since those times. The whole country, now dotted with smiling farms and quiet villages, traversed by railroads and telegraph wires, was then a wilderness, which stretched from the ocean westward to remote and undiscovered recesses.

To narrate the history of succeeding generations of the Preston family would be to give the history of Harford County, for as the county has grown and developed, the family has been prospered. The father of our subject, Hon. James B. Preston, is a man of prominence in the political world, and among other offices held that of representative in the state legislature for two terms. He married Mary A. Wilkes, a native of the city of Baltimore, and daughter of James Wilkes, Jr., a Scotchman, who was one of the well-known hardware merchants of Baltimore. She died in 1874. Our subject was born on the home farm, situated on Deer Creek, Harford County, January 14, 1863. His education commenced in the public schools, was continued in St. John's College, Annapolis, where he matriculated in 1877, and was further prosecuted in Princeton, from which he graduated in 1881, with the degree of A. B. Three years later the degree of A. M. was conferred upon him.

Turning his attention to the study of law, Mr. Preston entered the law department of the University of Maryland, from which he graduated in 1883, with the degree of LL. B. Immediately afterward he opened an office in Bel Air and began to practice at the bar here. Having thoroughly studied the principles of law, his judgment on legal questions is excellent. For public speaking he is well fitted, for he posesses an excellent voice, a fine presence, and ease of motion; but in addition to these gifts he has one still greater, and without which the others would be vain, viz.: a capacity for hard work. With a fine command of language, a broad fund of information and retentive memory; deeply read in local and general history, thoroughly informed upon the issues of the day, logical in thought and eloquent in utterance, his opponents in debate have found him a foeman "worthy of their steel."

In politics Mr. Preston is a member of the Democratic party, and believing in its principles, he has always zealously advocated them. He has done good service for his party in campaigns, and his speeches, delivered during pre-election times, have won votes for the men and measures he espoused. In 1888 he was elected to the Maryland legislature, and, although the youngest member of the house, he took a leading part in the deliberations of that body, and served on several committees. He was re-elected to the session of 1890, in the latter term serving as chairman of the judiciary committee and committee on claims. In 1891 he was elected prosecuting attorney for Harford County, and at the expiration of his term, in 1895, the people showed their appreciation of his able services by re-electing him to the office. He is recognized as one of the most able prosecutors the county has ever had, and all reputable citizens, irrespective of party, unite in praising him for what he has accomplished in the interests of law and order. Fraternally he is connected with the Odd Fellows and Masons, and is past master of Mt. Ararat Lodge at Bel Air. In 1892 he married Lillie Pue Hall, of Harford County, and their home is one of the most attractive residences in Bel Air.

LAWSON EWING is one of the extensive land owners and leading citizens of District No. 2, Harford County. He has been an active promoter of the business interests of this county, but is now practically living retired, merely looking after his property interests. Widely and favorably known, he well deserves mention in this volume, and with pleasure we present the record of his life to our readers.

Dr. Ewing, as he is called, is a native son of Harford County, born near Hopewell Cross Roads, March 2, 1827. He is a representative of one of the old families of this section of the state. His grandfather, Joseph Ewing, who was probably born in this county, lived here for many years and reached an advanced age. William Ewing, the father, opened his eyes to the light of day in District No. 2, and spent his entire life upon a farm, his death occurring at the age of seventy-five years. His early political support was given the Whig party, and on its dissolution he joined the ranks of the Democracy. In his church relations he was a Presbyterian. His wife, who bore the maiden name of Elizabeth Russell, was also a representative of one of the early families of the county, and died in her native locality at the age of sixty-three.

Dr. Ewing is the only survivor of a family of five sons and two daughters. No event of special importance occurred during his boyhood and youth, which were quietly passed upon the home farm and in attendance at the common schools, where he acquired a good practical education. After attaining his majority he engaged in fishing and working at the cooper's trade for two years. Later he spent one summer in Pennsylvania, then taught one winter in Virginia (now West Virginia), and afterward went to Ohio, where he taught one term of summer school in 1854. Subsequently he removed to Maysville, Ky., where he engaged in teaching a district school for two and a-half years. His next place of residence was Pike County, Mo., where he followed the same profession for two years, after which he crossed the Mississippi River to Pike County, Ill., and was numbered among the successful educators of that locality from the fall of 1856 until the spring of 1862. At the expiration of that period hs turned his attention from professional to mercantile pursuits, and for six years conducted a store at Pleasant Hill, Pike County. On selling his property there, he opened a general mercantile establishment in Milton, Ill., where he remained until 1873, when he again sold and resumed farming near Holden, Johnson County, Mo. In 1875, however, he disposed of his land in the west and returned to Harford County to assume the management of two farms which had been left to himself and brother by his father.

Dr. Ewing devoted his energies to agricultural pursuits until 1885, when he rented his land and embarked in general merchandising at Hopewell Cross Roads, but after continuing business at that point for three years he placed his store in charge of his sons, took up his residence upon one of his farms and has since practically lived retired. He is now the owner of four valuable farms, deriving therefrom a good income. He possesses excellent business ability and executive force, sound judgment and determined purpose, and by the exercise of these qualities has so conducted his business interests as to bring to him a handsome competence.

In 1861 Dr. Ewing married Miss Sarah J. Shultz, who died at the age of fifty years, leaving three children: William E., a farmer of District No. 2; Solomon Russell, who is represented elsewhere in this work; and Florence, at home. In 1896 the doctor married Mrs. Elizabeth McKindless. His political support is given the men and measures of the Republican party, and for eight years he served as postmaster at Hopewell Cross Roads. He is a man of broad general culture, of pleasant manner and social disposition, who wins friends wherever he goes, and has the happy faculty of drawing them closer to him as the years pass by.

HENRY C. McDOWELL. While the stock business is not the most prominent industry of Cecil County, it is at present receiving a greater proportion of the attention of the people than in former years. Among those who are contributing to the development of this industry, and who have in it gained a commendable degree of material success, mention should be made of Mr. McDowell. The increased interest now taken in this department of agriculture is due, to no small extent, to his energetic efforts. As a citizen he is well and favorably known in various enterprises, contributing to the growth of his district, and his influence is always given when progressive measures are presented for adoption.

Prospect Hill farm, where Mr. McDowell makes his home, consists of one hundred and nine acres of well-improved land, and is situated in District No. 5, near Principio. The visitor to the place soon notices the fine head of Jersey cattle, and is made aware of the fact that the owner is interested in the raising of fine stock, particularly cattle. However, his attention is not given exclusively to this business. As a general farmer he has been quite successful, and upon his place may be found all the cereals to which the soil and climate are adapted.

In the city of Philadelphia Mr. McDowell was born September 29, 1844. His paternal grandfather, James, a native of Bucks County, Pa., and a soldier in the War of 1812, was a son of Alexander McDowell, who came to America from the north of Ireland, his ancestors having been among those Scotch families who sought refuge in Ireland during the days of religious persecution. Alexander bore arms in the Revolutionary War in defense of the principle of freedom for which the colonists struggled, and he had a brother-in-law, Samuel Smith, who was a general in the American army.

David McDowell, father of our subject, was born in Bucks County, Pa. Like his ancestors he was a man of intense loyalty to the country, and possessed undaunted courage. At the opening of the war with Mexico he raised a company of men in Philadelphia and took them to New Jersey, where they enlisted for service, he being selected as their captain. He remained at the front until the war was ended, and afterward, in 1849, went to California, where he witnessed all the excitement connected with the discovery of gold and endured the hardships associated with the deprivation of the comforts to which he had been accustomed. While making his home in Philadelphia he engaged in the mercantile business, but after going to the far west he became chief of the Sacramento fire department of Sacramento and was otherwise connected with public affairs in that city. His death, which occurred in January of 1857, resulted from a cold contracted while trying to subdue a fire. Politically he voted the Whig ticket, and in religious belief was a Presbyterian. His wife, who died when quite young, was Susan, daughter of Samuel Runner, of Philadelphia; their only child was the subject of this sketch.

The patriotism so characteristic of the family was imbedded in the spirit of H. C. McDowell. After the completion of his education, which was obtained in the public schools of Bucks County and a boarding-school at Carversville, Pa., he enlisted in the Union army when but eighteen years of age. In February, 1864, his name was enrolled in the Third Pennsylvania Heavy Artillery at Philadelphia. For a year he was engaged principally on gunboat service on the James River, and in November, 1865, he was honorably discharged from the army. He then came to Cecil County and began as a farmer. Purchasing a place in District No. 9, he began its cultivation, and to keep house for him brought his grandmother, who had reared him and cared for him in childhood. After five years, in the spring of 1871, he went to the oil regions of Pennsylvania, but in 1874 returned to Cecil County and resumed farming. In the fall of 1893 he purchased Prospect Hill farm, where he has since engaged in farming and cattle raising. He is a member of the Grange, and in religious belief is identified with the Presbyterian Church. Politically he has always voted the Democratic ticket, as he believes in free trade and the free coinage of silver.

The marriage of Mr. McDowell occurred May 21, 1873, and united him with Mary J., daughter of Benjamin Gifford, of Cecil County. They became the parents of six children, of whom all but one are living. They are David, Laura B., Thomas K., James N. and H. Clayton, all intelligent and well educated. The pleasant personality and genial manner of Mr. McDowell have brought him the respect of others. He enjoys the reputation for uprightness and strength of character that distinguishes the residents of Cecil County, and not alone for these admirable qualities is he known, but also for the attributes that make him a congenial and welcome companion.

GEORGE I. SMITH. For solid worth and reliability, no resident of Cecil County is deserving of more honorable mention than the gentleman with whose name this sketch is introduced, and who has made a good record as a citizen and a farmer. It is now more than thirty years since he came to District No. 4 and purchased one hundred acres, constituting one of the oldest farms in the county. Here he has since engaged in general farming and in the dairy business. He and his wife are a genial, kindly couple, and by their warm hospitality render their home pleasant and comfortable to the many friends whom they welcome within its walls from time to time.

The family of which our subject is a member was first represented in America by his grandfather, John, who came from Ireland and settled in Chester County, Pa. The father, William, was reared there, and in youth learned the trade of a stone mason and contractor. He was among the first contractors on the Frenchtown Railroad, built about 1830. In addition he followed agricultural pursuits through much of his life. In 1832 he removed with his family to Delaware, where he was afterward prominently identified with public affairs. Elected to represent his district in the state legislature, he was re-elected at the expiration of his first term, and so satisfactory was his service that he was further honored by election to the position of state senator. At one time he was a member of Governor Thorpe's staff. In fact, his closing years were spent entirely in the public service. His death occurred at his home in Delaware when he was sixty-nine years of age.

The mother of our subject was Mary DeHaven, a native of Chester County, Pa., and a daughter of Jesse DeHaven, who was a descendant of an old family of that locality. They became the parents of ten children, and of these all but one are still living. They are named as follows: Sarah, George I., Mary J., wife of William Armstrong; William H., postmaster at Newark, Del.; Jacob R., whose home is in Philadelphia; James P., of Cecil County; Dr. Samuel, of Ohio; Elizabeth, who married John W. Kennedy, and resides in Chester County, Pa., and Winfield S., of Fair Hill, Cecil County. Our subject, who was next to the eldest member of the family, was born in Chester County, Pa., August 1, 1826, and received his education in the common schools of Delaware, to which state he accompanied the other members of the family when he was a boy of six years. On completing his studies he began to assist actively in the management of the home farm in Delaware, also having charge of his father's property in Pennsylvania for a time. In 1865 he removed from Delaware to District No. 4, Cecil County, and bought the farm which he still owns and operates.

In 1849 occurred the marriage of Mr. Smith and Miss Anna E. Riddell, of Newcastle County, Del. Their three children are named as follows:

Mary E., who is the wife of James H. Foard; Hosea R. and George H., who reside in District No. 4. In former years Mr. Smith was identified with the Grange and the Odd Fellows, but no longer retains active membership in these organizations. He has maintained a warm interest in religious work, and as a deacon in the Presbyterian Church for twenty years or more, he has done all in his power to advance the cause in his locality. He is a man of excellent habits and sterling principles, is prompt and reliable in his business dealings, and as a citizen has identified himself with local enterprises, contributing his quota to the progress of the district and county.

JAMES C. CROTHERS. One of the special lines of labor in which many residents of Cecil County successfully engage is that of fishing. The fishery business has long been a prominent one, and those who have followed it have found it remunerative. If long experience in this industry brings a knowledge of its every detail, then Mr. Crothers may certainly be considered one of the best-informed men in that line that the county contains, for he has been engaged in the business since 1850. During the fishing season, from April 1 to May 30, he gives employment to forty men. In addition to this work, he has the superintendence of the old homestead, a valuable place comprising two hundred and five acres and lying in District No. 9.' Of it he has been the owner since the death of his father.

Upon the place where he now resides, situated two miles from the village of Calvert, J. C. Crothers was born June 5, 1829. He is a descendant, in the second generation, of John Crothers, a native of Ireland, who upon coming to America selected for his home the property that is still in the possession of the family. On this place was born James Crothers, our subject's father, who was long a resident here and identified with the best interests of the neighborhood. His life covered much of the nineteenth century, during which time he witnessed the gradual upbuilding of our national government and the development of local industries. Politically he was first a Whig and afterwards an adherent of Republican principles. For years he acted as county commissioner, rendering able service in that capacity. He and his family were connected with the Presbyterian Church. In every action he endeavored to be consistent and honest, doing unto others as he would be done by. When seventy-four years of age he passed away, July 7, 1873. Years before that, in 1847, he had lost by death his wife, Rachael, daughter of James Cameron, of District No. 6, this county. They had three children, of whom there survive our subject and his sister, Elizabeth B., widow of Benjamin F. Kirk, of District No. 6.

At the age of eighteen our subject considered his schooling sufficiently good to permit him to begin the battle of life in earnest. First he worked in the employ of his father, continuing in that way until the death of the latter, when he inherited the old homestead. This place he has since cultivated, carrying on general farming pursuits. He owns two hundred and forty-five acres of land where he fishes, at Red Point, about six miles from North East. His personal affairs have called for his close attention and he has given little time to public affairs, although a pronounced Republican in sentiment. In 1877 he was elected county commissioner, and this office he held for two years. The Methodist Episcopal church represents the doctrines to which he gives allegiance, and he is an active worker in the denomination. For twenty-five years he has been a trustee of the Woodlawn camp-meeting. In former days he was identified with secret organizations, but no longer retains his membership in these. His first wife bore the maiden name of Hannah E. Burns, and by her he had a daughter, Rachel L., now the widow of Rufus Foster, of Calvert. The only child born of his marriage to Rebecca Burns, his second wife, died when young. In 1861 he was united in marriage with Hannah Thompson, daughter of Ezekiel Thompson, of Theodore, this county. Eleven children were born of this union, of whom eight are living:

William J., of Leslie; John E., who is a storekeeper at Calvert; Rebecca J., who married Turner Cameron, and lives in Calvert; Hannah Elizabeth, Mrs. Thomas Mearns, living on the home farm; Alfred, Anna Mary, Curtis and Lawrence, who remain with their parents.

A L. DUYCKINCK. The career of him whose name heads this review illustrates most forcibly the possibilities that are open to a young man who possesses sterling business qualifications. It proves that neither wealth nor social position, nor the assistance of influential friends at the outset of his career are necessary to place him on the road to success. It also proves that ambition, perseverance, steadfast purpose and indefatigable industry, combined with sound business principles, will be rewarded, and that true success follows individual effort only. Mr. Duyckinck has gained recognition and prestige as one of the influential and representative business men of Cecil County, and has advanced to honorable distinction in business circles.

The birth of our subject occurred at Lamington, Somerset County, N. J., March 7, 1852, but when four months old he was brought by his parents to Maryland, where he grew to manhood upon a farm. He was educated in the common schools and at Nottingham Academy, and remained with his father upon the home farm until 1873, when he entered the warehouse at Rising Sun, Cecil County, as a clerk, serving in that capacity for six months. On the 25th of March, 1874, however, he became a partner of Mr. Briscoe, in that business, and a year later became sole proprietor. In the spring of 1876 he also purchased an interest in the warehouse at North East, and for one year was interested in the lumber and sawmill business at that place. In 1882 he admitted Mr. Passmore to a partnership in the business at Rising Sun, and he remained a member of the firm until his death, which occurred in 1889, when J. M. Starrett purchased his interest and is still connected with our subject. They do an extensive business as dealers in hay, grain, fertilizers, coal and lumber, and are numbered among the most progressive and wide-awake business men of the county. Mr. Duyckinck purchased a tract of land on the Baltimore & Ohio Railroad, where is now the village of Leslie, and made many valuable improvements, but a few years later sold his interest there to Messrs. Crothers and Hambleton.

In January, 1879, was solemnized the marriage of Mr. Duyckinck and Miss Willemenia M. Reed, who was born near Rising Sun. They have three children: Horace, now seventeen years of age, who is attending the Cheltenham Military Academy; Emily, fourteen; and Mabel, twelve. Politically Mr. Duyckinck has always been identified with the Democratic party, and religiously he is an active and prominent member of the West Nottingham Presbyterian Church, in which he has served as elder for the past five years, and trustee for twelve years. A man of unswerving integrity and honor, one who has a perfect appreciation of the higher ethics of life, he has gained and retained the confidence and respect of his fellow-men, and is distinctively one of the leading citizens of Rising Sun, with whose interests he has so long been identified.

SAMUEL A. S. KYLE. During the years that Mr. Kyle resided in Harford County he made many warm friends among its best citizens. After having been long connected with a business firm in Baltimore, in 1878 he purchased the Booth place, near Bel Air, and here he continued to reside until he passed away, in 1893. The place is well improved and constitutes an attractive country home. The residence, built by the Booth family in 1855, is substantial, roomy and comfortable; and the other farm buildings are also well adapted to their various purposes. The two hundred and fifty acres comprising the place are divided and subdivided into fields of convenient size, for the raising of grain or the pasturage of stock, and all the improvements of a first-class estate have been introduced.

The Kyle family is one of the large number of American families that trace their ancestry to Scotch-Irish progenitors. During the time of the religious persecution in Scotland, some of them fled to Ireland in order to seek a refuge for themselves and their families. They were people of prominence in the ministry, the royal navy and the East India service. The succeeding generations remained residents of the island that lies like a beautiful green emerald in the setting of the mighty Atlantic. The Covenanter faith, implanted in the hearts of those who lived in Scotland, was the religion of their descendants in Ireland, most of whom held membership in the Presbyterian Church. The subject of this sketch was born in Ireland, being the son of George Kyle, a lieutenant in the royal navy. At the age of fourteen he came, alone, to the United States, and joined his uncle, Adam Kyle, who was a merchant in Baltimore, and a member of the firm of Dinsmore & Kyle, established in 1805. With this concern he remained for forty-six years, retiring at the age of sixty.

The first marriage of Mr. Kyle, occurring when he was twenty-eight, united him with Ann E. Fendall, who died, childless, in 1876. Three years afterward he was united in marriage with Ella V. Harward, daughter of C. W. Harward, of Harford County. Two children, Grace and Annie, blessed this union. In religious belief Mr. Kyle was a member of the Episcopal Church, always interested in its work, and for some years before his death he was a member of the vestry of Holy Trinity Church. He had the unqualified respect of the whole congregation, and of the entire community. From his very nature he was a Christian gentleman; a life marked by courtesy, scorning any ignoble action, or a word savoring of untruth or profane jest; always just, honest and true. A man of upright character, he is remembered with affection by his family and, indeed, by all with whom business or social relations brought him into contact. Since his death his estate has been superintended by Mrs. Kyle, who is a lady of considerable business ability; she is also an admirable housekeeper, one who looks well to the ways of her household, providing bountifully for its inmates and for those friends or strangers who may happen to cross the threshold of her comfortable home.

JOHN COULSON HINDMAN, a well-known and influential citizen of Rising Sun and a leading auctioneer of Cecil County, was born near that village, in District No. 6, on the 28th of October, 1845, a son of Hiram and Rachel (Coulson) Hindman. His maternal grandfather, Eli Coulson, was a representative of one of the old and prominent families of District No. 6. Our subject is the only one in a family of five children now living. He attended the common schools to a limited extent during his boyhood and youth, but is almost wholly self-educated. His business training, however, was not so limited, and he early began to assist in the labors of the home farm.

In 1867 Mr. Hindman was appointed constable of District No. 6, in which capacity he continuously served until 1886, with credit to himself and to the satisfaction of his constituents. He was then appointed postmaster of Rising Sun, and served through President Cleveland's administrations having the honor of being the first presidential postmaster of the place. He is an ardent Democrat in politics and was elected president of the board of commissioners of Rising Sun in 1896. He has proved a most able and trustworthy official, is prompt and faithful in the discharge of his duties, and has won the commendation of even his political enemies. Since 1867 he has engaged as an auctioneer, and has done an extensive and profitable business along that line. Although not a member of any religious denomination, he attends and contributes to the support of the Presbyterian Church. Being endowed with a genial, hospitable manner, he receives the respect and confidence of the entire community and has made many warm friends.

In 1868 Mr. Hindman married Miss Rachel A. Edmondson, by whom he had two children: Ella J., now the wife of Lewis R. Kirk, Jr., a druggist of Malvern, Chester County, Pa.; and L. Blanche. After the death of his first wife he was again married, in 1891, his second union being with Miss Mary E. Haurand, and they have one child, John C., Jr.

JESSE HOSKINS. That our subject was an intelligent and energetic farmer is shown by the success that crowned his efforts, and that enables him now, in his advancing years, to live in retirement from active labors. The property which he acquired is a monument to his enterprise in the affairs of life and the good judgment that characterized his efforts. His high standing among his fellow-men is an equally satisfactory proof of his worth as a neighbor and citizen. He makes his home on a farm in District No. 3, Harford County, where he has resided since a young man of thirty years.

The father of our subject, Nathaniel Hoskins, removed from Chester County, Pa., to Baltimore County, Md., and thence in 1821 came to Harford County, settling upon the farm now occupied by R. C. Lee. Here the remainder of his life was spent in the occupation of a farmer. In early years he learned the trade of a stone mason, but never followed it to any extent after settling in this county. By his marriage to Elizabeth Cheyney ten children were born, and of these four survive: Jesse; William, of Baltimore County; Sarah A. and Phœbe H. The father died at the age of sixty-six years.

Born in Chester County, Pa., in 1810, the subject of this sketch accompanied his father in the various removals of the family. His education was limited to a brief attendance at the common schools, and he was obliged to learn from observation and experience what the boys of these days learn from text-books. When thirty years of age he bought the eighty-acre tract where he has since resided, though since 1886 he has not had charge of the place, having practically retired from agricultural pursuits.

Miss Angeline Johnson became the wife of Mr. Hoskins in 1840, and nine children were born of their union, namely: George W. and Sarah M., deceased; Hattie, wife of David Preston; Philena; Joseph A., deceased; Catherine, Mrs. Daniel Hollingsworth, deceased; Cornelia H., wife of Charles L. Vail, of Forest Hill; Joseph B., who married Miss Anna I. Hollingsworth, and they have one son, Raymond H.; and Fannie C., deceased, the youngest of the children. The family is identified with the Society of Friends.

The homestead is now conducted by Joseph B. Hoskins, who has always resided with his parents and since attaining manhood has managed the property with unqualified success. He brings to the consideration of all subjects connected with the management of the place a cautious and sound judgment, and maintains the high order of improvements instituted by his father. While he is a quiet, retiring man, he is an influence for good in the community, where his entire life has been passed. Of father and son it may be said that every deed and act are guided by the highest principles of integrity and morality.

JOSEPH L. WELLS. While the history of the Wells family in the years of its early settlement in America is unknown, owing to the fact that no record has been preserved, yet it is known that some of the name have been identified with the growth of Elkton during the entire nineteenth century. Probably in colonial times they sought homes here, witnessing the rapid development of local industries subsequent to the Revolution, participating in some of the exciting scenes of the War of 1812, and in the no less trying experiences of the '60s. In this village in

1818 occurred the birth of our subject's father, Joseph Wells, who was for many years in the employ of the government as a mail contractor, his first contract being from Elkton to Easton. When a boy he carried the mails for Joseph Mahan, who was then a large contractor. That was in the days preceding railroads, when the mails were carried on horse-back, and on the "fast" mail routes they had relays of horses every five miles. It is said that he "broke the record" as to time, making the trip from Elkton to Wilmington, a distance of eighteen miles, in fifty-two minutes. But his greatest achievement in that line was when he made the trip from Baltimore to Philadelphia in five hours, the fastest time ever made for so long a distance. He continued in the mail contracting business for many years, and during this time he established, with his son, John C., the store now owned by our subject. During the construction of bridges across the Susquehanna River he supplied large quantities of goods to the Pennsylvania Railroad. In 1886 he was succeeded in business by his son, our subject.

For a time during the progress of the Civil War, Joseph Wells acted as a scout for General Sherman, on the eastern shore of Maryland. He was a strong Union man and took an active part during the early part of the conflict. In local politics he was interested, and his recognized ability led to his frequent selection for public office, though his duties in business were such as to preclude much participation in local affairs. For two years he held the position of tax collector, and under the administration of President Harrison he was postmaster of Elkton. His prosperity was well merited, for with nothing to depend upon but his own exertions he became one of the substantial citizens of the community. Among his fellow-citizens he was respected, as he possessed the integrity of character that enabled him to live uprightly and in accordance with the teachings of the Golden Rule. He died in April, 1897. Upon another page reference is made to his brother, Benjamin, who was for fifty-five years agent for the Pennsylvania Railroad at Elkton, holding the position at the time of his death in 1894.

By the marriage of Joseph Wells to Cornelia Corouch, of Elk Neck Creek, who is living at the age of seventy-four, the subject of this sketch, John C., Edwin E. and Anna R., wife of Dr. J. W. Cooper, were born. John C., who was his father's partner for many years, later became a wholesale merchant of Philadelphia, and is now living in that city, retired from business. Edwin E. is chief clerk in the city tax office of Philadelphia. Our subject was born in Elkton, April 16, 1853, and received a public-school education. At the age of sixteen he went to Philadelphia, and learned telegraphy, after which he was employed for two years as operator at Chester, Pa. He then received an appointment in the Baltimore custom house as liquidating clerk, receiving a good salary and remaining there for five years, when he resigned to succeed his father in business. Since that time, 1886, he has been one of the successful business men of Elkton, as well as one of its leading citizens. For three terms he was a member of the town council, and for eight years held the position of treasurer of the town. As a Republican he takes an active part in politics and has been a member of the Republican state central committee. In March, 1878, he married Florence, daughter of George F. Harlan, who was for many years superintendent of the McCullough iron works. They are the parents of two sons and one daughter, named as follows: George Harlan, a student in Delaware College; Edwin Webster and Ada Cornelia.

JOHN H. McCRACKEN. The subject of this article is certainly entitled to be considered among the respected and honored residents of Cecil County. In his career we find that of a man whose course in life has been such as to commend him in a marked manner to the esteem and confidence of his fellow-citizens. Upright in his dealings, generous and public spirited, he has, as a citizen of North East, exerted a good influence upon those around him, and furthered the enterprises calculated to upbuild the better elements of society. His ancestors, both maternal and paternal, were closely identified with the growth and early history of this part of the state, and he is worthily wearing the mantle of his honored forefathers.

The McCracken family had its origin in Ireland, whence William, grandfather of our subject, crossed the Atlantic, hoping to better his financial condition in the new world. He settled in Cecil County, and as an active, energetic man, bore a part in the advancement of agricultural enterprises. After his death, his wife, Ruth (Richardson) McCracken, became the owner of the "North Star," a large sloop. This ship was captured near North East by the British fleet and though she hastened down to the Chesapeake Bay and obtained an interview with the commander of the fleet, her most urgent entreaties failed to induce the British general to return the sloop, which was transferred to Halifax.

John McCracken, father of our subject, was born on the Shawner farm in Cecil County, and, early gaining familiarity with agricultural pursuits, chose farming for his life work, and in it he continued to engage as long as he lived. He assisted in the organization of the Methodist Episcopal Church of North East and was a trustee of the congregation for years. First an old-line Whig, the disintegration of that party found him ready to join the Republican ranks. He died in 1863. The mother of our subject was Martha J. Cazier, a native of Cecil County, who died here in 1873. She was a member of an old and honored family of the county. Her father, Thomas Cazier, of North East, raised a company in this village and the surrounding country, and at the head of his men, engaged in service in the War of 1812.

Born in North East, January 11, 1840, the subject of this notice was educated in the local schools, where he was a student until seventeen. Afterward he assisted in the farm work until the outbreak of the war. Desiring to enlist, he availed himself of the first opportunity to do so, and August 12, 1862, his name was enrolled as a member of Company A, Eighth Maryland Infantry, he being the color bearer of his regiment. He continued in active service until the battle of Laurel Hill, Va., May 8, 1864, where he was wounded and lost a limb; captured by the opposing army, he was sent to Lynchburg and Richmond, where he was imprisoned for four months, after which he was exchanged, discharged and returned to his home. The injury received while in service prevented him from enjoying the active life he had hoped to lead, and he was obliged to seek employment requiring little manual labor. For a time he was employed as a clerk in the revenue office at Elkton. Himself a Republican, he was honored by his party January 1, 1879, when, under the administration of President Hayes, he was appointed postmaster of North East. This office he filled with efficiency until 1894, when he resigned, and at present is engaged in fishing. He has never married, preferring, doubtless, the independence of single life. He is a charter member of Fellowship Lodge No. 42, K. of P., in which he has held all the offices. An active Grand Army man, he has held the various offices of the local camp and is identified with the Maryland State Encampment.

WILLIAM PENN HAINES, Jr. While Mr. Haines has not been long at his present location, it must not be supposed that his experience as a merchant has been of but brief duration. On the contrary he has been engaged in business for a number of years and has proved himself a capable, energetic and judicious business man. In 1896 he came to Conowingo, Cecil County, where he erected a store building and near it a residence. Embarking in business, he stocked the place with a supply of all the requisites for a country store, and soon built up a fair trade among the people of District No. 8, whose confidence he won by his fair dealings and accommodating disposition.

The ancestry of the Haines family is given in

the sketch of H. H. Haines, upon another page of this volume. The father of our subject, William Penn Haines, Sr., was for a long time engaged in the mercantile business at Kirks Mills and Pleasant Grove, Lancaster County, Pa., where he occupied the position of postmaster, succeeding his father, who had filled the office from 1828 until 1872. Now, however, he is living retired, and makes his home in Pleasant Grove. At the age of seventy-one he is in the enjoyment of good health. By his marriage to Mary Kirk he had four children, namely: Eugene M., who lives at Pleasant Grove; Jeremiah B., of Philadelphia; Mabel, wife of Joseph P. Griest, of Reading, Pa.; and William Penn, Jr. The last-named was born at Kirks Mills in 1862 and received his education principally in the public school of Pleasant Grove. At the age of seventeen he went to Philadelphia, where he secured a position as inspector of yards for John Wanamaker, remaining in that place for two years. He then returned to Pleasant Grove, and for the five ensuing years clerked in the employ of his brother, Eugene M., after which the two formed the firm of E. M. & W. P.,Haines, Jr., in the canning business in Lancaster County, Pa. In 1888 our subject bought a one-half interest in the store at Pleasant Grove, and in 1892, selling his interest in the canning business, he purchased his brother's interest in the store, which he continued to superintend until disposing of it to Herr Brothers in 1895.

Meantime, in 1894, Mr. Haines had purchased the store owned by John A. Richie, in Pilot Town, but in 1896 he removed to his present location. In June, 1897, he was appointed postmaster of Pilot. There is not a department or detail of the mercantile business with which he is not familiar. His long experience, both as clerk and partner in the business, has given him a thorough knowledge of the occupation, the best markets, etc. He gives his attention to the business and post-office to the exclusion of all other matters. It is his ambition to establish his finances upon a solid footing and gain a competency before he becomes old. Having this aim in life he has not cared to identify himself with public affairs. However, he keeps posted upon politics and is a Republican by preference and by training. December 30, 1890, he married Gertrude E. Gillespie, of Cecil County. He adheres to the doctrines of the Society of Friends, while Mrs. Haines has always been identified with the Presbyterian Church.

EDWARD T. MONKS. A native of Harford County and one of its lifelong residents, Mr. Monks is deeply interested in all enterprises having for their object the promotion of local welfare and the advancement of the people. Probably no citizen of Kalmia has done more than he for the development of its material resources and the enlargement of its business interests. In 1867 he purchased property in this village and the following year opened a general mercantile store, beginning upon a very small scale, but gradually increasing his stock of goods as the demand justified. His store is now the largest in the place and he has a profitable trade among the people of this part of the county.

Near his present place of residence Edward T. Monks was born June 16, 1831, being the son of James P. and Mary A. (Tredway) Monks. His grandfather, John Monks, was born in England, whence he emigrated to the United States and settled in Abingdon, Md., opening a mercantile store. He was also a large land owner and gave a good deal of attention to farming; in these occupations he was engaged during the remaining years of his life. James P. was also an agriculturist, and remained a resident of District No. 3 until his death, which occurred in 1873, at the age of seventy-three. His wife passed away when sixty-seven years of age. Of their sixteen children, five are now living, namely: Edward T.; William, who resides at Gibson, District No. 3; Cassandra, of Baltimore; Addie, wife of William S. Smith; and Eliza, widow of Thomas L. Grier.

At the age of eighteen Edward T. Monks left school and began to learn the hoopmaker's trade, which he followed for ten years. With a desire to enter an occupation more remunerative, in 1865 he succeeded J. E. Tredway as proprietor of a general store, which he conducted for two years, and then bought property and put up the buildings which he now occupies at Kalmia. He lends his influence to the advancement of local measures, and in politics gives his vote in favor of the Republican party. In religious belief he is identified with the Methodist Protestant Church, in which he is a trustee, and has held various other positions. In the selection of a helpmate he was particularly fortunate, his wife being a lady who looked well to the ways of her household and those little details that have so much to do with the happiness of a home. Mrs. Monks was, prior to her marriage in 1866, Ellen C. Tredway, and the family from which she is descended is among the oldest of Harford County. Her death occurred August 21, 1879. Mr. Monks has two daughters, one of whom, Amy D., married William D. Jones, of Forest Hill, and the other, Sallie A., is the wife of Harry E. Harkins, of Kalmia.

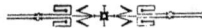

WILLIAM B. HOPKINS. Occupying a pleasant location in Harford County, apart from the distracting influences of city life, the visitor notices the comfortable home of Mr. Hopkins, who is one of the successful farmers and well-known public men of District No. 2. From youth he has been engaged in acricultural pursuits, and he has a thorough knowledge of the best methods of rotating crops and fertilizing the soil. The farm, which his wife inherited from her uncle, Col. William B. Stephenson, consists of two hundred and sixty acres of land, two hundred of which is tillable, and is one of the most valuable pieces of property in the locality.

The Hopkins family is one of the oldest in Harford County and is of Welsh extraction. The great-grandfather of our subject, Joseph Hopkins, was born here and attained an advanced age, rearing a large family. One of his sons was Joseph, grandfather of our subject, who was a native and large landowner of Harford County. It is thought that he took part in the War of 1812, but the length of his service is not known. In public affairs he was active, and his influence was always felt on the side of right and justice. His death occurred when he was about seventy years of age.

Our subject's father, J. Lee Hopkins, was born in this county and here spent his life as a prosperous farmer, dying when fifty-eight. In political faith he was a Whig. His wife, Amanda, was born in Baltimore, Md., a daughter of Joseph Dallam, who was a native of Harford County. Mention of the Dallam family is made in the sketch of Richard Dallam, her second cousin, upon another page of this work. She was sixty-eight at the time of her death. In religion she was an earnest member of the Methodist Episcopal Church. Her five children were named as follows: William B.; Edward, who owns the old homestead in District No. 5, Harford County; Josephine, wife of Richard Davis, of Burlington, Iowa; Cassandra, who is unmarried and resides on the old homestead; and Charles, who died at twenty-one years.

On the home farm in District No. 5, the subject of this notice was born August 2, 1842. When he was seventeen his father had a paralytic stroke and he being the oldest took charge of the farm, overseeing its management and looking after the welfare of the younger members of the family. When he was twenty-nine he married and rented a farm in District No. 5, where he made his home for ten years. His wife, Lizzie, was the adopted daughter of Col. William B. Stephenson, who was born on the farm our subject now owns and here made his home as long as he lived. A man of considerable prominence, he was held in the highest regard by the people of the county, and was especially active in the ranks of the Democratic party. Honoring his party, he was in turn honored by it with election to the Maryland legislature, where he represented his district for several terms. The family of which he was a member is mentioned in the sketch of his father, James. In his later years his health was poor and for a long time before his death, which occurred when he was in his eighty-third year, he was unable to personally superintend the management of his large property interests. He therefore appreciated the services and helpfulness of Mr. Hopkins, who relieved him of all responsibility, taking charge of the farm and attending to other interests. Colonel Stephenson having no children, he bequeathed his property to his adopted daughter.

Mr. and Mrs. Hopkins are the parents of four children, namely: Francina; J. Lee, who graduated in 1897 from the medical department of the University of Maryland with honors and was immediately chosen resident physician of the Maryland University Hospital; Annie, who is with her parents; William Stephenson, who assists in the management of the home place. In his fraternal relations Mr. Hopkins is connected with Stephenson Lodge No. 36, A. F. & A. M., of Lapidum, which was named in honor of Colonel Stephenson. An active Democrat, he was in 1889 elected to the legislature and during his term of two years he served on the committees on incorporations and the Chesapeake Bay and its tributaries. Since nineteen years of age he has been a member of the Methodist Episcopal Church, in which he has filled all the important offices, and is now recording steward of this circuit.

JOHN E. ALEXANDER. Even a cursory view of the business establishments of Elkton will reveal the fact that they are in charge of men of energy and good judgment. In quality of stock, in price of goods and in the honorable, courteous way of treating customers, they vie with the stores of larger places. One of these flourishing establishments is the hardware store owned and conducted by Mr. Alexander, who has built up a large trade since first embarking in the business some time in the '70s. Having spent his entire life in Elkton, he naturally maintains a deep interest in its welfare and feels the greatest pride in its progress. He was born February 14, 1838, in the house where he now resides, near the county jail. The family of which he is a member is one of the oldest in Cecil County, but the date of its settlement here is not known.

The father of our subject, Andrew Alexander, was born in this county and was successfully engaged in the blacksmithing business throughout his entire life, having his shop adjoining his house. He built the fine old family residence in Elkton, and here his life was brought to a close in 1862. His wife bore the maiden name of Harriet Aldrich and was born in Elk Neck, this county, being a member of one of Cecil's old families. She died some years prior to the demise of her husband. Her family consisted of four sons and two daughters, one of the latter dying at the age of fifteen years, while the other, Louise, married William T. McCauley, of Ellicott City, Howard County, Md., and died in 1896. One of the sons, William, died young; another, Andrew, is a traveling salesman; and Harry was a partner of his brother, John E., at the time of his death, October 1, 1886.

Of this family John E. was the eldest. He had but little schooling, but at an early age learned the blacksmith's trade in his father's shop, continuing the business after the death of his father until 1869, when he opened a hardware store. As a business man he has been successful, having gained the confidence of the people and accumulated a considerable amount of this world's goods. In addition to his business enterprises, he has taken an interest in public affairs and has filled various minor offices of honor and trust, among them those of town commissioner for about ten years and trustee of the county alms house for some time. However, he is not a politician, and aside from voting the Democratic ticket is not actively connected with his party.

In 1862 Mr. Alexander married Miss Martha Robinson, of Elk Neck, daughter of Capt. William Robinson, who was master of a packet on Chesapeake Bay. Their family consists of five

JAMES LEE.

children: Henry T., who is connected with his father in the hardware business; Harriet J., Lydia L. and Lillie V., who are with their parents; and William A., who married Lydia Hartgrave, of Deland, Fla., and is engaged in the drug business in Chesapeake City, this county. The oldest child, Henry T., married Miss Catherine Anthony, of Vienna, Dorchester County, and they have two children, Miriam and John.

JAMES LEE. For the valor of its men and the graces of its female representatives, the Lee family has long had a more than local reputation. Concerning the history of its founders in America and the place of the original settlement, little that is authentic can be obtained. However, it is known that they came from England and that all of the name in the United States are descendants of the three brothers who founded the family here. Several of the name rose to prominence, notably Gen. Robert E. Lee, the gallant leader of the Confederate cause. As far back as the pre-Revolutionary period the name of Lee was a synonym for valor and dauntless courage. When the question concerning the independence of the states arose, Parker H. Lee, Sr., grandfather of our subject, was one of those who thought that the American eagle would be strong enough to use its own wings and make its own way in the world; he therefore took his place as a soldier in the American army and served creditably as a lieutenant in General Smallwood's regiment. It was his privilege to live to see the cause of liberty triumph, not only then, but later, when a second war with England arose. When death came to him, June 6, 1829, at the age of seventy-one, the country in whose service he had fought so valiantly was becoming a power felt throughout the entire world.

The first wife of Lieutenant Lee was Elizabeth Dallam. After her death he married Mrs. Mary Munnikhuysen, née Howard, who survived him many years, passing away in 1860, at eighty-four years of age. Their children were: Parker H., Jr., Henry Hall, Olivia Jane and James Carvil. The father of this family was buried in the family cemetery at the old homestead, and the mother was buried at Rock Springs. Parker H., Jr., was born and reared on the home farm, where he spent his entire life, engaged in farming. He was identified with the Rock Presbyterian Church, in which he was an official for some years. He married Mary E. Bryarly, daughter of James Bryarly, of Virginia. They became the parents of five children, named as follows: Elizabeth M., deceased, formerly the wife of Harris Archer; Parker H., deceased; Mary, who has also passed away; James, and Bryarly, deceased. The father of these children died at the old homestead, September 18, 1896, when eighty-five years of age. He was a man well known for his piety, and his death was much regretted by his host of friends. He retained his faculties unimpaired to the last.

The only surviving member of the family, who is the subject of this notice, was born in 1847, in the house where he now resides. On the completion of his education he began to assist in the cultivation of the homestead, to the management of which he succeeded at the age of twenty-five, and he has since had charge of the place, engaging in general farm work and in stock-raising. In addition to the management of this property, which comprises two hundred and twenty-six acres, he has charge of about twenty farms in Harford County, this being done in the interests of S. A. Williams and his clients. Besides other duties, he is a director in the Harford National Bank, which position he has held since its organization. He is one of the best-known residents of District No. 3, and the majority of the people living here are acquainted with him. In 1889 he married Miss Mary E. Whitaker, member of an old family of Harford County. They are identified with the Episcopal Church and for some years he has held the office of vestryman. An earnest promoter of every cause which he deems to be just and beneficial, in everything calculated to benefit the community he is a leading worker, and as such stands committed before the community. Under his intelligent supervision his property presents an appearance of thrift and prosperity. The broad acres well tilled, the pastures with the grazing cattle, the substantial farm buildings, and the residence with its air of home happiness, seem always to offer the rest sought by the tired toiler at the close of the day.

Mrs. James Lee is a great-granddaughter of Col. Nathaniel Ramsey, who received his title in the Revolutionary War, having fought at Monmouth.

T. EDWARD SWARTZ. The ancients had a proverb "Call no man happy until he is dead." This saying owed its origin to the fact, as well known in modern times as in ages long gone by, that often men who, in middle life, were rich, influential and blessed with every comfort heart could desire, are in later life poor, friendless and forgotten. Of those who have passed away we may truly say their lives were happy, if they were surrounded by the affection of relatives, regarded with esteem by friends and blessed with good health. The life of Mr. Swartz was not an eventful one, and was quietly passed in District No. 3, Harford County. While it was quiet, it was by no means useless or aimless, but the cultivation of his farm, the discharge of his duties as a citizen, the oversight of his varied interests and the provision for the needs of his family, consumed his entire time and made every day a busy one.

Near Abingdon, this district, Mr. Swartz was born October 5, 1852, being the youngest child and only son of Basil and Frances E. (Cochran) Swartz. He had three sisters, Marion, Mary and Sophia. His father was born and reared on the old homestead and engaged in the cultivation of this place until 1889, when he retired from active labors and removed to Bel Air. There his death occurred in October, 1893, at the age of eighty-two years. He and his wife were a worthy couple, kind to all, generous to the needy, and devoted to the welfare of their children. The influence of their noble lives surrounded the earliest days of our subject and continued through the years when he was better able to grasp its meaning.

In the country schools and in Churchville, T. Edward Swartz was a student during much of his boyhood. While he did not gain a broad classical education, he acquired a general knowledge that proved very helpful to him in his subsequent life. Agriculture was his chosen occupation and in it he engaged from an early age. In 1892 he established his home upon the Rogers farm in District No. 3, and here he carried on general farming until his earth life ended. In politics he was a Democrat, and by the members of the party was considered one of its faithful friends and firm adherents. To round and complete his character, religion gave its gentle, uplifting influence. With an unwavering faith in the doctrines of Christianity, he aimed to live up to its beautiful teachings, and in his life he showed its fruits. His membership was in the Methodist Protestant Church at Bel Air, and he served the congregation as steward for some time, always maintaining the deepest interest in all that would promote the cause of Christ.

January 18, 1882, occurred the marriage of Mr. Swartz and Miss Nannie C. Crossley, who was born on the eastern shore of Maryland and is a lineal descendant of the Hewitt family, of Baltimore. The four children born of their union are Edward R., James M., John R. and Clara C. When still a young man, Mr. Swartz passed from earth, February 2, 1896, and was laid to rest in Mt. Zion cemetery. His upright character and beneficent spirit find a eulogy more eloquent than any word picture could present in the esteem in which he was universally held and the regret everywhere expressed when the tidings of his death were heard. Harford County lost one of its best citizens when he passed away.

The farm now occupied and owned by Mrs. Swartz became hers by inheritance from her uncle, Roland John Rogers, whose grandfather, Roland Rogers, purchased the place from one Captain

Matthews, an Englishman. Roland Rogers (1st) married a Miss Jarvis. Roland Rogers (2d), father of Roland John, married Catherine Rogers, and they had ten children, namely: Lilburn, Lawson, William, Elijah, Roland John, Lucinda, Jane, Catherine, Hannah E. and Anna M. Roland John Rogers married Miss Elizabeth Hewitt, of Baltimore. He died February 5, 1892, and his wife passed away February 14, 1897.

JAMES M. CASHO. Located in District No. 4 lies one of the fine farms of Cecil County. Here Mr. Casho has resided since 1878, meanwhile bringing the property under excellent cultivation. Buildings have been erected and other improvements introduced which prove his thrift and enterprise as an agriculturist. The place comprises two hundred and twenty-seven acres, upon which are raised the various cereals to which the soil is adapted. Judicious management has brought the owner a good competency; while he is well-to-do, he has not become so at the expense of others, but has ever been just in his dealings and generous to those less fortunate than himself.

Newcastle, Del., is Mr. Casho's native county, and January 16, 1843, the date of his birth. As indicated by the name, the family is of French origin. The first to come to America was his great-grandfather, Jacob Casho, who crossed the ocean prior to the Revolution and served during the war under Lafayette He settled in Maryland, where Isaac Casho, our subject's grandfather, was born. He also served as lieutenant in the War of 1812, under Captain Mackey. George A., son of Isaac, was born in Newcastle County, Del., and is still living there, being now (1897) seventy-nine years of age. Through his active life he has been engaged in general farming and in trading, and has become well-to-do. He has never been active in local affairs, but always votes the Democratic ticket and takes an interest in party matters. By his marriage to Eliza Mote, he became the father of the following-named children: James M.; Anna; George J., who resides in Delaware; and Margaret, who is the wife of John L. Hanna, of Baltimore.

The district schools of Newcastle County afforded the subject of this sketch such educational advantages as he received. At the age of sixteen he left school and began to learn the trades of carpenter and millwright, which he followed for many years and in different places. In 1878 he purchased the farm in District No. 4, where he has since resided. The land is taken care of in the best possible manner and yields large harvests in return. The political questions of the age have received from him the consideration which they deserve. While favoring the general policy of the Democratic party, he is inclined to be independent, especially at the local elections, where he votes for the best man, irrespective of politics. He gives his aid to all public measures having for their object the promotion of the welfare of the people, and may be relied upon to assist in behalf of all that is morally and intellectually uplifting. He has never sought public office, though well fitted to discharge such duties satisfactorily, should he consent to enter public life. In 1879 he was united in marriage with Miss Sarah Evans, daughter of Hon. John Evans, at one time a member of the legislature. They attend the Presbyterian Church and are also connected with all the activities of the congregation.

DAVID E. WILSON. Prominent among the energetic, far-seeing and successful business men of Harford County is the subject of this sketch, who is successfully engaged in milling in District No. 5. In the house where he still resides, he was born in December, 1822, a son of William and Rachel (Smith) Wilson. William Wilson, Sr., the grandfather, came from Scotland, his native land, and located near Glenville, Harford County, where he devoted his remaining years to agricultural pursuits. His son William succeeded to the old homestead, on which he was born and reared, and in connection with its cultivation, also engaged in milling, owning and operating the Stump Mills on Deer Creek for many years. His home was near the mill, and he was prominently identified with the improvement and development of this region. He departed this life in 1840, at the age of sixty years. Of his five children two are deceased, and those living are David E., Ruth and Mary.

The common schools of Harford and Cecil Counties furnished our subject good educational privileges, and his business training was obtained with his father. Becoming a thorough and practical miller, he has since successfully followed that vocation at his father's old mill. He was married in 1855, the lady of his choice being Miss Mary Wilson, by whom he has five children, William, Gilpin, David E., Jr., Mary and Margaret. The family attend the Episcopal Church, and in his social relations Mr. Wilson is a member of Stephenson Lodge, F. & A. M. The thoroughness and persistency with which he applied himself while learning the trade has characterized his entire business career, and has been supplemented by careful attention to details, and by honorable, straightforward effort that has gained him a most excellent and enviable reputation.

EWBERRY A. S. KEYSER, M. D. An able physician in general practice, Dr. Keyser is a model physician. His cheerful confidence in the sick chamber is often as potent as his medicines, and he has been and still is a student in his profession, ever grasping after new truths in science. He keeps thoroughly posted in his profession, his diagnoses being quickly made and very rarely incorrect, while his kindness and consideration at all times cannot fail to be recognized and appreciated. He was born in the city of Baltimore, January 16, 1860, a son of Charles M. Keyser, also a native of Baltimore.

The paternal grandfather was Derrick Keyser, a native of Germantown, Pa., whose ancestors came to this country from Amsterdam, Holland, in 1688, and settled at Germantown. They were Dunkards in religious belief, which body is opposed to warfare, but this did not stand in the way during the Revolution, for some of the members of the family took an active part in the struggle of the colonists for independence, and also in the War of 1812.

Charles M. Keyser was a man of more than ordinary intellect and force of character, and consequently became prominent in political affairs in his state. He was a member of the upper house of the legislature for two years, and throughout life was interested in the organization and progress of charitable institutions. He was one of the organizers and the second president of the Baltimore House of Refuge, holding the latter position twenty years, and also that of director. He was captain of the Eutaw Infantry, the finest company in Baltimore before the war, commanded them during the '40s, and was frequently called out to quell mobs at that place. His chief calling in life was that of wholesale dealer and importer of queensware, which, under his management, proved both important and profitable.

Mr. Keyser was married twice, first to a Mrs. Monroe, whose maiden name was Armstrong, and next to a daughter of William Wilson, of Baltimore. He died in 1874 and his widow in 1892. He was the father of the following children: Anna, wife of James R. Edmonds, cashier of the Bank of Commerce, Baltimore; Martha, who died after her marriage to Joshua Levering; Margaret, who also married Mr. Levering, the Prohibition candidate for president during the campaign of 1896; Wilson, cashier of the Commercial and Farmers' National Bank of Baltimore; Charles M., of Baltimore; Grace K., now Mrs. Frank E. McIntire, of Philadelphia; and Mary, the deceased wife of Charles A. Keyser, of Los Angeles, Cal.

Dr. Newberry A. S. Keyser, another child of the above couple, first attended the Friends' high school of Baltimore, later the Johns Hopkins University, and finally the University of Maryland.

He received his degree of M. D. in 1883, and at once entered upon the practice of his profession at Baltimore, remaining there until 1890, when he came to his present location. Although he has resided here a comparatively short time, his practice is large and has been so from the first. He married Louise, daughter of Dr. Altvater, of Baltimore County, but in December, 1894, was called upon to mourn her death. She left two children, Allen Dirck and Mary Louise. One of Dr. Keyser's uncles, George Keyser, was a very prominent man of Baltimore, and was interested in military affairs, being major of engineers in the regular army during the War of 1812, so it may be seen that the doctor comes of fighting stock, notwithstanding the fact that his people were Dunkards.

JUDGE JAMES McCAULEY was for many years one of the most important factors in the business, political, educational and moral life of Cecil County. His name is inseparably interwoven with its history, and the part which he took in its substantial development classes him among those to whom the county will ever be indebted for the broad foundation, upon which will be raised the superstructure of its future prosperity.

Judge McCauley was born August 23, 1809, in the old stone house known as Lowry's, which stood on a tract of land near Mechanics Valley. It was an old historic place, having been erected during the Revolutionary War by Jethro Baker, one of whose daughters, Francina Baker, became the wife of Daniel McCauley, and the mother of Elizabeth McCauley. The latter married her cousin, John McCauley, and the judge was one of their children. The family has throughout the existence of the Republic been prominent in affairs in Cecil County.

The educational privileges of Judge McCauley were limited to instruction in the three branches, reading, writing and arithmetic, taught in Maffit's schoolhouse. Later he had ten lessons on English grammar. His studious nature overcame the lack of educational privileges and he was ranked among the well-informed men of the district. He became an expert surveyor and, unaided, constructed a compass and chain which he used in his work. The section of the country in which he lived was thickly wooded with fine oak timber, and the manufacture of barrels was a leading industry there. He learned, and for a short time followed, the cooper's trade, but his tastes lay in the direction of mathematics and were put to a practical test in surveying. After attaining his majority in 1830, he was for a time with the corps of engineers employed on the construction of the Baltimore & Ohio Railroad at Sykesville, Md. In 1833 he began the manufacture of portable threshing machines, personally attending to all the wood and iron work except the iron turnings and the castings.

In 1841 Mr. McCauley was appointed county surveyor by Governor Pratt, and as there was a large number of land cases unsettled at that time, he was engaged for several years in locating disputed boundary lines. In 1857 he was elected register of wills, and held that office for six years, his term extending into the exciting period of the Civil War. His business interests were ever prosecuted with vigor and energy and he carried forward to successful completion whatever he undertook. His official duties were discharged with the same fidelity and ability, and in public office he won the commendation of all concerned. When the south seceded he ardently espoused the cause of his native land and was a prominent figure in the meeting held in Elkton, early in the conflict, when the resolution was adopted that Cecil County should stand by the Union if all the rest of the state seceded. He gave to the service his son, Lieut. John McCauley, who did considerable recruiting service, and on the battlefield displayed his valor and his loyalty to the Union cause.

Honored and respected by all, Judge McCauley was chosen a member of the house of delegates of Maryland and served as chairman of the committee on education, which reported the new school law of 1865, one of the most important measures for the advancement of education ever adopted in the state. For a number of years he had taken an active part in the organization of public schools in Cecil County, and in 1851 was a member of the committee which framed the school law for the county. From 1834 he was a tireless worker in the cause of temperance and while in the legislature was a leader in securing a law closing drinking houses on election day. In the special session of the legislature in 1866 he made the first motion to exempt mortgages from taxation. In 1868 he was appointed school commissioner for the third district, and served as president of the board of school commissioners until December of that year, when he was appointed by the governor as chief judge of the orphans' court, serving out an unexpired term of nearly three years. He was afterward elected judge for six consecutive terms of four years each, his last term expiring in November, 1895.

Judge McCauley was married November 27, 1834, to Miss Sarah Beard, who died in 1846, leaving five children: Elizabeth, widow of Richard G. Reese; Mary, her twin sister, and the wife of R. T. Crouch; John; Rachel; and Hannah Louise, who married J. T. Yates. In 1849 Judge McCauley married Miss Melicent R. Price, who was a daughter of Jacob Price and who died in April, 1890, leaving three children, Helen A., James J. and Hattie S. James J. married Miss Etheland Gallagher, and they, with their two children, Elsie R. and Jay Hayes, reside in District No. 3. Miss Helen A. McCauley is a graduate of the Maryland State Normal School, and was principal of the Leeds school for several years, but is now conducting a private class in Latin. She has made a specialty of botany and has prepared a collection of the plants of Cecil County, containing over five hundred specimens, properly classified. Her intellectual attainments are of a high order. She is a member of the Methodist Protestant Church and has been superintendent of the Sunday-school for three years.

Rev. James Andrew McCauley, D.D., LL. D., ex-president of Dickinson College in Pennsylvania, was a first cousin of Judge McCauley. He was born in Mechanics Valley, Cecil County, October 7, 1822, and died December 12, 1896. For sixteen years he was president of Dickinson College, and his death was deeply mourned by all who knew him.

Judge McCauley was a man of deep religious feeling, a very active member of the Methodist Protestant Church at Leeds, and in 1885 he was instrumental in securing the erection of a new house of worship. Through his efforts largely, in 1895 a monument was erected in the Leeds cemetery to the memory of Miss Sarah Wilson, who in 1816 organized the first Sunday-school in Cecil County. When a young man he commenced to write poetry, and during the last half-century of his life contributed many articles in prose and a number of poems to the newspapers of the county. July 4, 1876, he delivered the centennial oration at Elkton, Md., which received the commendation of the press and all who heard it. He held friendship inviolable, home ties sacred, was true to every trust committed to his care, and over his life record there falls no shadow of wrong. He passed away January 25, 1897, and the memory of his useful life remains as a benediction to all who knew him.

WESLEY CLAYTON. In the spring of 1866 Mr. Clayton came to Maryland and purchased two hundred and ninety acres of land in District No. 2, Cecil County, where he has since engaged in general farm work. The family of which he is a member is an old and honored one and has furnished many generations of industrious men, mainly farmers, to assist in the development of the resources of the east. Nor is he less able and proficient than those who have preceded him. It has been his aim to surround his family with every comfort and to live an honorable, upright life, and this noble ambition has been gratified.

The Claytons were among the earliest settlers of Pennsylvania, their arrival in the state antedating that of William Penn. William Clayton, of Clayton Hall, England, came to this country in 1617, and settled near the present city of Philadelphia, where he took up large tracts of land. A portion of his property is comprised within the present limits of the city. Following him were William, Jr., Richard and Richard, Jr., then Powell, our subject's grandfather, a native of Pennsylvania and a farmer by occupation. The family were closely related to Dr. Joshua Clayton, first governor of Delaware, and one of the most prominent men of Revolutionary days, whose history is briefly outlined in the sketch of Charles S. Ellison, upon another page. The parents of our subject, Nelson and Jemima (Booth) Clayton, were born in Pennsylvania, and had a family of thirteen children, of whom the survivors are Phebe Ann, Wesley, Nelson N., Powell F. and Thomas A.

Upon the farm in Delaware County, Pa., where he was born February 27, 1835, our subject grew to manhood, meantime attending the district schools and one term in Wilmington, Del. In the spring of 1857 he went to the west and made Leavenworth, Kan., his headquarters for a period of about three years. During seven months of this time he was employed in the government survey in Kansas and Nebraska, and during the remainder of the time he was deputy surveyor and engineer of the city of Leavenworth. In 1859 he returned to Pennsylvania, and in 1863 went to Philadelphia, where he was employed in a wholesale shoe house about three years. At the time of the battle of Antietam he was held as a member of a reserve force of ninety thousand, to be brought into requisition if more troops were needed. In the spring of 1866 he came to Cecil County, where he has since given his attention to the development and cultivation of his farm. Politically he is in sympathy with the Republican party upon the tariff question, but is an advocate of the free coinage of silver. He has never sought official positions, and does not actively identify himself with politics, preferring to devote his time to personal affairs. In religious connections he is a member of the Methodist Episcopal Church. November 20, 1862, he married Mary P. Goodley, who was born and reared in Delaware and received her education at Greenwood, Del., and Marshallton, Pa. Like her husband, she is a Methodist in religion. She is a daughter of Samuel and Elizabeth R. (Stidham) Goodley, and a granddaughter of Samuel Goodley, who was born in Germany and in an early day settled upon a farm in Delaware. Mr. and Mrs. Clayton are the parents of eight children, namely: Calmar E., Samuel G., Elizabeth G., Mary E., Anna W., Wesley, Jr., Ervin G. and Bertha, of whom Elizabeth, Mary and Bertha are deceased.

EDWARD P. HOLLINGSWORTH, of District No. 3, Harford County, is a descendant of English ancestors, settlers in America during the days of its colonial history. Upon the farm now occupied by his brother Daniel, he was born December 12, 1849, the son of Amos W. and Lois P. (Clement) Hollingsworth, and the grandson of Robert Hollingsworth. His father, who remained a resident of this district until his death, was a farmer by occupation and a carpenter and builder by trade, both of which callings he followed with success. His children, six in number, were named as follows: Daniel; Elizabeth, wife of W. S. B. Preston; Edward P., Rebecca, Cyrus C. and Dr. Charles A.

In the common schools near his home and a boarding school at Glen Cove, the subject of this sketch obtained a good education. From the age of eighteen until twenty, he worked on his father's farm, after which he rented Longwood farm and remained there for one and one-half years. He then removed to Baltimore County and conducted a large dairy business for three years, later returned to Longwood farm and remained until his father's death, when he purchased the Wilna farm and here he has since engaged in the raising of cereals and of cattle. In addition, he has been the agent for farm machinery, and formerly engaged in the fertilizer business. His possessions have been accumulated by energy and perseverance, united with economy and excellent business qualifications, and the youth who may peruse this sketch can do no better than emulate his example. He has never sought public office, and his connection with politics is limited to the casting of a straight Republican vote at elections.

In December, 1870, Mr. Hollingsworth married Hannah F. Moore, by whom he has two sons, Robert A. and David F., both of whom, with their parents, hold membership in the Friends' Church. The older son married Elizabeth Atkinson, of Pennsylvania, and they have a daughter, Marie. This is one of the representative families of the county and of its members old Harford may well be proud. Energetic, honest and upright, they are the kind of people who will promote the welfare of any locality and bring it to a high rank among the other sections of the state.

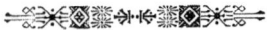

SERUCH TITUS KIMBLE, the eldest son of Henry Harding and Mary (Titus) Kimble, was born in Buckingham Township, Bucks County, Pa., April 21, 1849. On his father's side he traces his ancestry to Gov. John Carver, of the Plymouth colony, while his maternal ancestors were of Roman descent. His grandfather, Seruch Titus, was a man of prominence as a lecturer and musician and also took an active part in the public life of Bucks County, which he represented in the legislature of Pennsylvania. He had a brother, John Titus, who became a successful lawyer and for many years was chief justice of Arizona. Seruch Titus was named in honor of a brother of his father, so the name has been handed down through several generations.

William Titus, the great-grandfather of our subject, married Mary Torrents, of Bucks County, who remembered having seen General Washington when he visited Bridge Valley, Pa., about 1777. This lady was noted for her personal attractions, as well as her ability as a housekeeper. She died at the age of eighty-five years. Her grandfather was killed in the famous battle of the Boyne, which was fought in Ireland in 1690. His son, John Torrents, who came to America, married Nellie Williams, and their daughter, Mary, became the wife of William Titus.

In 1855 Mr. Kimble removed from Bucks County to Cecil County, Md. When a boy he was diligent and acquired a broad fund of information, though he did not attend a high school or academy. When a young man he taught school and subsequently was engaged in farming. Talented in music, many of his happiest hours were passed in the cultivation of this taste. He was leader of a musical band at eleven years of age, having previously learned to play on the violin, fife and drum. He was a popular teacher of vocal music and an excellent leader of brass bands and orchestras. His interest in music continued from 1860 until 1881. He played all instruments in brass and string bands with facility and ease, gave lessons on the piano and organ, and was engaged as professor of music in the academy at Newark, Del. On several occasions he and his brother furnished music for the commencement exercises at Delaware College and for many excursions and entertainments. In fulfilling engagements he was always prompt. His professional work extended through lower Chester, Newcastle and Cecil Counties. In addition to his musical interests, he was active in literary and debating societies and contributed many articles to the county newspapers. As a citizen he was patriotic; as a man, upright; as a friend, highly esteemed.

In March, 1874, Mr. Kimble married Ada, daughter of Isaac Slack, a well-known resident of Toughkenamon, Pa. They were the parents of two children, one of whom died in infancy; the other, Fanny Titus, with her mother, survives him. In 1882 he was afflicted with paralysis and spinal disease, which was a source of constant pain and rendered him unable to walk. The best physicians were consulted, but medical skill proved of no avail. After three years of intense suffering, he passed peacefully away, February 8, 1885. He was an exemplary Christian, cheerful and hopeful at all times. In the midst of suffering no word of complaint escaped his lips. He would speak rather of the comforts he enjoyed and the kindness of his friends. During his last hours he was entirely conscious and looked forward joyfully to the happiness of heaven. He was a member of Head of Christiana Presbyterian Church, and the pastor, Rev. J. L. Vallandigham, conducted the funeral service, which was attended by a large concourse of friends.

The following stanzas are quoted from a poem, written in memory of Mr. Kimble, by his brother, John H. Kimble:

> The shade of death had haunted him
> Through many a weary day;
> With dread disease his youthful frame
> Was wasting slow away.
> He took his violin and sighed,—
> "I am too weak to play."
>
> With failing strength he strikes at length
> His favorite—"Home, Sweet Home;"
> His dreamy spirit ceases with
> The pleasing past to roam,
> And through the future seems to rise
> Up, up to heaven's high dome.
>
> The last sweet note of that sweet tune
> Within the room has died—
> And now he's playing on the harp
> Upon the other side
> Of death's dark river, safe and free,
> Among the glorified.

CHARLES A. HOLLINGSWORTH, M. D. The record of the Hollingsworth family, both in England and in America, is one of which the present representatives may well be proud. Of direct Saxon descent, they showed in their lives the virtues of that race. For centuries, from generation to generation, has been handed down the valuable estate, comprising six hundred and twenty-five acres, and situated in the northeastern part of Cheshire, England. This property came into the possession of the family in 1022, during the days of Saxon prosperity, thirty-three years before the battle of Hastings was fought and sixty-five years before the death of that illustrious monarch, William the Conqueror, whose reign had been one of warfare and bloodshed.

The country seat in Cheshire continued to be the home of the family notwithstanding the many changes wrought by time and by war. Valentine Hollingsworth, Sr., was born there in 1630, and married Catherine, daughter of Henry Cornish, high sheriff of London, who was unjustly executed in 1685, during the reign of James II. Being a member of the Society of Friends, Mr. Hollingsworth became acquainted with the celebrated Quaker, William Penn, with whom he and his family came to America in 1682, settling in what is now Newcastle County, Del. Afterward he filled many prominent positions in the colony, among others being elected a member of the assembly in 1683, 1687 and 1695. He obtained a patent to nine hundred and eighty-six acres of land in Brandywine, and soon became one of the prominent landowners and citizens of his locality. In 1695 he was chosen to serve as justice of the peace, and at other times held various offices of trust and responsibility.

During the Revolutionary struggle the family identified themselves with the cause of the patriots, and one of their number, Colonel Hollingsworth, became famous through his masterly leadership of his soldiers. All who bore the Hollingsworth name were active in the cause of American liberty. They were awake to the insults heaped upon the colonies and during the unequal contest which followed, against a king affluent in the resources of war, they were among the patriotic men who helped to make permanent the declaration of that immortal instrument which its bold drafters courageously signed. The memories of the Revolutionary heroes may well be cherished by all who love their country. Their descendants to-day have just cause for revering their memories; for, from their constancy and brave endurance of hardships, a national prosperity unprecedented has sprung up. Colonel Hollingsworth stood high in the esteem of his co-laborers and acted as confidential agent for the continental army. He was regarded as a friend by General Washington, who visited him at his home in Elkton, when on his way to Brandywine. The old mansion where these illustrious men met and counseled regarding the war, still stands, a link between the dim and fast-receding past and the active present; the property is now owned by John Patridge, a descendant of the colonel.

Nathaniel Hollingsworth was born September 4, 1755, his birthplace probably being Center County, Pa. In 1806 he removed to Harford County, Md., where his death occurred October 2, 1834. In 1783 he married Abigail, daughter of Robert Green. Their son, Robert Hollingsworth, was born in Harford County in 1784 and in 1809 was united in marriage with Elizabeth West. He died in Maryland in 1863, during the progress of the Civil War. Amos W., his son and our subject's father, was born in this county in 1820, and in early life followed the occupation of a builder, but afterward engaged in farming, and was the owner of large tracts of land. In public affairs he took an active interest and held a place among the influential citizens of the county. Here he died in February, 1884. His wife, Lois P., daughter of Cyrus Clements, was born in Woodstock, Vt., a descendant of a family identified with the early history of the Green Mountain State. After her marriage she became a member of the Quaker Church, to which her husband belonged, and the lofty teachings of this sect she has since endeavored to follow in her life. A lady of excellent education and retentive memory, possessing a cheerful, winning disposition, she attracts friends, and is beloved by all who know her. In her family are four sons and two daughters, namely: Charles A., who was born at Fallston, Harford County, in May, 1857; Daniel P., a successful farmer and the owner of a creamery; Elizabeth, Mrs. William S. B. Preston, of Fallston; Edward P., who married Hannah Moore and resides in Harford County; Rebecca, who is unmarried and resides with her mother; and Cyrus C., a farmer, who married Miss Jane Hanway.

By private tuition at home, afterward at the Oakland boarding school, the subject of this sketch received his literary education. Taking up the study of medicine under the preceptorship of Dr. R. D. Lee, he made rapid progress in the acquirement of medical knowledge and in 1881 graduated from the medical department of the University of Maryland. A year after coming to Bel Air he began his professional practice, in addition to which he added the business of a druggist, but sold out his drug store in 1888. His life here has been passed busily and happily, with no break in professional work, except in 1897, when he met with a serious accident that necessitated the amputating of a limb. In 1888 he married Miss Ada Roberta Young, daughter of the late Col. William Young, of Bel Air. They have four children, Karl A., William Y., Edward W. and John S.

HON. GEORGE Y. MAYNADIER. The family represented by this well-known citizen of Bel Air is of French origin, but for many years has been identified with the history of Maryland, the first of the name in this country having settled in Talbot County on the eastern shore. It has given to the United States many men of prominence in business and professional life, especially in the ministry, several Episcopal clergymen having been in successive generations of the family. Bravery in battle is a family characteristic. The genealogical record shows that Col. Henry Maynadier, grandfather of our subject, was an officer in the Revolutionary War and was one of the most influential men of his day.

William M. Maynadier, our subject's grandfather, was born in Talbot County, Md., August 1, 1776. His first recollections were of warfare and bloodshed. When he was a child of seven years the Revolution was brought to an end and his father returned home. Much of his boyhood was spent in Virginia, whither the family removed from Maryland. At the outbreak of the War of 1812 he enlisted in the American service, and his commission as lieutenant was signed by James Madison. His career as a business man proved that he possessed more than ordinary ability, and in civic affairs, as in war, he was ever faithful to duty. About 1800 he engaged in business in the city of Baltimore as a member of the firm of Harrison & Co., importers of dry goods for the wholesale trade. In the interests of the firm he visited Europe, representing the house, especially in Great Britain. His later years were spent upon a farm in Harford County, Md., where he died in 1855. He married a daughter of Dr. William Brown, of Alexandria, Va., a Scotch physician, and a graduate of the Medical College of the University of Edinburgh, Scotland. During the Revolution Dr. Brown acted as surgeon in the colonial army and expended a large part of his private fortune in securing medical stores and relieving the sufferings of the patriots; for this he was partially reimbursed by congress and a vote of thanks was passed by that honorable body. After the death of his first wife and when well advanced in years, William M. Maynadier married a second daughter of Dr. Brown, and moved to Maryland, such marriage being contrary to the laws of Virginia. His son, William, who was a graduate of West Point, was stationed for many years and during the late war at Washington, D. C., in the ordnance bureau, with the rank of brigadier-general in the regular army.

The father of our subject, Henry G. Maynadier, was born in Alexandria, Va., and when a young man, in 1824 or 1825, he came to Maryland, where he engaged in agricultural pursuits until his death, in Harford County, in 1842. Had his life been spared, he would undoubtedly have gained prominence among the people of the county. He married Elizabeth Yellott, a native of Baltimore County, and sister of ex-Judge George Yellott, of Towson. She long survived her husband, dying in 1890, at eighty-four years of age. In her family there were five sons. William C., the eldest of the number, was a farmer and lawyer, having read law with his uncle, Judge Yellott. John H., who was a soldier in the Confederate army during the Civil War, afterward became a prominent business man of Baltimore, being a member of a well-known commission house of that city. Jeremiah Y., a farmer by occupation, resides at Woodbrook, Baltimore County. J. M., who died in 1878, was a soldier in the Confederate army during the war, being attached to the command of Fitzhugh Lee.

The youngest of the five brothers was the subject of this article. He was born near Bel Air, Md., January 10, 1839, and was only three years of age when his father died. Reared upon a farm, he was given good educational advantages, attending Bel Air Academy, at that time taught by Edwin Arnold, LL. D., an Englishman and graduate of Oxford, and an accomplished scholar, with a wide reputation. Having determined to become an attorney, he took up the study of law, which he carried on with the late Otho Scott and Henry D. Farnandis, two of the most able members of the Harford bar. His readings were prosecuted with diligence, and in 1861 he was admitted to the bar. He entered upon professional practice in Bel Air, where his ability soon brought him into prominence. In 1870 he was appointed circuit judge to fill a vacancy caused by the resignation of Judge Bateman. At the expiration of the time for which he was appointed he retired from the bench and resumed the practice of law. The possession of qualities that admirably fitted him for public office led to his election as state's attorney, in which capacity he served eight years. For ten or more years he served as auditor of the circuit court. In every place that he has filled and in every duty he has been called upon to perform, he has been characterized by keen discrimination, broad intelligence and mental acumen, and both by natural gifts and acquired knowledge he seemed adapted for professional work. He has had little time to bestow upon matters not directly connected with his professional or public duties, although for some years he was an editor of the *Intelligencer*, of Bel Air, in connection with F. W. Baker, its publisher.

In 1870 Judge Maynadier married Miss Laura P. Moores, daughter of Aquilla P. Moores, of Harford County. They are the parents of two sons and a daughter, namely: Henry G., a promising young man, now employed as teller in the Second National Bank of Bel Air, and fraternally identified with the Masonic order; P. Moores, who for some years has been connected with the Harford National Bank of Bel Air; and S. Roberta, who is now being educated. The family attend the Episcopal Church, in which the judge was vestryman for several years. In fraternal relations he has been connected with the Masons for thirty years. As an attorney he is an indefatigable worker, a close student, possessing an analytical mind and logical reasoning faculties, and has established a reputation as a capable and successful advocate.

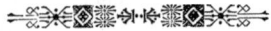

WILLIAM CARSINS, deceased, was one of the representative farmers of District No. 2, Harford County, and left the impress of his individuality upon the community. His life was marked by fidelity to duty, honesty of purpose and energy in business, and all who knew him entertained for him high regard.

Mr. Carsins was born July 28, 1822, on the same farm where his widow now resides, and was a son of John and Ann (Coen) Carsins. His father was also a native of Harford County, and when a young man purchased the old family homestead in District No. 2, where he carried on agricultural pursuits for many years. He was a prominent and influential citizen, and was elected sheriff of Harford County, in which position he was serving at the time of his death, which occurred when he was about sixty years of age. His wife was also a native of the same district, and died at the advanced age of eighty-two years. She held membership in the Methodist Episcopal Church.

William Carsins, whose name introduces this review, spent his early life on the home farm, and obtained his education in the common schools. He served as deputy sheriff under his father when only sixteen years of age, but after attaining to man's estate his entire life was passed upon the farm, with the exception of two years, from 1865 until 1867, when he lived in Bel Air, and discharged the duties of county sheriff, to which position he was elected in the former year. He proved a capable and efficient officer, fearless in the discharge of his duties, and won the confidence and commendation of all. His political support was given the Democracy and he warmly espoused its principles. To farming, however, the greater part of his time and attention was devoted, and he met with a fair degree of success in his undertakings. He took pride in keeping abreast with the progressive spirit of the age, and his place showed many evidences of the careful supervision of the owner.

On the 30th of December, 1847, Mr. Carsins was united in marriage to Miss Martha J. Maxwell, who was born in Havre de Grace, Harford County, November 20, 1824, a daughter of John and Elizabeth (Coen) Maxwell. Her father was also a native of District No. 2, and spent his entire life in Harford County, where he followed the occupation of carpentering. He passed away at the age of eighty-two, and his wife, also a native of the same district, died at the age of eighty-four. William Carsins and his wife were the parents of eight children, namely: George, who died in infancy; James, who died at the age of twenty-five; Mary C., widow of S. D. Jewens, of District No. 2, Harford County; Elizabeth Jane, wife of Wesley Butts, of the same district; Anna Etta, who died at the age of twenty-six years; Laura, at home; John William and Edward E.

The last-named was reared on the home farm, remaining with his parents until he had attained his majority. To the common-school system he is indebted for his educational privileges. When he had reached man's estate he married Miss Hattie V. Wells, of Aberdeen, Md. She is a member of the Methodist Episcopal Church, and a most estimable lady. By their marriage were born six children, five of whom are now living, namely: Grace, Belle, William W., Harry M. and Webster S. One daughter, May, died at the age of six years.

Edward Carsins now owns eighty acres of rich

and arable land, where he carries on general farming, but his efforts have been by no means confined to one line of operation. He is a man of resourceful business ability, and has connected himself with other enterprises, whereby he has added to his income. He is now engaged in canning tomatoes, renting and operating a canning factory at Forest Hill, Harford County. He also owns a small gristmill and grinds feed. He possesses great energy, is enterprising and progressive, and his sound judgment has carefully guided his business interests to a successful termination. He is numbered among the leading citizens of this community.

AMOS MARTINDALE. The farming community of Cecil County recognizes in the subject of this article one of its representative citizens and agriculturists. He is the owner of a fine estate lying in District No. 9, and, by a course of unflagging industry and wise economy, he has not only retained the full amount of his inheritance, but has increased the value of his possessions. The district where he lives has been his home throughout the greater part of his life and here have centred his closest interests. The occupation that he follows, farming, is the one in which for several preceding generations his ancestors engaged, and in it he has been prospered.

The subject of this sketch is a namesake of his paternal grandfather, the son of an Englishman and a native of Bucks County, Pa. Ross R. Martindale, father of our subject, for some years carried on farming and general merchandising in Bucks County, his native place, but in 1852 removed from there to Cecil County and settled in District No. 9. His death was a sad one, being the result of accident, and was deeply mourned by all who knew him. He was killed on the railroad at North East when fifty-two years of age. By his marriage to Ellen S. Singley, of Bucks County, he had seven children, namely: Samuel, who resides in Oxford, Pa.; Mary, Ellen S., Alice, Rebecca, Hannah and Amos.

In 1844, during the residence of his parents in Bucks County, the subject of our sketch was born. At the age of eight years he accompanied the family to Maryland, where he has since resided, his home being on the place purchased by his father at the time of coming here. In the various departments of farm labor he is energetic, shrewd and industrious, and from the raising of cereals and garden truck obtains a good revenue from his farm. In religious belief he and his family are Presbyterians and for some time he was a trustee of the church. In 1872 he was united in marriage with Gertrude Vanarsdale, who was born in Cecil County, and is a daughter of Isaac and Mary (Smock) Vanarsdale. Of the children born to their union three are now living, namely: Ross V., who assists his father in the cultivation of the farm; Harry, who is in Philadelpha; and Gertrude, at home. In his political views Mr. Martindale is a Republican. He has never sought office, but has devoted his energies principally to the welfare of his family and to his duties as a private citizen.

HON. E. M. ALLEN. The history of a county is best told in the record of the lives of the people. Their successes mean the advancement of the community and the enlargement of local industries; their reverses, the retarding of progress and the thwarting of enterprises. Reading between the lines of their biographies, one may learn much concerning the early days of a locality, its settlement, the experiences of its pioneers, the gradual development of its material resources, the introduction of improvements, the enlarging of commerce and the various transforming influences that have so much to do with the growth of any section of country. While the biographies in this volume are principally those of men now living or but recently deceased, yet the records of their ancestors incorporated therein do much to throw light upon days long past, and largely enhance the value of the work.

There are perhaps few of the residents of Bel Air who cherish a deeper affection for the place and its people than does the subject of this article. A busy man of affairs, he yet finds opportunity to keep in touch with every local measure and all village improvements. It is but natural that the place should be dear to him, for this was his birthplace. He represents the third generation of the family that has been identified with the history of Harford County, the first of the name to settle here having been his grandfather, Rev. John Allen, a native of Wexford, Ireland, a graduate of Trinity College, and from 1795 to 1815 rector of St. George's parish, which at that time embraced all of the county. He died in 1830. Concerning the remote history of the family little is known, except that, during the reign of Queen Elizabeth, some of the name accompanied the Earl of Essex from Scotland to Ireland, which afterward remained their home. The homestead, three miles from Wexford, has remained in the family for three hundred and fifty years.

Dr. Richard N. Allen, father of our subject, was born in Harford County, and was a man of marked ability and talent. In young manhood he became an attorney, and would undoubtedly have risen to prominence in the profession had it not been for an unfortunate accident. While speaking in public upon one occasion, he burst a blood vessel, and the injury sustained debarred him from further practice at the bar. He then began the study of medicine, but died soon afterward, in 1835, when his children were small. Had he lived to mature years, he would doubtless have made a name and enviable reputation for himself. He had a brother, William H., who was an unusual man, both physically and mentally. In height he was six feet and six inches, and his mental attainments were as remarkable as his physical. At one time he held the office of territorial governor of Florida.

The mother of our subject was Adeline Miller, a native of Harford County and the daughter of Edward Miller, who was born in England and became a woolen manufacturer of Maryland. She died within less than a year after the death of her husband, leaving three orphaned sons, of whom Edward M. is the eldest. Richard N., the second son, became a lawyer, and died in 1870. Henry L. is engaged in farming near Dallas, Tex. The subject of this article was reared in the home of a wealthy aunt, who sent him to Darlington Academy and would have given him a college education had he so desired. But the bent of his mind was in the direction of business affairs, rather than literary attainments, and he preferred to take charge of her estate, which he did very successfully. When twenty-three years of age he married Miss Sallie E. Wilson, half-sister of the late Judge John H. Price, with whom Mr. Allen studied law. Though often identified with professional, political and business affairs, he still makes his home on a farm in the northern part of the county.

In 1881 Mr. Allen was elected, upon the Republican ticket, to represent this district in the state senate, and during his term of office was chiefly remarkable for his aggressive disposition. He made a strong fight for low taxes and for the reduction of the fees of county officers, which naturally brought to him the enmity, or at least the determined opposition, of some politicians. Nevertheless, feeling that he was in the right, he persisted in his advocacy of reform movements, and now, though no longer in office, he still does all within his power to bring about the culmination desired. In 1890 he was admitted to the Bel Air bar, where he has since practiced, and prior to that time he had also done much legal business for his neighbors. He is a member of the Maryland Historical Society and strongly favors every means for perpetuating the memory of our early settlers and famous men. Fraternally a Mason, he is identified with Mt. Ararat Lodge of Bel Air. For more than forty years he was a vestryman of the Episcopal Church, but finally resigned from the position, in which he was succeeded by his son. He and his wife have four children. His son, E. M., Jr., is a prominent manufacturer and business man of Harford County. J. A. Greme, who resides at Davis, W. Va., is president of one company that has a capital of $70,000, manager of another with $120,000 capital, and of still another with a capital of $150,000.

With a desire to perpetuate the names and faces of our once distinguished residents, Mr. Allen, assisted by friends, but without expense to the county or the general public, placed in the court room at Bel Air, oil paintings of many men who were natives of Harford County and who attained distinction. Among them are the following: Dr. J. A. Preston, who was a member of congress and a man of influence in public affairs; Capt. John A. Webster, who commanded the six-gun battery that defeated the British fleet at Ft. McHenry in 1814; Dr. John Archer, the first graduate of a medical college in the United States, later a surgeon in the Revolutionary War and several times representative from his district in congress; Commodore Rogers, U. S. N., and his son, Admiral John Rogers, U. S. N.; Gen. William P. Maulsby, who was a general in the Union army and also a judge; Henry D. Farnandis, who is one of the most distinguished members of the Harford County bar, and refused the nomination for governor of Maryland when it was equivalent to an election; Otho Scott, a member of the Bel Air bar and a man of remarkable gifts intellectually; Judge James D. Watters, the present judge of the circuit court; Judge Stevenson Archer, chief justice of Maryland; Judge William Paca, one of the signers of the Declaration of Independence; Judge J. L. Bartol, who was chief justice of the Maryland Court of Appeals; Judge Hugh I. Jewett, who was a member of congress and a judge, and formerly president of the Erie Railroad; Judge John H. Price, ex-judge of the circuit court and brother-in-law to Mr. Allen; Henry W. Archer, one of the legal lights of the Harford bar; Col. E. H. Webster, who filled many positions of trust and honor in the county and state; Dr. David Harlan, who spent most of his life in the United States navy and who was the father of Henry D. Harlan, now chief justice of the superior court of Baltimore; Col. Robert S. Rogers, an officer in the Union army; and Edwin Booth, the famous tragedian, whose first performance was given in the court house at Bel Air. These portraits were painted in oil by a leading artist of Washington, and their presence in a public building may well serve as an inspiration to young men starting out in life, reminding them of the success that almost invariably crowns diligent effort and application.

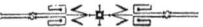

NICHOLAS P. MANLY. Among the residents of Cecil County who display a high order of ability in connection with agricultural affairs, and whose personal characteristics have brought them added prominence, the subject of this article is conspicuous. With steady purpose, energy and determination, he attended to his chosen calling through all the years of youth and early manhood, and his industry enabled him to accumulate a competency, so that he is now living retired, in the enjoyment of the fruit of the labor of former years. His home is in Elkton, within a mile of which village he was born April 16, 1834.

The father of our subject was Capt. Nicholas Manly, a native of Elk Neck, born May 3, 1795, and a seafaring man by occupation. Prior to the age of forty years he commanded vessels on the Chesapeake Bay and its tributaries, after which he purchased a farm near Elkton and spent his remaining years in the cultivation of the place. Personally he was of a quiet and retiring disposition, with little interest in public affairs, content rather to devote himself to his private business duties. His industry and energy brought him a small fortune and he was well-to-do at the time of his death, which occurred March 18, 1864. His father, whose name was Nicholas G., was born in Cecil County and made his home in District No. 5, where he successfully carried on a farm. He also engaged in hotel keeping in North East. He died December 8, 1826. The mother of our subject was Sarah W., daughter of John Highland, and was born in Chestertown, Kent County, Md.

By her marriage to Captain Manly, which took place May 10, 1831, a son and daughter were born, the latter being Anna E., widow of Thomas Drennen and mother of Manly Drennen, treasurer of Cecil County. Mrs. Sarah W. Manly died December 12, 1856. Our subject's father had two brothers, John and Stephen, both of whom served in the War of 1812; John died unmarried.

The years of boyhood and youth were spent by our subject on the home farm. On the death of his father the estate was divided between him and Mrs. Drennen, he taking a farm two miles from the place where he was born. In 1885, renting this place, he retired from farm work and moved to Elkton, where he owns a comfortable home. February 13, 1862, he married Miss Louise J. Simcoe, of North East, daughter of Hon. William Simcoe, a farmer by occupation, and a member of the Maryland legislature in 1842. He died when Mrs. Manly was quite small. She has two brothers, George, of Bay View, and John S., of North East. By her marriage two children were born: Sarah Rebecca and Elizabeth L., the latter of whom remains with her parents, brightening their declining days with her attention and devotion. The elder daughter is the wife of George McCauley Reese, grandson of the late Judge McCauley, and at this writing an employe in the Baltimore custom house; they have two children, Louise M. and Richard George.

CHARLES H. JAMES. Many of the native sons of Harford County have become known as successful farmers and efficient men of business, and among these is none more worthy of mention than Mr. James, a business man of Aberdeen and the owner and occupant of a well-improved farm situated about four miles west of the village. He was born in this district (No. 2) May 19, 1829, being the son of Jacob and Sarah (Gilbert) James, also natives of the same district. His father, who was a farmer and turner, was fairly successful in life, and was a hard-working, persevering man. He died when about seventy years of age. He did not take an active part in public affairs and never sought official distinction, contenting himself with casting a Republican vote at elections. His wife lived to be ninety years of age.

The parental family comprised ten children, named as follows: William, whose home is in Indiana; Jarvis G., a farmer, also residing in Indiana; Charles H.; George B., who carries on a farm and is interested in a canning business in District No. 3, Harford County; John L., a farmer of Baltimore County, this state; Jacob M., who is connected with our subject in the mercantile business; Catherine, Elizabeth, Susie and Jennie. The demands of this large family obliged the parents to husband with care their resources and to see that each child was doing his share of the work. The sons early learned the truth of the trite sayings, "No pains, no gain. No sweat, no sweet." "He that would eat the kernel must crack the nut." As they grew toward manhood, the sons went out into the world for themselves, the most of them selecting agriculture for their life work. Our subject, however, learned the carpenter's trade in his youth and for twenty-two years followed it and contracting. A careful workman, he was considered reliable and efficient, and met with commendable success. On retiring from his trade, he purchased a farm near Aberdeen, where he has since engaged in farming and the canning business. In 1895 he opened a flour, grain and feed store in Aberdeen and has since spent a portion of his time here. This is not done to the detriment of his farm, as he continues its cultivation and improvement the same as before. His possessions consist of his store and three small farms in District No. 2, these representing his own earnings and the fruit of his toil.

While Mr. James has never taken an active part in politics, this does not mean that he is uninterested in public events or deaf to his duty as a citizen. A thoughtful student of the times, of late years he has had an increasing realization of the evils of the liquor traffic. Believing that prohibition is the only remedy for the disease that gnaws at the vitals of our nation

LEWIS B. ROBINSON.

and threatens even the perpetuity of the government, he has become a Prohibitionist and casts the regular party ticket at elections. In religious belief he is connected with the Methodist Episcopal Church. By his marriage to Maria J. Cole, of this county, he has six children, named as follows: Lemuel C., a farmer in District No. 2; Lulu A., C. Harry, A. Minnie, Cornelia H. and J. C. Hagey.

LEWIS BOLIVAR ROBINSON was born upon the family homestead in District No. 3, Harford County, July 4, 1825, and died at the same place, of paralysis of the heart, May 9, 1890, when little less than sixty-five years of age. The family to which he belonged came to this state from Pennsylvania. His father, William, was the son of the original member of the family in Maryland and was a man of earnest Christian character, an industrious farmer and an intelligent citizen. By his marriage to Margaret Pierce, there were born four sons and two daughters, all deceased but two sons, Lewis Bolivar and Alphonso, between whom the estate was divided, the former receiving the tract that contains the buildings. Here his whole life was passed, with the exception of a few years spent in Baltimore County, where he also owned a farm.

Reared in a Christian home, the son of upright, intelligent parents, the subject of this sketch was the recipient of a goodly heritage. He was endowed with a bright mind and the capabilities that grasped every opportunity. Entering upon an occupation, he chose the calling with which he was most familiar and became a farmer. In addition to the raising of cereals, he became interested in other departments of agriculture. For some years, during the latter part of his life, he engaged in the canning business, putting up fruits and tomatoes, in which line he met with success. For thirty years he was in the dairy business, in which line he was also successful.

Twice married, the first wife of Mr. Robinson was Ellen Holland, who bore him three children. Only one is now living, Adelaide, who is the wife of J. W. Archer. His second wife was Marion I. Smith, of Harford County, a lineal descendant of the Levering family, who were pioneers of Baltimore and have always been prominently connected with the business interests of that city. By his second wife Mr. Robinson had three children, Jesse Levering, Charles Carroll and Olivia Smith. His death occurred very suddenly, while he was at work in the field, on the 9th of May, 1890, and was a deep bereavement to his family. For many years before his death he was an earnest member of the Methodist Protestant Church, the services of which he attended regularly and in which he was long a steward. In politics he was a Democrat.

WILLIAM E. CHANDLEE. The life of any man is of benefit to his community, when his energies are directed toward advancing its interests, and when he lives in accordance with principles he believes to be right. Mr. Chandlee is one of this class. His residence in Darlington, which covers a long period of years, has brought him intimate acquaintance with many people here and the regard of those with whom he has business and social relations.

The grandfather of our subject, John Chandlee, was the son of a Frenchman, who spent his life principally at Brick Meeting House, Cecil County, where he was an extensive farmer and large land owner. The father of William E. was Allison Chandlee, who, it is thought, was a native of Cecil County, but whose life was principally passed in York County, Pa., where he followed the trade of a tailor at Delta. His death occurred in 1868, at the age of fifty-nine. His wife, Mary, daughter of Adam Anderson, a soldier in the War of 1812, survived him many years, passing away in 1893, at the age of sixty-five. In their family were six children, but only three are now living, namely: William E.; Mary, wife of John Dorton; and Charles, who makes his home in Delta.

Near Texas, in Lancaster County, Pa., the subject of this notice was born in 1848. When a small child his parents removed to Peach Bottom, York County, and later settled in Delta, where he was a pupil in the public schools. In 1867 he came to Maryland and learned the trade of a harness-maker with a cousin, John Chandlee, at Brick Meeting House, Cecil County. Afterward he went to Zion, in the same county, where he followed his trade for two years. He also spent a short time in Wilmington, Del. In 1871 he settled near Pylesville, Harford County, where he made his home for three years, and later spent a short time in Philadelphia. Coming to Darlington in 1876, he opened a harness manufactory and repair shop, which he has since had in charge. In 1894 he erected the building which he has since utilized as his shop.

In 1871 Mr. Chandlee married Rachel Dorton, and their family consists of seven children, all at home, namely: George, Charles, William, Herbert, Allison G., Harry A. and Grace. The parents and the three eldest sons are members of the Methodist Episcopal Church, to the maintenance of which Mr. Chandlee contributes regularly. He takes pride in being a Democrat of the strongest type and adheres with fidelity to his political views and party principles. Fraternally he is connected with the lodge of Odd Fellows at Rising Sun.

THE CHANDLEE FAMILY, which is an old and honored one of Cecil County, was founded in America by Benjamin Chandlee, a native of France, who, with his father's family, fled from that country to a sea-port town on the coast of Ireland to escape religious persecution. This was during the reign of Louis XIV, when many thousands of Protestants, known as French Huguenots, left France and spread over Europe or came to America. Benjamin Chandlee was probably born about 1685 and came alone to the new world in 1699 or 1700, leaving the rest of the family on the Emerald Isle. He located at Philadelphia, which at that time was a mere village, having only been founded in 1682, and there bound himself as an apprentice to Abel Cottey, a watch and compass maker, who belonged to the Society of Friends.

Sometime after completing his apprenticeship, Benjamin Chandlee married Miss Sarah, daughter of Abel and Mary Cottey, the wedding being performed at the Friends' meeting house in Philadelphia, March 25, 1710. In 1702 Nottingham, Cecil County, Md., was laid off in farms of from four hundred to six hundred acres each, and one of these (located near the Brick Meeting House) was taken up by Randel Janney, who gave it the name of Randel's Prospect. This place he sold in 1706 to Abel Cottey of Philadelphia, who at that time had Benjamin Chandlee in his employ. Soon after his marriage the last-named came to Nottingham and located at Randel's Prospect, thus establishing the family in Cecil County. Here he was employed at his trade and also did iron work for neighboring farmers.

As Mrs. Chandlee was born in Philadelphia, her parents were probably among the colonists who founded the city. Abel Cottey also owned a small farm adjoining the Brick Meeting House at Nottingham, which property his widow, Mary Cottey, left by will to her daughter, Sarah Chandlee. The will was dated June 18, 1713, and proven and registered at Chester, Pa., March 3, 1714. In this document are mentioned her grandsons, Abel Cottey and Cottey Chandlee, and also ten acres were to be given John Cottey, "if he comes into these parts again."

The children of Benjamin and Sarah (Cottey) Chandlee were all born at Nottingham, Md., and were as follows: (1) Cottey, born between eleven and twelve o'clock in the morning of February 2, 1713, lived, married and died at Nottingham, passing away October 9, 1807, at the advanced age of ninety-four years, five months and three weeks. He was a faithful member of the Society of Friends. (2) Mary, born June

27, 1715, married, and lived at various places, being last heard of in York County, Pa., in 1773. (3) Hannah was born about four o'clock in the afternoon of March 24, 1718, but nothing is known of her history. (4) William, born at sunset, June 29, 1721, wedded Mary Elagar in 1748, and died January 28, 1806, at the age of eighty-five. (5) Benjamin, born a little before day on January 22, 1723, became the great-grandfather of William E. Chandlee, of Darlington, whose sketch appears in this work. (6) Abel, born about eleven in the morning of July 12, 1726, was married in 1760, and lived at Sassafras, Md. These children were all born at Randel's Prospect, where the parents continued to make their home for thirty years, but in 1741 sold the place to Joseph Trimble.

Benjamin Chandlee, Jr., took up his residence upon the property adjoining the Brick Meeting House, at Nottingham, Cecil County, which was left by will to his mother, and occupied the old Benny Chandlee house, known in olden times as the Arc. In 1749 he was united in marriage with Miss Mary Folwell, a daughter of Goldsmith Edward Folwell, of Wilmington, Del. Mr. Chandlee died between one and two o'clock, September 18, 1791, at the age of sixty-eight years and six months; and his wife October 6, 1806, at the age of seventy-seven years and six months.

Five children were born to Benjamin Chandlee, Jr., and wife, namely: (1) Goldsmith, born May 18, 1751, became a resident of Baltimore, where he followed the trade of watch and compass making until the latter part of his life, which he spent at Winchester, Va., dying there in 1821, at the age of seventy years. His son Benjamin remained in charge of the business in Baltimore, where he died in 1822. (2) Sarah, born April 10, 1753, died August 5, 1808, at the age of fifty-five years and four months. (3) Ellis, born June 11, 1755, married Elizabeth Giles Oldham, a daughter of Nathan Oldham, of Cecil County, and spent his entire life at Nottingham, where he died in 1816, at the age of sixty-one years and seventeen days. His children were as follows: Maria; Evan; Sydney, who married a Miss Price, of Nottingham, and had a number of children, among whom were William, of Washington, D.C., and Henry, of Baltimore, Md.; Absalom; Lilbern; Veasey; Eliza; Gainer; Edwin; Courtland, who married Elizabeth Pierce, of Wilmington, Del., and had one son, David Wollford, who died at the age of thirteen years; Mira, who married Rawlins Abrahams and had a number of children, and Ellis Goldsmith, who married Ann Eliza, daughter of Robert and Sarah Brown, of Cecil County, and had several children. (4) John, born July 10, 1757, is mentioned more fully below. (5) Isaac, born September 12, 1760, at Nottingham, died December 9, 1813, at the age of fifty-three years. He never married and lived in the old Benjamin Chandlee house known as the Arc, which was sold some time after his death. His maternal aunt, Susan Folwell, kept house for him.

John Chandlee, son of Benjamin and Mary (Folwell) Chandlee, spent his entire life at Nottingham, where he died August 12, 1813, at the age of fifty-five years and ten months. He was three times married, his first wife being Miss Sarah Brown, of the same place, by whom he had one child, Edward G., born at four o'clock in the afternoon of September 13, 1792. The son died at Rockford, Del., August 15, 1851, when about fifty-nine years of age. He had married Jane Walker, and to them were born three children who died in infancy. After the death of his first wife John Chandlee married a Miss Kinky. He became acquainted with his third wife, Miss Rebecca Ward, in Wilmington, Del. Three children blessed their union, all of whom were born at Nottingham in the white house standing between the Brick Meeting House and Lombardville. (1) Horatio Ward, born at three o'clock Saturday morning, August 6, 1803, married Lucinda Barnum, of Baltimore, and had two children, Frances Anna and Sarah Jane, both born in Ohio. He was in Baltimore in 1832 and for some years was at Havre De Grace, Md., with his father's cousin, Benjamin Chandlee, but spent most of his life in the west. (2) Mary, born about ten o'clock P. M., Tuesday, September 17, 1805, became the wife of James Fulton, of Steuben County, N. Y., who at the time of their marriage was living near Wilmington, Del. All of their four children were born at Rockford, Del., namely: Edward A., who died in 1880 of wounds received at the battle of Antietam; William Thomas, who died in infancy; Anna Rebecca, who married J. Darnell Gifford, of New Jersey; and Sarah Caroline, who married George Wright, of Pennsylvania, and has three children living, Joseph F., Emma Leola and James. James Fulton, the father of these children, died in Chicago, Ill., in 1855, while traveling with his son, Edward A., then a boy, who brought the body back home for burial. His widow survived him for many years, dying at the old homestead at Rockford, near Wilmington, Del., in 1893, aged eighty-eight years and four days. (3) Allison Chandlee, the youngest child of John and Rebecca (Ward) Chandlee, was born at five P. M., Tuesday, August 22, 1809, in Nottingham, but spent the greater part of his life in York County, Pa., following the tailor's trade in Delta. He died in 1868, at the age of fifty-nine. In early life he wedded Mary Anderson, a daughter of Adam Anderson, a soldier of the War of 1812, and she survived him many years, dying in 1893, at the age of sixty-five. In their family were six children, but only three are now living: William E.; Mary, now the wife of John Dorton; and Charles, who makes his home in Delta.

SAMUEL J. ARBUCKLE. In making note of the life of Mr. Arbuckle it is proper to mention the fact that he is looked upon as one of the most public-spirited men of Cecil County. He has a pleasant country home, built up by his industry and enterprise, assisted by his capable wife. His homestead comprises sixty-nine acres of excellent land and has all the facilities for the successful prosecution of general farming and dairying. The dwelling, as well as the surroundings, gives evidence of the cultured tastes of the owner.

A gentleman still in the prime of life, Mr. Arbuckle was born in Montgomery County, Pa., in 1845. His grandfather, Daniel, came to this country from Ireland and settled in Philadelphia County, Pa. Daniel, Jr., father of our subject, was born in Montgomery County and for thirty-three years engaged in the manufacture of cotton and woolen goods. On retiring from active life he came to District No. 3, Cecil County, where the last twenty-four years of his life were passed. Here he died in 1891, at the age of seventy-eight. In early days he was a Whig, and upon the disintegration of that party and the organization of the Republican, he joined the latter, to the principles of which he afterward adhered. Frequently he was solicited to accept positions of local trust, but having no taste for public affairs and wishing to devote himself exclusively to business, he invariably refused. By his marriage to Mary S. Magargle, of Philadelphia County, he had nine children, four of whom are still living, namely: Samuel J.; Daniel T., of Cecil County; Paul T., also a resident of this county, in District No. 4; and Philip R., of Cherry Hill.

In the common schools of Philadelphia County the subject of this sketch received his education. At the age of sixteen his studies were discontinued and he began to assist his father in the factory owned by the latter. Gaining a thorough knowledge of the business, he became an invaluable assistant in its management. After spending five years there, he began in the flour and feed business in Philadelphia County, and for five years carried on an enterprise of his own. Coming to Maryland in 1872, he established his home at Cherry Hill, in District No. 3, and here he has a large farm, equipped with necessary buildings and divided by good fencing into fields and pastures of convenient size. In 1866 he married Catherine M. Kuhn, daughter of Jacob and Rebecca A. Kuhn, of Philadelphia County, and a lady of estimable character, who shares with him in the respect of acquaintances. Her father had a machine shop at Manayunk for a number of years, and was the inventor of the double box loom. In politics Mr. Arbuckle is in harmony with the Republican party and gives stanch adherence to the party of his choice. With his wife he attends religious services at the Methodist Church. He is connected, fraternally, with Roxborough Lodge No. 135, F. & A. M., at Manayunk, Pa. The high position he occupies is due not alone to his management as a farmer, but also to his general intelligence and firm principles.

In 1863 he enlisted in Company A, Thirty-first Pennsylvania Volunteers. He is now connected with Grant Post No. 10, G. A. R., at Cherry Hill.

WILLIAM D. BRATTON. In the line of public journalism, more than in any other vocation, success is not gauged by the accumulation of money, but by the influence exerted upon a community, the progressive measures fostered and the public-spirited enterprises originated. Among the newspapers that have exerted a marked influence in the upbuilding of Cecil County, prominent mention justly belongs to the *Cecil News* of Elkton, which has a large circulation among the people of this section and influences in a marked degree the educational, commercial, moral and material interests of the locality. While the subject of this sketch has been connected with it for a comparatively brief period only, yet he has proved the possession of the traits of character that mark the true journalist, and is building up a reputation as an editor. The high standard of journalism which he has set has met with a corresponding appreciation on the part of the people, so that to-day his paper commands a wide influence, and his editorials, clear, logical and pointed, are widely read. Every important national event or question is treated in the columns, and the people are enlightened as to the right or wrong, the justice or injustice, of proposed measures.

The editor of this paper is a native Elktonian, born near this village June 8, 1868, the son of Daniel and Susan (Reese) Bratton, natives, respectively, of Delaware and Cecil Counties, Md. His father, who was of Irish descent, started in life a poor man, but by industry and economy accumulated a fortune in the mercantile business and became the owner of large tracts of valuable land. He died March 5, 1882. His widow is still living on the estate in the suburbs of Elkton. She is the mother of four sons, Daniel, Samuel, Howard and William D. Daniel was, for some years before his death, the owner and editor of the *Cecil News*. Samuel is a civil engineer in Texas. Howard graduated from the medical department of the University of Pennsylvania, and is a practicing physician of Elkton.

In 1889 the subject of this sketch graduated as a civil engineer from Princeton, and afterward for several years was in the employ of the Pennsylvania Railroad Company as civil engineer, but ceased professional work at the time of the death of his brother, Daniel, in May of 1895. He succeeded to the management of the *Cecil News*, which he has since published. He is a young man of high scholastic attainments, fitted for the responsible work of a newspaper editor. Not only is he an able and forcible writer, but as a business man he also possesses ability, and is qualified to carry on the management of the journal with success. He is unmarried and resides with his mother and sisters.

WILLIAM THOMAS BRICKLEY, a thorough and skillful farmer, and a business man of more than ordinary capacity, was born May 11, 1829, in the house which he still occupies, in District No. 6, Cecil County, and is a son of Andrew and Mary (Campbell) Brickley. The birth of both the father and grandfather, Joachim Brickley, occurred on the same farm, which was first owned and occupied by Joachim Brickley, Sr., the great-grandfather of our subject, who was of German descent. The family has been prominently identified with the entire growth and development of this region, and its members have been numbered among the leading and influential citizens of Cecil County.

During the War of 1812, Andrew Brickley faithfully served as a soldier in the American army. He never left the old home farm, which he continued to operate up to the time of his death, which occurred in 1870, when in his seventy-sixth year. The mother of our subject passed away in 1883, at the age of seventy-nine. Both were earnest Christian people and the mother a devout member of the Methodist Episcopal Church.

Our subject was an only child and was reared upon the home farm, which he assisted his father to cultivate and improve until the latter's death, when he assumed entire charge of the place. He acquired a good practical education in the common schools, and by reading and observation in later years has become a well-informed man. He successfully carries on general farming and is the owner of a valuable and well-improved tract of one hundred acres.

Mr. Brickley led to the marriage altar Miss Mary L. McCall, and to them was born one child, who died at the age of five years. The only nephew our subject has of the Brickley name is T. Ernest Brickley, son of Theodore Brickley. Mrs. Brickley is a consistent member of the Methodist Episcopal Church, and, like her husband, she is held in the highest regard by all who know her. He holds membership in the Grange, and is one of the most earnest adherents of the Republican party. No man takes a deeper interest in the prosperity of Cecil County, and it is safe to say that few have contributed in a larger degree to bring about this result.

JOHN G. WILLIAMS, clerk of the circuit court of Cecil County, was born near Principio, District No. 5, Cecil County, May 21, 1849. His father, Thomas Williams, was born on the same farm in 1818 and throughout life followed agricultural pursuits on the place where he was born. In 1882-83 he held the office of tax collector, but never cared for public positions, his inclinations being rather for the quiet retirement of home life. He died on the old homestead in April, 1891. His father, Jesse Williams, who spent his life principally upon the same farm, was a son of Thomas Williams, who came from Wales and founded the family in Cecil County.

The mother of our subject was Catherine Thompson, a native of Cecil County and daughter of John Thompson, of one of the old families here. She is still living on the old place. Two of her children died in infancy, but she had five sons and three daughters who attained mature years. William M., a mechanic, lives in Baltimore; Jesse T. is a wheelwright; Sarah L. is the wife of James Buchanan, a farmer; Lizzie married John H. Thompson, a farmer of this county; Joseph R. is a farmer and resides on the old homestead with his mother; Edward T. is a painter by trade; Rebecca is single and lives in Philadelphia. The eldest of the family is our subject, who received a good public-school education, thus becoming fitted for the practical activities of life. In youth, following the good old custom of learning a trade, he became a painter and paper-hanger, and was a reliable, efficient workman. In 1886 he served as a committee clerk in the state legislature, the first time on the house side, and in 1890 on the senate side, in that way gaining practical experience that was of great value to him in later years. In 1892 he entered the county clerk's office as deputy under James T. Graham, and continued in the position under the late William P. Howard, who died August 2, 1896. On the death of that gentleman, Mr. Williams was chosen to succeed him.

As a citizen Mr. Williams has ever maintained a deep interest in the welfare of the people and the progress of the county, and his labors have been instrumental in securing the advancement of local enterprises. Having been the incumbent of official positions, he has been situated so as to render the people valuable service, and with justice it may be said that few citizens have accomplished more for the development of the resources of the county than has he. He is unmarried, and resides in Elkton, but still considers the old place his home and spends each Sunday with his mother there. Fraternally he is connected with the Knights of Pythias. He has met with success, a fact that is due to his energy and common sense, and as a citizen and official he has the respect of all.

SAMUEL M. JOHNSON, ex-sheriff of Cecil County, is one of the representative farmers and prominent citizens of District No. 5. Believing that "from labor, health, from health, contentment springs," he has bent every energy toward perfecting his agricultural projects, and has proved himself eminently one of the best citizens of the community. He began his earthly career in District No. 5, Cecil County, March 25, 1836, and upon the same farm, his father, Benjamin F. Johnson, was also born. For many years the family has been prominently identified with the agricultural and industrial interests of the county, the grandfather, Charles Johnson, being one of its pioneer settlers. Here he established Johnson's grist and woolen mills, which later became known as the Crawford factory. For some time the father engaged in their operation, and he also successfully followed farming and school teaching. He spent his entire life in District No. 5. By his marriage with Miss Mary McCollough, he had three children: Joseph, now a contractor and builder residing in Baltimore; Charles L., who lives in Cecil County; and Samuel M., of this review.

Our subject was reared in much the usual manner of farmer boys, becoming a thorough and skillful agriculturist. His education was such as the district schools of the locality afforded and on laying aside his text books he devoted his entire time to his chosen calling. When a young man he assumed charge of the home farm, and afterward purchased a portion of the same, which he successfully operated until his election as sheriff, when he removed to Elkton. On the expiration of his term two years later, he took up his residence upon his present fine farm, which he has placed under a high state of cultivation and greatly improved.

On attaining to man's estate, Mr. Johnson married Miss Caroline Nowland, and to them were born five children: Benjamin F., now station agent at Perryman, Harford County, Md.; Otho, who is a merchant of the same place; Charles H., teller in the Second National Bank of Elkton; George A. M., a telegraph operator, connected with the Philadelphia, Wilmington & Baltimore Railroad; and William W., who is engaged with his brother Otho in business.

Since the organization of the Republican party, Mr. Johnson has been one of its ardent supporters, and on that ticket was elected sheriff of Cecil County in 1888. He proved a most efficient and satisfactory official, and left office as he had entered it, with the respect and confidence of all who know him.

J T. BROWN, M. D., one of the leading physicians and surgeons of Cecil County, residing in District No. 6, is a native of this county, and was born February 4, 1844, in District No. 9, but when quite small he accompanied his family on their removal to Chester County, Pa. There he grew to manhood and acquired his primary education in the public schools. He completed his literary training, however, in the Nottingham Academy, and at the age of eighteen began the study of medicine with Dr. Worthington, of Westchester, Pa., with whom he remained for one year. Going to Philadelphia, he continued the preparation for his chosen profession under the direction of Drs. Levick and Hunt, and in 1866 graduated from the medical department of the University of Pennsylvania.

Dr. Brown at once opened an office in the village of Principio, Cecil County, Md., where he remained until 1879. He then purchased his present farm of sixty-eight acres in District No. 6, and in connection with its cultivation still continues the prosecution of his profession. He enjoys a large and lucrative practice and has met with excellent success in the treatment of the various cases that have been placed in his care. For thirty-one years he has been identified with the medical fraternity of Cecil County and he stands deservedly high among his professional brethren.

In 1866 Dr. Brown was united in marriage with Miss Martha Touchton, by whom he has three children: Clara, now the wife of Clifton Miller, of Woodlawn, Md.; Howard, a medical student of the University of Richmond, Va.; and John F., who is now studying dentistry. The doctor is an honored and prominent member of the Cecil County Medical Society, is a pronounced Democrat in politics, and both he and his wife are active members of the Methodist Episcopal Church. Both have the warmest esteem of the entire community for their many admirable virtues and for their genial manners.

HON. JAMES D. WATTERS. Ever since society was organized its enemies have lived, and to enforce laws calculated to protect mankind from the doers of evil has always been a serious duty of the judge. The philosopher and the social reformer may indulge in speculations as to the causes of vice and lawlessness, but, dealing with these grave social problems in a practical as well as a beneficent spirit, it has been the aim of the makers of law to devise such measures as will punish the individual law breaker as well as deter his fellows from like wrongdoing. The office of the judge who faithfully discharges his duties and permits no innocent man to suffer and no guilty man to escape, is one of honor and dignity. No other place within the gift of the people is more conspicuous and important. It should be filled by a lawyer of unquestioned ability, as well as sterling integrity, and in the election of James D. Watters to the bench the people have secured an intelligent, energetic and faithful officer, who has proved a terror to wrong doers, not only because it is his duty to do so, but because he has no sympathy with crime or criminal. Withal he is humane and just, and the scales of justice in his hand are balanced with care and circumspection.

Judge Watters was born in Harford County, Md., six or seven miles from Bel Air, January 11, 1834, a son of Henry G. and Mary (Clendenin) Watters, and a grandson of John Clendenin. His paternal grandfather, as well as his father, was born in the same place as himself, and both were worthy tillers of the soil. Henry G. Watters was a leader in the affairs of his section, and held the office of county commissioner and other official positions of responsibility. He was a soldier of the War of 1812 and a worthy member of the Methodist Episcopal Church, with which he and his family were the first to unite in this section. He died in 1865. One of the ancestors of Judge Watters, William Watters, was the first native American Methodist Episcopal minister in this country.

Judge Watters was one of four children. His brother, Dr. John H. Watters, was a young man of much promise and bright prospects. He went to St. Louis, became a professor in a medical college of that city, but at the breaking out of the Civil War he entered the Confederate service as a surgeon, in which capacity he served throughout the war. He died in 1872. The other brother, Godfrey Watters, was a farmer and is now deceased. The sister is still living. The early life of Judge Watters was spent in healthful farm work and in attending the district schools. After a time he entered Bel Air Academy, then Dickinson College, of Carlisle, Pa., and from the latter institution graduated in 1856 with the degree of A. B. For one year thereafter he was tutor in Latin and Greek in Brocket's school at Alexandria, Va., and afterward for one year taught a small private school in Chester County, Pa.

In the latter part of 1858 Mr. Watters made his way to St. Louis, where he entered the law office of Krum & Harding, and in January,

1861, was admitted to the bar. In the summer of that year he returned to Harford County, Md., and the following year joined the First Virginia Confederate Regiment, but was soon transferred to the Maryland Cavalry, under Col. Ridgeley Brown. In 1864 he was made lieutenant, and this position he held until the close of the war, when he returned to Harford County and commenced the practice of law. In 1868, in company with William Bauldin, he established the *Harford Democrat*, and this he edited until 1871, at which time he was elected to the office of judge of the circuit court, and has ever since been on the bench. This fact alone would be sufficient to illustrate his competence and popularity without further remark.

In 1868 Judge Watters married Miss Fannie H., daughter of John A. Munnikhuysen, of this county, and they have one child, Anna M., a student at the Woman's College of Baltimore. Judge Watters is a prominent Mason. During the winter season, while his daughter is at school, he makes his home in Baltimore, while his summers are spent at Bel Air.

JAMES A. GRIER, who was a resident and business man of Washington for a quarter of a century, has for some time made his home in Harford County, residing with his son, who owns a valuable farm of one hundred and thirty acres situated in District No. 3. In whatever line of work he has engaged, his honorable and straightforward record has brought him many friends. Ever true to each duty, he has through his long life maintained the confidence of all with whom he has been brought in contact, either through business or social relations.

The first representative of the Grier family who made settlement in the United States was James Grier, son of John, and father of our subject. From his native country, Ireland, he crossed the ocean to this country and established his home in Chester County, Pa., where he afterward engaged in farming, and also carried on a pottery near Oxford, Pa. His death occurred on the home farm in Chester County when he was eighty-two years of age. Twice married, his first wife, who was in maidenhood Elizabeth Patterson, bore him five children, as follows: Eliza and J. Patterson, deceased; Mrs. Helen Johnson, of Saratoga, N.Y.; Caroline, deceased; and James A., who was born February 26, 1817, and was bereft of a mother's care a few days afterward, his mother passing away March 4. The second marriage of James Grier united him with Martha Hindman, and they had the following children: Melinda, wife of John Hooker; Franklin, deceased; Mary Ann; Martha, who is married and lives in Illinois; William, also a resident of Illinois; and Thomas, formerly of Martin's Ferry, Va., but now deceased.

In his native place, Chester County, Pa., the subject of this biography was reared and educated. At the age of sixteen he began an apprenticeship to the trade of a carpenter in Philadelphia, and at the expiration of his term of three years he continued in that city, following his trade for two years. He then went to Baltimore County, settling near Towson, where he was similarly employed a number of years. Later he removed to Washington, where he remained about twenty-five years, being there during the entire period of the war. In 1861 he built for Barnett Clark the house where he now resides, which is the property of John P. Grier, and hither he removed from Washington in 1894.

Mr. Grier married Mary Jane Thomas, of Harford County. Nine children were born of their union, namely: Sultina, wife of J. T. Harkins; Mortimer, deceased; James, who makes his home in Winchester, Va.; John P., a prosperous farmer, with whom our subject resides; Ralph, who resides in Washington; Mary, who married Edgar Tuchton; Lorenzo, of Chestnut Hill; Elmore, residing in this district; and Emantos, now in Colorado. Fraternally Mr. Grier is connected with Mt. Ararat Lodge of Masons, at Bel Air, and in the days before the war he was associated with the Independent Order of Odd Fellows, but has not continued his membership. An active worker in the Methodist Protestant Church, he has been superintendent and a teacher in the Sunday-school for some time, and maintains a deep interest in every department of church work. His duties of citizenship have always been faithfully performed.

ABEL MEARNS. Cecil County lost one of its best citizens when Abel Mearns died here in 1848. His life had been replete with useful deeds, deeds which have benefited his fellow-men and materially added to the resources of the county in whose advancement he took such pride. As he was not an old man when he died, he might reasonably have anticipated many more years of activity and years in which to enjoy the fruits of his constant labors. Born in District No. 9, where his entire life was passed, he had no factitious aids for advancement, but at an early age became inured to habits of industry and frugality. He learned, too, that there is no royal road to wealth in the United States, but he had the advantage of becoming imbued with the thought that men may become the architects of their own fortunes. With such an incentive to success, he labored diligently and perseveringly in the cultivation of his property and the management of his financial interests.

The son of Andrew Mearns, a native of Ireland and a farmer of Cecil County, the subject of this memoir was reared on the home farm and was early anxious to assist in its cultivation. The estate purchased by his father was very large, but subsequent division among the heirs has materially reduced the acreage of the old homestead, which now contains one hundred and thirty-two acres. As soon as he reached manhood he began farming for himself and as he was energetic he accumulated a competency in his chosen occupation. In politics he was a Democrat, but not active.

Mr. Mearns was happiest in his home, a loving wife and devoted children forming the household to which he could always turn for sympathy amid discouragements and with whom he could rejoice in prosperity. His wife, Mary, was a daughter of Robert Cameron, and eleven children were born to them, nine of whom attained mature years, and six are living, as follows: Frances, Vianna and Semilia, who reside at the old homestead; Josephine, who lives in Wilmington, Del.; Andrew F. and Robert A., who are farmers of District No. 9. The most of the children are connected with the Presbyterian Church.

Personally Mr. Mearns was a man of companionable nature, genial and kind in his intercourse with all. He was ever ready to respond to the calls of his fellow-men in any way that he could be of assistance. This district continued to be his home until his death, at the age of fifty-one years, and he was always interested in any measure that tended to enlarge the local resources. His life was not an exciting or eventful one, but was marked by simple acts of kindness and by strict integrity of character. He was less a man of words than of actions, and when he spoke it was for a purpose and with the firmness of convictions formed after careful study. He is affectionately remembered by the many who held him in the highest esteem.

LAFAYETTE BRADLEY, who resides in District No. 6, Cecil County, is one of the highly esteemed citizens of the community, and devotes his energies to general farming. He is a native of the neighboring state of Pennsylvania, his birth having occured in Chester County, near the town of West Chester, in 1824. He there lived until four years of age, when, on the death of his father, he was taken to Cochranville, the same county, and was there reared on a farm, early becoming familiar with all the duties that fall to the lot of the agriculturist. His education was acquired in both the common and subscription schools, and reading, experience and observation in later years have made him a well-informed man. He remained with the family on the farm until twenty-one years of age, and then followed farming and butchering on his own account. In 1869 he removed to Rowlandsville, where for the long period of twenty-two years he served as station agent, discharging his duties with promptness and ability, and to the satisfaction of all concerned. On the expiration of that period he purchased his present farming property in District No. 6, and since 1891 has continuously made his home thereon.

Mr. Bradley was united in marriage with Miss Nancy J. Smith, and their union has been blessed with a family of five children: Ira, who has charge of the station at Rowlandsville; Sarah C., Alfonso, Emma and Lizzie. Prompted by a spirit of patriotism, Mr. Bradley entered the Union service during the Civil War, enlisting in 1864 as a private of the Seventh Pennsylvania Cavalry, in which he served for one year. He was a brave and loyal soldier, and is alike true to his duties of citizenship in days of peace as he was in the time of war, when he followed the old flag on southern battlefields. His long service as station agent at Rowlandsville made him widely known in Cecil County, and his sterling worth gained him the high regard of all with whom he came in contact.

R. E. BROMWELL, M. D. Prominent among the professional men and leading citizens of Cecil County is this gentleman, whose name is found high on the rolls of the leading medical practitioners of northern Maryland. Those sterling qualities of character which everywhere command respect have brought to him the highest regard, and he has made an untarnished record and unspotted reputation as a business man.

The doctor was born on a farm which is still his home, in District No. 7, Cecil County, February 28, 1827, and is a son of William Bromwell, a native of Philadelphia, who spent the greater part of his life in Baltimore. The grandfather, also named William, resided for many years in Cecil County. The father was long engaged in the lumber business in Baltimore and in 1825 came to Cecil County, where he purchased the old homestead now owned by the doctor. He died in 1827, at the age of forty-nine, and his wife passed away in 1858, aged sixty-six years. They were the parents of eight children, namely: George, Thomas, Martha, Mary, Beulah, Deborah, Samuel and Robert.

Dr. Bromwell, the only survivor of this family, was reared on a farm and acquired his primary education in the common schools, after which he attended the West Nottingham Academy. When eighteen years of age he began teaching, and for eighteen months followed that profession. In the meantime he commenced reading medicine under the direction of Dr. Henry B. Broughton, and in 1848 entered the medical department of the University of Maryland, where, on the completion of a thorough course, he graduated in the class of 1850. In the winter of 1851 he pursued a post-graduate course in the same institution, and throughout his career he has been a close student of his profession, gaining by his extensive reading and study a comprehensive and accurate knowledge of the science of medicine. From the beginning he has enjoyed a large practice, and his skill and ability have gained him high rank among his professional brethren. He has always made his home upon his farm, which comprises seventy-five acres of rich and arable land, and personally superintends its cultivation.

Dr. Bromwell was married in 1860 to Miss Josephine Evans, daughter of Levi H. Evans. They had three children. Mary, the eldest, died at the age of ten years. William is a graduate of Johns Hopkins University, in which he also took a post-graduate course with the degree of Ph. D., and is now a professor of chemistry. Florence is a graduate of Mrs. Carey's College and Southern Home School of Baltimore. The doctor's home is noted for its hospitality, and forms the center of a cultured society circle. He is a member of the Cecil County Medical Society. In politics he is a Democrat, and on that ticket was elected county commissioner in 1873. In all places and under all circumstances he is loyal to truth, honor and right, justly valuing his own self-respect as infinitely more to be preferred than wealth, fame and position. In those finer traits of character which combine to form that which we term friendship he is royally endowed.

ELI S. SENTMAN. Strong hands, a clear head, tireless energy, and a correct idea of the importance of economy and honesty to the young man who seeks financial success, constituted the sum total of Mr. Sentman's capital at the beginning of his business career. The prosperity which he has gained demonstrates and emphasizes the value of such endowments. He is now the owner of a well-improved farm in District No. 7, Cecil County, where he makes his home; also several houses in Perryville, this county, and considerable real estate. In addition, he has gained a reputation as one of the most reliable contractors in northern Maryland. Thoroughly familiar with the carpenter's trade and reliable and honest in even the smallest details, his services are sought not only in this county, but elsewhere. Among the contracts he has had may be mentioned those for several large business blocks and residences in Philadelphia, a factory at Marion, Ind., the remodeling of the opera house at Havre de Grace, and the building of the schoolhouse at the same place, the latter costing $20,000; Isaac Hecht's new hotel; also architect and builder of New Myer's store, and some of the principal stores and dwelling houses of Harford and Cecil Counties.

The birth of Eli S. Sentman occurred near New London, Chester County, Pa., April 25, 1833, his parents being Michael and Catherine (McMillan) Sentman, natives, respectively, of Berks and Chester Counties. His father, when quite small, accompanied his parents to Chester County, where he engaged in farming until 1838, and then came to Cecil County. Here he operated as a renter until he died, at eighty-two years. During the War of 1812 he served in the defense of Baltimore, and was there at the time Ross was killed. Politically he was a stanch Democrat. His father, Lawrence Sentman, was born in Lorraine, Germany, whence at the age of eighteen he came to America with a brother and settled in Berks County, purchasing a farm there. The remainder of his life was given to farm work, with the exception of the eight years that he served in the colonial army under Capt. Alexander. He was present at the battle of Brandywine and at other struggles that made the Revolutionary War notable. His death occurred when he was fifty-six years of age.

The mother of our subject was a daughter of John McCauley, a native of Dublin, Ireland, who emigrated to America and settled in Pennsylvania just six weeks before his daughter was born. She died at the age of eighty-four, and was survived by her entire family of nine children, the youngest of whom was then thirty-five years of age. John, the eldest, died when seventy; Lawrence was sixty-five when he passed away; Adelia, Mrs. George Peterson, was about sixty-three at the time of her death. Mary Ellen married Jonathan Sentman; Robert attained threescore and ten years; Margaret A. is the wife of John Ewing; Evan G. owns and occupies a farm at Principio, Cecil County; Eli S. is the next to the youngest of the family; Phineas B. resides in District No. 7, Cecil County.

When eighteen years of age our subject began to learn the carpenter's trade and served an apprenticeship of three years, after which he entered the employ of the Philadelphia, Wilmington & Baltimore Railroad Company, and was foreman for them about two years. Since that time he has engaged in contracting. April 18, 1855, he married Sophia Jackson, of Cecil County. They have seven children, namely: Robert Newton, an employe of the Baltimore & Ohio Railroad Company; Norman M., a carpenter, employed as foreman for his father; Alderman B., by trade a ship joiner and car builder; Laura M., wife of William Blackson; Victor, a carpenter, connected with his father in business; Alexander J., who is engineer on the Philadelphia, Wilmington & Baltimore Railroad; and Charles Arthur, a painter by occupation.

While Mr. Sentman has been conservative in business matters, yet he is not too much so, but is quick to see an advantage to be gained by investment. All his business transactions are characterized by the strictest integrity and the most scrupulous honesty. A Democrat in politics, he was commissioner of Cecil County in 1884-85, but with that exception has refused public office. Fraternally he is identified with Harmony Lodge No. 53, A. F. & A. M., at Port Deposit. Personally he is a man of prepossessing appearance, with a face so free from the usual indications of age that few would suppose him to be as old as he really is. In all respects he is an exemplary citizen. Simple in his tastes and devoted to his interesting family, he finds his greatest happiness in the quietude of his home circle. He is a thorough master of his business and interested in anything looking toward its advancement.

STEPHEN ATKINSON. For many years Mr. Atkinson has enjoyed a reputation as a substantial farmer and progressive citizen. In that part of Cecil County where he makes his home he is well and favorably known, and his long experience in agricultural affairs renders his judgment sound and his advice valuable. While his farm is not as large as many others in the county, it is so well improved that it brings the owner a fair income. The eighty-five acres comprising the place are situated in District No. 5, and, during the years they have been in the possession of the present proprietor, have been placed under first-class cultivation.

Alexander Atkinson, father of our subject, was born and reared in Ireland, whence in young manhood he emigrated to the United States and settled in Cecil County. His education was a good one, and he utilized it in his work as a school teacher, having charge of a school near Rising Sun. The broad information he possessed upon all topics of general interest rendered him a most companionable man, and his friends were many in this locality. The family of which he was a member ranked among the influential people in Ireland and a vast fortune in that country came to them, his share in the property being considerable. He was preparing to return to his native land to prove his claim to the estate, but was taken ill and soon afterward died, this being about 1825. Later the family attempted to secure the property, but every effort was futile. He was a man of sincere Christian belief and held membership in the Methodist Church. By his marriage to Elizabeth Mahoney he had eight children, but Stephen alone survives.

At the home farm in District No. 5, Cecil County, the subject of this sketch was born July 17, 1820. During boyhood years he attended school in the winter months, when work on the farm was impossible, but his summers were devoted to tilling the soil and harvesting the grain. Inheriting from his father a fondness for books and a desire for knowledge, he took advantage of every opportunity for increasing his fund of information, and is now well posted upon topics of historical and scientific nature. At the age of eighteen he secured employment as a farm hand, and saved his earnings until he had a sufficient amount to enable him to purchase property for himself. About 1855 he bought the place where he has since engaged in general farming. He has never mingled in public affairs and aside from voting the Democratic ticket has taken no part in local elections. In the Methodist Protestant Church he has been class leader and trustee for many years.

June 23, 1842, occurred the marriage of Mr. Atkinson and Hannah Maria, daughter of William Ramsey, of Bay View, Cecil County. Of the children that were born to this union, all but two are living. They are named as follows: Theresa, wife of Oliver Logan, a resident of District No. 5; William, who makes his home at Porter's Bridge, in District No. 8; Wesley, living in Pennsylvania; Martha Jane, wife of

John D. Barrett, of Port Deposit; Norris M., who lives near the old homestead; Benjamin T., living near his father's place; Ida; Emma, wife of I. Corsett, of North East; and Thompson R., who resides at Childs Station, this county. Those deceased are Stephen John and Millard R.

WILLIAM H. BOOTH was born May 18, 1853, in District No. 2, Cecil County, in what is called Back Creek Neck, near Chesapeake City. The family of which he is a member originated in England, the first of the name in this country being his grandparents. In 1829 they crossed the Atlantic, accompanied by eleven children, two others remaining in England, the oldest son, James, and a daughter. James spent his entire life in his native land, where he died, unmarried, at the age of ninety; the sister also died, unmarried, when about ninety years old. Of the eleven children that came to the United States, John was the oldest, and he engaged in agricultural pursuits until his death, which occurred near Leeds; Henry was a farmer in Chester County, Pa.; Charles was a miller and made his home in Chester, Pa.; William owned and cultivated a farm in Harford County, Md.; Mary Ann, who was twice married, was first the wife of Moses Whitworth, and afterward married David Fulton, dying near Leeds; Adam was a commission merchant in Baltimore, and was killed during the riots at the breaking out of the Civil War; George went to Pittsburg, Pa., where his descendants now live; Richard, who went to California in 1849, was reported to have made a fortune, but all trace of his whereabouts was lost; of Isaac, too, nothing is now known. The father of this family was a weaver in England, where he invented, and put in operation, in a crude way, the first power mill for weaving cloth. Instead of being regarded as a public benefactor, he was persecuted by all the weavers of his locality, and his buildings were burned down, this doubtless being one of the reasons that led him to emigrate to America. He continued weaving after his settlement in the United States, until advancing years rendered constant labor impossible. He died at the age of eighty-seven, and his wife, Elizabeth (Carter) Booth, when eighty-five.

The father of our subject, Joseph Booth, was born in Lancashire, England, April 9, 1811, and accompanied his parents to America in 1829. For many years he resided on the farm now owned and occupied by our subject, and here he engaged in farming and stock-raising. In addition, he was an extensive dealer in ice, and a large manufacturer of ice cream. His was a busy and useful life, and he maintained his activities until he passed away, December 20, 1891. The lady whom he married was Barbara Ann Schuh, who was born in Pennsylvania in 1820, and died in 1884. She had a brother, Emanuel, who entered the Union army as a member of the Third New Jersey Infantry and was killed in the two days' fight at the battle of Gettysburg, Pa.; she also had one sister, Hannah, Mrs. Michael Barry, who resided at Dobson's Mill, near Philadelphia, until her death, in 1879. Their father, Emanuel G. Schuh, was born in Germany, and at an early age accompanied his parents to America, settling in Philadelphia, where he was apprenticed to Barnard McMann, the well-known seedsman, and learned the gardening business, which he afterward followed. His last days were spent in Elkton and he died here September 3, 1880, at the age of eighty-four.

Of the eleven children of Joseph and Barbara Booth, we note the following: Hannah, born February 20, 1840, became the wife of William Quinn, of Philadelphia, and after his death married Robert Hamilton, of the same city. John E., who enlisted in the Union army in 1863, as a member of Parnell's Cavalry of Wilmington, Del., was killed by a sharpshooter in front of Petersburg June 22, 1864. Lydia Ann is unmarried and resides in Elkton. Ann Elizabeth died at the age of two years. George, born October 26, 1848, married, December 15, 1881, Mrs. H. M. Mack, of Philadelphia, and they have two children living, Edgar and Sadie; his home is now in Elkton, where he has been a prominent business man.

Isaac was born in 1850 and died in 1852. Mary Jeannette is married and has one son. Josephine is the wife of George W. Revell, a hatter in Baltimore, and they have two children, Leon L. F. and Josephine M. William H., of Elkton, in 1894 married Miss Ellen D., daughter of the late Daniel Bratton and sister of W. D. Bratton, of the *Cecil News;* they have two children, Susan Bratton and Henrietta. Joseph R. and Algemine D. both died young.

The homestead of fifty-seven acres William H. Booth has purchased, and in addition to the cultivation of this property he manufactures ice cream on a large scale, making about thirty-five hundred gallons a season. Politically he is independent. The family is identified with the Presbyterian Church.

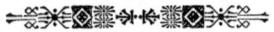

WILLIAM R. COOLEY, deceased, was for many years a leading and influential citizen of Cecil County. His sterling worth, his straightforward and honorable business methods and his many excellent traits of character commended him to the confidence and respect of all, and at his death the entire community recognized that a most valuable citizen had passed from their midst. He belonged to one of the old and honored families of the county, and was born on the Cooley homestead in 1847. His grandfather, John Cooley, was born in the vicinity of Manchester, N. H., and was the first of the name to locate in Maryland. He was of French lineage.

Corbin Cooley, the father of our subject, was born in Harford County, near Darlington, and in ante-bellum days was a large slave-owner and a very prominent and influential planter. One of his old slaves, Uncle George, as he is called, still lives with the family, and is now one hundred years of age. Corbin Cooley was united in marriage with Miss Mary Shaw, whose birth occurred almost within the shadow of Westminster Abbey, London, England. She crossed the Atlantic from England to America when seven years of age, and by her marriage she became the mother of eight children, four of whom are now living, namely: J. P., of South Dakota; Dr. C. O., of Minnesota; Emma, wife of D. W. Hutchinson, of Downingtown, Pa.; and Mary, wife of R. L. Christie, of Colora. The father of this family died on the old homestead November 13, 1876, at the age of seventy-six years. He gave his political support to the Democracy and did all in his power to promote its growth and insure its success, but never held public office.

William R. Cooley was liberally educated, pursuing his studies in West Nottingham Academy. He remained at home until about 1869, when he went to South Dakota, where he engaged in farming for one year, and in speculating in government land. In 1870, however, he returned to the old family homestead, where he lived until called to his final rest. He owned two hundred acres of rich and arable land, and was a progressive and enterprising farmer, whose careful supervision was indicated by the neat and thrifty appearance of his place. He dealt largely in stock, buying and selling cattle on an extensive scale, and his operations in this direction were very successful. By his energy, perseverance and fine business ability he was enabled to secure an ample competence. Systematic and methodical in business, his sagacity, keen discrimination and sound judgment made him one of the prosperous agriculturists and stock dealers of his county.

On the 8th of October, 1878, Mr. Cooley was united in marriage with Miss Charlotte Russell, daughter of Edward T. Russell, who belonged to one of the old families of Cecil County. Her mother was a descendant of the Ewing family, whose identification with the interests of northern Maryland dated back to the days of the Indian wars. Mr. and Mrs. Cooley had two children, Jenzie Coulson and Marion Russell.

Mr. Cooley exercised his right of franchise in support of the Democracy, and in 1885 was elected county commissioner, acceptably and faithfully serving in that capacity for three years. He was a member of the Farmers' Club, the Home Literary Society, and one of the leading members of the Nottingham Presbyterian Church. Cecil

County is indebted to him for the efforts he put forth on her behalf. Social, educational and moral interests were promoted by him, and anything that tended to uplift and benefit humanity secured his hearty co-operation. He was a true citizen, a good neighbor, a faithful friend and a loving husband and father, and all who knew him deeply mourned his death.

EDWIN E. EWING, editor and proprietor of the *Midland Journal*, of Rising Sun, is conducting his paper with signal success and ability, and also does an extensive business in job printing. He is a native of Cecil County, born in District No. 8, in 1824, and is a worthy representative of one of the prominent pioneer families of Maryland. His great-grandfather, Joshua Ewing, was a native of Scotland, and on crossing the Atlantic with his brother Nathaniel, he settled in District No. 8, Cecil County. He was a son of William Ewing, who spent his active life amid the beautiful hills of Scotland. Patrick Ewing, the grandfather of our subject, became one of the prominent and influential citizens of Cecil County, and for many years served as squire of Octoraro Hundred, as it was then called, now District No. 8. When the colonies resolved to throw off the yoke of British oppression he joined their ranks and was commissioned captain in the continental army.

Patrick Ewing, Jr., the father of Edwin E., was one of the representative and leading farmers of Cecil County, who took quite a prominent part in public affairs and served as county commissioner for some time. In politics he was a Jacksonian Democrat. His death occurred in 1864. As a companion on life's journey he chose Miss Isabella Evans, of Lancaster County, Pa., whose father was a prominent farmer, banker and merchant of that county. By their marriage they became the parents of seven children: Edwin E., of this review; Theodore, who resides on the old homestead in District No. 8, Cecil County; William P., a resident of New York; Jane Anne, of this district; Rebecca F. M., widow of W. J. Evans, and a resident of Rising Sun; E. Caroline, twin sister of Rebecca, and the wife of J. Nelson Black, of Charlestown, District No. 5, Cecil County; and Margaret I., wife of James Evans.

The boyhood and youth of Edwin E. Ewing were spent in attending school during the winter months and in assisting in the labors of the farm during the summer season until sixteen years of age, when he began devoting his entire attention to agricultural pursuits, remaining with his father until 1861. He then went to Elkton, where he purchased the *Cecil Whig*, an old-established newspaper, and carried on the printing and newspaper business for fifteen years. On selling out in 1876, he went to Topeka, Kan., where he conducted a grocery store for a short time and then, in partnership with Maj. J. K. Hudson, he purchased the *Kansas Farmer*, which they conducted until 1880. They also established the *Daily Capital*, which is still one of the best papers of that city. At the end of three years Mr. Ewing sold out his interest, and removed to Highlands, N. C., where he established the *Blue Ridge Enterprise*, a weekly journal. Three years later he returned to Rising Sun, Cecil County, and with his three sons purchased the *Rising Sun Journal* in 1885. They still conduct that paper, but have changed the name to the *Midland Journal*, which is published weekly, and is a bright, spicy paper. They also carry on general job printing and publishing. The journal has an excellent circulation, a good advertising list, and the editorials show deep culture and sound common sense.

In 1863 Mr. Ewing married Miss Clara Vaughan, of Camden, N. J., a daughter of Dr. Vaughan, and one daughter blessed this union, Clara, now the wife of George Beeson, of Columbus, Ohio. After the death of his first wife Mr. Ewing wedded Miss Emma McMurphy, of Elkton. They have three sons: Cecil, Evans and Halus, who are all in business with their father and are numbered among the steady-going and most reliable young men of Rising Sun. The family attend the Presbyterian Church. In his political affiliations Mr. Ewing is a Populist, and

WILLIAM HOPE.

he is an influential and prominent member of Cecil Grange, No. 3, of Rising Sun. During the Civil War he served as deputy assessor of internal revenue for his district, but he has never cared for the honors or emoluments of public office.

WILLIAM HOPE. This family was founded in America by James Hope, great-grandfather of the subject of this sketch, and a native of Scotland, whence in an early day he emigrated to this country, settling in Bucks County, Pa. In the development of a farm there, he spent a number of years. About 1771 he crossed the state line into Maryland, and established his home in Harford County, where he remained until death. A portion of his farm he donated to the Presbyterian Church for a building site and graveyard, and upon the lot now stands Bethel Church, a fine stone edifice, and the third house of worship that has been erected on the same site.

Thomas Hope, grandfather of our subject, was born in Bucks County, Pa., whence he came to Harford County and engaged in agricultural pursuits. He died March 20, 1815, at the age of seventy-two, and was laid to rest in the Bethel Cemetery. Thomas Hope, Jr., our subject's father, was born in Harford County, and was a man of prominence here, which fact is proved by his continuous service as a member of thirteen sessions of the Maryland legislature. During the War of 1812 he served in the American army. Farming was his occupation, and in it he was very successful, accumulating a large property. He married Catherine Hutchins, who was born in Baltimore County, Md., and unto their union were born eight children, of whom William and Ellen are the only survivors.

Near the farm which he now owns, in District No. 4, Harford County, the subject of this sketch was born January 9, 1818. Here he was educated, and here he has been content to spend his entire life thus far. Like his forefathers, he is a farmer, and the proprietor of large landed interests, his home place consisting of one hundred and thirty-four well-improved acres. In politics he has always been a Democrat of the "strictest sect," the principles and aims of his party ever being dear to his heart, and anything that seems to be an abandonment of them receives from him a most strenuous opposition. The only office he has ever held was that of state hay weigher in the city of Baltimore, to which he was appointed by Gov. Philip Thomas in 1843, serving for two years. He has never cared for official positions. It has always been characteristic of him to seek retirement rather than publicity, and for that reason he never occupied the public positions he was so well qualified to fill. From his youth he has been a professor of the Christian religion, and in the Presbyterian Church for years has been a member of the board of elders.

At the age of twenty-four Mr. Hope married Elizabeth E. Pocock, who was born in this district, the descendant of English ancestors who settled in America at a very early period of its history. She was a woman of many excellent qualities of head and heart, and attracted friends in every circle. In religious belief she was identified with Bethel Presbyterian Church. Her death occurred July 26, 1891, at the age of seventy-six, and was deeply mourned by him whose loving companion she had been through so many years.

JOHN S. MITCHELL. Those who have engaged in the canning business in Harford County have found it so profitable that without doubt it will soon become a very important industry, adding thousands of dollars to the annual incomes of the people. The subject of this article, and his brother, E. Lewis, are among the most extensive growers and canners of sweet corn in the county, and that they have found the business remunerative is shown by their present prosperity. Their possessions aggregate about five hundred and fifty acres, subdivided into four farms, all of the land being excellent and under cultivation. Their home farm, situated in District No. 2, is well improved, containing all the buildings necessary to a first-class estate, and in addition a small canning factory. Here the visitor will also notice some fine trotting horses, which are being raised for the market and the turf.

The father of our subject, Evan, was a son of Parker Mitchell, who was born in Harford County and spent his entire life upon a farm here. Evan was born in District No. 2 and was also an agriculturist by occupation, meeting with fair success in his ventures. His death occurred when he was sixty-four years of age. He was a man of considerable influence among his neighbors, who held him in the highest respect for his commendable traits of character. The Democratic principles received his support at the polls, but he did not take an active part in politics. His wife, who bore the maiden name of Frances Morgan, was born in Harford County and died here in 1866, when fifty-five years of age. Their family consisted of six children, named as follows: Thomas P., a farmer of District No. 2; Hannah J., who died at eighteen years; E. Lewis, who is in partnership with our subject in farming and the canning business, and is unmarried, making his home with his brother, John S.; Frances, who died at five years; and Morgan, a prominent farmer and canner residing in this district.

Born in this district in June, 1848, our subject remained at home, assisting in the management of the property until the death of his father in 1872, when he and his brother, E. Lewis, purchased the interests of the other heirs in the estate. They still own the place, and from time to time have added to their possessions until they now own four good farms. In all their enterprises they display cautious judgment, yet are not too conservative, having in their dispositions a happy medium between recklessness and business timidity. The success which they have already met is doubtless but a promise of what the future will bring to them in the management of their property and business, and unless something unexpected intervenes, it may safely be predicted that they will become wealthy.

In 1879 Mr. Mitchell married Sallie S., daughter of Lewis Todd, of District No. 2. They are members of the Grove Presbyterian Church and take an interest in its work. Their family consists of two sons, Howard and Malcolm. In matters political Mr. Mitchell always sympathizes with the Democratic party and votes for the men and measures it advocates. Fraternally he is connected with Aberdeen Lodge No. 187, A. F. & A. M.

WILLIAM H. EDER. The prosperity of a place is dependent upon the growth and development of its real-estate interests, and it is therefore a matter of the highest importance that these should be in the hands of reliable, energetic and efficient business men, who will use their influence, not alone for selfish ends, but to secure the improvement of the city. It may safely be said of the subject of this article that he has materially assisted in improving the condition of Elkton and in promoting its real-estate interests. Through his efforts he has contributed to the prosperity of the village and is therefore entitled to a place among its public-spirited citizens.

On a farm situated on the Bethlehem pike, twenty-one miles from Philadelphia, in Montgomery County, Pa., the subject of our sketch was born July 24, 1818. The family of which he is a member came to this country from Germany and settled in Pennsylvania, where his grandfather, Mathias Eder, was a farmer, four miles from Williamsport. His several sons became scattered in different parts of the United States, and nothing is known of their descendants by the branch of the family to which our subject belongs. One son, John, was born in Berks County, Pa., in 1785, became a carpenter, and followed that occupation in Montgomery County until his death, in 1852. For many years he was captain of militia there. He was a soldier in the War of 1812, for which services his widow was given a warrant for one hundred and sixty acres of government land.

The mother of our subject, Sarah, was a daughter of Col. William Hines, a Revolutionary hero, and was of Irish descent. The founder of the family in America, Matthew Hines, who came to this country from Ireland in 1720, was the son of Lord Matthew Hines, member of the Irish parliament from 1697 to 1710. Matthew Hines first settled at Whitemarsh, where he married Mrs. Ann Simpson, and became in time the owner of about five hundred acres of land. His stepson, John Simpson, was the grandfather of Gen. Ulysses S. Grant. Our subject's grandfather was a lieutenant in Captain Roberts' company of volunteers, later became colonel in command of a regiment of volunteers and as such served during the invasion of Philadelphia by the British. He died January 17, 1830, at the age of eighty. Dr. A. J. Hines, of Doylestown, Pa., is the only one of his sons now living. The mother of our subject died in 1867, at the age of eighty-one. She had three sons and an only daughter, Mary, who died at the age of eighteen years. One of the sons, Mathias, a carpenter, died in 1876; another son, John Q., now a resident of Lomanda Park, near Los Angeles, Cal., was for many years in the railroad postal service between New York and Washington.

With no aids to success other than a limited education and good health, the subject of this notice began for himself when quite young. His first work was as a clerk. In 1848 he came to Elkton, where he was engaged in the building business for twenty-one years. In 1861 he entered the United States railroad mail service, being one of the first mail agents appointed under the new system. He continued in the service between New York and Washington continuously from 1861 to 1883, when he resigned. Since that time he has been extensively engaged in the real-estate and insurance business in Elkton. He is a member of the board of managers of the Cecil County Mutual Fire Insurance Company and a member of the executive board. Other local enterprises receive his assistance, among them the Elkton Cemetery Association, of which he is a member. For thirty years he has been a trustee of the Methodist Episcopal Church and secretary of the board. In 1866 he was made a Mason, and is now the oldest member of Elkton Lodge. In 1852 he married Sarah, daughter of David Alexander, of Elkton. They have one son living, Fred, who lives on his father's farm and is connected with the Baltimore & Ohio Railroad. Their daughter, Mary, married Harry H. Simpson, secretary and treasurer of the South Malleable Iron Works, of Philadelphia; in that city she died in 1891, leaving a son, Thomas Eder Simpson, who makes his home with his grandparents.

ROBERT F. WRIGHT. There is no incident connected with the history of Cecil County more interesting to the people of to-day than that in which the illustrious Capt. John Smith was the central figure. Both in local and national history his name has an important place. His landing in America, his expeditions through the country, his capture by the Indians and his rescue from death by the Indian maiden, Pocahontas, all possess a unique interest to him who studies the events of early days. A visitor to District No. 8 will invariably be shown the old Smith fort farm, situated on the Lancaster and Port Deposit road, and the oldest farm in the county. Here it was that Captain Smith landed and here he established his headquarters, building, to protect himself from the savages, a stone fort, the remains of which may still be seen. Later the place became a trading post for barter and commerce with the Indians. In after years, when the Indians had sought homes in the distant west far from the scenes of their former conquests and defeats, and when the arrival of white settlers had brought all the refinements of civilization, the place became a farm, and where once man sought the life of his fellow-man, the soil was now made to yield its increase in fruit and grain.

On this farm, with its one hundred and seventy-five acres of well-cultivated land, Robert F. Wright makes his home. He bought and settled upon the property in 1891, and has since engaged in general farming here. He is a member of an old Pennsylvania family that was founded there by his great-grandfather, a native of Wales and a commissioned officer of the Revolutionary War. The grandfather, John Wright, was a native of Bucks County and attained the great age of one hundred and twelve years. Joseph, father of our subject, was born in Chester County and in youth learned the blacksmith's trade, but spent most of his life as a farmer upon his estate in Chester County. Politically a Republican, he was a prominent man in local affairs and wielded large influence among his neighbors. By his marriage to Martha McDowell Ford, of Chester County, he had a family of eight children, of whom three are living, namely: Robert F., Edward and George. His death occurred in 1885, when he was seventy-seven years of age.

In Penn Township, Chester County, Pa., the subject of this sketch was born in 1833. His education was obtained principally in New London Academy in his native county, where he was a student during the winter months. For two years he served an apprenticeship to the trade of wheelwright and coachmaker, and afterwards followed the carpenter's trade for a number of years, meantime working in Wilmington, Cleveland, Washington, Philadelphia and other cities. In 1862 he enlisted in Company I, One Hundred and Seventy-fifth Pennsylvania Infantry, under Capt. T. A. Hicks, and served for three and one-half years. Among the engagements in which he participated were those at Antietam, Hampton Roads and Harper's Ferry. At the expiration of his term of service he returned to Wilmington, where he was then employed as a carpenter. In 1891 he purchased his present home in District No. 8.

Shortly after his return from the war Mr. Wright established a home of his own, choosing as his wife Miss Mary E. Porter, an estimable lady, whose worth of character rendered her a fitting representative of one of the oldest families of Maryland. Her father, Robert Porter, was a descendant of a hero of the Revolution. She became the wife of Mr. Wright in 1866 and remained his efficient helpmate, sharing in his labors and rejoicing in his successes, until she passed away, June 8, 1893. In the midst of the scenes familiar to her in life and associated with all she held most dear, she was laid to rest, mourned by many friends.

HON. HENRY ROBINSON TORBERT, proprietor of the *Cecil Whig*, was born in Elkton, July 17, 1834. He is a member of a family formerly residents of Delaware, but for many years identified with the history of Cecil County. His grandfather, Rev. William Torbert, was a prominent Methodist minister of his day and belonged to the Philadelphia general conference, holding pastorates in Pennsylvania, Delaware and on the eastern shore of Maryland, where he was well and favorably known. One of his most noticeable traits was his enthusiasm in behalf of the Methodist religion. The denomination had in him one of its most earnest and eloquent exponents. He gave his time, his life, to the promotion of the cause, deeming no sacrifice too great that would advance the welfare of the church. To such men as he, the Methodist Church owes its wonderful prosperity of the present day.

The father of our subject, William Torbert, was born in Delaware, but in early life came to Elkton, of which place he became the leading merchant, and occupied an influential position among the citizens of the village a half-century ago. He imbibed much of his father's enthusiasm for the advancement of Methodism, and to him the church in Elkton is indebted more than to any other member. For forty years he was its most active worker, the one to whom all turned for counsel, and whose advice was sought in every enterprise inaugurated by the congregation. For an equally long period he was superintendent of the Sunday-school. He was a man of irreproachable character, integrity and sincerity, and no man was more esteemed than he by the people of Elkton and the surrounding country.

In June, 1832, William Torbert married Adaline Matilda, granddaughter of William Silver, of Christiana, Del. They had four sons, of whom our subject was the eldest. One of them, W. F. Asbury, was a man of ability and of broad intellect. At the outbreak of the war he joined the Second Delaware Infantry in the cause of the Union and was soon promoted to be major on the staff of General French, with whom he served during the whole peninsular campaign under General McClellan. In May, 1864, he was transferred to the navy department as acting assistant paymaster and was attached to the iron-clad "Lehigh," of the South Atlantic blockade squadron, from that time to the close of the war. He became assistant paymaster in July, 1866, during which year he was on special duty at Pensacola. In September, 1868, he was commissioned paymaster and was on duty on the supply steamer "Massachusetts," on the steam sloop "Wampanaag," on special duty on the practice ship "Savannah," and in 1870 was assigned to the "Idaho," at Yokahoma, Japan, where he remained until 1873. After his return from Japan he was assigned as paymaster of the receiving ship "Potomac," at the Philadelphia navy yard. During his service there he died, October 4, 1874, from congestion of the brain. His death was greatly lamented by his fellow-officers, who held him in the highest esteem. Another brother of our subject, John, entered the army as a private in Anderson's Cavalry of Philadelphia and was promoted to be lieutenant on the staff of his cousin, Gen. A. T. A. Torbert, and served until the close of the war. The fourth son, Edwin J., died at Germantown, Pa., in October, 1886.

The early education of our subject was obtained in Elkton Academy, and in 1851 he entered Dickinson College, Carlisle, Pa., where he graduated in June, 1855, carrying off the honors of the class.

He studied law in Elkton, and was admitted to the bar in the fall of 1857. Endowed by nature with more than ordinary advantages in personal appearance, voice and manner, he was a striking figure when he entered the bar of his native place, and had he continued in this profession no doubt he would have attained prominence at the bar, but he relinquished it temporarily to devote his time to the business interests of his father. In 1862 he resumed the practice and the following year was elected state's attorney, which office he filled with much credit to himself and satisfaction to his constituents. In January, 1866, he resigned to accept, at the hands of Judge John H. Price, an appointment as clerk of the circuit court, death having caused a vacancy in that office. He remained in the position until the next general election, in 1867.

At the outbreak of the war, Mr. Torbert was a Democrat, but he then espoused the Union cause, and by his eloquent public speeches did much to rally the people of his native county to the support of the Union. In 1868 he received the Republican nomination for congress, in the district embracing the eight counties of the eastern shore of Maryland, a territory intensely in sympathy with the Confederate cause. When he accepted the nomination there was not the slightest hope of electing any Republican to congress in the district, but he went into the campaign with the same zeal that has characterized him in all his undertakings through life. However, the odds were too great against him and his party, and he was defeated. In 1870 he was again the candidate for the position, but the same conditions confronted him and he was again defeated. In 1869 he was appointed deputy surveyor for the port of Baltimore and continued to discharge the duties of the office for nine years without having even the slightest suspicion cast upon his management of affairs, even by his most bitter political opponents. In 1876 he purchased the *Cecil Whig*, which he has since conducted as proprietor and editor. Under his able management the paper has grown to be the leading journal of the eastern shore. He is an able writer and the editorials that appear in the columns from time to time from his pen would do credit to editors of national renown. His classical education and literary tastes qualify him for a journalist and his articles are widely quoted. The building in which he has his office and its appointments are modern and all that could be desired. He takes a stand against all classes of immorality in his native county, more especially in his own town, and policy will not keep him from speaking his sentiments and presenting them to the people.

December 24, 1867, Mr. Torbert married Mary Rachel, daughter of Col. Edwin and Hannah E. (Megredy) Wilmer, the ceremony being performed by Bishop Levi Scott, of the Methodist Episcopal Church. They have two children. Victor Megredy, a young man of literary and journalistic tastes, is associated with his father in the management of the paper; Frances Elizabeth, the only daughter, is an accomplished young lady.

R. C. LEVIS. The student of human progress, and the youth who seeks, in the struggle for success, an example worthy of his emulation, will find in the life of Mr. Levis a proof that the road to prosperity is a plain and narrow path, which lies open to almost every ambitious man. Beginning for himself, with no other capital than good health and a determination to succeed, he worked his way ambitiously forward until he gained a position among the leading men of Cecil County. The establishment of which he is the proprietor ranks among the best equipped, not only in Elkton, but in the entire county as well, and the large trade which it receives is due to the energetic and honorable business methods pursued by the owner.

Near the village of Leeds, in this county, on the Little Elk Creek, the subject of our sketch was born, in 1840. His father, a native of Delaware County, Pa., and by name Norris Levis, came in early manhood to Cecil County, of which he became a pioneer paper manufacturer. Later he was the owner of a flour mill in the Walnut Valley, in which business he continued until his death. He had filled many places of honor and trust in the county, among them that of county commissioner, and fraternally was connected with the Masons. He married Amelia Kirk, who was born near the Brick Meeting House, and was reared by Quaker parents in that faith, but later became identified with the Rock Presbyterian Church. She died in Elkton. Her family comprised four sons and five daughters. William, the eldest of the number, became a paper maker, and was engaged in that business in Dayton, Ohio, at the time of his death; Eliza is the widow of I. D. Carter, formerly a paper maker of Walnut Hill, where she resides; Joseph K., who resides on the old homestead, operates the mill in Walnut Valley that was started by his father; Amelia K. is the wife of Slater B. Russell, of West Chester, Pa.; Harriet is the wife of V. K. Alexander, of Lancaster, Pa.; Mary L., the widow of Arthur W. Mitchell, resides in Elkton; Harry B. died in 1896.

In the schools of Leeds our subject received all the education he was privileged to gain. When quite young he began as a clerk in the store of Edward Brown in Elkton, and from time to time invested his earnings in such a way as to bring him fair returns. In 1861 he became a member of the firm of Levis & Marratt, and established the house of which he is now the sole proprietor, having succeeded to the business some years ago. His business interests are numerous and varied, not being limited to his mercantile establishment. He is a stockholder and director in the First National Bank of Elkton, a stockholder in the Second National Bank, director and treasurer of the Electric Light Company, director and treasurer of the Elkton Water Company, and sole owner of the Cecil Telephone Company, which is a flourishing concern. Though always taking an active part in any measure for the good of the place, he has never held office nor aspired to any political honors, but prefers to devote himself entirely to his personal interests. In religious belief he is connected with the Presbyterian Church. A prominent Mason, he has been treasurer of the blue lodge for thirty years, and on the anniversary of his admission to the lodge was presented by his fellow-members with a beautiful gold badge, as a token of their appreciation of his long service. He is also a Chapter Mason. June 12, 1885, he married Miss Hester C. Connor, of Dover, Del., his first wife, Lydia C. Biddle, having died some time before, leaving one child that died soon afterward. He has a family of three children, Ella C., Robert C. and Hester, in whose welfare he is deeply interested, and who will be given the advantages that will prepare them for honorable positions in life.

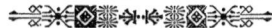

GEORGE R. ASH is the able editor of the *Cecil Democrat*, the leading Democratic paper of Cecil County. It is a newsy paper and enjoys a good circulation, not only in the village of Elkton, where it is published, but throughout the entire county. Avowedly Democratic in political sentiment, it has the majority of its readers and supporters from among the ranks of this party, but the fair and impartial tenor of its editorials, the broad and liberal spirit displayed in the reviews of public events, and the loyal devotion to county and state noticeable in every issue, have combined to bring to the journal the respect of even the most implacable political opponents. In addition to politics, it devotes considerable space to society happenings and local affairs, and is also used by business men as a medium of communication with the people of the county.

The editor of this paper was born in the village where he now resides, the date of his birth being March 21, 1861. His father, who was born three miles from Elkton, in 1832, was a dealer in agricultural implements throughout his entire active life, and never aspired to official positions, preferring to concentrate his attention upon business affairs. In the Presbyterian Church he was an active worker and the superintendent of the Sunday-school. He was a member of various secret societies in which he was interested. At the opening of the Civil War he enlisted in the Sixth Maryland Infantry, U. S. A., and held the position of adjutant, with the rank of captain, but resigned in 1863. He died in 1879. His father, Jacob Ash, was a farmer of Cecil County, where he was born, and was one of the founders of the Presbyterian Church in Elkton.

The mother of our subject, Emily, was a daughter of the late Col. George R. Howard, who was born in Lancaster County, Pa., but removed from there to Cecil County and engaged in the mercantile business in Elkton. Prominent in public life he was register of wills for the county and represented his district in the state senate. Although advanced in years when the Civil War broke out, his enthusiasm in the cause was so great that he organized the Sixth Maryland Regiment, of which he was chosen colonel. He led the fortunes of his regiment until 1863, when on account of failing health he resigned his commission. Returning to his farm on the Elk River, he spent several years there, but afterward purchased the Colonel Hollingsworth mansion, one of the most historic homes in Elkton, erected many years prior to the Revolution. It is said that General Washington spent the night within its walls once, when on his way to Brandywine. In this old place the closing years of the useful life of Colonel Howard were passed, and there he died in 1884. Possessing great force of character and decision of purpose, he was justly prominent among the citizens of Elkton. In his latter years, though possessed of an ample fortune that rendered labor unnecessary, he accepted the position of justice of the peace, more because he liked the work than from a desire to increase his income. By his first wife, a Miss Jones, he had several children, but all are deceased. His second wife was Mary H. Ash, sister of his son-in-law, Jacob B. Ash, and by her he had four children. The father of Colonel Howard was born in England, came thence to America and served in the Revolution, being in command as an officer at the battle of Trenton. Our subject's mother died in 1874.

George R. Ash had six sisters, four of whom are living: Helen, Mary, Flora and Charlotte.

He was educated in the Elkton Academy, but left school at fourteen years and for some time was employed by his father in the agricultural implement business. Later he was in the office of the county commissioners, and in 1884 was appointed deputy register of wills, which office he filled until 1890. In that year, in company with a number of leading citizens, he formed a company and purchased the *Cecil Democrat*. Of this company Hon. John S. Wirt was made president, while Mr. Ash became editor and manager, and as such has built up a large business. He is a clear and forcible writer, and also has ability as a business man, which fact is recognized especially by his business associates. In December, 1892, he was appointed school commissioner for Cecil County and continues to hold that office. He is interested in military affairs, being a member of the Third Battalion, Eastern Shore of Maryland, in which he was first sergeant, then second lieutenant and afterward adjutant with the rank of captain. Fraternally he is past grand in the lodge of Odd Fellows and member of the grand lodge of the state. He is also identified with the Knights of Pythias.

HENRY VINSINGER. In reviewing the history of any community there are always a few names that stand out pre-eminently among others because those who bear them are men of superior ability, sound judgment and progressive spirit. Such names and such men add to the prosperity of a place, elevating its moral tone and increasing its commercial importance. Their means, put into circulation in the home neighborhood, becomes a factor in the prosperity of every citizen, while their intelligence is a power that cannot be lightly estimated. The position occupied by Mr. Vinsinger among the business men of Elkton is one of importance and influence. For years he has been connected with the activities of the place and has been instrumental in promoting its material welfare.

In the neighboring county of Chester, Pa., Mr. Vinsinger was born November 21, 1849. His father, William, a native of Pennsylvania and a farmer, came to Cecil County in 1860 and settled six miles north of Elkton, where he engaged in farming until his death, in 1862. He married Levina Hill, who was born in Pennsylvania and from there accompanied her father to Maryland. She died in 1885, at the home of a daughter in Camden, N. J. One of her brothers, Joseph C. Hill, commanded the Sixth Maryland Infantry in the Civil War, and in 1869 entered the custom house in Baltimore, where he remained until his death, in 1897. The family of which our subject is a member consisted of four sons and four daughters, of whom three sons and two daughters survive. J. Spencer is employed as time-keeper in the Wilmington car shops; Franklin resides in Cecil County; Maria is the widow of J. Z. Finley; and Rebecca E. is the widow of Daniel Cummings, of Camden, N. J.

Educated in the public schools, our subject remained at home until eighteen years of age. In the spring of 1868 he became an employe in the flouring mill of Hill, Harlan & Co., of Elkton, his uncle, Colonel Hill, being the head of the firm. He continued there until August, 1871, when he became proprietor of the mill, and this he continued to operate until the spring of 1895. At that time, on account of failing health, he relinquished the business, his son and a Mr. Davis becoming proprietors under the firm name of Davis & Vinsinger. Prior to this, in 1893, he had established a furniture and undertaking business, and this he has since successfully conducted. His present possessions have been secured by hard work and economy, in connection with good management and sound judgment. He is considered an able, sagacious business man. By a judicious investment of his money he has acquired a valuable property and ranks among the well-to-do men of the village. Fraternally he is connected with the Ancient Order of United Workmen. He and his wife are active workers in the Methodist Episcopal Church, in which he is a trustee. December 28, 1871, he married Cordelia R. Strickland, daughter of William P.

Strickland, of Elkton. They are the parents of two children: William T., who succeeded his father in the mill; and H. Edward, a clerk in the National Bank of Elkton.

BENJAMIN M. WELLS. While Cecil County has much in the way of natural resources and commercial transactions to commend it to the public, the chief interest centers in the lives of those citizens who have achieved success for themselves, and at the same time benefited the community in which they reside. Prominent among these men is the subject of this sketch. Having spent his entire life in Elkton, he is naturally interested in its prosperity. The family of which he is a member has taken an active part in laying the foundation for the present development of the community, having had representatives here during the entire nineteenth century. It is, indeed, one of the oldest families of the county. In the possession of our subject there is a Bible, printed in 1770, that has been in the family since that year and contains the family record back to 1766.

The father of our subject, Benjamin Wells, was born in Elkton June 4, 1814, and in early life learned the coach-making trade. He was, however, best known by his long connection with the Pennsylvania Railroad as station agent at Elkton, for he was appointed to that position in 1839, and from that time up to his death, in 1894, he filled this responsible position, a period of more than fifty-five years. He was devoted to his work, and when the company offered to put him on the retired list with full pay, he refused to accept it, saying he would prefer to attend to the duties of the office as long as he lived. Therefore, the company retained him in active service and allowed him to follow out his desires and die with "the harness on." At the time of his death he was the oldest man in the employ of the company, in point of continuous service. No one was prouder than he of the prosperity of the road, and no one rejoiced more in its success than he. In religious belief he was an influential member of the Methodist Episcopal Church.

In January, 1841, Benjamin Wells married Rebecca J., daughter of Henry Alexander, member of an influential and old family of Cecil County. She died May 25, 1897, at the age of seventy-four years. In her family there were four children, H. A. Wells; Mary A., wife of W. J. Aldrich, of Elkton; our subject and Charles G. The oldest son, when a boy, learned telegraphy and became one of the most expert operators in the country; during the Greeley campaign he was made private operator of that famous statesman, whom he accompanied until the close of the campaign. Charles G., assistant agent of the Elkton station, married Daisy, daughter of A. J. Scott, and they have two children.

The subject of this article was born January 6, 1855, and received a common-school education. When a mere boy he entered the employ of the Pennsylvania Railroad Company under his father, and in 1879 was made agent of the Adams Express Company, which position he has continued to hold ever since. In 1882 he married Miss Mary H. Howard, daughter of the late Col. George R. Howard, of Elkton. They are the parents of one child, Helen H.

WILLARD G. ROUSE. The American bar offers the finest opportunities of preferment of any country upon the face of the earth, its members being privileged, if the talent is not wanting, to attain not only the greatest distinction in the profession, but it is the easiest way to approach to the highest official positions in the land. Furthermore, the American bar can show an array of eminent talent, of profound erudition and of judicial ability equal to that of England, France or Germany. The bar of Maryland has ever been famed for the learning and talent of its members, who know not the meaning of failure when pitted against lawyers from other states. A very bright and most promising young attorney is the subject of this sketch, Willard G. Rouse, who thus early in his career has attained a prominent place at the Harford County bar.

Mr. Rouse was born April 4, 1867, at Creswell, Md. He received his initiatory educational training in the public schools, later attended the Bel Air Academy, and finally entered Johns Hopkins University, from which institution he graduated in 1887. Two years later he was graduated from the law department of the University of Maryland, after which he was engaged in the practice of his profession for two years in Baltimore. He then returned to the place of his nativity, and in June, 1891, formed a partnership with Hon. Richard Dallam, who is now secretary of the state of Maryland. Their connection continued harmoniously until the election of Mr. Dallam to that office, when it was dissolved necessarily, and since that time Mr. Rouse has been alone. He has a lucrative and growing practice and has been identified with a number of important cases, in which his clients were defended with signal success.

While devoted to his profession, which he pursues unremittingly, Mr. Rouse has given some time to the social amenities of life. He is an active member of the Free and Accepted Masons and the Independent Order of Odd Fellows. In 1894 he married Miss Anna Stump Webster, a daughter of William Webster and a niece of the late Colonel Webster. They are attendants of the Presbyterian Church, and are favorites in the social circles of their locality.

JOHN T. BENNETT. Like many of the influential citizens of Elkton, Mr. Bennett began for himself without capital. When he started out in the world to fight life's battles on his own account, he went empty-handed, but he needed no other capital than his good health, clear brain and tireless energy, which have placed him in comfortable circumstances. His life record is a good one and is such as to commend him to the respect of the entire community. Connected for many years with the railway mail service, on retiring from that position he turned his attention to the mercantile business, in which he has since engaged in Elkton. He was born in this village December 5, 1844, and has always considered it his home, though circumstances or business duties have taken him temporarily to other points. The family of which he is a member settled in Cecil County at an early period of its history, and his grandfather, Henry Bennett, who was born here, was a slave owner and a soldier in the War of 1812.

The father of our subject, John P. Bennett, was born in Elkton, where he engaged in the fishery business for many years. During the progress of the Civil War, he served as provost-marshal, and at another time he was one of the commissioners of Cecil County. He died in Elkton. His wife, Martha, was a daughter of Moses Scott, a wheelwright, and died in this village. Their family was composed of four sons and two daughters. Two of the boys served in the Union army, Henry H. being a member of the Second Delaware Infantry; G. S., who was in the same regiment, was taken prisoner by Confederate forces and confined in Andersonville prison, where he died soon afterward. Another son, Alexander S., is a carriage-maker and resides in Wilmington, Del. The only living daughter, Ada, is the wife of Thomas Sharf, of Wilmington.

When the Civil War broke out, the subject of this sketch was a youth of little more than sixteen years. Notwithstanding his youth, he was so ardent in the Union cause that he determined to enter the service. Accordingly, in September, 1861, he joined the Fifth Maryland Infantry, with which he remained until the close of the war. For a time he was orderly sergeant, but from that was promoted to the rank of second lieutenant. He participated in many of the hard-fought engagements of the war, where bullets flew fast and thick, and life was in momentary peril. With his regiment he was in front of Richmond at the time of the surrender of General Lee, and they had the honor of being the first to enter the city after the war. When peace was declared, Mr. Bennett returned to his home in Elkton. Soon afterward he received an appointment to the postal mail service between Washington and New York and held this position for twenty years, when he resigned to enter the mercantile business in Elkton.

In 1870 Mr. Bennett married Mrs. Mary E. (Denny) Bennett. Mr. Bennett has never accepted office, preferring to devote his time to the duties of citizenship in a private capacity, and to assist as far as he is able in those measures that will add to the mental and material prosperity of the community. A public-spirited man, he takes great pride in conscientiously fulfilling the obligations of life both great and small. In religious connections he is identified with the Methodist Episcopal Church and contributes to its maintenance.

COL. OTHO S. LEE was born near Bel Air, December 6, 1840, the son of Richard Dallam and Hannah B. Lee, and the descendent of ancestors who bore an influential part in the early history of Maryland and in the wars that marked the colonial period. His paternal grandfather, Parker Hall Lee, who was born in January, 1759, was one of the brave men to whom we owe the freedom of our country from British domination and whose record in the army was that of a brave and dauntless officer. Enlisting with the patriots at the opening of the Revolution, he became a lieutenant in the Fifth Maryland Regiment and served loyally until the conflict ceased and peace was declared. During the battle of Monmouth, in which he bore a valiant part, he captured a sword from a British officer and this trophy of victory is now in the possession of our subject, by whom it is highly prized. On returning home from the war, he resumed farming operations and in time became one of the most extensive planters of Harford County, where he owned over one thousand acres of land, lying between Deer Creek and Thomas Run. He died May 6, 1829, and was buried at Jericho, in the private graveyard on that property, enclosed by a large stone wall. Jericho was one of the fine farms into which the estate was divided at his death. His son by his second marriage, James Carvil Lee, is still living, and makes his home on Deer Creek.

On the family homestead where he was born, Richard Dallam Lee spent his entire life, his attention being given chiefly to the supervision of the landed interests that had become his, by inheritance and purchase. He was a man of prominence in the county and held a number of local offices. Doubtless he would have been elected to positions of larger importance, had his life been prolonged, but he died at the age of forty-three years. Colonel Lee spent his early life on the home farm, but at the age of seventeen he came to Bel Air and secured a clerkship in a store. His education was largely received in the Bel Air Academy. When the Civil War began he was prosecuting his law studies with Henry W. Archer, but he immediately abandoned his books and joined Stuart's Confederate Cavalry, serving under Gen. Fitzhugh Lee in the army of northern Virginia, and participating in all the important campaigns in which that famous general led his forces. From the first battle of Bull Run until the surrender of Richmond, he bore a part in the struggles of the Confederacy, and in recognition of meritorious conduct was made a sergeant-major of Artillery near the close of the war.

Returning to Harford County at the close of the war, our subject was admitted to the bar in November, 1865, and has since been one of the leading attorneys of Bel Air. He was elected a member of the house of delegates of 1874, where he ably represented his constituents. He has been an examiner in chancery continuously since 1867 and counsel to the Harford County board of school commissioners. As an advocate of improvements that will promote the progress of the county, he has taken an active part in local affairs. He holds the office of president of the Bel Air Water and Light Company, and since its incorporation has been president of the Permanent

Building Association of Harford County. The title by which he is always called, was given him in 1876, when he served on the staff of Governor Carroll with the rank of colonel. He has always taken a great interest in the militia of the state and has been captain of two companies raised in the county. A prominent Mason, he is past master of Mt. Ararat Lodge, at Bel Air.

In 1867 Colonel Lee was united in marriage with Miss Sallie B. Griffith, only child of John L. Griffith, a prominent farmer of District No. 2, Harford County. They are the parents of eight children, named as follows: Helen M.; John L. G., a graduate of Johns Hopkins College and the University of Maryland law school, recently a member of the house of delegates, now assistant United States district attorney of Maryland, and one of the most promising young men of the state; Hannah B.; Elizabeth Dallam; Henry W. Archer; Alice; Cassandra; and Otho Scott Lee, member of the class of 1899, Princeton College.

R OBERT MARSHBANK. Within the limits of a brief biographical sketch it is impossible to render full justice to prominent men, and yet there are some whose names are so familiar to all that it is only justice to dwell upon what they have done. In a list of those once prominent in business circles of Elkton we find the name of Robert Marshbank, whose long and honorable connection with the best interests of the village entitled him to the respect in which he was held. It was in 1843 that he came to Elkton, and the following year he opened a furniture store, which he afterward conducted, in connection with the undertaking business. During this period of more than half a century he witnessed the many changes that have been made in Cecil County; the darkening days prior to the war, the perils of that great civil strife, the business depression that followed it, and the final return to prosperity. To secure the development of material resources he contributed his quota. While, in the management of his business, he never gained a fortune, he secured a competency and that which is even better, an enviable name as an efficient, honorable business man.

It was on Christmas Day of 1821 that the birth of Robert Marshbank occurred, his native place being Chester County, Pa., where also were born his parents, Robert and Ann (Lyle) Marshbank. His father, who was a member of a Scotch family, was a school teacher by occupation, but died at an early age, when his son and namesake was a boy of seven. His wife was a member of a family that engaged principally in the manufacture of paper. Their family consisted of two sons, our subject's brother being John D., who was a cabinet-maker by trade, but in later life owned a foundry at Harrisburg, Pa., and died in Chester County. The mother departed this life in Lancaster, Pa., at the home of her son. The death of the father leaving the family in straightened circumstances, our subject was unable to devote much time to study, but in boyhood was bound out to a farmer, with whom he remained until sixteen years of age. He then went to Baltimore and learned the cabinet-maker's trade. Coming to Elkton in 1843, the next year he opened a furniture store, and has also for more than fifty years been in the undertaking business, during which time he has had charge of the burial of more than five thousand persons.

The first wife of Mr. Marshbank, Eliza J. Short, at her death left a daughter, Eliza J., now the wife of George Crocker, of Laporte, Ind., a civil engineer, who is engaged in railroad construction in the west. The second marriage of Mr. Marshbank was to Eliza A. Lynch, who died July 31, 1887, leaving four children. The eldest of these is Maggie, wife of H. C. Wells, a druggist of Elkton. J. H., who is in business with his father, married Lidie Bennett, of Elkton, and they have five children, Robert, Flora, Hyland, Harry and Mary. Fannie is single and lives at home. The fourth child, Richard, is deceased. The third wife of our subject bore the maiden name of Mary D. Henry. Fraternally Mr. Marshbank was identified with the Independent Order of Odd Fellows for more than half a century, and filled all the offices in the local lodge, besides which he was a member of the grand lodge of the state. He was vice president of the Mutual Building Association for twenty years or more. During the existence of the Whig party he advocated its principles, and upon its disintegration became a Republican, the principles of which party he afterward supported by his vote and influence. Though he did not care to take a very active part in the political life of the village, the value of his citizenship was never questioned, and his death, July 11, 1897, was recognized as a public loss.

EDWARD A. BALDWIN. While this gentleman has been a resident of Darlington for a comparatively brief period only, yet he has many acquaintances in this portion of Harford County, for much of his life has been passed in the adjoining district, No. 2, of which his ancestors were pioneer settlers. He was born at Hopewell Cross Roads in 1857, the son of Samuel Tyler and Fannie (Loflin) Baldwin, natives of the same district. His paternal grandfather, Tyler Baldwin, was born there and spent his entire active life as a blacksmith. Samuel T., who followed the occupation of painter and glazier, was a man of some prominence in his community, an active worker in the ranks of the Democracy, and for some time the incumbent of the office of road supervisor. He passed away June 9, 1884, aged sixty-six; his wife died March 17, 1888, at the age of seventy. They were the parents of nine children, namely: John T., Sarah M., Annie C., George F., Eben N., Phoebe E., Edward A., Robert L. and Samuel T. All are living but the last named, who died in 1861.

The boyhood days of our subject were passed in attendance upon the common schools and in work at home. With a desire to see more of the world, and thinking a more favorable opening might be found elsewhere, he went to Texas, in February, 1877, and spent one year in Dallas.

However, he found the Lone Star state not equal to his expectations, and, with the belief that no state could surpass old Maryland, he returned to Harford County in 1878. Afterward he engaged in the canning business for three years in Hopewell precinct, and then spent five years in Kennedyville, Kent County. October 6, 1896, was the date of his arrival in Darlington. Here he at once established a cabinet, upholstery and undertaking business, in which he has embarked with every prospect of success.

The Democratic party stands for the principles in which Mr. Baldwin believes, and to it therefore he gives allegiance. In fraternal relations he is identified with the Aberdeen Lodge of Masons. In the lodge of Odd Fellows at Aberdeen he has passed all the chairs and is eligible to membership in the grand lodge of the state. The Senior Order of American Mechanics numbers him among its members. He is also connected with the Sons of Temperance at Hopewell Cross Roads and was treasurer of the organization for two years. Reared in the faith of the Methodist Protestant denomination, he has for years been associated with the congregation at Hopewell Cross Roads and at this writing is a trustee of the church.

RICHARD B. MERRITT. On one of the principal streets of the village of Warwick stands the general mercantile store owned and conducted by Mr. Merritt and of which he has been the proprietor for more than twenty years. He is an efficient business man, honest in every transaction, energetic and capable, and has built up a good trade among the people of his locality, who have learned to place confidence in his word. As boy and man, his entire life has been passed in Cecil County, and naturally he feels the deepest interest in its development and in the welfare of its people. He was born here February 5, 1850, and this county was also the birthplace of his parents, Joseph and Rachel

(Boulden) Merritt. In order of birth he was second among five children, the others being James, Mary, Anna, and Julius, who was accidentally shot and killed while out hunting deer, when he was a boy of eleven. Both the Merritt and Boulden families are old residents of Maryland, having resided here from an early period of its history. Richard Boulden, our subject's grandfather, and for whom he was named, took part in the Revolution in his early manhood, and again, when quite old, started out to defend our country against the encroachments of the British in the War of 1812. Afterward he received a pension from the government.

Reared upon a farm, our subject was given excellent advantages in boyhood and finished his education in the Middletown (Del.) Academy. In early years he devoted his attention principally to farming, but since then he has carried on a general store in Warwick. At the age of twenty-two he married Leota L. Wilson, of this county, and to their union were born five children.

Mrs. Merritt is a member of a family long resident in Maryland, and is a lady of estimable Christian character and an active member of the Methodist Protestant Church. Mr. Merritt is not only interested in business, but in politics as well, and is a firm Democrat in principle. For a time he held the office of collector, and in 1897 was his party's candidate for county treasurer. He is a public-spirited citizen and takes an interest in all measures for the benefit of the people of this section.

ROBERT KERR VANNEMAN. The social, financial and business history of Harford County is filled with the deeds of self-made men, and if by this word we understand that a man, solely through his unaided exertions, has risen from an unimportant position to one of influence, then certainly Mr. Vanneman may be called self-made. The family of which he is a member, though an old and honored one in this part of Maryland, has never been wealthy, and from an early age he was obliged by force of circumstances to earn his living. From his remote forefathers he inherits the traits of perseverance and honesty that have ever characterized the Swedish nationality, as well as the enterprise that is a trait especially peculiar to Americans. These qualities have enabled him to gain a position among the prominent men of Havre de Grace.

The First National Bank of Havre de Grace, of which Mr. Vanneman is cashier, was organized, largely through his instrumentality, in September, 1883, with Arthur Vosbury as president and himself as cashier. The president died in February, 1889, and was succeeded by A. P. McCombs. Mr. Vanneman is now the largest stockholder in the concern. Since the inception of the enterprise the bank has paid the stockholders a large percentage in dividends, and has added to its surplus an amount greater than the capital stock of $60,000. This flattering record is largely due to the management of Mr. Vanneman. The excellent condition of the institution is especially worthy of mention, after these last years of bank failures, stringency in the money market, and depreciation of values; but in times of panics elsewhere, the depositors in the First National have never had cause to feel the slightest concern regarding the safety of their moneys.

In considering the life of a man, it is always appropriate to dwell upon the lives and characters of his ancestry. The father of the gentleman named was Daniel Vanneman, who was born and reared in Port Deposit, Md., where for years he was employed as timber inspector and later owned a steamer line from Port Deposit to Havre de Grace, and from Church Creek to Baltimore (after the railroad was built to Port Deposit), carrying both freight and passengers. He built the "Isador," which, however, proved too large for these waters and was sold for navigation on larger rivers. Another steamer that he built was named the "Alice." The railroad taking away his custom was the cause of his financial reverses, and obliged him to sell his vessels. From that time he served as postal clerk on the Baltimore Central Railroad, which position he retained until his death, at the age of fifty-four. Politically he voted the Republican ticket, but was not active in local affairs and never displayed any partisanship in his opinions. His father, John P. Vanneman, came to Port Deposit in early manhood and was among the pioneer lumbermen of the place.

The mother of our subject, in maidenhood Caroline Isador Kerr, was born in Port Deposit. In 1884 she moved to Havre de Grace. She is now sixty-seven years of age. The birth of the subject of this sketch occurred in Port Deposit December 1, 1854, and his education was obtained in the public schools of the village. When about seventeen he began in life for himself and thenceforward was self-supporting. His first position, which he held for a year, was that of clerk in a hardware store in his native town, but afterward he was offered and accepted a position as runner in the Cecil National Bank. Soon afterward he was promoted and filled all the positions up to teller, but resigned August 1, 1883, to aid in the organization of the First National Bank of Havre de Grace.

In 1879 Mr. Vanneman was united in marriage with Miss Laura V., daughter of Samuel M. C. Nesbitt, of Port Deposit. They are the parents of five children, namely: Charles Reeve, Caroline Kerr, Arthur Vosbury, Ella Haines and Homer Nesbitt. The family attend the Methodist Episcopal Church of Havre de Grace, of which Mr. Vanneman and his wife are members. Politically a Republican, he has been an active factor in local politics and has been closely identified with the work of the party here. His fellow-citizens, realizing his fitness for public office, have three times elected him to fill the responsible position of mayor, and he is the present incumbent of this office. In the responsibilities of the position he is proving the possession of energy, tact and fidelity to duty, the qualities that have also brought him success in private affairs. For several years he held the position of town treasurer, and in 1892 was a member of the city council, but refused to serve again after the expiration of one term. In all matters tending to the advancement of the place he is interested, and his hearty co-operation may be relied upon. In the organization of the Havre de Grace Improvement Company he was a prime mover, and is its secretary and treasurer, and a director and stockholder, also secretary and treasurer of the Water Company, a director in the bank, stockholder and director in the Havre de Grace Shoe Manufacturing Company, director of the Harford Telephone Company, and secretary, treasurer, director and the largest stockholder in the Perryville Water Company, which is just across the river in Cecil County; also vice-president and a stockholder of the Havre de Grace Real Estate and Power Company, which bids fair to be the leading concern of this locality. Fraternally he is connected with Susquehanna Lodge No. 130, F. & A. M., of Havre de Grace, and Cecil Lodge No. 31, K. of P., at Port Deposit.

TAYLOR RAWLINGS. Concerning the genealogy of the Rawlings family but little definite information can be obtained. It is known, however, that the first representatives in this country came from either Scotland or Ireland; possibly Scotland was the original home of the family, but during the religious persecution they may have fled to Ireland for safety and from that island afterward crossed the ocean to America. Several succeeding generations have resided in Cecil County, and almost invariably they have been people of moral worth and great energy of character. The first to come here was Greenberry Rawlings, who settled in District No. 7, at what is now known as Battle Swamp.

John, son of Greenberry, had a son Robert, who was the father of our subject. Robert was born in Cecil County, where he spent his entire life, engaged in agricultural pursuits. On the home farm, in District No. 8, his death occurred when he was sixty-four years of age. By his marriage to Mary McVey he was the father of five children, named as follows: Elizabeth, John M., Z. Taylor, Hannah M. and Roberta E. The subject of this sketch was born in 1848, in the house which still remains his home. Educated in the common schools, and reared to habits of industry, he became a man of sound common-sense, practical knowledge of agriculture, and sterling traits of character. At the age of twenty-two years he assumed the management of the home farm, and of it he has since maintained a general supervision. The place is not as large as many of the farms of the county, but its eighty acres have been brought under such excellent cultivation that the best possible results are being secured from year to year.

While Mr. Rawlings is well informed regarding politics, yet his tastes do not lie in that direction, for he is a man whose inclinations are toward private rather than public life. However, he keeps posted regarding the issues before the people to-day, and gives his allegiance to the Democratic party. It has always been his opinion that protection tends to the building up of monopolies and the concentration of wealth within the hands of a few, while free trade is calculated to more equally distribute money among the people. He believes, too, that much of the financial depression from which the country has suffered during the past years is due to the incorrect standard of relationship between silver and gold; when this is rectified and the free coinage of silver an established fact, an era of prosperity will begin. Fraternally he was connected with the Knights of Pythias in former years, but does not retain his membership in the order. His marriage united him with Emma H. Reynolds, daughter of Jacob and Eliza Reynolds, of this county, and an estimable lady, who takes a part in the work of the Presbyterian Church and has many warm friends among the people of the district.

JOHN B. HANNA. Harford County may well be proud of the amount of brains and energy possessed by her representative business men, for, taken as a whole, there are none brighter, more intelligent, or with more ability and push in any direction than they possess. Among the number is John B. Hanna. Those who deal with him find him a very pleasant gentleman, courteous and affable, and in every respect a true man of business; a man whose experience and thorough knowledge of his work have placed him among the leading merchants of this thriving village. Mr. Hanna is a native of the town of Bel Air, where he was born May 16, 1867, son of William F. Hanna, who was born near the village of Churchville. The latter was a carriage manufacturer by trade, a member of the firm of John A. Hanna & Bro., and in every relation of life was the soul of honor, and a man who endeavored to "do as he would be done by." He was an elder in the Presbyterian Church, and died in that faith in 1875. His father, Stephen B. Hanna, was also born in Harford County, and a more complete notice of his life is given in the sketch of James Fulton. The maiden name of William F. Hanna's wife was Martha A. Barnes. She was born at Churchville, a daughter of John Barnes, who belongs to an old and leading family of this section. Mrs. Hanna is living in Bel Air.

John B. Hanna has three brothers: Edwin F., who is a successful insurance man of Baltimore; William F., a substantial business man of Bel Air; and Henry N., who is secretary of the Baltimore Blind Company. The subject of this sketch received his education in Bel Air Academy, and when still a lad began working as a clerk in the store of John G. Rouse, with whom he remained until 1887. By that time he had acquired a sufficient knowledge of business to make a venture on his own account and the result has proved most satisfactory. His trade is extensive and continually increasing, as it has every reason to do, for he keeps an excellent stock on hand and is reasonable in his prices. He has not confined his attention wholly to his business, however, for he has taken an active interest in local politics, is a leader of the Republican party in his section, and has had charge of every campaign therein since the fall of 1893. So intelligent and active has he proved himself in all matters pertaining to public affairs that in 1897

ISAAC TWINING.

he was the candidate of the second congressional district for collector of internal revenue for the district of Maryland. He is a director in the Fireside Building Association of Harford County.

He and his family have identified themselves with the Presbyterian Church, in which he has been a ruling elder since 1891. Fraternally he belongs to the Independent Order of Odd Fellows, in which he is district deputy. In 1888 Miss Martha Standiford became his wife. She was born in Harford County, and here their children have been born: John A., William F., Mary Fulton, and Horace, who died at the age of four years.

MISS MARTHA E. TWINING. The first member of the Twining family who sought a home in America was the great-grandfather of our subject, a native of Wales, but from an early age a resident of Pennsylvania, where he made settlement in Bucks County. Like the majority of the early settlers he engaged in farming, which he conducted in the usual crude manner of those days, and without the aid of the many modern improvements now considered indispensable. In spite of hardships and discouragements, he gradually added to his possessions, until he was one of the largest land owners of the county. The kind hospitality, genial manner, strict honesty and financial thrift characteristic of the Quakers in every age of the world were among his noticeable traits, and he was ever earnest in upholding the principles adopted by the Society of Friends.

Our subject's grandfather, David Twining, was born in Bucks County, Pa., and, like his father, was an extensive land owner, and a faithful member of the Friends' Church. Isaac Twining, father of our subject, was born in Bucks County, and shortly after attaining manhood he married Ann H. Hallowell, member of an old family of that county, whose representatives were by occupation principally farmers. They became the parents of seven children, namely: D. Hallowell; Martha E.; Horace B., who died in 1895; Isaac; B. Franklin, deceased; Caroline W., and Robert B., who was killed in the Union army at the second battle of Bull Run, in 1862.

Born in Pennsylvania, the subject of this sketch was brought by her parents to Harford County in 1845, and settled with them in District No. 4. Upon the death of her father and mother, she inherited the old homestead, and here she has since remained, having in all these years made many friends among the people of the vicinity. When her nephew, Joseph B. Twining, son of D. Hallowell Twining, was a boy, she took him to her home and there he has since remained, being reared under her careful training to habits of industry, perseverance and energy. He was given a good education and prepared for the responsibilities of life. In addition to looking after his aunt's place, he owns a farm of forty-three acres. At the age of twenty-seven he married Minnie S. Saurman, who was born near Philadelphia, Pa., and they have one child, named Martha E., in honor of her great-aunt.

The farm which Miss Twining owns and occupies consists of sixty acres, upon which have been placed the improvements that mark a model estate and so largely add to the comfort of its occupants. The well-tilled fields return large crops to reward the industry of the husbandman, and the granaries are filled each season. The active work of superintending the place falls upon her nephew, and his good judgment and enterprise have been of the greatest assistance to her in the management of her property interests. In religious belief she is loyal to the teachings of the Friends' Church, in which faith she was reared.

JOHN R. McELWAIN. This government of the people is no discriminator of persons, and its doors are opened wide for entrance into the business or professional arena of all such as possess the requisite qualifications to success.

It may be truthfully said that you may travel the world over and nowhere will you find better opportunities for a young man to advance in every way than under the shadow of the stars and stripes. This fact was early recognized by the subject of this sketch, and that his career has been a successful one is well known. He is distinctively American, as were his ancestors, both lineal and collateral, for generations, and farming was their occupation. Habitual frugality and industry were the fundamental principles and characteristic features of his parents, John S. and Rebecca (Webb) McElwain, whose native state was Pennsylvania. These characteristics have been inherited to a considerable extent by the subject of this sketch, who was third of the following-named children: William J., deceased; Mary, deceased; John R., subject of this sketch; Rachel E., Robert B., William, H. Clay, Mary S., Henrietta R., Margaret V., Ella M. and Daniel E. The paternal great-grandfather of John R. McElwain was a native of the north of Ireland, and when quite young came to the new world and made a settlement in Pennsylvania, where he successfully tilled the soil and became the owner of a large estate. He was a member of the colonial army during the Revolution.

John McElwain, the grandfather, was born on his father's fine country estate in Pennsylvania, and, like his father before him, devoted his attention to agricultural pursuits throughout life and reared his sons to a thorough knowledge of this pursuit. John R. McElwain was born in Pennsylvania June 10, 1854, and with the intelligent council and advice of his worthy father, he soon came to understand the details of farm work. His early education was obtained in the common schools of the rural districts and after reaching a suitable age he engaged in teaching school, and continued this occupation in the district schools for eight years. Both in teaching and farming his labors were crowned with success. The result of his efforts is an excellent farm comprising one hundred and twenty-four acres. This land is carefully tilled and well improved and is therefore valuable.

At the youthful age of twenty-one years Mr McElwain was united in marriage with Miss Almira Brooks, a native of the state of Pennsylvania, but her death occurred after the birth of a little daughter, Edith C., who also died when about one year old, in 1880. At the time of the mother's death, in the spring of 1879, she was but twenty-three years of age. For his second wife Mr. McElwain chose Edith J. Brooks, a sister of his first wife, who was also born in Pennsylvania, and is of Quaker descent. Both sisters united with the Presbyterian Church in early life, and with this church Mr. McElwain is also connected. His last marriage has resulted in the birth of the following children: Cora E., Olive M., J. E. Clifton, Lorenzo C., Harry E. and Ellis W. Mr. McElwain has always supported the Republican party, and for the past eight years he has been trustee of the district. He is of the stuff of which substantial citizens are made and he is most liberally helpful toward any movement having a tendency to benefit any considerable class of his fellow-men.

JOHN G. ROUSE. The reputation enjoyed by a city or village, throughout the surrounding country, depends largely upon the character of its merchants. The influence of the business man is far reaching, permeating all avenues of trade, and affecting important interests that are not reached by the professional man on the one hand, or the artisan on the other. No village of Harford County enjoys a more enviable reputation than Bel Air for the high character of her merchants, both as to strict commercial integrity and business enterprise; and among these merchants John G. Rouse stands prominent.

Mr. Rouse was born in Joppa, Harford County, Md., March 14, 1844, the son of C. Chapman and Mary G. (Day) Rouse. His father, who was born at the same place in 1807, engaged in farming and merchandising, and was a man of considerable local prominence. Among the official positions which he filled was that of county commissioner. A lifelong resident of Joppa, he died in that village in 1873. He was a son of John Rouse, an Englishman, who came to America in early manhood and settled in Maryland. In those days it was thought that the principal city of Maryland would be located at Havre de Grace, and as the travel between that place and Baltimore was very large, he conceived the idea of opening a hotel on the road between the two cities. This plan he carried into effect, opening a large hotel that for years was known as the Half Way House. It became the popular hostelry for people traveling in that part of the state and was constantly crowded with guests, the result being that he accumulated a good-sized fortune. The old Rouse homestead is now occupied by a sister of our subject, Mrs. James B. Hanway. The maternal grandfather of our subject was Goldsmith Day, the owner of large tracts of land in Gunpowder Neck, and at one time clerk of courts of Harford County.

The family of C. Chapman and Mary G. Rouse consisted of four sons and four daughters, all of whom attained mature years. There are now, besides our subject, one son living, William C., of the firm of Rouse, Hempstone & Co., merchants of Baltimore, and three sisters, Mrs. J. S. Richardson of Bel Air, Mrs. J. B. Hanway of Joppa, and Mrs. Martha Hanway, widow of Samuel Hanway. The early years of the life of our subject were spent in Joppa, where he was educated in the public schools. With a natural taste and fitness for business life, we find him, at the age of twenty-one, conducting a small cross-roads store. Being a young man of enterprise and energy, with plenty of sound common sense and good judgment, he gained the confidence of all, and his business ventures were successful from the first. Wishing a larger field for his energy, in 1877 he came to Bel Air and opened his present store. At first, however, it was conducted on a much smaller scale than at present, but by degrees he increased the amount of stock and the importance of the business, until now his store is the largest in the entire county, and would do credit to a place much larger than Bel Air.

In addition to this concern, Mr. Rouse was interested in several other stores in Harford County, his sales amounting to upwards of $200,000 per annum. By close attention to business, push and industry, he has made for himself a name that stands high for honesty, integrity and progressiveness. It is a noteworthy fact that, during his entire business career, with the responsibility of the management of his extensive business, he has enjoyed a credit that would enable him to buy goods in any market, without a reference. Many times, during periods of financial depression, when banks were failing and money scarce, he spent long and anxious hours in planning how to meet certain payments as they became due; but he always found a way to do so; of late years he has had no difficulty in this line, as he has been able not only to meet, but also to discount, his bills. For use in his business he has an account book, of his own invention, which is one of the most convenient for the purpose ever devised. Each bill is entered as it comes in, with date of purchase and date it falls due, by months and days. All that is necessary is to turn to a certain month, where he finds all of the bills due in that month. By systematizing his work, he has made of the business a science, and largely enhanced his financial success.

Aside from his extensive mercantile interests, Mr. Rouse is one of the directors in the Harford National Bank, and a director in various building and loan associations. He is looked upon as one of the foremost citizens of Bel Air, and is always ready to lend a helping hand to local measures. Fraternally he is past master of the Masonic lodge. He has no political aspirations and although his well-known business sagacity and prudence, which he has displayed in the conduct of his private affairs, would have been of great service to the community, his tastes and inclinations, as well as his devotion to his business, would never admit of his accepting public trusts.

Although a business man in the best sense of the term, Mr. Rouse does not allow the cares of business to intrude upon his hours of recreation or the enjoyment of home life. He has a pleasant home in one of the finest residences of Bel Air.

His wife, Harriet B., is a daughter of Thomas Hanway, one of the oldest families of Harford County. Five children were born of their union. Mention of the eldest, Willard G., an attorney of Bel Air, appears on another page. C. C. is engaged in business with his father, the firm name being Rouse & Son. Daisy is the wife of J. Wilson Richardson, son of the late Dr. Hall Richardson. Dora C. married Hon. J. Edwin Webster, whose sketch is presented elsewhere in this volume. Helen C., the youngest of the family, is with her parents, brightening the home by her presence and holding a prominent position in the best society of the place.

WILLIAM MORRIS, whose well-spent life commends him to the confidence and high regard of all with whom he has been brought in contact, is a farmer of District No. 1, Harford County. This is his native county, his birth having occurred on the 4th of July, 1817. He is the son of Lloyd and Beckie (Sheridan) Morris, also natives of the same county. The father learned the cooper's trade, but devoted the greater part of his life to agricultural pursuits. When the country became engaged in the second war with England, he joined the American army and did valiant service for his native land. His death occurred at the age of forty-five years; his wife, who long survived him, reached the advanced age of eighty-four years.

Under the parental roof William Morris was reared to manhood. No event of special importance occurred during that period, which was devoted to acquiring an education and pursuing his studies when the work of the farm was over for the season. He early became familiar with all the duties that fall to the lot of the agriculturist, and when twenty years of age he began work as a farm hand, being employed either by the month or day. This undertaking was the beginning of his business career. He later secured a position in a factory, where he was employed for sixteen years. His industry, perseverance and good management during that time enabled him to acquire the capital with which he purchased a tract of land of sixty-three acres. This has since been his home and he has made it one of the well-improved farms of the neighborhood, the land being placed under a high state of cultivation, while many excellent improvements have been added.

Mr. Morris has been twice married, his first union being with Miss Anna Wilson, by whom he had six children, all now deceased. After the death of his first wife he was joined in wedlock with Mrs. Andrews.

Mr. Morris gives his political support to the Republican party and warmly advocates its principles, believing that by their adoption the country's best interests will be promoted. He holds membership in the Methodist Episcopal Church, with which he has long been identified, and is very active in church work, doing all in his power to promote the cause of Christianity. He contributes liberally to its support, and is a generous benefactor to the poor and needy. Although he has reached a very advanced age, he still possesses his physical powers but slightly impaired, his age resting lightly upon him. His has been an honest, upright life, true to all the duties that have devolved upon him, and he has thereby won the respect of all with whom he has come in contact.

JOHN HENRY KIMBLE. To the memory of our beloved dead we rear stately monuments of marble and beautiful columns of granite. Over their last resting place we strew sweet-blooming flowers. The flowers soon wither and perish, and in time the massive marble grows discolored with age and crumbles away. But when these have passed away, the good that has been done, the influence that has been exerted, will continue to bless mankind through the ages yet to come. The influence of a noble life ends only when time itself shall be no more.

The years that have elapsed since Mr. Kimble entered into rest have not dimmed his memory in the hearts of the many to whom he was dear. His talents, of a wonderfully broad and comprehensive range, attracted all to him, and the impression first made by his genius was deepened by a growing knowledge of the pure and lovable spirit of the man. With the soul of the true poet, his ideals were high, his conceptions keen, his tastes cultured. Like all poets, he was a lover of Nature, a reverent worshipper at her shrine, and it would not be difficult to imagine that Nature mourned his death, as Sir Walter Scott says she mourns the death of every true poet.

> "Call it not vain:—they do not err
> Who say, that, when the poet dies,
> Mute Nature mourns her worshipper,
> And celebrates his obsequies;
> Who say, tall cliff and cavern lone,
> For the departed bard make moan;
> That mountains weep in crystal rill;
> That flowers in tears of balm distil;
> And rivers teach their rushing wave
> To murmur dirges round his grave."

The life of one who was held in such high regard by his fellow-men and whose influence over them was always manifest for good, will be of interest to our readers. It is unnecessary to dwell upon his ancestry, since that is given fully in the life of his father, Henry Harding Kimble, upon another page. Born in Buckingham Township, Bucks County, Pa., September 8, 1850, he was five years of age at the time the family removed from there to Cecil County, settling upon a farm near Fair Hill. The limited means of his parents rendered it impracticable for him to attend school regularly, but he was of an ambitious, aspiring disposition, with the student's love of knowledge, and through self-culture he acquired a fund of information not always possessed by a college-bred man. However, it was always a source of regret to him that his schooling was not more extended, and he advised young men to gain a good education, if possible. Like other members of the family, he possessed remarkable musical talent. As the age of eight he began to play the violin, and a few years later became the owner of a fife, with which he accompanied his brother Seruch on the drum. In 1865 his father purchased a melodeon, on which he soon learned to play, though he had no one to teach him the use of the instrument. Two years later a brass band was organized in the neighborhood and he mastered every instrument in it. His talent was of a comprehensive nature, that enabled him not only to render skillfully the compositions of others, but also to compose selections himself. For some years he taught vocal and instrumental music.

In 1869 Mr. Kimble became a member of a debating society organized near what is now known as Cowantown, and in this he soon gained prominence for logical skill in debating. From 1872 to 1874 he taught in the public schools of Cecil County, being a careful, conscientious and successful teacher. From the time of the appearance of his first poem in 1870, he was a frequent contributor to the local press. In 1875 he wrote "The Patrons of Husbandry," a serial poem which the Grange organ of Pennsylvania published in seven parts with illustrations. This attracted wide attention and was favorably noticed by the *New York World*, and other leading papers. Competent critics pronounced it among the "best and most natural descriptions of rural life ever written." In 1876 he wrote another serial, entitled "Two Granges." He wrote easily, without effort or mental labor, the thoughts flowing smoothly in rhythmic form, so that the effect was pleasing and the whole harmonious. When we consider the fact that he was a farmer, teacher, and busy man of affairs, and his reading was snatched between hours of hard work in other lines of employment, it is apparent that he possessed true native genius, or he could not so easily have adapted his mind to poetry. Undoubtedly, had his life been spared, he would have attained a place of prominence among our national poets. His tastes did not lead him into public affairs, but he was a patriotic citizen and a stanch Republican.

In December, 1873, Mr. Kimble married Sarah Teresa Gallaher, eldest daughter of John E. Gallaher, of Cherry Hill, District No. 4. Her mother was a member of the celebrated Chandlee family that emigrated to this country from Ireland more than a century ago. His estimable wife and their five children survive him, and their most valued keepsakes are the productions of his pen. The names of the children are Anna Mary Ellis, Ida Louisa, Evelyn Teresa, Henry Evans and Seruch Titus. While of a retiring disposition, he was quick to do good, eager to help the unfortunate, and anxious to discharge every duty as man and citizen. Writing in his journal at one time, he gave this as his life's aim: "I have no hopes of fame, only a desire to do good; to help just a little in the world from which we must soon be taken by death." A consistent Christian, for years he was a member of Rock Presbyterian Church, near Fair Hill, but on removing to Appleton, in 1880, he transferred his membership to Head of Christiana, a venerable church of the same denomination, just over the state line in Delaware. For several years he was organist in the church, and the Sabbath before his sudden illness he was in his place as usual. His death occurred August 3, 1887. Five days before, he was prostrated by heat while at work upon his farm, and was never fully conscious afterward.

George Johnston, the poet, and author of the History of Cecil County, was a personal friend of Mr. Kimble, and wrote the following tribute to his memory: "The funeral of J. H. Kimble at Head of Christiana cemetery on Sunday last (August 7, 1887) was attended by the largest concourse of people ever witnessed at that place within the memory of any person now living in the neighborhood. And probably no one of all the unnumbered host that sleep their last long sleep on the sunny slope of the historic old graveyard, which has been the resting place of the dead for nearly two centuries, had more sincere and honest friends to mourn their departure. Though comparatively young in years, Mr. Kimble was old in the practice of honest integrity and every virtue that adorns and beautifies the Christian character. Unostentatious and unobtrusive, his life was a beautiful exemplification of the religion of the Divine Master, whom he delighted to serve. The writer hereof knew him from childhood and has yet to hear the first word spoken derogatory of his integrity as a man or his sincerity as a Christian. Consequently, it was no wonder that the number of friends who came to testify to the high esteem in which he was held, was estimated at a thousand. The funeral services were conducted by his pastor, Rev. J. L. Vallandigham, assisted by Rev. J. F. Williamson. Mr. Vallandigham's sermon was a beautiful and honest tribute to the memory of the deceased, of whom he spoke in the highest terms. Thus ended the earthly career of John Henry Kimble, who will be long remembered wherever he was known, as an honest man, a sincere Christian, a skilled musician, and the "poet of the people." "The path of the just is as a shining light that shineth more and more unto the perfect day."

The following lines composed by Mr. Kimble in memory of his cousin, Daniel R. Titus, of Morris, Grundy County, Ill., seem so appropriate to himself that we quote them as a conclusion to this biography:

"His brief career
Was filled with noble deeds, and words of cheer
That won kind friends where'er he dwelt; for Truth
He worked with all the vigor of strong youth;
But ere his great life mission was complete,
Disease compelled him from his labor sweet.
Alas! and can it be his gentle voice
No more will make our weary hearts rejoice?
Ah, yes; the dismal silence of his room,
The vacant chair, the flowers he loved, that bloom
So brightly by our humble cottage door——
All answer, he has gone forever more!
His true heart feared not death; for purer life
His spirit yearned; and now where mortal strife
Is never known, he rests. God speed the time
When we shall meet him in those realms sublime!"

Below we insert a hymn, the words and music of which Mr. Kimble composed, but a short time before his death:

Shall we reach the home immortal
After death's impending night?
Shall we pass the golden portal
In the spirit land of light?
There no stormy tempest rages,
And our Saviour is the King;
And the saints of former ages
Join the songs the angels sing.

Shall we catch the glorious vision
  When the scenes of earth depart,
In our Father's house elysian
  Where no sorrow chills the heart?
O, to meet the friends we greeted
  Ere death took them from our side,
Where each life shall be completed,
  And each soul be satisfied!

Yes, ye faithful, Christ has said it;
  We may rise from prison chains.
Welcome death; why should we dread it,
  While the great beyond remains?
Soon the dark veil may be parted;
  We shall reach the glittering plains;
Cheer up, all ye broken-hearted,
  Labor while the light remains.

Never fainting, never fearing,
  Do thy duty every day;
Verily the end is nearing,
  When thy soul shall flee away;
Flee with seraphs through the portal,
  Where no sin can ever blight,
In the glorious home immortal,
  In the spirit land of light.

JOHN D. WORTHINGTON. Few men in Harford County are so well known as Mr. Worthington. Still fewer have a wider personal popularity and warmer friendships. In his official capacity as superintendent of schools of the county he has been instrumental in advancing the standard of education and the grade of scholarship, the result of his intelligent management being apparent in the improved condition of the schools. From youth he has been interested in the public-school system. The absolute necessity of universal education, wide in scope, complete in curriculum, practical in aim, has long been evident to him; he has, therefore, been deeply interested in educational matters and his sympathies are always given to matters connected therewith.

In the eastern part of Harford County, on the Susquehanna River, the subject of this article was born, December 2, 1856, the son of William and Mary (Dallam) Worthington. Both of these families have long been prominent in Maryland; the Worthingtons are descended from Quaker ancestors that came to America from England, and the Dallams date back in the history of Maryland to the first settlement. William Worthington died in 1859, and his wife in 1889. They had three sons, one of whom, Frank, who was a farmer, died in 1878; and another, Charles, is now engaged in a manufacturing business near Philadelphia. The boyhood years of our subject were spent on the home farm and in attendance at Darlington Academy. His studies were further prosecuted at St. John's Academy, Annapolis. Possessing a love of study, he acquired a broad fund of information. His bent of mind was such that it was easy for him to impart knowledge to others, and hence he chose the congenial occupation of teaching, his first term of school being taught in a country district in 1876. His success brought him in prominence in the locality, and his services were sought in positions more pleasant and remunerative. February 1, 1878, he was made assistant principal of the Bel Air school. The pupils advanced so rapidly under his instruction and the work moved along so systematically and smoothly that he was soon recognized as one of the best instructors Bel Air ever had. His success brought him promotion to the position of principal, in which capacity he remained until 1887, and then resigned to accept the office of superintendent of schools for Harford County. He had been a most thorough and competent teacher, and his elevation to the head of the schools of the county was but a just tribute to his ability.

As teacher and as superintendent the record of Mr. Worthington has been above criticism, and the schools of Harford County have never been in as good condition as now for effective work. In 1890 a further recognition of his ability was tendered him. This was his appointment, by Governor Jackson, as a member of the State Board of Education, a position of great responsibility, and one, too, that brought him prominently before the public. For four years he officiated in that capacity, and there, as in every other post of duty, he served the people faithfully and efficiently. He has had little time in his busy life for any matters not pertaining to education, though he has been a director in the Second National Bank of Bel Air, in which he is a stockholder, and he has held other positions that identified him with local interests and enterprises. In the Presbyterian Church, of which he is a member, he holds the office of trustee and ruling elder. As an active, public-spirited citizen, he has always endorsed the principles of the conservative Democratic party, though as the holder of an office which makes him peculiarly the servant of the whole people, he has never been identified with politics as an active partisan.

In 1882 Mr. Worthington married Theresa McCormick, a niece of the late Col. E. H. Webster. It is their happiness to be mutually compatible in disposition and tastes; their union has, therefore, brought a more complete felicity into both lives. They are the parents of four children, Malcolm McLean, Annie Laurie, Frank D. and John D.

COL. ISAAC D. DAVIS. The history of the Davis family in America is an interesting one. It begins with the year 1705, when John Davis emigrated from Wales and settled on Long Island, where he remained until his death, at an advanced age. In religious belief he was identified with the Quakers. His eldest son, Isaac, moved to Salem County, N. J., in 1725, and there reared his children, John, David, Hannah and Elizabeth. David, the second son, was appointed judge of the Salem County court and became prominent in his locality. He owned a tract of land near Pittsgrove and there built a brick house, which is still standing, and that place continued to be his home until death. He married Dorothy Cousins, an English lady, who was born in 1693, and their children were Sarah, Mercy, Amy, David and Incol.

David, the son of David and Dorothy Davis, born in 1730, was, like his father, a large landowner. His wife bore the maiden name of Martha Cole and they had several children. Isaac Davis, their eldest son, was born in 1762. In early life he commanded a sailing-vessel, trading into Philadelphia, and in the War of 1812 he commanded a company of Light Horse raised in the vicinity of Christiana, Del. He married Susanna Newman, daughter of John Newman, of Red Bank, N. J., and with his family came to Cecil County, Md., in 1820. His children were, Hannah, Rachel, Catherine and John Newman Davis. Hannah married Thomas McNeal, and they have descendants in Cecil County. Catherine married David Robinett, an officer of the United States navy. John Newman Davis married Rebecca Bolton in 1832, and resided near Elkton, where he engaged in farming. He was a retiring, unassuming man, of literary tastes, and led a consistent Christian life as a member of the Methodist Episcopal Church. His wife was a granddaughter of Hugh Bolton, who in 1764 was a shipmaster in the king's service and came from Glasgow, Scotland. Their children were Mary, Isabella, Isaac D. and William.

The subject of this article was born in Cecil County, near Elkton, December 31, 1841. He was educated at the Elkton Academy, and in 1861, at the outbreak of the Civil War, enlisted in the Federal army, serving in the army of the Potomac until the close of the conflict. Among the engagements in which he participated were the battles of Antietam, Winchester, Varina Landing, Ft. Harrison, Drury's Bluff, Fair Oaks and Petersburg. He was taken prisoner at Winchester by General Ewell's forces and confined for two months in Libby prison in the city of Richmond. After the surrender of General Lee's army in Virginia he was sent with Sheridan's command to Texas. During the Civil War several European forces had seized upon Mexico as a foothold for establishing a monarchy upon our continent. They placed the Archduke Maximilian of Austria on the throne as emperor of Mexico. This was a direct act of war against the United States by the powers engaged and was treated as such as soon as the Federal army was free of the war at home. After the surrender of Lee, therefore, General Sheridan was sent with a strong force to the Rio Grande, to be on hand should negotiations for the evacuation of Mexico by the European troops fail.

Concerning the connection of Colonel Davis with this episode of American history, the following may be appropriately quoted from the *Baltimore Sun:* "Col. I. D. Davis, cashier of the Second National Bank of Elkton, has the distinction of having commanded the only United States troops which crossed into Mexico to drive out the French who were upholding the Emperor Maximilian. Colonel Davis says: ' In the fall of 1865 I commanded the post at Clarksville, at the mouth of the Rio Grande River, in the state of Texas, being a part of the army under General Sheridan, stationed along the Mexico border pending negotiatious for the evacuation of Mexico by the French. The troops occupied that line from June, 1865, until January, 1866, with no indications on the part of the Mexican, Maximilian, that the demands of the United States would be complied with. The maintenance of this force, about thirty thousand men, was a great expense to the government and the object to be attained seemed as far off as at the beginning of the negotiations. All were heartily tired of this inactivity and anxious to strike a blow for the liberation of Mexico and the vindication of the Monroe doctrine. With the knowledge of this feeling on the part of all the officers, from General Sheridan down, I resolved to take the initial step toward bringing matters to a decisive focus. I had no official orders for what I did, but it was done with the full knowledge of General Weitzel, the corps commander. On the night of January 4, 1866, I crossed the Rio Grande River in an English schooner, with volunteers from my own troops and some ex-Confederates from Kirby Smith's command. I surprised and captured the forts at Bagdad, with two hundred Austrian infantry and four pieces of artillery, and confined the prisoners in the warehouses of the town. At daylight on the morning of the 5th, the French gunboat "Antonio," arrived from up the river and opened fire upon us, but was engaged by our captured cannon, disabled and driven off. Three French men-of-war were off shore in the gulf and daylight showed that they had steam up and ports open ready for action. After the "Antonio" retreated these three ships all opened fire on us with shell; but their gunnery was bad and they did us no harm. Seeing this they attempted to land a force in small boats, but we drove them back and held the town. Next day, the 6th, General Escabedo, the liberal officer of the Republican party of Mexico, arrived, and I turned the town over to him, recrossed the river and reported to General Weitzel. Within a month from that time our government received notice that the French troops would be withdrawn, and I claim that it was the direct effect of my invasion that brought this prompt result. In this engagement Federal and Confederate troops fought side by side; they met a double force, composed of the flower of European forces, and not only defeated, but captured and disarmed them. The audacity of the enterprise and the prompt evacuation of Mexico by the French afterward, show that the slow process of diplomatic negotiation is not suited to all cases.' "

For his distinguished services in this engagement Colonel Davis was complimented in general orders by General Sheridan and was offered a commission in the regular army. He was also offered by General Escabedo a brigadier-general's commission in the army of Mexico. He declined both, and the services of the troops being no longer required in Texas, he was mustered out of service in 1866. He returned to Cecil County and shortly afterward married Clara Miller, daughter of Rev. Joseph Miller, of this county. She died in 1894, leaving four children, namely: Henry M., attorney-at-law, of Elkton; William J., secretary of the Keys & Miller Lumber Company; John Newman, clerk to the Pusey & Jones Company, of Delaware; and Mary R., a student in school. The sons are married, Henry M. having married Araetta Anthony in 1896; William J. married Ada Steele in 1895; and John Newman married Bertha McNeal in 1896.

Colonel Davis is extensively engaged in business, being director and treasurer of the Keys & Miller Lumber Company, director in the Singerly

Pulp and Paper Company, and director and cashier of the Second National Bank of Elkton. He also manages his farm, a fine property near Elkton, on which he resides and which has been the home of four generations of the family. In educational matters he is deeply interested, and is a trustee of the Elkton Academy and of the West Amwell public school. Political matters receive his thoughtful consideration, and few men are better posted regarding public events than is he. However, he has never been an office seeker and never ran for office except once, when he was defeated for the legislature by a very small majority by the late Hon. James B. Groome. For two years, 1889-90, he was clerk to the board of county commissioners, and for twenty years he has been a member of the Republican executive committee for Cecil County. Since 1866 he has been identified with the Masonic fraternity.

A very large number of the old residents of Cecil County of the Davis name trace their ancestry back to David Davis, of Salem County, N. J., and also many of the name in Delaware and Pennsylvania. Some also reside in the west, and it is singular to note that while the old-fashioned names, such as Mercy and Susanna, have disappeared, the patriarchal names of David and Isaac are still used and seem to be the favorite names in the record running back nearly two hundred years.

ROBERT N. RAMPLEY. The family represented by this gentleman is favorably known in Harford County, and especially in District No. 4. Its members have contributed their efforts to the development of the resources of the community, and have ever been characterized by manliness and integrity. When James Rampley, who founded the family in the United States, came here from England, he settled upon the farm where our subject now resides. Capt. James, son of James, and father of Robert N., spent his life on this place engaged in its cultivation. During the War of 1812 he enlisted in the American army, and while in the service gained the title by which he was afterward known. He married Elizabeth Nelson, who, like himself, was a native of Harford County, and they became the parents of four children, Sarah, James, William and Robert N.

On the farm which has been his only home through life, the subject of this sketch was born June 25, 1817. In boyhood he became familiar with scenes common to the early half of the nineteenth century. His education was limited, for in those days schools were not as numerous as now. A large part of his time was devoted to manual labor, and from the time he was old enough to assist he was called upon to do his share of the farm work. On arriving at man's estate he entered for himself the occupation to which he had been reared, and with which he was most familiar. In it he continued until the approach of old age, and the possession of an ample income caused him to retire from active labors, though he still maintains the supervision of his interests. As he looks back over life's day, now in its sunset hour, he rejoices in the many improvements that have been made in Harford County; he notes with pleasure the enlargement of industries and the increased importance of its commerce and its agriculture. To secure this result he gave his quota, and when he was in his prime the district had no citizen more active than he.

At the age of thirty-two years Mr. Rampley married Frances R. Maul, of this county, member of a Pennsylvania family that followed farming pursuits. She is an active member of the Presbyterian Church, and has always been helpful to the needy and distressed. Mr. Rampley contributes to the Presbyterian Church largely, but is not a member of any denomination, though a believer in Christianity. On his farm, and now in use as a barn, stands the first Presbyterian Church ever built in District No. 4, it having been erected on the site now occupied by Bethel Church. The two children born of the union of Mr. and Mrs. Rampley were named: Cornelia and Mary E. The latter is deceased. The former became the wife of Capt. James C. Turner, by whom she has four sons and three daughters: Fannie M., Elizabeth N., Phillips C., Robert N., John M., Susan M. and James C. In politics Mr. Rampley is a loyal Democrat, and unswerving in his allegiance to the men and measures of the party. An energetic and industrious man, by good management he has acquired a sufficient capital to enable him to spend his remaining days in retirement from labor.

DAVID REA. America is indebted to the Emerald Isle for many of her best citizens. The sons of that country have come to the new world and with their versatile ability have been quick to see and take advantage of opportunities and work their way upward to success in the various callings to which they have devoted their energies. Among those of that nationality who sought homes in Cecil County and became allied with her best interests was Mr. Rea. He was born in the town of Bangor, County Down, Ireland, on the 14th of June, 1809, and having spent the days of his boyhood and youth in that country resolved to try his fortune in America.

It was in 1830 that Mr. Rea bade adieu to the land of his birth, and in a sailing-vessel crossed the Atlantic to New York City. In that place he learned the slater's trade, which he followed there until 1835, when he removed to New Orleans, continuing in the same line of business in the Crescent City for twenty years. In 1855 he came to Cecil County and purchased the farm on which his widow now resides. It was a tract of one hundred and fifty acres, and with characteristic energy he at once began to develop and improve the place, continuing his energetic labors until he had made it one of the valuable and attractive farms of the county. He was a man of great energy, of untiring purpose and resolute will, and these qualities were the essential factors in his business.

In 1838 Mr. Rea was united in marriage to Miss Mary Graham, who was born in New York City in 1822, a daughter of Robert Graham, a native of Scotland, who came to America in 1821. Mr. Rea was a progressive and public-spirited citizen, who manifested a deep interest in everything pertaining to the welfare of the community, and gave a liberal support to all objects tending toward the advancement and improvement of the county. All esteemed him for his sterling worth, and his circle of friends was extensive. He died in 1885, and his remains were interred in West Nottingham Cemetery. Since her husband's death, Mrs. Rea has continued to reside upon the farm, in District No. 7, which he left to her, and which provides her a comfortable support. For thirty-eight years she has been a faithful and consistent member of the Presbyterian Church of West Nottingham, and her consistent life, her kindly manner and her pleasant disposition have won her the love and regard of many.

J WILEY NORRIS, one of the leading and influential farmers of Harford County, residing in District No. 4, comes of a family that has been connected with Maryland from the days of its early development. His great-grandfather, John Norris, was born in England, and when a young man came with his brother George to the new world. They made their way direct to Harford County, and purchased eighteen hundred acres of land of Lord Baltimore, the first governor of the colony. A part of this tract is now in possession of our subject. From that early day down to the present the representatives of the Norris family have been prominent in the work of reclaiming the state from its primitive condition and making it one of the leading commonwealths of the Union. Harford County bears the impress of their individuality, and the town of Norrisville stands as a monument to the enterprise of Vincent Norris, the grandfather of our subject. He was a native of Harford County, devoted his energies to farming with much success, and laid out the village which bears his name.

John S. Norris, father of our subject, was numbered among the native sons of this county and followed farming as a life work. In early life he married Manda Z. Hutchins, who was born in the same locality, and their union was blessed with three children: J. Wiley, Robert R. and Richard M., the last-named now deceased. Mr. Norris, of this review, was born on the 7th of December, 1844, on the ancestral homestead, where his boyhood and youth were quietly passed. His elementary education, acquired in the common schools, was supplemented by a commercial course in Eastman's Business College, of Poughkeepsie, N. Y., and by a few terms' attendance at a select school. He was thus well fitted for life's responsible duties and in 1869, when twenty-five years of age, he embarked in general merchandising in Norrisville. After conducting his store for three years he resumed farming and has since devoted his time and attention to that pursuit. His landed possessions now aggregate one hundred and forty-five acres, and rich lands yield to him good returns for the care and labor he bestows upon the place.

·Believing thoroughly in the principles of Democracy, Mr. Norris identified himself with that party on attaining his majority and is one of the leading workers in its ranks in his district, doing all in his power to promote its growth and insure its success. His church relationship is with the Methodist Protestant denomination in Norrisville, and fraternally he is connected with Charity Lodge No. 134, A. F. & A. M., of Parkton, Md.

we find that in almost every instance they are those who have risen gradually by their own efforts, their industry and perseverance. These qualities are undoubtedly possessed by Mr. Reed, for without them he could not have secured the confidence and respect so universally given him.

The Reed family is among the oldest and most honored within the limits of Cecil County. The first representatives in this country came hither from Ireland at an early day, bringing with them very little capital, but an abundant supply of the sturdy qualities of heart and mind characteristic of the Irish people. The father of our subject, William Reed, was born in District No. 5, Cecil County, and grew to manhood here. Trained to farm work, he selected agriculture for his occupation, and was so uniformly prosperous that he became the owner of valuable property in the district. In addition to the management of his farm, he had charge of the building and opening of roads in the district, and his services in that capacity were of the greatest value in the development of the locality. Besides being road supervisor, he held other local positions of trust. The Methodist Protestant Church had in him a leading and generous member, and the carrying forward of this religious movement was largely due to his interest and assistance. In 1865, when quite advanced in years, he passed away, and was laid to rest near the spot where he had spent his busy life. He married Amy McVey, daughter of Jacob McVey, and of Welsh descent. They became the parents of five children, all but one of whom are living, namely: Joseph T., who is engaged in the mercantile business in Bay View; Benjamin M.; William, whose biography will be found upon another page of this volume; and Martha, now widowed, and residing near Calvert, Md

BENJAMIN M. REED. In studying the lives and characters of men, we are naturally led to inquire into the cause of their success or of their failure. Success is less the result of genius than of good judgment and hard work. When we trace the careers of those who have become well-to-do and influential, whether they are business men, or farmers, or public officials,

At the family homestead, and in a stone house standing one-quarter of a mile from his present place of residence, the subject of this sketch was born September 26, 1822. His earliest recollections are of sights and scenes in District No. 5, and he is attached to this locality by ties of long and intimate association. Studies in school occupied his attention in the winter and work on the

JESSE A. KIRK.

farm consumed the summer months. Thus uneventfully passed the years of youth. At the age of twenty-one he purchased the place where he has since resided. It is situated south of the property owned by his brother, William, and consists of eighty-two acres, which, though not constituting a large farm, are so productive that they return liberal profits to the owner.

In 1876 Mr. Reed was united in marriage with Christie McVey, adopted daughter of John and Hannah Riddell; she was born and reared in this county and received her education in local schools. Trained in girlhood to a knowledge of housework, she was qualified to take charge of a home of her own and manage it economically and successfully. Four children were born of this union, two of whom are now living, namely: Benjamin H. and Melvina L., both of whom are with their parents.

JOSEPH C. BOSLEY. This gentleman was for many years counted among the leading farmers of Harford County, and although he has now passed from earth's activities, it is but just that an outline of his life work be given, for he was one of those who did excellent service in bringing this section into its present splendid condition. All of his life was spent here, where he was born June 7, 1820. His parents, Joseph and Mary (Cathcart) Bosley, were also born here and in this section their earthly career ended. They were the parents of the following children: Jemima, Mary, Ann, Ellen, Rachel, Elizabeth, Vincent and Joseph C.

The early life of Joseph C. Bosley was spent in the same manner as that of the average farmer's boy; that is, he did chores about the home place, and later followed the plow, and to this occupation his attention turned after he commenced life for himself. At the age of twenty-six years he married Miss Anna Wiley, a native of Harford County, and they became the parents of nine children, named as follows: Mary A., Alice A., David W., Jemima E. (deceased), John J., Margaret C. (deceased), William R., Rachel E. (deceased), and Laura R. (deceased). Mr. Bosley's life was one of usefulness and activity. Being a man of excellent judgment and unbounded energy, he tilled his fine farm of one hundred and fifty acres to his profit, and improved it with substantial buildings. His interests were not confined to agriculture alone, for the welfare of his section was of moment to him, and everything pertaining to the advancement of Harford County received his support. He was a patron of worthy enterprises of all kinds, charitable in disposition, and his correct mode of living won him universal respect and esteem. He was for years prominently connected with the Methodist Episcopal Church, in which he was an active worker and a substantial supporter.

Mr. Bosley was always in sympathy with the principles of the Democratic party and supported its measures and candidates at each election, but was himself no office seeker, for his farming and other interests occupied his attention to the exclusion of all else. On the 21st of September, 1890, at the age of seventy years, his earthly career closed, but the good which he accomplished in his quiet way will live through the ages, long after his name has been forgotten. Such is the influence of a well-spent life.

JESSE ALLEN KIRK belongs to that class of citizens whose sterling worth, public spirit and progressiveness have been the means of procuring the substantial development of Cecil County. He belongs to one of the old and honored families of the county and was born in District No. 6, June 22, 1822. The founder of the family in America was Roger Kirk, who emigrated from Ireland in 1712, and settled in Chester County, Pa. His son, Elisha Kirk, was the father of Allen Kirk, who was born in District No. 6, Cecil County, in 1789, and became the father of our subject. He married Martha McCullough, and they had fourteen children: Evander, James R.; Benjamin F., Rebecca, wife of James Cameron; Elisha, Martha J., William A., John, of College Green; Mary A., Jesse A., Lemuel, and three who died in infancy.

Born and reared on the farm which is still his home, Mr. Kirk acquired his education in the common schools, and when twenty-one years of age began teaching, a profession which he followed until 1846, when he embarked in merchandising in Rising Sun with his eldest brother and Basil Haines. He continued in that line until 1850, when he sold his store. In 1852 he became a partner in the firm of Haines, Kirk & Stubbs. In 1857 he embarked in the hardware business, which he successfully continued until 1876. Since that time he has lived retired. He is a man of resourceful ability, of untiring energy and sound judgment, and carries forward to successful completion whatever he undertakes. In 1871 he was instrumental in organizing the National Bank of Rising Sun, and for the past ten years has served as its vice president, while from its establishment he has been a stockholder and director.

On the 21st of March, 1851, Mr. Kirk married Miss Hannah Mount, by whom he had one son, Mount E., the well-known hardware merchant of Rising Sun. After the death of his first wife he was again married, in March, 1887, his second union being with Mrs. Mary J. Warner.

In 1848 Mr. Kirk was appointed postmaster of Rising Sun. He has long been one of the most prominent citizens of Cecil County, and in 1864 was honored by an election to the state legislature, where he discharged his duties with marked ability. He was appointed school commissioner in 1886, serving for eight years, and in 1897 was re-appointed to fill out the unexpired term of F. S. Everist. His official duties have been marked by the exercise of good business judgment, absolute fidelity to the trust reposed in him and by courtesy to all with whom he has thus been brought in contact. He votes with the Republican party. To the Methodist Episcopal Church he has been a liberal contributor and withholds his support from no interest calculated to prove of public benefit. His well-spent life has won him the unqualified regard of all, and his name is high on the roll of Cecil County's eminent citizens.

JAMES H. QUINBY. The subject of this sketch has passed away, but this record shows that a man of Christian character, such as he possessed, is not soon forgotten. He was of English descent, his grandfather having emigrated from England some time during the eighteenth century and established a home in Morris County, N. J. There he was born in 1826, and there his early boyhood days were uneventfully passed, in school studies and farm work. During the Civil War he acted as private secretary to Col. John Smith. By occupation he was an agriculturist, and for twenty-five years prior to his death he resided upon a farm in District No. 3, Harford County, where he raised various cereals and carried on an extensive dairy business.

In 1856 occurred the marriage of James H. Quinby and Nancy B. Farrand, daughter of Samuel Farrand, a well-known real-estate owner of Morris County. Eleven children were born of their union and of that number five are now living, namely: Annie K., of Morris County, N. J., wife of C. W. Wingfield, of Richmond, Va.; Elizabeth; Carrie S., who married B. F. Howell; James H.; and Bertha A., Mrs. Thomas H. Hanway. Since the death of her husband, which occurred August 26, 1892, at the age of sixty-six, the widowed mother has made her home with her son, James H., Jr.

By the people of his community, Mr. Quinby is remembered as one of its solid citizens, a man of sterling character, and upright in his dealings with his fellow-men. Thoroughly absorbed in his farming interests, he never sought the honors of office or the responsibilities of public life. His ventures were crowned with success, and the results of his keen judgment and great energy netted him a competence. A man of strong convictions, and an earnest, public-spirited citizen, he held the regard of all his acquaintances.

James H. Quinby, Jr., was educated at St. John's College, Annapolis, and was a member of the class of 1887, with which he would have graduated had not the death of his two brothers made it necessary for him to return home and take charge of the farm. In 1895 he purchased the old homestead, which contains one hundred and fifty acres, and here he has since engaged in farming and the dairy business. In 1891 he was united in marriage with Emma H., daughter of Dr. A. S. Baldwin, of Baltimore County. They have one son, named James A. They are identified with the Presbyterian Church, of Bel Air, in which his father was a trustee for many years.

JAMES W. GLADDEN, the founder of the postoffice and station of The Rocks, is a prominent farmer and successful business man of District No. 5, Harford County. He is a descendant of Scotch-Irish ancestors, men and women of worth of character and firmness of convictions, a race that has had its influence upon the history of our nation. The first of the family in this country was his great-grandfather, who came to America in a very early day. The grandfather, William Gladden, was a native of York County, Pa., whence he removed to Harford County during the latter part of the eighteenth century. During the War of 1812 he served in the American army, and participated in a number of engagements with the enemy.

The father of our subject, Jacob Gladden, was born on the farm where James W. now lives, and here his life was actively passed in the cultivation of his land. By his marriage to Jane Wilson, who was born in this county, he had eight children, but only two are living, James W. and Hannah J., Mrs. Archibald Wilson, of this district. The occupation followed by the Gladden family, as far back as the record can be traced, has been that of agriculture. On the farm where he now resides, the subject of this sketch was born February 23, 1835. Here he was reared to a knowledge of farm work and an understanding of all its details. He has made agriculture his vocation and in it has gained prosperity. However, he has had other interests and at different times has engaged in other enterprises. As mentioned, he founded and built what is called The Rocks postoffice, and from the rental of the popular pic-nic grounds there, which he owned, he received considerable money. For three years he ran the Glen store and sawmill.

At the age of thirty-eight Mr. Gladden married Blanche Richardson, of this county. Eight children were born of their union, namely: Harry R., S. Walter, James W., William, Bertram, Margaret J., Anna E. and Harriet. The Gladden estate comprises two hundred and twenty acres, bearing good improvements, and devoted to general farming. The owner is a man of marked enterprise and executive ability, and in his business relations his energetic character and practical sagacity find abundant room for exercise. Throughout his life he has kept his powers of observation on the alert and has a fund of information that is quite valuable. He takes an active interest in politics and is a Democrat, first, last and all the time.

THEODORE EWING has been the proprietor of the Ewing homestead in Cecil County since 1869, and as a result of industry, prudence and frugality, has brought under excellent cultivation what is now one of the best farms in District No. 8. His landed possessions aggregate two hundred and fifty acres of land, with suitable farm buildings, some live stock, and the other appurtenances of a country estate. In his younger years he was a carpenter and for a long time followed that occupation, but since turning his attention to agriculture he has done no carpentering except such as is necessary in the conduct of his homestead.

The Ewings of Maryland are all descendants of Joshua Ewing, who was born in the north of Scotland, on the Dundee River, and from there crossed the ocean to America, making settlement in 1680 upon the place now occupied by Theodore. Little else is known of him save his name and the date of his emigration. However, it may safely be supposed that he was a man of courage and enterprise, fitted by nature to brave the hardships and inconveniences of life in a new country, in whose forests savages still lurked and wild animals roamed. Patrick, son of Joshua, had a son also named Patrick, who was the father of our subject. He was born on the old homestead, which he occupied throughout his entire life, engaging in its cultivation. Here his death occurred in 1869, when he was seventy-six years of age. By his marriage to Isabel Evans, of Pennsylvania, he had a family of seven children, named as follows: Edwin E., Theodore, William P., Jane Anna, Rebecca, Elizabeth and Margaret.

This old homestead was the birthplace of our subject, and he was born in 1826. When quite young he learned the carpenter's trade, which he followed for eighteen years in different parts of the south, especially in Georgia and Alabama. On the death of his father in 1869, he returned to Cecil County and has since carried on the home farm, which has been in the possession of the family since 1680. In 1858 he was united in marriage with Miss Elizabeth Matherson, who, like himself, is an earnest Christian and in sympathy with the doctrines of the Presbyterian Church. Their two daughters and one son are named as follows: Arabella, wife of William T. Frier; Georgia, who married Michael McKinney; and Albert, who remains on the home farm, to the possession of which he will succeed, thus retaining the property in the Ewing name. While living in Georgia, Mr. Ewing was identified with the lodge of Odd Fellows at Augusta. He is well and favorably known, not only as a representative of one of the oldest families of this section, but as a man who honors the name he bears, one who has unselfishly administered to the comfort of a large number of people, and who counts among his close friends the best people of the district. When he was young he did not have the educational advantages that Cecil County now offers its young people; the knowledge he possesses has been acquired by experience in the school of life and by contact with men in business affairs. To him and such as he, Cecil County owes much, for their labors have brought about the present encouraging condition of farming affairs and the enlargement of local industries.

THOMAS B. DALLAM. We are glad to present to the many friends of the late Thomas B. Dallam this sketch of his life, outlining the principal events in his career. A man of genial nature and conscientious character, he died when the shadows of life's brief day were beginning to fall toward the west and when the sun was sweeping in its orbit to the twilight's horizon. A loved and loving husband, his passing away, even though the quiet and happy close of a busy life, was a deep bereavement to his wife, who had ever been his affectionate helpmate and who by his death was left alone.

Many of the traits that seemed most admirable in the character of Mr. Dallam were his by inheritance, for he was a member of an old and honored Quaker family, and personally always held allegiance to the Society of Friends. His birth occurred in Baltimore in 1819, and his ancestors had been for several generations identified with the history of that city. There occurred the birth of his father, William, who was for many years a merchant in that place, and the residents of the city during the early part of the present century were quite well acquainted with him.

The family being well-to-do, the subject of this sketch was given excellent advantages in an educational way. He attended private schools in

Baltimore, and Newark, Del., and also prosecuted his studies for a time in the Friends' school at Westtown. When a lad he came to Harford County, and in early manhood he settled upon the farm now owned by James Andrews, making it his home for some time, and keeping "bachelor's hall." However, this kind of life was not entirely congenial, and he determined to change it for one happier and more agreeable. At the age of forty-five he chose as his wife Miss Ellen Hopkins, daughter of John W. Hopkins, and a most estimable lady, who brightened the declining years of his life by her care and attention. He continued to reside there until his death, which occurred in 1881, at the age of sixty-two.

JOHN FLETCHER PRICE, formerly superintendent of the Chesapeake and Delaware Canal, was one of Cecil County's most distinguished men. Personally he was genial, affable, and whole-souled, in intellect discriminating, in mental acumen keen and far-reaching, with a natural faculty for business pursuits. The long period of his connection with the canal company as assistant superintendent, and later as superintendent, proved the confidence reposed in him, a confidence that he never abused. His was not a life of stirring events, but was characterized by the quiet discharge of daily duties as business man and as citizen.

The Price family was founded in this country about 1726, their first home being in Delaware, where succeeding generations resided, engaged mostly in agricultural pursuits. Mr. Price was born in that state October 4, 1837, the son of John R. and Mary Price. His maternal grandmother bore the name of Hester Allman, and was the descendant of an old and aristocratic English family, whose first representatives in America came to this country from England in 1630. Mr. Price was given an excellent education in the seminary at Pottstown, Pa. In 1862 he was appointed assistant superintendent of the Chesapeake and Delaware Canal, and in 1877 was promoted to the position of general superintendent, which had previously been held by his father. In that capacity he continued to serve until his death, May 27, 1896, at the age of about fifty-nine years. Interested in public affairs, he was well posted concerning the issues of the age and always supported Democratic principles.

The lady who for years was the devoted wife of Mr. Price and who now survives him, bore the maiden name of Mary C. Clayton, and was born in Delaware April 20, 1855. She was given a good education at home, where she studied under a governess, and remained with her parents until she left their home for that of her husband. Like him, she is an earnest member of the Methodist Episcopal Church, and has many warm friends among the best people of Cecil County, where she makes her home in District No. 2.

The Clayton family was founded in America by Joshua Clayton, who accompanied William Penn to this country in 1682. His two sons were John and Joshua. The former, who was an influential public man, served as high sheriff, justice, captain of Kent County militia, and member of assembly. He and his wife, Grace, had a son, James, who in turn had three sons, Dr. Joshua, John and James. James had a son, John M., who married Sally Ann Fisher, a descendant of Thomas Fisher, private secretary to William Penn. John M. Clayton was a brilliant lawyer, politician and statesman, served as United States senator, held the office of chief justice of Delaware, and was secretary of state under President Taylor. Both of his sons, Charles and James, died when young and were buried in Dover, Del.

John, son of James Clayton, was also prominent in public life, being justice in 1777, member of assembly 1777–83, member of council 1782, high sheriff 1785, judge of court of appeals 1788, and judge of orphans' court 1788–92. Dr. Joshua, the eldest son of James Clayton, and direct progenitor of Mrs. Price, held many distinguished public offices, the most important being that of first governor of Delaware, under the constitution of 1789-96. He was also state treasurer, judge of court of appeals, member of the colonial congress, president of the council and United States senator. While ministering to the needs of yellow fever patients in Philadelphia he died, August 11, 1798, at the age of fifty-four years, and was buried in Cecil County, Md.

The three sons of Dr. Joshua Clayton were Thomas, Dr. James Lawson and Capt. Richard Clayton. The two last-named left numerous descendants, some of whom have gained prominence. The first-named was an eminent lawyer of Delaware, where his large talents brought him many positions of trust and high honor. He was attorney-general, congressman, United States senator and chief justice of Delaware. He had a son, Col. Joshua, and two daughters, Elizabeth and Jeanette. Elizabeth married Maj. N. Young, for many years in the United States army, commanding brigades in the Mexican war and against the Indians, also at one time state treasurer of Delaware. Jeanette married Robert Frame, a distinguished lawyer, and attorney-general for Delaware for a number of years. Col. Joshua Clayton, of Thomas, father of Mrs. Price, was a well-known lawyer and land owner of Delaware. Reference to his history appears upon another page, in the sketch of Charles S. Ellison.

CLEMENT G. BUTLER, who is engaged in the milling business in District No. 3, Harford County, traces his lineage to Irish ancestors who settled in this county at a period very early in its history. His grandfather, Clement Butler, won the title of colonel by his meritorious service in the Mexican War, and was a resident throughout life of District No. 4, where he owned a farm near Clermont Mills, on Deer Creek. Of his four children, the oldest, Thomas, was our subject's father and was a native of District No. 4, where in early manhood he bought a plantation and a few slaves. Farming was his life work, but he did not engage in it to the neglect of his duties as a citizen. He was always willing to help forward any progressive measure. In politics he was a strong Democrat, prominent in the party councils in this locality. For a long time he held the office of justice of the peace and for two years he was county commissioner.

The marriage of Thomas Butler united him with Cordelia, a daughter of James Streett, and six children were born of their union, namely: Maggie, who resides at the old home place; Clement G., of this sketch; James S., whose home is in Delta, Pa.; J. Thomas, who lives at The Rocks, District No. 4; May; and Harry, who is traveling salesman for a tobacco firm in Baltimore. The father of this family died at his home in May, 1893, aged seventy-two. His wife still remains on the old home farm, and is now about seventy years of age, but is quite hearty for one so far advanced in life.

Born at The Rocks, on Deer Creek, Harford County, in 1852, the subject of this sketch received a public-school education, and at the age of eighteen began to cultivate his father's farm, where he remained some years. Then entering Preston's mill at The Rocks, he began to learn the milling business, and spent four years in the one place, afterward working for a similar period at Rocks Run. In 1879 he bought the grinding mill owned by M. L. Mitchell, on Winter's Run, and this he has since operated. The mill is run by water power, of about eighteen-horse power. It is never operated to its fullest capacity, thirty barrels a day, but is usually run steadily at fifteen barrels per day.

For Mr. Butler there is no party but the Democratic party, and as long as strength of mind and body is vouchsafed him he will cast his vote for the men and measures of that organization, because in it he sees the principles that will best advance the prosperity of the people. For his uprightness of character and recognized intelligence, he would often have been chosen as the incumbent of some official position, but he has had no ambition in that direction. However, at one time he consented to serve as trustee of the public schools of his district, and in that capacity was instrumental in advancing the welfare of the common schools. In 1879 he married Laura L. Nagle, daughter of Emanuel Nagle, of one of the old families of the county. They have an only child, Thomas. In religious belief they belong to the Presbyterian Church of Bel Air, which they attend regularly, and in which they are regarded as earnest and loyal members.

WILLIAM WILSON. There are many citizens of Cecil County who are not well known beyond the limits of the community where they reside, but whose honesty, enterprise and perseverance are of such a striking nature that the results, which by the possession of these characteristics they have attained, are calculated to promote the best interests of the county. The record of the lives of such deserves to be perpetuated for the perusal of coming generations, to whom they set an example worthy of emulation. It is therefore with pleasure that we place before the reader the summary, brief and imperfect though it may be, of the life of Mr. Wilson. Doubtless there are many in this county who possess greater fortunes than he, for being of a generous nature he has never become wealthy, but he has that which is better than great wealth —the esteem of all with whom business or social relations have brought him in contact.

A native of Delaware, Mr. Wilson was born in the county of Newcastle, March 8, 1832. His father, Samuel D., and grandfather, Jacob Wilson, were also natives of Delaware, whence, in 1842, Samuel D. removed to Cecil County and settled in District No. 9. Here he purchased the old Kirk homestead, that had been built in 1797, and here he engaged in general farming during the remaining days of his life. In political opinion he supported Democratic principles. By his marriage to Mary Pearson, of Pennsylvania, he had seven children, all of whom are living, namely: Sarah, William, Amos, John P., Martha, Thomas J. and Ross W. He died in 1864, at the age of sixty-one, and his wife when eighty-three years of age.

The education of our subject, obtained in the common schools, was completed at the age of eighteen, and afterward he gave his attention to the cultivation of the home place, of which he took charge upon his father's death. The farm is situated in District No. 9, and consists of one hundred acres of land, devoted to mixed farming. He has never identified himself with political affairs, and aside from voting the Democratic ticket, takes no part in elections. In 1864 he married Mary F. Taylor, of this district. They became the parents of six children, as follows: Samuel D., who carries on a creamery; Mabel, wife of John Reynolds; Alfred T., who assists in the cultivation of the home farm; William, Jr., Hanson Z. and Bayard G. The family are members of the Society of Friends.

SENECA POINT FARMS. On a high knoll overlooking the waters of the bay stands the spacious mansion that is one of the most comfortable in Cecil County. Surrounding the mansion and extending westward from the bay are the spacious and well-kept grounds, adorned with shrubs and trees. The estate originally consisted of one hundred and seventy-five acres, which stretch out like a grand old park as far as the eye can see. The place is the pride of Cecil's residents. Visitors, too, are not wanting in exclamations of admiration, and all who love nature cannot but delight in gazing upon this, a most attractive specimen of her handiwork.

It is said by those who know the history of this old place that for many years the property belonged to James Hasson, a native of Cecil County and long a resident of District No. 5. Here, in 1837, he erected a substantial residence, and, surrounded by every comfort his ample means rendered possible, he made it his home for twenty-five years. Finally he disposed of the property to I. C. de Figanier, Portuguese minister to the United States, who made it his home for four years, and then sold it to Mr. Ogden, who occupied it as a summer residence. After two years he sold the place to twelve gentlemen, who had organized the Seneca Point Club, incorporated under the laws of the state of Maryland. The mansion, which had been the scene of so many brilliant gatherings, took on new life under their ownership. The members often visited the club house, and enjoyed a pleasant diversion from business duties, spending their time in fishing and in hunting geese and ducks. But later the members ceased to take an interest and subsequently this property, as well as the one adjoining on the south, making an acreage of upwards of four hundred, was purchased by Horace C. Disston, a saw manufacturer, and who had been a member of the club. Since then he has made many improvements in the place, and frequently comes here from Philadelphia.

TAYLOR GILBERT. Upon a farm situated four miles from Bel Air, Mr. Gilbert has made his home since 1883. A man, enterprising, industrious and of more than ordinary intelligence, he has the true conception of rural life and agricultural pursuits, and his place bears evidence of his painstaking care. The estate of one hundred and sixty-five acres forms one of the attractive spots in the landscape of this region. The buildings are of modern style of architecture and conveniently arranged; while on every hand may be seen the numberless features which none but the systematic and thorough-going farmer can secure, but which to him are absolutely indispensable.

In recording events in the life of a well-known man, it is but natural to revert to those from whom he drew his origin. Jarrett Gilbert, father of our subject, was a resident of Havre de Grace, where he carried on the manufacture of shoes, and in season also engaged in fishing. The firm of Gilbert & Saddler, of which he was a member, has been succeeded by another firm, and the business is still conducted at the old place. In addition to other interests, he also devoted some attention to farming. He married Sarah, daughter of George Moore, of Alexandria, Va., member of an old Virginian family. She died about 1876, and he ten years later, at the age of sixty-eight years. Of their eleven children seven are now living, namely: Jarrett W., a commission merchant of Baltimore; John, who resides in Havre de Grace; Mrs. Hettie Thompson; R. H., a grocer of Baltimore, where he also holds office as fire commissioner; Mrs. Henry Dilg, of Philadelphia; Z. Taylor; and D. R., who occupies the old homestead.

In the city of Havre de Grace our subject was born in 1847, and in the common and private schools there he was educated. At the age of sixteen he began to superintend the home farm, remaining there until he was twenty-one, when he bought property in District No. 2, Harford County, and embarked in the canning business. In 1883 he purchased a farm near Bel Air, and here he has since engaged in general farming and fruit raising. He finds the canning business profitable, and makes of it a special feature. The demands of his business are such as to engross his entire attention, and he has therefore never identified himself with public affairs. This does not mean, however, that he has no decided opinions of his own. On the contrary, he has opinions and the courage of his convictions under all circumstances. Believing that the sale of intoxicating liquors is the cause of much of the suffering and poverty that darkens the world to-day, he has allied himself with the prohibition party, and by precept and example aims to abolish the liquor traffic.

Mr. Gilbert and his wife have one daughter, Ethel. In former years Mr. Gilbert was identified with the Odd Fellows, but is not now a member of the lodge. In the Methodist Protestant Church he was long a member of the board of trustees. Perhaps his chief work, in religious matters, has been in the Sunday-school, over which he has long presided as superintendent.

The fact that he has successfully officiated in this responsible position proves that he possesses the qualities that go to make up a leader, the aptitude to intelligently convey instruction and the magnetism to win the confidence of those associated with him in the work.

JAMES G. McCAY. There are no rules for building character; there is no rule for achieving success. The man who can rise to a prominent position is he who can see and utilize the opportunities which surround the human race. He who takes advantage of these and by energy and perseverance overcomes the obstacles in his path will ultimately reach the goal of success, and the worth of such a man to the community in which he lives is widely recognized. To-day among the prominent business men of Cecil County stands Mr. McCay, who is accounted one of her leading agriculturists.

He resides in District No. 7, and in this neighborhood was born in 1823. He is a descendant of John McCay, a native of Scotland, and a descendant of the Scottish nobility, who came to America about 1775, locating near Rowlandsville. The father, James McCay, was a native of Maryland, and served his country in the War of 1812, with the rank of major. His life was largely devoted to farming and merchandising, and he followed the latter occupation in Port Deposit. His business was ably conducted and in his undertakings he won a well-merited success. He married Miss Mary Broughton, and died in 1881, on the old homestead, at the advanced age of eighty-eight years. Of his family of eleven children only four are now living, namely: Henry, of District No. 7; James G., Joshua and Marcus.

James G. McCay, whose name forms the caption of this article, supplemented his early education, acquired in the district schools, by a course in McGrow Academy, where he completed his studies at the age of eighteen years. He then entered upon his business career, and going to Baltimore, for several years he remained in that city, acquiring not only a good living, but also a valuable experience which fitted him for his own mercantile career. He began business on his own account in that city and was thus engaged for five years, after which, however, he returned to the pursuit to which he was reared, that of farming. In 1857 he purchased what is known as the Indian Queen farm in District No. 7, Cecil County, where he has resided since 1859. He has here forty-seven acres of rich and arable land and successfully carries on general farming, the well-tilled fields yielding to the owner a golden tribute for the care and cultivation he bestows upon them.

Mr. McCay was married in 1854, the lady of his choice being Miss Isabel C. Boughton, a native of Cecil County. They have a family of five children, as follows: Sophia, Mary R., Florence, Margaret, and Joshua P., of Elkton. Mr. McCay and his family attend the Presbyterian Church. They are people of the highest respectability, widely and favorably known throughout the entire county, and their circle of friends is extensive. Mr. McCay gives his support to the Democracy, and while he manifests an intelligent interest in political questions has never sought or desired official preferment. His life has been well spent in quiet but honorable pursuits and his marked characteristics are such as to commend him to the confidence and good-will of all.

WILLIAM H. HARLAN, attorney-at-law, of Bel Air, was born in Darlington, Harford County, Md., November 14, 1850. Tracing his history, we find that his father, Reuben S. Harlan, M.D., was a physician of Harford County, a man gifted in science and skilled in his profession, one who accomplished much, notwithstanding the fact that his life was short. He had a brother, Dr. David Harlan, an officer in the United States navy, whose son,

Henry D., is chief judge of the supreme bench of Baltimore. Dr. Harlan's father, Jeremiah Harlan, was a Quaker, with all the kindly traits and the integrity so characteristic of that sect; in early life he removed from Pennsylvania to Maryland, settling in Harford County, where he became a prosperous farmer, and also identified himself with the measures looking toward the development of the county. The history of the family in Pennsylvania dates back to the days of William Penn.

The mother of our subject was Elizabeth Schaefer, a native of the city of Baltimore and daughter of Rev. George B. and Frances (Hawkins) Schaefer. Mr. Schaefer was a minister in the Protestant Episcopal Church, and, as indicated by his name, of German ancestry. Mrs. Elizabeth Harlan is still living, and makes her home with her children, of whom seven are living. Esther, who married William L. Hawkins, of Louisiana, died, leaving two children. George S. is an insurance broker in Baltimore; he is married and has several children. Frances is the wife of Benjamin B. Hyde, who is living in Baltimore County. Henry, a farmer, owns and resides on the old Harlan homestead. Ellen is the wife of Edward S. Maxwell, and resides in Lancaster County, Pa. David, who was engaged in the mercantile business in Harford County, died in 1887. Reuben S. is unmarried and resides with his brother, William H. Hannah, the youngest of the family, is the wife of William L. Reynolds, a farmer of Harford County.

After completing the studies of the public schools, the subject of this sketch entered St. John's College, Annapolis, from which he graduated in 1872. The ensuing year was spent as a tutor in the same college, after which he was for two years principal in the Bel Air Academy, and for six years superintendent of public schools. Meantime he devoted his leisure hours to the study of law, and on retiring from educational work he formed a partnership with J. Edwin Webster, with whom he has since engaged in practice. He is connected with the Harford National Bank as a stockholder and director. Other local enterprises and institutions have felt the impetus of his influence and aid. In matters religious he is an Episcopalian, and assists his church by active service as a vestryman. When at leisure from professional and business cares, he may be found at his comfortable home, in the suburbs of Bel Air, where his happiest hours are spent in the society of his wife and children. The lady whom he married, in 1885, was formerly Bessie Webster, and is a sister of his law partner and a daughter of the late Col. Edwin H. Webster, at one time member of congress and collector of the port of Baltimore. Their family consists of three sons and three daughters, Edwin, Elizabeth, Caroline, William, Mary and Henry.

J HOWARD WATTERS. The entire life of this gentleman has been passed in District No. 4, Harford County, and he was born upon the farm where he now resides, October 13, 1823, being the oldest child of Walter and Mary (Kennard) Watters. An only son, he had four sisters: Eliza K., Mary F., Martha J. and S. Catherine, of whom the two last named are deceased. Both the Watters and the Kennard families are among the oldest of Harford County, in fact, they have been represented here from a period so early that the exact date of their settlement is not known. The Watters family came from England, the Kennards from Scotland, and their descendants possess the determination characteristic of the one nation and the thrift for which the other race is renowned. Rev. William Watters, a great-uncle of our subject, had the distinction of being the first American-born itinerant minister of the Methodist Episcopal Church in this country and was a man of much prominence in his day. His body lies buried in the cemetery near Alexandria, Va.

In youth the subject of this sketch gave promise of the same traits of character that have distinguished him in later life. He was a manly boy, of steady habits, energetic, active and industrious. His youthful years were uneventfully passed upon the old homestead, work upon which was alternated with attendance at the neighboring schools. While much of his time has been given to agriculture, he has not followed it exclusively, as he also has a general store on his place. His homestead comprises four hundred and twenty-five acres, upon which have been placed first-class improvements, with all the buildings to be seen upon a model farm. He has never identified himself with any political organization, but is independent in his views, supporting those whom he deems best fitted for office, no matter what their party affiliations may be. Like many of his family, he is a member of the Methodist Episcopal Church, and his contributions to religious work have been generous. At this writing he and his sister, George Rigdon, and his aunts, Sarah E. and Esther Y. Watters, are erecting a substantial stone house of worship, to be used by the Methodists here, and known as the William Watters Memorial, in memory of William Watters. He has always been a man of public spirit, and is well informed, keeping posted upon all that is being done in the fields of science, politics and public affairs.

JOEL C. HOLLINGSWORTH is a representative of one of the old families of Fallston precinct, District No. 3, Harford County. His paternal grandfather, Nathaniel Hollingsworth, a descendant of English ancestry, was born in Pennsylvania and after his marriage removed to Maryland, where he purchased a large tract of land in Harford County, and erected the residence now occupied by Silas and Thomas Hollingsworth. The remainder of his life was devoted to agricultural pursuits here. His son, Eli, father of our subject, was born in Goshen, Pa., and was quite young when he came to Harford County. On the death of his father, the property was divided among the eight children, and a portion of the home place fell to his share,

as well as the water right. For a time he devoted his attention largely to running a saw mill, but afterward added a grist mill, operating the two, also cultivating some farm land, during his entire active life. By his marriage to Edith Carter, of this county, he had three children, namely: Joel C., the eldest of the family, born December 26, 1831; Nathaniel, who is the present proprietor of the grist mill; and Jeremiah, who died in boyhood. The father passed away at the old homestead in 1879, aged eighty-six years, and his wife died in 1874, aged seventy years.

Reared on the home farm, at the age of fourteen years the subject of this sketch began to assist his father in the mill, and soon acquired a thorough knowledge of its workings. Up to the present he has continued to be interested in manufacturing. In 1879 he built the first carriage wheel, and now owns a fine plant, the operating power for which is furnished by Winter's Run and is equivalent to fifty-horse power. He is thoroughly informed regarding the business in which he is engaged and by managing it efficiently he has become the possessor of a competence. In 1856 he married Hanna C., daughter of Amor Carter, of Chester County, Pa. Their family consisted of four children, three now living, namely: Barclay E., Harrie J., and Maggie B., who is the wife of William F. Stubbs, son of Vincent Stubbs, of Delta, Pa. The two sons are connected with the father in the manufacture of spokes, wheels and rims. The oldest son, Curtis A., who died at the age of twenty-five years, was of a literary bent of mind, and before his health failed him he was assistant superintendent of the Institute for the Blind in Baltimore. The family are identified with the Society of Friends, with the exception of Harrie, who is a member of the Disciples' Church. All are stanch Prohibitionists, both by voice and ballot, believing the government should not be a legal partner in any business that destroys both body and soul.

Coming as he does from good old Quaker stock, Mr. Hollingsworth inherited all the physical and intellectual vigor of his ancestors, along with the prudence and good judgment that have always distinguished the sect. He has thus been quick to

H. H. HAINES.

perceive and grasp at an opportunity for profitable investment. His code of morals is of the Quaker type, impelling him always to a just consideration of the rights of all with whom he is brought into contact, and to a conscientious regard for and observance of all the proprieties of life. Thus he has won many friendships, which grow stronger with more intimate acquaintance.

GEORGE J. FINNEY. No name is more familiarly known in Harford County than that of Finney, and it has so long been connected with local history that a work of this character would be incomplete without reference to some member of this old family. The enterprising manner in which George J. Finney has conducted his affairs, combined with ability and strict probity, has but tended to enhance the respect with which the name of Finney is regarded in this county. For some time past he has been clerk of the board of commissioners of Harford County. He is a native of Churchville, Md., where his eyes first opened on the light of day August 28, 1830, his father being Rev. William Finney, for a notice of whom, see the sketch of Rev. E. D. Finney.

The subject of this sketch was educated in the local schools, and Hopewell Academy of Chester County, Pa. After finishing his education he returned home and turned his attention to agricultural pursuits, of which he had acquired a thorough and practical knowledge while growing up, and to this occupation the greater portion of his time and attention have been devoted ever since. He has met with a fair degree of success and is the owner of a good farm at Churchville on which he makes his home. He has always been quite active in political matters, a stanch Democrat in his views, and in 1856-57 was a member of the board of county commissioners. He served in the capacity of treasurer, and in 1893 was elected to the position of clerk of the board, a position he has filled with marked ability up to the present time. He has long been a member and is a trustee and treasurer of the Presbyterian Church at Churchville, to which positions he was chosen some twenty-six years ago.

On the 26th of April, 1865, Mr. Finney was united in marriage with Miss Louisa L. Webster, a daughter of Rev. Augustus Webster, of Baltimore, and a family of five children was given them: Walter, who is the cashier of the Second National Bank of Bel Air; William W., cashier of the Harford National Bank; George J., Jr., who died at the age of nineteen years; Edward, a machinist, in Philadelphia; and John C., who is attending school.

HENRY HARDING KIMBLE was born in the village of Bushington, Bucks County, Pa., October 13, 1824, and was the youngest child of John Kimble and Hannah (Carver) Kimble. He traced his ancestry back to the Pilgrim Fathers, who sailed from England and landed at Plymouth in 1620. His maternal grandfather, William Carver, who was born in Bucks County about 1750, was a lineal descendant of Gov. John Carver, whose name is inseparably associated with the early history of Massachusetts. John, a son of William Carver, and doubtless a namesake of his celebrated ancestor, was killed in the battle of Chippewa in the War of 1812.

The youngest of six children, the subject of this sketch was obliged to work hard from early boyhood, and attended school only during the winter months, being a student in Doylestown Academy for one term. At the age of sixteen years he began teaching public school and engaged in that profession for eight years, during the last two of which he studied law in leisure hours. However, before the completion of his legal course his health failed, and he was forced to seek an occupation less confining. After his marriage, in November, 1847, to Mary, eldest daughter of Seruch Titus, a farmer of Bucks

County, he purchased a small farm lying on the Neshaminy Creek, and there he followed agricultural pursuits for a number of years. In 1855 (having sold his farm in Bucks County) he purchased a farm near Fair Hill, Cecil County, Md., where he moved with his wife and two children, Seruch and John. The place was in every respect a neglected one and a great deal of hard work was necessary before the buildings were in good repair and the land ready for cultivation. However, Mr. Kimble was a willing worker. He possessed untiring industry, and from morning until night was busily engaged in the various details of farm life. His own industry and energy inspired others with greater enthusiasm. His sons often remarked that he always said "come on," not "go on" to work. While the days were spent in arduous toil, the evenings were devoted to recreation and music, and the friends who visited them in their hospitable home counted it not the least of their enjoyments when the family entertained them with vocal and instrumental music.

In 1873, having purchased a house and a piece of land at Fox Chase (now Appleton), and having erected an addition to the house, in the way of a store room, Mr. Kimble removed thither, and opened a general mercantile store, leaving his sons in charge of the farm at Fair Hill. He was one of the original incorporators of the Farmers and Mechanics' Mutual Insurance Company of Cecil County, and was secretary and treasurer from the time of its organization to the day of his death. He was also one of the charter members of Good Intent Grange No. 88, organized about 1875. During the last twenty years of his life he was an active member of the Republican party. He was public spirited and highly esteemed, but though prominent in politics, never held public office. At different times he taught school in this county and his work always proved satisfactory to this patrons. He was noted in debating circles, and was a frequent contributor to the press of Cecil County, the greater part of his writings being prose. He was a man of varied acquirements. Besides attending to his mercantile affairs, he superintended his two farms at Appleton and the one near Fair Hill, and satisfactorily discharged his duties in the fire insurance company. He was proficient in the writing of deeds, wills, etc., and was in frequent demand as a surveyor.

In 1885 Mr. Kimble began the erection of a new dwelling house opposite his store property at Appleton, but before its completion his wife and his eldest son were called from earth, so that whatever pleasure he might have experienced in the new home was turned into sadness. The final blow came when, in August, 1887, his only remaining child was laid to rest in the silent tomb. August 19, 1887, just two weeks and two days after the death of his son, he died of congestion of the brain. His death was a shock to the entire community, whose best interests he had always advanced. His funeral was held on the 23d, his pastor, Rev. J. L. Vallandigham, conducting the services, which were largely attended. He was a member of Head of Christiana Presbyterian Church, and his remains were interred in the cemetery adjoining.

Thus passed from earth the genial host, the patriotic citizen, the sincere and honest friend.

B. H. HAINES. Prominent among the business men of Cecil County is the subject of this sketch, who for over a quarter of a century has been closely identified with the history of the county, while his name is inseparably connected with its financial records. The banking interests are well represented by him, for he is to-day at the head of the National Bank of Rising Sun, the leading moneyed institution of this place. He is a man of keen discrimination and sound judgment, and his executive ability and excellent management have brought to the concern with which he is connected a high degree of success. The safe conservative policy which he inaugurated commends itself to the judgment of all, and has secured a patronage which makes the volume of business transacted over its counters of great importance. The success of the bank is certainly due in a large measure to him, and through it he has promoted the welfare of the town.

Mr. Haines was born in Fulton Township, Lancaster County, Pa., November 25, 1844, upon a beautiful farm of nearly two hundred acres known as "Hillside Home," adjoining the celebrated "Black Barren Springs" resort on the north, and lying along the Lancaster road running north from Pleasant Grove postoffice. His parents were Lewis and Sarah (Kirk) Haines, the latter a daughter of Jacob Kirk, of Kirks Mills, Lancaster County, Pa. For many generations his ancestors were prominent and leading members of the Society of Friends, and were also active in the affairs that were of public interest in the community where they resided.

In this connection may be mentioned a very unusual circumstance attending the location of Mr. Haines in Rising Sun. Within view of his residence is the original home of his great-great-grandfather, Joseph Haines, one of the progenitors of the family in America, who came to this country from England with his brothers on the ship "Amity" early in 1682, and after some thirty-two years' residence in New Jersey located in Cecil County, Md., in 1714. The name in the mother country seems to have undergone many changes. At one time it was Eaune, then Ayne, next Hayne, etc. Mr. Haines is not only near the early home of his paternal ancestors, but his maternal ancestors as well. On the banks of North East Creek, in Cecil County, within three miles of his home, lived his great-great-great-grandfather, Roger Kirk, who on coming from the north of Ireland located here in 1712.

Mr. Haines received his early education in the public schools, later attended the academies at Pleasant Grove, Chestnut Level, Lancaster County, Pa., and Concordville, Delaware County, Pa., and completed his literary training in the Pennsylvania State Normal School at Millersville. During the Civil War he enlisted in the Union army, first as a private in Company E, Twenty-ninth Pennsylvania Volunteer Militia, in 1863, and in 1864 became a non-commissioned officer of Company C, One Hundred and Ninety-fifth Pennsylvania Infantry.

In January, 1865, Mr. Haines left home to reside in Philadelphia, where he was engaged in the counting room of a wholesale drug firm, and later went to New York City to open a new set of books for the same firm. He resigned his position in order to engage in business on his own account and removed to his present home in Rising Sun, Md., to which point the railroad had just been completed. Associating himself with his older brother, they erected a store and dwelling on the corner of Walnut and Main Streets, and for the next four years conducted a general mercantile business under the firm name of Haines Brothers. His brother's health having failed, they disposed of the business in 1870, and of the real estate three years later.

In 1871 Mr. Haines, in connection with other prominent citizens, agitated the establishment of a banking institution at Rising Sun, which resulted in successfully opening the banking house of Evans, Wood & Co. upon the 1st of August of that year. The title was changed in July, 1873, to The Rising Sun Banking Company, and in July, 1880, was merged into the National Bank of Rising Sun. During its entire existence Mr. Haines had served as cashier of the organization, and in January, 1884, was elected president, which position he still occupies.

Mr. Haines was married in December, 1873, to Miss Ella Warner Rittenhouse, the daughter of Azariah and Mary J. Rittenhouse, of Rising Sun, and a member of a branch of the old and well-known family of that name in and around Philadelphia. In politics Mr. Haines has been from early boyhood a zealous and unwavering Republican, active and energetic in the affairs of the party, and while always refusing to take any place on the ticket, he is well and prominently known in state politics and enjoys the acquaintance and confidence of many national men in his party. He has also from early boyhood been identified with aggressive temperance work and temperance organizations. He is prominently connected with a number of secret societies, and is at present holding the position of Judge Advocate in the department of Maryland, Grand Army of the Republic. He is an extensive traveler with many and diversified interests in other states, and is known among those with whom he lives as a man of affairs, possessing untiring energy and indomitable perseverance.

WILLIAM CHANNELL. The subject of this sketch is a well-known citizen of Harford County, who has improved every opportunity for gaining knowledge and availed himself of every chance for the betterment of his condition, and more than this cannot be said of the most successful man who has ever lived. He has lived a life of peace with his neighbors, and has done unto others as he would have had them do unto him under similar circumstances. The family of which he is an honored member is of Scotch lineage. His paternal grandfather was born in "Bonnie" Scotland, but came to America at a very early day and made a home for himself and family in Pennsylvania. Here his Scotch shrewdness manifested itself, and he became the owner of a large and valuable estate. There is a tradition in the family that he was a member of the patriot army during the Revolutionary War. His son, Isaac Channell, was reared on his vast estates, and after reaching manhood gave much attention to agriculture and also devoted many years to teaching school, in which occupation he was very successful. He wedded Miss Mary Anderson, who, like himself, was a native of the Keystone state, and in the course of time six children were born to them: Anderson; William, the subject of this biography; Deborah, Margaret, Mary A. and James.

William Channell was born in Pennsylvania November 9, 1824, and was reared upon a farm, where he did all manner of work that came to hand. When the district school in the neighborhood of his home was in session he attended it and acquired a useful education. When he reached the age of twenty-eight years he came to the conclusion that "it is not good for man to live alone," and he wooed and won for his wife Miss Mary J. Herbert, who was born in Pennsylvania, and they at once established a home of their own.

Since that time Mr. Channell has devoted his attention indefatigably to tilling the soil, and the result of his efforts has been the accumulation of one hundred and fifty acres of land. He has improved and increased the value of this property very much by the erection of substantial and commodious buildings, good fences, etc., and his home is one of the most pleasant and hospitable in the district. His family consists of the following children: Sarah A., Richard, Elizabeth, Aaron B., Henrietta and Rebecca. Mrs. Channell is a member of a well-known Pennsylvania family, the male members of which have long been noted as thrifty and successful farmers. Both she and her husband have been members of the Presbyterian Church for years, and are generous contributors to its support; in fact, every enterprise which has for its object the betterment of mankind, finds in them liberal patrons. In his political views Mr. Channell has always been in sympathy with Democratic principles.

REV. D. F. HAUGH, S. J., priest in charge of St. Francis Xavier's Church in District No. 1, Cecil County, was born in Ireland November 27, 1840. At the age of nine years he accompanied his parents to America, landing in New York City, where he spent the years of his youth in attendance upon local schools. It was his ambition to become a Jesuit priest. At the age of sixteen he matriculated in Georgetown (D. C.) College. From Georgetown he entered the Society of Jesus and taught at the college for six years. He finished his course of philosophy and theology at the Jesuit College of Woodstock, Md., where he was ordained priest.

Father Haugh spent some time in California and Colorado, and built St. Patrick's Church in South Pueblo during the period of his service there. In 1877 he had charge of Petersville and Libertytown, Md. In 1890 he became pastor of St. Francis Xavier's Church in Cecil County, where he still resides. St. Francis Xavier's Church was organized about 1680, by virtue of the power in a warrant granted for Mary Ann O'Daniels and Margaret, her sister. The warrant comprised three hundred acres, but the amount was afterward increased from time to time, and now the Jesuits own about eleven hundred acres of well-improved land.

The attention of Father Haugh is given to the details of his work as priest, and he guards well the spiritual interests of his parishioners. However, he finds time to be posted upon public affairs of importance and is a pronounced Republican. As he considers himself a thorough American, he regards it as an insult to be called upon to proclaim his loyalty to our government and its institutions.

HENRY C. SCHILLING. The pages of history fail to disclose an older or more honorable calling than that of the farmer, and among its most honorable votaries is Henry C. Schilling, who is a native of Germany, born June 30, 1832. The estate, of which this progressive tiller of the soil is the owner, comprises one hundred and forty-five acres advantageously located near Shawsville, and this he has put in an excellent state of cultivation. His parents, Charles L. and Louisa (Billings) Schilling, were born in Germany, and in that country were reared, educated and married. Their five children were born in that country, two of whom died and were buried there. Those who survived and came to this country were Henry C., the subject of this sketch; William H., who became a soldier in the Union army, was captured by the enemy and died in Andersonville prison in 1864, at the age of thirty years; and Caroline, who is the wife of Dr. Charles Krause, of Cedar Creek, Wis., by whom she has two children.

While in his native land, Henry C. Schilling was placed in school, upon attaining a proper age, and there he obtained a practical education. He was an enterprising and ambitious young man, and in 1855 decided to seek his fortune in America. Upon landing in this country he made his way to Baltimore County, Md., and it was not long ere he had obtained employment in a woolen mill, and during his connection with the same he thoroughly learned every detail of the business. In 1860 he left the east, made his way to Missouri, and in the city of St. Charles secured employment at his trade, which he continued to follow for six years. With true German thrift, he saved a portion of his earnings, and when the six years had elapsed, he returned to the state of his adoption and purchased the woolen mill in District No. 4, Harford County, then owned by John R. Jackson. After the lapse of some time he felt that his circumstances admitted of his purchasing some real estate, and he became the owner of his present tract of land adjoining his mill.

Mr. Schilling turns out excellent woolen fabrics from his mill, which find their way to various portions of the country, but while so successfully conducting this establishment, he has not neglected his agricultural interests, for every portion of his farm is carefully looked after and judiciously tilled. He has by no means traveled in a rut in his journey through life, but he is one of those men who can have several irons in the fire and keep them all working. Although he is strictly a business man, he has always been interested in political affairs, and in his views is an ardent Republican. He at one time held the office of registrar, and discharged his duties admirably.

His wife, whom he married in 1857, was formerly Miss Emma Lawton, a native of England. She was brought to this country at an early age, and like Mr. Schilling, her adopted country has become very dear to her. Five children have been born to them, as follows: Charles L. (deceased); Louisa J. (deceased); Howard L., Hannah C. and John W. Mrs. Schilling was a devoted wife and mother. At the time of her death, which occurred in the winter of 1896, at the age of sixty-two years, she was a worthy member of the Methodist Episcopal Church. In his religious belief Mr. Schilling has ever leaned toward the Lutheran faith, but he is a member of the Methodist Church at the present time. He has always been in sympathy with secret organizations, and has shown his approval by becoming a member of Mt. Ararat Lodge No. 44, A. F. & A. M., of Bel Air, and Lodge No. 92 of the Knights of Pythias of Shawsville. He is a self-made man, and has reason to be proud of his substantial and honorable position in life.

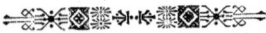

NICHOLAS BAKER, long one of the prominent farmers of Harford County, died on the 2d of April, 1896, and in his death the community lost one of its representative men and valued citizens. His life was passed in the quiet pursuits of business, but was characterized by those qualities which everywhere command respect. As a citizen he was true and faithful and gave his support to all measures which he believed would advance the general welfare.

Mr. Baker was born in District No. 2, Harford County, January 27, 1810, a son of Nicholas and Elizabeth (Cole) Baker. His father, who was born in the same district, was a farmer and merchant, carrying on a store in connection with his agricultural pursuits. He served in the War of 1812 in defense of his native land, and died on the 9th of February, 1845, when about sixty years of age. His wife, who was also a native of Harford County, had reached the ripe old age of eighty-three years when called to her final rest.

Nicholas Baker, of this review, spent the days of his boyhood and youth in his parents' home, and while acquiring his education in the public schools he received a liberal training in farm work by assisting in the development and cultivation of the old homestead. He also clerked in his father's store at times, and was thus trained to habits of industry which characterized his entire business life. On attaining his majority, he joined James Everett in the establishment of a small chair and furniture factory, operating the same for several years. About 1839 he purchased the farm whereon his widow now resides, and there spent the remainder of his life, giving the greater part of his time to agricultural pursuits, while also engaging in the manufacture of chairs and furniture materials on a small scale. In later life he added to his business another industry, that of canning vegetables, and for several years he successfully conducted that enterprise, adding considerable to his income thereby. He was a man of determined purpose, good business ability and executive force, and carried forward to successful completion whatever he undertook.

On the 2d of November, 1837, Mr. Baker was united in marriage with Miss Elizabeth Carsins, a sister of William Carsins. She died February 27, 1853, leaving six children, namely: Elizabeth, wife of George Everist, of District No. 2, Harford County; John C., a resident of Dover, Del.; Charles H., who died at the age of thirty-three years; Mary J., who married, but died at the age of twenty-eight years; Sarah F., who died at the age of thirty; and George H., who also died when about thirty years of age. On the 4th of March, 1855, Mr. Baker was again married, his second union being with Mary B. Greenland, who was born in District No. 2, July 10, 1819. By this marriage there were two children: Edmund, who died at the age of twelve years, and Winfield L., who is now at home engaged in the operation of the farm, and in the canning business.

Mr. Baker was a stalwart advocate of Republican principles, and was a prominent and active worker in the Methodist Episcopal Church, in which he held membership from the age of seventeen years. He belonged to the congregation which built the first church in Harford County. It was a log structure, primitive in style, and was the second Methodist Church in the state. He served as church trustee, steward and class leader, and did all in his power to promote the cause of Christianity. His life was in harmony with his profession and commanded the confidence and esteem of all. In his business he was fairly successful, and his property was all acquired through his own honorable and industrious efforts. He passed away April 2, 1896, and was laid to rest in Barr cemetery, near Aberdeen. His widow and three children are members of the church. They reside on the old family homestead and have the warm regard of all who know them.

WILLIAM W. VIRDIN, M. D. There are few homes in Harford County more beautiful than Brightwater. Its location is picturesque and attractive. On the east, within a short distance, flow the tranquil waters of the Susquehanna; and in every other direction stretch the fine farming lands of District No. 2. Here for many years Dr. Virdin resided, busily engaged in professional work, but a paralytic stroke in 1896 obliged him to relinquish his practice, and he lived in retirement from that time until his death, which occurred May 20, 1897. He was one of the most highly respected physicians of the county, and his skill in diagnosis and treatment of disease brought him the confidence of all.

Born in Baltimore August 11, 1829, the subject of this sketch was a son of Capt. William W. and Emily J. (Ash) Virdin, natives, respectively, of Caroline County and Baltimore, Md. His father, when fourteen years of age, went from his native county to Baltimore, where he resided for some time. He commanded the "Governor Walcott," which was among the first steamers that sailed from the port at Baltimore; in 1836 he resigned that command and entered the employ of the Philadelphia, Wilmington & Baltimore Railroad Company, as captain of the steamboat that carried the cars across the Susquehanna River from Havre de Grace to Perryville. Retiring from this position in 1851, he took up his permanent home in Baltimore, where he died at the age of sixty-eight. Politically he was an old-line Whig and a supporter of the Union. Successful in financial matters, he left an estate valued at $100,000, which was inherited by his only child, our subject, but the bulk of the property was lost in the vicissitudes of war. Our subject's mother died when only twenty-two years of age.

When Dr. Virdin was a boy of eleven, he entered West Nottingham Academy in Cecil County, where he was a student for five years. In 1845 he entered the sophomore class at Princeton College, with the intention of completing the entire course, but after a year he decided to go to Yale, and entered the junior class of that institution. Unfortunately, in a short time he was taken ill and had to abandon all literary work, being ordered south for his health. For two years he did no reading or study of any kind, but as soon as he became strong once more, he began to read medicine with Dr. N. B. Hill, of Hills Store, N. C., and later attended lectures at the University of Maryland, where he graduated in 1858. He at once began in professional practice, continuing at Hills Store, N. C., until the outbreak of the war. In 1861 he was commissioned assistant surgeon in the Confederate army, and the following year became surgeon for the state of North Carolina, with the rank of major of the Sixty-third Regiment, Sixteenth Brigade. At the close of the war he was a full surgeon of the Confederate States army and was a member of the examining board. He was brigade surgeon under Brigadier-General Leaventhorp, at Kingston, N. C., and occupied General Lee's extreme right. He was present at Seven Pines and in the seven days' fight around Richmond, under special order.

When the war ended Dr. Virdin went to Baltimore, where he spent the winter. In the spring of 1866 he came to Lapidum and settled on a farm of one hundred acres that his father had purchased in 1840. Here he engaged in continuous practice until a paralytic stroke in the left side rendered further work an impossibility. In 1867 he assisted in the organization of the Harford County Medical Society, of which he was secretary for several years. For a number of terms he was president of the Cecil County Medical Society. He was a member of the State Medical Faculty and of the first Pan-American Medical Society, that met in Washington, D. C.

In 1854 Dr. Virdin married Miss Kate E. L. Dunn, of North Carolina. They had nine children, namely: Phenix, who died in infancy; Emily J., wife of N. E. Ford, of the editorial staff of the *Baltimore Sun*; Lizzie, widow of Silas W. Barnes; James C., who resides in Colorado; Martha Lee, wife of Rev. E. D. Fitzgerald, of Cincinnati, Ohio; Carrie M., who died at fifteen years; Mary D., who resides at home; John McCoy, who died at twenty-two years; and Joseph D., a resident of Baltimore. Dr. Virdin was a member of the Presbyterian Church, to which his wife also belongs. In politics he was a Democrat, stanch and active in local affairs, but not an office seeker. He was made a Mason in North Carolina in 1855 and became a member of Balfair Lodge No. 188, and Montgomery Chapter, R. A. M., but later was identified with St. John's Chapter No. 19, R. A. M., of Baltimore.

JOHN W. COOPER, Jr., M. D. Of the numerous and various professions in which men may rise to distinction, there is none known to the civilized world that claims a higher place in the esteem of all than does the science of medicine. From the earliest times down to the present there has never been a class of men in whom greater confidence has been placed and who have occupied a higher place in the respect of mankind, than does the physician. No one more fully proves the truth of this fact than Dr. Cooper, who is recognized as one of the leading and efficient physicians of Elkton.

The Cooper family is one of the oldest in Delaware, and its members have been men and women of upright character and progressive spirit. Through the English records the lineage of the family is traced directly to William Cooper, of Hallam, England. His son, Benjamin, born in 1623, entered Merton College (now the University of Oxford) in April, 1641, became professor in 1652, and served as registrar of the college from 1659 to 1701. George, son of Benjamin, was born in 1667, entered Merton College in 1682, became professor and succeeded his father as registrar in 1701, holding that position until his death, in 1737. George (2d), son of George, was born in 1696, and entered Magdalene College, Oxford, in 1715. Two other sons of George, Benjamin and John, who were also students at the university, emigrated to Dorchester County, Md., where they patented land from King George. Benjamin died a bachelor. John married a Miss Smith, of Tuckahoe, Dorchester (now Caroline) County, and at his death left the following children: Thomas, who at the age of twelve was sent to England as heir of his uncle George, who was childless; George, Deborah, Ann and Richard. George's son John and Richard's daughter, Sarah, married July 24, 1787, and were the great-great-grandparents of Dr. Cooper.

Their son, Samuel B. Cooper, the doctor's great-grandfather, married Catherine Lowber, the only daughter of Peter Lowber and his wife, Mary Patton, and the great-granddaughter of Peter Lowber, who emigrated from Amsterdam and settled on a farm seven miles below Dover, Del., September 15, 1684. From there the family spread through Delaware and the eastern shore. The Lowbers were connected with the Gilders of Philadelphia and New York, Richard Watson Gilder being a second cousin. Through the Pattons the family is connected with Judge Wales, of Wilmington, Del., and Judge Benjamin Caton, who settled Catonsville, now Station G, Baltimore. Samuel B. Cooper and Catherine, his wife, had a son, Samuel B., Jr., the doctor's grandfather, who married Mary Cooper, daughter of Thomas Cooper, a son of Richard.

John W. Cooper, son of Samuel B., Jr., was born in Kent County, Del., in 1813, and married Susan Dill, daughter of John Dill. From the age of eighteen he made his home on his share of the estate, lying in Caroline County, Md., and Kent County, Del., until his death, in March, 1891, aged seventy-three. His wife is still living at the old homestead. She was the mother of seven children, of whom all but one are still living. Dr. Thomas H., a graduate of the University of Pennsylvania, is a physician of Chestertown, Md.; George F. is a farmer and occupies a portion of the old homestead in Delaware; Dr. Peter Cooper, a graduate of Hahnemann Medical College of Philadelphia, is engaged in practice in Wilmington, Del.; James C., a graduate of the law department of the University of Pennsylvania, and for a time a law student with Judge Arnold, of Philadelphia, is now deceased; Mary S. is the wife of John Dill, a farmer in Delaware; and Elizabeth married Frank Dill, a brother of John Dill, they being sons of Alexander Dill, who was a large land owner in Delaware. The ancestors of the Cooper family were identified with the Episcopal Church until the late Rev. Ezekiel Cooper embraced Methodism, since which time they have been divided between the two denominations.

Upon the home farm in Kent County, Del., the subject of this notice was born February, 16, 1850, and there the years of boyhood were uneventfully passed. His literary education was acquired principally in Felton Seminary, Kent County, while his commercial studies were prosecuted in Bryant & Stratton's Business College in Philadelphia, and his medical course taken at Hahnemann Medical College, a homeopathic institution in Philadelphia, from which he graduated March 25, 1884. After the completion of his medical studies he was engaged in practice with his brother in Chestertown for a year, and in 1886 came to Elkton, where he has since built up a large and lucrative practice. In addition to his private practice, he has filled the office of physician to the county almshouse and asylum, physician to the county jail, and examining surgeon of the pension bureau at Elkton. While he has given his attention principally to matters connected with his profession, he also takes an intelligent interest in public affairs and supports the principles of the Republican party, which he considers best adapted to our national prosperity. His father, who in early life was a Whig, became a Republican upon the organization of this party and was a sympathizer with the Union during the Civil War. While he did not join the ranks, he rendered valuable service to his neighbors in the cause of the Union.

In 1889 Dr. Cooper was united in marriage with Anna Wells, daughter of Joseph Wells, who at one time was the postmaster of Elkton. Two children blessed the union, but one died in infancy, the other, Helen, being now (1897) five years of age. Fraternally Dr. Cooper is connected with the Heptasophs, the Masons and the Ancient Order of United Workmen.

GEORGE B. KERFOOT, superintendent of the Singerly paper mills of Elkton, was born in Lancaster, Pa., 1834, the son of Dr. George B. Kerfoot. His father entered the medical profession when a young man and achieved considerable success in it, having his office at Lancaster, where he died many years ago. One of his sons, William D., is a prominent and wealthy real-estate man of Chicago.

When a boy of seventeen the subject of this sketch started out in life for himself. Going to Philadelphia, he secured a clerkship and gradually worked his way upward to a position of responsibility. For twenty-five years he was engaged in the shipping and commission business in Philadelphia, and gained many friends among the merchants of that city during the long period of his residence there. The fact that he had a brother in Chicago and that his own interests there were important led him to remove to that city, where for nine years he was connected with the board of trade. From there he went back to Philadelphia and again engaged in business. In 1887 he came to Elkton as superintendent of the Singerly paper mills, he having been acquainted with Mr. Singerly throughout his entire life and associated with him for a long time.

From the time of his first connection with the Singerly Pulp and Paper Company Mr. Kerfoot has proved himself to be an able and efficient business man, and by resolution and force of will, combined with unvarying industry and judicious management, he has won his way to a position of assured success, and now enjoys the respect of the people among whom he has transacted business during these past years. He married Julia E. Lippincott, of Philadelphia, and they reside in their recently completed home, which is one of the finest in Elkton. Fraternally he is a Mason, interested in the work of that order, and in religious connections he is identified with the Episcopal Church.

E. SAVAGE SHURE, a wide-awake and progressive merchant of Shures Landing, Harford County, is an important factor in business circles and his popularity is well deserved, as in him are embraced the characteristics of unbending integrity, unabated energy and industry that never flags. He is public spirited and thoroughly interested in whatever tends to promote the moral, intellectual and material welfare of the community.

Mr. Shure was born at Shures Landing in 1863, and is a grandson of Michael Shure, who was a colonel in the War of 1812 and spent his entire life in Perry County, Pa. Daniel Ferree Shure, our subject's father, was born in Liverpool, Pa., March 11, 1817, and for many years had charge of a store at that place for the father of William T. Waters, of Baltimore. In 1842 he was sent by Simon Cameron, William T. Waters and others from Harrisburg, Pa., to the old Worthington Landing on the Harford side of the Susquehanna River, to act as superintendent of the Susquehanna and Side Water Canal. Here he spent the last fifty-five years of his life, and became prominently identified with the upbuilding and development of this region, establishing what is now known as Shures Landing.

Daniel F. Shure was united in marriage with Miss Jane McDarah, by whom he had twelve children (ten still living): Charles A., a practicing physician of Port Deposit, Md.; Harry W., deputy revenue collector at Baltimore; Miriam A., wife of A. J. Colwell; Daniel F., Jr.; Jeanie, deceased; John M.; James B.; George W.; William J.; Edward Savage; Arthur E., and Robert Lee, deceased. Daniel F. Shure became one of the influential and prominent citizens of Harford County, and as an ardent Democrat took quite an active interest in public affairs, but cared nothing for political preferment, in fact refused several nominations to official positions of honor and trust. He was an honored member of the Masonic fraternity, and in all the relations of life was found true to every trust reposed in him. He passed away February 5, 1891, at the age of seventy-four years, and is survived by his wife and ten children.

In the schools of Darlington, E. Savage Shure acquired a good practical education, and on laying aside his text books returned to his boyhood home at Shures Landing, where he still lives with his widowed mother. At the age of twenty he entered his father's general store at that place, which had been established in 1845, and since the latter's death has assumed charge of the business and other property. He is also interested in farming to some extent, owning a good place of one hundred and fifty acres on the Susquehanna River, which he has under a high state of cultivation. He is a business man of more than ordinary ability, and is meeting with a well-deserved success in his undertakings. Like the other members of the family, he is identified with the Episcopal Church.

DENNIS H. STANDIFORD. The name of Standiford is connected with the agricultural development of Harford County and with its advancement in other directions, since the early days of its settlement. Both in this and in Baltimore County its members have taken an active part in farming interests, and have gained prominence in their chosen calling. The Standifords were first represented in America by the great-grandfather of Dennis H., who was born in Wales and in youth crossed the ocean, settling in Baltimore County, Md., where he gave his attention to the cultivation of a farm. Little is known concerning his life and character, but he must have been a man of energy, determination and force of will, for he came alone to the new world and sought his fortune among strangers in a strange land. His son, Jacob, grandfather of Dennis H., was born in Baltimore County and always engaged in general farming except the period of his service in the War of the Revolution.

Claudius Standiford, our subject's father, was born in Baltimore County, and when very young took part in the War of 1812, being present at the battle of North Point, Baltimore. By his marriage to Cordelia Hitchcock, a native of District No. 4, Harford County, he had nine children, but all are deceased excepting Dennis H. The latter was born in this district October 31, 1818, and when quite young attended the local schools. However, the advantages then were quite inferior to those of the present day and he had none of the helps in acquiring knowledge that the children of to-day enjoy. When twelve years of age he began to work in a cotton factory at Warren, Baltimore County, and during his three years there he rose early each day and worked late. His pay was very small, and he was pleased when a more favorable opening for work presented itself. With his parents he came to District No. 4, where, at seventeen years, he commenced to learn the blacksmith's trade, serving an apprenticeship of three years. For four years afterward he worked at the trade, but failing health forced him to turn his attention to employment of a different nature. From that time he engaged in general farming, which he carried on until the approach of old age, and then transferred the management of the property to his adopted son.

At the age of thirty-one, Mr. Standiford married Susanna Engle, who was born in Delaware; her father, John Engle, was a native of Pennsylvania, of German descent, and by occupation was a farmer. In religious connections Mr. and Mrs. Standiford are identified with the Evangelical Church, in which he holds the office of steward. They have no children of their own but adopted a boy, William K., whom they carefully trained in youth and who is now married and in charge of the home farm. The political affiliations of our subject are with the Democratic party, which has no adherent in this section more loyal than he. In his native county he takes a patriotic interest and all feasible plans for its advancement are sure of his approval and material assistance in putting them into execution.

MRS. R. BELLE STIFLER is a lady of much intelligence, energy and executive ability, and is in every way competent to be a leader in society, as she is in her home circle. She was born in District No. 4, Harford County, Md., September 24, 1845, one of the four children of William and Martha (Gillespie) Gailey, both of whom were natives of Pennsylvania. They removed to Harford County, and here reared their family, whose names are as follows: Mary A., Simon G., R. Belle and Martha L. The paternal grandfather, Rev. John Gailey, was a minister of the Methodist Episcopal Church and for many years was located at Prospect, Pa., where he pursued his ministerial labors and at the same time tilled the soil successfully.

Mrs. Stifler's girlhood was passed on the farm. She received good educational advantages, and after imbibing all that could be learned in the common schools she entered the Normal School of Baltimore, which institution she attended for two years. At the end of that time she returned home and began teaching school, and during the three years that she pursued this occupation the district schools were her sphere. At the age of twenty-three years she married William H. Stifler, a Pennsylvanian by birth and a foundryman by occupation, at which business he made a good living. As time passed by, eight children were born to bless their union and were named as follows: Bertha L., who is married; William C., Rosa G., Silas H., Robert S., James M., Dora M. and Anna Adelle.

Mr. Stifler was a man of good principles, a useful, law-abiding citizen, and for many years had been a consistent member of the Methodist Episcopal Church, with which Mrs. Stifler is also connected. His death occurred in the prime of manhood (forty years), December 26, 1890, and in his demise society lost one of its most useful members. He was patriotic and public spirited, and from the time his first vote was cast until his death, the Democratic party received his support. His record as a citizen is untarnished and in all the affairs of life he bore himself in an upright manner and was recognized as a man of true worth. His widow still lives in Norrisville with her children, four of whom are successfully engaged in teaching school.

HOWARD A. LEVERING. In the history of Maryland there is no name more honored than that of Levering. Coming to the state at a very early period in its settlement, they identified themselves closely with every advance movement, and for generations have borne an active part in business enterprises. Of the subject of this sketch it may be said that in every respect he is worthy of the honored name he bears. While his inclinations were in the direction of a business life, poor health obliged him to seek an occupation less confining, and it was thus that he decided to come to Harford County. Here he settled upon Woodlawn farm in District No. 3, where he and his only surviving sister, Sarah R., are surrounded by every comfort that can enhance the pleasure of existence. The farm contains one hundred and twenty-six acres and is operated by a tenant.

In the city of Baltimore Mr. Levering was born in 1827, being a son of Jesse, and grandson of Enoch Levering, the latter a lifelong resident of Leverington, Pa. Jesse Levering was a ship builder by occupation, but in his early years he met with an accident that prevented him from following the trade. For more than fifty years he was engaged in the wholesale grain business in Baltimore, being associated with his brothers. During the War of 1812 he was a staff officer in the Fifth Regiment, Maryland militia, and two of his sons, Enoch and Peter, also participated in the war as members of the same company with himself. At the battle of Bladensburg, while loading his gun, he was wounded in the right hand, and the lead ball which was taken from the wound is still in the possession of our subject. He married Sarah Brown, a native of Baltimore, and they had twelve children, but only two survive. He died in Baltimore in 1832, at the age of fifty-nine; and his wife passed away in 1848, aged sixty-five. In the Civil War their son, Alexander T., served in the Federal army, as did also their grandson, Jesse.

On account of delicate health, which rendered constant study an impossibility, the subject of this sketch spent very little time in school; however, thoughtful reading and observation have to a large degree atoned for the deficiencies of his early education. In youth he was for a short time employed as a machinist at Ellicott Mills, but the confinement of indoor work was injurious to his health and so weakened his constitution, none too robust at best, that he decided to seek another occupation. For two years he was engaged as clerk in a general store for Ellicott & Palmer. In 1848, accompanied by his five sisters, he came to Harford County and purchased Woodlawn farm, where he now resides. While he maintains a general oversight of the place and its one hundred and twenty-six acres, the active work of tilling the soil and harvesting the grain is done by the tenant, Mr. Levering leading a practically retired life. He is not a member of any denomination, but attends the Fallston Presbyterian Church, to which his sister belongs. In politics he is a Republican, but has never mingled in public affairs or sought official position. His sister is the author of a volume entitled "Memoirs of Margaret Jane Blake, of Baltimore, and Selections in Prose and Verse." Their home is a place of contentment, and they have won the regard of neighbors and friends on account of their mental and social qualities. They cherish and preserve the good name handed down to them, and their lives point the moral that an upright career always brings with it the approval not only of conscience, but also of acquaintances and associates.

JOHN C. TUCKER. Harford County has its full quota of vigorous, enterprising farmers, whose popularity is based upon their well-known integrity and business activity. Among those residing in District No. 3 perhaps none is better liked than the subject of our sketch, who owns and occupies a part of the old Tucker homestead of sixty-eight acres. Here he carries on general farm pursuits, including the raising of cattle, in which line of work he has become interested.

Upon the place where he still resides, John C. Tucker was born March 19, 1835. His father, David, Jr., and grandfather, David, Sr., were born in Bucks County, Pa. (the former in 1800), and from there removed to Harford County about 1812. By occupation both were farmers, which calling was also followed by John Tucker, father of David, Sr. When our subject's father came to this county, he was a boy of twelve. He grew to manhood upon a farm in District No. 3, where afterwards he engaged in farming and market gardening until his death, in February, 1881, at the age of eighty-one.

The marriage of David Tucker, Jr., and Sarah Carter resulted in the birth of twelve children, namely: Elizabeth, Mrs. Amos Benson; Sarah J., who married Mortimer Smith; Hannah, Mrs. John England, deceased; Isabel, wife of John C. Stonebraker; Mary A., Mrs. John Strithoff; Margaret C., who married David Deaver; William H., deceased; Ellis J., who is living near Darlington; John C.; David L.; Samuel R., deceased; and Margaret E., who died in infancy. The mother of this family passed away in 1889, when eighty-three years of age.

The entire life of our subject has been passed on the old homestead, of which he has had charge since the age of twenty-one. Politically he favors the Republican party, and upon that ticket was elected collector of taxes, filling the office for two years. At one time he was connected with the lodge of Odd Fellows at Bel Air. In 1861 he married Emma L. Smith, daughter of William Smith, of Baltimore County. Seven children were born of this union, namely: Mary, who married William Kessinger; Eugene Seymour and Morris, who live in New Jersey; Bertie; Allen; Herbert, and Harry, deceased. The family attend the Methodist Episcopal Church. In all matters relating to the welfare of the community Mr. Tucker takes an active interest, and his sympathy and support may be relied upon in promoting plans for the benefit of the people of this section. He believes thoroughly in maintaining agriculture up to modern standards, is an advocate of good roads, substantial bridges and first-class local improvements. Land, he believes, should be thoroughly cultivated and systematically fertilized by the use of proper agencies and by a rotation of crops. Were each farmer to do his share toward securing the best results, as it has been his endeavor to do, then, indeed, Harford County would stand without a peer as an agricultural center.

JOHN W. STRAWBRIDGE. Enterprise and square dealings usually lead to more flattering results than the practice of sharp and unscrupulous business measures, and when these qualities are combined with a thorough knowledge of the business engaged in, they are sure to bring a legitimate and well-deserved reward. A provision for the material wants of life is one of the most important of callings, and without the aid of the merchant the whole public would find itself in a tangled dilemma from which extraction would be impossible. The mission of the merchant is so important that he is an indispensable member of society at large. One of the foremost merchants of Norrisville is John W. Strawbridge, who is a native of District No. 4, Harford County, Md., his birth occurring on the 8th of November, 1851. His parents, Henry M. and Elizabeth (Almoney) Strawbridge, were natives of District No. 4 also, and the occupation to which they devoted their attention throughout life was tilling the soil. A sketch of this worthy couple may be found in this volume.

The early life of John W. Strawbridge was spent in the healthful occupation of farming, this active out-door life doing much to improve him physically, but while acquiring a knowledge of agriculture, the improvement of his mental faculties was by no means neglected and a thoroughly practical education was acquired in the common schools near his home. After imbibing such knowledge as these institutions afforded he began teaching school and continued this occupation very successfully for about two years, at the end of which time he engaged in the general mercantile business at Norrisville, and has continued the same successfully up to the present time. His establishment is well stocked with an excellent line of goods, and his courtesy and fairness in dealing with his patrons and the reasonable figures at which he disposes of his commodities, have met with substantial returns.

At the age of thirty-seven years Mr. Strawbridge married Miss Louisa J. Schilling, a native of St. Louis, Mo., but their short married life ended in the death of Mrs. Strawbridge, January 27, 1890, at the age of twenty-eight years. She left an infant daughter, now seven years of age, to whom the name of Louisa J. was given in honor of the mother. Mrs. Strawbridge was a worthy member of the Methodist Protestant Church, as is also Mr. Strawbridge. The latter chose for his second wife Miss Abbie J. Jenkins, who was born in York County, Pa., and they have a very pretty and comfortable home in Norrisville. He is a shrewd and practical man of affairs, ready to take advantage of every opportunity for bettering his financial condition, but withal is strictly honorable in his business dealings, generous and kindly disposed. The part he has taken in the business affairs of life has been such as to redound to his credit and well worthy the imitation of others. He has ever been a stanch Republican politically and during the administration of President Harrison he was made postmaster of Norrisville, and discharged the duties of this position with his usual ability and good judgment. He still holds the incumbency under President McKinley. At one time he was a member of the Knights of Pythias fraternity, but is not connected with that order at the present time. For a number of years he has been an active worker in the Methodist Protestant Church, of which he is one of the trustees and was formerly Sunday-school superintendent.

P. B. HOUSEKEEPER, M. D., is an eminent and successful physician of Cecil County, who has for many years engaged in practice in North East. His talent and culture have gained him an honorable position in the medical profession and he enjoys an extensive practice. He was born in Chesterville, Lancaster County, Pa., March 28, 1847, and was reared on the farm until the removal of the family to North East, Md.

The doctor obtained his primary education in the district schools near his home, and was later a student in the Lititz Academy, near Lancaster, Pa., where he completed his literary course. At the age of seventeen he began reading medicine, and subsequently entered the Jefferson Medical College of Philadelphia, graduating from that institution in 1866. Soon afterward he opened an office in North East, where he has since engaged in the prosecution of his chosen profession with remarkable success.

In 1877 Dr. Housekeeper was united in marriage with Miss Verquir Veasey, and they have one child. The mother is a consistent member of the Episcopal Church, and a most estimable lady, who is held in high regard by a wide circle of friends and acquaintances. The doctor is an honored and prominent member of the Cecil County Medical Society, belongs to the Masonic lodge of Elkton, and the Knights of Pythias fraternity of North East. The Democratic party finds in him a stanch supporter, and he has served his fellow-citizens in the capacity of physician for the Cecil County almshouse and insane asylum for about eight years, discharging his duties in a most creditable and efficient manner.

HENRY M. STRAWBRIDGE. Biography should be written for the sake of its lessons; that men everywhere may place themselves in contact with facts and affairs, and build themselves up to and into a life of excellence, where they may keep and augment their individuality. For this reason a sketch of Henry M. Strawbridge is here given, his career having been both honorable and useful. Industry, frugality and honesty were the principles instilled into the life of their son by the parents of Mr. Strawbridge, and who can doubt but these principles have had much to do with his success. He was born in Baltimore County, Md. May 12, 1831, to Joseph and Rebecca (Manifold) Strawbridge, both natives of York County, Pa., and farmers by occupation. The children born to them were named as follows: Isaac, Henry M., William F., Joseph, Lydia A., and Rebecca J. There were also two children that died in infancy. The paternal grandfather, Isaac Strawbridge, was a native of Pennsylvania and all his life gave his attention to tilling the soil. His father, Joseph Strawbridge, was born in England, but in early manhood came to America and was a patriotic, law-abiding citizen.

Henry M. Strawbridge was born on the parents' farm in Baltimore County, and there his boyhood days were spent in various duties and in becoming familiar with the work of tilling the soil intelligently. His ancestors for three generations before him were farmers, and it is therefore not to be wondered at that upon commencing for himself he should choose the same occupation. His labors were interrupted, however, by the opening of the Civil War, but it was not until October 3, 1864, that he enlisted in the service, becoming a private in Company A, Purnell's Cavalry Maryland Volunteers. He served until the close and received his discharge at Fortress Monroe, Va., July 28, 1865, and although he did not participate in any engagements he showed his willingness to give his life for his country.

At the early age of twenty years, Mr. Strawbridge married Miss Elizabeth Almoney, who was born in Harford County, Md. As the years rolled by, ten children were added to their household, two of whom died in infancy unnamed. Those who reached maturity were named as follows: John W., Rebecca C., Mary J., deceased; Lydia A., Sarah A., A. Sherman, Benjamin A. and Joseph H. The farm owned by Mr. Strawbridge contains one hundred and thirty-two acres, well improved with good buildings and tilled in a careful and intelligent manner. He is a strictly self-made man, is actively interested in all public matters, and can at all times be relied on to give aid where it is most needed. A strong Republican politically, he is also a member of the Wann Post, G. A. R., of Forest Hill, Md. He and his wife have for some time been members of the Methodist Protestant Church.

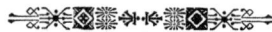

THE FOARD FAMILY. The history of the Foard family in America dates back to the seventeenth century. About 1680 the first of the name in this country crossed the Atlantic and settled in Maryland, obtaining from Lord Baltimore a grant to a tract of land adjoining the property of the Roman Catholic Church on Sassafras Neck. This place has since been in possession of the family. Not only was it one of the oldest, but also one of the largest families on

Bohemia Manor. Previous to 1741 Richard Foard married Mary, the daughter of Richard Boulding, of Back Creek Neck. For a time he lived in the old and now decayed dwelling, but after ten years or more he leased the tract of land now occupied by Erving Griffith (then called "Husband's Choice," but now known as "Bacon Hall,") on condition that he should annually pay three pounds to Peter A. Bouchell and John A. Lawson at the ancient manor house, on Bohemia River.

The family of Richard and Mary Foard consisted of eight children, some of whom attained very advanced years. Five of them were sons, namely: Jeremiah, who died young; Edward, Hezekiah, Josiah and Richard Boulding. Three were daughters, as follows: Tamson, Mrs. Alexander; Lydia, Mrs. Lawrenson; and Letitia, who married John Mansfield. Of the sons, there is a tradition in the family that Jeremiah was killed while fighting in the Indian wars. Edward, who married Sarah Mansfield, purchased the Great House farm from John Hodge Bayard and Col. John Bayard in 1788, and there resided until his death, January 24, 1822, at the age of seventy-nine years. Three days later his remains were interred in the Bohemia churchyard. His wife survived him about three years and died when more than fourscore years of age. They had two daughters, Jemima and Mary. Jemima married James Blackstone, and their descendants are the Blackstones and Naudains, of Kent and Newcastle Counties. Mary married Dennis James Nowland and they resided at the old homestead on Sassafras Neck until his death, in 1807, after which she and her children returned to her father's home. Her family consisted of Edward F. and Mary R. (twins), Augustus J. and Sarah J. (twins), Alfred C., Henry N. and Frisby M. (twins), Lambers D. and Louisa H., nine in all, of whom three are buried in St. Augustine churchyard, three sleep in death elsewhere, and three yet sojourn in the land of the living.

Hezekiah, the third son of Richard Foard, enlisted in the Revolutionary War and participated in many of the hard-fought engagements of that desperate struggle. In recognition of valor and ability, he received the title of major-general. At the close of the war he returned to the old home on Bohemia Manor and continued to reside there, and elsewhere on the Manor, until 1833, when he passed away at an advanced age. By his marriage to Mrs. Sarah Lawrenson he had several children, namely: Andrew; Richard, who married Sarah Craig; Josiah, who married Harriet Thompson; Hezekiah, who chose as his wife Araminta Hyland; and Harriet, who became the wife of Hyland Freeman and the mother of William R. Freeman, now of Back Creek mill.

Josiah, the fourth son of Richard Foard, married Hannah Lawrenson, and they resided on the farm now owned by John J. Williams; their home, the old hipped-roof house, still stands. Having no children, they adopted Hannah L. Bayard as their daughter, and gave her every advantage their means could provide. She became the wife of John W. Bouchell, and some time previous to the death of Mrs. Foard, which occurred September 22, 1831, she was given a farm on Morris Neck, the present home of her family.

Richard Boulding Foard, fifth son of Richard, was an officer in the Revolution, at the close of which he returned to his farm situated at the head of Back Creek Neck. There he remained until his death. He had three children, Mary, James and Levi G. Mary became the wife of Nathan Boulding. Levi G., at the age of eighteen years was an ensign in the army and later took part in the War of 1812, holding the position of captain of a company of soldiers raised on Bohemia Manor. His wife, Ann, was the eldest daughter of Samuel Bayard. At his death, in 1814, he left four children, Samuel B., Richard J., Edward L. and Mary, wife of Capt. Lambert D. Nowland.

The present generation of Foards is descended from colonial and Revolutionary stock, on both the paternal and maternal sides. Richard Boulding Foard's son, Maj. James Foard, was an officer in the colonial army during the Revolution. He married a Miss Logue for his first wife and they had two children, Dr. Josiah and Ann J. His second wife, Mary, was a daughter of Major McDonough, of Revolutionary fame, and sister of Commodore McDonough of the War of 1812, who after his victory on Lake Champlain, in 1814, was presented by congress with a golden sword set with jewels. Four children were born of this marriage, Mary, Lydia, Kate and Wilhelmina. Dr. Josiah Foard married Lydia Caulk, the granddaughter of Maj. Thomas McDonough, who was a Revolutionary soldier and later became judge of the orphans' court in Kent County, Del. Dr. Foard had nine children. James L., who was the father of the present generation, was born on Bohemia Manor in 1816, and came to Elkton, where he married Miss Martha Rebecca Hyland. She was the daughter of Stephen Hyland, a colonel in the War of 1812, and granddaughter of Col. Stephen Hyland, a friend of the patriots, who entertained Lafayette at his mansion and did much to advance the Revolutionary cause. Col. Stephen Hyland married Maria Kankey March 9, 1812, and they became the parents of five children: John, Lambert, Harriet, Martha Rebecca and Arminta. After the death of his first wife, Colonel Hyland married Miss Mary Mauldin, and the seven children born of their union were Benton, Stephen, Henry, Albert, Martha, Elonora and Mary.

When but a youth James L. Foard came to Elkton, in 1831, and afterward became prominent in business and agricultural circles here. By all who knew him he was held in the highest esteem, and, had he consented, he would often have been chosen to serve in public offices. In religious belief he was connected with the Episcopal Church. He died in 1894, having survived his wife four years. The large estate which he had accumulated through intelligent management and industrious application was at his death divided among his six children. They are named as follows: James H., a farmer of Cecil County; Charles R., who is one of the most successful business men of Elkton; Lydia C., Mary Elizabeth, Ruth Anna and Martha Jane.

Of the brothers and sisters of James L. Foard, we note the following: Ann married Dr. George Gordon; Mrs. Sarah Church went to California in 1849; Mary, who is unmarried, resides in Camden, N. J.; Emily became the wife of James Mulford; John joined the tide of emigration westward at the time of the California gold excitement in 1849; Martha married Joseph Casperson; and Lydia became the wife of Thomas Cavender; Thomas accompanied his sister and brother to the Pacific Coast at the time of the discovery of gold in '49.

THE HYLAND FAMILY were identified with the history of North Elk Parish, Cecil County, at least as far back as 1710, and doubtless their arrival in the locality considerably antedated that period. They were descendants of John and Nicholas Hyland, natives of England, the former being a colonel in the British army, who resigned his commission in order to come to America. First seeking a home in Maryland, he found, however, that the province being under the royal government, it was impossible for him to secure a valid grant to land, and on this account he crossed over into Pennsylvania, where he obtained a patent to one thousand acres. Later he purchased additional property in New York state. On the restoration of the province of Maryland to Lord Baltimore he returned here, and secured the grant of a large tract of land, a part of St. John's Manor in Elk Neck. This property he named John and Mary's Highland, this name being chosen not only on account of his own and his wife's names, but also by reason of the elevation of much of the land. His oldest son, Col. Stephen Hyland, was born on Elk Neck February 23, 1743, and died March 19, 1806. During the Revolutionary War he raised a company of soldiers for the protection of private property in Cecil County and subsequently was commissioned by the national government as colonel of a regiment and assigned to duty at Annapolis. In 1781 he entertained General Lafayette and the officers of the French fleet at his old family mansion, which was called Harmony Hall.

WILLIAM C. McCURDY, M. D. The entire professional life of Dr. McCurdy has been passed in Harford County, where he owns and occupies a pleasant home in District No. 4. He was born in the neighboring state of Pennsylvania, in York County, near Delta, February 27, 1846, and is a son of Alexander C. and Mary A. (Turner) McCurdy, natives, respectively, of Scotland and the city of Baltimore. His grandfather, Rev. Alexander C. McCurdy, came to America from his native Scotland and first touched our shores at the old emigrant landing place, Castle Garden, New York. He was a preacher in the Baptist Church, in the early days of the history of that denomination, when its friends were obliged to defend its principles in the face of the most critical opposition. It is said that he officiated at the first baptism by immersion ever administered in Peach Bottom Township, York County, Pa. Gen. George B. McClellan, of Civil War fame, was a distant relative of the McCurdy family.

At the time of coming to America Alexander C. McCurdy, Jr., was a youth of sixteen years. His after years were passed in York County. Of his fourteen children ten are deceased, the survivors being Martha A., Alice J., Dr. William C. and Dr. Alexander C. Our subject received an excellent education in the public schools and Bryansville Academy in York County. At the age of seventeen he began the study of medicine at Bryansville, where he remained for two years, and afterwards spent a similar period in the College of Physicians and Surgeons in Baltimore, from which he graduated. Immediately afterward he commenced the practice of medicine in District No. 4, Harford County, where he has since built up a profitable practice. In earlier years he united with the Presbyterian Church and has ever since retained connection with that branch of the Christian church, to which his wife and daughter also belong. He is a firm and consistent believer in the doctrines held by that denomination and has ever lived up to his profession. In politics he is a thorough Republican, believing firmly in the principles advocated by that party, never yielding what he considers to be right at any time for present success. In addition to the management of his practice, he has other important interests, notably that of president of the Harford Creamery Company, which he organized and with which he has long been connected.

Dr. McCurdy was united in marriage with Hannah Stansbury, of this county, and one child blesses their union, a daughter, Madonna, to whom every advantage has been given, and who is popular in social circles. Dr. McCurdy secured the establishment of the post-office at Madonna, naming the place in honor of his daughter. He was the first and has been the only postmaster here. He is a man of great energy, and could not be idle if he would. As a citizen he is respected for his love of justice, as a Christian he is God-fearing; as husband and father, kind and thoughtful; as a physician, accurate and painstaking. Such in brief is Dr. McCurdy, who, without means or influential friends in his youth, has worked his way forward until he has won prosperity and the regard of many friends.

GEORGE N. WILEY. It would be difficult to conceive an industry which is more important or requires more painstaking care than does that of milling. If bread is made from an inferior grade of flour it is far from being the "staff of life," and should be avoided. Mr. Wiley has shown that he possesses a special adaptability to the business of milling and therefore he has been successful. His mill is largely patronized and turns out a grade of flour second to that of no other similar establishment in the country. In addition to this he has carefully looked after his farming interests, which are of no small importance, and both enterprises have been carried on in a manner to reflect the highest credit upon his good judgment, push and energy.

Mr. Wiley comes of Irish stock, for his paternal great-grandfather was born on the Emerald Isle and there attained manhood. The new world possessed great attractions for him and hither he came and made his home the remainder of his days. He reared a family, of whom Matthew Wiley was a member. The latter was born in Chester County, Pa., became a very wealthy farmer and was at one time the owner of over two thousand acres of land. His son, Matthew, was reared on this farm, became thoroughly familiar with all its duties and eventually became a farmer also. He married Miss Charlotte A. Norris and as the years passed by a family of nine children gathered about their hearthstone: Andrew Jackson, Elizabeth, Rebecca, Hannah, Mary Susan, William, George N., Caroline J. and Thomas H.

George N. Wiley is a native of District No. 4, Harford County, and was born September 21, 1837. His boyhood was spent in activity, for on a farm there is always something for a lad to do, but the work done by him in the pure open air improved both brain and brawn and taught him lessons of energy and push, without which no one can be successful in the accumulation of worldly goods. He was also early trained to a knowledge of milling and may be said to have been reared in the business, a secret, no doubt, of his success in this branch of human endeavor. While busily employed at these occupations his education was not neglected and in the common schools in the vicinity of his home he secured a practical education, sufficient to fit him for the ordinary duties of life. He has been especially successful as a miller, his training in this respect being received under his father, who followed the occupation before him, as did the grandfather also. His fine farm comprises two hundred and thirty acres, well improved and carefully cultivated. He is possessed of more than an average amount of financial ability, and while keenly alive to his own interests, has the satisfaction of knowing that he has wilfully wronged no man.

When about thirty-eight years of age Mr. Wiley married Miss Zanna I. Wiley, a native of the same state and county as himself, and to them was born a daughter, Dora M., who is living with her parents. Mr. and Mrs. Wiley united with the Bethel Presbyterian Church, in which they are earnest workers. He is a member of Parkton Lodge No. 134, A. F. & A. M., and Home Secret Lodge No. 92, K. of P., of Shawsville, Md. The men and measures of the Democratic party have always received his cordial support.

THOMAS A. AMOS, a farmer residing in District No. 4, Harford County, was born in District No. 3, October 19, 1819, the son of Lemuel and Rachel P. (Pearson) Amos, natives, respectively, of District No. 3, Harford County, and Chester County, Pa. The family of which he is a member comprised twelve children, named as follows: Alfred P.; Susan G., who is deceased; Thomas A., of this sketch; Melinda P., and William W., deceased; Milton; Lemuel H., who passed away some years ago; E. Pearson, Oliver C., Henry C., Howard and Ann Elizabeth.

The grandfather of our subject, William Amos, Jr., was born in this county, where he became an extensive farmer. He was a son of Rev. William Amos, a native of England, who, emigrating to America in early manhood, settled on a farm near Fallston, and became an extensive land owner and wealthy farmer, as well as a prominent minister in the Quaker Church. During the early part of his life, while exercising the functions of his office in the militia, it was revealed to him that the kingdom of Christ was a "peaceful kingdom." Therefore he resigned his commission and united with the Friends' Church. During his subsequent years he was a promoter of justice and a friend of peace. In 1806 he called a meeting of his descendants in America, and over one hundred and forty gathered in the Friends' meeting house on Lombard Street, Baltimore, on which memorable occasion one of his great-great-grandchildren was present. This venerable patriarch was the father of a numerous progeny. As correctly as can be ascertained, the number of his descendants was as follows: Children, sixteen;

grandchildren, ninety-two; great-grandchildren, one hundred and thirty-eight; and great-great grandchildren, eight; total, two hundred and fifty-four. He died in Harford County, February 26, 1814, at the advanced age of ninety-seven.

Upon the home farm near Fallston the subject of this sketch grew to manhood, receiving in the schools a fair education. At the age of thirty-two he married Angeline V. Wetherall, who was born in Bucks County, Pa. Their six children are, Ida, Anna, Emmett (deceased), Rachel, Hattie and Ella. Mrs. Amos and the children are identified with the Methodist Episcopal Church, while Mr. Amos clings to the Quaker teachings of his ancestors. Though he has never desired to enter public life nor wished office, yet he believes every true American citizen should inform himself concerning the issues of the age and vote as he is led, by the dictates of his conscience and the opinions formulated after careful thought. For himself he believes stanchly in Republican principles, and the grand old party has in him a loyal supporter. As a farmer he has been successful and his place is one of the best in the district.

when he was ninety, and his body was laid to rest in Bethel cemetery. Our subject's father, who was likewise a farmer, was successful in life, a Democrat in politics, and a Presbyterian in denominational preference. He died at the age of seventy and was buried in Bethel cemetery.

In attending school and working on the home farm our subject spent his early years. At the age of twenty-four he married Cornelia S. Haile, who was born in Baltimore County, the daughter of Capt. Charles T. and Sarah (Deets) Haile, natives of the same county. The family of which she was a member consisted of eight children: Hannah C., Susanna, Amanda, Cornelia S., Laura, George M., Wilson and Frederick D. Of her marriage eight children were born, Minna B., Charles W., Edgar A., Sarah E., Laura J., G. Wilson, Walter H. and Mary C. All are at home except Charles W., who is a graduate of the Maryland Agricultural College and a lieutenant in the United States revenue marine service. Sarah E. graduated from the Maryland State Normal School of Baltimore and is a teacher by profession.

In 1887 and 1888 Mr. Cairnes represented his district in the office of tax collector. In addition to farming, his services are sometimes called into requisition as an auctioneer. At this writing he is a director in the Harford Mutual Fire Insurance Company. With his family he belongs to the Presbyterian Church, and in the congregation officiates as an elder. Politically he is a Democrat.

GEORGE A. CAIRNES, whose farm of two hundred and fifty acres lies in District No. 4, Harford County, was born in this district July 5, 1846, the son of William and Elizabeth (Vance) Cairnes, natives of the same place as himself. The family of which he was the youngest consisted of seven children, the others being named Louisa, Mary A., Rebecca J., Hannah E., Margaret E. and Franklin (deceased). The first of the family to locate in America was the grandfather, George Cairnes, a native of Ireland, who was brought by his parents to this country when a child of four years, and soon after landing at Philadelphia was brought to Harford County, his subsequent home. Farming was his life work, and in it he engaged until so old as to render manual labor impossible. In religion he advocated the Presbyterian faith. His death occurred

MRS. RACHEL M. STRONG. This worthy and intelligent woman comes of an ancestry of which she has every reason to be proud, for her progenitors fought for the freedom and rights of this country on many a field of battle during the Revolution and the War of 1812. Her husband also was an active participant in the great civil strife in which this country was engaged, and held the rank of lieutenant in the Union army. More than this, her ancestors were industrious, law-abiding and useful citizens, actively engaged in agricultural pursuits, and were universally respected. Mrs. Strong is the younger of two daughters (the other being Alice P.) born to Ezekiel and Mary (Payne) Slade, natives, respectively, of District No. 4, Harford County, Md., and the state of Pennsylvania. Mrs. Strong's paternal grandfather, Thomas Slade, is supposed to have been born in Ireland, and to have come to this country in his youth. At least it is known that he became a loyal citizen, and here ended his days. The maternal grandfather, John Payne, was born in England, and in early manhood crossed the Atlantic ocean to seek a home in America. So great was his love of liberty, and so thoroughly did he identify himself with the land of his adoption, that when the colonists flew to arms after the battle of Lexington, he joined the colonial forces and fought for the freedom of this country until independence was gained.

Ezekiel Slade followed the peaceful pursuit of farming throughout life, but when war was declared against England in 1812, he cast aside personal interests and enlisted in the service. His daughter, Mrs. Strong, was reared on his farm in Harford County, Md., where her birth occurred, and in the vicinity of her childhood's home she pursued her studies in the common schools. Upon reaching womanhood she united her destinies with those of Joseph W. Strong, a native of the state of New York, and with him settled in a comfortable home in Harford County, Md. Here their four children were born, named as follows: Mary M., Amanda A., Ezekiel S. (deceased), and Emma E., who became the wife of J. R. Strawbridge. She was born in District No. 4, of this county, and bore her husband three children: Mary M., Nettie R. and Emma V. She died January 18, 1897, at the age of thirty-nine years, having long been an earnest member of the Methodist Protestant Church of Norrisville. Amanda A. married Thomas Hawkins; and they have four children living, the eldest of whom, Mary G. Hawkins, makes her home with her grandmother.

Mr. Strong was a public-spirited man, who was respected by all for his many worthy traits of character. His war record was an honorable one also, and he became an officer of Company A, Maryland Volunteers. Since the death of her husband Mrs. Strong has conducted her affairs with intelligence and foresight, and her kindly heart and generosity have made her universally beloved and respected. She is a consistent Christian, a member of the Presbyterian Church, and earnestly strives to "do as she would be done by."

RICHARD N. WILEY. A study of biography leads one to the inevitable conclusion that like conditions produce like results, that success depends upon certain qualities, chiefly close application, earnest purpose and a ready adaptability of one's opportunites to the ambition and purpose of their lives. This fact illustrates most aptly one of the salient features of our American civilization, that an opportunity is offered under our emblem of liberty for every human being to work out and develop the best there is in him. This Mr. Wiley has done, and success has rewarded him, so that he is now classed among the well-to-do citizens of Harford County.

He was born on the farm which is now his home, in District No. 4, on the 12th of January, 1845. It was the play-ground of his youth and the training school for his business career. Habits of industry and perseverance were strongly encouraged by his parents, and until sixteen years of age he largely spent his youth in working on the farm, and in acquiring an education in the common schools of the neighborhood. He then began learning the miller's trade, which he has followed continuously since, in connection with agricultural pursuits. He is a man of firm purpose, not easily deterred from accomplishing that which he sets out to do. In business circles he merits the confidence of all, and has won the warm regard of many with whom he has thus been thrown in contact. Although he stanchly advocates Democratic principles he has never sought political preferment, desiring rather to give his attention to his chosen life work.

Mr. Wiley was married at the age of thirty-three years to Miss Josephine Forder, a native of Philadelphia, and to their union have been born four children, namely: Clarence B., Olive V., Willard J. and Carl N.

GILBERT S. HAWKINS, a rising young lawyer of Bel Air, was born July 28, 1869, at Thomas Run, about seven miles east of Bel Air, in Harford County. His father, Capt. William L. Hawkins, was a native of Louisiana, and for years engaged in the cotton business at New Orleans. In 1865 he removed to Harford County, and in June of the following year he married Etta Harlan, daughter of Dr. Reuben S. Harlan, a prominent physician of this county. Two children were born of this union, namely: Anna L. and Gilbert S.

The Hawkins family are of English descent, and the lineage can be traced in an unbroken line from the noted John Hawkins, the bold sea captain, who lived and flourished in the days of "Good Queen Bess." On the maternal side our subject is of German origin. His great-great-grandfather was Balzaac Schafer, who resided in Heidelberg, and whose title was that of count.

At an early age our subject accompanied his parents to Louisiana, and there gained the rudiments of his education at home under private tutors. He passed his boyhood days in the Crescent City and was engaged in various occupations there and in Texas until 1887. Returning then to Maryland, he was engaged in the management of his mother's estate, his father having died in 1886. His mother died in 1891. He commenced the study of law in the office of Harlan & Webster in 1889, but two years later, through failing health, his studies were interrupted for some months, but were later resumed. In 1892 he was admitted to the bar upon the motion of Hon. Thomas H. Robinson.

Believing that a more southern clime would better suit his weakened constitution, Mr. Hawkins returned to the home of his youth, and opened an office for the practice of his profession in Covington, La. Possessing the qualifications of ability and indefatigable industry, he soon had a successful practice, and was identified with a number of important cases, which were decided favorably to his clients. In 1893 he returned to Bel Air and opened an office in connection with Hon. Thomas H. Robinson, where he still continues his practice with unabated vigor and marked success.

June 19, 1895, Mr. Hawkins married Miss Lillian E. Evans, of Covington, La., daughter of the late Edgar D. and Mamie A. (Kennedy) Evans, the former a prominent cotton broker of New Orleans.

Mr. Hawkins has always been an ardent Democrat and is identified with his party in all the leading movements of the day. With his wife, he resides in a pleasant home on Broadway, Bel Air.

HENRY HARLAN. Prominent among the agriculturists of Harford County is Mr. Harlan, who, throughout his entire life, has been closely identified with the history of this locality, while his name is inseparably connected with its business records. He is a man of keen discrimination and sound judgment, and his executive ability and excellent management have brought him a fair degree of success.

Mr. Harlan was born at Hopewell, Harford County, in 1848, a son of Dr. Reuben S. Harlan, and grandson of Jeremiah Harlan. His childhood was passed at Hopewell, on the farm where Mr. Naffler now resides, and he early became familiar with the duties that fall to the lot of the agriculturist. He was provided with excellent educational privileges, having attended a private school in Baltimore, and an Episcopal academy in Philadelphia, where he completed the prescribed course of study at the age of sixteen. Soon after his return home he took charge of the farm, which he continued to operate until 1879, and then removed to the old Henry Harlan place, near Stafford, which he is still successfuly cultivating. It is a valuable tract of one hundred and eighty acres of rich and arable land, and the well-tilled fields and neat appearance of the place indicate the progressive spirit of the owner. His sound judgment and well-known integrity have been the means of having him appointed administrator of many estates, including that of Henry S. Harlan, and it is superfluous to state that his duties have always been satisfactorily and conscientiously discharged. His political support is always given to the men and measures of the Democratic party, and in religious belief he and his family are Episcopalians.

In 1878 Mr. Harlan was united in marriage with Miss Hettie F. Turner, of Newport, R. I., who belongs to one of the most distinguished and honored families of this country. Her father was Commodore Turner, of Philadelphia, and she is a sister of Capt. William J. Turner, of the Second Regiment of United States Infantry. Another brother, Daniel Turner, was for many years consul to Japan. Mr. and Mrs. Harlan have two children, Hettie F. and James T., twins, born in 1881.

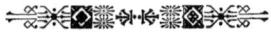

J WILSON MOORE. It is difficult in a few words to accurately describe a character. Only the most salient features can be fitly expressed—the lights and shades can be understood only by those who come in contact with the man under various circumstances. It is difficult, also, to point out the exact traits to which a man owes his success. Suffice it to say that energy and tenacity of purpose have been Mr. Moore's principal traits, and have in a large measure contributed to his present prosperity. He is a well-known farmer of District No. 3, Harford County, and has been as successful in agricultural pursuits as he was previously in his mercantile enterprises.

In the house where he still lives Mr. Moore was born in 1844, the son of Benjamin P. and Mary G. (Jones) Moore. His father was born in Caroline County, Md., but when a few months old was taken to Talbot County, Md. He traced his lineage to Scotch-Irish ancestors, being a son of Robert, who came from the north of Ireland, and whose father, William Moore, a native of Scotland, fought in the famous battle of Londonderry. On coming to America, Robert Moore settled in Talbot County, where for many years he was a practicing physician, but his death occurred in Philadelphia. Benjamin P. Moore was born in 1791, and grew to manhood in Talbot County, whence he removed to Baltimore, and embarked in the grocery business in partnership with Johns Hopkins, whose name is known throughout the entire country on account of his munificence in educational gifts. In 1842 Mr. Moore came to Harford County, having in 1841 bought the farm now owned by our subject, and originally known as Bond's Forest. Here his remaining years were spent, his death occurring in 1875, when he was eighty-four years of age, and both of his wives and family were members of the old Friends' Church.

Twice married, the first wife of Benjamin P. Moore was Mary Hopkins, and their union was solemnized May 21, 1817. Nine children were born to them, three of whom survive, viz.: Mrs. Elizabeth H. Walton; Deborah H., at the old homestead; and Benjamin P., an attorney of Baltimore. The first wife died July 29, 1834, and on the 24th of June, 1840, Mr. Moore was again married, choosing as his wife Miss Mary G. Jones, who bore him five children. She died August 13, 1896, at the age of ninety years. Three of their children survive, Caleb J., John Wilson and Theodore R.

In youth our subject was given good advantages, being a pupil in the common schools, later a student in a private school in charge of the Friends and afterward attending a boarding school in Virginia. In 1863 he went to Baltimore, where for four years he was an employe of the firm of Reese Bros., but in 1867 he went west to Milwaukee, Wis., thinking, perhaps, prospects were more flattering in that city. Four years were spent in the grain business there and a short time in Kansas City, after which he took a position on the road as salesman for a wholesale agricultural implement house. Resigning his position in the fall of 1878, he returned to the old home county, and at Fallston opened a store and warehouse, continuing the same until 1888, when he sold out. Since then he has given his attention to the cultivation of his farm of one hundred and fifty-three acres. Politically he favors Republican principles. In 1876 he married Estelle Nelson, of Pennsylvania, and they had one child, Mary, who died in infancy.

THOMAS J. AYRES, Jr., belongs to one of the prominent old families of Harford County, and makes his home on a farm in District No. 4. The name of Ayres is inseparably connected with the development and improvement of this county, and the gentleman whose name heads this sketch, like others of the family, is always ready and willing to support any cause which will enhance the welfare of the community. On the farm which is now his home, he opened his eyes to the light of day, May 28, 1859. His parents were John and Elizabeth (Perdue) Ayres, the former a native of District No. 4, Harford County, the latter of Baltimore County, Md. They had a family of eight children, namely: Mary C., William, Amanda, James B., Thomas J., John, Hannah and Elizabeth.

Thomas J. Ayres was reared under the parental roof and obtained a common-school education. He assisted in the labors of the home farm and early manifested the business ability and energy that have characterized his entire career and have been important factors in his business. His interests are well managed and he is progressive, following the most approved methods of farming. He now owns a valuable tract of land of two hundred and twenty-seven acres near Shawsville, and the neat and thrifty appearance of the place indicates his careful supervision. A good residence, barns and outbuildings stand in the midst of well-tilled fields, and his energy and labor have brought to him a well-merited success. The spirit of self-help is the source of all genuine worth in the individual and this same spirit has been the guiding power of his life.

When thirty-two years of age Mr. Ayres married Miss Sallie M. Carlin, a native of Baltimore County, and they have two children: Charles C. and Clara M., aged five and three years respectively. Mrs. Ayres is a representative of an old family of Maryland. The Carlins are of Irish lineage, and at an early day established a home in Baltimore County, where they became well-to-do farming people. Her grandfather, William Carlin, was born in Maryland, and his father was a native of New Jersey. Josiah Carlin, the father of Mrs. Ayres, was a native of Baltimore County, as was his wife, who bore the maiden name of Asenath Lytle. They have three children: Laura, Sallie M. and Elizabeth E.

Mr. and Mrs. Ayres are active members of the Methodist Episcopal Church, constant to its teachings and faithful in its work. He is now serving as trustee of the church. He exercises his right of franchise in support of the Democracy and his study of political issues has enabled him to give clear and decided reasons for his faith in the tenets that are promulgated by his party.

JOHN C. ROBINSON. In the following sketch is strikingly illustrated the force of well-directed energy, steadfast purpose and never-ceasing effort to the accomplishment of worthy ends, and the successful overthrow of those obstacles which beset the progress of every young man who sets out to combat life's stern realities and hew his own way to success. The career of such a man presents an example worthy of consideration and earnest emulation, and without doubt does much to promote industry, integrity and consistent manhood.

Mr. Robinson is of Scotch lineage, although himself a native of District No. 4, Harford County, Md., born March 28, 1841. His paternal great-grandfather, John Robinson, was born in Scotland, but in early manhood came to America. His son, Joseph Robinson, was born in the state of Delaware, but came to Harford County, Md., about 1808, and throughout life was engaged in milling and farming. His son, William Robinson, married Miss Mary Kirkwood, both natives of Harford County, Md., and their union resulted in the birth of seven children: Robert K.; Joseph; Rebecca J.; William T.; John C., the subject of this sketch; Mary E. and Rachel B. Rebecca J. and her husband are deceased, leaving a family of six children: Mary E., deceased; Agnes Belle; Annie Blanche, Levisa Rebecca, Ida Nelson and Janie Robinson Wiley. The last-named is the adopted daughter of our subject, in whose family she has been since she was five weeks old.

John C. Robinson was born and reared on a farm and in the public schools near by he received his rudimentary education, which was later completed in Stewardstown Academy, where he pursued his studies for two terms. Realizing that his country needed the services of all her able-bodied citizens he, at the age of twenty-one years, enlisted in Company A, Seventh Regiment of Maryland Volunteers, for three years or during the war, and served until the close of hostilities. On September 1, 1864, he was promoted to the position of hospital steward, and while in the service participated in the battles of the Wilderness and Spottsylvania. After the last-mentioned engagement he was detailed to carry the United States mail, and did so until his promotion to steward. He received his discharge May 31, 1865, at Arlington Heights, and returned home to once more take up the peaceful pursuits of agriculture and carpentering. The former occupation has received his attention ever since, and he owns a fine farm of one hundred and five acres. This land is well improved and under his able management brings him in a goodly income. His attention has been given to the general mercantile business also, which likewise has proved successful. In the management of his affairs he has shown much discernment and good judgment, and his methods for the advancement and improvement of his interests are most practical.

When about thirty years of age Mr. Robinson married Miss S. Emma Robinson, a native of the county, and daughter of Joseph and Eliza (Howlett) Robinson. They had seven children: M. Florence, L. Bertha, R. Belle, E. Maude, and J. T. Calvin, living; and two children who died while babes. Mr. and Mrs. Robinson have long been connected with the Bethel Presbyterian Church. As regards his political views Mr. Robinson has always supported the principles of the Republican party. He has never been a political aspirant, but at the present time holds the office of magistrate. His life and its success afford evidence that industry, economy and integrity constitute the key-note to honorable competency, and it is truthfully said of him that no citizen more useful makes his home in the county.

ROBERT F. HANNA. One of the successful and thrifty farmers of Harford County is the gentleman whose name stands at the head of this sketch. He is a descendant of one of those families that have come from another land and found in this country a prosperity impossible elsewhere on account of the overcrowded condition of the population. His property, situated in District No. 3, comprises one hundred and thirty-five acres of land and is devoted to general farming.

The great-grandfather of our subject was John Hanna, a native of Ireland, and an early settler of Maryland. Alexander, son of John, was a farmer in district No. 3, and his property in turn descended to his son William, father of our subject. By the marriage of William Hanna and Jane McGaw, nine children were born, but only three are now living namely: Hannah E., wife of M. Patterson; Susan R., widow of James Forward; and Robert F., the youngest of the family. The father died on the old homestead at the age of

S. D. McCULLOUGH.

ninety, and the mother in 1877, aged seventy-six. Their bodies are interred in the family cemetery at Churchville.

On the place where he now lives, Robert F. Hanna was born in 1840. Through the medium of the public and private schools, and by thoughtful reading of books and newspapers, he was enabled to acquire a fair education. Of this education and the knowledge he gained of men and business, he made use, endeavoring to work to the best advantage. While much of his property has come to him by inheritance, yet he deserves credit for his energy, frugality and good management that have enabled him to conserve his own financial interests. Everything about his place indicates the thrift of the owner and shows that his reputation as a practical farmer is not undeserved. Politically he is independent, voting at elections for the man he deems best qualified to represent the people. He and his wife have three children, William S., Zenolia and Lizzie S. With his family he attends the Presbyterian Church, which is near their home and is one of the oldest in the state. He is an encourager and promoter of every scheme that will enhance the material progress of the county or district where he resides, or that will serve to elevate their moral and social status.

SAMUEL D. McCULLOUGH. A resident of North East throughout the principal part of his life, Mr. McCullough is one of the most influential business men of the place. He is known as a public-spirited citizen who has been identified with its iron interests for many years. By his energetic and resolute force of character and steady industry, he has given an impetus to the business established by his father and has been actively identified with forwarding the advancement of this locality.

The McCullough family is of the Scotch-Irish origin, notable for steadfast integrity and honorable character. Several succeeding generations were identified with the history of Delaware. The grandfather of our subject, Enoch, was a carpet maker and weaver, and the carpets that he made were noted throughout all that locality for their durability. For many years engaged in the business in Newark, Del., he died there March 2, 1827. His son, our subject's father, Jethro Johnson McCullough, was born at White Clay Creek, Newcastle County, Del., March 8, 1810, and when only six years of age was put to work in the Rosedale cotton factory, where he remained for two years, afterward beginning to work for his father. As may be supposed, he had limited advantages; in fact the education that he obtained was secured by self-culture and in the face of many disadvantages that would have discouraged a man less resolute. Working for his father until he was seventeen, he then turned his attention to the millwright's trade, which he followed for three years in the employ of others and afterward on his own account. For nine years he traveled through Cecil County, Md., Chester County, Pa., and Newcastle County, Del., building up a very large trade and giving employment to many men.

In 1842 Mr. McCullough purchased an interest in the Red City rolling mill in Newcastle County, and this he carried on, in partnership with C. J. and J. Marshall, for five years. February 2, 1847, he purchased the North East forge and on the 16th of March began to operate the plant. In 1861 the concern was incorporated and then reincorporated in 1865 under the name of the McCullough Iron Company. In 1853 he purchased the West Amwell works near Elkton, and three weeks later bought the Stony Chase property in North East, the same year building the Shannon mill on the property. This increased the capacity to eight hundred and eight tons per annum. In 1857 the Rowlandsville mill was purchased, and in 1863 a steam mill at North East was established for the manufacture of bar iron. In 1853 he introduced the manufacture of galvanized iron into the United States, sending to Europe for a man familiar with the work. The total capacity of the mill was four thousand tons of iron per annum, the forges having a capacity of five thousand tons. In the possession of the company there were books to show that George Washington's father and brother and Sir Henry Crewe owned the mill at North East prior to Revolutionary days.

Upon the organization of the Republican party Mr. McCullough joined its ranks and ever afterward supported its principles. In 1855 and 1859 he held the office of county commissioner, and about the close of the war, 1865-66, he represented his district in the state legislature. About the same time he established his home in Wilmington, Del., moving there from North East, where he had resided since 1847. An active supporter of the temperance cause, he gave time and money for its advancement. His death occurred May 25, 1878. His life was one of sobriety and integrity, and he was a consistent member of the Methodist Episcopal Church. January 2, 1834, he married Elizabeth, daughter of John Tull, of Cecil County. Ten children were born of their union, four of whom are living: Enoch, a farmer living one-half mile from Liberty Grove, Md.; George, who is engaged in the iron business in Wilmington, Del.; John and Samuel D., residents of North East. George, Jethro and John were soldiers in the war. The mother passed away in January, 1885, having survived her husband seven years.

August 29, 1855, the subject of this article was born in a house that stood on the opposite side of the street from where he now resides. He attended the schools of North East and Wilmington, and at the age of sixteen began to learn the trade of a machinist, at which he was employed in Wilmington for seven years. Thence he went west to Wyoming and tried the life of a ranchman for two years, having a place stocked with sheep and cattle. The adventurous life of hardships was, however, not entirely congenial to his tastes, and in 1882 he returned to the east, settling in North East, where he has since been assistant manager of the iron business. An active Republican, he was elected to the office of town commissioner, serving four terms, and has been town treasurer for three years. Fraternally he has been a member of Union Lodge No. 48, F. & A. M., at Elkton, since 1883, and belongs to St. John's Chapter No. 1, K. T., at Wilmington; Fellowship Lodge No. 42, K. of P., and is retired captain of Fellowship Division No. 11, Uniformed Rank. Personally he is a man of genial manner, accommodating and generous, willing to help those in need, and desirous of advancing the best interests of the community. His marriage, which took place February 20, 1884, united him with Miss Sarah Martindell, of Cecil County, daughter of Lewis Martindell, who came to Maryland from Bucks County, Pa. They are the parents of five children: Ethel E., Carrie E., Margaret, George W. and Nettie Ray.

CAPT. THOMAS BUTLER was a resident of Harford County almost his entire life and was particularly well known in District No. 4, where he owned and occupied a valuable farm. Agriculture was his occupation, though in youth it was his ambition to become a physician, and with that profession in view he studied medicine in Pennsylvania for two years. However, before his graduation his health failed and he was obliged to give up all hopes of engaging in practice. Knowing that an occupation that would give him more exercise and outdoor employment was better fitted for his physical constitution, he adopted farming as his vocation, and at the time of his death he had the old homestead of one hundred and thirty acres under excellent cultivation. In his community he was a man of prominence, and frequently he was called to fill offices of trust and honor. For six years he was commissioner of Harford County, for some time held the position of justice of the peace, also acted as register and census enumerator. His title was gained through services as captain of a militia in Harford, his native county. In politics he always stanchly upheld Democratic principles, and in religious belief he was a Catholic. His death occurred in May, 1893, when he was seventy-one years of age. It is a noteworthy fact that his father, Col. Clement Butler, and grandfather, Thomas Butler, both of whom were farmers, served in the Revolutionary War, the former being an officer in the army.

The lady who was Captain Butler's cherished companion and helpmate through all the years of their married life bore the maiden name of Cordelia Streett, and was born in Harford County, being a daughter of James and Margaret (Miles) Streett. She was the youngest of four children, the others being Rebecca, Martha J. (deceased) and John J. Reference to the history of the family is made in the sketch of J. M. Streett, of Bel Air, a cousin of Mrs. Butler. She was reared on the home farm and at the age of nineteen became the wife of Thomas Butler, whose subsequent success was due to her energy no less than his own ability. They became the parents of six children, named as follows: Clement G., James S., John T., Harry W., Margaret and May M. The oldest son, who is a miller by occupation, owns and runs a mill at Waterville. The second son is engaged in the mercantile business in Delta, Pa. John, who remains with his mother, manages the home farm. Harry is employed as traveling salesman for Fink Bros., a wholesale tobacco firm of Baltimore. The sons and daughters were reared in the faith of the Catholic Church, to which their mother belongs.

GEORGE W. NORRIS. The gentleman whose name heads this sketch is a public-spirited citizen, in harmony with advanced ideas, intelligent progress and the best methods of benefiting agricultural pursuits, and promoting the good of his country generally. There are few who show as much fitness for their avocation as does he, or are more wide-awake, experienced, reliable and energetic. Born in Baltimore County, Md., September 4, 1835, he is a son of Edward and Elizabeth (Seitz) Norris, the former a native of Harford County, and the latter of Baltimore County. Their marriage resulted in the birth of eleven children, whom they named as follows: James W., Mary A., Edward, Daniel, Andy, George W., Elizabeth, William, Jonathan, Eliza J., and Benjamin.

The paternal grandfather, George Norris, was born in this county also, and here devoted his life to the occupation of farming. His patriotic spirit led him to enlist in the War of 1812, and he was always a very patriotic, enterprising and public-spirited citizen. His father was the founder of the town of Norrisville, was very successful in the accumulation of worldly goods and was at one time the owner of three thousand acres of land in and around the town. His energetic spirit and the excellent example he set did much to build up Harford County, and in the various affairs of the section he took a leading part, his support at all times being given to those enterprises which had for their object the upbuilding of the county.

On a farm in Harford County the subject of this sketch was reared and obtained a thoroughly practical knowledge of agricultural pursuits. At the same time his studies were pursued in the district schools and a practical education acquired. At the age of twenty-three years he married Miss Mary E. Wiley, whose birth occurred in this county, and the young couple at once settled on a farm and began tilling the soil on their own account. Mr. Norris' efforts have met with a reasonable degree of success and he is now the owner of about one hundred and ten acres of fine farming land. The place is well improved with good buildings, and the neatness and order which prevail indicate the thrift and energy of the owner. Politically he has always been an ardent Democrat. He and his wife are earnest members of and workers in the Methodist Protestant Church. He has held the position of class leader for twenty-one years and has aided the church with both influence and means ever since his connection with it.

Mr. and Mrs. Norris have an interesting family of six children: Edward W., Joseph M., Agnes E., Elva I., Nelson and George W. A history of Mrs. Norris' people may be found in the sketches of George N. and Thomas Wiley. Mr. Norris is an excellent citizen, a man of practical and intelligent views, and as a natural result is in good financial circumstances. He is public spirited, as were his ancestors before him, and commands universal respect.

CONRAD P. COOK is the enterprising owner of a valuable farm of two hundred and sixty-five acres, pleasantly located three and a-half miles from Havre de Grace, in District No. 2, Harford County, and is a prominent representative of the agricultural interests of this section of the state. Germany has furnished to America many of her best citizens, who, leaving the fatherland, have identified their interests with those of the Republic, becoming important factors in the business life of the communities with which they are connected. Such a one is Mr. Cook, who on the 9th day of September, 1826, was born in Nedar, Hesse-Darmstadt, Germany. He was reared to manhood there and during his boyhood and youth worked with his father, who was a farmer and baker. When twenty-three years of age, he determined to try his fortune in America and bidding adieu to friends and native land took passage on a sailing-vessel which did not reach the American shore until sixty-nine days later. During the voyage they encountered some severe storms.

Mr. Cook at once made his way to Baltimore, where he worked at the baker's trade for about eighteen months, and then removed to Havre de Grace, Md. He was there employed in a bakery for three months, after which he began business on his own account, establishing a bakery which he successfully conducted for about nineteen years. He enjoyed a good trade and his liberal patronage brought to him a comfortable competence. He then purchased the farm on which he now resides and has since engaged in its cultivation in connection with stock dealing. He is a man of excellent business capacity, capable of carrying out his well-formed plans, and his resolute purpose and honorable dealing have brought to him success.

On the 7th of April, 1852, Mr. Cook was united in marriage with Miss Catherine A. Schreitz, daughter of John and Margaret Schreitz. She was born August 25, 1829, near Frickburg, Germany, and came to America with her parents when three years of age. Mr. and Mrs. Cook have two children: John L., a bookkeeper in Baltimore; and William F., who is with his parents on the home farm.

Mr. Cook exercises his right of franchise in support of the men and measures of the Democratic party, and is a firm believer in its principles, but prefers to support his friends for office rather than to seek the same for himself. He belongs to Morning Star Lodge No. 20, I. O. O. F., Havre de Grace, and is a member of the Episcopal Church. He has never had occasion to regret his determination to seek a home in America, for here he has steadily worked his way upward and has secured a handsome property and the warm regard of many friends.

MRS. MARY J. HUTCHINS. The subject of this sketch is a woman of ripe intelligence, large benevolence and broad sympathies. Since the death of her husband, which occurred June 18, 1880, at the age of sixty-seven years, she has had control of a large amount of property, and so ably and intelligently has she managed it that its value has been considerably enhanced. She was born in District No. 4, Harford County, Md., February 28, 1828, a daughter of John and Susan (Thompson) Hawkins, who were natives of this county also, and who became the parents of eight children, four of whom are living at the present time: Mary J. (Mrs. Hutchins), Dr. John A., Edwin and Thomas W. The paternal grandfather, Nicholas Hawkins, was born in England, but when very young he took passage on board a sailing-vessel for the new world and became a loyal, law-abiding citizen of this country. His attention was devoted almost exclusively to farming, and in this occupation he showed great discernment and sound judgment and eventually became a very extensive land owner. When the colonists rebelled against the tyranny of England he heartily espoused their cause and was an active participant in the Revolutionary War.

Mrs. Hutchins spent her girlhood days on the fine farm owned by her parents and received such educational advantages as the common schools afforded. At the age of seventeen years she became the wife of John S. Hutchins, a native of District No. 4, Harford County, and a man of more than ordinary intelligence and good judgment, possessed of keen business instincts. His efforts to obtain a competency were crowned with financial success, and at the time of his death he was considered wealthy. He owned a large and valuable estate, well improved in every way and stocked with the various domestic animals, and all this valuable property was willed to his widow at the time of his death, the place where she lives being the homestead that had been in the Hutchins family for three generations. The entire life of Mr. Hutchins was spent as a tiller of the soil, his knowledge of the work being obtained on his father's farm while growing up. He secured a practical education in the common schools, which he greatly improved in later years by contact with business men and judicious reading. He was well informed on all topics of the times and although a stanch Democrat in politics never desired or sought office. His marriage resulted in the birth of twelve children: Martha J., Susan M., Ann R., Laura, Alvarda (deceased), William B., Charles L., Gertrude, Zanie, Elizabeth, and Estella and Maud (twins).

Mr. Hutchins' death occurred after a long illness of three years, and was caused by cancer of the stomach. The county lost in his demise a most useful and valued citizen. He was one of her public-spirited citizens, upright and honorable in all his business transactions, and liberal in his contributions to a worthy cause. Since his demise his widow has conducted her large estate in a manner to reflect the greatest credit upon her good judgment and her sex, and has entirely overthrown the old idea that women are not adapted for business life. Like her husband she is generous in the use of her means and has always been very charitably inclined. She has long been an active member of the Episcopal Church (as was her husband) and is a worthy Christian woman and one who commands universal respect.

NATHANIEL HOLLINGSWORTH, deceased, was for many years an honored and valued citizen of Harford County, and one of its leading farmers. He belongs to an old and distinguished family of the Keystone State that was founded there in 1682 by Valentine Hollingsworth, of England, who came with William Penn and settled in Delaware County, locating a grant of nine hundred and eighty-six acres of land on the Brandywine and there spending his remaining days. He held many important official positions in those early days, being a member of the Pennsylvania Assembly in 1695. He was still living in 1710, but we have no record of his death.

Following Valentine Hollingsworth in line of succession were Thomas, Sr., Thomas, Jr., and Nathaniel, the latter born in Westtown, Pa., in 1755, married Abigail Green in 1783, and removed from Chester County, Pa., to Harford County, Md., where he became a large land owner. He had a family of ten children, of whom Nathaniel was, in 1834, united in marriage with Mary Warner, daughter of Silas and Miss Sarah Warner. The history of the Warner family in Maryland dates from 1771, when Joseph and Ruth (Hayhurst) Warner came to this state from Wrightstown, Bucks County, Pa. They were the parents of six sons, three of whom died in youth. Their son, Silas, was born June 14, 1766, and married, December 3, 1807, Miss Sarah Warnock, daughter of Philip Warnock, who came to this country from Ireland. They became the parents of seven children: Mary and Ruth, twins; Joseph, Philip, William, Edward and Jane. Joseph married Margaret Pyle, and they had three children. Philip and William kept the old homestead and carried on general farming, entertaining at their comfortable abode a great many friends at different times, and maintaining a high place in the regard of all. They, like their father, were men of noble character and manly attributes.

During his boyhood Nathaniel Hollingsworth, of this review, came to Harford County, Md., locating on Winter's Run, where he successfully followed agricultural pursuits until called to the world beyond. As a companion and helpmate on life's journey he chose Miss Mary Warner, of Darlington, Harford County, and by their marriage they became the parents of seven children, as follows: Silas W., Thomas, Sarah, Rebecca G., Mary, Nathaniel, deceased, and Edward. The family hold membership in the Society of Friends and are numbered among the representative and prominent citizens of this community. Mr. Hollingsworth departed this life in 1851, at the age of sixty years, and his wife in 1848. He was one of nature's noblemen, and the world is better for his having lived. Standing under the light and life of a character like this, and viewing the ground in which they had germinated and on which they grew, one cannot but feel that the best type of manhood is created and developed on American soil, and what one has done worthily another may attempt.

CHARLES A. McGAW, proprietor of the Old Eagle Hotel of Bel Air, is a wide-awake, progressive business man, and comes of a family that has long been connected with the history of Harford County. He was born January 6, 1846, in the old Bush Tavern, one of the historic landmarks in this section of the state. George Washington and Andrew Jackson were both entertained there and it was the scene of many of the most important events which form the annals of Harford County. The grandfather of our subject, Robert McGaw, was a native of Scotland, and, crossing the Atlantic to America, took up his residence in Harford County many years ago. His son, Robert McGaw, Jr., was born on Red Hill, in District No. 1, and during his early life followed the miller's trade. He purchased a farm of three hundred acres where the town of Bush now stands and also bought the celebrated Bush Tavern in 1830. For twenty-five years he carried on that hotel and as its proprietor became widely known. Later in life he engaged in farming, following that pursuit until his death. From 1848 until 1850 he filled the position of sheriff, and for years served as constable at a time when it was an honor to hold that office. He was also extensively engaged in fishing interests for many years, and his was a very busy and useful life. He voted with the Whig party until its dissolution and then joined the ranks of the Democracy, being regarded as one of its leaders and as a man of much personal influence. He also supported the Presbyterian Church. His death occurred in 1877, when he had reached the age of seventy-two years. His wife, who bore the maiden name of Elizabeth Henson and was a daughter of Thomas Henson, of Harford County, died in 1878. They had five children: Matilda, who is living in Abingdon; James, of Prince George County, Md.; Thomas, who is engaged in merchandising in Baltimore; Charles A.; and Sallie J., of Abingdon.

Mr. McGaw, of this sketch, acquired his elementary education in the district schools and afterward attended the Bel Air Academy. At the age of seventeen he began farming with his father and the business relation between them continued for fifteen years. Our subject then turned his attention to the canning business, and for eleven years conducted a canning establishment at Bel Camp. The enterprise proved a successful one, and he did an extensive business, which yielded to him a good income. In 1889 he was elected sheriff of the county on the Democratic ticket, and acceptably discharged the duties of that position for two years, retiring from office, as he had entered it, with the confidence and good-will of the general public.

On his return to private life Mr. McGaw built a store in Abingdon, stocked it with general merchandise and for a year continued operations along that line. Through the succeeding three years he conducted a canning factory in Salem County, N. J., after which he resumed farming at Abingdon, and was thus occupied until May 1, 1897, when he embarked in the hotel business in Bel Air. He is enterprising and progressive, keeps abreast with the times in all particulars, has a pleasant, genial manner, and, possessing these essential qualities of a good host, he will probably win success in his new undertaking. He is a member of the Order of the Golden Chain. He married Miss Ella J. Griffin, a daughter of William E. Griffin, and a representative of one of the old and prominent families of Harford County.

BENJAMIN A. AYRES. History shows that the strongest nations have been those in which agriculture has been the chief pursuit of the majority of their people, and the strength of the American republic lies largely in this class. While the statesman forms an important part in controling the destiny of the country, it is his constituents at home, the reliable and trustworthy business men, who form her real power.

Mr. Ayres of this review is numbered among the leading agriculturists of Harford County, and comes from a family that has long been identified with the farming interests of Maryland. He was born in the district where he still lives on the 7th of April, 1841, and in the usual manner of farmer lads was reared to manhood, performing the work of field and meadow from an early age. He obtained his elementary education in the public schools and later spent one year in study in the high school of Stewartstown, Pa. He then returned to the farm and has since engaged in tilling the soil. He now owns one hundred acres of rich and productive land, and gathers from his fields good harvests. Upon his place are substantial buildings, improved machinery and all the accessories which are in harmony with the progressive spirit of the age. In addition to his farming interests, he owns stock in the Harford Creamery Company, at Bradenbaugh, and is its treasurer. He is a man of progressive ideas who began life with a definite purpose in view, worked faithfully, honestly and with a will for its accomplishment and now enjoys a comfortable competence as the reward of his labors.

When forty years of age Mr. Ayres was united in marriage with Julia Shrodes, a native of District No. 4, Harford County. Her grandfather, Henry Shrodes, was a native of Germany, and at an early day in the history of America took up his residence in the city of Baltimore, where he followed the hatters' trade. Charles Shrodes, the father of Mrs. Ayres, was born in Baltimore, learned the stone mason's trade in early manhood and for many years followed that pursuit. On arriving at years of maturity he married Sarah J. Taylor, a native of Harford County.

Mrs. Ayres is a member of the Presbyterian Church. In his political views Mr. Ayres is a Democrat, and is deeply interested in the success of his party, although he has never sought or desired the honors or emoluments of public office. His attention has been given to his business, wherein close application, resolute purpose and energy have brought to him success.

GEORGE D. WHITELOCK. While "the race is not always to the swift, nor the battle to the strong," the invariable law of destiny accords to tireless energy, industry and ability a successful career. The truth of this statement is abundantly verified in the life of Mr. Whitelock, who is one of the prosperous general merchants of Darlington. He is a native of Harford County, born on Swan Creek in 1845, and a son of James Whitelock, of Darlington, whose sketch appears elsewhere in this work. The family is one of the oldest and most prominent in Maryland, the founder, a native of England, having crossed the Atlantic in 1630 and taken up his residence in Cecil County. John Whitelock, our subject's grandfather, followed farming in that county until 1824, when he removed to Harford County, locating near Hopewell, where he made his home until his death, at the age of seventy-three years. Of his eleven children, James was the seventh in order of birth, and only three are now living: James; Eveline, widow of William Brown; and A. J.

James Whitelock was born at Perryville, Cecil County, in 1822, and was therefore but two years old when taken by his parents to Harford County. In early life he engaged in milling, but now owns and operates a farm in District No. 5, Harford County. He was married in 1846 to Caroline Bowman, and to them were born nine children, but only three are now living: George D., of this review; Euphemie, wife of Charles H. Stamford; and Emma, widow of R. E. Spencer. Andrew Gorrell, a great-uncle of our subject, aided the colonies in their struggle for independence during the Revolutionary War, and lost an arm in the service.

The first two years of his life our subject passed at his father's mill on Swan Creek, but at the end of that time was taken by his parents to Cecil County, remaining there until 1861, when he returned to Harford County. In the public schools at Rockland, he acquired a good practical education, which has fitted him for business life. On leaving the parental roof at the age of twenty-five, he embarked in mercantile pursuits in Avondale, where he remained for three years, but in 1876 opened a general store in Darlington, where he carries a full and complete line of dry goods, groceries, etc., and by fair and honorable dealing receives from the public a liberal patronage. June 4, 1879, occurred the marriage of Mr. Whitelock and Miss Annie Hopkins, a daughter of Henry W. Hopkins. They now have three children, Beulah, Mary and Marjory. In politics Mr. Whitelock is a stanch Democrat, and in his church relations is identified with the Methodist Episcopal denomination, and is now serving as trustee of his church. For twenty-one years he has been identified with the business affairs of Darlington, and the social, educational and moral interests of the village have all been promoted by him, while anything that tends to uplift and benefit humanity secures his hearty co-operation.

HENRY G. WHEELER, a well-known resident of District No. 4, Harford County, was born in this county, January 16, 1833, and is a son of Joseph A. and Henrietta (Green) Wheeler. The family of which he is a member consisted originally of nine children, named as follows: Elizabeth A., deceased; Susan; Joseph and Thomas, deceased; Bennett L.; Henry G., of this sketch; Helen, Maria and William. The grandfather, Joseph Wheeler, also a native of this county and a farmer by occupation, was a large land owner in District No. 3 and exerted considerable influence in local enterprises, being held in high regard as a man of intelligence and ability. His father was, it is thought, a native of Ireland, but at an early day he emigrated to the United States and settled in Maryland.

After completing a common-school education, our subject began to learn the wood-worker's trade, at the age of seventeen years, and for a time was employed at Jarrettsville. From 1849 until 1869 he followed that trade, but in the year last named he turned his attention to agriculture and purchased the farm where he now resides. The place contains one hundred and eight acres of land, all of which is improved. To its cultivation he gives his entire attention and through his labors it is made to return a fair income. In politics he is an ardent Democrat and always takes an interest in plans for the success of the party's principles. For three years he held the position of tax collector, in which office he rendered efficient service.

At the age of twenty-one years Mr. Wheeler married Miss Mary A. Cairnes, who was born and reared in this district and is a sister of George A. Cairnes, mentioned elsewhere in this volume. Nine children were born to the union of Mr. and Mrs. Wheeler, and of these six are living, namely: Virginia; William A., who is engaged in the mercantile business at Pylesville, Harford County; H. Elizabeth, Mary, Anna L. and James A. Mrs. Wheeler is a member of Bethel Presbyterian Church, in the work of which our subject assists, though not a member of the congregation.

HENRY C. JENKINS is a member of a family that has been identified with the history of Maryland since the days of Lord Baltimore, his great-great-grandfather, William Jenkins, a native of Wales, having come to America in 1634 in company with the famous proprietor of the colony, and made settlement in St. Mary County, where he became an extensive land owner. The great-grandfather, Ignatius Jenkins, was born in Maryland and here engaged in farm pursuits, as did also the grandfather, Oswald Jenkins. The father of our subject, Ignatius W. Jenkins, was born in Baltimore County, but spent much of his active life as a farmer in Harford County, where he married Anna M. Brown. The three children born of their union are Samuel O., who is unmarried and resides with his younger brother; Henry C. and Mary J. Henry C. was born in Baltimore County, August 30, 1850, and was reared upon a farm. At the age of fifteen he entered the college at Ellicott City, where he carried on his studies for two years.

Farming has been Mr. Jenkins' life occupation and of it he has made a success. His property lies in District No. 5, Harford County, and consists of two hundred and twenty acres of land as choice as can be found in the precinct. On the property, in which he takes justifiable pride, are farm buildings and substantial improvements, and everything is kept in excellent repair. The fine condition of the place is due to the efforts of the energetic owner, who is resolved to make the farm one of the best in the district, and if he continues to improve it as much in the future as he has in the past, there is no doubt but that he will succeed. Some of the land is devoted to cereals, and the remainder to pasturage for stock.

At the age of thirty-two, Mr. Jenkins married Catherine L. Jenkins, who was born in Adams County, Pa., a member of an old family, prominent in the agricultural circles of that section. Seven children were born of the union, but three died in infancy, and the others are Jane R., Mary J., Ignatius W. and Catherine C., all at home. The family attend the Catholic Church, and at the time of the erection of St. Mary's Church Mr. Jenkins was a member of the building committee. In politics he is a firm adherent of the principles of the Democratic party, and loyally supports its principles and measures, firmly upholding its doctrines upon all occasions and under all circumstances.

ANEELY HENDERSON. One of the well-known residents of District No. 4, Harford County, is the subject of this sketch, who has spent his entire life here and is ranked among the skillful veterinary surgeons and large land owners of this section. His early training led him to adopt farming as his vocation, while his natural inclinations were along the line of veterinary surgery. Not being able to gain the knowledge desired by education, he "picked it up" here and there, and the fact that he is now well informed in his chosen specialty, proves that he is an energetic man, with considerable force of character. He is a son of Thomas Henderson, one of the prominent old residents of Black Horse and a man whose life has been filled with deeds of helpfulness and kindly acts. To his sketch upon another page the reader is referred for the family history.

The subject of this sketch was born on the home farm, September 13, 1849. In boyhood he had many opportunities for acquiring an education, but on account of ill health it was impossible to take advantage of them. He established domestic ties at the age of twenty-three, when he married Miss R. Ann Patterson, a native of District No. 4, and of Welsh descent. The five children born of their union are named as follows: Ross C., Ellwood S., Alice C., Mary E. and Martha P. The family reside on the well-improved farm of two hundred acres owned by Mr. Henderson, who, in addition to its cultivation, has an extensive practice as a veterinary surgeon. In his youth he was disciplined in a hard school, but it taught him habits of self reliance, which have been of service to him in every subsequent step in life. Whatever success he may have achieved is the result of energy and hard work. He is known for his sound common sense, for his judgment as a business man and for his honesty and integrity. Together with his family he holds membership in the Methodist Episcopal Church and attends its services. He is a trustee of the Black Horse schools and has held other local offices of trust.

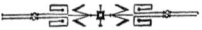

ELLIS L. DUYCKINCK. The friends of Mr. Duyckinck know him to be a successful farmer, and, more than that, a man who is earnestly striving to make the world better for his presence in it. He is not only a factor in agricultural circles, but he is constantly endeavoring, so far as lies in his power, to promote the welfare of others and the advancement of local measures. He owns the old family homestead in District No. 9, Cecil County, where he has lived since 1892, having resided upon an adjoining farm for some years prior to that time. Devoted to the welfare of this locality, he is one of the class of citizens who believe in the resources of the county, in its future and its limitless possibilities. While some seek new homes amid strange surroundings, he has been content to remain in the east, believing that the soil here, if properly cultivated, will bring returns as satisfactory as in any other part of the Union.

The founder of the family in America, Levi Holden Duyckinck, was born in Holland, January 12, 1754, and came to America in the service of the Spanish government. Afterward for some years he was proprietor of a stationery, book and music store in New York City. Little is known concerning his personal characteristics, save that he was very fond of music and had great talent in that art. His son, Richard B., resided in New Jersey, where he owned and cultivated a farm. Horace H. Duyckinck, son of the latter and father of our subject, was born in Somerset County, N. J., in 1819, and spent his youth and early manhood in his native place, but in 1852 removed to Cecil County and settled upon the farm in District No. 9, now owned by our subject. Here he spent the remainder of his days in the occupation of a farmer. An active worker in Zion Presbyterian Church, he officiated as an elder in the congregation. He chose as his wife Emily Longstreet, of New Jersey, and their union was blessed by the birth of four children, namely: Anna, now the widow of William Haines; Ellis L.; Aaron L. and Magdalene, wife of John J. Pennell. The father died at the homestead April 8, 1891, when seventy-two years of age.

While the family still resided in Somerset County, N. J., the subject of this sketch was born in 1846. He was quite small when brought to Cecil County, and here he grew to manhood, meantime obtaining his education in the common schools, and Millersville and West Nottingham Academies. On starting out for himself he established his home on a place that adjoined his father's, but upon the death of the latter, he returned to the homestead, where he has since resided, cultivating the one hundred and eighty acres that compose the estate. Politically he is a Democrat. In 1883 he was united in marriage with Catherine, daughter of Jonathan Smock, and member of an old family of New Jersey, where she was born. Their only son is Bancker, now a student in school. Mr. Duyckinck is a man of public spirit, and material success has not been his sole achievement, for he has become known as a capable citizen. With others who have contributed to the development of the county, he is building for himself a monument that will outlast shafts of marble, and is carving his name upon the hearts of his associates in a more enduring manner than those written in letters that perish.

WILLIAM A. DURHAM, county commissioner, and the owner of a well-improved farm in District No. 4, Harford County, was born here February 25, 1831, the son of Abel and Sarah (Devoe) Durham. The family of which he is a member originally comprised six children, namely: David, Sarah A., John D., Elizabeth F., William A. and Mary E., of whom he and his sister, Sarah, are the sole survivors. His grandfather, David Durham, a native of this county and a farmer by occupation, was a son of Samuel Durham, whose father emigrated to this country from his native land, England, in an early day and settled near Bel Air, becoming the owner of large tracts of land. Members of the family participated in the Revolution and the War of 1812.

At the age of seventeen our subject left school and began to learn the carpenter's trade, which he followed for ten years. At the age of twenty-seven he married Rachel A. Gladden, who was born in Harford County, was identified with the Episcopal Church, became the mother of two children, and died in 1865, at the age of twenty-six. Their daughter, Mrs. Elizabeth F. McNorris, became the mother of two children and died at the age of thirty-three. The son, Jacob, married Evalina Hannah, of this county, and they have a daughter, Mabel. In 1868 our subject was united with Matilda E. Lowe, a native of Maryland. Five children were born of this union, namely: John, C. Howard and F. Pierce (twins), M. Alice and Sarah A. (twins). Mrs. Matilda E. Durham died in November, 1874, aged thirty-nine years. In 1880 Mr. Durham married Martha S. Richardson, who was a lifelong resident of this county, a faithful member of the Methodist Episcopal Church, and who died in 1884, at the age of thirty-nine. The only child of this union, George S., was accidentally killed by the upsetting of an ox cart when he was six years of age. The present wife of our subject, whom he married in 1894, was Mrs. Marion V. (Forwood) Bull, widow of John E. Bull, of this county. One son, William F., blesses this union.

For thirteen years Mr. Durham was interested in the canning business, but with this exception, since he abandoned work at his trade, he has devoted his attention entirely to farming. He has met with his share of misfortunes, losses through placing confidence in those unworthy of it, losses through droughts and through floods, losses through the depreciation of the value of land, losses through the prevalence of hard times and financial depression; but in spite of discouragements, he has worked patiently and industriously, and is now well-to-do, his farm of one hundred and twenty-five acres being as well improved as any in the district. Politically a Democrat, on that ticket, in the fall of 1895, he was elected county commissioner to serve for a term of six years, and his efficient service in this capacity has won the commendation of all.

WILLIAM E. DAVIDSON owns and occupies a farm lying in the northern part of District No. 5, Cecil County. He is a native of this county, born in District No. 3, February 14, 1843. His father, John W. Davidson, was born and reared in Pennsylvania, and upon moving to Cecil County, in 1825, settled upon a farm, where he afterward dwelt, devoting his attention exclusively to the raising of cereals and stock. He was an industrious and hard-working man, but never became wealthy, obtaining, however, by honest effort, an amount sufficient to provide well for his family. In early life a Whig, he became a Republican on the organization of the party and ever afterward voted that ticket. He was a public-spirited citizen and kept intelligently posted regarding both local and national issues. His death occurred in this county in 1868.

The mother of our subject bore the maiden name of Eliza Weaver and was a daughter of John Weaver, of Bucks County, Pa. She long survived her husband, her death occurring in 1887. Of her family of eight children five are still living. They are named as follows: John, whose home is in District No. 9, Cecil County; William E.; Hannah, who is married and lives in Wilmington, Del.; Mrs. Rachael Wildy, also of Wilmington, and Susan, who married William Hall and lives in Chester County, Pa.

Educated in the local schools, at an early age, the subject of this sketch entered the employ of Hugh M. Cameron, with whom he remained for the long period of twenty years. In 1873 he purchased the Stony Chase place of forty acres and here he has since engaged in general farm pursuits. He has never desired to enter public life and does not care to hold office. Politically he favors the policy of the Democratic party. February 16, 1873, he married Letitia Lynch, daughter of Harrison Lynch, of this county, and, like himself, an earnest member of the Methodist Protestant Church. Their four children are named as follows: Martha, who is married and makes her home in Wilmington, Del.; Rachael L., Mrs. Thomas Van Pelt, of Cecil County; William H. and M. Vernon, who are with their parents.

WILLIAM B. SELFE, proprietor of a hardware store and blacksmith shop at Darlington, was born in Havre de Grace in 1857. The family to which he belongs has been identified with the history of England as far back as the genealogical record can be traced. His father, James Selfe, was born in Chilcompton, England, and there spent the years of youth, emigrating to the United States in 1855 and settling in Havre de Grace. It was, doubtless, an unfortunate time for him to seek a home in the new world, for already the dark clouds of civil strife were hanging over the nation, and a few years later war burst in all its fury upon the people, dividing asunder families and bringing sorrow and death into many homes. By occupation he was a machinist. For ten years he held a position as engineer on the Philadelphia, Wilmington & Baltimore Railroad, running between Baltimore and Wilmington. He was not permitted to see old age or even to attain middle life, as his death occurred when he was thirty-two, the date being January 6, 1866, shortly after the end of the war. His wife, whose maiden name was Catharine Moon, was also born in Chilcompton, England. She died in Maryland, January 5, 1897, aged sixty-seven, after a life of Christian fortitude and patience under trials, and of kindly deeds toward others, which is an inspiration to those who knew her best. Of their five children, two are living, William B. and Henry E.

In his native village of Havre de Grace the first twelve years in the life of our subject were passed. They were eventful years and he recalls even now, over the chasm of the intervening years, the excitement incident to the war and the later grief occasioned by the death of his father. At twelve he secured employment on a farm near Perryman, where he worked for a period of five years. In 1877 he came to Darlington and learned the trade of a blacksmith (with J. S. Gorrell), becoming thoroughly familiar with the occupation in which he has since engaged. In 1888, he established a hardware store, and of this he has since been the proprietor. Since exercising the right of suffrage he has been a stanch adherent of the Democratic party. In 1884 he married Louise W. Webster, daughter of the late Isaac Lee Webster, of the Harford family of that name. They have had four children, Serena Webster, Catharine, Louise Eleanor, and Lee Webster, of whom three survive, Louise Eleanor having died in infancy.

In his fraternal relations Mr. Selfe is a Mason,

belonging to Stephenson Lodge No. 135, in which he has been through all the chairs; and is also connected with Deer Creek Lodge of Odd Fellows, in which he has held the office of secretary for some time. He and his family are members of the Episcopal Church and at this writing he is warden of the congregation. All local enterprises having for their object the benefit of the people receive his warm sympathy and cordial support.

JAMES W. HANNA. Those residents of Harford and Cecil Counties who have given attention to the canning industry have found it a source of revenue and a congenial occupation. It opens a field for the cultivation of fruit, to which many farmers are giving considerable attention; and not only small fruits, but vegetables as well, may be raised here to advantage, the products being used for canning purposes. Mr. Hanna gives especial attention to the raising of tomatoes, having fourteen acres planted to this vegetable. His long experience in this line and careful study of the best modes of treatment and quality of soil, make his opinion on the subject very valuable. He does not, however, confine his attention to this business, but is engaged in general farm work upon his farm of one hundred and fifty acres, situated in District No. 3, Harford County.

On the William O. Michael farm, about one mile from his present place of residence, our subject was born in 1830, being a son of Robert and Elizabeth (Jervis) Hanna, also natives of Harford County. The first of the Hanna family to come to America was John Hanna, who crossed the ocean from Ireland and settled upon a farm in Harford County. Alexander Hanna, our subject's grandfather, spent the larger part of his life on the farm now owned by Edward W. Mitchell, and there his death occurred. Prior to that he divided the place between his three sons, Robert, William and Stephen B. Upon the portion that fell to his share Robert engaged in general agricultural pursuits, sowing, plowing, harvesting, storing crops in the granary, etc. He attained an advanced age, dying in 1867, at the age of eighty-one.

Of eight children comprising the parental family the sole survivor is James W. Hanna. He was reared in District No. 3, where he attended the common schools. For twenty years he operated a part of the old homestead, after which, in 1877, he purchased the St. George farm, where he has since resided. In 1857 he was united in marriage with Miss Anna M. Hanna, a lineal descendant of William Hanna. They have no children; an aunt, Mrs. Hannah N. Hanna, makes her home with them. In religious belief they are of the Presbyterian faith, and take an interest in all the work of their church. In politics Mr. Hanna is always loyal to the Democratic party, to which he unwaveringly lends his influence and gives his suffrage.

THOMAS HENDERSON, A. M. To show that the subject of this article is a man of versatile talents it is but necessary to state that now (though seventy-five years of age), he is proprietor of a general store at Black Horse, Harford County, postmaster at that place, local minister in the Methodist Episcopal Church, preaching almost every Sunday, and owner of more than two hundred acres of fine farming land, the supervision of which he personally overlooks. Much of the active years of his life were given to the occupation of a school teacher, and his work in that line has more than temporary value, owing especially to his publication of an English grammar and a new development of algebra. In spite of his advanced years, he is very active physically and mentally; in fact, his powers have showed no sign of diminution, but he is as able to discharge his multiform duties as at any time in the past. This is the more remarkable when it is known that at the age of fourteen he had strong symptoms of consumption, and at twenty-one he was given up by all the doctors of the neighborhood as a hopeless victim of bronchitis, with no prospect of recovery.

Robert T. and Margaret (Brown) Henderson, parents of our subject, were natives of District No. 4, Harford County, and had a family of nine children, but the only survivor is Thomas. He was born within half a mile of his present place of residence, December 2, 1821, and was reared on the home farm, receiving only such advantages as inferior district schools afforded. Though he never attended college a day in his life, he is an excellent Hebrew scholar, has read the Hebrew Bible through, and prepared a Hebrew grammar, which, however, he has not published. He is also well versed in mathematics and the sciences. At the age of sixteen and a-half he began to teach school; and after having charge of country schools for a time taught for three years in the city of Baltimore. As an educator he was thorough and efficient, and many who gained their first glimpses into the wonderful realm of thought under his careful oversight are to-day prominent in business or the professions. In about 1870 he retired from teaching, and after that embarked in the mercantile business at Black Horse, which he has since carried on, besides being postmaster of the village.

At the age of twenty-seven Mr. Henderson married Alice A. Henderson, of District No. 4, daughter of Thomas and Jane Neely (Lutes) Henderson, natives, respectively, of Harford County and Lisbon, Pa. Three children were born to this union, but one died in infancy; those living are Alfred Neely, a veterinary surgeon, and M. Emma. The wife and mother was a devoted member of the Methodist Episcopal Church, and, cheered by her Christian faith, she entered the unknown world at the age of about fifty-one years. The second marriage of Mr. Henderson united him with Susan T. Meredith, a native of Baltimore County. This union was childless. For forty years or more Mr. Henderson has been a local preacher in the Methodist Episcopal Church, and frequently preaches, endeavoring to reclaim the lost and cheer the sorrowing. At funerals his services have often been called into requisition. During the war he was in sympathy with the Union cause, and many a poor Union soldier was fed and helped by him. His life has been a very active one. Laziness is intolerable to him; he is fond of action and most happy when busy and useful in the service of his fellow-men and his God.

CHARLES S. M. BESLER. The farmers of Maryland who have come from Germany have invariably brought with them such traits and habits of life as have been of the greatest assistance to them in their new home. Their industry, frugality and perseverance have helped to achieve such a degree of success as enhances the prosperity of their neighbors. Such a one we find in Mr. Besler, who began life a poor boy and is to-day one of the well-to-do citizens of District No. 4, Harford County. His estate consists of one hundred acres of finely improved land, upon which have been placed all the necessary buildings, including the family residence that is one of the most comfortable homes in the district. The valuable homestead has been secured by the persistent industry of the owner, seconded by the efforts of his capable wife.

In Germany, November 27, 1817, the subject of this sketch was born to the union of Christian H. and Rachel J. (Snell) Besler, also natives of that country. He was the older of the two children, his sister being Johanna S. E. W., who died, unmarried, September 16, 1890, at the home of her brother. Reared in Germany, our subject received his education in the excellent schools of his native land. At the age of fifteen years he accompanied his father to America, landing in Baltimore, August 30, 1832, and upon the 17th of the following month settled upon the farm in Harford County where he now lives. He was unacquainted with our language and with the customs of the people, but soon became fluent in the use of English and familar with local and national problems. It was necessary for him to work hard after settling upon the new place and he therefore had few opportunities for increasing his knowledge by attendance at school, but through self-culture he has largely made up for his early lack of advantages. Whatever success he may have had in life is due not a little to the energy and wise co-operation of his wife, whom he married at the age of twenty-seven, and who bore the maiden name of Christiana Seaman. Like himself, she was born in Germany and accompanied her parents to America at the age of about fifteen. This was in the year 1840, and from that time until her marriage she resided in Baltimore. Though having no children of their own, they have reared four boys and one girl, to whom they have given good educational advantages, carefully training them for positions of responsibility in life.

Bethel Presbyterian Church is fortunate in having in its membership such active workers and liberal givers as Mr. and Mrs. Besler, who are ever ready to devote their time, efforts and means to promote its interests and the cause of religion. Although in no sense of the word a politician, Mr. Besler has been stanch in his adherence to the principles of the Democratic party, ever since the time he became a voting citizen of the United States. He carefully superintends the management of his property and the neat appearance of his home indicates his intelligent oversight.

MARTIN L. JARRETT, M. D. As a physician the success of Dr. Jarrett has been such as to give him an influential position in the medical fraternity of Harford County. Since the completion of his medical studies he has been engaged in professional practice at Jarrettsville and has built up a wide reputation for skill in the diagnosis of disease and its treatment. His prominence, however, is by no means of a professional nature entirely. In various lines of business activities he has proved the possession of discrimination, tact, efficiency and large executive ability. He is president of the Jarrettsville Creamery Company, an enterprise that has done much for the upbuilding of the place and is one of the most important local industries.

The Jarrett family originated in England and has been represented in Maryland for many generations. Luther M., the doctor's father, was born in Harford County, where his father, Jesse, was a farmer. By his marriage to Julia A. Scarff, of this county, six children were born: James H., M. D.; William B., Thomas B., Sarah E., Martin L., M. D., and Joshua W. The subject of this sketch, who was next to the youngest of the family, was reared on the farm where he has since resided, and for a time attended Bethel Academy, at Cathcart, Md. Beginning the study of medicine, he was for two years with his brother, Dr. James H. Jarrett, and afterward for two terms was a student in the medical department of Maryland University at Baltimore, graduating in 1864. Since that time he has conducted his practice in and around Jarrettsville. He is now in the prime of life, having been born November 18, 1841, and has many years of usefulness yet before him. That the reputation which he has established as a skillful physician shall increase with the passing years and the broadening knowledge acquired by further experience, may safely be predicted of him.

January 31, 1867, when twenty-five years of age, Dr. Jarrett married Sarah F. Glenn, of Harford County, the descendant of Scotch-Irish ancestors who came to this country in an early day, and, as farmers, acquired large possessions. Mrs. Jarrett was reared upon a farm and received a good education in the local schools. She takes an active interest in the work of the Presbyterian Church, to which she belongs. The doctor is a Methodist and is officiating as steward of the church. The political question is one in which he is deeply interested, and he is a stanch Democrat, upholding the principles of free trade and free coinage of silver. He is an active friend of the public school system and holds the office of school commissioner at this writing. Among his interests is that of director of the Second National Bank of Bel Air. Fraternally he was formerly connected with the Knights of Pythias and is now identified with Mt. Ararat Lodge No. 44, A. F. & A. M., at Bel Air. He is a man of keen perception, of strict integrity, of great energy and of more than ordinary ability; a man who is devoted to the interests of his community and has contributed very largely to its development.

ROBERT J. GILBERT is devoting his energies to agricultural pursuits in Harford County, which has been the home of his ancestors since colonial days. His great-great-grandfather was a native of England and sought a home in the new world while this land was still under the domination of Great Britain. His son was born in District No. 1, and was one of the heroes who fought for the independence of the nation in the Revolutionary War. His son, Micah, was born near Avondale, and the latter's son, Michael Gilbert, the father of our subject, was born near Avondale. Thus for six generations the family has been connected not only with the history of Harford County, but has been represented in the district where Robert J. now makes his home.

Michael Gilbert made farming his life work and led a busy and useful life. He voted with the Whig party until the organization of the Republican party, when he joined its ranks. He held the office of both magistrate and constable. An attendant at the Presbyterian Church, he did all in his power to promote its cause and was one of the valued citizens of the community. On the 23d of May, 1839, he was united in marriage with his cousin, Miss Elizabeth Gilbert, and they became parents of six children. The father died February 17, 1879, but the mother is still living at the age of eighty-six.

Robert J. Gilbert was born near Carson Run, August 27, 1842, and was reared to farm labor. He attended the district schools until twenty-one years of age, after which he learned the carpenter's trade, following that vocation until his father's death. He is now following that pursuit near Creswell, where he has a good tract of land under a high state of cultivation. Following in the footsteps of his father, he became a Republican, and to the principles of that party his sound judgment gives a hearty sanction. In 1896 he was appointed magistrate and is creditably discharging the duties of that office. As a member of the Methodist Protestant Church, he has been very active in its work and upbuilding, and has served as trustee and as secretary of the quarterly conference.

On the 2d of February, 1881, Mr. Gilbert was united in marriage with Miss Anna, daughter of Amos Gilbert, of District No. 1, and they have four children: James Amos, Mary, Robert Channing and Helen Ann.

JACOB GROSS, who owns and cultivates a farm in District No. 4, Harford County, was born in Germany, September 6, 1820, and was the third among eight children, the others being Catherine, Margaret, George, John, Ellen, Mary and Julia A. His father, Jacob, Sr., was born, reared and married in Germany, and in his native land, when a young man, served for seven years in the army. After his marriage to Catherine Cooper, he operated a small farm and also followed his trade, that of a manufacturer of hemp. When his son, our subject, was a child of seven years, in the fall of 1827, he brought the family to America and at once purchased a farm in District No. 4, Harford County. Here his remaining years were busily passed, and at the time of his death he was quite well-to-do.

Of his native land the subject of this sketch has little recollection, as his life has been passed principally in the United States. He was reared on the farm that he now owns, and has always followed farm pursuits. At the age of twenty-six he married Keziah Bryley, a lady of many noble attributes of character and a faithful member of Bethel Presbyterian Church. Her entire life was spent in this district, and here her death occurred

JAMES T. GRAHAM.

in February, 1896, when she was eighty years of age. Her body was laid to rest in Bethel cemetery. The six children born of her marriage are all living and are intelligent and prosperous. They are by name, William, Thomas, Richard, Frank, Luther and Martha J. All are married but Richard, who remains at home; the others occupy adjacent farms and are in good circumstances. They have been given good starts in life by their father, each son being presented with a fine farm, while Mr. Gross himself retains the ownership of one farm comprising four hundred acres. In religious belief he is a member of the Evangelical Association. Though not active in politics, he is a firm Democrat, true to the principles for which the party stands.

THEODORE GRAHAM was numbered among the leading citizens and native-born sons of Cecil County. At his death he left to his family the rich legacy of an untarnished name and the memory of an upright, honorable life. He was born in District No. 7, in 1829, and on the farm where his eyes first opened to the light of day he passed the years of boyhood and youth. It was his playground and also the field wherein he was trained for business cares. He secured a fair education in the common schools, and after attaining to man's estate he began farming on his own account. He made his start in life, however, by working as a farm hand by the month, and his industry, economy and perseverance enabled him to engage in the same pursuit on his own account at a later date. Through good management his land was placed under a high state of cultivation, and the well-tilled fields always gave evidence of the thrift and enterprise of the owner. In addition to farming he also dealt in hay and grain. Tireless energy, keen perception and honesty of purpose were among his chief characteristics and led to his success, making him one of the prominent business men of his district.

The marriage of Mr. Graham and Miss Eliza J. Caldwell was solemnized in 1851. They became the parents of a large family, concerning whom we note the following: Mary is now deceased; Addie died in infancy; Ella M. is also deceased. James T., who was but ten years of age at the time of his father's death, was, however, an exceedingly manly and bright boy, and from that early age he assumed control of home affairs and the protection of his mother and sisters. His opportunity for study was therefore limited, but by close application and observation he acquired a practical education. He became a member of the Eureka Fertilizer Company of Perryville, and in 1890 was elected clerk of the courts of Cecil County, continuing to fill the office until his death, which occurred in 1893, at the age of thirty-three. Fraternally he was connected with the Masonic lodge at Port Deposit and in politics supported Democratic principles. His death, when in the prime of usefulness, was deeply mourned by all who knew him. The other members of the Graham family are as follows: Catherine, wife of John Green, of Rowlandsville; Alice, who married Charles Burke, of Philadelphia; Rose, wife of Lucius G. White, of Port Deposit; Elliott, of Conowingo; Roberta, at home, and Matilda, deceased.

A member of the independent order of Odd Fellows, Theodore Graham was highly regarded by his brethren in that fraternity. In all local enterprises he took a warm interest, aiding in their progress in every way that lay in his power. He died in 1871, and the community mourned the loss of one of its most valued citizens.

PATRICK CALLAHAN, who resides in District No. 1, Harford County, is one of the successful farmers and canners of the community. At an early age he started out in life for himself and has since been entirely dependent upon his own efforts; he has met obstacles and difficulties, but has overcome these by determined purpose and has worked his way steadily upward to prosperity. He is recognized as one of the leading citizens of the community, and is well deserving of the success that has come to him.

One of Ireland's sons, Mr. Callahan was born in that country March 18, 1831. His father, Timothy Callahan, was a cattle dealer, and in 1845 crossed the Atlantic to America, taking up his residence at Harford Furnace, where he made his home until his death, in 1885. He was a Democrat in his political affiliations and a Catholic in religious belief. His wife, who bore the maiden name of Mary Lynch, was also a native of Ireland, and is still living, at the advanced age of ninety-two years. They had a family of five children: Patrick; Mary, wife of John Lynch, of Harford Furnace; Farrell, who resides in Level, Harford County; Daniel, of Kansas City; and Terry, deceased.

Mr. Callahan, whose name introduces this review, began his education in the schools of the Emerald Isle, pursuing his studies there until he was thirteen years of age, when he came to America, prior to the emigration of his parents. Here he supplemented his early training by attendance at the public schools at intervals for a few years, and at the age of sixteen he began life on his own account. He worked for others until he had accumulated a small capital, after which he purchased a little place and began selling milk. He soon built up an excellent trade and at one time kept forty cows. At length abandoning that industry he turned his attention to the canning business, in 1877, being one of the first to embark in the enterprise in this section of the state. He has since been engaged in canning tomatoes, and has met with signal success in his undertakings. Owing to the excellent quality of his goods he readily finds a market, and has now a large trade. In 1880 he purchased a farm of two hundred and fifty-five acres, and has made it one of the valuable and productive places of the neighborhood.

Mr. Callahan married Miss Ann Ready, of Baltimore, who died in 1896. They had the following-named children: Daniel, who is living in District No. 1; John, deceased; Joseph, at home; David, who has served as tax collector; Timothy, who is studying medicine; Mary and Ann, at home.

Mr. Callahan votes with the Democracy, but has never sought or desired political preferment. He is a communicant of the Catholic Church. His life has been well spent, and among his leading characteristics are unflagging industry and enterprise. He has been the architect of his own fortune and has builded wisely and well.

Joseph Callahan, who now has the management of the home farm, was born January 29, 1868, in Harford County, and is indebted to the public schools for his elementary education, which was supplemented by an academic course in Bel Air. At the age of twenty he became his father's active assistant in the cultivation of the home farm, and some years afterwards, owing to his father's ill health, he assumed the management of the farm, and has since superintended it. He is a young man of excellent business and executive ability, possessing those traits which always insure success. He has the progressive spirit of the age and will undoubtedly work his way steadily upward. He was married in December, 1896, to Miss Josie, daughter of Ed Johnson, of Hopewell, Harford County.

JOHN H. BAKER. The varied occupations in which Mr. Baker has engaged with success prove him to be a man of resources. As an agriculturist he has been energetic and industrious; in the canning business, a pioneer; as a merchant, progressive; and as a local preacher in the Methodist Episcopal Church, earnest, sincere and conscientious. His home has been in Aberdeen since 1893 and his business interests are centered in this locality.

On the old Baker homestead, situated two and one-half miles from Aberdeen, John H. Baker was born in 1849, a member of a well-known family which is referred to in the sketch of his brother, George A. His boyhood and youthful years were spent on the home farm and in attendance at the local schools. When about twenty-one years of age he went to Baltimore and secured employment in a factory for the manufacture of tin cans. After a few months in that position, he formed a partnership with his cousin, Charles H. Baker, and embarked in the milk and ice cream business, but eleven months later he sold his interest in the business and returned to Harford County. From that time he remained at home, engaged in farming and the canning business, until the death of his father, when he purchased a farm, and to the cultivation of the property gave his attention until his removal to Aberdeen in 1893. He still owns the estate and continued its management until 1897, since which it has been rented.

In 1892 Mr. Baker opened a ladies' furnishing store, under the firm name of Baker & Ivins, but after two years the junior member sold his interest to Mr. Baker and it has since been conducted by G. P. Pyles, a son-in-law of Mr. Baker under the firm name of G. P. Pyles & Co. When twenty-two years of age Mr. Baker united with the Methodist Episcopal Church, in which, about 1883, he was licensed as an exhorter, and two years later became a local preacher. For the past ten years he has been superintendent of the mission Sunday-school of the Aberdeen Church, at Boothby Hill, and for three years superintended the Aberdeen Methodist Episcopal Sunday-school. He is interested in the work among young people and rendered efficient service as first vice-president of the Epworth League, which office he held for three years. For some years he has voted the Prohibition ticket, believing it his duty to support principles that tend to the betterment of mankind and the extermination of the liquor traffic. In 1893 he received the nomination for state senator, but withdrew in favor of his brother, William B., who was the successful candidate and the Republican nominee. Fraternally he is connected with the Senior Order of American Mechanics.

The marriage of Mr. Baker took place in February, 1872, and united him with Elizabeth Smith, of Baltimore. She was an estimable lady, and her death, May 29, 1892, was a heavy bereavement to the family. Four children were born of the union, namely: Viola Estelle, wife of G. P. Pyles, who is connected with Mr. Baker in business; Margaret L., an accomplished young lady; Warren L., a student in the Medical College of Baltimore; and William Reid, who died at fifteen months.

THOMAS J. AYRES is a well-to-do citizen of District No. 4, Harford County, where he is engaged in farming and dairying. He is a splendid type of our best American manhood. He comes of the sturdy Scotch race, characterized by reliability and firmness of purpose and with these qualities he combines the energy and progressiveness of the typical American. Honored and respected by all, there is no man in Harford County who occupies a more enviable position in business circles than Mr. Ayres, not alone on account of the success he has achieved, but also because of the honorable, straightforward business policy he has followed. His present farm was his birthplace, and his natal day was March 9, 1833.

His grandfather, Thomas Ayres, was a native of Scotland, and, crossing the Atlantic to the new world, took up his residence in Harford County, where he became owner of a large estate, including the farm which is now the property of our subject. He at one time owned more than one thousand acres of land, and conducted his farming operations on a very extensive scale, deriving a handsome profit therefrom. When the colonies proclaimed that they were henceforth to be a free and independent nation, he and two of his sons went forth to establish this statement by the force of arms, and valiantly aided in the war whereby was ended English rule in the United States. Thomas J. Ayres, father of our subject, and his wife, Elizabeth (Albany) Ayres, were both natives of District No. 4, Harford County, where they reared their family of seven children, as follows: John, Elizabeth, Darkness, Thomas J., Anna, Mary and Benjamin.

Thomas J. Ayres, whose name introduces this review, lived upon the home farm through his minority and his choice of a life work fell upon the occupation to which he was reared. He was here educated and was trained to the labors of field and meadow. He now owns over five hundred acres of the original Ayres homestead and carries on general farming and dairying. He is an excellent financier and his well-managed business interests are evidenced by his handsome property. He possesses untiring energy, is quick of perception, forms his plans readily and is determined in their execution; and his close application to business and his excellent management have brought to him the high degree of prosperity which is to-day his.

When thirty-two years of age Mr. Ayres was united in marriage with Alice A. Norris, a native of Baltimore County, and their union has been blessed with six children, namely: John T., E. Elione, Mary A., B. Franklin, J. Upton and Nicholas M. Mrs. Ayres and her children are members of the Methodist Episcopal or Methodist Protestant Church. Mr. Ayres gives his political support to the Democracy, and during the years of his life he has been looked upon as a model of honor and an example of the truly honest business man.

MRS. SALLIE E. CAIRNES is a member of the Jarrett family, one of the oldest and most influential in Harford County. Her parents, Luther M. and Julia A. (Scarff) Jarrett, were born in this county. After their marriage they removed to Taylor, where the father engaged in farming and merchandising for several years. In 1835 he removed to this place and conducted a hotel and store, after which he purchased the farm whereon our subject now resides. Through economy and industry he and his wife gained possession of a competency that enabled them to enjoy every comfort in old age, and also to provide for the temporal welfare of each of their children. In the family there were five sons and one daughter, namely: James H., M. D.; William B.; Thomas B.; Sarah E.; Martin L., M. D.; and Joshua W. To the sketch of Dr. Martin L. Jarrett, the reader is referred for further mention in regard to the family history.

Joshua W. Jarrett was born and reared on the old homestead where he still resides. When a boy he attended school at Mount Airy, Carroll County, Md., and his education was thorough and practical. Wishing to acquire a commercial education he entered a business college at Baltimore when twenty years of age and took a course of five months there. On his return home he began active agricultural pursuits, in which he has since engaged. He has never married, but finds a pleasant home with his sister, Mrs. Cairnes. In politics he has never allied himself with party leaders, but has maintained an independence of thought, supporting the best men and measures, irrespective of partisan ties. He is identified with the Methodist Episcopal Church, South, and has striven to lead a consistent, upright Christian life.

Across the road from the old homestead where she now resides, the subject of this article was born September 25, 1839, and here her early childhood days were passed. At the age of thirteen she went to Oxford, Chester County, Pa., and for two years was a student in the female seminary there. Returning home, she remained with her parents until her marriage, at twenty years, to Benton Nelson, a native of Harford County, a man of energetic disposition, in politics a Democrat, and by occupation a farmer. He was only thirty-three when, in 1868, he was called from earth. Of the three children born to this union, Julia, Harry and Laura, the last-named alone survives. The second marriage of our subject united her with C. F. Cairnes, M. D., who was born in this county. He died in October, 1895. In religious belief Mrs. Cairnes is a member of the Presbyterian Church. She is of a charitable disposition, generous to those in need, never refusing practical assistance to worthy people in distress. From year to year of her life in this locality she has drawn friends around her and is well known for the genial hospitality that welcomes beneath her roof both rich and poor.

HON. PATRICK H. RUTLEDGE, attorney-at-law, Harford County. The first paternal ancestor of our subject of whom we have any definite knowledge was Abraham Rutledge. He settled upon a portion of My Lady's Manor, a tract of about two thousand acres of land in Baltimore and Harford Counties, for which he paid a small annual rental to Lord Baltimore. Next in the line of descent was Jacob, son of Abraham, born in Maryland and a lifelong farmer of Harford County, near the line of Baltimore County. He married Monica Wheeler, daughter of Col. Ignatius Wheeler, who rendered valiant service as an officer in the Revolution. John W., son of Jacob, and father of our subject, was born in District No. 4, Harford County, upon a portion of the landed estate of his grandfather. Upon attaining manhood, he selected agriculture for his occupation and carefully cultivated his eight hundred acres of good land. Like his ancestors he was an Episcopalian in religious belief, and he and his wife held membership in St. James' Church. By his marriage to Julia A. Ward, he had ten children, of whom the following survive: Martha J., Patrick H., John R., Monica A., Dr. Charles A. and Henrietta M. Of these none is married excepting Charles. All remain at the old homestead, which is divided into six separate farms, and like their forefathers, they have identified themselves with the Episcopal Church.

The best educational advantages which the country afforded were placed within the reach of the subject of this sketch. In boyhood he attended the common schools of District No. 4, in the vicinity where he was born and reared. At the age of eighteen he matriculated in Princeton College, where he took the regular four years' course of study and graduated with an excellent record as a student. On the conclusion of his literary course, he engaged in reading law under the preceptorship of the well-known attorney, Otho Scott, of Bel Air, and in 1857 he was admitted to practice at the bar. Since that time he has been engaged in practice, though not constantly, as his large property interests consume considerable of his time. In former years he was prominent in public life, ranking among the influential Democrats of the county. Elected state's attorney in 1867, he filled that responsible position for four years, and in 1876 he was elected to represent his district in the legislature, where he remained for two years. The honors that he received in the way of official position were unsought by him, but came to him as the natural reward of deserved merit. He is a keen reader and an intelligent thinker, a man whose faculty of observation has been well cultivated and whose knowledge of law renders his legal opinions valuable.

SAMUEL G. SCARFF. The life of this venerable resident of Harford County covers the greater part of the nineteenth century, and has been spent entirely within the limits of District No. 4. As may be supposed, he has seen many changes in this locality, the cultivation of its farms, the erection of substantial buildings, the introduction of improvements, the building of railroads, and the enlargement of every industry through which men earn their livelihood. Starting for himself without a dollar, his only capital being two strong arms, he succeeded beyond many possessing greater advantages. No one stands higher in the community than he, and his reputation as an upright man is the result of a life of Christian living.

In this district Mr. Scarff was born March 13, 1816, the son of John and Martha (Garrison)

Scarff, natives, respectively, of this district and Pennsylvania. He was the eldest of seven children, named as follows: Samuel G., Sarah A., Edwin and John, who are deceased; Charles T., Eunice and Thomas. The grandfather, John Scarff, was a native of Harford County, and engaged in farming. The educational advantages of our subject were very limited, and consisted only of occasional attendance at the common schools. For his life calling he chose agriculture, and to it all his active years were given, the result being that he became well-to-do. At the age of forty-two he married Hannah Walker, who was born in this county, the youngest of seven children, named as follows: Thomas, Mary, Elizabeth, Eliza, Ellen, Serena and Hannah, of whom Thomas, Elizabeth and Serena are deceased. The parents of these children were Thomas and Hannah (Wise) Walker, natives, respectively, of England and Hagerstown, Md., the latter of Irish descent. The former learned the trade of a piano manufacturer, which he followed after coming to the United States. Mr. and Mrs. Scarff are the parents of three children: Josephine, Elizabeth A. and Philip G., but the last-named alone survives. The family are identified with the Methodist Church, in which Mr. Scarff is a trustee and prominent worker.

When Mr. Scarff began life for himself he had but little of this world's goods, but he had the courage and determination necessary to success, and these qualities, combined with cautious judgment, placed him in the front rank of the farmers of District No. 4. That he has been successful as an agriculturist is evinced by the farm on which he resides, one of the best improved and most carefully managed in this locality. In his ventures he has made few mistakes, and if he errs, it is on the safe side. In his neighborhood he is regarded as a man of excellent judgment. He has not identified himself with any political organization, but has maintained an independence of views characteristic of him in every department of life. In 1862 he was elected commissioner of Harford County, and held the position for two years, but with that exception he has not been an office holder, nor has he at any time sought positions of prominence. As a citizen he stands high in the community in which he has ever resided, being a good neighbor, and a benevolent man, one who would be trusted implicitly by stranger or friend.

NATHANIEL C. KIRKWOOD. In the twilight of his long and useful life, the subject of this sketch is surrounded by the comforts secured through years of industrious toil and is in the possession of an ample competence. While he no longer engages in manual labor as in years past, he is still active and energetic, capable of superintending efficiently the management of his well-improved farm of two hundred and sixty-five acres that lies in District No. 4, Harford County. His entire life has been passed in this district and here he was born February 28, 1816, the son of Robert and Rebecca (Bell) Kirkwood, natives, respectively, of Delaware and Harford County, Md. The family originally consisted of seven children, but two died in infancy, the following attaining mature years: Robert, John B., Mary, Jane Ann and Nathaniel C. The maternal ancestors came from Ireland and have been represented in this country since an early day; farming has been their principal occupation and longevity has been a noticeable characteristic. The grandfather, John Bell, was a hero of the Revolution. One of the members of the family, Dr. Ephraim Bell, was a celebrated physician and made his home at New Market, Baltimore County, Md., where he died about 1876, aged eighty-two.

The Kirkwood family was founded in America by our subject's grandfather, Robert Kirkwood, a native of Ireland, who accompanied his mother to America about 1730 and settled in Delaware, where he engaged in farming. During the Revolution he assisted the colonies, as did also an uncle, William Kirkwood. Perhaps one of the most eminent members of the family was our subject's cousin, Hon. Samuel J. Kirkwood, fifth governor of Iowa, and a native of Harford County, born December 20, 1813; he went west to Ohio in 1835 and in 1843 was admitted to the bar there, remaining in active practice in that state until his removal to Iowa in 1855. The following year he was elected to the state senate, and in 1859, upon the Republican ticket, was elected governor of Iowa by a majority of three thousand. In October, 1861, he was re-elected by a majority of eighteen thousand. Later he was United States senator, and in 1875 was again chosen governor, but resigned in 1877 to become United States senator, serving four years and resigning to become secretary of the interior under President Garfield.

In the days when our subject was a boy educational advantages were exceedingly limited and he attended school very little, but having a retentive memory and keen perceptive faculties he is a well-informed man. He has never married, being content to live the independent existence of a bachelor. Politically, like the most of his relatives, he is a pronounced Republican. He has served on the jury in Harford County. The confidence of those with whom he has come in contact he has won by his straightforward course of action, his self-reliance and the interest he has taken in enterprises calculated to aid in the advancement of the community and its upbuilding.

WILLIAM M. AND JOHN W. BARTON. To be successful in business depends upon character as well as upon knowledge, it being a self-evident proposition that honesty is the best policy. Harford County has a fine body of men engaged in agricultural pursuits, and very prominent among the number who have the respect and esteem of the entire community are the twin brothers, William M. and John W. Barton, whose success affords another evidence that industry, economy and integrity constitute the keynote to honorable competency. These gentlemen were born in District No. 4, Harford County, February 2, 1847, to John and Mary A. (Morris) Barton, who were natives of this section also, and here were reared, educated and married. Thirteen children were born to them: Washington, Joshua, Amanda, Sophronia, William M. and John W. (twins), Elijah, Franklin, Susanna, Canada, Charles and Andrew J. (deceased) and James R. The paternal grandfather of these children, William H. Barton, was a native of England, and in his youth came to America to make his home, and the rest of his life was spent in Harford County. He was an industrious and intelligent farmer, and through good management became the owner of a large tract of land. The maternal grandmother of our subjects came to America from the old country and lived to be ninety-six years of age.

The boyhood days of William and John Barton were spent in the healthful outdoor occupations of the farm, and they acquired a knowledge and love of the calling which have remained with them to the present time. The public schools afforded them their early educational opportunities, after leaving which John completed his education at Stewartstown and for one year pursued his studies at Glen Rock. At the age of twenty-nine years he married Miss Anace A. Watters, who was born in York County, Pa., and they have one child, Minnie E., who is at home with her parents. Mrs. Barton's people were farmers of the Keystone State, and were well and favorably known in the section in which they resided. William Barton received a practical education and has remained unmarried. He and his brother John W. have always lived together and have been very successful in their farming operations, being the owners of an admirably tilled farm of three hundred and forty acres. The place is nicely improved with excellent farm buildings and a thrift and orderliness is observable which at once stamps the brothers as intelligent and energetic farmers.

The brothers are stanch Democrats in politics. William has taken considerable interest in political matters and has very successfully filled the office of justice of the peace since 1890. He has shown his approval of secret organizations by becoming a member of the Knights of Pythias fraternity, Fawn Lodge No. 377, of Fawn Grove, Pa. John W. Barton and his wife are members of the Presbyterian Church and are highly respected in the community where they have so long made their home. The brothers have so conducted themselves throughout their business career as to gain the confidence and respect of all who know them, and, being strictly honorable and possessing excellent business qualifications, they are valuable members of society.

SAMUEL A. S. KYLE. During the years that Mr. Kyle resided in Harford County he made many warm friends among its best citizens. After having been long connected with a business firm in Baltimore, in 1878 he purchased the Booth place, near Bel Air, and here he continued to reside until he passed away, in 1893. The place is well improved and constitutes an attractive country home. The residence, built by the Booth family in 1855, is substantial, roomy and comfortable; and the other farm buildings are also well adapted to their various purposes. The two hundred and fifty acres comprising the place are divided and subdivided into fields of convenient size, for the raising of grain and the pasturage of stock, and all the improvements of a first-class estate have been introduced.

The Kyle family is one of the large number of American families that trace their ancestry to Scotch-Irish progenitors. During the time of the religious persecution in Scotland, some of them fled to Ireland in order to seek a refuge for themselves and their families. They were people of prominence and it is said that not a few were ministers. The succeeding generations remained residents of the island that lies like a beautiful green emerald in the setting of the mighty Atlantic. The Covenanter faith, implanted in the hearts of those who lived in Scotland, was the religion of their descendants in Ireland, most of whom held membership in the Presbyterian Church. The subject of this sketch was born in Ireland, being the son of George Kyle, a lieutenant in the royal navy. At the age of fourteen he came, alone, to the United States, and joined his uncle, Adam Kyle, who was a merchant in Baltimore, and a member of the firm of Dinsmore & Kyle, established in 1805. With this concern he remained for forty-six years, retiring at the age of sixty.

The first marriage of Mr. Kyle, occurring when he was twenty-eight, united him with Miss Fendall, who died, childless, in 1876. Three years afterward he was united in marriage with Ella V. Harwood, daughter of C. W. Harwood, of Harford County. Two children, Grace and Annie, blessed this union. In religious belief Mr. Kyle was an Episcopalian, always interested in church work, and for some years before his death he was a member of the vestry of Holy Trinity Church. A man of upright character, he is remembered with affection by his family and, indeed, by all with whom business or social relations brought him into contact. Since his death his estate has been superintended by Mrs. Kyle, who is a lady of considerable business ability, and is also an admirable housekeeper, one who looks well to the ways of her household, providing bountifully for its inmates and for those friends or strangers who may happen to cross the threshold of her comfortable home.

MILTON E. SMITH. Success in any walk of life is an indication of earnest endeavor and persevering effort, and these characteristics are possessed by Mr. Smith, who has for many years been honorably and prominently connected with the agricultural and educational interests of Harford County. He resides in District No. 4, his birth occurring August 19, 1853, on the farm which is still his home. The Smith family of which he is a representative had its origin in England, and was established in America in colonial days. The great-grandfather of our subject was a soldier of the Revolution. The grandfather, Isaac Smith, was a native of New York, and in his business career followed both merchandising and farming. In the Empire State Buell J. Smith was born, and after attaining to years of maturity married Miss Sarah Field, a native of Connecticut, who belongs to the same family as Cyrus Field. She is a member of the Baptist Church, and at the age of eighty years is living with her son, Milton. She had nine children, namely: Ellen A., Florence A., F. Eva, H. Melville, J. Egbert, Milton E., A. Augusta, Emma L. and C. Adelle.

Milton E. Smith spent the days of his youth on the farm which is still his home, and the work of the place soon became familiar to him. A broad and liberal education fitted him for life's practical and responsible duties. He attended the Stewartstown Academy for three terms, and is a graduate of the Maryland University of Law of the class of 1891. He has never practiced that profession, but his knowledge of jurisprudence aids him in successfully conducting his business interests. He is prominently identified with the schools of Baltimore and Harford Counties, and for seventeen years has been numbered among their successful teachers. He has the ability to impart readily and clearly to others the knowledge that he has acquired, his methods are progressive, and the schools of which he has had charge have made substantial advancement. In connection with his professional duties he also owns and superintends the management of his farm of one hundred and fourteen acres, which is under a high state of cultivation and well improved with all modern accessories and conveniences.

Mr. Smith is a member of the Baptist Church, and in politics is an ardent Republican, warmly advocating the principles of reciprocity, protection and sound money. He has made a close study of the issues which divide the two great national parties and is recognized as one of the leaders in Republican ranks in his district. He is a man of strong determination and noble purpose, and never acts except from honest motives.

In all his varied relations in business affairs, and in social life, he has maintained a character and standing that have impressed all with his sincere and manly purpose to do by others as he would have them do by him.

HON. THOMAS B. HAYWARD, M. D., is not only well known as a skillful physician of Harford County, but through his efficient supervision of his farm he has acquired a reputation as an agriculturist, and through his championship of all progressive measures has become known as a public-spirited citizen. His name is inseparably associated with much that has contributed to advance the material interests of district and county and to promote their welfare in a higher sense. He resides upon his large and well-improved farm, lying in the eastern part of District No. 4, where he established his home upon first coming to the county in 1859. In the Democratic party he is one of the local leaders, and upon that ticket was chosen to represent the district in the state legislature, where he remained from 1892 to 1896.

The genealogical record of the Hayward family shows that they came from England in an early day and settled in South Carolina, removing thence to Pennsylvania. Thomas Hayward, the doctor's grandfather, was born in South Carolina and engaged in farming there in early life, but later removed to Pennsylvania. Joseph J., our subject's father, was born in Philadelphia and became a physician, engaging in professional practice in York County, Pa., for many years. He married Sarah Briarly, a native of Franklin, Pa., and nine children were born of their union, of whom the following survive: Margaret J., Maria A., Amanda N., Thomas B. and Samuel H. The doctor, who was the older of the two sons, was born in York County, Pa., May 4, 1838, and received his primary education in the schools of his native place, after which he was for a year a student in Dickinson College, an old institution that was founded at Carlisle, Pa., in 1783. Later he attended Cumberland Institute for a year, but afterward returned to Dickinson College, where he was a student two years. After a short time spent in teaching school, he began preparations for his life work, the practice of medicine, at the age of nineteen. For three years he read under the preceptorship of Dr. James W. Kerr, of York, Pa., and afterward took a course of lectures in the Pennsylvania Medical College, Philadelphia, from which he graduated in 1859, receiving the highest grade of any member of his class.

Immediately after his graduation, Dr. Hayward came to Harford County and began the practice of his profession at his present location. Soon he built up a good practice, the care of which, together with the supervision of his farming property, required his entire time. In 1864 he married Helen M. Bussey, who was born in Harford County, of French descent. The ten children born of their union are named as follows: Thomas S., Francis S., Charles J. (deceased), Augustus O., Edward B., James F., Eugene H., Florence M., Helen R. and Lillian J.

STEVENSON A. WILLIAMS. The occupation by which Mr. Williams is best known and the pursuit of which has secured for him a competency and an honorable position in the world, is that of attorney-at-law. However, his energies have by no means been limited to the legal profession, but in other lines of labor he has also won commendable success. He is president of the Harford National Bank of Bel Air and has aided in placing the finances of this institution upon a solid basis amongst leading concerns of the kind in the state.

The Williams family originated in Wales and was first represented in America by John Williams, who settled in Harford County towards the middle of the last century. William Williams, grandfather of our subject, was a prominent contractor at Havre de Grace, where his death occurred in 1848. Like other members of the family, he was known as a man of unwavering integrity, excellent business ability and shrewd judgment. His son, Dr. Lewis J. Williams, who was our subject's father, was born in Harford County, in 1819, received an excellent literary and medical education, and became an eminent physician. Entering the United States navy in early years, his entire active life was spent in the service of the government. He died at Baltimore in 1888.

While his father was stationed in the naval hospital in Brooklyn, the subject of this article was born there, May 6, 1851, being one of three children. His sister, Mary, resides in Baltimore, while his brother, Frederick R., is an attorney, associated with him in practice at Bel Air. The mother of this family was Harriet H. Archer, who died in 1871. Her father was Stevenson Archer, late chief justice of the court of appeals of Maryland. She had three brothers, namely: James, who settled in Mississippi; Dr. John, who became a prominent physician in Louisiana; and Stevenson, who was a successful attorney and at one time a member of congress from Maryland.

When less than a year of age the subject of this notice was brought by his parents to Harford County, which is the only home he remembers. His parents gave him the best educational advantages the country afforded. After carrying on his studies in private schools for some years, he matriculated at Princeton, and from that celebrated institution graduated in 1870, receiving the degrees of A. B. and A. M. from his alma mater. In 1872 he entered the law department of the University of Maryland, from which he graduated in 1873, with the degree of LL. B. At once returning to Bel Air, he opened an office and has since practiced law there. In local politics, too, he has been quite prominent, wielding an influence among other members of the Republican party. This being the minority party in Harford County, his candidacy upon the ticket for various offices has been unsuccessful.

Mr. Williams in 1875 married Miss A. E.

Streett, daughter of the late John Rush Streett of Harford County. They have four children: Elise, Harriet A., Elizabeth Rush and Lewis J. In religious belief Mr. Williams is an Episcopalian. He is now in the prime of life, with many years of usefulness before him, and undoubtedly added honors will come to him as the years go by.

JAMES H. AMOS, who resides in District No. 4, Harford County, is a son of B. Scott and Sarah (Amos) Amos, all natives of this district. He is next to the youngest of five children, his sister and brothers being Martha, Zachariah, Robert and Isaac. His father, who was a son of Robert Amos, grew to manhood upon the home farm in this district, and upon attaining mature years adopted agriculture as his vocation, and to it his entire active life was devoted. During the War of 1812 he was one of the many heroic Marylanders who enlisted to defend their state from the encroachments of the British and their country from subjection to foreign rule. Among the public positions which he held were those of tax collector of the district and county commissioner, in which latter capacity he was retained for more than twenty years.

It was natural that, upon attaining man's estate, our subject should select for his occupation that in which his forefathers had engaged and with which he himself was most familiar. As an agriculturist, he has superintended and managed his farm in District No. 4, maintaining a high grade of improvements and building such structures as are necessary for the proper management of the farm. In matters political he is a Democrat, true to the principles for which the party stands. He has been identified with the Independent Order of Odd Fellows, but is no longer active in the fraternity.

At the age of thirty Mr. Amos married Mary E. West, an estimable lady, who was born in this district and has spent her entire life here. She is a daughter of Stacy and Mary (Dallam) West, natives, respectively, of Bucks County, Pa., and District No. 5, Harford County, Md., and is the eldest of three children, the others being S. Augustus and Wilson D. Her grandfather, Thomas West, was born in Bucks County, Pa., where he engaged in farming for some years, but in an early day he removed to Harford County and purchased a tract of more than one thousand acres of valuable land. His ancestors were of English origin and Quakers in religion, and as a rule were agriculturists by occupation. In religious belief Mrs. Amos is identified with the Methodist Episcopal Church, in the work of which she takes an active interest, and by the members of which she is held in the highest esteem. All who know her have the highest regard for her estimable Christian character and amiability of disposition, qualities which have won for her the admiration of all with whom she has an acquaintance. The six children born of her marriage are named as follows: Mary A.; Sarah, wife of George Rigdon; Caroline E., who married Benson Gable, of York County, Pa., Eugenia; Henry S., who married Virginia W. Ensor and resides in District No. 4; and Charles D., deceased.

REV. ALPHEUS S. MOWBRAY. This active and public-spirited man is regarded as one of the most influential citizens of Cecil County, and it is but just to chronicle in this volume some of the events that mark his life as one of usefulness. Although his material wealth is not inconsiderable, yet it is so far overbalanced by his riches of character, his ability and his virtues and the herculean efforts he has put forth to raise the standard of life and thought in the communities in which he has lived, that to mention his worldly wealth would be but a waste of time. Mr. Mowbray comes of a fine old English family who trace their ancestry back to the days of William the Conqueror. The Mowbray family tree first took root on American soil at the time Lord Baltimore came to this country, two Mowbray brothers accompanying him hither. They settled at Dorchester County, which has been the birthplace of nearly all the members of the family. The paternal grandfather, Levin Mowbray, was born there and in that region became very well and favorably known. He was at one time an extensive merchant and owned a line of boats that plied on the Chesapeake Bay and its tributaries. His son, William H. Mowbray, father of the subject of this sketch, was born in Dorchester County, Md., but later removed to Denton, Md., where he followed the occupation of carpentering and still makes his home. His wife was Anna Sparklin, daughter of Daniel Sparklin, of Caroline County, who was for sixteen years judge of the county orphans' court. He was of Scotch ancestry, was active and prominent in church affairs, and a leader of public thought in his section.

Rev. Alpheus S. Mowbray was born in Denton, Caroline County, Md., December 30, 1858, and was one of the family of three sons and four daughters born to his parents. His two brothers are, like himself, Methodist ministers. Rev. W. R. received his education in Wilmington College and is stationed at Smyrna, Del. Rev. E. T. was educated in Western Maryland College, of Westminster, Md., and is now a member of the Baltimore conference. About the time that the subject of this sketch needed assistance in securing an education, his father, who had previously been a successful business man, met with some severe reverses of fortune, and could, therefore, render him but little aid. Being a young man of determination and anxious to acquire an education, he determined to make his own way through school notwithstanding ill fortune, but his manly deportment soon attracted the attention of men of prominence and won him their regard and interest. He was tendered, and gladly accepted, assistance by Prof. James Swann, who was an instructor in the Conference Academy of Dover, Del.

This institution young Mowbray attended until he was eighteen years of age, when he began teaching, and at the age of twenty entered Dickinson College at Carlisle, Pa., from which he received his degree of A. M. In 1883 he joined the Methodist Episcopal Conference held at Cambridge and presided over by the famous Bishop Simpson, and was afterwards stationed at Oxford for two years. He was then at Marydell for the same length of time, four years at Pocomoke City, four years at Newport, Del., and in 1895 was sent to Elkton, where he has since been pastor of the Methodist Episcopal Church. He is one of the most brilliant and eloquent members of the Methodist conference.

In 1892 his scholarly attainments, energy and ability as an organizer were rewarded by the Methodist Episcopal conference and he was made secretary of that body, a position that has greatly increased his labors and responsibilities. Each year he publishes a full report of the proceedings of the conference. Mr. Mowbray is a most agreeable gentleman to meet, for he is at all times courteous and has a kind word and a smile for everyone. He is extremely popular, not only with his own church people, but with all who known him, who can but recognize his good intentions and his earnest desire to aid his fellows. He has devoted his life to the good of others and his unselfishness and disinterestedness will surely be rewarded. He was married in May, 1883, to Miss Stevenson, of Dover, Del., and they have one daughter and two sons: Agnes L., Edwin Stevenson and Alpheus.

MRS. HANNAH A. McCLUNG resides in Norrisville, in a pleasant home and in the midst of many friends. She is a representative of one of the oldest families of Harford County, and one whose identification with the best interests of the locality has been as honorable as it is long. Her great-grandfather, Joseph Cathcart, was a native of Ireland, but in early life left the Emerald Isle and sought a home in America. For many years he followed farming in Harford County, and his well-directed business interests brought to him a handsome estate. The grandfather, William Cathcart, was born in Harford County, and also devoted his time and energies to agricultural pursuits. When the country became engaged in its second war with England he went to the scene of battle as a defender of the Republic.

The parents of Mrs. McClung were John P. and Eliza J. (Wiley) Cathcart, both natives of Harford County, and their family numbered six children, all daughters, namely: Hannah A., Jemima J., Mary A., Rebecca, Laura and Rebecca. The last three named are deceased. Thus coming from a family whose history is indissolubly connected with that of her native county, Mrs. McClung well deserves representation in this volume. Then, too, the part which the women have borne in advancing the best interests of the community must not be overlooked. Although their labors have been of a more quiet character, they are none the less important, and their influence in producing a higher and better development is felt and acknowledged by all.

Mrs. McClung was born in District No. 4, June 21, 1843, and spent her girlhood days in her parents' home, the time being quietly passed after the manner of the girls of that period. When twenty-one years of age she gave her hand in marriage to Robert R. McClung, a native of the same district, and presided over his home until he was called to his final rest. Mr. McClung was a farmer by occupation, and a man of great energy and business ability. In his dealings he was ever honorable and straightforward, and his word in all business transactions was considered as good as his bond. His well-managed interests brought to him a good return, and he became the possessor of a large estate, which thus enabled him to leave his family in very comfortable circumstances.

In politics Mr. McClung was a stalwart supporter of the Democracy, and kept well informed on the issues of the day. He held membership in the Methodist Protestant Church of Norrisville, was prominent in its work, served as trustee, and held official positions in the Sunday-school.

As a citizen he was true to his duties, and never withheld his support from any object that would promote the material or moral welfare of the community. He passed away November 17, 1881, at the age of fifty-four years, and left to his family the record of a blameless life.

Mr. and Mrs. McClung had seven children, Benjamin F. W., Columbus P., Mary E., Rosa F., Samuel J., Elsie M. and Pearl R. With her children Mrs. McClung resides in Norrisville. Like her husband, she is a member of the Methodist Protestant Church, and is deeply interested in all that pertains to its advancement and growth. She is a lady of many excellent qualities, of kindly disposition and genial manner, and has the warm regard of many friends.

HON. THOMAS H. ROBINSON. That success in life is not wholly a creature of circumstances, but the result of natural ability to seize upon circumstances and turn them to advantageous account, is exemplified in the life of the above-named gentleman. While he had the advantages of good birth, honorable ancestry and an excellent education; yet these have been merely factors in, not the cause of, his success. While his reputation and prosperity have been won principally through his labors as an attorney, he has also been connected with various business enterprises. As a politician he has been influential in the Democratic party, both in his county and state. As a public official, he has faithfully and ably represented the people whose interests he has ever had at heart; and as a financier he finds a field for action in his position as president of the Second National Bank of Bel Air.

Three miles from his present home in Bel Air, the subject of this article was born March 2, 1859, to the union of Dr. Samuel S. and Mary C. (Prigg) Robinson, natives, respectively, of Baltimore city and Harford County. Both represented old families of Harford County, whose members have always taken a leading part in business and politics. Dr. Robinson removed from Baltimore to a farm in Harford County in 1856, and there continued to reside until his death, in 1888. He was a son of Thomas Robinson, member of the firm of T. &. S. Robinson, wholesale dry-goods merchants of Baltimore; the latter in turn was a son of Joseph Robinson, a native of Harford County.

The only son of his parents, our subject was given every advantage within the means of the family. He began to study law with Hon. Henry D. Farnandis, of Bel Air, with whom he continued until he was admitted to the bar, May 11, 1882, and since that time he has been engaged in active practice. The Democratic party has in him one of its most ardent supporters. Since his entrance upon professional life he has also been closely identified with political affairs, being perhaps one of the most prominent members of his party in Harford County, and is a member of the state central committee. In 1891 he was nominated by his party to represent the county in the state senate and was elected by a large majority. During his term in that body he served on a number of important committees, as chairman of the executive, nominations, railroads and canals committees, and as a member of the finance committee.

In 1884 Mr. Robinson married Miss Clara C., daughter of Judge J. M. Cain, of the orphans' court. They have five children, namely: Lucile, Madeleine, Elizabeth, Thomas Hall and Clara.

THOMAS H. WILEY, an enterprising and progressive farmer of District No. 4, Harford County, is highly respected throughout the community, and the record of his life cannot fail to prove of interest to our readers. He was born in District No. 4, on the 22d of March, 1828, and is descended from good old Revolutionary stock. The ancestry of the family can be traced back to Ireland, where the great-grandfather, David Wiley, first opened his eyes to the light of day. The new world, with its many opportunities and possibilities proved to him an irresistible attraction and he therefore bade adieu to the land of his birth and sought a home beyond the Atlantic. Locating in Chester County, Pa., he there followed farming for many years and founded a family which was for several generations associated with that region. His son, Matthew Wiley, was born in Chester County, and learned the miller's trade, which he followed in connection with agricultural pursuits. He was among those who aided in casting aside the yoke of British tyranny and as a colonial soldier valiantly fought for American independence. He adhered to the Presbyterian faith, and at his death, which occurred at the advanced age of eighty-eight years, he was laid to rest in Bethel churchyard, near the present home of our subject. His wife, who bore the maiden name of Rebecca Nelson, was a native of Harford County, also a member of the Presbyterian Church, and when called to the home beyond was laid to rest by the side of her husband, near the old meeting house where she worshiped.

The parents of our subject, John and Elizabeth (Hutchins) Wiley, were both natives of Harford County, and here they reared their family of ten children, of whom six are yet living, as follows: Thomas H., Hannah E., Mary A., Caroline M., Zana Idelett and Richard N. To the common schools near his home Thomas H. Wiley is indebted for his educational privileges. He remained with his parents during his boyhood and youth and assisted his father in the cultivation of the old homestead. At the age of twenty-six years he was united in marriage with Rebecca Wiley, who was born in the same district as her husband. They became the parents of nine children, who in order of birth are as follows: Thomas H., Richard H., Harry F., Charles L., Caroline B., Robert L., Franklin M., Elizabeth A. and Rebecca J. The mother of this family passed away in 1890, at the age of sixty-one years, and was buried in Bethel cemetery. She was long a faithful member of the Bethel Presbyterian Church, and was beloved by all who knew her.

Although Mr. Wiley has devoted the greater part of his life to agricultural pursuits, he was for a time engaged in business in Baltimore, whither he removed in 1856. There he engaged in running an omnibus line for nine years. On the expiration of that period he returned to Harford County, in 1865, and purchased one hundred and nineteen acres of land, constituting the farm on which he now resides. It is called Brown's Choice, and is a very valuable and desirable property, the excellent buildings and substantial improvements indicating the careful supervision of the owner. Mr. Wiley's political affiliations are with the Democracy. Fraternally he is connected with Home Secret Lodge No. 92, K. P., of Shawsville. He is an active and influential member of the Bethel Presbyterian Church, and for many years has served as one of its trustees.

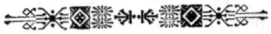

NELSON O. MERRYMAN. Personal popularity, it cannot be denied, results largely from industry, perseverance and close attention to business, which one displays in the management of any particular line of trade; and in the case of Mr. Merryman this is certainly true, for he has adhered so closely to farming and helped in so many ways to advance all worthy enterprises in this community that he is classed among the representative men of Harford County. On starting out for himself, he very naturally preferred the occupation to which he had been reared, rather than to attempt something foreign, and in agricultural pursuits he has continued up to the present time. That he has been successful cannot be questioned for a moment, when a glance is cast over his well-improved place in District No. 4. Careful and painstaking in the cultivation of his land and thorough in everything connected with its management, it is, perhaps, not to be wondered at that he is meeting with success.

In the district where he now resides Nelson O. Merryman was born May 6, 1850, the son of Nelson and Sarah (Davis) Merryman, natives, respectively, of the county and city of Baltimore. He was one of seven children, the others being Joseph D., Henry S., Margaret E., John R., Eleanora and Sarah J. His great-grandfather was a native of England, and established the family in America, coming to this country and settling upon a farm in Baltimore County. The grandfather, Joseph, was a native of Baltimore County. The youthful years of our subject were uneventfully passed, in the routine of farm work and the acquirement of a common-school education. At the age of twenty-six he married Miss S. Alice Gemmill, a native of Pennsylvania. The six children born of the union are named as follows: Howard D. and Bertie J., both deceased; Walter G., C. Marvin, Mary E. and Sarah A., the latter deceased. Mr. Merryman stands well in the estimation of his neighbors and is a worthy member of the Methodist Episcopal Church, to which his family also belongs. He is a great temperance worker, in theory and practice opposing the saloon, and carries this principle into politics, giving his support to the Prohibition party.

JOSHUA G. LUCKEY. Harford County has among its citizens many men of more than average ability and intelligence, who are doing a great work for its advancement. Prominent among these is the subject of our sketch, a well-known resident and enterprising farmer of District No. 4. He owns and operates one hundred and sixty acres of valuable land, which he has placed under a high state of cultivation and improved with all the accessories and conveniences of a model farm. It is pleasantly located near the postoffice of Black Horse and is one of the desirable farms of the neighborhood.

In the district where he now resides Mr. Luckey was born November 4, 1826, the eldest child of James and Martha (Guyton) Luckey, also natives of this district. He had two brothers and a sister, namely: Dr. John B., deceased; Elizabeth and Prof. George J. The family is an old and honored one and has given to this country brave soldiers in times of war and public-spirited citizens in times of peace. Our subject's grandmother was related to President Buchanan's ancestors, and one of her sons was a soldier in the Revolution. His grandfather, Rev. George Luckey, was born in June, 1750, at Fagg's Manor, Chester County, Pa., and was reared under the ministry of Rev. Samuel Blair and under the literary instruction of Professor Ross, author of the Latin grammar. After teaching for a time in Virginia, where he boarded with James Madison's father, he entered Princeton College and carried on his studies there until his graduation, in 1772. He was a classmate of Aaron Burr and Rev. John McMillan, the father of Presbyterianism in western Pennsylvania. For years afterward he was president of a classical academy, in which were educated many men who later attained prominence. In addition to educational work he was engaged in preaching the Gospel and was a well-known minister. He died December 23, 1823, at the age of seventy-three, and was buried in the Bethel cemetery. His father, a native of Ireland, emigrated to America at an early day and settled in Pennsylvania, where he operated a farm.

On the farm where he now lives, our subject passed his early boyhood years. He received his education in the private schools of his neighborhood. Agriculture has been his life work, and both in general farming and in stock-raising he has met with success. In political belief he allies himself with the Democratic party and always supports the principles of this political organization. For more than thirty years he has held the office of magistrate and still serves in this capacity, in addition to which he has been assessor of the county, and for one term served as county commissioner. While not connected with any denomination, he is a believer in Christianity and usually attends services at the Bethel Presbyterian Church, while his wife is a member of the Methodist Episcopal Church. At the age of twenty-five he married Mary Lytle, a native of Baltimore County and of Irish descent. Thirteen children were born of the union, nine of whom are now living, namely: Octavia A., James B., Edward T., Ella, Lue, Laura, Bessie, Jennie and Clara, all of whom are married, excepting Laura and Bessie.

OLIVER T. ROGERS. The legal profession has many able representatives in Harford County, men who have combined native gifts of a high order with thorough study of the best authorities in the law, and who, by reason of these two qualifications, have gained a fair measure of success. In the list of well-known attorneys we place the name of Mr. Rogers, of Havre de Grace, who, in addition to the management of his practice, has held the office of justice of the peace since May of 1896. He is a man of excellent education, a concise, logical reasoner, and is thoroughly informed regarding every legal point or technicality of his cases. In all his transactions he is exact and accurate, never failing to bestow painstaking care even upon seemingly unimportant items.

In the city where he now resides the subject of this article was born in 1859, upon the day dear to all Americans as the anniversary of national independence. His father, George W. Rogers, was born in Cecil County, Md., and was reared upon a farm there, making it his home until about thirty years of age. He then came to Havre de Grace and worked at the trade of a shoemaker in this place. Though now (1897), seventy-four years of age, he still follows his chosen occupation and is quite active for one so advanced in life. In political belief he is a thorough Republican, but has never sought office nor cared for public prominence. His wife, Caroline (Metzger) Rogers, was born in Havre de Grace and is now sixty-three years of age. Since girlhood she has been identified with the Methodist Episcopal Church and one of its consistent members.

Educated in the public schools, our subject early determined to enter the legal profession, and with this object in view he read law under William M. Marine, late collector of the port of Baltimore. Upon the completion of his studies he was admitted to the bar in Baltimore County in 1885, and during the three ensuing years he was connected with his former preceptor in Baltimore. From that place he came to Havre de Grace and has since been in continuous practice at this place. In addition to his private practice, he is acting as justice of the peace and for a number of terms has rendered efficient service as city attorney. The Republican party contains the principles to which he pledges his adherence and which he believes will best advance the welfare of our country. While supporting the policy of that party, he has at no time sought political prominence and the positions to which he has been chosen have come to him because the people believe that he can fill them with efficiency. He possesses an analytical mind and is well equipped for his profession. In other ways than as a lawyer he is helpful to his community, the best interests of which he ever seeks. In 1888 he was united in marriage with Miss Jennie Magowan, of Havre de Grace, and they are the parents of a daughter, Laura Annie.

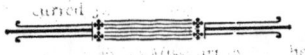

SEPTIMUS D. SEWELL. The family of which this gentleman was an honored representative has been identified with the history of Maryland for many generations and has been a potent factor in the development of the state's resources. The first of the name to settle in Harford County was the father of our subject, Col. Charles S. Sewell, a native of Queen Anne County, but through much of his life a resident of Harford County, where he owned thousands of acres of land. The title by which he was always called was given him in recognition of meritorious service in the War of 1812. His fellow-citizens, recognizing his large talents and fitness for public service, elected him to represent this district in the United States congress, and in that honored body he was a leading member. He is remembered as one of the best citizens the county has ever had and one who, by his ability and fidelity to the people's interests, won the position for himself.

The subject of this sketch was born in District No. 1, Harford County, April 26, 1822, and died at the same place August 5, 1869, having devoted his entire active life to the cultivation and improvement of the old homestead. In youth he attended the local schools, which being far inferior to those of the present day, did not assist him so much in preparing for life's activities as did his own powers of observation and his experience. While he superintended the farm personally, he did not engage actively in its cultivation, but rented out the land to others. He was thus enabled to devote much of his time to the consideration of public affairs and to the enjoyment of the amenities of life. In early manhood a Whig, upon the disintegration of that party he became a Democrat and was ever afterward loyal to the principles of that organization. It was never his desire to hold office, but he used his influence to secure the election of men who wished to serve the public as officials and whom he deemed fully competent to do so. He was the possessor of a fine voice and often sang in the choir of the Episcopal Church at Perryman, of which he was an active member and a vestryman. Fraternally he was connected with the Odd Fellows.

In 1850 Mr. Sewell was united in marriage with Maria L. Smith, daughter of Fielder B. Smith, and a member of an old family of Maryland. She is still living, being now (1897) sixty-four years of age. They were the parents of eight children, the oldest of whom, Charles S., died at Milledgeville, Ga., September 7, 1884; and the second, Lucy E., who married a gentleman of Baltimore, departed this life July 4, 1894. Catherine is the wife of M. D. Wilson, a resident of Frizellburgh, Carroll County, Md.; Mary S. resides with her mother; C. K. and William H. occupy the old homestead, of which the latter has had charge since he was fifteen years of age; L. Louise is the wife of J. P. Heard, of Gainesville, Ga.; the youngest child, Fielder B., died in childhood. The family is highly esteemed and well known in this locality, and a station on the Baltimore & Ohio Railroad is named in honor of them. C. K., who is a man well known in public affairs, held the position of tax collector in 1891-92 and again in 1897. He and his brother are agents for farm machinery and fertilizers, the utility of which has been acknowledged by those best fitted to judge. He has the energy and intelligence of his father and is a young man of great promise.

MARTIN E. RIDGELY. The family represented by this prosperous farmer of District No. 3, Harford County, originated in England, but its members have been long identified with American history. His grandfather, Commodore Daniel B. Ridgely, of the United States navy, was conspicuous among the American officers during the War of 1812. Dr. Nicholas G. Ridgely, our subject's father, was during most of his life a resident and practicing physician of Baltimore, where he built up a large practice and gained a name as a skillful and reliable physician. In that city his death occurred in 1892, on the day sacred to loyal citizens as the anniversary of American independence. His wife survives him, and makes her home with her only living son. They were the parents of six children, and at this writing, besides our subject, four of the family survive: Martha E.; Henrietta M.; Elizabeth D., wife of S. R. Reed; and Mary E.

Graduating from school at the age of nineteen, the subject of this sketch afterward removed from his native city of Baltimore to New York City, where he became interested in the banking and brokerage business. However, after one year he went back to Baltimore, firm in the opinion that it far surpassed the metropolis of the new world,

if not in population, at least in everything that goes to make a city a desirable place of residence. In 1894 he purchased the Woodside farm, near Bel Air, of which Robert Brown had previously been the owner. Bringing his mother and three unmarried sisters with him, he established his home here. The place contains one hundred and fifty acres, upon which, through his management, first-class improvements have been made, and through the cultivation of which he has been financially prospered. When residing in Baltimore, he and the other members of the family were identified with Grace Episcopal Church. The Democratic party has a strong adherent in him, and his vote and influence are given to that party. However, he has never sought office nor identified himself with political affairs, and has lived so quietly since coming to Harford County that the great questions causing so much discussion in the United States do not disturb him in his rural home. Unlike many who seek notoriety, he has always preferred the quiet discharge of personal duties to the excitement of public life. The fame of his deeds may never reach the outside world, yet, after all, no higher praise can be bestowed upon any man than to say truthfully that his life is upright, and that no one was ever wronged by him. Such may, in truth, be said of Martin E. Ridgely.

HON. WEBSTER WHITE. Although yet a young man, Mr. White has already made a success of life, both as a teacher and farmer. At this writing the latter occupation engages his attention, and he is interested in the cultivation of an eighty-acre farm lying in District No. 9, Cecil County. This is a portion of the old family homestead that has been in the possession of succeeding generations for many years, in fact, since an early period in the history of Maryland. Naturally he is fond of the old place, and will keep from passing into strange hands the property that his ancestors hewed out of the wilderness. In the supervision of the estate, he aims to improve the soil with each rotation of crops by the application of science in the husbanding of nature's boundless resources of fertility.

The family from which Mr. White descends in the paternal line is of good old English stock, well known for their good character and their industry. John White, who founded the family in America, received a warrant to two hundred acres of land from Lord Baltimore. His son, Israel, had a son, Milton, who was born in 1802, in District No. 9. The former was a blacksmith and farmer, and owned the property formerly belonging to his father; the latter was for a time employed in carrying the mail from Port Deposit to Perryville, also worked in a warehouse at Columbia, and later taught school in Chester County, Pa., for twenty years, being an instructor in the New London Academy for a part of the time. When forty-five years of age he settled upon the homestead, where he spent the remainder of his life, dying in 1892, at the age of ninety years. In political sentiment he was a stanch Republican. His wife, who was Martha Caldwell, of Farmington, Md., bore him seven children, five of whom are living.

At Calvert, formerly known as Brick Meeting House, in a house that stood opposite his present home, the subject of this sketch was born in 1860. He was educated in the public schools, West Nottingham Academy and the Friends' select school. At the age of eighteen he secured employment in the iron works at Wilmington, Del., where he was occupied as shipping clerk for one year. Then entering upon the teacher's profession, he had charge of schools in Cecil and Chester Counties from 1880 to 1892, becoming known meanwhile as an efficient and successful instructor. In the latter year he bought the old homestead, and has since engaged in farming and dairying here. A Republican in politics, he was upon that ticket elected a member of the legislature in 1896, serving for one term in that responsible position. He married Annie Ramsey, daughter of John Ramsey, and they have two children, Esther and Elizabeth. Fraternally he assisted in the organization of Banner Council No. 11, Junior Order of American Mechanics, in which he has passed through all the chairs, and is still an active member. He is a representative to the state council, which met at Cambridge in June, 1897, and also to the Junior Order of American Mechanics at Oxford. As a citizen he is progressive and enterprising, and all measures for the benefit of the people receive his support. His reputation is that of a reliable citizen, and as such he is accorded the respect of others.

DR. CHARLES M. ELLIS, the third son of Francis Asbury Ellis and Eliza Ann Howard, was born at Elkton, Md., on the 13th of December, 1838. His early education was acquired at the Elkton Academy, under Principals Thorpe and Getty. In 1852 he was sent to New London Academy, one of the earliest foundations in Pennsylvania, and before his sixteenth year was one of the teachers thereof. Returning to Elkton he assisted his father, who for nearly fifty years was secretary-treasurer of the Mutual Fire Insurance Company of Cecil County.

Before he was of age Dr. Ellis was elected secretary and treasurer of the board of school commissioners of Cecil County. In the spring of 1858 he began the study of law in the office of Hon. Alexander Evans, but in the fall of the same year he matriculated in the medical department of the University of Pennsylvania, of which institution his great-great-grandfather was an original incorporator. He pursued a graded three years' course, and graduated in the class of 1861, amidst the din and turmoil of the early days of the Civil War. He immediately entered the military service of the United States as assistant surgeon of Rush's Lancers, a favorite Philadelphia organization, subsequently known as the Sixth Pennsylvania Cavalry. Three of his brothers, Howard, Rudulph and Philip, were also officers of the same regiment. He served with the Army of the Potomac, and in May, 1862, was detached by order of Gen. Philip St. George Cooke in command of the cavalry division of the army, to take charge of the hospital of the division located by General Cooke on the "Johnson" farm, near the Chickahominy. He was captured, with his hospital, by the advance of Stonewall Jackson's corps the day after the battle of Mechanicsville, which ushered in the Seven Days' fight on the peninsula. His hospital, being immediately in the rear of the rebel lines, was overrun by wounded Confederates, to whom he rendered surgical aid. Before his removal to Richmond he went into that city through the Confederate lines in disguise and made known to General Reynolds (then a prisoner at the Spotswood Hotel) the starving condition of the officers and wounded prisoners on the battlefields. His mission, although one of great danger, was entirely successful through the courtesy of General Winder, Provost-Marshal of Henrico County. He was subsequently removed with many others to Libby prison and occupied his time continuously in devoted attention to the wounded prisoners in Castle Thunder and other prison houses, a service that attracted the favorable comments of the Richmond press.

Returning to Elkton Dr. Ellis became associated in the practice of his profession with the late Dr. Henry H. Mitchell in 1864, a co-partnership which terminated ten years later. Dr. Ellis has acquired a moderate fortune, owning the town hall, half interest in the gas works, a handsome residence, and is largely interested in agriculture, owning a number of farms. He has been an active promoter of many of the business interests of the community, taking especial pride in the success of the Mutual Building Association of Cecil County, of which he was the founder in 1870, and of which he has been the president for nearly twenty-five years. He has been a liberal contributor to the periodical literature of his profession. He has been for many years surgeon to the Pennsylvania Railroad, was a member of the first State Board of Health of Maryland, is a member of the American Medical Association, an honorary member of the Medical Society of Delaware, and an active member of the Medical and Chirurgical Faculty of Maryland, which has this year honored him by promoting him to its presidency.

In very early life Dr. Ellis married Miss Mary E. Cantwell. He has no children.

The Ellis family is connected through many lines with colonial and revolutionary ancestry. The first one of this family coming to America was Rowland Ellis, a Welsh gentleman and a priest of the Established Church. He was sent to America by the still existing society for the diffusion of Christian knowledge. Locating in Burlington, N. J., in 1701, he became early connected with the famous St. Mary's Church, of which, for one hundred and seventy-five years, in direct line, his descendants were wardens, the line terminating with the death of Dr. Charles Ellis, the cousin of Francis A. Ellis. The vestry of St. Mary's has recently erected a monument to the memory of this Rowland in its beautiful cemetery.

Francis A., the father of Dr. Ellis, was the child of Rowland Ellis and Elizabeth Rudulph. He is thus connected with the Rudulph family, which contributed Majors John and Michael Rudulph to the Revolution. They were known for their desperate courage as the "Lions of Lee's Legion," having early in the contest gone to Virginia to join Lightfoot Harry Lee's Legion. The mother of Elizabeth Rudulph was Esther Synge, one of the daughters of Philip Synge, the "patriot silversmith of the Revolution." This remarkable man, a German, landed as a youth in 1701 (the same year the first Rowland Ellis arrived in America) at Annapolis, Maryland. He was soon in Baltimore, and thence removed to Philadelphia, where he became well known as a silversmith and maker of mathematical instruments. He was the intimate personal friend of Franklin; made for him all the instruments used by him in the study of electricity, and pursued the subject long after Franklin abandoned it. He was associated with Franklin in all his educational enterprises, and was an original incorporator of the University of Pennsylvania and of the American Philosophical Society. The silver inkstand which was used by the colonial congress, and which contained the ink used in signing the

Declaration of Independence, was made by him, and is now preserved in Independence Hall at Philadelphia, among the cherished relics of the Revolution. Among his many distinguished descendants were Philip Synge Physick, the father of American surgery, and Commodore Connor, of the United States navy.

Dr. Ellis' mother's grandfather was Maj. John Howard, an English Catholic priest, who, eschewing celibacy, married Miss Evans, a descendant of Governor John Evans of Pennsylvania. Major Howard died at Valley Forge during the war, of camp fever. His mother was the daughter of Jacques Casho, an Alsatian, who came to America to serve the cause of popular liberty and enlisted in the Delaware line. His musket and accoutrements are preserved by the Delaware Historical Society.

JOHN B. SLICER, M. D. Success in any occupation can be attained only through industry and study, and the good physician must necessarily be the most painstaking of workers and the best of students. Of Dr. Slicer it may be justly said that he is a most conscientious physician, and whatever he undertakes is done thoroughly. The welfare of a patient is ever in his mind, and by careful diagnosis and accuracy of treatment he endeavors to restore the body to its wonted vigor and health. He keeps pace with every onward movement made in his profession, and aims to take advantage of every improvement in the science which he has adopted for his life work. Since completing his course of study he has engaged in practice, and during all this time, with the exception of a year at Principio, has had his office in District No. 9, Cecil County.

In this district Dr. Slicer was born in 1858, a son of John T., and grandson of Thomas, who in turn was a son of John T. Slicer, a native of Germany. The last-named was one of three brothers who crossed the Atlantic in early manhood and settled in Maryland, near the city of Baltimore. The father of our subject followed the occupation of a farmer from boyhood until death, and was a man of great energy and untiring industry. In political belief he was a Democrat. He married Martha J. Read, of District No. 5, Cecil County, a member of an old family of this locality. They became the parents of five children, namely: William, who resides in Harrisburg, Pa.; Sabina C., Annie M., John B. and H. Emily. The father died in this district in 1892, at the age of sixty-six years.

The subject of this article began his studies in the common schools of the district, and afterward attended West Nottingham Academy. His commercial education was obtained in Eastman's Business College, in Poughkeepsie, N. Y. However, it was not his intention to enter the field of business activity, as he preferred a professional life. With this object in view, he matriculated in the College of Physicians and Surgeons, of Baltimore, from which he graduated in 1884, with the degree of M. D. On the close of his studies in college, he practiced at Principio, Cecil County, but after one year, removed from District No. 6 to No. 9, in 1885, and here has since conducted a general practice. He has patients not only in this district, but also in the adjoining Districts Nos. 5, 6 and 7, and some across the state line in Pennsylvania. He is well known in this section of the county, and is popular, both professionally and socially. Gifted by nature, he has cultivated his endowments, and through indefatigable labor has gained a place among the successful physicians of the locality. Fraternally he is connected with Excelsior Lodge of Odd Fellows, in which he has passed all of the chairs. He is also Senior Warden of Harmony Lodge, A. F. & A. M., at Port Deposit, a member of Chapter No. 21, R. A. M., at Baltimore, and Maryland Commandery, also of Baltimore. His parents reared him in the faith of the Methodist Church, and he is in hearty sympathy with the work of this denomination and is interested in all movements looking to the welfare and advancement of his fellow-men. In matters political he favors the policy and platform of the Democratic party.

When he began in practice he was a poor man, but possessing self-reliance and being determined to succeed, his enterprise and industry overcame the difficulties in his path and he is now numbered among the successful physicians of the county.

JAMES W. HARKINS, M. D. The value to any community of a professional man is not marked merely by his learning and skill, his proficiency in medical and surgical practice, but also by his character, both private and professional, his honorable adherence to medical ethics and his personal integrity and benevolence of purpose. These characteristics are combined in Dr. James W. Harkins, who is one of the foremost professional men of his section. All his life has been spent in Harford County, Md., and here he was born to William and Martha O. (Bassford) Harkins, who were natives of Maryland also. This worthy couple were actively engaged in agricultural pursuits throughout their lives, as was also the paternal grandfather, John Harkins, and the native state of the latter was Maryland. The paternal great-grandfather was Aaron Harkins, a native of the Keystone state and a tiller of the soil. The children born to William and Martha Harkins numbered ten, of whom at the present time five are living: Thomas A., William A., Richard R., Hannah J. and Dr. James W., the immediate subject of this sketch.

The youthful days of Dr. James W. Harkins were spent in following the plow and in discharging the various duties of the farm, but when the time came to choose a life occupation for himself, he deviated from the established custom of the Harkins family, and instead of becoming a farmer he began reading medicine under Dr. Richard Mitchem, of Pleasantville, Md. He pursued his medical researches very energetically from the time he was twenty-four years of age until he graduated from a medical college in Baltimore, and he is still an indefatigable student of his profession. He considers it the duty of every physician to keep abreast of the progress made in that science, and carefully studies and considers each and every one of his cases that is in any degree complicated, with the result that few medical practitioners have had better success in alleviating the pains and ailments to which the human family is heir than has he. He is cheerful and encouraging at the bedside of his patients, and is, in fact, a model family physician. That his services are appreciated is demonstrated by the large practice which he commands and by the comfortable competency and beautiful home which he has acquired.

Soon after his graduation Dr. Harkins located in Norrisville, opened an office, and it was but a short time ere he was one of the busiest physicians of the county. He found a worthy helpmate in Miss Mary E. Gibson, whom he married in early manhood. Mrs. Harkins is a Pennsylvanian by birth and her early life was spent on her parents' farm in that state. The doctor and his wife are active members of the Presbyterian Church. In his political views the former has always been independent, and particularly in local matters, voting for the candidate whom he considers best fitted to fill the office creditably. His life has been an exceptionally active one, as is that of all successful physicians, and in every relation of life he has acquitted himself creditably and as a gentleman.

PROF. E. B. FOCKLER. There are many who claim, and not without excellent reason, that the public-school system of the United States surpasses that of any other country in the world. Certainly it is true that in no other land are there so many efficient, educated young men devoting their attention to the instruction of youth as may be found in our own country. One of this class is the subject of our sketch, who holds the responsible position of principal of the public school of North East, and who, since coming to this place, has evinced talent and the possession of those qualities without which a teacher cannot hope to gain success.

The subject of this article was born March 24, 1865, in Cavetown, Washington County, Md., which was also the birthplace of his father, Benjamin. The latter was an honest, hard-working man, a shoemaker by trade, in politics an advocate of Democratic principles, and in religion a member of the German Reformed Church. Honored by all who knew him, he passed from earth in 1886. His wife, who bore the maiden name of Louisa H. Colliflower, died in 1892. She had a brother, Rev. William Colliflower, who was pastor of the Reformed Church in Frederick, Md., at the time of his death; another brother, Henry, who is a retired merchant and prominent citizen of Hagerstown, and a third brother, George, who resides at Chambersburg. In her family there were ten children and seven of the number are living, namely: John T., principal of the public school at Chewsville, Md.; George S., teacher in the public schools of Washington County, this state; Harry L., who is a railway postal clerk, with residence in Hagerstown, Md.; E. B., of this sketch; Catherine, who resides with her brother Harry; Susan B., wife of William O. Fahrney, of Hagerstown; and Ella S., who married George Shetrone, of Columbia, Pa. The Fockler family is of German extraction.

In the public schools of Washington County and the high school of Smithsburg our subject received his education, and he graduated from the latter in the spring of 1884. At once he began to teach in Pinesburg, Washington County, where he remained for two years, and afterward for three years he was principal of the public school at Ringgold, Washington County. In the fall of 1889 he became assistant principal of the school at Clear Spring, the same county, and after two years there, in 1891, received an appointment as assistant principal of the high school at Waynesboro, Pa. The following year he was assistant principal of the Emmettsburg high school in Frederick County. In 1894 he was selected from among fifty-six applicants, as principal of the North East school, which position he has since filled. Brought up in the belief that the Democratic party contained the principles that are best for our country, he has never changed the opinion instilled in his mind when young. Fraternally he is a member of Acacia Lodge No. 155, A. F. & A. M., at Fairmount, Md., chancellor of Fellowship Lodge No. 42, K. P.; secretary of Fellowship Division, Uniformed Rank, and a member of Council No. 5, Junior Order of American Mechanics, at Hagerstown. In youth he united with the German Reformed Church and afterward officiated as superintendent of its Sunday-school, but as there is no church of that denomination here, he attends the Methodist Episcopal Church and is a teacher in its Sunday-school.

HON. CHARLES C. CROTHERS. Cecil County has among its citizens a number of men eminent in the annals of the state, men of ability, energy and honor, who, in the duties of public and private life, have ever been true and loyal. Such a one is the subject of this article, who has been a prominent member of the Elkton bar for years. Soon after entering upon active practice he was elected to the office of prosecuting attorney, which first brought him into public and political life. The efficient manner in which he discharged every duty connected with the position and the large talents of which he gave evidence, led the people to believe that he was qualified to represent them in offices of great trust and responsibility. When, therefore, his party (the Democratic) selected him as their nominee for state senator in 1893, he was given a very gratifying majority at the election, and is the present representative of the district in the senate.

The family of which Mr. Crothers is a member has long been identified with the history of Cecil County. The first of the name here were two brothers, James and William, natives of Ireland, and early settlers of this county. William was a sea captain, and on one of his voyages was lost at sea; his descendants live in Baltimore. James had a son, John Lawrence, our subject's grandfather, who was born in District No. 9, and engaged in farming until his death, at an early age. One of his sons, Richard H., was a very prominent man here and for some years held the office of commissioner of Cecil County. Another son, Alpheus, our subject's father, was born in this county, May 17, 1820, and was a lifelong farmer, an honored citizen, and a man of quiet, retiring disposition. He never aspired to political honors, but was elected to the offices of justice of the peace and collector of taxes. At the age of seventy-seven, he died suddenly, of heart disease, at his home in District No. 8, on the evening of March 26, 1897.

The mother of our subject was Margaret Orelia, daughter of John Hart Porter, member of one of the oldest families of the county and formerly a prominent farmer of District No. 8. One of her brothers, William E. Porter, was for a time connected with the Baltimore & Ohio Railroad, and later was superintendent of the West Virginia Central Railroad. Another brother, Charles C. Porter, was a wealthy resident of Louisville, Ky. She was the mother of eight sons, of whom we note the following: William E., went to California many years ago and still resides there; Dr. R. R., a graduate of the University of Maryland, is a practicing physician at Colora, Cecil County; Alpheus, owns and operates a farm in District No. 8, this county; John L. is superintendent of construction of the Baltimore & Ohio Railroad, and lives in Baltimore; Ranville W. is a carpenter and builder in Lancaster County, Pa.; A. L. is an attorney in Elkton, where he was state's attorney from 1890 to 1895, and also counsel to the county board of commissioners; Dr. A. C., a graduate of the University of Maryland, is now engaged in practice at Port Deposit.

Near the village of Conowingo, in this county, Charles C. Crothers was born March 28, 1857. His education was obtained in the public schools and West Nottingham Academy, after which he studied law in Elkton and was admitted to the bar. The following year he was elected state's attorney, and this office he filled for four years. The honor was tendered him, in 1893, of election to the state senate, in which illustrious body he has been a conspicuous figure. He was at one time the Democratic nominee for attorney-general of Maryland, but suffered defeat in a general "landslide." Fraternally he is identified with the Knights of Pythias and Independent Order of Odd Fellows. As a lawyer, he takes front rank at the bar of the county. He is a man of liberal education and scholarly attainments. At all times he has been a close, thoughtful student. His libraries, law and miscellaneous, are filled with works by standard authors. He possesses natural aptitude for the profession he has selected for his lifework, being a logical thinker and a concise reasoner. Every case, together with the laws governing it, he has well in hand. As a member of the senate he has sought to perform his arduous duties conscientiously, ever bearing in mind the welfare of his constituents. A man of positive convictions, he is never afraid to take a stand that he considers right, and has the courage of his convictions under all circumstances. In perplexing problems he argues from primal causes to sequence, and grasps the matter at issue in its various phases. He has the deepest affection for old Maryland, and the greatest faith in her people, her institutions and her future; and certainly the welfare of the state is immeasurably promoted by the able efforts of such citizens as he.

HENRY MITCHELL McCULLOUGH is engaged in the practice of the legal profession in Elkton. His entire life has been passed here and since early manhood he has been identified with the professional and material interests of the place, to many of the enterprises of which he has contributed by his recognized progressive spirit. His firm, quiet reasoning faculties, which are his by education and training, enable him to grapple with the salient points of a case and the technicalities of legal jurisprudence, and have secured for him a position of prominence at the bar of Cecil County.

James T. McCullough, father of the subject of this article, was long one of the most prominent men of Maryland, where much of his life was passed as a member of the Elkton bar. He was born on Rosedale farm, in Newcastle County, Del., in December, 1816, and received a thorough education in Delaware College. Entering upon the practice of the legal profession, his talents soon brought him distinction at the bar. His reputation was by no means limited to Elkton, where he had his office, but he was well known throughout the state. For some years he was a member of the Maryland senate, and his services in that distinguished body were such as to increase his reputation. He was a delegate to the convention that nominated Bell. During the administration of President Lincoln he held the office of collector of internal revenue in his district. While the Civil War was in progress, he took an active part at the time of the draft riots. Not alone was he prominent in his profession, but in religious enterprises as well. Long a leading member of the Presbyterian Church, he officiated as an elder and repeatedly represented the church in the general assembly. He continued in professional practice up to the time of his death, which occurred January 19, 1888. His father, James McCullough, was a native of Delaware and from that state went to Missouri, where he died.

The mother of our subject, who bore the maiden name of Catherine W. Mitchell, is still living and resides at the old homestead in Elkton. She had two sons and two daughters, but one of the sons, Andrew H., was drowned in the creek, March 4, 1889. Delia is the wife of a banker and large real-estate owner of Harrisburg, Pa. Mary is the wife of a merchant in Elkton.

In Elkton, where he was born September 24, 1858, the subject of this sketch gained the rudiments of his education. His studies were afterward continued at Princeton, where he graduated in the class of 1879. Under the preceptorship of his father he carried on his legal studies and in June, 1881, was admitted to practice at the bar,

since which time he has had his office in Elkton. He is regarded as one of the leading attorneys and rising political leaders of his locality, and his name has been mentioned as the Republican candidate for state's attorney. Fraternally he is connected with the Independent Order of Odd Fellows, and is past grand of the local lodge and a member of the grand lodge. February 25, 1896, he was united in marriage with Miss Carrie, daughter of H. H. Brady, of Chesapeake City.

HUGH T. HEAPS. The farm which this gentleman owns and operates is especially dear to him, because it is his birthplace and was the home of his ancestors for several generations. It lies in District No. 5, Harford County, and contains a fine set of buildings and other desirable improvements. A portion of the property is devoted to the raising of cereals, while the remainder is utilized for the pasturage of stock, Mr. Heaps giving some attention to both of these departments of agriculture.

Born in 1830, our subject is the second son of John and Martha (Alexander) Heaps, natives of this district. The family of which he is a member consisted of six children, his brother and sisters being William A., Sallie A. (deceased), Eliza J., Mary M. (deceased) and Belle V. His grandfather was born in Harford County, and in 1800 bought five hundred acres, a portion of which is included in our subject's farm. Farming was his life work, and being a man of energy he was fairly successful. During the Revolution he rendered service in the American army, and his son, our subject's father, was a lieutenant in the War of 1812, and afterward a captain in the service. The great-grandfather, Robert Heaps, was born in England, but emigrated to America prior to the Revolution and settled in Harford County, where he developed and cultivated a farm. Agriculture has been the occupation of the family as far back as the record can be traced.

As a tiller of the soil, our subject has led a busy

and useful life. His education was gained rather from observation than from text books, but it has been none the less serviceable for that reason. He married Maggie Barton, of York County, Pa., an estimable lady and a successful school teacher, and they have three children. The Barton family originated in England, whence the great-grandfather of Mrs. Heaps came to America and settled in York County. Members of the family participated in the Revolution and the War of 1812, and they have always been patriotic and loyal to the institutions of our government.

During 1874 and 1875 Mr. Heaps held the office of county commissioner, in which capacity he was always alert to promote the best interests of old Harford. Politically he is a staunch Democrat, decided in his views, and not easily turned from his convictions when once assured he is in the right. Fraternally he is connected with Mt. Ararat Lodge No. 44, A. F. & A. M., at Bel Air. He and his wife hold membership in the Presbyterian Church, in which he officiates as a trustee and elder. He is a man of sound principles and has the respect of his fellow-citizens.

JACOB BRILLHART. Among those of German descent who have developed a high order of ability in connection with the agricultural affairs of Harford County, and whose personal and social qualities have given them added prominence, Mr. Brillhart is conspicuous. With steady purpose, energy and a full comprehension of the many duties of his calling, he has pushed to the front and is justly respected in the county of his adoption. He traces his ancestry back through four generations to his great-great-grandfather, who was born in Germany, and came to this country in the early part of his life. He settled in York County, Pa., where he became a very extensive land owner. His son, Isaac Brillhart, was born there, and, like his father, was engaged in farming, but when the Revolutionary War opened, left the plow to enlist in the colonial army, with which he served throughout the war. York County was also the birthplace of his son, David Brillhart, and farming was his life occupation. Joseph Brillhart, son of the last named, was a product of the same county as himself, and farming was his occupation throughout life. He eventually became the owner of a fine farm of two hundred and forty acres, and on this homestead were born to himself and wife, Elizabeth (Strayer) Brillhart, the following children: Jacob; Mary, deceased; Henry S.; John W.; Elizabeth, deceased; Sarah; Noah; Joseph and Catharine, both deceased.

Like each and every one of his lineal ancestors, back to his great-great-grandfather, Jacob Brillhart was born in York County, Pa., and like them he was reared to a knowledge of farm life. His birth occurred January 25, 1831, and his youth was spent in doing various chores about the home place and in acquiring an education in the district schools. At the age of twenty-eight years, Miss Elizabeth Venus, a native of York County, Pa., became his wife. Her mother, whose maiden name was Ann Sykes, was a native of England, while her father was of French extraction. As the years rolled by a family of four children was given them, named as follows: Edward L., Ellen A., Minnie S. and Jacob C., deceased. The mother, who was a devoted member of the Evangelical Church, was called from this life in January, 1888, at the age of forty-six years. She was a kind and devoted wife and mother, and her death was lamented by all who knew her, as well as by her own immediate family.

Although Mr. Brillhart was reared to the occupation of farming, he followed milling and lumbering for over thirty years in various parts of Missouri, Ohio, Arkansas, Maryland and Pennsylvania, and while thus engaged he traveled over the western part of the United States, and became thoroughly familiar with the topography of that region. His experiences were many and varied while thus employed, and he experienced numerous financial ups and downs, but never relaxed his efforts to better his financial condition, and is now in good circumstances. He has always been a faithful and enthusiastic Republican in politics, and has held the offices of assessor and justice of the peace, the latter for three years. He was formerly a member of the Improved Order of Red Men. Like his ancestors for generations, he is a member of the Evangelical Church.

THOMAS FASSITT. Of the residents of Cecil County, there are perhaps few who have traveled as extensively in our country as has Mr. Fassitt, of District No. 9. His occupation of a civil engineer, in which for years he was actively engaged, took him to different points, and at various times he has been a resident of twenty-three states. Finally, wishing to enter an occupation that would enable him to establish a permanent home, he turned his attention from engineering to farming, and has since operated a farm of one hundred and fifty acres. While he had no previous experience as an agriculturist, his sound common sense enabled him to succeed in the occupation.

As nearly as can be ascertained, the founder of the Fassitt family in Maryland was Ralph Fassitt, who was a native of France, and a descendant of the illustrious Huguenots. The grandfather of our subject, James, and the great-grandfather, William, were born in Worcester County, this state, whence the former removed to Philadelphia in 1790, and embarked in business there. Alfred Fassitt, our subject's father, was born in Philadelphia in 1800 and spent his life there, engaged in business as a wholesale jobber and merchant. In politics he was a Whig, and in religion a member of the First Presbyterian Church, always being deeply interested in religious enterprises. As his wife, he chose Margaret Barclay, of Philadelphia, daughter of John Allen, a soldier in the Revolution, and for years chief clerk to Stephen Girard. They became the parents of nine children, but only three are now living: John B., of New York City; Thomas and Marcelena. The father of this family died in Philadelphia in 1874, when seventy-four years of age.

Born in Philadelphia, Thomas Fassitt was educated there and in Maryland. He learned civil engineering while in the employ of the Pennsylvania Railway Company and followed the occupation for many years. In 1872 he was united in marriage with Miss Catherine Van Sant, of Bucks County, Pa., and afterward bought the old Kirk Brown farm in District No. 9, Cecil County, where he has since engaged in general farming and the dairy business. He has four children, the eldest of whom, Alfred, assists in the management of the home place; John Barclay, Loraine F. and Kathleen Mary are at home. They attend the Zion Presbyterian Church, while Mr. Fassitt holds membership in St. Mary Anne's Episcopal Church, at North East. While connected with the church at Oxford, he officiated as vestryman for some years. He is a veteran of the late war, in which he enlisted in 1862, as a member of the Second Pennsylvania Cavalry, and served about one year. Interested in local affairs, he stands well among his fellow-citizens. His social ways and kindly manner toward all with whom he comes in contact, his hearty appreciation of the merits of others and his enjoyment in whatever brings happiness to them, all these things have won for him a position among the people of the community, which is one of the greatest prizes of life.

CAPT. JOSEPH HENRIQUES. On the banks of Chesapeake Bay, in District No. 2, Harford County, lies the fertile and well-improved estate of five hundred and fifty acres, where, in the twilight of a very busy and active life, Captain Henriques is living retired from business cares. Could his biography be given in full, with its many thrilling incidents and perilous experiences, it would read like a page from romance. He has traveled extensively, both in foreign lands and in our country, and has thus gained a cosmopolitan culture that can be acquired in no other way; he has also gained a knowledge of men and countries, the customs of peoples and their relations with the United States.

The life here chronicled began at Kingston, Jamaica, June 18, 1825. Of the place of his birth, however, the captain retains no recollection, for he was only six weeks old when his parents removed to New York City. His father, Moses, was born and reared in London, England, and in early life was successfully engaged in trading in the West Indies, where he met and married Sarah Nunes, a native of Kingston, West Indies. They became the parents of ten children, but only three are living, viz.: Joseph, the eldest; William H., a stock broker, of New York; and Lavinia, widow of Col. Alfred W. Taylor, of New York. The father removed to New York in 1825, and remained there about three years, after which he traveled in Europe until 1832, when he returned to New York and became an agent for the banking house of Rothschild. For many years he carried on a banking business on Wall Street. A speculator in lands, he owned considerable property where now stands the city of Chicago.

When our subject was two years of age, the family went to Europe and spent two and one-half years in travel upon the continent, then returned to New York City, where his early schooling was obtained. For a time he was a student in the New York Lyceum, where he took a seven years' course in French and Spanish, also carried on other studies. Afterward for three years he attended a private school in Boston, taught by Rev. D. M. P. Wells, and then spent two years in Columbia College, in New York. His first employment was that of clerk in the dry-goods store of A. T. Stewart & Co., in New York, where he remained three years. On the breaking out of the Mexican War in 1847, he became sergeant of the first regiment that was organized in New York and at once marched to the scene of warfare. When the army finally entered the city of Mexico, he was placed on the staff of the major-general as secretary and interpreter, and continued in that capacity until the treaty of peace was signed. During that time he was commissioned to officiate as interpreter and translator to the peace commission, headed by Nicholas P. Twist. When the American army evacuated the city of Mexico, he returned to the United States. Twice during the war he was wounded, once by a gun shot in the left limb and at another time in the head by a sabre. On his return he was presented with a medal by the city council of New York City, and this he still has in his possession, one of his most valued souvenirs of the war.

In January, 1849, Captain Henriques was one of a party of one hundred gentlemen organized to go to California. En route to the west he passed through Mexico, where he acted as interpreter. After the city of San Francisco was chartered, he was chosen deputy county clerk and also served as public administrator of the county, secretary to the United States land commissioners and interpreter to all the courts. He also held the position of secretary to the judiciary committee of the legislature. For a short time he prospected for gold and also dealt in sugar. On two occasions he has officiated as second in duels, being Graham's second in the duel with John Nugent, of San Francisco. While in the west he became identified with San Francisco Lodge No. 1, I. O. O. F., and passed through all the chairs. He was also identified with Lebanon Lodge No. 49, A. F. & A. M., of San Francisco, which was the first lodge instituted by the Masons in that city. In 1857 he returned to New York via steamer.

From 1857 to 1861 Captain Henriques was employed as a translator in the liquidating department of the New York custom house, except during the year 1858, when he was sent by the government to Cuba to investigate some fraudulent sugar deals. When the Fourth New York Infantry was organized, under Col. Alfred Taylor, he raised a company and was chosen captain. The regiment, about one thousand strong, went to Newport News, where five weeks were spent in perfecting the organization and in drilling. They were then ordered down the line of the Philadelphia, Wilmington & Baltimore Railroad, between Perryville and Baltimore, and Captain

Henriques was placed in command of five companies at Havre de Grace, as senior captain. Later he was sent to protect a bridge at Gunpowder River, thence to Ft. McHenry, from there to Suffolk, Va., Washington, D. C., and through Maryland to Antietam. There he received a wound in his left hand that disabled him from further service. Returning to New York, he accepted a position as clerk in charge of French correspondence for the house of H. B. Claflin & Co., and was also made secretary of the New York Stock Exchange, of which his brother was vice-president. This position he held from 1865 to 1869, when he came to Harford County and took up his residence upon Wilton farm, the property inherited by his wife from her parents. She bore the maiden name of Sarah B. Hoke, and was born on the place she now owns. Jacob Hoke, who was a native of York County, Pa., came to Harford County with his father, Peter Hoke, and settled upon this farm in 1814. The marriage of Captain Henriques and Sarah B. Hoke took place October 22, 1863, and one child was born of the union, Peter H., who died in 1873. Mrs. Henriques is a member of the Episcopal Church, which the captain attends. In politics he has always been a stanch Democrat, and is warmly interested in party matters.

I HENRY FORD. It has been said that the "worth of a state in the long run is the worth of the individuals composing it." This being accepted as true, the presence of a public-spirited, talented man, of superior mental traits, is of the greatest value to the state. But, while the state is benefited, the especial benefit falls upon the village or locality, the immediate center from which the influence radiates. We find this to be the case in studying the life of Mr. Ford, of North East. At an early age he displayed the earnestness of purpose that has since been one of his chief characteristics and that has largely been the means of his success. A review of his life will be of interest to the people in Cecil County, of which he is a native and to which he returned, after an honorable and successful career as an attorney in Washington, D. C.

The Ford family is thought to be of Irish extraction, but the genealogy is not clear upon this point. It is certain that it has been identified with the history of America from a very early period of its settlement. Patriotism has always been a marked family characteristic. Col. John Ford, great-grandfather of our subject, took part as an officer in the Revolutionary War and was present at the battle of Long Island. While in active service he captured, from a conquered foe, a Hessian musket, that is now in the possession of our subject and highly prized by him. John, father of I. Henry Ford, was born at Oldfield Point, Cecil County, and became a farmer, which occupation he followed, together with work as an itinerant Methodist preacher, as long as he lived. In politics he was first an old-line Whig, and later a Republican. He was a descendant of Francis Mauldin, who came to this country about 1687, and settling on Elk Neck took up a large tract of land, some of which is still owned by the descendants. The marriage of John Ford and Elizabeth Simpers resulted in the birth of eleven children, of whom seven are living, namely: Charles, who has been a very successful man and resides in Washington, D. C.; John Fletcher, of North East; Capt. Samuel, who is a resident of Washington, D. C.; Margaret, who is unmarried and resides in Philadelphia; Alfred, of Washington; I. Henry, and Sarah M., who resides with our subject and has charge of his home. The father of this family attained an advanced age, dying in 1891, and the mother passed away in 1876. They were a worthy couple, honest in even the smallest details, kind and generous to those in need, and respected by all who knew them.

At the family home in North East, I. Henry Ford was born October 21, 1845. His father being well-to-do, he was given the best educational advantages it was possible to secure, and of these he availed himself to the utmost, as he was ambitious to gain a wide fund of knowledge. He attended the private schools of his native town, after which for four terms he was a student in Ft. Edward Institute near Albany, N. Y., and then prepared for college at Suffield, Conn. The fall of 1867 found him a student in classic Yale, from which institution he graduated in 1871 with the degree of Bachelor of Arts. Beginning the study of law, in the law department of the same college, he graduated in 1873 as a Bachelor of Laws. Immediately afterward he opened an office in Washington, D. C., where he conducted a general practice for twenty years, meeting with fair success in his profession. Failing health at last obliged him to seek an entire change of occupation, and in 1893 he returned to the old homestead in Cecil County, where he has since resided, superintending the management of a part of the property and renting the balance to tenants. He also rents another farm that he owns in this county. He belongs to the Greek letter societies, is a friend of religious movements, and always votes the Republican ticket, though at no time a candidate for office. During the campaign of 1896 he was president of a sound-money club. As a citizen he is progressive and consistent, and always identifies himself with movements tending toward the benefit of town and county.

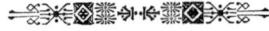

JOHN DUNNIGAN. Among the representative and prominent citizens of Harford County, there are many of foreign birth, who have come to this country with the hope of bettering their financial condition and in this free land of ours have succeeded in securing a good home and comfortable competence as the reward of their industry, perseverance and economy. In Mr. Dunnigan we find a worthy representative of this class.

He began his earthly career in Ireland, and was the eldest of the five sons of John Dunnigan, the others being Patrick, James, Bernard and Andrew. When our subject was a young man the father brought his family to the new world and took up his residence in Harford County, Md., where he spent the remainder of his life engaged in agricultural pursuits, dying in 1865.

The boyhood and youth of Mr. Dunnigan, of this sketch, were spent on the Emerald Isle, where in early life he learned the stone mason's trade, and this occupation he successfully followed for a number of years after coming to America. It was in 1863 that he crossed the Atlantic, and he has since been numbered among the leading citizens and wide-awake business men of Harford County. He is the owner of a good farm of sixty acres in District No. 5, which he has placed under a high state of cultivation and operates in connection with his son Daniel J., a promising young man of thrifty and industrious habits.

As a companion and helpmate on life's journey Mr. Dunnigan chose Anna Clark. Five children have blessed their union: John, now a resident of Darlington; Mary, wife of Theodore Crew; James, of Lapidum; Daniel J. and Andrew. The family is one of the highest respectability and worth and its members are all communicants of the Catholic Church.

DR. DAVID O. BOTTS, who has had long and successful experience as a dentist at Darlington, Harford County, was born in this village in 1853, the son of Isaac H. and Mary (Sheridan) Botts. He is a descendant on his mother's side, from one of the old and honored families of the county. His father was for fifty years engaged in the practice of dentistry at Darlington, where his death occurred in 1887, at the age of seventy-five years. His wife died in 1872. Eight children were born of their union and of these five are now living, namely: Mary E., wife of George Murphy; George and John, who reside in District No. 5, Harford County; David O., of this sketch; and Thomas, also a resident of District No. 5.

In the academy at Darlington our subject obtained a practical education, completing his literary studies at the age of twenty-one. When a mere boy he became interested in dentistry and nothing pleased him more than to be given an opportunity to visit his father's office, where he studied the dental instruments, their varied uses, the treatment of patients, and all the work connected with the profession. As soon as he acquired a thorough knowledge of the occupation, he began in practice for himself and has since carried it on among the people residing in and near Darlington.

The Democratic party finds in Dr. Botts a firm and loyal supporter, whose views upon matters relating to the government have been adopted only after thoughtful study of men and the times in which we live. In religious belief he and his family are Methodists. In 1876 he married Sallie B. Smith, and they have two children. Mrs. Botts is the daughter of Thackery and Sarah Smith, natives of England, who came to America in 1848 and settled in Chester County, Pa., but from there removed to Harford County in 1853 and settled upon a farm. Mr. Smith died here in November, 1893, aged eighty-three, and his wife passed away in August, 1896, at the age of seventy-eight. Their family consisted of seven children, and of these all but one are living. They are named as follows: Richard, residing in Castleton, this county; John, also a resident of this county; Harry, who lives in Kansas; Samuel, of Darlington; Sarah, wife of Dr. Botts; and Esther, who married Samuel Love and makes her home in Castleton.

HARVEY H. MACKEY. The service which in the past Mr. Mackey has rendered his fellow-citizens in Cecil County, and which he is now rendering the people in the responsible office of sheriff, entitles him to rank among the influential men of the county. As an honored member of an honorable family, connected through many generations with the history of this locality, he is adding lustre to the name he bears, and in the efficient discharge of his duties is winning a high reputation. It is fitting, therefore, that in this volume mention should be made of his ancestry and life.

A lifelong resident of Cecil County, Mr. Mackey was born in District No. 9, September 11, 1868, the son of Robert and Lydia (Yerkes) Mackey, natives, respectively, of Rock Church, Cecil County, and Bucks County, Pa. His father, who in youth learned the trade of a wheelwright, has long been a man of prominence in this part of the state, and for one term held the office of sheriff, in which position he enforced the law with a vigilance that made him a terror to evil doers. At this writing he is engaged in business in Fairview, District No. 4. His father, whose name was David, was also a native of this county. Our subject's maternal grandfather, Andrew Yerkes, was a member of an old and leading family of Bucks County, Pa. In the Mackey family there were three sons: Harvey H.; Andrew Jarrett, a farmer and wheelwright; and David Clinton, who is now in school.

When two years of age, the subject of this sketch was taken by his parents to Fairview, where he received his education in the common schools. He was a youth of seventeen when his father was elected sheriff of Cecil County, and, though so young, he served as deputy sheriff with the greatest efficiency. In fact, he proved so helpful in the office that he was retained as deputy under three sheriffs. In this way he gained thorough familiarity with every duty connected with the office, and as a natural result he became the people's choice for sheriff. In 1895 he was nominated, on the Democratic ticket, for the position, and was elected by a fair majority. Since boyhood he has taken an active part in local politics, and his influence as a politician reaches to all parts of the county. In personal appearance he is striking, possessing a fine physique, and being in height six feet and four and one-half inches. He entered upon the discharge of the duties of his office with the best wishes of a host of friends, and has acted in this capacity with credit to himself. He is a very energetic man, quick to see an emergency, and equally quick to devise means of overcoming it, in fact, this energy is one of the most noticeable traits of his character. Fraternally he is connected with the Independent Order of Odd Fellows and the Junior Order of American Mechanics. His marriage took place November 12, 1896, and united him with Margaret M. Biles, daughter of Charles R. Biles, a prominent farmer residing near Fairview.

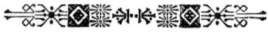

JAMES H. KENNEDY, M. D. To those who wish to make a success in any business or profession, the most thorough preparation is absolutely necessary. Especially is this true of the medical profession. The day has gone by when the "quack" of great pretensions but no learning can cope with the growing demands of the science, which calls for the most careful study and training on the part of its members. It may with justice be said of Dr. Kennedy that he prepared himself for his profession by most careful study in the university and has since kept abreast with every development in the science, having spared neither time nor pains in the acquirement of knowledge.

In looking up the genealogical history of the Kennedy family, we find that their first representative in America was the doctor's great-grandfather, John Kennedy, who came from the north of Ireland and settled in Harford County some time in the eighteenth century. It is probable that he rendered service as a patriot in the Revolution. His son, James, was born in this county and became a large land and slave owner here, his possessions including some valuable property that made him well-to-do. He served in the War of 1812 and was present at the battle of North Point. While he led a busy life, he found time for some recreation, and was known for miles around as the champion fox hunter in the neighborhood. Silas Baldwin Kennedy, the father of our subject, was born and spent his entire life in Harford County, and was a farmer by occupation. In 1834 he was appointed captain of the state militia, which position he filled for several years. In political belief he was a typical Democrat, true to the free-trade policy adopted by the party in its platform. Feeling that the institution of slavery was unjust, prior to the war he set free the many slaves that he owned. He possessed a splendid physique, and was active and strong until shortly before his death, which occurred when he was eighty-nine. His wife, who bore the maiden name of Eliza Cory, was a daughter of James and Hannah Cory, the former of whom was killed when in middle life. She is still living and is now about eighty years of age. Of her five children, two died young; the others are Elmira and Samuel L., who is a farmer and stockraiser of this county.

At Upper Cross Roads, Harford County, the subject of this sketch was born September 3, 1848. From an early age he displayed an aptitude for learning and a love of study that plainly indicated a professional bent of mind. The common schools furnished him with his primary education. At the age of sixteen he entered the Bethel Academy, where he took a course in Latin, Greek and mathematics. He then entered Washington University College of Physicians and Surgeons and conducted his medical studies there until his graduation with the class of 1874. For a few months afterward he was engaged as resident physician in a hotel at Afton, Va. In the fall of 1874 he opened an office in Aberdeen, where he has since been in continuous practice. For several years he has been president of the Harford County Medical Association and he is also a member of the state faculty. In things political he is a Democrat, but not active in public affairs. Fraternally he is identified with Aberdeen Lodge No. 187, A. F. & A. M.

Dr. Kennedy married a daughter of Dr. Thomas and Elizabeth (Hunter) Elliott. For many years Dr. Elliott was engaged in active practice in Aberdeen and here he died in 1872; Mrs. Elliott is still living and is seventy-five years of age. The three children of Dr. and Mrs. Kennedy are Elise, Ethel and Douglas Elliott. While professional matters have taken the principal portion of Dr. Kennedy's time and attention, he yet maintains close sympathy with all enterprises for the public good. Possessing the tastes of a naturalist, many of his leisure hours have been devoted to a study of birds and animals, and his knowledge concerning the fowl native to its locality is perhaps exceeded by none. He is an interesting writer and frequently writes for papers and magazines. Harper's Magazine, of April, 1897, contains an article from his pen, entitled, "Wild Things in Winter," which shows that he has been a thoughtful observer of the habits of canvas-back ducks, squirrels, crows, blue-jays, and many other species of wild fowl and birds known in this section of country.

LABAN LOW. Harford County is well known for the energy, enterprise and push of its farmers, and Laban Low stands in the van in this industry, and has shown much wisdom and good judgment in the conduct of agricultural affairs. He has led a quiet unobtrusive life, but he has done fine work in his own community and has devoted the greater part of his time and attention to the cultivation of his fine farm of two hundred acres and development of the resources of his vicinity. Such men deserve more mention than they ordinarily receive, and it is a privilege to here give a brief notice of the life of this wide-awake man of affairs. His entire life has been spent within the confines of Harford County and District No. 4, his birth having occurred here April 4, 1838, to Jeremiah and Rebecca (Fife) Low, both natives of Pennsylvania, for history of whom see the sketch of Rufus Low elsewhere in this volume.

The home farm was the scene of Laban Low's early labors, and a thorough and practical knowledge of agricultural affairs was acquired under the guidance of his father, who was a thrifty and intelligent tiller of the soil. Agricultural life was congenial to him and upon commencing life for himself he wisely chose it as his future work,

and to it he has ever devoted his attention. He has wisely increased the value of his property by making many improvements, and the neatness of his buildings and fences shows that he has not mistaken his calling. His financial prosperity has been due to his own efforts and his farm has been made a garden spot in the great commonwealth of Maryland. At the age of thirty-four years he married Miss Margaret A. Taylor, a native of this district, and to this union thirteen children have been given: Cora (deceased); Rebecca, Maud, Bessie, Clayton, Brittie, Ora B., J. Blaine, L. Ross, Anna, Martin, Milton and Chauncey. John Taylor, father of Mrs. Low, was a native of Harford County and here followed the occupation of farming for years.

Mr. Low has always been a staunch supporter of the principles of the Republican party and though he has never, in any sense of the term, been an office seeker, he has held the office of census enumerator and at the present time is the efficient postmaster of Corea. He has also held the position of school trustee in School No. 11, District No. 4. He discharges his duties in a capable and praiseworthy manner, as he has ever met all his responsibilities, and to the satisfaction of all concerned.

WILLIAM A. BRICKLEY. Many of the prominent citizens of Cecil County have spent their entire lives within its borders, and from the cultivation of the soil have accumulated a competency. One of this number is Mr. Brickley, an influential citizen and capable farmer residing in the northern part of District No. 5. The farm on which he resides consists of seventy-eight acres and he has two other farms of fifteen and thirty acres, which were purchased by him after the war. The property has been brought to its present cultivation through his untiring efforts, and is deservedly classed among the valuable estates of the district. It is provided with a set of buildings, each of which is adapted to its special purpose. Improved farming machinery has been introduced and the agricultural operations are conducted upon the basis of modern appliances and developments.

The Brickley family came to America from Germany and has been represented here for many generations. William, father of our subject, was a son of Joseph Brickley, both natives of this county. The former was a blacksmith by trade and carried on a shop for many years near the old homestead. He was seventy-six years of age at the time of his death. Politically he was a Republican after the organization of that party. Among the local offices which he held were those of road overseer and constable. A member of the Ebenezer Methodist Episcopal Church, he was ordained a local preacher and frequently had charge of services in his neighborhood. He was a member of the order of Knights of Pythias and held all the offices in his lodge. By his first wife, Margaret McMullen, he had five children, but two alone survive: David G. and William A., both residents of District No. 5. His second wife was Mrs. F. Lee, by whom he had six children, three living: George, in Virginia; Franklin, in this district; and Mary Elizabeth, wife of James Armour.

Within one-half mile of his present place of residence, the subject of this article was born July 22, 1833. In youth he learned the trade of a blacksmith under his father, but afterward turned his attention to farming. In September, 1861, he enlisted as a member of the Parnell Legion from Baltimore and served for two years and seven months, afterward re-enlisting in the First Maryland Infantry, and serving until he was discharged, in July, 1865, at the close of the war. While taking an active part in the battle of Five Forks, in September, 1864, he was wounded in the hip, but not seriously. When the war was over he bought the place where he has since engaged in general farming.

The political issues of the day receive the earnest attention of Mr. Brickley, who is a thoughtful student of current events. He has made somewhat of a study of politics, and gives his preference to the Republican party, the principles of which are, in his opinion, best calculated to promote the welfare of the people of the United States. A member of the Methodist Episcopal Church, he contributes liberally to religious and benevolent enterprises and his sympathies are with all Christian efforts. March 5, 1867, he was united in marriage with Miss Rachel Maxwell, daughter of David Maxwell, and a resident of District No. 6, this county. They are the parents of three children, two of whom are living, Nettie E. and Howard Newton, both at home.

DR. CROTHERS, M. D., has for twenty years been numbered among the leading physicians of Cecil County. Ability and energy have won him high rank in his profession, and his genuine personal worth has gained him the esteem of a large circle of friends. He was born in Rock Springs, Cecil County, in 1845, and on a farm was reared to manhood. He attended the district schools, where he familiarized himself with the elementary branches of learning, after which he became a student in West Nottingham Academy, and then entered the normal school in Millersville, Pa., where he was graduated in 1873. Desiring to enter the medical profession, he began his preparatory study in the office and under the direction of Prof. N. R. Smith, of Baltimore, and a year later entered medical college, where he graduated in the class of 1874. The following year he continued his medical studies in Bellevue Hospital College of New York City.

Dr. Crothers began the practice of medicine in Rowlandsville, Md., where he remained for three years, after which he spent eleven years as a successful and able practitioner of Colora. He remained at Vinegar Hill for one year, and then purchased his present farm of one hundred and seventy acres in District No. 6, Cecil County, where he has since maintained his residence. He is excellently qualified for the practice of medicine; his professional knowledge is extensive and accurate, and in his work he has met with gratifying success. His ability has secured to him a liberal patronage and his professional brethren accord him a high place in the ranks of the medical fraternity.

In 1883 the doctor married Miss Fannie Christie, and they have two interesting children, Roman R. and John C. Dr. Crothers belongs to the Presbyterian Church, to the Odd Fellows' lodge at Rising Sun, to the Oxford Medical Society and to the Cecil County Medical Society. He is a man of pleasant address, genial in manner and kindly in disposition. His sterling qualities of mind and heart have won him high regard and he is a welcome addition to the best circles of society.

FRED EMMORD. The old saying that "There is no excellence without great labor" has proved true in very many instances, and particularly so as regards the husbandman, for if he be successful in this line of human endeavor it necessitates earnest and persistent effort on his part extending over many years, as well as economy and prudence in his expenditures. A descendant of thrifty German stock and a farmer by inheritance, Mr. Emmord also possesses those principles of industry, integrity and determination that have ever been characteristic of the Teuton, and as a natural sequence his reward has been of a substantial nature, and he is now the owner of a fine farm of one hundred acres, which he carefully tills.

Mr. Emmord was born in Magnolia, Harford County, Md., November 27, 1854, and was named in honor of his father, who was born in Hanover, Germany, in 1813. In his boyhood days the latter accompanied his parents to this country, and the first home of the Emmords was established in the city of Baltimore, where Fred Emmord, Sr., secured employment on the Baltimore & Ohio Railroad when work was commenced on that line. He was an intelligent, well-educated German, who had previously practiced the profession of law, but after the lapse of a few years turned his attention to other pursuits. For about nine years he was overseer of a large farm in District No. 1, Harford County, but eventually purchased a tract of one hundred and one acres, in the same district, the interests of which he was actively engaged in looking after until his death, which occurred in 1883. Besides this farm he purchased the Collrain place, consisting of one hundred and thirty-five acres, in 1875. He always supported the principles of the Democratic party, but was never a political aspirant.

In his religious views Mr. Emmord was a follower of Martin Luther, was a liberal contributor to and a worthy member of the Lutheran Church, and for years was president and a member of the board of trustees. The upright life which he led won him universal respect, and in his own immediate neighborhood he wielded great influence for good, for in precept and example his aims were high and noble. In his early manhood he led to the altar Miss Louisa Bauersfeld, a daughter of John Bauersfeld, a native of Saxony, Germany, the result of which union was the birth of eight children: Henry, a merchant of Perryman, District No. 2; Fred; Molly, wife of Charles Kammer, a farmer of Harford County; Amelia, wife of Herman Hanson; Louisa, wife of Rev. A. R. Kuldell, of Allegeny, Pa.; and three deceased. The mother of these children is still living and has reached the age of seventy-four years.

The subject of this sketch received his initiatory training in the public schools of District No. 1, but later was placed in the public schools of Baltimore and still later attended a business college for some time. Having learned telegraphy, he secured a position as operator at the age of nineteen years, and followed this occupation successfully for four years. At the end of that time he returned to the parental roof and has since had charge of the home farm, which he conducts in a most satisfactory manner. The place is devoted to general farming, but much attention is also given to dairying, the milk being shipped to Baltimore. Mr. Emmord is a wide-awake, progressive young man, and to one of his temperament success is a fore-gone conclusion. He is unmarried.

WILLIAM S. NOBLE. Among the leading, wide-awake and successful business men of Harford County is the subject of this sketch, a well-known miller of Darlington. His life history most happily illustrates what may be attained by faithful and continued effort in carrying out an honest purpose. Integrity, activity and energy have been the crowning points of his success, and his connection with various business enterprises and industries has been of decided advantage to his section of the county, promoting its material welfare in no uncertain manner.

Mr. Noble first opened his eyes to the light in 1853, in Stafford, and his father, Benjamin Noble, also a native of Harford County, was born at Swansburg, near Havre de Grace. The family, which is of English origin, was founded here at an early day by Mark Noble, who located near Aberdeen; and James Noble, the grandfather of our subject, was born near Havre de Grace.

Throughout his entire business career Benjamin Noble followed milling at different places, including Wellington and Brandywine, Md., the old city mill in Baltimore, and also at Montgomery, Ala. In 1860 he came to Darlington and began operating the mill which his son William S. still conducts. He married Susannah Silver, a daughter of David Silver, and to them were born two children: Mary E., now the wife of David Hanway, of Bel Air, and William S. The father died in 1894, at the age of seventy-four years, honored and respected by all who knew him. The mother still survives, making her home with her son.

During his boyhood and youth, William S. Noble pursued his studies in both the public and private schools of Harford County, and at an early age began assisting his father in the mill, where he soon mastered the business in all its details. In 1869 they purchased of Jarrett Gover the milling property which our subject still owns, known as the Deer Creek Mill, it being situated on Deer Creek, near Glenville and Darlington, in District No. 5. For many years it was an old-fashioned burr mill, but in 1888 rollers were put in and the plant was entirely remodeled, so that it is now one of the best grist mills in the locality. It now has a capacity of forty barrels every twenty-four hours, and the product turned out is first-class in every particular. It is run by water equal to forty horse power, and is successfully operated by Mr. Noble, who is one of the most thorough, practical and reliable millers in this section of the state. In politics he is a stanch Democrat, and in religious belief is a Presbyterian, holding membership in Harmony Church. His life has been one of industry and perseverance, and the systematic, honorable methods he has followed have gained for him the confidence and esteem of the entire community.

HENRY W. GUILFOYLE, justice of the peace, and a business man of Whiteford, District No. 5, Harford County, was born in Ireland, October 16, 1846, and is the son of William and Eliza (Henderson) Guilfoyle, also natives of the Emerald Isle. Of a family of six children, he and his brother, Capt. John F., are the only survivors. Both his father and grandfather took an active part in the rebellion of 1798 in Ireland. In 1848, the father, accompanied by his wife and their two children, Henry W. and Mary E., crossed the Atlantic and settled in Baltimore, where he found employment in a lumber yard. In that city he continued to reside until his death. During the Civil War he was a soldier in the Union army.

The subject of this sketch has no recollection of his native land, as he was but two years of age at the time the family sought a home in the

United States. When he was about sixteen his parents died and thenceforward he was dependent upon his own resources. For a time he was employed by Frank Hamway, a woolen manufacturer of Harford County, but after working at that trade for two years he turned his attention to blacksmithing, which occupation he has since followed. At the age of twenty-one he married Maggie E. Hildt, who was born in Harford County, and a member of a Pennsylvania family. Their three children are John H., Priscilla E. and Mamie E., all of whom are married and doing well in life.

A man of excellent habits and fine principles, possessing in a large degree the traits of character that commend him to the confidence of all about him, Mr. Guilfoyle was the choice of the people for justice of the peace and was commissioned to that office by Governor Lowndes in 1896. Politically he has always been pronounced in his allegiance to Republican principles. He and his wife are active members of the Methodist Protestant Church and take an interest in the work of the congregation.

MANLY DRENNEN. The men who from time to time have been chosen to represent people of Cecil County as their officials have been almost invariably public-spirited citizens and men of intelligence. Of Mr. Drennen it may be said that in genuine public spirit, in untiring vigilance, in strict integrity and unfailing accuracy, he is the peer of them all. Since he first became connected with his present office, he has discharged its duties in a manner highly satisfactory, even to those who oppose him politically. The same accuracy and energy which characterized his private life are now manifested in his official capacity as treasurer of Cecil County, and while his influence was apparent in former years, it is naturally more noticeable in his present important and responsible position.

Like many of the well-known citizens of Elkton, Mr. Drennen is a native of this village, he having been born here February 3, 1864, the only son of Thomas and Anna E. (Manly) Drennen. His grandfather, Jonathan Drennen, was born in Newark, Del., in 1806, and learned the wheelwright's trade, which he followed for many years, and in addition he filled a number of local offices of responsibility. For several years he was postmaster of Newark, and at different times held minor offices. In the Methodist Church he was an active worker. From Delaware he removed to Maryland and his last years were passed in Cecil County.

Thomas Drennen was born in Newark, Del., in 1834, and in early manhood came to Elkton, where for many years he was the proprietor of a large dry-goods establishment, in this way accumulating a small fortune. In 1880 he retired from the mercantile business in order to accept the position of secretary and treasurer of the Cecil County Fire Insurance Company, and in the latter capacity he was employed until his death, in May, 1896. He was a man highly respected by all who knew him and had the full confidence of the people. His connections, religiously, were with the Presbyterian Church, in which he acted as a trustee. His wife was a daughter of Capt. Nicholas Manly, who in early life was commander of a vessel, but later retired to a farm near Elkton and there passed the remaining days of his life. (For a more complete history of the family, see sketch of Nicholas P. Manly, in this work.) Mrs. Drennen and her daughter own and occupy a beautiful home on North Main Street, Elkton. Her other daughter, Annie Highland, is the wife of John M. Tucker, who succeeded his father-in-law as secretary and treasurer of the Cecil County Mutual Fire Insurance Company.

The education received by the subject of this sketch in the Elkton Academy and Eastman's Business College was of a practical nature, fitted to qualify him for business pursuits. For four years he was interested in the mercantile business and then embarked in the fire and life insurance business, in which he built up a large patronage. In 1894 he was appointed county treasurer, and the following year he was tendered the position by election upon the Democratic ticket. He is one of the most popular officials the county has ever had, for he is genial, thorough and efficient. In local affairs he takes an interest, especially in regard to educational matters, and is now treasurer and trustee of the Elkton Academy. Fraternally he is connected with the Independent Order of Odd Fellows. November 26, 1883, he was united in marriage with Alice S. Donnell, daughter of Andrew Donnell, a retired business man of Newark, Del. Mrs. Drennen is well educated and refined, and is a member of the Episcopal Church. Two children bless the union, Manly and Elizabeth G.

MISS ESTHER ELIZABETH EWING is a representative of one of the prominent and highly esteemed families of District No. 6, Cecil County. Her great-grandfather, Samuel Ewing, a native of Glasgow, Scotland, was the founder of the family in the new world, and on his arrival here he located on the farm now owned and occupied by our subject. He bore an important part in the early development and upbuilding of the county and experienced all the trials and hardships of pioneer life. Establishing a grist and sawmill, he engaged in their operation in connection with farming and met with a well-deserved success in his undertakings. He was married in the Second Presbyterian Church of Philadelphia, which was attended by the president and members of congress when Philadelphia was the seat of government. The pastor of this church was Rev. John Ewing, D. D., one of the most eminent divines of his day.

Amos Ewing, Jr., the father of our subject, was born on the old homestead July 21, 1793, a son of Amos Ewing, Sr., whose birth also occurred on that place. There the former continued to engage in agricultural pursuits and milling throughout life, having erected a new saw and grist mill. He married Miss Mary Steel, and they became the parents of four children. Ambrose, like his father, followed both the occupations of farming and milling. He died in 1890, leaving a widow and three children. Miss Ewing, of this review, is next in order of birth. John S., who resided on the old homestead, died in 1891, leaving a family of four children. Mary R. is the wife of William E. Gillespie, of Hazleton, Pa. The father was called to his final rest in 1872, at the age of eighty, and his estimable wife died in 1886. Both were members of the Presbyterian Church, in which he was an elder for more than fifty years. They merited and received the warmest confidence and esteem of their fellow-citizens, who appreciated their sterling worth and many excellent traits of character.

After the death of the father the sons took charge of the old homestead until they, too, were called to the world beyond. The place is now owned by Miss Ewing. It embraces two hundred and seventy-five acres of farming land as rich as can be found in the county, and is ably managed by its present owner. She is a consistent member of the Presbyterian Church, and is much beloved by everyone with whom she comes in contact.

STEPHEN H. FORD. For some men once prominent in the public affairs of Cecil County the curtain of death has fallen, the battle of life is finished. The place that once knew them knows them no more. But the men among whom they labored, the needy whom they assisted and the friends to whom their noble characters endeared them, have not forgotten them. Judged by weeks and months, a long time has elapsed since the subject of this review passed from the scenes of time, but his memory is still green in the hearts of all who knew him, and the frequent mention of his name, even at this time, shows how indelibly his life work was stamped upon the history of his locality. He was not an old man (being forty-six years of age) when death came to him, April 25, 1884; but life is rightly measured, not by years, but by intensity; and judged by that standard his life was a long one.

A native of Maryland, Mr. Ford was given a good education, attending school in Pottstown, Pa., and Newark, Del. He was a young man when the dark cloud of war overshadowed our nation. His sympathies were with the south in the struggle and he enlisted in the Confederate service, becoming identified with the navy. During the period of his service he endured all the hardships and perils of war, but received no injury. At one time, however, he was taken prisoner by the northern troops, being captured under the tree where, years before, the Indian maiden, Pocahontas, had saved the life of Captain Smith. After the war was ended he settled upon a plantation in District No. 1, Cecil County, to the supervision of which his remaining years were given. He always voted the Democratic ticket and took an interest in public affairs. For a time he was tax collector of District No. 1.

In 1870 Mr. Ford married Lenette A. Ellison, who was born in Delaware February 25, 1845, the daughter of Lewis P. and Susan M. (Suckert) Ellison, natives, respectively, of New Jersey and Pennsylvania. The Ellison family consisted of twelve children and seven of these are living: Susan T., Cecilia A., Lenette E., James S., Priscilla T., Lydia D. and William S. Mrs. Ford's grandfather, James Ellison, was born in New Jersey, and was by occupation a farmer, which was also the calling of his father, James, Sr., a soldier of the Revolution. William Suckert, the maternal grandfather of Mrs. Ford, was a physician in Philadelphia and also proprietor of a drug store there. His brother, George Suckert, was a soldier in the Revolutionary War and was stationed near the present home of Mrs. Ford. At the age of eleven years Mrs. Ford was brought to Maryland by her parents and here she has since resided, with the exception of three years spent in a boarding school at Oxford, Pa. Her five children are Mary S., Lenette E., J. Arthur,

Stephen H. and Susan S. In religious belief she is connected with St. Stephen's Episcopal Church. The Ford estate, upon which she resides, contains six hundred acres of well-improved land and is divided into two farms, known, respectively, as Dividing and Ford's Landing, each with three hundred acres, the latter being the home of Mrs. Ford. She is a lady who has many warm friends in this community. Whether entertaining in her pleasant home those who are proud to call themselves her friends, whether mingling with refined and aristocratic men and women in select social circles, or going upon errands of mercy to the suffering and the sad, at all times and under all circumstances she shows that nobility of character that is always its possessor's greatest charm.

WILLIAM L. SMITH, M. D., is a leading and successful physician of Jarrettsville, Harford County. Fortunate is he who has back of him an honorable ancestry, and happy should he be if his lines of life are cast in harmony therewith. The doctor is a representative of one of the oldest and most prominent families of Maryland, whose history is inseparably connected with the annals of the state.

Richard Smith, the first of the family of whom we have record, died at Hall's Croft in 1667. He came to the state about 1649, and his wife, Eleanor, about 1651. As appears from the land records in Annapolis under date of October 7, 1662, Richard Smith, Gentleman, entered rights for one hundred acres of land with dwelling house on the west side of Solomon's Creek. May 27, 1655, he was appointed attorney-general for the province of Maryland, and held office until 1660. He represented Calvert County in the provincial legislature from April 16, 1661, until his death, in 1667. His son, Richard Smith, Jr., married three times. His second wife was Barbara Rousby, widow of J. Rousby, of Calvert County, and afterwards Mrs. Maria Johanna Lawther, widow of Mr. Lawther of the Queen's Life

Guards, and a daughter of Charles Somerset, and granddaughter of Lord John Somerset, Marquis of Worcester.

Col. Walter Smith, the second son of Richard and Eleanor Smith, served as vestryman of All Saint's parish from 1702 until April 2, 1711. Walter Smith, Jr., son of Col. Walter Smith and his wife, Rachel, was made vestryman April 16, 1716, but refused to take the oath of office. He was afterward appointed and qualified, May 6, 1729. His son, Dr. Clement Smith, married Barbara Ann, daughter of Dr. Patrick and Mary (Brooke) Linn, and they became parents of ten children, namely: Patrick Linn; Dr. Walter, who married Esther Belt; Richard, who married Miss Peter and left three daughters, Barbara, Harriet and Carni; Alexander Lawson, who commanded the militia of Calvert County about 1787, and married Miss Griffith; Dr. Clement, who was born in 1756, and was married; Dr. Joseph Simlee, of Frederick County, who married Elizabeth, daughter of Dr. T. Price, and died in Taneytown; John Addison, who died unmarried; Mary Smith, who became the wife of Henry Hunt; Susan, who died unmarried; and Rachel.

Dr. Walter Smith died about 1795. He married Esther Belt, who died in Georgetown August 29, 1796. Their son, Joseph, by his wife, Lucy Smith, had two sons, William and Anthony. The former died May 22, 1809. He married Middleton Belt, daughter of Middleton and Mary Ann Belt, of Montgomery County, December 29, 1796. Their children were as follows: Emily, born December 9, 1797, died December 14, 1808; Mary Ann, born August 27, 1800, died October 14, 1812; Lucy Middleton, born December 20, 1802, married F. B. Smith, and her second husband was R. Estep; Elizabeth, born March 20, 1806, became the wife of Mr. Bootes; Annie Maria, born September 30, 1808, married Anthony Hyde; William Emily, born December 9, 1809, married Dr. Granville Farquaher. After the death of the father of this family his widow married his brother, Anthony Smith, in December, 1813, and by that marriage had three children: Mary Sophia, born October 14, 1814, died October 6, 1818; David Porter, born June 26, 1817, died November 3, 1853, of yellow fever, at Bagdad Mills, Fla.; and his wife, Emma Wood, of Vermont, died October 18, 1853, of the same disease, as did also their infant child; and Sophia Middleton, born April 18, 1821, died January 14, 1838.

The Belt family, with which the Smith family intermarried, is also one of prominence in Maryland. Records show that Middleton Belt and Mary Ann Dyer were married at St. John's Church, Surrey, England, March 25, 1763. Their daughter, Anna Maria, was born in Bristol, England, on the 24th of November, 1771. Another daughter, Middleton, the great-great-grandmother of our subject, was born in Virginia, April 24, 1777. Others of the same family are Mary Ann, who was born in Fairfax, Va., March 29, 1779; Clarissa, born in Georgetown, Md., November 10, 1781; Middleton, a son, born in Georgetown, September 13, 1785; William Dyer, born in Montgomery County, Md., February 26, 1788; and James Harrick, born January 31, 1792, in Montgomery County. The father of this family died January 15, 1807, aged sixty years; and his wife died in Georgetown, December 18, 1830, aged eighty-five. Their eldest daughter died in Chillicothe, Ohio, in April, 1808. Mary Ann died in Georgetown, September 17, 1783.

Mordecai Smith, the great-grandfather of Dr. Smith of this review, was born December 9, 1737, and married Phœbe Finch, born November 3, 1740. Their son, Mordecai Finch (known as General Smith), born November 25, 1777, married Miss Kent, of Calvert County, and died July 19, 1834. Fielder Bowie Smith, the doctor's grandfather, was born November 14, 1775, and was married June 22, 1802, to Sallie S. Plummer. Their children were: Mordecai, who was born in 1803, and died July 19, 1834; Sarah Ann, Mrs. Nathan Childs, born September 15, 1805, died March 14, 1826; Mrs. Eliza Ann Boswell, born February 8, 1809, died February 9, 1826; and Mrs. Phœbe Finch Boswell, born in June, 1810, died in October, 1872.

Fielder Bowie Smith married Lucy Middleton Smith, September 22, 1824. Their children were:

Elizabeth Ann, born October 6, 1825, and died October 2, 1827; Fielder Bowie, Jr., born February 5, 1828; William Daniel, born March 18, 1830; Maria Louisa, born July 26, 1832; Eleanor Stewart, born October 6, 1834, and died April 28, 1835; Mordecai Finch, born May 14, 1836, and died May 21, 1836; David Porter, born November 27, 1838; Mary Sophia, born May 13, 1841, and died February 9, 1864; Henry Clay, born May 7, 1844, and died June 20, 1845. Of this family Fielder Bowie married Rebecca Bradley, March 14, 1850; Maria Louisa became the wife of Septimus D. Sewell, April 30, 1850; William Daniel married Adeline Bradley, September 16, 1856; David Porter married Martha L. Chaney, October 20, 1863; Mary S. married Charles W. Owens, October 16, 1864. Fielder Bowie Smith, the grandfather of our subject, died in June, 1844, and his widow was married August 22, 1848, to Richard Estep. She died August 17, 1877, aged seventy-four years.

The parents of Dr. Smith have a family of four children: Fielder B., Mary L., Andrew P. and William L. The last-named was born in Maryland, December 18, 1862, and was reared and educated on a farm in Calvert County. At the age of seventeen he entered the Maryland Agricultural College in Prince George County, where he pursued his studies for two years, after which he returned home and began reading medicine under the direction of Dr. Lewis A. Griffith. He also attended the College of Physicians and Surgeons of Baltimore, and was graduated from that institution in the spring of 1887. He is now successfully engaged in practice in District No. 4, Harford County. He has made a close study of his profession, his knowledge is comprehensive and accurate, and he ranks among the skilled and leading physicians in this section of the state.

In the fall of 1887 Dr. Smith married Miss Eleanor O. Smith, a native of Calvert County. Her father, Dr. John S. Smith, also a native of that county, practiced medicine at Smithville with excellent success for many years. His children are Frank O., Gertrude, Eleanor O., R. Percy and Allen W. The doctor and his wife had two children, but lost the younger, Anna B., at the age of three years. Miriam L. is still at home. Dr. and Mrs. Smith hold membership in the Methodist Episcopal Church South. His political support is given the Democracy. He is a young man of superior ability, of sterling worth and of noble purpose. His courteous, genial manner has won him the regard of all, and he has a large circle of friends in Harford County.

THOMAS M. TYSON was born October 27, 1843, upon the farm where he now resides, in District No. 5, Cecil County. He is one of a family of twelve children, of whom six are living, those besides himself being Emily C., who is married and resides in Conshohocken, Pa.; Margaret J., a widow, living in Media, Pa.; Sarah K., who is married and lives near the old home; John P., a resident of Pennsylvania; and I. B., of Media, Pa. The father of this family, John W. Tyson, was a member of an English family that settled in Maryland many generations ago. Throughout life he engaged in farming here. Politically he was first an old-line Whig, later a Democrat, and finally a Republican. At one time he held the office of constable. He was identified with the Methodist Episcopal Church and was one of its influential workers. His death occurred November 29, 1896. His wife, Sarah Jane, was a daughter of Cloud Carter, a farmer of Cherryhill, Cecil County; she died in September, 1891.

In the schoolhouse near his father's home, our subject gained the rudiments of his education, and later he was a student at Southampton, in this county. August 13, 1862, he enlisted as a member of Company A, Eighth Maryland Regiment, and served from that time until he was honorably discharged, June 28, 1865. After his return home he farmed the old place, after which he bought the store that he has since conducted. He makes his home at Mechanics Valley, and gives his attention to the management of his business. Politically he is a Republican, fraternally is identified with the Independent Order of Odd Fellows, and in religious connections is associated with the Methodist Episcopal congregation, being church and parsonage trustee. December 8, 1869, he married Lydia Field, daughter of John R. Field, of this county. They have one daughter, Mamie, wife of William K. Blake.

JOHN A. LAMBERT, of North East, was born at the family home near this place October 13, 1844. He was a son of Adam Lambert, a native of Lancaster County, Pa., and an iron worker and farmer by occupation. At the age of seventy-six, he is now living in Chester County, Pa. Politically he is a Democrat, and in religious belief holds connection with the Methodist Episcopal Church. He married Mary Reed Adams, a descendant of George M. Reed, of Delaware, one of the signers of the Declaration of Independence. She was a daughter of John Adams, who moved to Cecil County in 1840, but six years later went to Pennsylvania. She is still living and is now eighty-one years of age. Her family consists of the following children: Susan, wife of Benjamin Farnan, of Kimballville, Pa.; John A.; Mary A., who married Knox Reed, of Hickory Hill, Chester County, Pa.; Martha; Matthew Watson, of Lewisville, Chester County, Pa.; Lydia, Mrs. Harry Lemon, of West Grove, Pa.; Robert, of Easton, Md.; and Caleb, of Oxford, Chester County, Pa.

For one year our subject was a pupil in the public school at Pine Grove, Chester County, Pa. He then attended school in this district, near Mechanics Valley, for one year, and for a short time was a pupil in the school at North East, also at Oak Grove. His attendance at school was limited to the winter months, as in the summer season he was obliged to assist in the cultivation of the farm. Like his father, he learned the trade of an iron worker. From the time he was sixteen years until he was forty-eight he was employed in the McCullough iron works, and during most of that time was a shingler or iron drawer, being considered a first-class mechanic and skilled workman. In 1892 he resigned his position and since then has been town bailiff, tax collector and auctioneer. In politics he is a Republican, in religion a member of the Methodist Episcopal Church, and fraternally is connected with the Junior Order of American Mechanics and the Knights of Pythias.

The first wife of Mr. Lambert, who died in 1871, was Georgianna, daughter of Robert Barrett, of North East. The only child of this union is Ida M., who is married and lives in West Grove, Chester County, Pa. Afterward Mr. Lambert married Emily Veach, of District No. 1. She died in 1886, leaving a daughter, Laura, who is now engaged in teaching school. The present wife of Mr. Lambert is Harriet L., daughter of Enoch Johnson, of College Green.

D. H. RICHARDSON, M. D., of District No. 9, Cecil County, was born in 1851, in District No. 8, and is a son of Joseph and Margaret (McCullough) Richardson, of the same place. During the Revolutionary War three brothers by the name of Richardson came from England to America, one of whom settled on the Elk River, another near Wilmington, Del., and the third in Kent County. The doctor is a descendant of the first of these. Throughout the most of his life Joseph Richardson followed the carpenter's trade in District No. 6. The Democratic party received his vote, but he was not active in public affairs. By his marriage ten children were born, of whom six are now living: D. H.; William, of District No. 6; Elizabeth, wife of Zachariah Leonard; George, of District No. 6; Annie, Mrs. Robert Aiken; and Joseph P., of Wilmington. The father still resides in District No. 6, and though eighty years of age is still in the enjoyment of good health.

Dr. Richardson was educated in West Nottingham Academy, and completed his course of study at the age of twenty-one, after which he taught for five years in the academy and for seven years in public schools. He then began the study of medicine under a physician in Rising Sun, and on the completion of his studies he commenced to practice in this district, going one year later to Brick Meeting House, where he has resided since 1886. In politics he affiliates with the Democrats. By his marriage to Miss M. A. Williamson of Chester County, he has two children, Daisy C. and Margaret A. In fraternal relations he is connected with the Senior Order of American Mechanics, and has been through all the chairs and served as representative to state and national council. He is a member of the Zion Presbyterian Church, which his family also attend.

HON. ALBERT CONSTABLE, one of the most prominent attorneys of Elkton, was born in the city of Baltimore October 24, 1838, the son of Albert and Hannah (Archer) Constable, natives respectively of Kent and Harford Counties. Both the Archer and Constable families have been prominent in their respective localities for a number of generations and have been noted for superior intelligence and culture. Dr. John Archer, an ancestor of our subject, was the first graduate of medicine in the United States and attained prominence in the profession. Albert Constable, son of John Constable, was born June 3, 1805, and spent his boyhood days on the home farm. On arriving at manhood he entered the legal profession, which he followed in Bel Air, then in Baltimore. From 1851 to 1855 he was circuit judge for the district comprising Harford and Baltimore Counties; and held the office at the time of his death, August 22, 1855. A Democrat in politics, he was elected to the legislature on the party ticket and served in that body in 1846-47. His influence was felt in many public measures and was potent in the advancement of local enterprises. His wife, who, like himself, was a member of the Episcopal Church, died in 1866. Of their family Albert and his sister, Isabel S., are the survivors, two daughters being deceased. Isabel S. is the wife of S. E. Gittings, of Washington; Johanna died unmarried; Alice became the wife of John C. Gittings, of Baltimore County.

When a boy our subject was the recipient of excellent advantages. He attended school in Norwich and New London, Conn., and Newark, Del. In the year 1861 he began in legal practice at Towson and two years later removed his office to Elkton, his present location. In 1876 he was elected to the legislature, where he was chairman of the judiciary committee and prominent in his advocacy of all progressive measures. In 1866 he married Elizabeth Black Groome, who was born in Elkton, daughter of Col. John C. Groome, a prominent lawyer. Eight children were born of the union that are still living, four being deceased. The survivors are Albert, an attorney; John Groome, Henry Lyttleton, Reginald, William P., Arline, Catherine and Mary.

JTHOMAS WEBSTER, who is engaged in the canning business at Harford Furnace, Harford County, was born in District No. 3 of this county. He is the son of John Lester and Susan (Brown) Webster, natives, respectively, of Districts Nos. 3 and 2, the former of whom died in September, 1869, and the latter in June, 1885. His paternal grandfather was John Webster, and his maternal, Jacob Brown, of Primrose. The family of which he is a member consists of six children, those besides himself being Jacob B., of District No. 3; William E.; Mary E.; Martha A. S., Mrs. J. F. Mitchell; and Sarah, all of the same district.

At the age of twenty years the subject of this sketch married and rented a farm, upon which he began agricultural pursuits. In 1849 he was given charge of the old Harford Furnace property, where he remained until 1887, and from that time was in charge of the farm owned by Mrs. Walsh, until March, 1897. At this writing he is engaged in canning tomatoes. Politically he is a Democrat, but is not narrow in his views, voting for the man rather than the party. In the Presbyterian Church he holds the office of elder.

April 18, 1867, Mr. Webster married Susannah Mitchell, daughter of Alfred Mitchell, of Churchville. They have three daughters, namely: Carrie M.; Ann L., who is engaged in teaching in Alabama; and Harriet, at home.

HON. CHARLES E. BEATTY, judge of the orphans' court of Cecil County, was born October 8, 1843, on Elk River, about six miles from North East, his present home. His father, William, was a son of Arthur and Caroline Beatty, the former a native of County Tyrone, Ireland. William, who was born in Delaware, removed to Cecil County, and at different times was variously employed. In his youth he was a contractor and engaged in railroad work. By trade he was a millwright. In 1848 he entered the drug business in North East, establishing the first drug store here. Politically he was a Democrat and for ten years served as magistrate. In the Methodist Episcopal Church he officiated as class leader, trustee and superintendent of the Sunday-school for many years. He died in 1882, at the age of eighty-two.

After having attended the public schools for some years, the subject of this sketch entered Port Edward Institute in Washington County, N. Y., where he remained for two years. In 1861 he went to Baltimore and secured employment in a retail drug store, where he remained for six years, meantime learning the business. Going to St. Louis in 1867, he took a position with the medical purveying department of the United States army, and remained there as a druggist for two and one-half years, having in his charge $3,000,000 in supplies. His next position was with the wholesale drug house of E. C. Pike, for whom he traveled in Illinois and the northwest. In 1871, when Mr. Pike sold his patent medicine business to the Collins Drug Company, Mr. Beatty entered the employ of this concern, and for them traveled in the south and later in the southwest and west, remaining with them for nine years. The increasing feebleness of his father caused him to return to Maryland in 1880, and he then took charge of the drug business owned by his father.

Fraternally Judge Beatty is a member of the Independent Order of Odd Fellows and is recording secretary of the lodge, in which he is the oldest member in the town. Politically he is a Democrat. For seven years he was register of voters, and since 1895 he has served as judge of the orphans' court. With many of the departments of work connected with the Methodist Episcopal Church he is closely identified, and at this writing is secretary of the missionary society and secretary and librarian of the Sunday-school. October 7, 1875, he married Margaret Kelly, of St. Louis, Mo., the daughter of parents who came to this country from the Isle of Man. She died in December, 1892, leaving five children, namely: Arthur, who is engaged in the drug business in Philadelphia; Annie, Drew, Laura and Margaret.

REV. GILES BUCKNER COOKE has been rector of North Elk parish, diocese of Easton, since July 18, 1891. The church to which he ministers and whose welfare is so dear to his heart is one of the oldest in Maryland. The bricks used in the construction of the house of worship were brought from England and it is said that the Bible, prayer book and communion set were donated by Queen Anne of England. The original building was erected in 1690, and on the same site the present structure was built in 1734. Many are the changes that have been made since those days, and could the old walls, now gray with age, speak in human voice, what a story they might tell of days of terror when the land was infested by the hated "redcoats;" of the early days of the government when the foundation of our nation was laid; of years of progress and advancement; then of darker days, when the soldiers in the blue and those in the gray met on many a blood-stained battlefield.

The Cooke family was first represented in America by Mordecai Cooke, who came from England in 1650 and was sheriff of Gloucester, Va., in 1698. John K. Cooke, father of our subject, was a lumber merchant and a man of means. Politically he was a Democrat and a leading politician of Portsmouth, Va., of which place he was at one time postmaster. He went to the Mexican War as first lieutenant of Company F, Virginia Regiment, and was made provost marshal after reaching the front. He was also in the southern army during the Civil War and served as postmaster of General Lee's army, the army of northern Virginia. After the war he returned to Portsmouth and retired to private life. His death occurred February 6, 1887. He married Fannie Bracken, of Gloucester County, Va.; she died in 1867, leaving a son and three daughters, namely: Giles Buckner; Margaret, wife of Littleton White, of Portsmouth, Va.; Ella Mason, Mrs. J. W. Chandler, of Caroline County, Va., and Betty P., wife of J. W. Palmer, of Brunswick County, Va.

The subject of this sketch was born in Portsmouth, Va., May 13, 1838. He graduated from the Virginia Military Institute in 1859 and afterward taught school and read law until April, 1861, when he entered the Confederate army as a private. Afterward he was promoted successively to lieutenant, captain and major, and also served on the staff of several generals as assistant adjutant. From November, 1864, to the close of the war, he was on the staff of Gen. Robert E. Lee. The uniform which he wore while in service was given, after the surrender, to his nephew, Rev. John K. White, and the latter afterward wrote a poem, "The Old Gray Coat," that was inspired by the sight of the uniform and a recollection of the dark war days. The poem has fifteen stanzas and is beautiful in thought and effective in rhythmic harmony. Since the close of the war Mr. Cooke has devoted himself to the preaching of the Gospel, and by his noble Christian life, no less than by his earnest preaching, has led many to accept the Gospel of Christ. October 19, 1870, he married Mrs. Martha F. (Mallory) Southall, who remained his devoted helpmate until her death, January 2, 1894.

HON. R. L. THOMAS was born in Newcastle County, Del., June 30, 1809, and died in Elkton, Md., June 17, 1888, when lacking only a few days of being seventy-nine years of age. He was a son of Samuel and Hannah Thomas, the latter of Scotch ancestry. When he was a small child, his father engaged as manager for General Foreman on the latter's elegant estate, known as "Rose Hill," situated in Sassafras Neck, Cecil County, where the family continued to reside for some years. The earliest recollections of our subject are associated with the passing of the British barges, under Admiral Cockburn, up the Sassafras River, and the burning of Georgetown, on the Kent side of the river, in May, 1813. When fifteen years of age he was apprenticed to a woolen manufacturer at Stanton, Delaware, but after three years his employer failed and he was thrown upon his own resources. During all of this time he had the benefit of only forty days' schooling, and in later years acknowledged himself as chiefly indebted to the home and Sunday-school for the instruction he received.

Until 1834 Mr. Thomas worked at his trade in Cecil County. In that year he established his home in North East, where he embarked in the mercantile business in 1842, and for many years remained the leading merchant of the town. Honesty in business transactions was his motto as a business man. He was persevering and energetic and gave close attention to every detail of the work. During all periods of business depression he maintained an unshaken credit and enjoyed the confidence of the wholesale men with whom he dealt as well as of the community where he resided. Always a Democrat, he was appointed postmaster under President Tyler and again under President Polk. As an official he was obliging and faithful. Though he had neither time nor inclination to be a politician, he was nevertheless an active worker for his party and his judgment was highly respected. In 1849 and 1854 he was chosen a member of the Maryland legislature. In the former session he took an active part in securing the passage of the charter for the Cecil Bank at Ft. Deposit, and was an advocate of the act providing a convention for the framing of a new constitution for the state. In 1854 he was a zealous supporter of all measures before the legislature for the promotion of temperance. As a legislator he was esteemed for his business qualifications, his integrity and devotion to the interests of his constituents.

During his apprenticeship Mr. Thomas became the subject of deep religious convictions, and in 1830 he connected himself with the Methodist Episcopal Church, of which he has since remained a useful member, always active and liberal in contributions to its benevolences. In 1830 he married Sarah Jane, daughter of Charles and Mary Johnson, of Cecil County. She died childless in 1838. In 1854 he married Ruth Ann, daughter of John and Martha Jane McCracken, of North East. This lady died in 1867, leaving the following-named children: Martha Ruth, who married Philip Ricards; Sarah Rebecca, wife of Dr. Theodore A. Worrell; Mary Ann, Mrs. Thomas W. Harnon; Elizabeth, wife of Theodore Blackwell; Richard L., Emily and Ida.

JOHN S. SIMCOE, of North East, was born at Carpenters Point, Cecil County, May 18, 1831, and he is a descendant of George Simcoe, a Scotchman, who upon coming to America settled in Cecil County. The father of John S. was William Simcoe, a farmer and a man of prominence in public affairs, having served his district in the legislature and holding other offices of trust. For many years he was a steward in the Methodist Church. He married Rebecca Cazier, a native of Cecil County, and a member of a prominent family here; her father was one of the defenders of Baltimore during the War of 1812. The family of William and Rebecca Simcoe consisted of thirteen children, of whom the following survive: George, of Bayview; John S.; Louise and Nicholas.

At the age of sixteen John S. Simcoe began to work upon his father's farm, and continued there until 1863, when he entered the mercantile business at North East, remaining in this business for five years. Since then he has not been engaged in business, but still owns a farm and considerable property in town. A Democrat in politics, he has been a power in local affairs, but has never sought office for himself. In religious belief he is identified with the Episcopal Church and is one of its vestrymen. December 6, 1881, he married Mary Jones, of Cecil County.

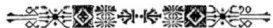

HAROLD WALSH, a lawyer by profession and a member of the Harford bar, is, however, giving his attention principally to the management and cultivation of the old family homestead, where he was born and where he still resides. It is situated at Jerusalem Mills, District No. 1, Harford County, and contains two hundred and fifty acres, in addition to which, Mr. Walsh has a farm of six hundred acres lying on the Gunpowder River.

The first of the Walsh family in this country was the grandfather of our subject, John Walsh, who was born in Ireland and settled in Baltimore, where he engaged in the lumber business. John Carroll Walsh, father of our subject, was born in Baltimore, and at the age of seventeen went to Ft. Madison, Iowa, where he bought land and remained for four years. In addition, he also purchased property in Illinois. On returning to Maryland, he bought the place in Harford County where he continued to reside until December 1, 1894, the date of his death. He was one of the leading men of his district and was active in politics as a member of the Democratic party. In 1868 he was elected to the state senate, where he served so efficiently that he was re-elected at the expiration of his term. For many years he was a director of the Baltimore & Ohio Railroad Company. He was one of the founders of the Maryland Agricultural College, in which he was a trustee until he died. For many years he was president of the Mutual Fire Insurance Company of Harford County. His membership was in the Catholic Church and to its doctrines he always faithfully adhered.

The marriage of John Carroll Walsh united him with Amanda Lee, daughter of Dr. Ralph Lee, one of the leading physicians of Washington, D. C. She is still living and is now seventy-eight years of age. Besides her son, she has a daughter, Mary Alice. Our subject received his education in the district schools and Washington and Lee University, at Lexington Va., from which he graduated in 1876. Politically he votes the Democratic ticket.

GEN. A. W. EVANS. A man's reputation is the property of the world. The laws of nature have forbidden isolation. Every human being submits to the controlling influence of others, or as a master spirit wields a power either for good or evil on the masses of mankind. There can be no impropriety in justly scanning the acts of any man as they affect his public and business relations. If he is honest and eminent in his chosen field of labor investigation will brighten his fame. Prominent among the men who have devoted the best years of their life to the service of their country is General Evans, of Elkton, Cecil County, Md.

He was born in that place July 6, 1829, and is a son of Amos A. Evans, M. D., who was born in 1785, and was a graduate of Hahnemann Medical College, and also Dr. Ruskin's College, University of Pennsylvania. In 1817 he opened an office in Elkton, where he successfully engaged in practice until his death. From 1808 until 1824 he served as ensign in the United States navy under Commodore Bubridge, was a strong Whig in politics and took quite an active and prominent part in public affairs. He died in January, 1848. His father, John Evans, was born in 1760, and departed this life in 1823. He was one of the leading business men of Cecil County, making his home on the Big Elk, where he followed farming and also engaged in the manufacture of iron. Robert Evans, the father of John, was born in Cecil County, became a large land owner of this locality, and was quite well off at the time of his death, in 1775. He was the son of John Evans, who was probably born in Wales in 1680, and settled at Iron Hill, Newcastle County, Del., in 1725. His death occurred at Nottingham, Md., in 1738. The mother of our subject, who bore the maiden name of Mary Oliver, was born in Beverley, Mass., in 1795, was reared in Boston, and died January, 1881.

During his boyhood General Evans attended the Elkton Academy, and later entered Harvard College, where he pursued his studies until the death of his father. Entering West Point in 1848, he graduated from that institution with the class of 1852, and as a member of the United States Cavalry served for several years in Indian Territory. During 1858 and 1859 he was stationed in Utah under Gen. Albert Sidney Johnston, was then in New Mexico until 1863, and was later in Virginia until the surrender of Lee, after which he was ordered to Texas, and subsequently to New Mexico and Arizona. Later he served in the department of the Platte, being located at different times in Nebraska, Wyoming and Dakota. He was in active service until 1883, when he retired and returned to his boyhood home in Elkton. Members of his family have taken quite a prominent part in the political history of the state; including his brother, Alexander Evans, a well-known lawyer, who was born in 1818 and died in 1888. In early life he was a surveyor and helped to lay out the railroad through Elkton, and later represented his district for three terms in congress.

General Evans was united in marriage with Miss Susan A. Duite, of Elkton, a daughter of Aaron G. Duite, who was born in County Longford, Ireland, and belonged to an old and prominent family of that country. He accompanied his father, Ed Duite, on his emigration to the new world, and located first in Cincinnati. He became quite well-to-do and was widely and favorably known. The general and Mrs. Evans occupy a high position in social circles and have the respect and esteem of all who know them.

REV. WILLIAM A. WISE, of North East, was born in Newcastle, Del., November 5, 1862, and is the son of James M. and Eliza Wise. His father, who was a resident of Cecil County prior to going to Delaware, has for years held the position of assistant freight agent of the Pennsylvania Railroad at Newcastle. Politically he is a Republican. Active in church work, he serves as local preacher in the Methodist Episcopal denomination, and is steward and class leader in his church and superintendent of the Sunday-school. His wife died November 17, 1894, leaving seven children: Arthur M., William A., John S., Loomis O., Sallie R., Thomas D. and Lizzie.

Until fourteen years of age William A. Wise attended the common schools of Newcastle, after which he was a student in a private school in New Orleans, La., and later completed his education and took a theological course in Newark, Del., under a private tutor, finishing in 1883. He was licensed to preach by the Newcastle quarterly conference, and by the same body was recommended to the Wilmington annual conference, where he was received on trial. In March, 1884, he was assigned to King's Wood Church in the city of Wilmington, Del., of which he was the first regular pastor, and which he served in 1884-85. His next charge was at Redlion, in Newcastle County, where he remained during 1886-87. The two ensuing years were spent at Cape Charles, Northampton County, Va., after which he served for one year in a circuit in Worcester County, Md. When he was assigned to Cape Charles, the church had but sixteen members, and although there were only twenty-four when he left, yet during his pastorage a church costing $3,350 was built and paid for.

In 1891-92 Mr. Wise had charge of the church at Pocomoke City, Md. He was ordained a deacon at Elkton, in March, 1886, and two years later was ordained an elder by Bishop C. D. Foss, in Wilmington, Del. While holding a pastorate in Wilmington, in 1893-94, the present large granite church, corner of Woodlawn and Lancaster Avenue, was built at a cost of $25,000. In the spring of 1895 he came to North East, where he has since won many friends, who have been attracted to him by his earnestness, perseverance and tireless energy in the Lord's work.

April 5, 1888, Mr. Wise married Fannie, daughter of Jesse and Sarah Sherwood, of Newcastle, Del. They are the parents of three children, Edna M., Allen D. and Harold J. Fraternally Mr. Wise belongs to Crescent Lodge No. 178, A. F. & A. M., at Pocomoke City, Md., and is also identified with the Heptasophs.

JOHN P. WILSON, of District No. 9, Cecil County, was born in Newcastle County, Del., in 1836, and is the son of Samuel D. and Mary (Pearson) Wilson, both natives of Delaware. The Wilson family was founded in America by four brothers who came here from England and made settlement in Delaware on the historic Brandywine. Three of them were Jacob, John and Samuel; the name of the fourth is unknown. They were sons of Christopher Wilson, of England. Samuel D., son of Jacob Wilson, removed from Delaware to Cecil County, Md., in

1842 and continued to reside here until his death, which occurred at the age of sixty-two years. Politically he was a Democrat. His seven children are still living, namely: Sarah; William and Amos, who live in this county; John P.; Martha, widow of H. B. Cameron; Thomas J., and Ross W., of Chester County, Pa.

At the age of seventeen our subject discontinued his studies in the common schools and began to learn the carpenter's trade, which he followed for six years. Afterward he became interested in farming and this occupation he has since followed, being at this time the owner of one hundred and sixty acres devoted to dairying purposes and the raising of cereals and vegetables. Politically he is a Republican and always rejoices when the party scores a grand victory. By his marriage to Louisa B. Bates, he has two children, namely: Charles, who resides in Washington, D. C.; and Sarah. In religious connections he is a member of the Presbyterian Church, in which he was ruling elder for twenty years and for fifteen years superintendent of the Sunday-school.

R EV. WILLIAM FRANCIS BRAND, rector of the Episcopal Church at Emmorton, Harford County, was born in New Orleans, La., June 17, 1814, and is a representative of one of the old and distinguished families of that state. His grandfather, Joseph Brand, a native of Scotland, came to America at an early day and located in Hanover County, Va., where he engaged in merchandising during the Revolutionary War. There his son William, the father of our subject, was born and reared. The latter must have gone to Louisiana previous to the year 1800, as he arrived there when that territory was still under Spanish rule, before the French had secured possession. He was a prominent architect and builder, and during his residence in Louisiana became a great friend of General Jackson, whom he greatly assisted during the War of 1812 by his knowledge of the country. Subsequently he established, at his own expense, a hospital for soldiers injured in that struggle, and General Jackson, recognizing and appreciating this, appointed his youngest son a midshipman in the United States navy. He died in 1850, in the faith of the Episcopal Church, of which he was a consistent member, and was a man of great influence in his community. By his marriage with Miss Hettie Reed, of Pennsylvania, he had five children who reached years of maturity.

Just before the celebrated battle of New Orleans, General Jackson attended the christening of our subject, who was also taken to see the fight, he "being in arms." As soon as he reached a sufficient age he entered the schools of Kentucky, where he pursued his studies until eleven, and then matriculated at the University of Virginia. Subsequently he studied law in New Orleans and was admitted to the bar, but only practiced a short time. Being religiously inclined he resolved to enter the ministry of the Episcopal Church, and was ordained in 1844 as deacon. He was transferred to New York, and was later sent by Bishop Whitting to Anne Arundel County, Md., where he remained for six years.

At the end of that time Rev. Brand came to Emmorton, where his wife's family had built for him a church, paying the entire expenses with the exception of $35, which was donated by others. It is one of the finest country churches in Maryland, the windows being of the best English glass, and the interior adorned with valuable oil paintings. It was consecrated in March, 1851, at which time it was entirely free from debt. Here Rev. Brand has since labored earnestly and persistently in the Master's cause, and is not only beloved by the people of his own congregation, but is held in the highest regard by all who know him, people coming from many miles around to attend his services.

On the 25th of May, 1842, Mr. Brand was united in marriage to Miss Sophia Hall, a daughter of Henry Hall, who was a native of Carpenters Point, Cecil County, Md., and to them was born one son, McHenry. During the war Mr. Brand had charge of the education of two of Jefferson Davis' sons, and at the end of the struggle was visited by the Confederate president. Mr. Brand is a man of fine personal appearance, whose long snow-white hair adds dignity to his clear-cut features, and although he is now in his eighty-fourth year he is still quite active, being a tireless worker in the Master's vineyard.

GEORGE W. JANNEY, deceased, late of District No. 9, Cecil County, was born in District No. 5, near Bayview in 1824, and was a son of Eli and Hester (Lackland) Janney. His grandfather, Thomas, came to America from England in company with the great-grandfather, Thomas, Sr., and settled in District No. 5, this county. The entire life of Eli Janney was passed in farm pursuits and he owned a farm in District No. 5. By his marriage he had nine children, but only five of these are living, namely: Jesse, who occupies the old place formerly owned by his father; Rebecca E.; Hester, who is married to John Fitzgerald; Nathan L., and Rachel, wife of John White. The father died at the old homestead in 1875, aged eighty years.

Until of age our subject remained on the home farm. He then removed to a farm near Zion, purchasing the property which he afterward owned and cultivated. In politics he affiliated with the Democratic party. He served his district as tax collector for some years, and held other local offices of trust. His marriage united him with Elizabeth A. Nolan, daughter of John Nolan, and three children were born of their union, namely: Wilbur, of Bayview; John, of this district; and Eli, who carries on the old home farm of eighty-eight acres of land. The family attend the Methodist Episcopal Church at Bayview.

INDEX

ABRAHAMS, Mira Chandlee 425; Rawlins 425

ADAMS, Alexander 157; Amanda Reasin 157; Catherine Brown 176; Hannah Catherine 176; John 574; John Quincy 167; Margaret 167; Mary Reed 574; William 176

ADY, Mary 278; Mary Ayres 278; Samuel 277; Thomas 277*; William 277

AHRENS, Adolph 301; Ella Hanway 301

AIKEN, Annie Richardson 574; Robert 574

ALBANY, Elizabeth 535

ALDRICH, Harriet 402; Mary A. Wells 449; W. J. 449

ALES, Sarah 292

ALEXANDER, Addie 317; Andrew 402; Benjamin 154; Catherine Anthony 405; David 443; Eliza Jane Benjamin 316; Harriet Aldrich 402; Harriet J. 405; Harriet Levis 352, 446; Harry 402; Henry 449; Henry T. 405; John 405; John E. 402*; Julia Ann 298; Lillie V. 405; Louise 402; Lydia Hartgrave 405; Lydia L. 405; Martha 557; Martha Robinson 402; Mary A. 335; Miriam 405; Rebecca J. 449; S. S. 154; Sarah 443; Tamson Foard 503; V. K. 446; V. R. 352; Washington 316; William 402; William A. 405

ALLEN, Adeline Miller 418; Bessie I. 382; E(dward) M. 417*; E(dward) M., Jr. 256, 418; Elizabeth Rudolph 382; Frederick H. 382; Henry L. 418; J. A. Greme 419; James C. 382; John 418, 559; John R. 381*; Margaret Barclay 559; Mary A. 382; Mattie D. 382; Patrick 381; Richard N. 418; Rudolph S. 382; Sallie E. Wilson 418; Sarah D. Hall 382; Thomas C. 381, 382; William H. 418

ALLISON, Susan 127

ALLMAN, Hester 477

ALMONEY, Elizabeth 501, 502

ALRICHS, Jacob 181; Peter 181; Sarah E. 181

ALTVATER, (Dr.) 409; Louise 409

AMOS, Alfred P. 506; Angeline V. Wetherall 507; Ann Elizabeth 506; Anna 507; B. Scott 543; Caroline E. 543; Charles D. 543; E. Pearson 506; Ella 507; Emmett 507; Eugenia 543; Hannah 272; Hattie 507; Henry C. 506; Henry S. 543; Howard 506; Ida 507; Isaac 543; James H. 543*; Lemuel 506; Lemuel H. 506; Martha 543; Mary A. 543; Mary E. West 543; Melinda P. 506; Milton 506; Oliver C. 506; Rachel 507; Rachel P. Pearson 506; Robert 543; Sarah 543; Susan G. 506; Thomas A. 506*; Virginia W. Ensor 543; William 506; William, Jr. 506; William W. 506; Zachariah 543

ANDERSON, Adam 423, 426; Andrew 227*; Ann J. 334; Anna B. 334; Cassie F. Whiteford 286; Clara 334; E. Milton 389; Elizabeth 334; Ellen McKelvey 334; Fred 286; George 227; Henrietta 334; Henrietta Register 334; Henry 227; John 227, 334; John C. 389; Laura B. McClung 389; Margaret 272; Mary 334, 423, 426, 489; Mary E. 334; Mary E. Gardy 227; Nellie V. 227; Patrick 334*; Raymond 389; Rebecca 227, 334; Robert 334; Robert H. 334; Sarah Winters 227; Susan E. 334; William 227, 334

ANDREW, Abram 238; Annie T. 272; Benjamin F. 238; Charles A. 238, 278*; Estelle K. 281; Georgia K. 238; Hannah E. 238; J. Robert 238; John 272; John W. 238*, 278;

583

Joseph 272*, 281; Joseph F. 238;
Julia A. Jackson 281; Maggie Cook
Willis 272; Mary 238, 281; Mary
E. Keene 238; Nancy McVay 238;
Quila 238; William H. 238

ANDREWS, (Mrs.) 462; Catherine
268, 274, 348; James 477

ANTHONY, Araetta 467; Catherine
405

ARBUCKLE, Catherine M. Kuhn 426;
Daniel 130, 426; Daniel, Jr. 426;
Daniel T. 130*, 426; Ella May
130; Kate Culp 130; Mary S.
Magargle 130, 426; Mary Spratt
130; Paul T. 130, 426; Philip
130; Philip R. 426; Raymond 130;
Samuel J. 130, 426*

ARCHER, (& Van Bibber) 157;
Adelaide Robinson 423; Elizabeth
M. Lee 405; G. W. 323; Hannah
575; Hannah C. 164; Harriet H.
542; Harris 405; Henry W. 126,
419, 451; J. W. 423; James 542;
John 133, 164, 419, 542, 575;
Stevenson 164, 419, 542

ARMOUR, James 566; Mary Elizabeth
Brickley 566

ARMSTRONG, (Miss) 408; Addie G.
285; Amelia E. 285; Ann Booth
284; Anne M. 352; Catherine 285;
James 285; John 384; John R. 285;
Martha Henderson 384; Mary 285;
Mary D. 285; Mary J. Smith 393;
Mary Smith 285; Susan 285; T. H.
285; Walter 352; William 284*,
393

ARNOLD, (Judge) 494; Edwin 415;
Henry 193; Mary 193

ASH, Charlotte 447; Emily Howard
447; Emily J. 492; Flora 447;
George R. 447*; Helen 447; Jacob
447; Jacob B. 447; Mary 447; Mary
A. 296; Mary H. 447

ASHE, Daniel Heinrich 119; Rachel
119

ATKINSON, Alexander 435; Benjamin
T. 436; Elizabeth 412; Elizabeth
Manoney 435; Emma 436; Hannah
Maria Ramsey 435; Ida 436; Martha
Jane 435; Millard R. 436; Norris
M. 436; Stephen 435*; Stephen
John 436; Theresa 435; Thompson
R. 436; Wesley 435; William 435

AYNE (surname only) 488

AYRES, Alice A. Norris 536;
Amanda 511; Anna 536; B. Franklin
536; Benjamin 536; Benjamin A.
521*; Charles C. 511; Clara M.
511; Darkness 536; E. Elione 536;
Elizabeth 511, 536; Elizabeth
Albany 535; Elizabeth Perdue 511;
Hannah 511; J. Upton 536; James
B. 511; John 511, 536; John T.
536; Julia Shrodes 521; Mary 278,
536; Mary A. 536; Mary C. 511;
Nicholas M. 536; Sallie M. Carlin
511; Thomas 278, 535; Thomas J.
511, 535*; Thomas J., Jr. 511*;
William 511

BAGLEY, Sarah 331

BAHN, Dorothy 147; Frederick 147

BAILEY, Cassie Hetrick 306;
Elizabeth Spencer 379; George
379; George W. 306; Mary 243;
Priscilla Bowman 242; Sarah 376;
William 242

BAKER, (Capt.) 321; Alice C. 364;
Austin L. 361; Bertha 357; Beulah
361; Charles H. 491, 535; Charles
W. 357, 361*, 364, 372; Charlotte
145; Edmund 491; Elizabeth 491;
Elizabeth Carsins 491; Elizabeth
Cole 491; Elizabeth Greenland
364; Elizabeth J. 218; Elizabeth
Smith 535; Ellen 218, 332; Emma

F. Michael 361; F. W. 415; Fannie Richardson 357; Francina 409; Frank Emerson 361; George A. 357, 361, 363*, 372, 535; George H. 491; George W. 364; Harold 357; Henry 218; Hollis R. 373; James B. 357*, 361, 364; Jeremiah 144, 145; Jessie M. 373; Jethro 409; John C. 491; John H. 364, 534*; Lydia 375; Lydia C. 364; Margaret 321; Margaret L. 535; Mary A. 141, 145; Mary B. Greenland 491; Mary C. Hollis 373; Mary J. 491; Mary W. Sumption 364; Maude 357; Nettie F. 373; Nathan 375; Nicholas 364, 491; P. Tevis 361; Rebecca Maulden 145; Sarah F. 491; Sarah R. 364; Susie E. 364; Viola Estelle 535; Warren L. 535; William B. 364, 372*, 535; William H. 321; William Reid 535; Winfield L. 491;

BALDWIN, A. S. 473; Annie C. 453; Eben N. 453; Edward A. 453*; Emma H. 473; Fannie Loflin 453; George F. 453; H. Streett 201; Hannah 233; Harry W. 201; John T. 453; Margaret 201; Mary E. Whiteford 201; Phoebe E. 453; Robert L. 453; Samuel T. 453; Samuel Tyler 453; Sarah M. 453; Tyler, 453

BARCLAY, Margaret 559

BARNES, Amos 377; Arabella Gilbert 377; Avarella Fulton 214; Belle E. Black 126; Charles F. 165; Clifford C. 165*; Edith R. 125; Eliza B. 125; Emily E. 125; Emma M. 126; Frederick M. 125; George W. 125*, 197; Harry H. 126; Harry R. 125; Henry 378; Hosea 377; John 214, 456; Lizzie Virdin 493; Martha A. 456; Mary Frances Noble 165; Mary G. 125, 197; Perry K. 125, 126; Rachel 374; Rachel L. Kirby 125; Richard 125; Richard A. 165; Richard K. 125; Robert L. 125; Sallie E.

378; Sarah Gilbert 377; Sarah Jane Morgan 125; Silas W. 493; W. L. 165

BARNUM, Lucinda 425

BARRETT, Georgianna 574; John D. 436; Martha Jane Atkinson 435; Robert 574

BARROLL, (family) 257; Ellen 258; Henrietta J. 258; Henrietta J. Bedford Hackett 258; Hopewell H. 258; James E. 258; Jonn Leeds 258; Jonn Leeds, Jr. 258; Laura 258; Morris K. 258; S. Rose 258; Sallie 258; Sir Knight 258; Victoria 258; William 257, 258

BARROW, Eliza Bull 173; James 173

BARRY, Hannah Booth 436; Michael 436

BARTOL, J. L. 419

BARTON, A. C. 157; Amanda 539; Anace A. Watters 539; Andrew J. 539; Canada 539; Charles 539; Elijah 539; Franklin 539; James R. 539; Jonn 539; John W. 539*; Joshua 539; Lida Gorrell 157; Maggie 558; Mary A. Morris 539; Minnie E. 539; Sophronia 539; Susanna 539; Washington 539; William H. 539; William M. 539*

BASSFORD, Martha O. 554

BATEMAN, (Judge) 415; Martha 343; William 343

BATES, Louisa B. 581

BATTON, Sarah J. 295; William 295

BAUERSFIELD, John 567; Louisa 567

BAULDIN, William 431

BAYARD, Ann 503; Francina 212; Hannah L. 247, 503; John 503; John Hodge 503; Samuel 503; Thomas 212

BAYLESS, Elizabeth 168

BAYLEY, James Roosevelt 321

BAYNES, Beulah McCay 379; John H. 379

BEAMAN, Susan 226

BEARD, Sarah 410

BEATTY, Annie 576; Arthur 576; Caroline 576; Charles E. 576*; Drew 576; Laura 576; Margaret 145; Margaret Kelly 576; William 576

BEDFORD, Gunning 258

BEESON, Clara Ewing 438; George 438

BELL, Catherine Wygart 265; Ephraim 538; Georgietta 263; Henrietta Spurrier 263; Isaiah 263; John 263, 538; Nicholas R. 263*; Rebecca 538

BELT, Anna Maria 572; Clarissa 572; Esther 572; James Harrick 572; Mary Ann 572; Mary Ann Dyer 572; Middleton 572; William Dyer 572

BENJAMIN, Albert 316; Anna S. 197; Charles A. 197; Deborah 316; Eliza Jane 316; Emeline 197; Emmaline 317; George 197, 316; Henry T. 316; Indiana 197; Isaac 317; James E. W. 197; Jeremiah John 316; John 316; Joseph 197, 198, 316, 317; Lavinia A. 316; Martha E. 316; Mary A. Johnson 197; Minnie 198; Orlando W. 197*; Sarah 197; Sarah J. Mahoney 316; Sarah Taylor 316; Thomas 316; William 315*; William W. 316; Winfield Scott 316; Zella A. 197

BENNETT, Ada 450; Alexander S. 450; Elizabeth 235; G. S. 450; George W. 247; Henry 450; Henry H. 450; John P. 450; John T. 450*; Lidie 452; Martha Scott 450; Mary E. Denny 451

BENSON, Amos 362, 500; Anna Reynolds 262; David T. 262; Elizabeth Tucker 362, 500; Rachel 271

BESLER, Charles S. M. 528*; Christian H. 528; Christiana Seaman 529; Johanna S. E. W. 528; Rachael J. Snell 528

BEST, Alma 384

BETTLEY, Caroline 379

BEVARD, Alethia 257; Charles 257; E. M. Streett 257; George 257; Harry 257; Howard W. 257; James 257; Louisa 257; Marion 257; Mary 257; Mary Wallace 257; Samuel 257; Wakeman H. 257*

BIAYS, Joseph 168; Rachel 168

BIDDLE, Frances A. Perkins 343; George 212, 343*, 365; Jacob T. 365*; John 343; Katherine Kettell 344; Lydia C. 447; Margaret Savin 212, 343; Martha Bateman 343; Mary 343, 365; Mary Amanda 343; Mary Egner 365; Mary Mouned 343; Mary Savin 343; Peregrine 212, 343; Rensselaar 365; Stephen 343; Susan 343

BILES, Charles R. 564; Margaret M. 564; Samuel S. 301; Sarah E. Dean 301

BILLINGS, Louisa 490

BILLINGSLEA, Julia 181

BIRD, Andrew 306; Susan 306

BIRMINGHAM, Catherine E. 207; Mary 195

BISSELL, Margaret Webster 168; Mary White 206; William 168

BLACK, Belle E. 126; Catherine Porter Evans 128, 196; E. Caroline Ewing 438; Edith C. 125, 197; Elizabeth 237; J. Nelson 125, 196*, 438; Mary 197, 236; Mary B. 125; Mary G. Barnes 125, 197; W. W. 128, 196; William W. 197

BLACKSON, Laura M. 434; William 434

BLACKSTONE, James 503; Jemima Foard 503

BLACKWELL, Elizabeth Thomas 578; Theodore 578

BLAIR, Samuel 548

BLAKE, Mamie Tyson 574; Margaret Jane 500; William K. 574

BOARMAN, Benjamin W. 325; Robert 325; Sylvester 324

BODDIN, Johanna 201

BOEHM, Anthony William 120

BOLDEN, Jesse 156; Margaret 156

BOLTON, Hugh 466; Rebecca 466

BOND, Frank A. 168; Phineas 236; Rachel Cassandra Webster 168; Thomas 236

BOOTES, (Mr.) 572; Elizabeth Smith 572

BOOTH, (family) 396; Adam 436; Algemine D. 437; Ann Elizabeth 436; Ann Schuh 284; Barbara Ann 436 Charles 436; Edgar 436; Edwin 419; Elizabeth Carter 436; Ellen D. Bratton 437; George 436; Hannah 436; Henrietta 437; Henry 436; Isaac 436, 437; James 436; Jemima 411; John 436; John E. 436; Joseph 436; Joseph R. 437; Josephine 437; Lydia Ann 436; Mary Ann 436; Mary Jeannette 437; Richard 436; Sadie 436; Susan Bratton 437; William 436; William H. 436*

BOSLEY, Alice A. 471; Ann 471; Anna Wiley 471; David W. 471; Elizabeth 471; Ellen 471; Jemima 471; Jemima E. 471; John J. 471; Joseph 471; Joseph C. 471*; Laura R. 471; Margaret C. 471; Mary 471; Mary A. 471; Mary Cathcart 471; Rachel 471; Rachel E. 471; Vincent 471; William R. 471

BOSWELL, Eliza Ann Smith 572; Phoebe Finch Smith 572

BOTTS, Anna Miller 365; Archie M. 366; Asel M. 366; Avarilla 366; David O. 562*; George 562; Goldsmith 365*; Isaac H. 562; John 562; John B. 365; Lester 366; Libbie 366; Mary E. 562; Mary Sheridan 562; Melissa Gardner 366; Sarah (Sallie) B. Smith 563; Thomas 562; Winfield 366

BOUCHELL(E), Alice Cannon 247; Caradora 247; Hannah L. Bayard 247, 503; John W. 247, 503; Lege de 247; Mary E. Simpers 158; Peter 247; Peter A. 503; Sarah C. 223; Thomas 247; Wilmer 158

BOUGHTON, Isabel C. 481

BOULDEN, Alice M. 236; Carlisle 236; D. Palmer 236; Elizabeth 236; Elizabeth Bennett 235; Emma Doble 236; Fannie 236; Harry 236; James A. 235*; Laura 236; Levi 235; Mary E. Clark 236; Nellie E. 236; Rachel 453; Richard 454

BOULDING, Mary Foard 503; Nathan 503; Richard 503

BOWEN, Benjamin D. 245, 522; Louisa Frances Hess 245

BOWMAN, Caroline 267, 522; Charles C. 243; David Thomas 243; Eliza 242; George W. 242, 243; Henry 242; Henry C. 242; James H. 243; James L. 243; John 243; John B. 243; John H. 243; Lee 336; Mary Ann 242; Mary Bailey 243; Mary Emma 243; Mary Grafton 336; Priscilla 242; Priscilla Keen 242; Rachel 242; Rebecca 243; Rebecca J. 242; Sophia Ann 243; William S. 242*, 243

BOYCE, Catherine 372

BOYD, Martha Ann Dean 301; Rebecca 186; Schuyler 301

BOYLE, Cromwell 338; David B. 303; Granville 338; Hannah Harland 338; Hannah M. 338; John 338; John E. 338; Patrick 338*; Roberta E. Rawlings 303; Sarah J. Hill 338; Steward L. 338

BRACKEN, Fannie 577

BRADBURY, Mary Reasin 157

BRADLEY, Adeline 573; Alfonso 433; Emma 433; Ira 433; Lafayette 432*; Lizzie 433; Nancy J. Smith 433; Rebecca 573; Sarah C. 433

BRADY, Carrie 254, 557; George F. 253; H. H. 557; Henry H. 253*; Henry H., Jr. 254; James 253; Lucy Cooper 254; Margaret McCrone 253; Rebecca Cooper 253; Samuel 253; William 253

BRAND, Hettie Reed 581; Joseph 581; McHenry 581; Sophia Hall 581; William 581; William Francis 581*

BRATTON, Daniel 427, 437; Ellen D. 437; Howard 427; Samuel 427; Susan Reese 427; W. D. 437; William D. 427*

BREUNINGER, Dora Kraut 226; Frederick 226; George 226; Henry 226; J. Henry 226*; Jacob F. 226; Josie Eckott 227; Lizzie Sommer 226; Louis E. 227; William 226

BRIARLY, Sarah 541

BRICKLEY, Andrew 427, 428; David G. 566; Mrs. F. Lee 566; Franklin 566; George 566; Howard Newton 566; Joachim 427; Joachim, Sr. 427; Joseph 566; Margaret McMullen 566; Mary Campbell 427; Mary Elizabeth 566; Mary L. McCall 428; Nettie E. 566; Rachel Maxwell 566; T. Ernest 428; Theodore 428; William 566; William A. 565*; William Thomas 427*

BRILLHART, Catharine 558; David 558; Edward L. 558; Ellen A. 558; Elizabeth 558; Elizabeth Strayer 558; Elizabeth Venus 558; Henry S. 558; Isaac 558; Jacob 558*; Jacob C. 558; John W. 558; Joseph 558; Mary 558; Minnie S. 558; Noah 558; Sarah 558

BRISCOE, (Mr.) 395

BROMWELL, Beulah 433; Deborah 433; Florence 433; George 433; Josephine Evans 433; Martha 433; Mary 433; R. E. 433*; Robert 433; Samuel 433; Thomas 433; William 433

BROOKE, Mary 572

BROOKS, Almira 460; Edith J. 460; Mary 293

BROUGHTON, Henry B. 433; Mary 379, 481

BROWN, (Judge) 144; Alice Reynolds 337; Amanda M. 291; Anna M. 523; Ann Eliza 425; Beulah M. 277; Carrie Elizabeth 276; Catherine 176; Clara 430; Edith L. 277; Edward 291, 446; Eleanor 276; Elizabeth Rawlings 303; Emeline 318; Emma 380; Evaline Whitelock 267, 522; George C. 277; George W. 276; Godell 276; H. M. 327; Howard 430; Hugh 318; Isborn 208; J. T. 429*; J. Warren 276*; Jacob 575; Jesse 276; John 303; John F. 430; John William 276; Kirk 559; L. K. 208, 272; Laura Knight 277; Lizzie Reynolds 282; Margaret 528; Maria Theresa 231; Martha 291; Martha Kirk 208; Martha Touchton 430; Mary A. Lee 276; Mary A. Smith 295; Mary Carter 327; Mary Eleanor 276; Ridgely 347, 431; Robert 425, 550; Samuel 325; Sarah 425, 499; Susan 345, 575; T. B. 295; Thomas 337; U. Grant 282; William 267, 415, 522

BRYARLY, James 405; Mary E. 405

BRYLEY, Keziah 530

BRYSON, Rachael 233

BUCHANAN, James 428; Sarah L. Williams 428

BUDDY, Isaiah 315; Rachel A. Haines 315

BUFFINGTON, (Mr.) 305

BULL, Alberta 152; Bessie 173; Carrie P. 152; Charles 173; Charles A. 152; Clara 173; Cordelia Hollingsworth 173; Edmund L. 151; Elisha 153; Eliza 173; Elizabeth 153; Elizabeth Ruff 173; Elma 173; Emma V. 152; Eugene 173; Hannah 173; Harry 173; Henry 151; Irene W. 152; Irving 173; Jacob E. {150}, 151*; John 151, 173; John E. 525; John F. 173*; Lillie T. 152; Margaret Gay 151; Marion V. Forwood 525; Mary 152, 173; Mary Susan 151; Mary Tustin Sunderland 151; Milton 173; Priscilla D. 162; Richard S. H. 151; William 173; William W. 152

BULLOCK, Margaret 157

BURKE, Alice Graham 533; Augusta 360; Charles 533

BURKLEY, Elizabeth 161; Fred 161

BURNS, Annie 164; Hannah E. 394; Michael 164; Rebecca 394

BURTON, Sadie 241

BUSSEY Edw. F. 325; Helen M. 542

BUTLER, Clement 478, 517; Clement G. 478*, 517; Cordelia Streett 478, 517; Harry 478; Harry W. 517; J. C. 145*; J. Thomas 478; James S. 478, 517; John 325; John T. 517; Laura L. Nagle 479; Louisa S. King 145; Maggie 478; Margaret 517; May 478; May M. 517; Oceolo 145; Reuben 145; Reuben M. 145; Thomas 478, 479, 516*, 517; Thomas F. 145; Victor King 145

BUTTS, Elizabeth Jane 416; Wesley 416

CADWALADER, John 234

CAIN, Clara C. 546; J. M. 546; James M. 325; Matthew 325

CAIRNES, C. F. 536; Charles W. 507; Cornelia S. Haile 507; Edgar A. 507; Elizabeth Vance 507; Franklin 507; G. Wilson 507; George 507; George A. 507*, 523; Hannah E. 507; Laura J. 507; Louisa 507; Margaret E. 507; Mary A. 507, 523; Mary C. 507; Mary Virginia 225; Minna B. 507; Rebecca J. 507; Sallie E. Jarrett 536*; Sarah E. 507; Walter H. 507; William 507

CALDWELL, David 327; Eliza J. 533; Ellen M. 346; Harvey 346; Joseph 236; Martha 551; Thomas 346

CALLAHAN, Ann 255; Ann Ready 255, 534; Daisy Kahoe 255; Daniel 254*, 534; David 255, 534; Farrell 534; Frank 255; Helen 255; John 255, 534; Joseph 255, 534; Josie 534; Mary 255; Mary Lynch 534; Patrick 255, 533*; Terry 534; Timothy 255, 534

CALVERT, Charles, 3rd Lord Baltimore, 324

CAMERON, Abel C. 321; Alice M. 318; Amor 318; Anna (Annie) L. Craig 218, 318; Andrew 355; Belle M. 268; Emeline Brown 318; George N. 321; H. B. 581; Hugh B. 318; Hugh M. 526; James 268, 394, 472; James N. 218, 318*; Lydia 268; Margaret 321; Margaret Elizabeth 318; Martha Wilson 581; Mary 432; Murray H. 321; R. H. 308; Rachael 394; Rachael Miller 355; Rebecca J. Crothers 395; Rebecca Kirk 472; Robert 318, 432; Ruth H. 321; Simon 497; Turner 395; Virginia Smith 308; William A. 321

CAMPBELL, Lavinia A. Benjamin 316; Mary 427; William R. 316

CANNON, Alice 247

CANTWELL, John 158; Mary E. 552; Rachael J. McCauley 158

CARLIN, Asenath Lytle 511; Elizabeth E. 511; Josiah 511; Laura 511; Sallie M. 511; William 511

CARMAN, Mary E. 195

CARROLL, Harry 234; Lizzie Rembold 234

CARSINS, Ann Coen 416; Anna Etta 416; Belle 416; Edward E. 416; Elizabeth 491; Elizabeth Jane 416; George 416; Grace 416; Harry M. 416; Hattie V. Wells 416; James 416; John 416; John William 416; Laura 416; Martha J. Maxwell 416; Mary C. 416; May 416; Webster S. 416; William 416*, 491; William W. 416

CARTER, Amanda C. 305; Amor 483; Annie 327; Charles 327; Cloud 573; Daisy 327; Edith 483; Edward 266; Eliza Levis 327, 352, 446; Elizabeth 436; Emily 327; Hanna C. 483; Hannah Reynolds 337; Hannah S. 283; Harriet 266; Harry L. 327; Helen 327; Henry R. 265*; Howard 378; I. D. 326*, 352, 446; Israel 266; John 266; Joseph 266; Lottie 266; Lydia 266; Lydia Levis/Lewis 266, 326; Mary 266, 327; Mary Janney 192; Mary Reynolds 266, 326; Nellie S. Walker 378; Philip 337; Robert 266, 326; Robert C. 266; Robert D. 327; Sarah 362, 500; Sarah Jane 573; Silas 192; William 266

CARTY, John 364; Sarah R. Baker 364

CARVER, Charles 163; Hannah 484; Irene Wilkinson 163; John 412, 484; William 484

CASHO, Anna 407; Eliza Mote 407; George A. 407; George J. 407; Isaac 407; Jacob 407; Jacques 553; James M. 407*; Margaret 407; Sarah Evans 407

CASPERSON, Joseph 504; Martha Foard 504

CATHCART, Eliza J. Wiley 545; Hannah A. 545; Jemima J. 545; John P. 545; Joseph 544; Laura 545; Mary 471; Mary A. 545; Rebecca 545; William 545

CATON, Benjamin 493

CAULK, Lydia 504

CAVENDER, Lydia Foard 504; Thomas 504; Willie R. 261

CAZIER, Martha J. 399; Rebecca 383, 578; Thomas 399; Thomas 383

CHANDLEE, (family) 424*, 463; Abel 425; Absolom 425; Allison 423, 426; Allison G. 424; Ann Eliza Brown 425; Benjamin 424, 425; Benjamin, Jr. 425; Benny 425; Charles 424, 426; Cottey 424; Courtland 425; David Wollford 425; Edward G. 425; Edwin 425; Eliza 425; Elizabeth Giles Oldham 425; Elizabeth Pierce 425; Ellis 425; Ellis Goldsmith 425; Evan 425; Frances Anna 425; Gainer 425; George 424; Goldsmith 425; Grace 424; Hannah 425; Harry A. 424; Henry 425; Herbert 424; Horatio Ward 425; Isaac 425; Jane Walker 425; John 423, 424, 425; Lilbern 425; Lucinda Barnum 425; Maria 425; Mary Anderson 423, 426; Mary (2) 424; Mary Elagar 425; Mary Folwell 425; Mira 425; Rebecca Ward 425, 426; Sarah Brown 425; Sarah Cottey 424; Sarah Jane 425; Sydney 425; Veasey 425; William 424, 425; William E. 423*, 425, 426

CHANDLER, Ella Mason Cooke 577; J. W. 577

CHANEY, Martha L. 573

CHANNELL, Aaron B. 489; Anderson 489; Deborah 489; Elizabeth 489; Henrietta 489; Isaac 489; James 489; Margaret 489; Mary A. 489; Mary Anderson 489; Mary J. Herbert 489; Rebecca 489; Richard 489; Sarah A. 489; William 489*

CHASE, Eliza 128; Samuel 128; Thomas 128

CHEAIRS, John T. 253

CHEYNEY, Elizabeth 397

CHILDS, Nathan 572; Sarah Ann Smith 572

CHRISTIE, Anna 284; Cornelia 284; Fannie 284, 567; Frank S. 284; George M. 283*; India S. 284; James 283; John S. 283; Mary Cooley 437; Mary J. 284; Priscilla G. Stevenson 284; R. L. 437; Robert L. 284; Sophia Logan 283

CHURCH, Sarah Foard 504

CHURCHILL, John, Duke of Marlborough 129; Sara Jennings 129

CLARK, Anna 562; Barnett 431; James 352; Mary A. 352; Mary E. 236; R. L. 202; Robert 202; Sallie R. Green 202

CLAYTON, Adelaide Young 328, 331; Anna W. 411; Annie 313; Bertha 411; Calmar E. 411; Charles 477; Edgar 331; Elizabeth 331, 478; Elizabeth G. 411; Ervin G. 411; Eugene Y. 331; Fannie 331; Grace 477; Henry 313, 331; James 328, 477; James Lawson 478; Jeanette 478; Jemima Booth 411; John 328, 477; John M. 477; Joshua 328, 331, 411, 477, 478; Lydia A. 331;

591

Macomb 331; Martha E. Lockwood 331; Mary C. 477; Mary E. 411; Mary P. Goodley 411; Mary W. 331; Nelson 411; Nelson N. 411; Phebe Ann 411; Powell 411; Powell F. 411; Richard 331, 411, 478; Richard, Jr. 411; Sally Anne Fisher 477; Samuel G. 411; Thomas 328, 331, 478; Thomas A. 411; Wesley 410*; Wesley, Jr. 411; William 411; William, Jr. 411

CLEAVER, Anna Jeffreys 366; Cornelia H. Karsner 222, 369; Harry Archer 369; Peter 366; Thomas J. 222, 366*

CLEMENT(S), Cyrus 414; Lois P. 411, 414

CLEMSON, Elizabeth N. 245; Harry E. 223*; Oliver P. 223; Sarah Louisa Rea Wilson 223

CLENDENIN, John 430; Mary 430

CLINE, Helen Holden 156; John 156

CLYNE, Frederick 254; Mary Dollman 254

COALE, Alice 291; Amy 291; Charles 129; Clara 291; Cornelia 291; Eliza 129; Eliza Chase Dugan 128; Eliza M. 128; Ella 291; Ella Loflin 291; Harriet 129; Harry D. 129; Howard 291; Ida 291; Ira 291; Isaac 128; Isaac W. 128*; Joseph 291; Joseph R. 291; Maria 291; Martha 129; Martha Davis 128; Philip F. {290} 291*; Roy 291; S. Chase 128; Sadie 291; Skepwith H. 128, 129; Skepwith H., Jr. 128; Thomas C. 128; Walter 291; William 128, 291; William F. 128, 129;

COCHRAN, Frances E. 406; Mary E. 187; Sarah 146; William 277

COCHRON, Mary Jane Grafton 277; Rebecca 198

COEN, Ann 416; Elizabeth 416

COLBURN, Alfred A. 293; Alice B. 293; Edward A. 144, 292*; Edward H. 293; Elizabeth Knight 293; Fletcher 293 Florence P. 293; George S. 293; Hannah Rogers 293; Harvey 293; James R. 293; Mary Brooke 293; Mary R. 293; Rollinson 293; William H. 293

COLE, Cornelia A. 281; Elizabeth 491; Fannie 253; Hannah E. 252; James 201; Joseph R. 281; Maria J. 423; Martha 466; Sarah 201; Sarah Ann Watson 281; Susan 363

COLLIFLOWER, George 555; Henry 555; Louisa H. 555; William 555

COLWELL, A. J. 497; Miriam A. Shure 497

CONARD, Mary 371

CONNOR, Hester C. 447

CONSTABLE, Albert 575*; Alice 575; Arline 575; Catherine 575; Elizabeth Black Groome 575; Hannah Archer 575; Henry Lyttleton 575; Isabel S. 575, Johanna 575; John 575; John Groome 575; Mary 575; Reginald 575; William P. 575

COOK, Abbie 358; Catherine A. Schreitz 518; Charles H. 254; Clifford 335; Conrad P. 518*; George P. 226; Helen England 335; John L. 518; Joseph 241; Lucy Cooper Brady 254; Maggie 272; 358; Sarah Gifford 241; William F. 518

COOKE, Betty P. 577; Ella Mason 577; Fannie Bracken 577; Giles Buckner 576*; James 146; John K. 577; Margaret 577; Martha F. Mallory Southall 577; Mordecai 577; Sarah 356; Sarah Gifford 146

COOLEY, Ambrose 176, 187*; C. O. 437; Caroline Hughes 176; Charlotte 437; Clara A. Hughes 188; Corbin 437; Daniel M. 188; Emma 437; Harriet Wiles 188; J. P. 437; Jenzie Coulson 437; John 188, 437; Marion Russell 437; Mary Shaw 437; William R. 437*

COOLING, Benoni 233; Mary Jane Cooper 233

COOPER, Ann 493; Anna R. Wells 398, 494; Benjamin 493; Bert 233; Catherine 530; Catherine Lowber 493; Charles P. 233; Cecil C. 233; Deborah 493; Edith 233; Elizabeth 211, 494; Ella 233; Ezekiel 494; George 493; George F. 233, 494; Helen 494; Herbert 233; J. W. 398; James C. 494; Jane Little 233; John 233, 493; John, Jr. 233; John W. 493; John W., Jr. 493*; Joseph 253; Margaret 253; Mary 493; Mary Jane 233; Mary Lizzie 233; Mary S. 494; Peter 494; Rachael Bryson 233; Rebecca 253; Rebecca Jane 233; Rebecca Small 253; Richard 493; Samuel B. 493; Samuel B., Jr. 493; Sarah 493; Susan Dill 493; Thomas 493; Thomas H. 494; William 253, 493; William Charles 233*; William H. Seward 233

CORNER, Mary 225

CORNISH, Catherine 413; Henry 413

COROUCH, Cornelia 398

CORSETT, Emma Atkinson 436; I. 436

CORY, Eliza 564; Hannah 564; James 564

COSKERY, Henry B. 325

COTTEY, Abel 424; John 424; Mary 424; Sarah 424

593

COUDON, Alice E. Wroth 275; Anna 275; Henry Stump 274, 275; Joseph 274, 275; Martha 275; Martha B. Levering 274; Wilson Levering 274*

COULSON, Eli 396; Rachel 396

COURTNEY, C. R. 364; Ellen Baker 332; George 158; George H. 332; George W. 332; Hollis, Jr. 332*; Hollis, Sr. 332; Lydia A. Foster 332; Matilda 158; Susie E. Baker 364

COUSINS, Dorothy 466

COX, Elida Enfield 207; William 207

COYLE, Benjamin A. Henderson 384; George 384

CRAIG, Aldridge B. 218; Anna Elizabeth 297; Anna L. 218, 321; Bessie Pauline 218; Christopher 218; Elizabeth A. Sentman 218; Elizabeth J. Baker 218; Ella M. 218; George Ferris 218; George W. 217*; Henrietta C. 218; Laura E. 218; Martha Washington 218; Merryman D. 218; Philip 218; Sarah 503; William 217, 321; William Evan 218

CRAMER, Ludwig 264; Margaret 264

CRAWFORD, Catherine A. Reading 347; Charles 347; Henry Van Bibber 347*; Margaret Price 347; William Hazlett 347

CRESWELL, Alice 264; Ann 119; Charles C. 264; Charles E. 263*; Ellen 264; Emma 264; H. J. Richardson 125; Hannah 264; Harry 264; James 264; Jane M. 119; John 119; John A. J. {118} 119*, 256, 288; Laura V. Granger 264; Margaret 264; Margaret Cramer 264; Martha 119; Mary 119; Mary

C. 264; Rebecca E. (Webb) 119; Robert 119; Samuel 119; William 264

CREW, Mary Dunnigan 562; Theodore 562

CREWE, Sir Henry 516

CROCKER, Eliza J. Marshbank 452; George 452

CROSSLEY, Nannie C. 406

CROTHERS, (Mr.) 395; A. C. 556; A. L. 556; Alfred 395; Alpheus 556; Anna Mary 395; Charles C. 555*; Curtis 395; Elizabeth B. 394; Fannie Christie 284, 567; Hannah E. Burns 394; Hannah Elizabeth 395; Hannah Thompson 394; James 394, 555; James C. 394*; Jonn 394; John C. 567; John E. 395; John L. 556; John Lawrence 556; Lawrence 395; Margaret Orelia Porter 556; R. R. 284, 556, 566*; Rachael Cameron 394; Rachel L. 394; Ranville W. 556; Rebecca Burns 394; Rebecca J. 395; Richard H. 556; Roman R. 567; William 555; William E. 556; William J. 395

CROUCH, Mary McCauley 410; R. T. 410

CRUIKSHANK, George W. 228; Henrietta W. 302; Sarah E. Morgan 303; Thomas C. 303

CUDDY, George 172; Sarah James 172

CULBERTSON, Ann Eliza Haines 235; William 235

CULP, Kate 130

CUMMINGS, Daniel 448; Henry Clay 287; James 287*; James F. 287; Jane McColgan 287; John 287; Lewis 287; Margaret 287; Rebecca E. Vinsinger 448; Samuel R. 287; Thomas H. 287; William Penn 287

CUNNINGHAM, (family) 211; George K. 217; Keziah 217

CURRY, Anna P. 195; John B. 195; John B., Jr. 195

DAVIS, (Mr.) 448; Ada Steele 467; Amy 466; Ann A. 302; Araetta Anthony 467; Bertha McNeal 467; Catherine 466; Clara Miller 467; David 302, 466; David P. 302*; Dorothy Cousins 466; Elizabeth 466; Emmaline L. Wickes 302; George C. 166; George N. 302; Hannah 466; Henrietta W. Cruikshank 303; Henry L. 302; Henry M. 467; Henry Winter 121; Incol 466; Isaac 466; Isaac D. 466*; Isabella 466; James A. 389; James L. 302; Jefferson 153; John 255, 466; John Newman 466, 467; John O. 302; Joseph 129; Josephine Hopkins 401; Lambert W. 303; Louisa M. 302; Martha 128; Martha Cole 466; Mary 466; Mary P. 303; Mary R. 467; Mercy 466; Mary V. 302; Rachel 466; Rebecca Bolton 466; Richard 401; Sarah 466, 547; Sarah E. 303; Susan 166; Susanna Newman 466; Susanna R. 302; William 466; William J. 467

DAY, Charles H. 257; Goldsmith 461; Louisa Bevard 257; Mary G. 460

DEAN, Ann Rebecca 298; George Herbert 301; Israel R. 298*; Jacob 298; Joel H. 301; John 298; John H. 301; Julia Ann Alexander 298; Martha Ann 301; Mary J. 298; Minerva 301; Minerva A. Scotten 301; Moses 298; Sarah E. 301; Susan 298; William G. 298; William S. 301

DEAVER, D. 362; David 500; Margaret C. Tucker 362, 500

DE BAUGH, Adam 175*; Elizabeth Passett 176; Mary Untonia 175; Philip 175

DEETS, Sarah 507

DE FIGANIER, I. C. 480

DALLAM, Amanda 401; Amanda M. Prigg 130; Charles 130; Elizabeth 174, 405; Elizabeth (Betty) Martin 129, 380; Ellen Hopkins 474; Frederick 130; Jefferson A. 130; John 129; Jonn S. 129*, 380; Joseph 129, 381, 401; Joseph W. 129; Josephine Evans 381; Josephine Webster 168; Laura 130; Mary 465, 543; Mary A. 129; Mary C. Maulsby 381; Rebecca 381; Richard 129, 380*, 401, 450; Sallie 130; Samuel 129; Sarah Wallis 129; Thomas 272; Thomas B. 474*; William 129, 168, 474; William H. 129, 183, 380; Winston 129

DAVIDSON, Eliza Weaver 526; Hannah 526; John 526; Jonn W. 525; Letitia Lynch 526; M. Vernon 526; Martha 526; Rachael 526; Racnael L. 526; Susan 526; William E. 525*; William H. 526

DAVIES, Elizabeth 178

DEHAVEN, Jesse 393; Mary 393

DELLONE, Gregg 147; Kate Strasbaugh 147

DELMAS, Francis 325

DENNISON, Barbara H. 388; William 388

DENNY, Mary E. 451; Sarah 127

DERICKSON, Catherine I. Miller 182; Emma 182; Florence I. 182; John P. 182; Joseph 182; Laura 182; Lillian M. 182; William L. 182*

DEVER, Addie 193; Benjamin 193; Carrie 193; Charles 193; David 193; Edwin 193; Ella 193; George V. 193*; Hattie 193; Mamie 193; Margaret Forsythe 193; Mary Arnold 193; Nancy Vandergrift 193; Samuel 193

DEVLIN, David 365; Mary Biddle 365

DEVOE, Sarah 525

DEWULF, D. 325

DIDERICK, Bernard 324

DIETRICH, Alexander 196; C. 195; C. W. 196; Caroline 196; Caroline Farish 196; Catherine 196; E. A. 195*; Josephine 196; Louise 196; Mary 196; Mimika 196

DILG, Mrs. Henry 480

DILL, Alexander 494; Elizabeth Cooper 494; Frank 494; John 493, 494; Mary S. Cooper 494; Susan 493

DISSTON, Horace C. 480

DIVERS, Adaline 171; Elizabeth Osborn 171; William Holland 171

DIX, Susan 194

DOAN, Frank M. 164; Lucretia Van Bibber 164

DOBLE, Budd 236; Emma 236

DOCHEZ, Josephine Dietrich 196; L. A. 196

DOLLMAN, Charles 254; Christina 254; Christina Heim 254; Hettie 254; John 254; John G. 254*; Mary 254

DONNELL, Alice S. 570; Andrew 570

DORSEY, Algernon S. 168; Mary Alice Webster 168

DORTON, John 424, 426; Mary Chandlee 424, 426; Rachel 424

DOUGHERTY, J. E. 382; M. Allie 347; Mary A. Allen 382

DRENNEN, Alice S. Donnell 570; Anna E. Manly 420, 569*; Annie Highland 569; Elizabeth G. 570; Jonathan 569; Manly 420, 569; Thomas 420, 569

DUGAN, Eliza Chase 128

DUITE, Aaron G. 580; Ed 580; Susan A. 580

DUNN, Ballard S. 154; Cornelia 153; Kate E. L. 493

DUNNIGAN, Andrew 562, Anna Clark 562; Bernard 562; Daniel J. 562; James 562; John 562*; Mary 562; Patrick 562

DURHAM, Abel 178, 525; C. Howard 525; D. D. 292; David 525; Elizabeth F. 525; Evalina Hannah 525; F. Pierce 525; George S. 525; Jacob 525; John 525; John D. 525; M. Alice 525; Mabel 525; Marion V. Forwood Bull 525; Martha S. Richardson 525; Mary E. 525; Matilda E. Lowe 525; Rachel A. Gladden 525; Samuel 525; Sarah A. 178, 525; Sarah Devoe 525; Sarah E. T. 292; William A. 525*; William F. 525

DURKEE, Mary T. 181

DUYCKINCK, A. L. 395*; Aaron L. 524; Anna 524; Bancker 524; Catherine Smock 524; Ellis L. 524*; Emily 395; Emily Longstreet 524; Horace 395; Horace H. 524; Levi Holden 524; Mabel 395; Magdalene 524; Richard B. 524; Willemenia M. Reed 395

DYER, Mary Ann 572

EARL, Caroline H. McCormick 184

ECKOTT, Josie 227

EDEN, Joseph (Edenschinck) 324

EDER, Fred 443; John 442; John Q. 443; Mary 443; Mathias 442, 443; Sarah Alexander 443; Sarah Hines 443; William H. 442*

EDMONDS, Anna Keyser 408; James R. 408; Ruth 146, 241

EDMONDSON, Rachel A. 397

EDWARDS, Prudence 255

EGNER, Mary 365

ELAGAR, Mary 425

ELLIOTT, Elizabeth Hunter 564; Thomas 564

ELLIS, Charles 552; Charles M. 551*; Eliza Ann Howard 551; Elizabeth Rudolph 552; Francis Asbury 551; Howard 551; Mary E. Cantwell 552; Philip 551; Rowland 552; Rudulph 551

ELLISON, Addie Y. 328; Adelaide Young Clayton 328; Cecelia A. 571; Charles S. 411, 478; Charles Scott 328*; Charles S., Jr. 328; Clayton L. 328; Edgar 328; Emma L. 328; Harry C. 328; James 571; James, Sr. 571; James S. 571; James T. 328; Jonathan L. 328; L. Frank 328; Lenette A. 571; Lewis P. 571; Lizzie B. 328; Lydia D. 571; Mary C. 328; Nellie 328; Priscilla T. 571; Sallie 328; Sara D. Scott 328; Susan B. 328; Susan M. Suckert 571; Susan T. 571; William S. 571

ELY, Isaac J. 317; Joseph 317; Joseph R. 317*; Mary R. 318; Sarah 317; Sarah Rogers 317

EMACK, George M. 347

EMMONS, Annie 379

EMMORD, Amelia 567; Emelie 204; Fred 567*; Fred, Sr. 567; Frederick 204; Henry 567; Louisa 567; Louisa Bauersfield 567; Molly 567

ENFIELD, Alice 207; Bertha 207; Dora 207; Elida 207; Eliza 207; Estella 207; Harry 207; Jacob 207; James 207; John 207; John S. 207; Julia A. 207; Mary 207; Nancy 207; Nancy Howlett 207; Tacy A. Weeks 207; William 207*; Willametta 207

ENGALL, Clara 307

ENGLAND, Deborah 335; Elisha 208; Hannah P. 335; Hannah Tucker 500; Helen 335; Isaac 335; John 335, 500; Joseph T. 335*; Leroy 335; Maria Haines 335; Mary A. Alexander 335; Mary E. 335; Reuben H. 335; Samuel 335; Sarah T. 193

ENGLE, John 498; Susanna 498

ENSOR, Virginia W. 543

EPPELSHEIMER, Lida P. 354

ESCH, Daniel Heinrich 119

ESTEP, Lucy Middleton 572; Richard 572, 573

EVANS, (Miss) 553; A. W. 579*; Alexander 127, 551, 579; Amos A. 579; Amos S. 126; Amos Alexander 127, 579; Amos Standly 128; Andrew P. 127; Andrew Wallace 127, 579; Ann 127; Catherine P. 196; Catherine Porter 127, 128; David 127; Edgar D. 509; Emily 126; Frank B. 126; Harry C. 126; Isabel 474; Isabella 438; James 126, 127, 438; James F. 126; James H. 126; James Hugh 128; James M. 127; Jane 127; Jennie Frazer 126; John 126, 127, 381, 407, 553, 579; John P. 126; John Patterson 128; Josephine 381, 433; Levi H. 433; Lillian E. 509; Mamie A. Kennedy 509; Margaret 127; Margaret I. Ewing 438; Margery Evans 127; Martha 127; Martha Gillespie 127, 128; Mary 185; Mary Oliver 579; Mary Patterson 128; Miss 553; Oliver 256; Rebecca M. F. Ewing 438; Rebecca S. 126; Rebecca Steel 126, 128; Robert 126, 127, 579; Sarah 127, 407; Sarah Denny 127, 407; Stanley 126; Susan A. Duite 580; Susan Allison 127; Susan Evans 127; W. J. 438; William 127; William James 128; William S. 296; William S., Jr. 126; William Steel 126*

EVERETT, James 491

EVERIST, Elizabeth Baker 491; F. S. 472; George 491

EWEN, Richard 125

EWING, (family) 437; Albert 474; Ambrose 570; Amos, Jr. 570; Amos, Sr. 570; Arabella 474; Cecil 438; Clara 438; Clara Vaughan 438; E. Caroline 438; Edwin E. 438*, 474; Elizabeth 474; Elizabeth McKindless 391; Elizabeth Matherson 474; Elizabeth Russell 391; Emma McMurphy 438; Esther Elizabeth 570*; Evans 438; Florence 391; G. E. N. 130; Georgia 474; Halus 438; Isabell(a) Evans 438, 474; Jane Anne 438, 474; John 434, 570; John S. 570; Joseph 391; Joshua 438, 474; Lawson 387, 391*; Margaret 474; Margaret A. Sentman 434; Margaret I. 438; Mary 434; Mary R. 570; Mary Steel 570; Nathaniel 438; Patrick 438, 474; Rebecca 474; Rebecca F. M. 438; Sallie Dallam 130; Samuel 570; Sarah J. Shultz 391; Solomon Russell 384*, 391; Theodore 438, 473*; William 391, 438; William E. 391; William P. 438, 474

FAHRNEY, William O. 555

FALLS, Elijah 296, 375; Emily E. 376; Emily Elizabeth 297; Emily Riddle 296; Hugh 296; J. W. 376; J. Wesley 296*; Rachael T. 297; Rachel Thompson 297; Wilmer J. 297

FARISH, Caroline 196; Edward 196

FARNAN, Benjamin 574; Susan Lambert 574

FARNANDIS, Henry D. 144, 415, 419, 546

FARQUAHER, Granville 572; William Emily Smith 572

FARRAND, Nancy B. 472; Samuel 472

FASSITT, Alfred 559; Catherine Van Sant 559; James 559; John B. 559; John Barclay 559; Kathleen Mary 559; Loraine F. 559; Marcelena 559; Margaret Barclay Allen 559; Ralph 559; Thomas 559*; William 559

FENDALL, (Miss) 540; Ann E. 396

FERGUSON, Anne M. 256; James 152; Margaret Matilda 152

FIELD, Cyrus 541; H. Y. 262; John R. 574; Lydia 574; Sarah 541

FIFE, Rebecca 565

FIFER, Rebecca 245

FINCH, Phoebe 572

FINLEY, J. Z. 448; James 231; James Brown 231; Maria Theresa Brown 231; Martha {230} 231*; Samuel 231

FINNEY, (Mr.) 151, 215; Anna L. Parker 191; Charles McL. 188; E. D. 188*, 484; Edward 484; Elizabeth McCormick 191; George J. 188, 484*; George J., Jr. 484; John C. 484; John M. 188; John M. T. 191; Louisa L. 484; Walter 484; William 188, 484; William Parker 191; William W. 484

FISHER, Charles 234; Elizabeth 374; Katie Rembold 234; Sally Ann 477; Thomas 477

FITZGERALD, E. D. 493; Elizabeth E. Reed 152; George W. 152; Hester Janney 582; John 582; Martha Lee Virdin 493

FLETCHER, Carpenter 345; Sarah J. 345

FLOUNDERS, Benjamin 376; Eliza J. Lynch 376

FOARD, (family) 502*; Andrew 503; Ann 504; Ann Bayard 503; Ann J. 503; Araminta 503; Charles R. 504; Edward 503; Edward L. 503; Emily 504; Emily J. Virdin 493; Hannah Lawrenson 503; Harriet Thompson 503; Hezekiah 503; James 503; James H. 394, 504; James L. 504; Jemima 503; Jeremiah 503; John 504; Josiah 503, 504; Kate 504; Letitia 503; Levi G. 503; Lydia 503, 504; Lydia C. 504; Lydia Caulk 504; Martha Jane 504; Martha Rebecca Hyland 504; Mary 503, 504; Mary Boulding 503; Mary E. Smith 394; Mary Elizabeth 504; Mary McDonough 504; N. E. 493; Richard 503; Richard Boulding 503; Richard J. 503; Ruth Anna 504; Samuel B. 503; Sarah 504; Sarah Craig 503; Sarah Lawrenson 503; Sarah Mansfield 503; Tamson 503; Thomas 504; Wilhelmina 504

FOCKLER, Benjamin 555; Catherine 555; E. B. 554*; Ella S. 555; George S. 555; Harry L. 555; John T. 555; Louisa H. Colliflower 555; Susan B. 555

FOLEY, John S. 321

FOLWELL, Goldsmith Edward 425; Mary 425; Susan 425

FORD, Alfred 561; Charles 561; Elizabeth Simpers 561; Emily J. 493; I. Henry 561*; J. Arthur 571; John 561; John Fletcher 561; Lavina 341; Lenette A. Ellison 571; Lenette E. 571; Margaret 561; Martha McDowell 444; Mary S. 571; Milicent 256; N. E. 493; Samuel 561; Sarah M. 561; Stephen H. 570*; Susan S. 571

FORDER, Josephine 509

FOREMAN, (General) 577

FORSYTH, Margaret 193

FORWARD, James 512; Susan R. Hanna 512

FORWOOD, Hannah E. Andrew 238; John F. 151; Marion V. 525; Mary Susan Bull 151; P. F. 238; Parker 166; W. S. 151; William S., Jr. 166*; William Smithson, Sr. 166

FOSTER, Ann 163, 218; Carrie 221; Dora 221; Edna 221; Elizabeth Rutter 218, Elizabeth Talley 221; Elizabeth Holden 156; Ellis 221; Ernest 221; Ethel 221; James 221; Jesse 163, 218; John 221; Lemuel 156; Lydia A. 332; Rachel L. Crothers 394; Raymond 221; Rufus 394; Washington 218*; William 221; William T. 221

FOWLER, Francis M. 322, 326

FOX, George H. 374

FRALEY, Harry 147; Susie Strasbaugh 147

FRAME, Jeanette Clayton 478; Robert 478

FRANKLIN, Adele 165; Benjamin 302

FRAZER, Eva C. Scott 297; J. F. 297; James 126; James H. 126; Jennie 126

FREDERICK, John M. 321; Joseph Alphonse Aloisius (320) 321*, 326; Margaret Ann Hild 321

FREEMAN, Harriet Foard 503; Hyland 503; William R. 503

FRIER, Arabella Ewing 474; William T. 474

FULTON, Anna Rebecca 426; Avarella 214; Bridget McGonigal 214; David 214, 436; Edward A. 426; Elizabeth 158; Jacob 158; James 187, 214, 425, 426, 456; James A. 214*; John 214, 215; John C. 214; Joseph M. 214; Margaret 214; Mary 187, 214, 436; Mary Chandlee 425; Philip 214;

Sarah Caroline 426; Susan 215; Susan Trego 214; Thomas 214; William 214; William H. 214; William Thomas 426

GABLE, Benson 543; Carolyn E. Amos 543

GAILEY, John 498; Martha Gillsepie 498; Martha L. 498; Mary A. 498; R. Belle 498; Simon G. 498; William 498

GALLAGHER, Elizabeth 355; Etheland 410

GALLAHER, John E. 463; Sarah Teresa 463

GALLEN, Joseph A. 326

GALLION, Jacob J. 336; James B. 242; Rachel Bowman 242

GARDNER, Melissa 366

GARDY, Mary E. 227

GARESCHE, A. J. 196; Caroline Dietrich 196

GAREY, Addie Alexander 317; Alfred 316; Carrie 316; Emmaline Benjamin 317; Frank 316; George O. 316*; George W. 316; Milton 316; Walter 316

GARRETT, Robert 185

GARRISON, Alfred S. 195; Anna P. Curry 195; Cornelius 195; Elsie 195; Ernest B. 195; Frank B. 195; James B. 195; John 195; John B. 195*; Martha 537; Mary A. 195; Mary Birmingnam 195; Mary E. Carman 195; Philip M. 195; Sannie S. 195; William M. 195

GAY, Margaret 151

GEMMILL, S. Alice 547; Sarah 202

GEORGE, A. Hamilton 352; Alexander Hamilton {350} 351*; Anthony 351; Anthony, Jr. 351; Harriet Lucinda 352; Lucinda Hamilton 351; Louis O. 352; Louisa 351; Mary A. Clark 352

GETTY, Alethia 257; G. A. 257

GIBSON, (Senator) 212; Mary E. 554

GIFFORD, Anna Rebecca Fulton 426; Benjamin 393; Catherine Janney 147, 192; Ellen 146; Ellen E. 241; George 241; George W. 147; Gertrude 242; Grant 147; Harry M. 242; Ida 147; J. Darnell 426; James 146, 147, {240} 241*; James, Jr. 241; Jesse 147; John W. 192; John Wesley 146*; John W. 192; Joseph 241, 242; Lotta 147; Mary J. 393; Rhoda A. Scarborough 241; Ruth Edmonds 146, 241; Samuel 146, 241; Sarah 146, 241; Viola 147; Wesley 241

GILBERT, (Miss) 168; Amos 376, 377, 530; Anna 530; Arabella 377; Bennett 148, 376; D. R. 480; Elizabeth 377, 530; Ellen McComas 377; Ethel 480; George 376*; Helen Ann 530; Henrietta Laughlin 377; Hettie 480; Ida B. 148; James 377; James Amos 530; Jarrett 480; Jarrett W. 480; Jarvis 172; John 480; Lucy Virginia Hughes 176; Martha 148; Martin 176; Mary 376, 530; Micah 530; Michael 530; Mickey 376; Quiller 376; R. H. 480; Robert Channing 530; Robert J. 530*; Sarah 172, 377, 420; Sarah Bailey 376; Sarah Moore 480; Z. Taylor 480*

GILDER, Richard Watson 493

GILLESPIE, E. A. 383; E. W. 294; Ellen E. Gifford 241; Ellen Gifford 146; Gertrude E. 400; Lulu R. Simcoe 383; Martha 127, 498; Mary E. Porter 294; Mary R. Ewing 570; Thomas 147, 241; William E. 570

GILLINGHAM, J. P. 154; Margaret A. 154

GILPIN, C. Monteith 341; Sally 341; Thomas 341

GITTINGS, Alice 575; Isabelle S. Constable 575; John C. 575; S. E. 575

GLADDEN, Anna E. 473; Bertram 473; Blanche Richardson 473; Hannah J. 246, 473; Harriet 473; Harry R. 473; Jacob 473; James W. 246, 473*; Jane Wilson 473; Margaret J. 473; Rachel A. 525; S. Walter 473; William 473

GLENN, Sarah F. 529

GLOYD, John 325

GOODLEY, Elizabeth R. Stidham 411; Mary P. 411; Samuel 411

GORDON, Ann Foard 504; George 504; Jonn 178; Mary T. Macklem 178

GORRELL, Abram 267; Alice O. 175; Andrew 522; Ann 267; Charles E. 157; Charles L. 157; Frank E. 156*; George P. 157; Henry C. 157; Hiram D. 157; J. S. 526; John 243; Joseph W. 157; Lida 157; M. Alice (Gorrell) 157; Margaret Bullock 157; Sophia Ann Bowman 243; Theodore 157

GOSWEILER, Emma Smith 161; William 161

GOVER, Cassandra 194; George P. 205; Jarrett 568; Juliet E. 205

GRAFTON, Alexander 277; Ann Elizabeth Hines 277; Ann L. 277; Basil 277*; Bennet 336; Corbin 335*; Corbin (Crobin) M. 277, 333; Eliza Ward 336; James 335; James O. 336; Georgia A. 333; Hannah Lee 277; Jesse 336; Liza 277; Maggie L. 277; Margaret C. 336; Martha H. 277; Martin 277; Mary 336; Mary Jane 277; Nathan 277; Phoebe 336; R. L. 277; Sarah Maud 277; William 336; William 277

GRAHAM, Addie 533; Alice 533; Caroline Richardson 211; Catherine 533; Charles 211; Eliza J. Caldwell 533; Elizabeth Cooper 211; Ella M. 533; Elliott 533; Helen 211; James T. 428, {532} 533; John B. 208*; John C. 211; Lafayette 211; Mary 469, 533; Matilda 533; Rebecca Lewis 211; Robert 469; Roberta 533; Rose 533; Theodore 533*; William 208; William H. 211; Zachariah Butcher 208, 211

GRANGER, Laura V. 264; William 264

GRAVES, Maggie Holden 156; Robert 156

GRAY, Eliza Bowman 242; George 242

GREEN, Abigail 414, 519; Catnerine Graham 533; Clement 325; Henrietta 522; John 533; John S. 202; Joshua R. 202*; L. May 202; Mollie E. 202; Moses I. 202; Robert 414; Robert C. 202; Sallie R. 202; Sarah Rankin 202

GREENLAND, Elizabeth 364; Mary B. 491

GREME, Mrs. Angus 325; Augustus I. 325; J. A. 419

GRIER, Caroline 431; Eliza 431; Eliza Monks 400; Elizabeth Patterson 431; Emantos 431; Elmore 431; Franklin 431; Helen 431; J. Patterson 431; James 431; James A. 431*; John 431; John P. 431; Lorenzo 431; Martha 431; Martha Hindman 431; Mary 431; Mary Ann 431; Mary Jane Thomas 431; Melinda 431; Mortimer 431; Ralph 431; Sultina 431; Thomas 431; Thomas L. 400; William 431

GRIEST, Joseph P. 400; Mabel Haines 400

GRIFFIN, Ella J. 521; Georgia A. 307; William E. 521

GRIFFITH, (Miss) 572; Erving 503; I. G. Jr. 236; Jonn L. 452; Laura Boulden 236; Lewis A. 573; Sallie B. 452

GROOME, Eliza Jeannette 237; Elizabeth Black 575; Elizabeth Black (Wallace) 237; James B. 468; James Black 237; John 237; John C. 237, 575; Samuel W. 237

GROSS, Catherine 530; Catherine Cooper 530; Ellen 530; Frank 533; George 530; Jacob 530*; Jacob, Sr. 530; John 530; Julia A. 530; Keziah Bryley 530; Luther 533; Margaret 530; Martha J. 533; Mary 530; Richard 533; Thomas 533; William 533

GROVES, Rebecca A. 384

GRYMES, Ella J. 177

GUILE, Samuel 133

GUILFOYLE, Eliza Henderson 568; Henry W. 568*; John F. 568; John H. 569; Maggie E. Hildt 569; Mamie E. 569; Mary E. 568; Priscilla E. 569; William 568

GUINN, Ann 262

GUNTHER, Frederick 204; Sophia 204

GUYTON, Martha 547

GWINN, Caroline F. 225

HACKETT, Henrietta J. Bedford 258; Major 258

HAILE, Amanda 507; Charles T. 507; Cornelia S. 507; Frederick D. 507; George M. 507; Hannah C. 507; Laura 507; Sarah Deets 507; Susanna 507; Wilson 507

HAINES, Alice 235; Amanda M. Brown 291; Ann Eliza 235; Anna Duyckinck 524; Basil 472; Charles H. 288; Cornelia H. 288; Edwin 374; Eli 288; Eli, Jr. 314; Eli, Sr. 314; Elizabeth Jackson 315; Ella Warner Rittenhouse 488; Estella 291; Eugene M. 400; Frank 235; Frederick Taylor 315; George 235; Gertrude E. Gillespie 400; H. H. 400, {486} 487*; Hannah Jane Harris 235; Hannah Marshall 315; Harriet Kirk 288; Harry 235; James 235; Jeremiah B. 400; Job 314; Joe Edward 235; Joseph 288, 314, 488; L. Marshall 314*; Lewis 488; Mabel 400; Margaret 314; Maria 335; Mary Ann Rockwell 235; Mary C. 291; Mary E. 288; Mary Kirk 400; Rachel A. 315; Reuben 287*, 288, 335, 370; Richard 314; Robert 288; Samuel 234, 314, 315; Samuel E. 315; Sarah Kirk 488; Thomas 234; Warren Jackson 315; Will 235; William 524; William H. 234*; William L. 288; William Penn, Jr. 399*; William Penn, Sr. 400

HALL, (Colonel) 262; Ann Gwinn 262; Anna 262, 294; Christiana J. 346; Elisha 262; Henry 581; James C. 382; Lillie Pue 391; Margaret Mitchell 262; Richard 294; Richard D. 262*; Sarah D. 382; Sophia 581; Susan Davidson 526; Washington 262, 294; Washington H. 262; William 526

HALLOWELL, Ann H. 459

HAMBLETON, (Mr.) 395; Carrie 371; Frank 371; Harry 371; Jesse W. 370*; Joseph 370; Mary 371; Rachel Lewis 371; Samuel 370, 371; William C. 371

HAMILTON, Alexander 351; Lucinda 351; H. 147; Hannah Booth (Quinn) 436; Ida Gifford 147; Robert 436

HAMWAY, Frank 569

HANBY, John W. 174; Mary Jane Mitchell 174

HANNA, Alexander 512, 527; Anna M. 527; Edwin F. 456; Elizabeth Jervis 527; Hannah E. 512; Hannah N. 527; Henry N. 456; Horace 459; James W. 527*; Jane McGaw 512; John 512, 527; John A. 456, 459; John B. 214, 456*; John L. 407; Lizzie S. 515; Margaret Casho 407; Martha A. Barnes 456; Martha Standiford 459; Mary Fulton 214, 459; Robert 527; Robert F. 512*; Stephen B. 214, 456, 527; Susan R. 512; William 512, 527; William F. 456, 459; William S. 515; Zenolia 515

HANNAH, Evaline 525; James 208; Rebecca 208

HANSON, Ada 204; Amelia 204; Dena 204; Emelie Emmord 204, 567; Emmord 204; Herman 567; Herman W. 204*; Irene 204; Lucy 204; Martha 215; Ruth 204; Sophia Gunther 204; Thomas 204

HANWAY, B. F. 301; Bertha A. Quinby 472; Carroll 337; David 165, 301, 568; E. C. 301; Ella 301; George William 301; Harriet B. 462; Mrs. James B. 461; Jane 414; Joseph B. {300} 301*; L. Littleton 146; Libbie A. Morgan 337; Lillian 337; Martha Rouse 461; Mary E. Noble 568; S. E. Rouse 302; Samuel 461; Sarah 146; Sarah Ann Keen 336; Sarah B. 301; Sarah Keen 301; Stanley 337; T. Littleton 336; Thomas 301, 336*, 462; Thomas H. 472; Timothy L. 301; Walter 337

HARKINS, Aaron 554; Hannah J. 554; Harry E. 401; J. T. 431; James W. 554*; John 554; Martha A. Bassford 554; Mary E. Gibson 554; Richard R. 554; Sallie A. Monks 401; Sarah 162; Sultina Grier 431; Thomas A. 554; William 554; William A. 554

HARLAN, Bessie Webster 184, 482; Caroline 482; David {132} 133*, 419, 481, 482; David E. 144; Edwin 482; Elizabeth 482; Elizabeth Schaefer 482; Ellen 482; Esther 482; Esther Stump 133; Etta 509; Florence 398; Frances 482; George 133; George F. 398; George S. 482; Hannah 482; Henry 419, 482, 509*; Henry D. 144, 419, 482; Henry S. 510; Herbert 144, 145; Hettie F. 510; Hettie F. Turner 510; James T. 510; Jeremiah 133, 482, 509; Joseph 333; M. 265; Margaret Rebecca (Herbert) 141, 144; Mary 482; Michael 133; Oleita 144; Reuben S. 481, 482, 509; W. Beatty 143, 144, 145; William 482; William H. 184, 481*

HARLAND, Hannah 338

HARNON, Mary Ann Thomas 578; Thomas W. 578

HARPER, Anna 186; Samuel 238

HARRIS, Alice McMullen 235; Hannah Jane 235; Wilder 235

HARRISON, Caroline H. Webster 184; E. P. H. 184

HARRY, Martha J. 268

HARTGRAVE, Lydia 405

HARTMAN, John 252; Mary 252

HARWARD, C. W. 396, 540; Ella V. 396, 540

HASSON, James 479

HAUGH, D. F. 489*

HAURAND, Mary E. 397

HAWKINS, (Professor) 388; Amanda A. Strong 508; Anna L. 509; Arvilla 174; Edwin 518; Elizabeth E. James 172; Esther 482; Etta Harlan 509; Frances 482; Gilbert S. 509*; Jonn 509, 518; John A. 518; Lillian E. 509; Mary G. 508; Mary J. 518; Nicholas 518; Phil 172; Susan Thompson 518; Thomas 508; Thomas W. 518; William L. 482, 509

HAWKS, Rev. Dr. 324

HAYHURST, Ruth 519

HAYNE, (surname only) 488

HAYS, Mary 332

HAYWARD, Amanda N. 541; Augustus O. 542; Charles J. 542; Edward B. 542; Eugene H. 542; Florence M. 542; Francis S. 542; Helen M. Bussey 542; Helen R. 542; James F. 542; Joseph J. 541; Lillian J. 542; Margaret J. 541; Maria A. 541; Samuel h. 541; Sarah Briarly 541; Thomas 541; Thomas B. 541*; Thomas S. 542

HAZLETT, William 347

HEADLEY, Huldah Michener 264; James D. 264

HEAPS, Belle M. Cameron 268; Belle V. 557; David H. 268; Eliza J. 557; Hugh T. 557*; Ida B. 268; John 557; Laura L. Tate 268; Maggie Barton 558; Martha Alexander 557; Martha J. Harry 268; Mary C. 268; Mary M. 557; Nathan W. 268; Osborne H. 268; Robert 267, 268, 557; Robert L. 267; Sallie A. 557; Sarah C. 268; Sarah Stokes 268; William A. 557; Zephaniah 267*

HEARD, J. P. 550; L. Louise Sewell 550

HEARNDON, Henry 206; Maria 206

HEATZIG, Adolph 224; Charles A. 224; Eleanor Stein 224; Emma 224; John 224; Laura 224; William B. 224*

HECHT, Isaac 434

HECK, Cassandra 278; Cassandra E. Morgan 278; Charles Henry 278; Charles L. 278*; Elizabeth E. 278; Elizabeth Hoffman 278; Laura 278; Louisa 278; Martha P. 278; Mary 278; Philip 278; Philip Martin 278; Philipine 278

HEIM, Christina 254

HELMBOLD, (Rev.) 372

HENDERSON, A. Neely 523*; Alfred Neely 528; Alice A. 528; Alice C. 524; Alice J. 384; Alma Best 384; Ann 384; Anna B. Smith 384; Armstrong 384; Benjamina 384; Eliza 568; Elizabeth 184; Ellwood S. 524; Emily 384; Gustavus 384; Helen 384; J. 384; James 384; Jane Neely Lutes; John 383; John S. 384; John T. 384; M. Emma 528;

Margaret Brown 528; Martha 384; Martha P. 524; Mary 384; Mary E. 524; Nora 384; R. Ann Patterson 524; Rebecca A. Groves 384; Robert T. 528; Ross C. 524; Susan 384; Susan T. Meredith 528; Thomas 523; 527*, 528; William 384; William C. 383*

HENRIQUES, Joseph 559*; Lavinia 560; Moses 560; Peter H. 561; Sarah B. Hoke 561; Sarah Nunes 560; William H. 560

HENRY, Mary D. 452

HENSON, Elizabeth 520; Thomas 520

HERBERT, James 153; James Beatty 141, 144; John 144, 145; Margaret Beatty 145; Margaret Rebecca 141, 144, 145; Mary A. Baker 141; Mary J. 489; William Paul 144, 145

HERING, Mary Eleanor Brown 276; W. S. 276

HERMAN, Augustine 343

HESS, Christian 244; Christian, Sr. 244; Elizabeth N. Clemson 245; Elizabeth Roop 245; George E. L. 245; Henry 244*; Henry C. 245; Hiester 245; Louisa Frances 245; Maria E. 305; Maria Elizabeth 245; Moses 244

HESSEY, Anna Sutton 251; Ellen H. 251; Ellen M. 251; Frank H. 251; George W. 251; Henry 251; John H. {250} 251*; Laura E. Morgan 251; Mary A. 251; William S. 251

HETRICK, Adam 306*; Annie 306; Cassie 306; Catherine Wendt 306; Clara 306; Elizabeth Rator 306; Jane 306; John 306; John C. 306; Mary V. Walker 282; Mollie V. Walker 306; Nicholas 306; Susan Bird 306; Theodore J. 282, 306

HEWITT, Elizabeth 407

HICKS, Thomas H. 121

HIGGINBOTHAM, Ann 344

HIGHLAND, John 419; Sarah W. 419

HILD, Georgius 321; Margaret Ann 321

HILDT, Maggie E. 569

HILL, (Col.) 448; Joseph C. 448; Levina 448; N. B. 492; Sarah J. 338

HINDMAN, Eliza M. 303; Ella J. 397; Hiram 396; John Coulson 396*; John C., Jr. 397; L. Blanche 397; Martha 431; Mary E. Haurand 397; Rachel A. Edmondson 397; Rachel Coulson 396

HINES, A. J. 443; Ann Elizabeth 277; Ann Simpson 443; Anna Webster 214; John T. 277; Matthew 443; Sarah 443; William 443; William H. 214

HITCHCOCK, Cordelia 498

HOFFMAN, Allen 204*; Elizabeth 278; Henry 325; John 204; Sallie R. Sheridan 205

HOGSMAN, Annie 158

HOKE, Jacob 561; Peter 561; Sarah B. 561

HOLDEN, Anna 156; Charles 156; Clementine 156; Elizabeth 156; George 156; Harriet 156; Helen 156; Henry W. 156; Jacob 156; John H. 156; Maggie 156; Margaret Bolden 156; Mary Ann 156; Mitchell 156; Sophia 156; Talitha Mahoney 156; Theodore B. 156; William 156; William T. 156; William W. 155*

HOLLAND, Catherine Armstrong 285; Ellen 423; William 285

HOLLINGSWORTH, (Col.) 413, 447; Abigail Green 414, 519; Ada Roberta Young 414; Amos 271*; Amos W. 411, 414; Anna I. 397; Catherine Cornish 413; Catherine Hoskins 397; Charles A. 411, 413*; Barclay E. 483; Cordelia 173; Curtis A. 483; Cyrus C. 411, 414; Daniel 397, 411; Daniel P. 414; David F. 412; Edith Carter 483; Edward 334, 520; Edward P. 411*, 414; Edward W. 414; Eli 483; Eliza 271; Elizabeth 411 414; Elizabeth Atkinson 412; Hanna S. Carter 283, 483; Hannah F. Moore 412, 414; Harrie J. 483; Jane Hanway 414; Jeremiah 483; Joel C. 283, 483*; John {270} 271; John S. 414; Karl A. 414; Lois P. Clements 411, 414; Lydia 271; Maggie B. 483; Margaret 271; Marie 412; Mary 334, 520; Mary Warner 334, 519; Nathaniel 271, 283; 333, 334, 414, 483, 519*, 520; Nathaniel T. 283*; Rachel Benson 271; Rebecca 411, 414; Rebecca G. 334, 520; Robert 411, 414; Robert A. 412; Samuel H. 283; Sarah 334, 520; Silas 483, 271; Silas W. 283, 334, 383, 520; Thomas 271, 333*, 520; Thomas, Jr. 519; Thomas, Sr. 519; Valentine 519; Valentine, Sr. 413; William 271; William Y. 414; Zebulon 236

HOLLIS, Mary C. 373

HOLLOWAY, Abbie Cook 358; Albert S. 357*; Edwin 358; Eliza D. 358; Hester N. Stump 358; Hugh S. 357; Margerie 358; Mary R. 358; Richard 357; Rowland 358; Samuel S. 358; William R. 358

HOLLOWELL, Sarah A. 327

HOLT, Andrew 163; Andrew W. 163*; Ann Foster 163, 218; Annie Burns 164; Charles 164; Gertrude 164; Isaac Lumsdon 163; Lizzie 163; May 163, 164; Washington 163, 218; Woodall 164

HOOKER, Ann L. Grafton 277; Ed. 277; John 431; Melinda Grier 431

HOOPES, Elizabeth Tucker 362; Price 362

HOOPMAN, Catherine 281; Christian 281; Mary E. 185

HOPE, Catherine Hutchins 441; Elizabeth E. Pocock 441; Ellen 441; James 441; Thomas 441; Thomas, Jr. 441; William {440} 441*

HOPKINS, Amanda Dallam 401; Amanda V. Reasin 158; Anna Harper 186; Annie 402, 522; Annie Hetrick 306; B. 158; Cassandra 401; Charles 401; Edward 401; Ellen 477; Ezekiel 274; Francina 402; Frank 186; George W. 378; Grace 346; Henry W. 522; J. Lee 401, 402; John W. 477; Johns 274, 510; Joseph 401; Joseph R. 344; Josephine 401; Lillie M. 186; Lizzie Stevenson 401; Maria McCausland 344; Mary 346, 510; Mary H. 274; Melissa R. 344; Priscilla 375; Samuel G. 306; Sophy Spencer 378; William B. 401*; William Stephenson 402

HOPPER, Henry Barnes 378; Helen 378; James 377*; John 377; Kate Mathews 378; Keziah Hufsee 377; Mabel Leslie 378; Sally E. Barnes 378; Seth 377; Thomas 377

HOSKINS, Angeline 397; Anna I. Hollingsworth 397; Catherine 397; Cornelia H. 397; Elizabeth Cheyney 397; Fannie C. 397; George W. 397; Hattie 397; Jesse 397*; Joseph A. 397; Joseph B. 397; Nathaniel 397; Philena 397; Phoebe H. 397; Raymond H. 397; Sarah A. 397; Sarah M. 397; William 397

HOUSEKEEPER, P. B. 501*; Verquir Veasey 501

HOUSTON, Ella Mackie 274; Frank 274; Susan Armstrong 285; William 285

HOWARD, Eliza Ann 551; Emily 447; Ethel 341; Eveline 341; George R. 447, 449; Guy 341; H. D. M. 338*; Helen H. 449; Henry M. 341; John 553; Lavina Ford 341; Lydia C. Baker 364; Mary 405; Mary H. 449; Sally (Gilpin) 341; Veleska 341; Wesley 364; William P. 428

HOWELL, B. F. 472; Carrie S. Quinby 472

HOWLETT, Eliza 512; Nancy 207

HUDSON, J. K. 438; Margaret 166

HUFSEE, Keziah 377

HUGHES, (Sheriff) 188; Amos 178; Amos H. 171, 176*; Annie 176; Caroline 176; Charlotta Catharine 176; Charlotte Mitchell 176; Clara A. 188; Elizabeth T. Macklem 178; Eugene Lee 176; Hannah Catherine Adams 176; Hannah Emma 176; Henrietta 176; John 176; John Hall 176; Lucy Virginia 176; Mary 176; Mary C. 171; Mary H. McCleary 355; Robert Henry 176; Scott 176; William 355; William Oliver 176

HUNT, (Dr.) 429; Edwin M. 282, 314; Ella 282; Inez White 206; Henry 572; Mary Smith 572; William 206

HUNTER, Elizabeth 564; Ida M. Webster 184; J. Abell 184

HURST, Mary Smith 308; Matthias 308

HUSBAND, Hannah P. 216; Herman 216; Joshua 216*; Joshua, Sr. 216; Margaret Jewett 216; Ruth W. Pennock 216; Thomas J. 216; William 216; William P. 216

HUTCHINS, Alvarda 519; Ann R. 519; Catherine 441; Charles L. 519; Elizabeth 519, 546; Estella 519; Gertrude 519; John S. 519; Laura 519; Manda Z. 470; Martha J. 519; Mary J. Hawkins 518*; Maud 519; Susan M. 519; William B. 519; Zanie 519

HUTCHINSON, D. W. 437; Emma Cooley 437; Sarah Elizabeth 168

HYDE, A. L. 202; Annie Maria Smith 572; Anthony 572; Benjamin B. 482; Eveline 311; Frances Harlan 482; Hazen 202; Molly E. Green 202; Rosa 202

HYLAND, (family) 504*; Albert 504; Araminta 503; Arminta 504; Benton 504; Elonora 504; Harriet 504; Henry 504; John 504; Lambert 504; Maria Kankey 504; Martha 504; Martha Rebecca 504; Mary 504; Mary Mauldin 504; Nicholas 504; Stephen 504

IRELAND, John M. 288; Mary E. Haines 288

JACKSON, Elizabeth 315; Ella M. Coale 128; Frederick D. 128; J. T. 315; John R. 490; Julia A. 281; Sophia 434

JAMAR, Henrietta Barroll 258; Laura C. 258; R. E. 258; Victoria Barroll 258

JAMES, A. Minnie 423, Annie 172; B. W. C. 172; C. H. 291; C. Harry 423; Catherine 420; Charles H. 172, 420; Clara Coale 291; Cornelia H. 423; Elizabeth 420; Elizabeth E. 172; Emma E. 172; George B. 172*, 420; J. C. Hagey 423; J. Gilbert 172; J. L. 291; Jacob 420; Jacob M. 172, 420; James 172; Jarvis G. 420; Jarvis Gilbert 172; Jennie 420; John L. 172, 420; Joseph 172; Lemuel C. 423; Lulu A. 423; Maria (J.) Coale 291, 423; Mary C. 172; Paul C. 172; S. S. 172; Sarah E. Keithley 172; Sarah Gilbert 172, 420; Sarah S. 172; Sophia Jane 172; Stephen G. 172; Susie 420; William 420; William Joseph 172

JAMISON, Archibald 148; Oleita G. Michael 148

JANNEY, Annie M. 193; Catherine 147, 192; Charlotte 192; Charlotte M. Reed 193; Eli 582; Elizabeth A. Nowland 582; George W. 582*; Hester 582; Hester Lackland 582; J. Kirk 193; J. Taylor 192*; Jesse 147, 192, 582; John 582; Mary 192; Maria Taylor 192; Nathan L. 582; Rachel 582; Randel 424; Rebecca E. 582; Sarah T. England 193; Thomas 192, 582; Thomas Sr. 582; Wilbur 582

JARRETT, (Capt.) 167; Archer Hays 225*; Ida Virginia 225; James H. 529, 536; James Henry 225; Jesse 529; Joshua W. 529, 536; Julia A. Scarff 529, 536; Luther M. 529, 536; Margaret McMaster 225; Martin L. 529*, 536; Mary Virginia Cairnes 225; Mary Virginia Streett 225; Sallie E. 536; Sallie Liona 225; Sarah E. 529; Sarah F. Glenn 529; Thomas B. 529, 536; William B. 529, 536; William Bosley 225; William Hope 225

JARVIS, (Miss) 407

JEFFREY, Joseph 234; Mary Rembold 234

JEFFREYS, Anna 366

JENKINS, Abbie J. 501; Anna M. Brown 523; Catherine C. 523; Catherine L. 523; Edward 214; Henry C. 523*; Ignatius 523; Ignatius W. 523; Jane R. 523; Mary J. 523; Oswald 523; Samuel O. 523; William 523

JENNINGS, Charlotte Reed 244; Jesse Taylor 244; Sara (Duchess of Marlborough) 129, 380

JERVIS, Elizabeth 527

JEWENS, Harriet E. 191; Mary C. Carsins 416; S. D. 416

JEWETT, Hugh I. 419

JEWITT, Margaret 216

JOHNES, (Miss) 157

JOHNSON, Angeline 397; Benjamin F. 429; Caroline Nowland 429; Charles 429, 578; Charles H. 429; Charles L. 429; Ed. 534; Enoch 574; Frederick 120; George A. M. 429; Harriet L. 574; Helen 431; Jethro 197; Joseph 429; Josie Callahan 534; Mary 578; Mary A. 197; Mary McCullough 429; Otho 429; Samuel M. 429*; Sarah Jane 578; William 323; William W. 429

JOHNSTON, George 464

JONES, (Miss) 447; Amy D. Monks 401; Harriett B. 264; Mary 578; Mary G. 510; Sarah A. 333; William D. 401; William J. 315

KAHOE, Daisy 255; Michael 255

KAMMER, Charles 567; Mollie Emmord 567

KAMMERER, Jacob 162; Mollie 162

KANKY, Maria 504

KARSNER, (Dr.) 369; Cornelia H. 222, 369; Daniel 222, 369; Eleanor 369; Eleanor F. Millechop 222; Elsie Eleanor 223; Sarah C. Bouchelle 223; William C. 222*

KAY, Alexander B. 285*; Bradford Ramsey 286; Charlotte 286; Ellen 286; Elizabeth Talmadge 286; Howard B. 286; John 286; Lewis D. 286; Robert H. 286; Stewart W. 286

KEAN, James 325; John 325

KEATING, Thomas J. 343

KEEN, Priscilla 242; Sarah 301; Sarah Ann 336; Timothy 301

KEENE, Annie L. Walker 282; Mary E. 238; Quila 238; Rebecca 378; William J. 281

KEETLEY, Martha J. 328

KEILHOLTZ, Ada B. 343; Amos E. 343; Charles M. 343; Clara C. 343; Ella N. 343; Ellis H. 343; Emma Beatrice 343; Henry C. 343; John 342*; Lillie R. 343; Martha E. Kirk 343; Mary 343; Mary A. 343; Sarah Mossey 343; William K. 343

KEITHLY, Sarah E. 172

KELLY, A. J. 197; Indiana Benjamin 197; Margaret 576

KENDALL, James A. 334

KENLY, George W. 145, 146; Harriet 146; James 301; James F. 145*; Jessie 146; Julia 146; Lemuel 146; LeRoy 146; Marion 146; Mary 146; Mary E. 146; Rebecca Rouse 145; Sarah 146; Sarah (B.) Hanway 146

KENNARD, Mary 482

KENNEDY, Douglas Elliott 564; Elise 564; Eliza C. 564; Elizabeth Smith 393; Elmira 564; Ethel 564; James 564; James H. 564*; John 564; John M. 373; John W. 393; Mamie A. 509; Samuel L. 564; Silas Baldwin 564

KENT, (Miss) 572

KERFOOT, George B. 494*; Julia E. Lippincott 497; William D. 494

KERR, Caroline Isador 455; James W. 542; John 325; Melissa McCleary 355; William 355

KERSEY, William 266

KERWIN, C. R. 148; Lydia Michael 148

KESSINGER, Mary Tucker 500; William 500

KESSLER, May W. 352

KETTELL, George F. 344; Katherine 344

KEYS, Ann M. Spedden 273; Charles 273; Mabel 274; Mary H. Hopkins 274; Samuel 273; Samuel J. 273*

KEYSER, (family) 127; Allen Dirck 409; Anna 408; Charles A. 408; Charles M. 408; Derrick 408; George 409; Grace K. 408; Louise Altvater 409; Margaret 408; Martha 408; Mary 408; Mary Louise 409; Newberry A. S. 408*; Wilson 408

KIDD, Charlotte Janney 192; T. W. S. 192

KIMBALL, Coulton 282; Frank 163; Mary J. Reynolds 282; Rosie Wilkinson 163

KIMBLE, Ada Slack 412; Anna Mary Ellis 464; Evelyn Teresa 464; Fanny Titus 412; Hannah Carver 484; Henry Evans 464; Henry Harding 412, 463, 484*; Ida Louisa 464; John 484, 487; John H. 413; John Henry 462*; Mary Titus 412, 484; Sarah Teresa Gallaher 463; Seruch 463, 487; Seruch Titus 412*, 464

KING, Henry S. 145; Louisa S. 145

KINKY, (Miss) 425

KIRBY, Eliza 125; Fannie 360; Rachel L. 125; Zebulon S. 125

KIRK, Ada 387; Adrianda Reynolds 261; Alexander 261; Allen 471; Amelia 446; Ann T. Reynolds 305; Anna E. 282; Annie E. Reynolds 387; Benjamin F. 394, 472; Elisha 471, 472; Elisha England 207*; Eliza 352; Elizabeth B. Crothers 394; Ella J. Hindman 397; Ellis P. 387; Eugene 208; Evander 472; Hannah Mount 472; Harriet 288; Harry 208; Hattie 208; Isabelle Taylor 208; J. P. 282; Jacob 305, 488; James 208; James R. 472; Jesse A. 472; Jesse Allen [470] 471*; John 472; Josiah 387; Josiah P. 387; Lemuel 472; Levi 208; Levi B. 358; Lewis 387; Lewis R., Jr. 397; Martha 208; Martha E. 343; Martha J. 472; Martha McCullough 472; Mary 400; Mary A. 472; Mary J. Warner 472; Mary R. Holloway 358; Mount E. 472; Rebecca Hannah 208; 472; Roger 471, 488; Sarah 488; Sherwood H. 387; Walter 208; Walter B. [386] 387*; William 288, 382; William A. 472; William M. 208

KIRKPATRICK, John 127

KIRKWOOD, Ed C. 257; Elizabeth McNamee 327; Jane Ann 538; John 327; John B. 538; Mary 512, 538; Mary Bevard 257; Nathaniel C. 538*; Rebecca Bell 538; Robert 538; Samuel J. 538; William 538

KITTERLINUS, Daisy Carter 327; Eugene 327

KNIGHT, Elizabeth 293; John Wesley 277; Laura 277; Lydia 304; Nellie 228; William 228

KOSHER, John 147; Lucy Strasbaugh 147

KRAUSE, Caroline Schilling 490; Charles 490

KRAUT, Dora 226

KROH, Eliza Light 252; Frank 252; Philip 252; Sophia 252

KUHN, Catherine M. 426; Jacob 426; Rebecca A. 426

KULDELL, A. R. 567; Louisa Emmord 567

KYLE, Adam 396, 540; Ann E. Fendall 396; Annie 396, 540; Ella V. Harward 396, 540; George 396, 540; Grace 396, 540; Samuel A. S. 395*, 540*

LACKLAND, Hester 582

LACOFLIN, P. 172; Sophia Jane James 172

LAMAR, Charles Augustus Lafayette 119; Gassaway B. 119; Jane M. Creswell 119

LAMBERT, Adam 574; Caleb 574; Emily Veach 574; Georgianna Barrett 574; Harriet L. Johnson 574; Ida M. 574; John A. 574*; Laura 574; Lydia 574; Martha 574; Mary A. 574; Mary Reed Adams 574; Matthew Watson 574; R. C. 316; Robert 574; Susan 574

LANTZ, Fred 204; Lucy Hanson 204

LARZELERE, Annie Scarborough 187; Robert C. 187

LATOUR, Eliza J. 360

LAUGHLIN, Henrietta 377

LAWRENSON, Hannah 503; Lydia Foard 503; Sarah 503

LAWSON, John A. 503

LAWTHER, (Mr.) 571; Maria Johanna Somerset 571

LAWTON, Emma 490

LEE, Alice 452; Amanda 579; Anna Wilson 193; Bryarly 405; Cassandra 194, 452; Cassandra Gover 194; D. M. 346; Elizabeth Dallam 405, 452; Elizabeth M. 405; Mrs. F. 566; Fannie 194; Hannah 277; Hannah B. 451, 452; Helen M. 452; Henry Hall 405; Henry W. Archer 452; James 193, {404} 405*; James Carvil 405, 451; John 194; John L. G. 452; Laura 194; Lycurgus 194; Lydia 194; Mary 405; Mary A. 276; Mary E. Bryarly 405; Mary E. Whitaker 405; Mary Howard (Munnikhuysen) 405; Nathaniel 276; Olivia Jane 405; Otho S. 451*; Otho Scott 452; Parker H. 193, 405; Parker H., Jr. 405; Parker H., Sr. 405; Parker Hall 451; Priscilla 194; R. C. 397; R. D. 414; Ralph 579; Richard 257; Richard Dallam 451; Sallie B. Griffith 452; Samuel 193; Samuel M. 193*; Sophia Warner 346; William 194; William D. 193

LEIB, Mary Jane 389

LEIGH, (Lt.) 139

LEMON, Harry 574; Lydia Lambert 574

LEONARD, Elizabeth Richardson 574; Zachariah 574

LESTER, William 174

LEVERING, (family) 423; Alexander T. 499; Enoch 275, 499; Gerhard 275; Howard A. 499*; Jesse 499; Joshua 408; Margaret Keyser 408; Martha B. 274; Martha Keyser 408; Peter 499; Rosier 275; Sarah Brown 499; Sarah R. 499; Thomas W. 275; Wigard 275

LEVICK, (Dr.) 429

LEVIS, Amelia K. 352, 446; Amelia Kirk 446; Anna M. Armstrong 352; Eliza 327, 352, 446; Eliza Kirk 352; Ella C. 447; Emma A. 352; Harriet 352, 446; Harry B. 446; Hester 447; Hester C. Connor 447; Joseph K. 352*, 446; Joshua 327; Lydia 266; Lydia C. 447; Mary 352; Mary L. 446; May W. Kessler 352; Norris 327, 352, 446; Norris K. 352; R. C. 446*; Robert C. 352, 447; William 352, 446

LEWIS, Lydia 326; Rachel 371; Rebecca 211

LIGHT, Adam 251; Eliza 252; George 252; James 252; John 251*, 252; Joseph 252; Mary 252; Mary Hartman 252; Nicholas 252; Robert 252; Samuel 252; Sophia Kroh 252; Thomas 252; William 252

LIGON, T. Watkins 265

LILLEY, Ella Coale 291; Robert 291

LINCOLN, Anna Reynolds 261; Charles S. 261; John 282; Lydia 282

LINN, Barbara Ann 572; Mary Brooke 572; Patrick 572

LIPPINCOTT, Julia E. 497

LITTLE, Jane 233

LLOYD, Elizabeth 120; Thomas 120

LOCKWOOD, Adelaide Morton 181; Blanche E. 182; Edward 181; Edward Wilson 181; George I. 182; George W. {180} 181*; Grace A. 182; Harry M. 182; James Booth 182; Julia E. M. 182; Marie T. 182; Martha E. 331; Robert 181; Sarah E. Alrichs 181

LODGE, Catherine 258

LOFLIN, Ella 291; Fannie 453; William 291

LOGAN, Minnie Benjamin 198; Oliver 435; Robert 283; Sophia 283, 284; Theresa Atkinson 435; Walter B. 198

LOGUE, (Miss) 503

LONG, Gamma 195

LONGSTREET, Emily 524

LORAINE, Catherine Lodge 258; Elizabeth W. 258; Henry W. 258; John C. 261; Kate I. 258; Ruth E. 258; Toward 258; Toward N. 258*; Toward N., Jr. 261; Willie R. Cavender 261

LOUDMAN, Christina Dollman 254; Daniel F. 254

LOVE, Esther Smith 563; Samuel 563

LOW, Amon 245; Anna 565; Benjamin F. 245; Bessie 565; Brittie 565; Chauncey 565; Clayton 565; Cora 565; David 245; Ennis 245; Festus 245; Grace 245; Harriett 245; Henry M. 245; Hulo 245; J. Blaine 565; Jeremiah 245, 565; Jeremiah L. 245; John 245; John F. 245; L. Ross 565; Laban 245, 565*; Lizzie M. 245; Margaret A. Taylor 565; Martin 245, 565; Maud 565; Milton 565; Obediah 245; Ora B. 565; Rachel A. Marstiller 245; Rebecca 565; Rebecca Fifer 245; Rebecca M. 245; Rezin 245; Rufus 245*, 565; Simon G. 245

LOWBER, Catherine 493; Mary Patton 493; Peter 493

LOWE, Andrew 338; Jane 292; John 292; Joshua 292; Joshua R. 292; Matilda E. 525; Sarah Ales 292; Sarah D. 292; Sarah E. T. Durham 292; Silas J. 291*

LUCKEY, Bessie 548; Clara 548; Edward T. 548; Elizabeth 548; Ella 548; George 548; George J. 548; James 547; James B. 548; Jennie 548; John B. 548; Joshua G. 547*; Laura 548; Lue 548; Martha Guyton 547; Mary Lytle 548; Octavia A. 548

LUM, Mary 237

LUMSDON, see page 163

LUSSON, Charles Leander 324

LUTES, Jane Neely 528

LYLE, Ann 452

LYNCH, Alice Haines 235; Anna E. 376; Clinton 376; Edmund 376; Eliza A. 452; Eliza J. 376; Emily E(lizabeth) Falls 297, 376; George W. 376; Harrison 526; Helen B. 376; Herbert W. 376; John 375, 534; John T. 376; Joseph 235; Letitia 526; Lydia 375; Mary 534; Mary Callanan 534; Nettie C. 376; Percival F. 376; Rachel 376; Stephen 376; William 375; William H. 297, 375*; Wilmer J. 376

LYON, Susanna 353

LYTLE, Asenath 511; Mary 548

MACATEE, Henry 325

613

McCALL, Margaret Fulton 214; Mary L. 428

McCAULEY, (Judge) 420; Daniel 370, 409; Elizabeth 369, 409, 410; Elsie R. 410; Etheland Gallagher 410; Francina Baker 409; Hannah Louise 410; Hattie S. 410; Helen A. 410; James 369, 370, 409*; James Andrew 410; James J. 410; Jay Hayes 410; John 158, 369, 409, 410, 434; Louise Alexander 402; Mary 410; Melicent B. Price 410; Rachel 410; Rachel J. Simpers 158; Sarah Beard 410; William T. 402

McCAUSLAND, Andrew J. 341; Ann Higginbotham 344; George W. 344; Inez 344; John C. 344; Marcus H. 344; Maria 344; Mary J. 344; Melissa R. Hopkins 344; Paul C. 344; Robert 344; Sarah A. 344; Thomas Jefferson 344*

McCAY, Annie Emmons 379; Beulah 379; Caroline Bettley 379; Cora B. 379; Ella V. 379; Elma 379; Emily G. 379; Eva C. 379; Florence 481; George B. 379; George P. 379; Henry 481; Henry B. 379*; Isabel C. Boughton 481; Isabella C. 479; James 379, 481; James G. 379, 481*; John 379, 481; John, Jr. 379; John J. 379; Joshua 481; Joshua P. 379, 481; Laura S. 379; Marcus 379, 481; Maggie Pennington 379; Margaret 481; Mary 379; Mary A. 379; Mary Broughton 379, 481; Mary R. 481; Sophia 481; Washington N. 379; William B. 379

McCLEARY, Ann Robinson 354; Annie 355; Elizabeth Gallagher 355; Elmira 355; Emma 355; John 354*; Joseph 354; Mary 354; Mary H. 355; Melissa 355; Robert J. 355; Theodore F. 355; William 354

McCLELLAN, Geo. B. 505

McCLUNG, Amanda Z. 389; Benjamin F. W. 545; Benton N. 389; Columbus P. 545; Cynthia J. Strawbridge 389; Elsie M. 545; Ephraim B. 389*; Hannah A. Cathcart 544*; Hannah E. Wiley 389; John P. 389; John T. 389; Joseph 389; Laura B. 389; Lizzie M. 389; Lovisa R. 389; Margaret C. 389; Mary C. 389; Mary E. 545; Mary Payne 389; Morgan E. 389; Pearl R. 545; Robert 389; Robert R. 389, 545; Rosa F. 545; Samuel J. 545; Webster C. 389; Wiley P. 389

McCOLGAN, Jane 287

McCOMAS, C. N. 217; Ellen 377; George W. 217*; H. G. 217; Henry Clay 217; Henry G. 217; Isabelle 217; Keziah Cunningham 217; Nona Mary 217; Virginia G. Norris 217; William 217

McCOMBS, A. P. 454; Abram P. {340} 341*; Elizabeth 341; Ellen Prizer 341; George T. 341; H. S. 336; James 341; Maria C. Schott 342; William 341, 342

McCONNELL, Jacob D. 285; Mary Armstrong 285

McCORMICK, Caroline H. 184; Elizabeth 191; Elizabeth Henderson 184; James, Jr. 184; Theresa 466

McCRACKEN, John 399, 578; John H. 398*; Martha J. Cazier 399; Martha Jane 578; Ruth Richardson 399; Ruth Ann 578; William 399

McCRERY, A. T. 245; Albert 304*; Florence 305; Harriet 304; James 304; Jonn 304; John, Sr. 304; John T. 304; Louise 305; Maria E(lizabeth) Hess 245, 305; Mary 304; Samuel 304; Sarah 304; Sophia Perry 304; William 304

McCRONE, Margaret 253

McCULLOUGH, Andrew H. 557; Carrie Brady 254, 257; Carrie E. 516; Catherine W. Mitchell 557; Delia 557; Elizabeth Tull 516; Enoch 515, 516; Ethel E. 516; George 516; George W. 516; Henry M. 254; Henry Mitchell 556*; Hiram 247, 284, 296; James 557; James T. 557; Jethro 516; Jethro Johnson 515; John 516; John Tull 516; Margaret 516, 574; Martha 472; Mary 429, 557; Nettie Ray 516; Samuel D. {514} 515*; Sarah J. 355

McCURDY, Alexander C. 505; Alexander C., Jr. 505; Alice J. 505; Hannah Stansbury 505; Madonna 505; Martha A. Turner 505; Mary A. Turner 505; William C. 505*

McDARAH, Jane 497

McDEVITT, James 325

McDONOUGH, (Commodore) 504; Thomas 504; Mary 504

McDOWELL, Alexander 392; David 392, 393; H. Clayton 393; Henry C. 392*; James 392; James N. 393; Laura B. 393; Mary J. Gifford 393; Susan Runner 392; Thomas K. 393

McELWAIN, Almira Brooks 460; Cora E. 460; Daniel E. 460; Edith C. 460; Edith J. Brooks 460; Ella M. 460; Ellis W. 460; H. Clay 460; Harry E. 460; Henrietta R. 460; J. E. Clifton 460; John 460; John R. 459*; John S. 460; Lorenzo C. 460; Margaret V. 460; Mary 460; Mary S. 460; Olive M. 460; Rachel E. 460; Rebecca Webb 460; Robert B. 460; William 460; William J. 460

McFADDEN, Sarah A. 268

McFARLAND, Mary 185; Matilda 370; Richard 370

McGAW, Charles A. 520*; Elizabeth Hanson 520; Ella J. Griffin 520; James 520; Jane 512; Matilda 520; Robert 520; Robert, Jr. 520; Sallie J. 520; Thomas 520

McGINNIS, Amanda C. McClung 389; M. Tidings 389

McGONIGAL, Bridget 214

McGROW, James 264

MACHEN, A. W. 144

McINTYRE, Frank E. 408; Grace K. Keyser 408

MACK, Mrs. H. M. 436

MACKALL, William H. 297

McKELVY, Ellen 334

MACKENZIE, John P. 133

MACKEY, (Captain) 407; Andrew Jarrett 563; Barton Hurst 352; Catherine 271, 274; Cornelia 348; David 271, 352, 563; David Clinton 563; David Levis 352; Elizabeth 271; Emma A. Levis 352; Harvey H. 563*; Lydia Yerkes 563; Margaret M. Biles 564; Robert 563

MACKIE, Alfred A. 274; Amos 271; Arthur A. 274, 348; Catherine Andrews 268, 274, 348; Clement L. 274; Cornelia J. Read 348; David 274; David A. 274, 348*; Dora 271; Elizabeth Mackey 271; Ella 274; Emma 352; Eugene 271; Frank H. 274; Franklin T. 268*, 274, 348; Harry M. 274; J. Alfred 268, 274*, 348; James A. C. 274; John 268, 274, 348; John, Jr. 274; John C. 274; Lillie 271; Mary McVey 274; Nellie 271; Osborne 271; Robert 274

McKINDLESS, Elizabeth 391

McKINLEY, J. W. 236

McKINNEY, Georgia Ewing 474; Michael 474

MACKLEM, Annie M. 178; Bessie V. 178; Elizabeth Davies 178; Elizabeth T. 178; John 177; John M. 177*; John W. 178; Lavinia D. 178; Lucy B. 178; Mary 177; Mary Thompson 178; Rebecca J. 178; Sarah L. 178; William 177, 178; William J. 178

MACKLIN, Sadie Walker 282; William J. 282

McMANN, Barnard 436

McMASTER, Annie McCleary 355; Caroline E. Gwinn 225; David 355; Joseph 354; Margaret 225; Mary McCleary 354; Robert 225

McMILLAN, Catherine 434; John 548

McMULLEN, Alice 235; Margaret 566

McMURPHY, Emma 438

McNABB, Anna M. 203; David G. 203; David Paul 204; Hannah J. Scarborough 204; Isaac 203; James 203; James W. 203*; John 203; Joseph Martin 203; Laura Thomas

204; Luther H. 203; Nancy Martin 203; Sarah E. Savin 203; Thomas 203; William 203

McNALLY, John Joseph 325

McNAMARA, Jonn 197; Saran Benjamin 197

McNAMEE, Berenice 328; Cecil 328; Cornelia J. 327; Elizabeth 327; Francis 327; Frederick 327; Martha J. Keetley 328; Merritt S. 327*; Sarah A. Hollowell 327; Stephen D. 327; William A. 327

McNEAL, Bertha 467; Hannah Davis 466; Thomas 466

McNORRIS, Elizabeth F. Durham 525

McNUTT, Alice Enfield 207; William 207

McVAY, John 238; Nancy 238

McVEY, Amy 152, 243, 470; Benjamin F. 376; Christie 471; Jacob 470; Mary 274, 303, 455; Rachel A. Lynch 376; Rebecca Anderson 227

MAGARGLE, Mary S. 130, 426

MAGOWAN, Jennie 549

MAHAN, Joseph 398

MAHONEY, Cornelius 324; Elizabeth 435; John 326; Sarah J. 316; Talitha 156; William R. 156

MALLORY, Martha F. 577

MALONEY, Dena Hanson 204; William 204

MANIFOLD, Rebecca 502

MANLY, Anna E. 420, 569; Elizabeth L. 420; John 420; Louise J. Simcoe 383, 420; Nicholas 419, 569; Nicholas G. 419; Nicholas P. 419*, 569; Sarah Rebecca 420; Sarah W. Highland 419; Stephen 420

MANSFIELD, John 503, Letitia Foard 503; Sarah 503

MARINE, William M. 549

MARKLAND, Alice E. 357

MARSHALL, C. J. 515; Hannah 315; Humphrey 315; J. 515; James W. 121

MARSHBANK, Ann Lyle 452; Eliza A. Lynch 452; Eliza J. 452; Eliza J. Short 452; Fannie 452; Flora 452; Harry 452; Hyland 452; J. H. 452; John D. 452; Lidie Bennett 452; Maggie 452; Mary 452; Mary D. Henry 452; Richard 452; Robert 452*

MARSTELLAR, Rachel A. 245

MARTIN, Elizabeth 129, 380; Indiana O'Neill 359; Jonn 359; Luther 203; Nancy 203

MARTINDALE, Alice 417; Amos 417*; Ellen S. 417; Ellen S. Singley 417; Gertrude 417; Gertrude Vanarsdale 417; Hannah 417; Harry 417; Mary 417; Rebecca 417; Ross R. 417; Ross V. 417; Samuel 417

MARTINDELL, Lewis 516; Sarah 516

MASON, George 177

MASSEY, Charles H. B. 343; Mary Amanda Biddle 343

MATHER, Mary E. Kenly 146; Thomas W. 146

MATHERSON, Elizabeth 474

MATHEWS, Kate 378; Samuel H. 238

MATTHEWS, (Captain) 406; Ignatius 324;

MATTING, George 211; Helen Graham 211

MAUL, Frances R. 468

MAULDEN, Rebecca 145

MAULDIN, Francis 561; Mary 504

MAULSBY, J. D. 381; Mary C. 381; William P. 381, 419

MAXWELL, David 566; Edward S. 482; Elizabeth Coen 416; Ellen Harlan 482; John 416; Martha J. 416; Matilda Courtney 158; Rachel 566; William 158

MAYNADIER, Elizabeth Yellott 415; George Y. 414*; Henry 414; Henry G. 415, 416; J. M. 415; Jeremiah Y. 415; John H. 415; Laura P. Moores 415; P. Moores 416; S. Roberta 416; William 415; William C. 415; William M. 414, 415

MEARNS, Abel 432*; Andrew 432; Andrew F. 432; Frances 432; Franklin 355; Hannah Elizabeth Crothers 395; Josephine 432; Mary Cameron 432; Robert A. 432; Sarah Miller 355; Semelia 432; Thomas 395; Vianna 432

MEDCALF, Charles 258; Henrietta J. Barroll 258

MEGREDY, Hannah E. 446

MEREDITH, Susan T. 528

MERRITT, Anna 454; James 454; Joseph 453; Julius 454; Leota L. Wilson 454; Mary 454; Rachel Boulden 453; Richard B. 453*

MERRYMAN, Bertie J. 547; C. Marvin 547; Eleanora 547; Henry S. 547; Howard D. 547; John R. 547; Joseph 547; Joseph D. 547; Margaret E. 547; Mary E. 547; Nelson 547; Nelson O. 547*; S. Alice Gemmill 547; Sarah A. 547; Sarah Davis 547; Sarah J. 547; Walter G. 547

METZGER, Caroline 548

MEVAY, Martha 372

MICHAEL, Ann M. Mitchell 171; Annie F. Smith 191; Balchior 148; Daniel 148; Emma F. 361; Georgie Bell 148; Ida B. Gilbert 148; J. Colvin 171; Jacob 148; John 148; Jonn C. 148; John M. 191; Lydia 148; Martha Gilbert 148; Martha Mitchell 148; Oleita G. 148; William B. 361; William O. 148*, 527

MICHENER, A. J. 264*; Amanda M. 265; Amos J. 264, 265; Esther Reynolds 265; Harriet 264, 265; Huldah 264; John D. 264, 265; Joseph 264; Martha J. Reynolds 265; Mary J. 264; Sarah 264

MILBURN, A. Virginia 372; Amy A. Ramsey 372; Benjamin 372; Catherine Boyce 372; Mattie J. 372; Nicholas 371*

MILES, Margaret 201, 517

MILLECHOP, Eleanor F. 222

MILLER, (Mr.) 273; Adeline 418; Andrew T. 355; Ann Simpers 355; Anna 365; Annie M. 355; Annie Whitson 355; Benjamin 158; Catherine 355; Catherine I. 182; Charles 355; Clara 467; Clara Brown 430; Clifton 430; Edward 418; Edwin M. 297; Ella M. Scott 297; Elva 355; Frank 355; George H. 355; Georgia K. Andrew 238;

Harriet R. Rose 154; Harry 355; Hester 355; James 355; Jane 158, 355; John E. 355; John W. 355; Joseph 154, 355, 467; Mary 355; Mary Ellen 225; Mary F. Rose 154; Philip 355; Rachel 355; Rebecca 355; Samuel 355; Sarah 355; Sarah J. McCullough 355; Thomas 154, 158, 355; W. E. 238; William A. 355; W. T. 355*; William W. 355

MINKER, Alice M. Cameron 318; Jacob 318

MINOR, Anna S. Benjamin 197; W. B. 197

MITCHELL, A. W. 352; Abram D. 262; Adaliza White 388; Alfred 576; Alice O. Gorrell 175; Ann M. 171; Arthur W. 446; Arvilla Hawkins 174; Carrie G. 171; Catherine 174; Catherine W. 557; Charlotte 176; E. Lewis 441, 442; Edward W. 527; Elijah 174; Elizabeth Silver 168; Evan 442; Frances 442; Frances Morgan 442; George L. 243; George W. 174; Hannah J. 442; Henry H. 552; Howard 442; J. F. 575; Jerusha 171; John 148, 168; John A. 388; John Archer 171; John O. 171; John S. 441*; John T. 174; Joseph 345; Madison 171; M. L. 478; M. Sophia Webster 345; Malcolm 442; Margaret 174, 262; Martha 148; Martha A. S. Webster 575; Mary Aleicia 216; Mary C. Hughes 171, 176; Mary E. 171; Mary Emma Bowman 243; Mary Jane 174; Mary (L.) Levis 352, 446; Morgan 442; Parker 168, 442; Rachel 171; Richard 221; Robert 174; Robert H. 171; Robert L. 174*; Robert P. 168*, 176; Sallie S. Todd 442; Samuel B. 174; Sarah (Mitchell) 171; Susan 221; Susanna 171; Susannah 576; Thomas P. 442

MITCHEM, Richard 554

MONKS, Addie 400; Amy D. 401; Cassandra 400; Edward T. 400*; Eliza 400; Ellen C. Tredway 401; James P. 400; John 400; Mary A. Tredway 400; Sallie A. 401; William 400

MONROE, Mrs. -- (Armstrong) 408

MOON, Catherine 238, 526

MOORE, Alexander 198; Annie 261; Archer 201; Benjamin P. 510; Bertha H. 295; Caleb J. 510; Charles G. 201; David 282; Deborah H. 510; Elijah 201; Elizabeth H. 510; Estelle Nelson 511; Ethel J. 295; George 201, 480; Hannah 414; Hannah F. 412; Harry 201; Henrietta Shaw 295; India S. Christie 284; J. Wilson 510; James 198, 201; James H. 295; Jane Stewart 294; Jarrett B. 198*; Johanna Boddin 201; John 226; John C. 295; John T. 294*; J(ohn) Wilson 510*; Lulu May 295; Mary 511; Mary G. Jones 510; Mary Hopkins 510; Mary O'Neill 359; Phoebe 282; Robert 510; Sarah 282, 480; Sarah Cole 201; Theodore R. 510; Van Buren 201; William 510; William H. 284; William L. 359; William T. 295; William V. 294

MOORES, Aquilla P. 415; Laura P. 415

MORGAN, Cassandra E. 278; Frances 442; Josiah 278; Laura E. 251; Libbie A. 337; Louisa Heck 278; Sarah E. 303; Sarah Jane 125

MORRIS, Anna Wilson 462; Arabella 266; Beckie Sheridan 462; James 266; John 266*; Lloyd 462; Lydia Price 266; Mary A. 539; Mary E. 266; Mary Tate 266; Panola 266; Ruth 266; William 462*; William H. 266

MORRISON, Anna E. 294; William 294

MORTON, Adelaide 181; Hamilton 181; Mary T. Durkee 181

MOSSEY, Sarah 343

MOTE, Eliza 407

MOUNED, Mary 343

MOUNT, Hannah 472

MOWBRAY, Agnes L. 544; Alpheus 544; Alpheus S. 543*; Anna Sparklin 544; E. T. 544; Edwin Stevenson 544; Levin 544; W. R. 544; William H. 544

MULFORD, Emily Foard 504; James 504

MULLEN, Esther 359

MUNNIKHUYSEN, Fannie H. 431; John A. 431; Mary Howard 405

MURPHY, George 562; Mary E. Botts 562

MYRES, Florence E. Tucker 333; Walter O. 333

NAFFLER, (Mr.) 509

NAGLE, Emmanuel 479; Laura L. 479

NAUDAIN, (family) 503

NAUDAINE, Caroline Whitaker 185

NEALE, (Archbishop) 323; Benedict (Bennet) 323, 326; Henrietta Maria 326; James 323

NEELY, Jane 528

NEFF, Victoria 234

NELSON, Benton 536; Elizabeth 468; Estelle 511; Harry 536; Julia 536; Laura 536; Rebecca 546; Sallie E. Jarrett 536; Mrs. William B. 381

NESBITT, Laura V. 455; Samuel M. C. 455

NEUMANN, Dr. --- (Hatzig) 225

NEWMAN, John 466; Susanna 466

NICE, John 282; Sarah Reynolds 282

NICHOLS, Charles 206; Helen White 206

NOBLE, Benjamin 568; James 568; Mark 568; Mary E. 568; Mary Francis 165; Susannah Silver 568; William S. 568*

NOCK, Alan Page 195; Gamma Long 195; Ivan Finney 195; John Dix 195; John W. 194; Littleton 194; Littleton H. 194; Nicholas N. 194*; Susan Dix 194

NOLAN, Elizabeth A. 582; John 582

NORRIS, Agnes E. 517; Alice A. 536; Alice Creswell 264; Amanda Taylor 155; Andy 517; Benjamin 517; Cardiff 217; Charlotte A. 506; Daniel 517; Edward 517; Edward W. 517; Eliza J. 517; Elizabeth 517; Elizabeth Seitz 517; Elva I. 517; Frank C. 155; George 469, 517; George W. 517*; George W., Jr. 517; J. Wiley 469*; James W. 517; John 469; John A. 264; John S. 470; Jonathan 517; Joseph M. 517; Manda Z. Hutchins 470; Mary A. 517; Mary E. Wiley 517; Nelson 517; Rheshea 155; Richard M. 470; Robert R. 470; Sophia 221; Susan E. 155; Vincent 469; Virginia G. 217; William 517; William B. 221

NOWLAND, Alfred C. 302, 503; Ann 347; Augustus J. 503; Caroline 429; Dennis James 503; Edward F. 503; Frisby M. 503; Henry N. 503; Joseph W. 355; Lambers D. 503; Lambert D. 503; Louisa H. 503; Mary Foard 503; Mary R. 503; Nettie Scarborough 187; Rebecca Miller 355; Sarah J. 503; Walter A. 187

NUNES, Sarah 560

NYMAN, Ann Rebecca Dean 298; Isaac 298

O'BRIEN, Mrs. A. H. 381; Timothy 325

O'CONNOR, Patrick Francis 325

O'DANIEL, Ann E. Scarborough 186; John 186

O'DANIELS, Margaret 490; Mary Ann 490

OGDEN, (Mr.) 480

OLDFIELD, Alice Wilkinson 163; Edward 163

OLDHAM, Cyrus 127; Elizabeth Giles 425; George W. 343; Nathan 425; Susan Biddle 343

O'LEARY, Charles 196; Louis Dietrich 196

OLIVER, Mary 579

O'NEAL, Mary 331

O'NEILL, Augusta Burke 360; Charles Z. 359; Eliza J. Latour 360; Esther Mullen 359; Fannie Kirby 360; Harry F. 360; Henry E. 358*; Indiana 359; John 358, 359, 360; J(onn) William 360*; Mary 359; Mary B. 360; Martha 359; Thomas 325; Virginia 359; Warren E. 360; William 360

ORDMAN, Elizabeth 163

OSBORN, Charles B. 171; Elizabeth 171; Jerusha 171

OSBORNE, Charles T. 346; Christiana J. Hall 346; Edward L. 346; Emma 346; Grace Hopkins 346; Groom 346; Louis H. 345*; Mary 346; Mary F. 346

OWENS, Charles W. 573; Mary S. Smith 573

PACA, William 419

PALMER, Betty P. Cook 577; J. W. 577

PANNELL, Isabella W. 148; James E. 148; William F. 147

PARKER, Anna L. 191; Rachel Price 133

PASQUET, W. 324

PASSETT, Elizabeth 176

PASSMORE, (Mr.) 395

PATRIDGE, John 414

PATTEN, Sarah Evans 127; William 127

PATTERSON, Elizabeth 431; Emily Carter 327; Hannah E. Hanna 512; Henry L. 327; John 128; John C. 168; Laura Archer Webster 168; M. 512; Mary 128; R. Ann 524

PATTON, Mary 493

PAXSON, Sarah 294

PAYNE, John 508; Mary 389, 508

PEACH, John 304; Laura L. 304

PEARCE, Ann J. 213; Anne Rebecca 213; Benjamin C. 213; Eliza Jeannette Groome 237; Matthew C. 237

PEARSON, Mary 479, 580; Rachel P. 506

PENN, John 127; Richard 127; Thomas 127; William 164, 284

PENNELL, Magdalene Duyckinck 524; John J. 524

PENNING, Alice E. Markland 357; Elsie M. 357; John 356; Oliver P. 357; Sarah Cooke 356; Sarah E. 357; Sylvester E. 356*; Thomas Jefferson 356; William E. 357

PENNINGTON, Maggie 379

PENNOCK, Ruth W. 216

PEOPLES, Hannah M. Rawlings 303; William 303

PERDUE, Elizabeth 511

PERSHING, Fredericka 234

PETER, (Miss) 572

PETERSON, Adelia Sentman 434; George 434

PHILLIPS, Anna A. 261; Emeline A. Benjamin 197; George W. 197

PHINEZY, John 119; Martha Creswell 119

PHYSICK (PHIPSIC), Philip Syng(e) 237, 553

PIERCE, Elizabeth 425; Margaret 423

PIKE, E. C. 576

PLANK, Levi 372; A. Virginia Milburn 372

PLEASANTS, see p. 168

PLUMMER, Sallie S. 572

POCOCK, Elizabeth E. 441

POE, John P. 144

POINSETT, Elizabeth 383

POIST, Annie C. 351; Charles D. 351; Elizabeth A. White 351; Fannie 351; George H. 351; George W. 348*; Harry 351; Mary 351

POOLE, Eveline Hyde 311; Georgia Scarboro 311; John 308; John Sprigg 308*; Mary 311; Thomas 308, 311

PORTER, A. Lee 294; Andrew 127, 293; Anna E. 294; Anna Hall 262, 294; Anna M. 294; Augustus H. 294; Catherine 127; Charles C. 556; Elizabeth 294; George 294; George H. 294; Harry 262; Henry T. 294; James 293; John H. 293, 294; John Hart 556; Margaret Celia 556; Mary E. 294, 444; Mary Toy 293; Robert 294, 444; Sarah Paxson 294; William 294; William E. 262, 293*, 556

POTTS, Mary Ann Holden 156; William 156

PRESTON, David 397; Elizabeth Hollingsworth 411, 414; Elizabeth Pue 153; Elizabeth Tucker 333; Fannie 177; George W. 333; Hattie Hoskins 397; J. A. 419; James B. 390; John W. 333; Lillie Pue Hall 391; Mary A. Wilkes 390; Mary Robinson 226; Rebecca Tucker 333; Robert 226; W(illiam) S. B. 411, 414; Walter W. 153, 390*

PRICE, (Judge) 133, 353; (Miss) 425; Ann Nowland 347; Anna 363; Anna W. 362; Belle Veach 363; Cornelia C. 237; Elizabeth 572; Ellen 362; Ellen A. 363; Emily 363; Eugene 362; Fredus 362; Fredus A. 362; Jacob 410; Jeremiah C. 362*, 363; Jeremiah C., Jr. 362*; J. Fletcher 331; John Fletcher {476} 477*; John H. 418, 419, 445; Mrs. John H. 256; John N. 347; John R. 237, 477; John V. 347; Lindsey 363; Lydia 266; Margaret 346; Margaret C. 347; Mary 477; Mary A. Lum 237; Mary C. Clayton 477; Mary W. Clayton 331; Melicent R. 410; Rachel 133; Richard 255; Susanna 347; T. 572; T. K. 387; Thomas 347

PRIGG, Amanda M. 130; Mary C. 545; Robert E. 318; Mrs. S. T. 318; Sarah Ely 317

PUE, Arthur 153; Barthena 154; Caleb 153; Clara 154; Cornelia Dunn 153; E. H. D. 153*; Elizabeth 153, 154; Elizabeth Bull 153; Joshua 153; Michael 153, 154; Michael E. 153; Richard 153

PUGH, Evan 373

PYLE, Margaret 520

PYLES, G. P. 535; Viola Estelle 535

QUINBY, Annie K. 472; Bertha A. 472; Carrie S. 472; Elizabeth 472; Emma H. Baldwin 473; James A. 473; James H. 472*; James H., Jr. 472, 473; Nancy B. Farrand 472

QUINN, Hannah Booth 436; William 436

RACINE, Charles 156; Harriet Holden 156

RAMBO, Rachael T. Falls 297; Worden 297

RAMPLEY, Cornelia 468; Elizabeth Nelson 468; Frances R. Maul 468; James 468; James C. 469; Mary E. 468; Robert N. 468*; Sarah 468; William 468

RAMSEY, Amy A. 372; Annie 551; Hannah Maria 435; John 551; Martha Mevay 372; Nathaniel 406; William 372, 435

RANKIN, Hannah J. 202; Margaret A. 202; Moses 202; Robert G. 202; Samuel 202; Sarah 202; Sarah Gemmill 202

RAPHEL, Stephen I. 325

RATOR, Elizabeth 306

RAWLINGS, Eliza M. Hindman 303; Elizabeth 303, 455; Emma H. Reynolds 456; Emory C. 303; Greenberry 455; Hannah M. 303, 455; John 303, 455; John M. 303*, 455; Llewellyn H. 303; Marion 128; Mary McVey 303, 455; Mary P. 303; R. Lee 303; Robert 303, 455; Roberta E. 303, 455; Z. Taylor 303, 455*

REA, David 469*; Mary Graham 469; Sarah Louise 223

READING, Catherine A. 347

READY, Ann 255, 534

REARDON, Jack 324

REASIN, Amanda 157; Amanda V. 158; Annie Hogsman 158; Claude Nelson 253; Dooley 253; Duty 157; Fannie Cole 253; Florence Aline 253; Gertrude 253; Hannah E. Cole 252; James F. 157, 158; Jennie

253; Martha 157; Mary 157; Matilda Courtney Maxwell 158; Samuel W. 157; Wesley 157; William 157; William F. 157*; William H. 252, 253; William H., Jr. 252*

REED, Amy McVey 152, 243, 470; Annie M. Janney 193; Benjamin H. 471; Benjamin M. 152, 244, 470*; Charlotte M. 193; Charlotte McVey 244; Christie 471; Elizabeth E. 152; Elizabeth Ridgely 550; George M. 574; Hettie 581; I. A. Russell 244; Joseph T. 152, 193, 243*, 244, 470; Knox 574; Mabel V. 152; Martha 152, 244, 470; Margaret Matilda Ferguson 152; Mary A. Lambert 574; Melvina L. 471; Pocahontas 244; Russell 193; Russell James 244; Ruth R. 244; S. R. 550; Thompson R. 152; Virginia 152; Willemenia M. 395; William 152*, 243, 244, 470, 471; William J. 152

REES, Anna E. Sevil 307; Annie E. 307; Georgia A. Griffin 307; John R. 307; Lizzie V. Woolford 307; Ralph H. 307; Thomas A. 306*; William 307

REESE, Elizabeth McCauley 410; George McCauley 420; Louisa M. 420; Richard G. 410; Richard George 420; Sarah Rebecca Manley 420; Susan 427

REGISTER, Henrietta 334

REID, James 325

REMBOLD, August 234; Charles 233*, 234; Frank 234; Frederick Pershing 234; Henry 234; John 234; Katie 234; Lizzie 234; Mary 234; Rebecca 234; Victoria Neff 234

REVELL, George W. 437; Josephine M. 437; Josephine M. Booth 437; Leon L. F. 437

REYNOLDS, A. O. 265; Adrianna 261; Alfred 337; Alice 337; Alva 337; Amanda C. Carter 305; Amanda M. Michener 265; Andrew 337; Ann T. 305; Anna 261, 262, 337; Anna A. Phillips {260} 261; Anna E. 282, 337, 387; Annie Moore 261; Arthur 337; Barclay 305*; Barclay, Jr. 305; Benjamin 305; Benjamin C. 261; Charles 305; Charles T. 305; David 282, 308; David M. 264; E. H. 282*; Edward H. 387; Eli 337; Eliza 305; Eliza Taylor 456; Elizabeth 282; Ella 282; Elmer 305, 337; Emma H. 456; Esther 261, 265; Eugene A. 305; Granville T. 261; H. Mitchell 305; Haines 282, 387; Hannah 337; Hannah Harlan 482; Henrietta 305; Henry 282; Hetty 305; Howard H. 305; Isobel 308; Jacob 261, 282, 305, 456; Jacob, Jr. 305; Jacob H. 261; Jannette 282; John 337, 479; John T. 305; Jonathan 282; Joseph T. 261; Joseph W. 337*; Josiah 337, 362; Kirk E. 337; Kirk S. 337; Lizzie 282; Lydia Lincoln 282; Mabel Wilson 479; Maggie 282; Margaret 337; Margaret A. Tucker 337; Martha J. 265; Mary 266, 326, 337, 362; Mary J. 264, 282; Mary Swagert 337; Mel(l)issa 337, 362; Mercy A. 261; Morris 337; Narcissa 262; Phoebe 282; Phoebe Moore 282; Reuben 282; S. Rosine 282; Samuel 337; Samuel T. 305; Sarah Moore 282; Sophia C. 305; Stella 337; Stephen J. {260} 261*; Susan J. 261; Taylor 305; Theodore 282; Tyson 337; Walter 337; William 262; William L. 482; William M. 261

RICARDS, Martha Ruth Thomas 578; Philip 578

RICAUD, James B. 343

RICHARDSON, Annie 574; Blanche 473; Caroline 211; D. H. 574*; Daisy C. 575; Daisy Rouse 462; Elizabeth 574; Fannie 357; George 574; Hall 462; Hannah Robinson 225; Henry 211; H. J. 125; Mrs. J. S. (nee Rouse) 461; J. Wilson 462; Joseph 574; Joseph P. 574; M. A. Williamson 575; Margaret A. 575; Margaret McCullough 574; Martha S. 525; Robert 125; Ruth 399; Samuel 226; William 125, 574

RICHIE, John A. 400

RIDDELL, Anna E. 393; Bridget 296; Hannah 471; John 471

RIDDLE, Bridget Shannon 296; Emily 296; Humphrey 296; Mary 296; William 296

RIDER, George 325

RIDGELY, Daniel B. 550; Elizabeth D. 550; Henrietta M. 550; Martha E. 550; Martin E. 550*; Mary E. 550; Nicholas G. 550

RIGDON, George 483, 543; Sarah Amos 543

RITTENHOUSE, Azariah 488; Ella Warner 488; George S. 353*; Lida P. Eppelsheimer 354; Mary J. 488

ROBERSON, Elijah H. 161; Sarah C. 161

ROBERTS, (Capt.) 443; (Mr.) 137; Edmond 135, 137; George H. 166; John B. 166; Margaret 166; Susan Davis 166; Thomas H. 165*; Thomas H., Sr., 166; William G. 166

ROBINETT, Catherine Davis 466; David 466

ROBINSON, (surname only) 221; Adelaide 423; Alphonso 423; Ann 354; Charles Carroll 423; Clara 546; Clara C. Cain 546; Clayton 263; E. Maude 512; Edwin 225, 226; Eliza Howlett 512; Elizabeth 546; Ellen Holland 423; Emily B. 226; Ernest 263; George 263; Georgietta Bell 263; Hannah 225, 226; J. T. Calvin 512; James Corner 225*; Jesse Levering 423; John 512; John C. 511*; Joseph 512, 546; L. Bertha 512; Lewis Bolivar {422} 423*; Lucille 546; M. Florence 512; Madeleine 546; Margaret Pierce 423; Marion I. Smith 423; Martha 402; Mary 225, 226; Mary C. Prigg 545; Mary Corner 225; Mary E. 512; Mary Kirkwood 512; Nannie H. 226; Olivia Smith 423; Priscilla Spencer 379; R. Belle 512; Rachel B. 512; Rebecca J. 512; Robert K. 512; S. Emma 512; Samuel S. 545; Susan Beaman 226; Thomas 379, 546; Thomas H. 509, 545*; Thomas Hall 546; William 402, 423, 512; William T. 512

ROCKWELL, Mary Ann 235

ROCKY, Benjamin R. 298; Mary J. Dean 298

ROGERS, (Commodore) 419; -- Jarvis 407; Anna M. 407; Caroline M. Metzger 548; Catherine 407; Catherine Rogers 407; Elijah 407; Elizabeth Hewitt 407; George W. 548; Hannah 293; Hannah E. 407; I. T. 372; Jane 407; Jennie Magowan 549; John 419; Laura Annie 549; Lawson 407; Lilburn 407; Lucinda 407; Mary 120; Mattie J. Milburn 372; Oliver T. 548*; Robert S. 419; Mrs. Robert 262; Roland 406, 407; Roland John 406, 407; Sarah 317; William 407

ROMAN, Absolom 315; Samuel T. 315

ROOP, Elizabeth 244

ROSE, A. P. 147; Alfred D. 154; Aquilla P. 154; Caleb V. 155; Edward W. 154; Elizabeth D. 154; Fred E. 155; George G. 154; H. C. 154; Harriet R. 154; J. P. 154; John 154; Lucy Jane 155; Margaret A. Gillingham 154; Marion E. 155; Marvin B. 155; Mary F. 154; Randall W. 154*; Rufus B. 155; S. S. Alexander 154; Timothy V. 154; Viola Gifford 147; William C. 155

ROSS, (Professor) 548; Margaret Evans 127; William 127

ROUSBY, Barbara 571; J. 571

ROUSE, (name not given) 461; Anna Stump Webster 450; Annie Stump 216; C. C. 301, 462; C. Chapman 460, 461; Daisy 462; Dora C. 184, 462; Harriet Hanway 462; Helen C. 462; J. G. 301; John 146, 461; John G. 184, 456, 460*; Martha 461; Mary G. Day 460, 461; Rebecca 145; S. E. 302; Sarah Cochran 146; Willard G. 216, 449*, 462; William C. 461

ROWLAND, Annie 380; Emma Brown 380; Emma H. Strickland 380; Ernest 380; R. J. 379*; William L. 379

RUDOLPH, Charles J. 389; Elizabeth 382; Mary White 389; William 382

RUDULPH, Elizabeth 552; Esther Synge 552; John 552; Michael 552

RUFF, Elizabeth 173; Henry 173; Priscilla A. 232

RULEY, Elizabeth Warburton 370; John P. 370

RUNNER, Samuel 392; Susan 392

RUSCHENBERGER, (Dr.) 136, 137

RUSSELL, Amelia K. Levis 352, 446; Anna 363; Charlotte 437; Edward T. 437; Elizabeth 391; I. A. 244; James 244; Mary 312; Slater B. 352, 446; Thomas 312

RUTLEDGE, Abraham 537; Charles A. 537; Henrietta M. 537; Jacob 537; John R. 537; John W. 537; Joshua 215; Julia A. Ward 537; Martha J. 537; Monica A. 537; Monica Wheeler 537; Patrick H. 537*; Phoebe Smith Webster 215

RUTTER, Elizabeth 218; John 218

SADDLER, Charles 221; Priscilla Webster 221

SAPPINGTON, Earl Neilson 332; Florence 331; John {330} 331*; Mark 331; Mary Hayes 332; Mary O'Neal 331; Richard 331; Sarah Bagley 331; Walter 331; Walter H. 332; William F. 332

SAURMAN, Minnie S. 459

SAVIN, Mary 343; Sarah E. 203

SCARBORO, Georgia 311; Hannah J. 204; Silas 311

SCARBOROUGH, Amos H. 187; Ann E. 186; Annie 187; Francina Spence 186; Hugh F. 186*; Isaac 292; Jane Lowe 292; Joseph 186; Joseph S. 186; Mary S. 186; Nelson 207; Nettie 187; Rebecca Boyd 186; Rhoda 241; Sarah Smith 186; Sutton 241; Willametta Enfield 207

SCARFF, Charles T. 538; Edwin 538; Elizabeth A. 538; Eunice 538; Hannah Walker 538; John 537, 538; Josephine 538; Julia A. 529, 536; Martha Garrison 537; Philip G. 538; Samuel G. 537*; Sarah A. 538; Thomas 538

SCHAEFER, Elizabeth 482; Frances Hawkins 482; George B. 482

SCHAFER, Balzaac 509

SCHILLING, Caroline 490; Charles L. 490; Emma Lawton 490; Hannah C. 490; Henry C. 490*; Howard L. 490; John W. 490; Louisa Billings 490; Louisa J. 490, 501; William H. 490

SCHOTT, Louis 342; Maria C. 342

SCHREITZ, Catherine A. 518; John 518; Margaret 518

SCHUH, Barbara Ann 436; Emanuel 436; Emanuel G. 436; Hannah 436

SCOTT, A. J. 449; Anna Elizabeth Craig 297; Bessie F. 297; Daisy 449; David 297, 298; DeLancey 298; Edith W. 298; Elizabeth 298; Ella M. 297; Eva C. 297; Frank R. 223, 297*; Helen 297; Henry D. 297; John Wirt 298; Levi 446; Martha 450; Mary J. Wilson 297; Moses 450; Otho 183, 205, 415, 419, 537; Rachael 298; Rachel J. Wilson 223; Susan D. 328

SCOTTEN, Minerva A. 301

SEAMAN, Christiana 529

SEITZ, Elizabeth 517

SELFE, Catharine 526; Catharine Moon 238, 526; Edith 241; Henry E. 238*, 526; James 238, 241, 526; Lee Webster 526; Louise Eleanor 526; Louise W. Webster 526; Sadie Burton 241; Serena Webster 526; Walter 241; William B. 241, 526*

SENECA, (ref. to Point Farms) 479*

SENTMAN, Adelia 434; Alderman B. 434; Alexander J. 435; Catherine McMillan 434; Charles Arthur 435; Eli S. 434*; Elizabeth A. 218; Evan G. 434; John 434; Jonathan 434; Laura M. 434; Lawrence 434; Margaret A. 434; Mary Ellen McCauley 434; Michael 434; Norman M. 434; Phineas B. 434; Robert 434; Robert Newton 434; Sophia Jackson 434; Victor 434

SEVIL, Anna E. 307

SEWALL, Charles 324; Henry 324

SEWELL, C. K. 549, 550; Catherine 549; Charles S. 549; Fielder B. 550; L. Louise 550; Lucy E. 549; Maria Louise Smith 549, 573; Mary S. 549; Septimus D. 549*, 573; William H. 549

SHAFFER, Elizabeth Porter 294; P. S. 294

SHANNON, Bridget 296

SHARF, Ada Bennett 450; Thomas 450

SHARP, Rebecca R. 247

SHAW, Henrietta 295; Mary 437

SHEA, John Gilmary 323; Thomas 323

SHERIDAN, Beckie 462; James 172; Mary 562; Mary C. James 172; Richard C. 205; Sallie R. 205

SHERWOOD, Fannie 580; Jesse 580; Sarah 580.

SHETRONE, Ella S. Fockler 555; George 555

SHORT, Eliza J. 452

SHRIVER, Catherine Dietrich 196; M. O. 196

SHRODES, Charles 521; Henry 521; Julia 521; Sarah J. Taylor 521

SHULTZ, Sarah J. 391

SHURE, Arthur E. 497; Charles A. 497; Daniel F., Jr. 497; Daniel Ferree (496) 497; E(dward) Savage 497*; George W. 497; Harry W. 497; James B. 497; Jane McDarah 497; Jeanie 497; John M. 497; Michael 497; Miriam A. 497; Robert Lee 497; William J. 497

SILVER, Adaline Matilda 445; Annie E. 286; Benjamin 185; Benjamin H. 185*; Benjamin Stump 186; David 568; Effie 185; Elizabeth 168; Elizabeth A. 286; Elizabeth Bayless 168; Gashen 168; Jeremiah 185; John 185; Lillie M. Hopkins 186; Mary E. Hoopman 185; Philip W. 286; Susannah 568; William 445

SILVERS, Charlotte Catharine Hughes 176; George 176

SIMCOE, Benjamin P. 383; C. Annie 383; Elizabeth Poinsett 383; George 382*, 383, 420, 578; J. S. 383; John S. 420, 578*; Louisa J. 383, 420; Louise 578; Lulu R. 383; Mary Jones 578; Nicholas 578; Rebecca Cazier 383, 578; Thomas C. 383; William 383, 420, 578; William H. 383

SIMLEE, Elizabeth Price 572; Joseph 572

SIMMONS, Eliza Ann 185

SIMMS, Ann Creswell 119; William 119

SIMPERS, Altha A. 161; Ann 355; Anne M. Ferguson 256; Annie M. 256; C. T. 256; Charles R. 161; Charles W. 158*; Edward E. 256; Elizabeth 158, 561; Elizabeth Fulton 158; Elizabeth Holliday 161; Gertrude 256; Gertrude Jane 161; Hattie Kirk 208; Henry E. 158; J. Scott 256; James A. 158; Jane Miller 158; Jesse H. 158; Jesse K. 158; John 208, 256; John F. 256*; John W. 158; Johnson 256; Joseph W. 158; Mary E. 158; Millicent Ford 256; Rachael E. Whitaker 256; Rachael J. 158; Sam B. 158; Sarah C. 161; William 158, 355; Wilmer F. 158

SIMPSON, (Bishop) 544; Ann 443; Harry H. 443; John 443; Mary Eder 443; Thomas Eder 443

SINGERLY, (company) 494; William M. 130

SINGLEY, Ellen S. 417

SLACK, Ada 412; Isaac 412

SLADE, Alice P. 508; Elizabeth 201; Ezekiel 508; Mary Payne 508; Rachel M. 507, 508; Thomas 508

SLICER, Annie M. 553; H. Emily 553; John B. 553*; John T. 152, 244, 553; Martha J. Read 553; Martha Reed 152, 244; Sabina C. 553; Thomas 553; William 553

SMALL, Rebecca 253, 254

SMITH, (Miss) 493; -- Griffith 572; -- Kent 572; -- Peter 572; A. Augusta 541; Addie 400; Adeline Bradley 573; Alexander 161; Alexander Lawson 572; Allen W. 573; Andrew P. 573; Ann W. 308; Anna 161; Anna B. 384, 573; Anna E. Riddell 393; Anna J. 295; Anna Whitaker 308; Annie F. 191; Annie Maria 572; Anthony 572; Barbara Ann Linn 572; Barbara Rousby 571; Buell J. 541; C. Adele 541; C. C. 252; Carni 572; Christian {160} 161*; Clement 572; David Porter 572, 573; David R. 308; Davis P. 264; Eleanor 571, 572; Eleanor O. 573; Eleanor O. Smith 573; Eleanor Stewart 573; Eliza Ann 572; Elizabeth 393, 535, 572; Elizabeth Ann 573; Elizabeth Burkley 161; Ellen A. 541; Emily 572; Emily Henderson 384; Emma 161; Emma L. 500, 541; Emma Wood 572; Estelle 296; Esther 563; Esther Belt 572; F. B. 572; F. Eva 541; Fielder B. 549, 573; Fielder Bowie 572; Fielder Bowie, Jr. 573; Florence A. 541; Frank O. 573; Frederick 161; George 161, 174; George H. 394; George I. 393*; George P. 295; George W. 308; Gertrude 296, 573; H. Melville 541; Hanna Emma 176; Harriet 572; Harriet E. Jewens 191; Harry 563; Henry Clay 573; Hettie 353; Hosea R. 394; Isaac 541; Isabel Reynolds 308; J. Egbert 541; J. P. 384; Jacob R. 393; James 191, 295; James P. 393; John 393, 443, 563, 571; John Addison 572; John S. 572, 573; Joseph 572; Joseph Simlee 572; Julian C. 296; Lucy 572; Lucy Middleton 572; M. 362; M. F. 572; Maria Johanna Somerset Lawther 571; Maria L. 549; Maria Louisa 573; Marion I. 423; Martha L. Chaney 573; Mary 285, 308, 572; Mary A. 295; Mary A. Ash 296; Mary Ann 572; Mary B. 296; Mary Creswell 264; Mary DeHaven 393; Mary E. 394; Mary J. 393; Mary L. 573; Mary Light 252; Mary Sophia 572, 573; Middleton 572; Milton E. 540*; Miriam L. 573; Mollie Kammerer 162; Mordecai 572; Mordecai Finch 572, 573; Mortimer 500; N. R. 566; Nancy J. 433; P. Jenks 308; Panama W. 308; Patrick Linn 572; Phebe Finche 572; Phoebe 174; R. Percy 573; Rachel 407, 572; Rebecca Bradley 573; Richard 563, 571, 572; Richard, Jr. 571; Roger 325; Ross Reynolds 308*; Sallie B. (Sarah) 563; Sallie S. Plummer 572; Samuel 295, 325, 392, 393, 563; Samuel A. 308; Samuel C. 295; Sarah 186, 388, 393, 500; Sarah Ann 572; Sarah Field 541; Sarah J. Batton 295; Sarah (J.) Tucker 362, 500; Sophia Middleton 572; Stephen 295; Susan 572; Thackery 563; Thaddeus S. 295; Virginia 308; Walter 572; Walter, Jr. 572; William 176, 393, 500, 572; William A. {190} 191*; William Daniel 573; William Emily 572; William H. 393; William J. 295*; William L. 571*; William S. 400; Winfield S. 393

SMITHON, Amelia 272

SMITHSON, (family) 166; Priscilla 214; William 214

SMOCK, Catherine 524; Jonathan 524; Mary 417

SNELL, Rachel J. 528

SOMERSET, Charles 572; John 572; Maria Johann 571

SOMMER, Lizzie 226

SOUTHALL, Martha F. Mallory 577

SPAIN, W. H. 382

SPARKLIN, Anna 544; Daniel 544

SPEDDEN, Ann M. 273

SPENCE, Francina 186; Henry 186

SPENCER, Eli 379; Elizabeth 378, 379; Emma Whitelock 267, 522; Henrietta Hughes 176; Herman 176; Jarrett 378; John R. 378; John W. 378; Noah 379; Priscilla 379; R. E. 267, 522; Rebecca Keene 378; Sarah R. 378, 379; Silas L. 379; Sophy 378; William T. 379

SPRATT, Mary 130

SPURRIER, Henrietta 263

STAMFORD, Charles H. 267, 522; Euphemie Whitelock 267, 522

STAMP, Anna M. 203; Anna McNabb 203; William 203

STANDIFORD, Claudius 498; Cordelia Hitchcock 498; Dennis H. 497*; Jacob 498; Martha 459; Susanna Engle 498; William K. 498

STANSBURY, Hannah 505

STARRETT, J. M. 395

STEEL, Esther 128; Hugh 128; Mary 570; Rebecca 126, 128; Rebecca R. 247

STEELE, Ada 467; Bennett 247; Caradora Bouchell 247; Caroline 247; Dora B. 247; George A. 247; Harold 247; J. Groome 247; Joseph 247; Joseph H. 246*; Rebecca R. Sharp 247; Stanley 247

STEIN, Eleanor 224

STEPHENSON, Ann 375; Eliza 375; George 375; Hannah 375; James 374*, 375, 401; Lizzie 401; Margaret 375; Mary 375; Priscilla Hopkins 375; Rachel 375; Rachel Barnes 374; Robert 375; Susan 375; William 374, 375; William B. 401, 402

STERNSBURY, Smith 154; Tobias 154

STEVENSON, (Miss) 544; Agnes 284; Priscilla G. 284; Robert 284

STEWART, (Captain) 331; Jane 294; Sarah 362

STIDHAM, Elizabeth R. 411

STIFLER, Anna Adelle 499; Bertha L. 499; Dora M. 499; James M. 499; R. Belle Gailey 498*; Robert S. 499; Rosa G. 499; Silas H. 499; William C. 499; William H. 498

STONEBRAKER, Isabel Tucker 362, 500; John (C.) 362, 500

STOKES, Sarah 268

STRASBAUGH, A. Henry 147*; Dorothy Bahn 147; Harry P. 148; Isabella W. Pannell 148; Jacob 147; Kate 147; Lucy 147; Maria 147; Susie 147

STRAWBRIDGE, A. Sherman 502; Abbie J. Jenkins 501; Benjamin A. 502; Cynthia J. 389; Elizabeth Almoney 501, 502; Emma E. 508; Emma V. 508; Isaac 502; Henry M. 501, 502*; J. R. 508; John W. 500*, 502; Joseph 502; Joseph H. 502; Louisa J. 501; Louisa J. Schilling 501; Lydia A. 502; Mary J. 502; Mary M. 508; Nettie R. 508; Rebecca C. 502; Rebecca J. 502; Rebecca Manifold 502; Sarah A. 502; William F. 502

STRAYER, Elizabeth 558

STREETT, (family) 162*; A. E. 542, 543; A. J. 205; Ann R. 201; Cordelia 201, 478, 517; E. M. 257; Elizabeth 205; Elizabeth Slade 201; Geraldine 201; Hannah Baldwin 233; J. M. 205*, 517; J. Ruff 233; James 201, 478, 517;

James P. 201; James Ruff 232; John 162, 201, 205, 232*; John J. 201, 517; John Rush 543; Juliet G. 205; Margaret L. 201; Margaret Miles 201; 517; Martha J. 201, 517; Mary V. 162; Mary Virginia 225; Mattie C. 162; Merryman 162; Priscilla D. Bull 162; Priscilla D. Ruff 232; Rebecca 517; Samuel 225, 257; Mary Ellen Miller 225; Sophia Priscilla 232; Thomas 162, 232;

STRICKLAND, Cordelia R. 448; William P. 448, 449

STRICKLEN, Emma H. 380

STRIDEHOFF, John 362; Mary Ann Tucker 362

STRITHOFF, John 500; Mary A. Tucker 500

STRONG, Amanda A. 508; Emma E. 508; Ezekiel S. 508; Joseph W. 508; Mary M. 508; Rachel M. Slade 507*

STUBBS, Benjamin 282; Fannie Boulden 236; Maggie B. Hollingsworth 483; S. Rosine 282; Vincent 483; William A. 236; William F. 483

STUMP, Ann 275; Anna J. 216; Esther 133; Henry 133; Herman 313; Hester N. 358; John 133, 216; Margaret Wilson 353; Mary Aleicia Mitchell 216; Rachel Perkins 133; Reuben 133, 353

SUCKERT, George 571; Susan M. ; William 571

SUMMERILL, Altha A. Simpers 161; Joseph J. 161

SUMMERS, George W. 119; Mary Creswell 119

SUMPTION, Mary W. 364

SUNDERLAND, Mary Tustin 151

SURRATT, (Mrs.) 325

SUTTON, Ann 251

SWAGERT, Mary 337

SWANN, James 544

SWARTZ, Basil 406; Clara C. 406; Edward R. 406; Frances E. Cochran 406; James M. 406; John R. 406; Marion 406; Mary 406; Nannie C. Crossley 406; Sophia 406; T. Edward 406*

SWECKENDEIK, Ernest 264; Margaret Creswell 264

SWEETING, Eleanor 276; John 276

SYKES, Ann 558

SYNGE, Esther 552; Philip 552

TALLEY, Elizabeth 221; William 221

TALMADGE, Elizabeth 286

TATE, James 268; Laura L. 268; Mary 266; Sarah A. McFadden 268

TAYLOR, Albert G. 265; Alfred W. 560; Amanda 155; Annie M. 265; Benjamin F. 265; Clarissa J. 265; Curtis 233; Edward 355; Eliza 305; Emma McCleary 355; Eugene 265; George H. 265; Helen M. 265; Ida Virginia 225; Isaac R. 265*; Isabelle 208; James 155, 208; Jesse Clinton 225; John 565; Joseph E. 238; Laura R. 265; Lavinia Henriques 560; M. Harlan 265; Maria 192; Margaret A. 565; Mary F. 479; Mary Lizzie 233; Robert B. 155; Sarah 316; Sarah J. 521; Susan E. Norris 155; William L. 265; William P. 155*

THOMAS, Daniel P. 204; David Edwards 255*, 256; David Edwards, Sr. 255; Elizabeth 578; Emily 578; Hannah 577; Ida 578; Laura 204; Martha Ruth 578; Mary Ann 578; Mary Jane 431; Phoebe Edwards 282; Prudence Reynolds 255; R. L. 577*; Richard L. 578; Ruth Ann McCracken 578; Samuel 577; Sarah Jane Johnson 578; Sarah Rebecca 578; Seth 255; Webster 256; William 282

THOMPSON, Andrew 178; Catherine 428; Elizabeth 178; Ezekiel 394; Hannah 394; Harriet 503; Hettie Gilbert 480; John 428; John H. 428; Lizzie Williams 428; Martha E. Benjamin 316; Mary 177; Rachel 297; Susan 518; William F. 316

TITUS, Daniel R. 464; John 412; Mary 412, 484; Seruch 412, 484; William 412

TODRIG, Francis T. 325

TOLLINGER, Alice C. Baker 364; C. 364

TORBERT, A. T. A. 445; Adaline Matilda Silver 445; Edwin J. 445; Frances Elizabeth 446; Henry Robinson 444*; John 445; Mary Rachel Wilmer 446; Victor Megredy 446; W. F. Asbury 445; William 444, 445

TORRENTS, John 412, Mary 412, 484; Mary Torrents 412; Nellie Williams 412

TOUCHSTONE, James M. 247

TOUCHTON, Martha 430

TOY, Mary 293

TRADDELL, Anna M. Porter 294; Louis 294

TRAGO, Alice Coale 291; Susan 214; W. Arthur 291

TRAVERS, Emma Creswell 264; Wesley 264

TREACY, William P. 323

TREDWAY, Ellen C. 401; J. E. 401; Mary A. 400

TRIMBLE, Joseph 425

TRITES, (Dr.) 222

TUCHTON, Edgar 431; Mary 431

TUCKER, Allen 500; Alva J. 362; Annie Highland Drennen 569; Bertie 500; David 333, 361, 362; David, Jr. 500; David, Sr. 500; David L. 500; David R. 333; Elizabeth 333, 362, 500; Ellis J. 361*, 500; Ellis R. 362, 500; Emma R. Smith 500; Eugene Seymour 500; Florence E. 333; Georgia A. Grafton 333; Hannah 500; Harry 500; Herbert 500; Isabel 362, 500; John 500; John C. 362, 500*; John M. 569; Lester Winfield 333; Margaret 362; Margaret A. 337; Margaret C. 336, 362, 500; Margaret E. 500; Mary 500; Mary A. 500; Mary Ann 362; Mary B. 333; Melissa E. Reynolds 362; Morris 500; Rebecca 333; Samuel 336; Samuel R. 500; Sarah 362; Sarah A. Jones 333; Sarah Carter 362, 500; Sarah J. 500; Sarah Stewart 362; Willard LeRoy 333; William H. 333*, 500

TULL, Elizabeth 516; John 516

TUNIS, Sergeant 347

TURNER, (Commodore) 510; Cornelia H. Haines 288; Cornelia Rampley 468; Daniel 510; Elizabeth N. 469; Fannie M. 469; Hettie F. 510; Isabelle McComas 217; James 288; James C. 468, 469; John M. 469; Joseph 217; Mary A. 505; Phillips C. 469; Robert N. 469; Susan M. 469; William J. 510

TUSTIN see page 151

TWINING, Ann H. Hallowell 459; B. Franklin 459; Caroline W. 459; D. Hallowell 459; David 459; Horace B. 459; Isaac {458} 459; Joseph B. 459; Martha E. 459*; Minnie S. Saurman 459; Robert B. 459

TYDINGS, Mary B. O'Neill 360; Millard F. 360

TYSON, Emily C. 573; Deborah M. Benjamin 316; I. B. 573; John P. 573; John W. 573; Lydia Field 574; Mamie 574; Margaret J. 573; Sarah Jane Carter 573; Sarah K. 573; Thomas M. 573*; William B. 316

UNTONIA, Mary 175

VAIL, Charles L. 397; Cornelia H. Hoskins 397

VALLANDIGHAM, J. L. 413, 464, 487

VANCE, Elizabeth 507

VANNEMAN, Arthur Vosbury 455; Caroline Isadore Kerr 455; Caroline Kerr 455; Charles Reeve 455; Daniel 454; Ella Haines 455; Homer Nesbit 455; John P. 455; Laura V. Nesbitt 455; Robert Kerr 454*

VANORSDALE, Gertrude 417; Isaac 417; Mary Smock 417

VAN BIBBER, (see Archer); A. F. 165; Adele Franklin 165; George L. 164*; Hannah C. Archer 154; Harriett L. 165; Isaac 164; Jacob Isaac 164; Lena C. 165; Lucretia 164; Washington 164

VANDERGRIFT, Nancy 193

VANDERWEER, (Vandiver) Jacob 311, 312

VANDIVER, Alice 312; Annie Clayton 313; Dorothy 313; Ellen 312; George T. 312; Jacob 312; Martha 312; Mary Russell 312; Murray {310} 311*; Peter 312; Robert M. 313; Robert R. 312; Robert R., Jr. 312

VAN PELT, Rachel L. Davidson 526; Thomas 526

VAN SANT, Catherine 559

VAUGHAN, (Dr.) 438; Clara 438

VEACH, Belle 363; Emily 574; John 363

VEAZEY, Edward 248; John 248; John, Jr. 248; Mary Wallace 237; Sarah 237; Thomas W. 237; Thomas Ward 248*; Verquir 501

VENUS, Ann Sykes 558; Elizabeth 558

VINCEN, Annie Hughes 176; Thomas 176

VINSINGER, Cordelia R. Strickland 448; Franklin 448; H. Edward 449; Henry 448*; J. Spencer 448; Levina Hill 448; Maria 448; Rebecca E. 448; William 448; William T. 449

VIRDIN, Carrie M. 493; Emily J. 493; Emily J. Ash 492; James C. 493; Kate E. L. Dunn 493; Lizzie 493; John McCoy 493; Joseph D. 493; Martha Lee 493; Mary D. 493; Phenix 493; William W. 492*

VOKES, Ellen Creswell 264; H. A. 264

VOSBURY, Arthur 454

WALKER, Anna Russell 363; Annie L. 281; C. H. 291; C. Rebecca 378; Catherine Hoopman 281; Christian H. {280} 281*; Christopher H. 378; Cornelia 282, 291; Cornelia A. Cole 281; 291; Cornelius 363; Eliza 538; Elizabeth 363, 378, 379, 538; Ella H. 282; Ellen 538; George 205, 363*; Hannah 538; Hannah Wise 538; Jane 425; Mary 538; Mary L. 378; Mary V. 282; Merienne 363; Mollie V. 306; Nellie S. 378; Percival 363; Robert 281; Robert J. 378*; Sadie 282; Serena 538; Susan Cole 363; Thomas 538; William R. 363; Winfield Scott 281

WALLACE, Andrew 236; Ann 236; Cornelia C. Price 237; Elizabeth Black 237; Elizabeth Ward 237; Ellinor 236; George 236, 237; George F. 237; James 237; Jeannette 236; John Charles Groome 237; Joseph 236, 237; Joseph Veazey 236*; Laura V. 237; Lillie T. Bull 152; Margaret 236; Mary 237, 257; Mary Black 236; Mary C. Ward 237; Mary E. 237; Randall 257; Veazey Ward 238; William 152

WALLIS, Sarah 129

WALSH, Amanda Lee 579; Harold 578*; James 196; John 578; John Carroll 578; Mary Alice 579; Mary Dietrich 196

WALTER, Hannah Creswell 264; Jacob A. 325; Joseph 264

WALTERS, Anna Smith 161; George 161

WALTON, Elizabeth H. Moore 510

WARBURTON, (Bishop) 369; Charles E. 370; Elizabeth 370; Elizabeth McCauley 369; Emma 370; Hannah 370; Henry A. 370; Mary 370; Matilda McFarland 370; Thomas 369; Thomas H. 370; William T. {368} 369*

WARD, Eliza 336; Elizabeth 237; James R. 237; Joshua 237; Julia A. 537; Rebecca 425, 426; Sarah Veazy 237

WARNER, M. Allie Dougherty 347; Edward 346, 520; Ellen M. Caldwell 346; Frank 346; Henry 346; Henry E. 347; Jacob 346; Jane 520; Joseph 520; Margaret Pyle 520; Mary 334, 519, 520; Mary J. 472; Nelson K. 346*; Philip 520; Richard 346; Ruth 520; Ruth Hayhurst 519; Sarah Warnock 519; Silas 519; Sophia 346; William 346, 520

WARNOCK, Philip 519; Sarah 519

WASHINGTON, Lawrence 185

WATERS, William T. 497

WATKINS, John 277; Liza Grafton 277

WATSON, Abraham 291; Sarah A. 281, 291

WATTERS, Anace A. 539; Anna M. 431; Eliza K. 482; Esther Y. 483; Fannie Munnikhuysen 431; Godfrey 430; Henry G. 430; J. Howard 482*; James D. 419, 430, 479; John H. 430; Martha J. 482; Mary

Clendenin 430; Mary F. 482; Mary Kennard 482; S. Catherine 482; Sarah E. 483; Walter 482; William 430, 482, 483

WEAVER, Eliza 526; John 526

WEBB, Elizabeth 120; James 120; Jonathan 119, 120; Rachel Ashe 119; Rebecca 460; Rebecca E. 119; Richard 120; William 120

WEBSTER, (family) 173*; (Col.) 381, 450; (Miss) 353; Adeline Divers 171; Alisanna 174; Ann L. 576; Anna 214; Anna J. Stump 216, 450; Anna Stump 450; Augustus 484; Benjamin Franklin 215; Benjamin M. 168; Bessie 184, 482; Caroline H. 184; Caroline H. McCormick (Earl) 184; Caroline Henderson 216; Carrie M. 576; Dora C. Rouse 184, 462; Edwin 151; Edwin H. 214, 482; Edwin Hanson 183, 203, 215, 419, 466; Elizabeth 168, 174; Elizabeth Dallam 174; Franklin 214; George 174; George Smith 148*, 215; Harriet 576; Henry 151, 174, 183, 213, 214, 215; Ida M. 184; Isaac 167, 174, 215; Isaac Lee 526; Isaac Pleasants 168; J. Edwin 182*, 462, 482; J. Thomas 345, 575*; Jacob B. 345*, 575; James {170} 171*, 174, 345; James Biays 168; John 171, 173, 174, 345, 575; John A. 168, 419; John Adams 167; John L. 345; John Lester 575; John Stump 216; John W. 213, 214; John Wesley 215; Joseph 221; Josephine 168; Laura Archer 168; Louisa L. 484; Louise W. 526; M. Elizabeth 174, 215; M. Sophia 345; Margaret 168; Margaret Adams 167; Martha Ann 215; Martha A.S. 575; Martha Hanson 215, 216; Mary 171; Mary Aleicia 216; Mary Alice 168; Mary E. 345, 575; Mary F. Webster 171; Michael 174, 255; Noah 171, 221; Phoebe 171, 174, 215; Phoebe Smith 174, 215;

Priscilla 214, 221; Rachel Biays 168; Rachel Cassandra 168; Rachel Mitchell 171; Rachel Virginia 168; Richard 171, 174, 182, 183, 215, 221, 222; Richard E. {220} 221*; Richard Henry 215, 216; Sarah 174, 345, 575; Sarah Elizabeth Hutchison 168; Sarah Francis 215; Sarah J. Fletcher 345; Samuel 167, 174, 182; Sophia C. 222; Sophia Norris 221; Susan Ann 168, 345; Susan Brown 345, 575; Susan Mitchell 221; Susanna(h) Mitchell 171, 576; Wesley 174; William 151, 171, 174, 214, 215*, 450; William E. 345, 575; William Samuel 167*; William W. 171, 174

WEEKS, Tacey A. 207

WEISEL, Joseph P. 215; Susan 215

WELLS, Ada Cornelia 398; Alevia 373; Anna 494; Anna R. 398; Benjamin 398, 449; Benjamin M. 449*; Charles G. 449; Cornelia Corouch 398; D. M. P. 560; Daisy Scott 449; Edwin E. 398; Edwin Webster 398; Florence Harlan 398; George Harlan 398; H. A. 449; H. C. 452; Hattie V. 416; Helen H. 449; John C. 398; Joseph 398, 494; Joseph L. 397*; Maggie Marshbank 452; Mary A. 449; Mary H. Howard 449; Rebecca Alexander 449

WENDT, (Major) 306; Catherine 306

WEST, Elizabeth 414; Mary Dallam 543; Mary E. 543; S. Augustus 543; Stacy 543; Thomas 543; Wilson D. 543

WESTON, D. E. 352; Eliza Levis 352; Elizabeth 352; Levis Belknap 352

WETHERALL, Angeline V. 507

WHEELER, Anna L. 523; Benjamin 324; Bennet 325; Bennett L. 522; Elizabeth A. 522; H. Elizabeth 523; Helen 522; Henrietta Green 522; Henrietta Maria Neale 326; Henry G. 522*; Ignatius 324, 326, 537; James A. 523; Joseph 522; Joseph A. 522; Josiah 324; Maria 522; Mary 523; Mary A. Cairnes 522; Monica 537; Susan 522; Thomas 324, 522; Virginia 523; William 522; William A. 523

WHITAKER, (Mr.) 375; Anna 308; Caroline 185; Charles 178; Clara Engall 307; Clifford C. 185; Edmund S. 184*; Eliza Ann Simmons 185; Emily 307; George P. 184, 185, 256, 342; Hattie 307; Hilda 307; James S. 307*; Joseph 185; Maggie 307; Maria 307; Mary E. 405; Mary Evans 185; Mary F. Wilson 178; Mary McFarland 185; Nelson E. 185; Rachael E. 256

WHITE, Adeliza M. 388; Alfred 388; Anne 207; Annie Ramsey 551; Barbara H. Dennison 388; Bertie 389; Catherine E. Birmingham 207; Charles W. 389; Clinton J. 388*; Clinton Johnson, Sr. 388; Elizabeth 388, 551; Elizabeth A. 351; Elizabeth D. Rose 154; Emmett 389; Emmett T. 388; Esther 551; George 389; Harry 388; Helen 206; Henry 206; Herbert 207; Inez 206; Irene 207; Israel 551; Jefferson W. 388; John 154, 206, 388, 551, 582; John D. 388; John H. 206*; John K. 577; Levi 388; Littleton 577; Lorenzo 206; Lucius G. 388, 533; Maggie 389; Margaret Cook 577; Maria Hearndon 206, 388; Martha Caldwell 551; Martha F. Mallory Southall 577; Martha Williams 389; Mary 206, 389; Mary F. 388; Milton 551; Milton J. R. 388; Napoleon P. 388; Rachel Janney 582; Rhoda 207; Rose White 533; Rufus 388; Sarah Smith 388; Sidney 206; Silas 206; Webster 550*; William L. 388

WHITEFORD, Annie E. Silver 286; Cassie F. 286; Doddridge 286; Elizabeth A. Silver 286; Frederick T. 286; Horace F. 286; Hugh 286; James S. 201; Joseph S. 286; Margaret L. Streett 201*; Mary E. 201; Mattie 286; Michael 286; Philip D. 286; Sallie E. 318; Silas S. 286; William 286; William E. {200} 201; William H. H. 286*; William M. 201, 202

WHITEHEAD, John 197; Zella A. Benjamin 197

WHITELOCK, A. J. 267, 522; Ann Gorrell 267; Annie Hopkins 522; Beulah 522; Caroline Bowman 267, 522; Charles 267; Emma 267, 522; Euphemie 267, 522; Eveline 267, 522; George D. 267, 521*; James 267*, 522; John 267, 522; Marjory 522; Mary 522; Mary R. 318

WHITSON, Annie 355

WHITWORTH, Mary Ann Booth 436; Moses 436

WICKES, Alethea 302; Emmaline L 302; Lambert 302

WILDY, Rachael Davidson 526

WILES, Harriet 188; William 188

WILEY, Agnes Belle 512; Andrew Jackson 506; Anna 471; Annie Blanche 512; Carl N. 509; Caroline B. 546; Caroline J. 506; Caroline M. 546; Charles L. 546; Charlotte A. Norris 506; Clarence B. 509; David 546; Dora M. 506; Eliza J. 545; Elizabeth 506; Elizabeth A. 546; Elizabeth Hutchins 546; Franklin M. 546; George N. 505*, 518; Goldy 389; Hannah 506; Hannah E. 389, 546; Harry F. 546; Ida Nelson 512; J. Nelson 389; James D. (& Son) 226; Janie Robinson 512; John 546;

Josephine Forder 509; Levisa Rebecca 512; Lizzie McClung 389; Mary A. 546; Mary E. 512, 517; Mary Susan 506; Matthew 506, 546; Matthew Jr. 506; Olive V. 509; Rebecca 506; Rebecca J. 546; Rebecca J. Robinson 512; Rebecca Nelson 546; Richard H. 546; Richard N. 508*, 546; Robert L. 546; Thomas 518; Thomas H. 506, 546*; Webster L. 389; Willard J. 509; William 506; Zana Idelett 546; Zanna I. 506

WILKES, James, Jr. 390; Mary A. 390

WILKINSON, Alice 163; Arthur 163; C. Rebecca Walker 378; Charles 162; E. L. 378; Edmund 163; Elizabeth Ordman 163; Ella 163; George 163; George W. 378; Hannah 162; Irene 163; Joseph 162; Martha 162; Mary L. Walker 378; Rachel 162; Robert 163; Rosie 163; Sarah 162; Sarah Harkins 162; Thomas 162; Thomas M. 162*

WILLIAMS, A. E. Streett 542; Adelaide P. 304; Catherine Thompson 428; Edward T. 428; Elise 543; Elizabeth Rush 543; Fannie Clayton 331; Fletcher Price 238; Frank Edwin 237, 238; Frederick P. 304; Frederick R. 542; George 298; George P. 389; Harriet 304; Harriet A. 543; Harriet H. Archer 542; Howard P. 304; Jesse 428; Jesse T. 428; John 428, 542; John G. 428*; John J. 303*, 304, 503; Jonathan K. 304; Joseph R. 428; Laura L. Peach 304; Lewis J. 542, 543; Lizzie 428; Lydia Knight 304; Martha 389; Mary 542; Mary E. Wallace 237; Mary K. 304; Nathaniel J. 331; Nellie 412; Rebecca 428; Roger K. 304; S. A. 405; Sarah L. 428; Stevenson A. 542*; Susan Dean 298; Thomas 303, 428; Thomas W. 304; Wallace 238; William 542; William M. 428

WILLIAMSON, J. F. 464; M. A. 575

WILLIS, Maggie Cook 272

WILMER, Edwin 446; Hannah E. Megredy 446; L. A. 212; Mary Rachel 446

WILSON, Abel 178; Alfred T. 479; Amos 479, 581; Anna 193, 462; Anna L. 246; Archibald 246*, 473; Armenia H. 374; Bayard G. 479; C. D. 216; Cassandra 246; Charles 581; Charles W. 373*; Christopher 352*, 353, 580; Cyrus H. 246; David E. 353, 407*; David E., Jr. 408; Edna 374; Edward 353; Edward A. 246; Elizabeth Fisher 374; Emma E. 374; Fred C. 374; Gilpin 408; Hannah J. Gladden 246, 473; Hanson Z. 479; Harry S. 246; Henry 306; Hettie Smith 353; Howard M. 374; Humphrey 178; J. P. 178*; Jacob 479, 580; James 246; James J. 246; Jane 473; John 352, 353, 580; John P. 479, 580*; Julia Billingslea 181; Letitia J. 246; Leota L. 454; Louisa Bates 581; M. D. 549; Mabel F. 479; Margaret 353, 408; Margaret J. 246; Martha 479, 581; Mary 408, 479; Mary Aleicia Webster 216; Mary F. Taylor 178; Mary J. 297; Mary Pearce 479; Mary Pearson 580; Mary S. 353; Rachel J. 223, 298; Rachel Smith 407; Rhoda V. 374; Ross W. 479, 581; Ruth 408; Sallie E. 418; Samuel 246, 580; Samuel D. 479, 580; Sarah 410, 479, 581; Sarah A. Durham 178; Sarah Louise Rea 223; Susanna Lyon 353; T. J. 178; Thomas J. 479, 581; William 407, 408, 479*, 581; William, Jr. 479; William, Sr. 407; William F. 246; William H. 246

WINGFIELD, Annie K. Quinby 472; C. W. 472

WINTERS, Sarah 227

WIRT, Annie Rebecca Pearce 113; Francina Bayard 212; Henry Biddle 212, 227*; John S. {210} 211, 343, 448; John W. 212, 228, 343; Margaret Savin Biddle 212, 343; Nellie Knight 228; Samuel 211; Thomas 211; William Bayard 212

WISE, Allen D. 580; Arthur M. 580; Edna M. 580; Eliza 580; Fannie Sherwood 580; Hannah 538; Harold J. 580; James M. 580; John S. 580; Lizzie 580; Loomis O. 580; Sallie R. 580; Thomas D. 580; William A. 580*

WOOD, (Dr.) 337; Edward 152; Emma 572; Irene W. Bull 152; Margaret A. Tucker 337

WOOLFORD, Lizzie V. 307

WOOLEY, Charles 388; Elizabeth White 388

WOOLSEY, Catherine 198; Elizabeth 198; Harriet 198; Henry 198*; James 198; Jason M. 198; Joseph 198; Rebecca 198; Rebecca Cochron 198; Sarah 198; Sophia 198; William 198

WORRELL, Sarah Rebecca Thomas 578; Theodore A. 578

WORTHINGTON, (Dr.) 429; Annie Laurie 466; Charles 465; E. H. 265; Frank 465; Frank D. 466; Harriet J. Michener 265; John D. 465*, 466; Malcolm McLean 466; Mary Dallam 465; Theresa McCormick 466; William 465

WRIGHT, Amelia Smithon 272; Daniel 272; Edward 444; Emma E. James 172; Emma Leola 426; Emily 272; George 426, 444; George E. 172; Hannah Amos 272; James 426; John 444; John W. 272; Joseph 444; Joseph F. 426; Joshua W. 271*; Margaret Anderson 272; Margaret W. 272; Martha McDowell Ford 444; Mary E. Porter 444; Mary S. 186; Robert F. 443*; Sallie R. 272; Sarah Caroline Fulton 426; William 186, 272; William A. 272

WROTH, Alice E. 275

WYGART, Catnerine 263

WYSONG, Annie 177; D. P. 177; Ella J. Grymes 177; Fannie Preston 177; Frank 177; John 177; John B. 177*; John Mason 177; T. T. 177

YATES, Hannah Louise McCauley 410; J. T. 410

YELLOTT, Elizabeth 415; George 415

YERKES, Andrew 563; Lydia 563

YOST, C. Harry 389; Lovisa R. McClung 389

YOUNG, Ada Roberta 414; Caroline Steele 247; Charles 187; Elizabeth Clayton 478; Harry L. 187; James 187; John S. 187*, 214; Mary Fulton 187, 214; Mary E. Cochran 187; N. 478; William 187, 247, 414; William S. 187

YOUNKER, Elmira McCleary 355; William 355

www.ingramcontent.com/pod-product-compliance
Lightning Source LLC
Chambersburg PA
CBHW060219230426
43664CB00011B/1485